ROZELLE

Czar of the NFL

JEFF DAVIS

New York   Chicago   San Francisco   Lisbon   London   Madrid   Mexico City
Milan   New Delhi   San Juan   Seoul   Singapore   Sydney   Toronto

The **McGraw·Hill** Companies

Library of Congress Cataloging-in-Publication Data

Davis, Jeff, 1941–.
    Rozelle : czar of the NFL / Jeff Davis.
        p.   cm.
    ISBN-13: 978-0-07-147166-4 (alk. paper)
        1. Rozelle, Pete.   2. Football commissioners—United States—Biography.
    3. National Football League—Biography.   I. Title.

    GV939.R695D38   2007
    796.332092—dc22   2007023788

1 2 3 4 5 6 7 8 9 10 11 12 13 14 15 16 17 18 19 20 21   DOH/DOH   0 9 8 7

ISBN 978-0-07-147166-4
MHID   0-07-147166-9

All photos courtesy of Anne Marie Rozelle Bratton collection, except where otherwise noted

McGraw-Hill books are available at special quantity discounts to use as premiums and
sales promotions, or for use in corporate training programs. For more information, please
write to the Director of Special Sales, Professional Publishing, McGraw-Hill, Two Penn
Plaza, New York, NY 10121-2298. Or contact your local bookstore.

This book is printed on acid-free paper.

CONTENTS

FOREWORD

Ernie Accorsi

As I was driving to Baltimore on April 1, 1970, leaving a wonderful post at the Penn State University Athletic Department to begin my first job in the NFL—as public relations director for the Baltimore Colts—I was awed and excited by my good fortune. To be joining the National Football League, at that time, with Pete Rozelle as our commissioner was a momentous prospect. I remember thinking, this must have been what it felt like for the boys of the New Frontier when they went to Washington to start the John F. Kennedy administration.

I don't mean to suggest that running the National Football League is comparable to running the country, but for me the person who came closest to embodying the inspiring leadership and vision of John F. Kennedy in my lifetime was Pete Rozelle.

If you're lucky, you have one moment in your life when you are touched by greatness. Along with many others who worked for what I consider the greatest sports institution in American history—the National Football League—during its greatest years, I had that opportunity. I joined the Baltimore Colts organization 10 years after Pete Rozelle took office, and I worked in the league for the remainder of his administration. During 1975–76, I was privileged to serve in the NFL office as a member of Pete Rozelle's staff. I was able to work with him, observe him, and learn from him on a daily basis.

Rozelle has been described as a brilliant visionary, a risk taker, a consensus builder, a skillful communicator, and a tireless worker. Watching him do his job every day, I saw all of those aspects in action, but in my opinion, the two traits that defined his greatness were integrity and humility.

Through his unfailing credibility, he earned my total trust. When he spoke, in private or in public, I never doubted that he was being genuine and honest. There was also no doubt about his intelligence. One time during a staff meeting—the staff in those days consisted of about seven or eight people—Pete listened politely to all of our opinions on an issue for about an hour. Then he tied everything together in five minutes and, typically, concluded with a solution that none of us had considered but that made all the sense in the world. After the meeting, I asked Harold Rosenthal, who was the director of information for the American Football Conference and a well-regarded colleague, "Harold, how did Pete come up with the answer to that problem, which made so much sense and seemed so logical, and yet none of us ever thought of it?" "Ernesto," he said, "he's just smarter than all of us."

That was true, but it was his integrity, to which I was exposed every day, that made the deepest impression. During the height of the labor issues in the mid-'70s, Los Angeles Rams owner Carroll Rosenbloom signed Detroit Lions wide receiver Ron Jessie, who had played out his option. In accordance with league rules and practice at that time, Rozelle was charged with awarding proper compensation to the team that lost the player, in this case the Detroit Lions.

Pete asked for a joint recommendation from Nick Skorich, who was the assistant supervisor of officials and former head coach of the Eagles and Browns, and me, since I was the assistant to the president of the National Conference, in which the transaction took place. After collaborating on the problem for about a week, Nick and I settled on a solution that we thought was fair.

The Rams, we proposed, should give the Lions their number one draft choice and Cullen Bryant, a promising running back who was playing behind Lawrence McCutcheon at that time but who probably would start for the Lions. Our thinking was that although a first-round draft choice in itself was obviously valuable, it carried some risk and wasn't enough to replace Jessie, who was a top NFL receiver. Bryant was a good running back who might become a very good one, so he seemed to be the perfect complement to the transaction.

We took the recommendation to Rozelle and made our case. The following day, Pete met with Nick and me, along with his chief aide, Jim Kensil (the most underrated sports executive in history), and accepted our recommendation.

To appreciate the weight of this decision by the commissioner, you have to take into account that the executive negotiating committee of the NFL management council, made up of a select group of owners and council officials, was in Washington preparing to negotiate with the NFL Players' Association, led by Ed Garvey. These were tense times with the players' union. To make matters worse, Rosenbloom was not happy with Rozelle at this juncture, and there was no question he was not going to be happy with the compensation. This formula was called the Rozelle Rule. Kensil, as well as his staff and the rest of us, warned Pete that this decision was going to trigger an explosive reaction from the players' union and from Rosenbloom. Pete, of course, knew that, but he followed through with it anyway. You know why? It was the right thing to do. It was the fair thing to do. He could have skirted the issue by not moving a player and just sending two draft choices instead, but he knew that would not be fair to Detroit; the Lions by right should have received a player.

The result: Rosenbloom filed for a temporary restraining order from the courts, Bryant never went to the Lions, and the Rozelle Rule was never used again.

The integrity that Pete Rozelle showed in all of his dealings was equaled by his humility. I have said many times that the two biggest stars in football with the greatest humility whom I have known personally were Pete Rozelle and Frank Gifford. It's fitting that they were such close friends. Whenever I'd walk down a street in Manhattan with Pete, on the way to a press conference or a meeting, and people would recognize him, he was almost shy. He never sought attention for himself, though he certainly attracted it.

In his professional role, he never sought accolades for his outstanding accomplishments throughout his career. Even more commendable, he never railed against blatant injustice, let alone put his considerable power to use in revenge.

As I look at the landscape of the National Football League over the past 47 years, during 35 of which I was involved, I'm struck by how many great men contributed to the birth of the league, its survival during a depression and a world war, its growth, and its achievement as the pinnacle of sport. I am also convinced that for the National Football League to have become what it has become one event was indispensable: Pete Rozelle had to be the commissioner. There is no way, no possible way, all of this could have ever happened without him.

I was in the Marriott Hotel in New Orleans, working in the pressroom of Super Bowl IX, when I received a call from Jim Kensil, asking me to come to his office. My first thought was, what have I done wrong this week? When I walked into Kensil's office, he said, "Pete wants to talk to you about working for him in New York." Those were probably the most thrilling words I ever heard in my career.

Pete Rozelle was simply the greatest commissioner—the greatest sports executive—in the history of the United States. I was lucky enough to be along for the ride.

PREFACE

I was a college freshman at Northwestern University's Medill School of Journalism in early 1960 when the 12 crusty old-timers who ran the National Football League shocked the sports world by breaking a weeklong impasse on the twenty-third ballot to name Alvin Ray Rozelle, the 33-year-old general manager of the Los Angeles Rams, their commissioner.

Young Rozelle's election occurred only because the toughest old-timer of them all, the league's last surviving founder, George Halas—still owner and coach at age 64 of my hometown Chicago Bears—agreed to it. In those days none of his fellow owners dared challenge Halas, nor did anyone even ask him to change his vote. You don't plead with potentates; you can only hope to please them. And no one was bigger in his realm than Papa Bear.

Halas had stood fast through 22 ballots in a South Florida hotel. He withheld the ninth and deciding vote that would have elected front-runner Marshall Leahy, the San Francisco 49ers attorney, simply by passing on *every* ballot. Halas held no personal grievance against Leahy. He simply didn't think Leahy's stated intention to move the league office to San Francisco—the western edge of America, three time zones away from the country's eastern business centers and two away from the country's midwestern heart—was a good idea.

Not when the league had made huge inroads against the dominant American sport of baseball. Especially not when Halas had recently convinced the late Bert Bell—his longtime friend, deferential ally, and the previous summer's commissioner—to expand the league. Definitely not when a well-financed opposing league was starting up with a network television deal. Absolutely not when Halas had all but bounced his crosstown rival, the Cardinals, out of Chicago, leaving the city for him alone.

No, Halas knew that neither Marshall Leahy, nor the other candidates who failed to gain traction during those interminable ballots, had the right stuff to succeed his pal, Bell, who died at a football game in Philadelphia in October 1959.

George Halas had almost single-handedly carried the league through its first four decades, from its 1920 startup in a Canton, Ohio, auto showroom—when it comprised a cluster of towns in Ohio, Pennsylvania, Indiana, and Illinois—through the Depression, World War II, and an interleague war in the late 1940s. He had taken it to the promised land of television and its big-money potential.

It's not that he was tired; George Halas was never tired. He knew the time had come for a young man of vision, as he had been at age 25 in 1920, to take the league to new levels. He knew the game had reached the brink of overthrowing baseball's domination, and he wanted a man in charge who could do just that. He knew that to accomplish it, his National Football League had to go toe-to-toe with the New York financial zone, television networks, and their big advertisers, who powered the engine driving the American economy.

When Dan Reeves, Pete Rozelle's boss, offered Rozelle's name as a compromise to break the impasse, and fellow league movers and shakers Wellington Mara of New York, Paul Brown of Cleveland, and Carroll Rosenbloom of Baltimore vouchsafed for the young man, Halas came aboard. Befitting his position, Halas still passed on the now perfunctory 23rd ballot, but Papa Bear had given his blessing. He would challenge the new man early on in small ways to let him know who was boss. But when a showdown came in 1961 over criticism of officials and Rozelle calmly ordered Halas to meet him in his New York office, Papa Bear complied and afterward became Rozelle's most vocal and ardent ally.

That's the way it was with Pete Rozelle. And so it had been from his relatively humble origins in Los Angeles at the end of the Roaring Twenties to the Great Depression to his stint in the navy in the final year of World War II. He was quiet, smart, hardworking, and made friends easily. His great ambition was to become sports editor of the *Los Angeles Times*.

Sports was the operative word. He loved football, baseball, basketball, and track and field. He read about them in the papers, studied box scores, knew and felt at ease with their athletes, and kept fit himself. Rozelle was a superb judge of talent not just in athletics but also in business, politics, communications, and law. He had even touted classmate Edwin "Duke" Snider, who would become one of the best Hall of Fame baseball players in history with the Brooklyn Dodgers, in his school newspaper. But while Duke Snider was a great athlete, Rozelle was not.

It would have been quite unlikely in the late '30s and early '40s that good old Pete Rozelle from Compton, California, would become the impresario of the biggest jock kingdom of all, the National Football League. But he would make it the richest and most popular sports organization in America, creating year-round interest in the sport. In fact, under Rozelle, professional football would enjoy a year-round season whether or not it was being played.

George Halas knew to the end of his long eventful life that he had entrusted his baby, the National Football League, to the right hands. A pleasant, seemingly friendly man with a steel spine, Rozelle had the vision to accomplish great things.

This is the story of *the* commissioner, Pete Rozelle.

ACKNOWLEDGMENTS

Rozelle: Czar of the NFL is the product of the hard, dedicated efforts of many more people than this lone writer. That's the way it always is.

This project began in 2005 when my agent, Paul Bresnick, and I contacted McGraw-Hill editor and friend Mark Weinstein. When Weinstein, who guided us so capably through *Papa Bear* (my book on George Halas), left the company, his successor, Ron Martirano, never missed a beat. Martirano handled this book with a deft touch and unwavering patience, for which I am grateful. Julia Anderson Bauer and her crack production team have again polished the copy to a fine luster in preparing it for printing and binding.

Learning the life of Pete Rozelle presented an unusual challenge. I knew of George Halas from childhood and became even more familiar with him when I got into the news business. I was in college when Rozelle became commissioner of the National Football League, and I observed him most of those years as a television sports producer, writer, and reporter. I met him several times but did not truly know him. That knowledge, of course, changed dramatically through my months of research, interviews, and writing.

Every person I interviewed offered valuable contributions to the fabric of this narrative. A few deserve special mention. First is Pete Rozelle's daughter, Anne Marie Bratton, who kindly shared her time, lent scores of pictures, and, most important, provided significant and revealing observations that give text and texture to a man whom she has treasured deeply all her life.

Rozelle's brother, Dick, supplied photographs of their family and hours of rich detail, especially of those years before his older brother was elected commissioner. Dick led me to several of his brother's earliest friends, including Hall of Fame baseball player Duke Snider; his wife, Bev; and Pete's early mentor, the Hall of Fame basketball coach Pete Newell.

Dennis Kroner, a Chicago financial planner and accountant, friend of 40 years, and great sports fan, kicked off the interview process when he had me call Detroit priest Don Worthy, a baseball fanatic and loyal Lions backer. Father Worthy is a close friend of Lions Hall of Fame linebacker and former coach Joe Schmidt, the first person I interviewed for this book. His former teammate Alex Karras was next as they discussed the 1963 betting scandal and the resulting suspensions that made the country stand up and take notice of the way young commissioner Rozelle handled the situation.

Another branch of the phone tree began with Kathy Davis at NFL Films, who supplied many key videos, especially very early ones, as she steered me to Rozelle's close personal friends, including her bosses Ed Sabol, founder of NFL Films, and his son Steve, president of NFL Films, and Steve's sister, Blair. Blair led me to their uncle, Herb Siegel, which led me to pursue and land interviews with Frank Gifford, Pat Summerall, Sam Huff, and Chuck Mercein.

NFL executive vice president Joe Browne gave me a superb interview and help in many areas, especially securing an interview with former commissioner Paul Tagliabue. NFL vice president Greg Aiello always had quick, accurate responses when I called for assistance, and I thank him.

My longtime friend Bill Orr detailed the "Philadelphia story" of the Bert Bell days and the inner workings of NFL Films' antecedent, Tel Ra, and led me to such men as Dan Endy, Pete Retzlaff, and Tom Brookshier.

Former *Sports Illustrated* associate editor Lester Munson, a friend since our schooldays in Glen Ellyn, Illinois, provided many insights to the Rozelle reign as he helped me land Frank Deford and Bill Nack (like Charlie Jones, a Kappa Sigma fraternity brother—in Bill's case at Illinois, in Charlie's at USC).

Jones has been a friend since 1973, when we worked together at the NBC affiliate in Chicago. Nobody saw and did more with the old American Football League from the beginning through the merger than he did. He also led me to Herb Klein, who directed me to Jack Kemp.

Rex Lardner, a close friend since we met three-and-a-half decades ago while working for NBC, steered me to former NBC Sports president Chet Simmons and former CBS and Turner executive Bob Wussler. Lardner has given me invaluable help and advice throughout this process on a daily basis.

As with *Papa Bear*, Bill Jauss and his wife, Kenny, provided constant support, guidance, and friendship. Jauss again had me read every word of every chapter aloud to him as we made corrections and amendments on the fly. A superb reporter in his half-century of covering sports for three major Chicago dailies, Jauss was every bit the tough, demanding editor and teacher, as he has been to many outstanding journalists at our alma mater, Northwestern's Medill School of Journalism.

No single individual has contributed more material than Ernie Accorsi. We are the same age and it is no coincidence that we grew up watching and following pro football—he in Hershey, Pennsylvania, and me in suburban Chicago—long before we dreamed we would be so involved in this sport. Ernie's observations, insights, and views from an insider's vantage point as an employee for Pete Rozelle, Carroll Rosenbloom, Art Modell, and Wellington Mara make him, in my opinion, the NFL's MVP—most valuable professional. He knows everything because he has lived it. He is a true kinsman and friend, and he led me to two men whose contributions to this book were so vital and wonderful, the late Peter Hadhazy and Joel Bussert.

Jerry Vainisi came through with observations about Rozelle's relationship with George Halas and details on Jim Finks's near-election as commissioner in 1989.

Finally, my most important contributors and loving supporters are my wife and best friend, Kris; our kids, Elisabeth Case and Erik; son-in-law Dan Case; and grandsons, Willy and Charlie. They, as always, are my motivators.

ONE

"I COME TO YOU WITH CLEAN HANDS"

"All this started with Rozelle. Until then, it might as well have been in a hut in Montana."

—DAVE ANDERSON, *NEW YORK TIMES* SPORTS COLUMNIST, JANUARY 18, 2006

*T*he University of San Francisco's future–Hall of Fame basketball coach Pete Newell was out recruiting in late winter 1948 when he stopped by Compton Junior College, in Greater Los Angeles, to check out a couple of prospects. "There was a junior college tournament there; that's when I ran into him," the 90-year-old Newell said in the fall of 2005.

The man Newell "ran into" was a 22-year-old navy veteran also named Pete who was handling the publicity for the tournament. Pete Rozelle was a second-year student at Compton and lifelong resident of the next town up, Lynwood, in that cluster of small cities that tie Los Angeles proper southward to Long Beach. "You're very conscious of someone like him. Anything you wanted, he'd get, and that's very unusual. He was so efficient. I was a big coffee drinker at the time. I'd finish a cup, and he'd come back with another one," Newell said. "I had a friend."

1

A few months later when USF's athletic publicist quit—as Newell put it, "in a huff because they fired the football coach he liked"—the basketball coach urged the school's business manager to bring young Rozelle up from L.A. for an interview. "Pete sold Tommy Needham five minutes after he talked to him," Newell recalled. "Pete was a rare person. There was nothing phony about him."

A dozen years later, that same young man, Los Angeles Rams general manager Alvin Ray "Pete" Rozelle, accepted the job of his life: commissioner of the National Football League. He was only 33. "He was much more mature as a young man than the average person," Newell said. "He didn't go out of his way to try things; the jobs came to him."

Job hunting was the last thing on Pete Rozelle's mind when he flew to Miami on January 16, 1960, for the league meeting. His designated role was to protect the interests of the Rams and his boss, Dan Reeves. Period. Two items led the agenda for Reeves and his 11 fellow owners: election of a commissioner to succeed the late Bert Bell, who died the previous October, and George Halas's plans to finalize expansion.

In Los Angeles, the personal plans were set for the Rozelles. Wife Jane would drop off their 16-month-old baby, Anne Marie, with Pete's parents a few days later and then join him in Miami, from where, after the conclusion of league business, they would depart for a much needed weeklong getaway to the tropical delights of Jamaica.

Back in Miami as the meeting was set to begin, an escape to the Island in the Sun was the last thing on Rozelle's mind. A sense of urgency unlike anything the league had experienced in years, perhaps in all its 40-year history, pervaded this meeting, and he, like everyone else in the room, felt it deeply. The league to this point had focused on the games themselves, fashioning a product to make fans of the professional game and show its superiority over the college version. The late Bert Bell was all about games. The new leader had to be a football man, for certain, but he also had to be a man for the '60s and beyond.

The generation emerging into leadership had experienced hardening forces of the Depression in childhood, World War II, and the postwar era, when, for the first time, they had the opportunity to gain a college education, thanks to the GI Bill of Rights. By necessity, the new commissioner had to reflect the changing times.

The new commissioner would have to employ extraordinary command skills to wage an interleague war that, for better or worse, would define the future of the sport. He had to harness the power of communications elements from visual imagery that included television, film, and print, to sell the league. He had to know where the money was, how to get to it, and how to bring it in using extraordinary negotiating powers.

He had to take an open and leading position on race. Black athletes were about to enter the league en masse, and they wanted equality on the field and in the checkbook. When it came to economics, the players wanted better pay and better benefits for themselves and their families. Last, he would have to be mindful as never before that in a real world, sinister forces existed that wanted to take advantage of the situation, be they gamblers or something else not yet known but waiting to emerge down the line—drugs.

The first order of business was to elect a commissioner to cope with the dire situation to be faced in the coming days, weeks, months, and years. That was the very real challenge from the well-heeled new American Football League, with many dynamic younger men in charge. The emergent league was organizing in a hurry, willing and able to test new ideas and concepts. These young guys in their late twenties and early thirties were not just flashing real money but also spending it well to find nuggets and building blocks from an abundant talent pool that flowed from two sources.

Both leagues would shop and pick from the usual collegiate market. Only this time, competition would drive salaries upward, mostly for rookies. At the opposite end, the veteran talent pool was spilling over with National Football League journeymen, some of whom had been tossed onto the discard pile, others whose skills had gone unrecognized, along with younger, able players who did not make the cut to a 40-man league roster, a few returnees from Canada, and a substantial number of former NFL players who had retired before their time, decided they still wanted to play, and definitely believed they still had what it takes.

Every bit as poignant, there was an abundance of excellent, ready-to-go coaches out there, some from the NFL, some from Canada who wanted to come home, and others from the colleges who were ready to advance their careers. One of the elite coaches the new league had bagged was a proven success wherever he had been. He was just-named Los Angeles Chargers headman Sid Gillman, the master of the passing game, who, until the end of the 1959 season, had been Pete Rozelle's trusted coach with the Rams. Gillman told Rozelle after the 1958 season that all he needed to deliver a championship was a top-flight running back. So Rozelle went to the Chicago Cardinals and traded nine players for a man he had touted to America when he hustled athletic publicity at USF, perennial all-pro Ollie Matson.

Unfortunately for Rozelle and Gillman, the Matson of 1959, trying to operate somehow behind a line decimated by the trade, no longer dominated at the elite level of a Jim Brown or Lenny Moore. When the Chargers flopped at 2–10, owner Reeves fired Gillman after the last game of the dismal season.

Shortly after New Year's, Barron Hilton's recently hired general manager, Frank Leahy, the legendary former Notre Dame coach, hired Gillman. Leahy, the controversial and immensely successful protégé of the even more fabled Knute Rockne, was the biggest name in college football when he stepped down at age 45 for "health reasons" after going 9–0–1 in 1953. It had been loudly whispered for years on and about the South Bend campus that Notre Dame's young president, the Reverend Theodore Hesburgh, actually fired Leahy but let him "retire" to save the educational reputation he wanted to build for the university even as he de-emphasized football there after Leahy's departure.

Leahy had kept an eye on Gillman through the years, from his early coaching time and successes at Miami of Ohio and the nearby University of Cincinnati, through his often brilliant tenure with the Rams, highlighted by a Western Conference championship in his first year, 1955. From the Rams, Gillman imported top assistant Jack Faulkner and added a pair of bright young assistants named Al Davis and Chuck Noll. Also, he had maintained a strong working relationship with Rozelle.

Thus, as the owners gathered in Miami, just who Gillman's successor would be was on Rozelle's mind, as was the embarrassing failure to land his top draft choice, Heisman Trophy winner Billy Cannon, of Louisiana State. Several weeks before, Rozelle negotiated a secret $50,000 contract with Cannon. Had the signing been made public, Cannon, as a pro, would have been declared ineligible, forcing LSU to forfeit its season, let alone miss its rematch in the Sugar Bowl with Ole Miss. Rozelle knew that and kept quiet. Meanwhile, the AFL Houston Oilers made Cannon their territorial choice.

For weeks, the Oilers couldn't track down Cannon. When they finally did, owner Bud Adams put him in the hotbox. After some hemming and hawing, the Heisman winner confessed that he had signed with the Rams. The fast-thinking Adams told Cannon the Rams deal would be voided in court and then proffered a multiyear deal including a $20,000 signing bonus that added up to $110,000. Cannon signed with the same burst of speed that won him the Heisman.

The waiting game ended on New Year's Day at the Sugar Bowl game, in New Orleans. Three of the prime picks in the National Football League draft walked to the goalposts at one end of Tulane Stadium after Mississippi completed its surprising 21–0 upset rout of LSU. There, they signed contracts with the American Football League. In each case, the new league outbid the established NFL: Cannon signed with the Houston Oilers; his defensive-back teammate Johnny Robinson, the top choice of the Detroit Lions, walked into the arms of Lamar Hunt's Dallas Texans; and Ole Miss fullback Charlie Flowers spurned the New York Giants for Barron Hilton's money with the Chargers.

Bert Bell had taken the league a long way from the outlaw image of its early years to fiscal strength of sorts, thanks to getting its games on television every Sunday across the country. Now Bell's successor would have to fight and, if the league were to make it, win the third interleague war in its history. With the birth of the American Football League, in many ways, the next commissioner would arrive in the same position as Lincoln did when he took power a century before as the country was torn asunder by secession and bloodshed.

The games would go on, but this uncivil war would be fought in boardrooms, in public relations maneuvers, in the print media, and on television.

Among the first league power-brokers to greet young Rozelle when the owners took their seats on Wednesday morning, January 20, to start the commissioner's election process were Cleveland Browns founder, minority owner, and coach Paul Brown and his son Mike, who, at age 25, was not that far removed from the Dartmouth campus. "Pete was at the table on the other side of where my dad was," he said. "I was sitting on a chair against the wall. I remember looking at Pete, and again, the thought that would go into your mind was how young he was. He was young enough to be playing."

As the curtain was raised on act 1 of the Miami drama, two venerable league figures remained in their positions of respect bordering on downright fear. As longtime ABC sportscaster Keith Jackson observed 46 years later, "Some tough old buzzards ran the NFL at that time. I mean there were some tough guys around."

The toughest of the tough were league founder George Halas, approaching age 65, still the quite active owner-coach of the Chicago Bears and still chasing after a sixth championship as the winningest coach in league history; and Halas's ally in league matters, Washington Redskins owner George Preston Marshall, 63 and cantankerous. Halas and Marshall had pushed through the rules in 1933 that opened up the game to crowd-pleasing scoring, and they marched at the head of the crowd ever since, innovating and pushing ahead through the years.

Both were the leaders in pushing television and developing their own networks in the '50s. Marshall's network ran down the eastern seaboard from the Mason-Dixon Line to Miami. Halas's vast network, which he built and shared with the crosstown Cardinals, stretched from the Midwest to the East. A key player in his network was New York advertising rep Edgar Scherick, whose St. Louis–based client Falstaff Beer financed the operation.

Halas entered the television business in 1947 when he sold the rights to the Bears' six home games to pioneering Chicago station WBKB for $900 a game, $5,400 in all. In 1948, after Halas sold

51,000 tickets to the finale with the Cardinals at Wrigley Field to decide the Western Division title, he let two stations, WGN-TV and WENR-TV, run competing telecasts.

Halas held off again in 1949, agreeing to telecast the Bears-Cardinals game on WGN-TV only after it sold out. The weather was the one thing Halas could not control. Chicago nearly drowned on December 11 under an all-day rainstorm. Despite the sellout, only a corporal's guard of fans showed up to see the game, with the rest preferring to stay at home if they had television sets, or go to the corner tavern to see the game and celebrate the 51–21 Bears victory.

Never again, Halas vowed, would he give away the game at the expense of the gate. The Bears were not on television in 1950. But other teams, including the Cleveland Browns and Washington Redskins, had joined the television game. Out in Los Angeles, when the Rams averaged more than 50,000 fans a game in 1949 in the Coliseum and still lost money, Dan Reeves cut a deal with the Admiral Television Company to air his home schedule. It came, as Michael MacCambridge writes in *America's Game*, after the Rams' Tex Schramm's research indicated that television should spearhead a 10 percent increase in attendance.

Reeves got Admiral to agree to guarantee that 10 percent increase and compensate the Rams if that did not happen. The 1950 Rams had the highest-scoring team in league history but, thanks to television, saw attendance fall by nearly half to a 26,000 average. Admiral had to come up with a whopping $307,000 make-good payment.

Bell, with Halas's prodding and corroborating evidence from Reeves's 1950 debacle, took charge in 1951 when he instituted a 75-mile television blackout of home games. It took a couple of court tests before Bell's blackout took effect. Right away, he credited that policy as a major factor in putting fannies back in the seats.

Bell then inaugurated a limited package of Saturday-night telecasts in the East. They ran on the DuMont network as far west as Chicago through 1955, with announcers Ray Scott, Chris Schenkel, and Chuck Thompson calling the games. Fans were talking up the league now and wanted more. From the early days, the networks had reserved Sunday afternoons for cultural programming that, for the most part, attracted quality, thinking audiences, but no sponsorships. Fortunately for football, television networks are in business to make money.

The breakthrough for network sports came at 5:00 P.M. CDT on Wednesday, August 31, 1955. Americans stopped whatever they were doing, wherever they were—at home, on the way home, in a hotel bar, or in the corner saloon—to watch the most ballyhooed horse race in history. It was a match race from Washington Park, in Homewood, south of Chicago. An estimated fifty million TV sets turned to CBS at that hour as Preakness and Belmont Stakes champion Nashua and jockey Eddie Arcaro routed Kentucky Derby winner Swaps and Willie Shoemaker to take the $100,000 winner-take-all purse.

Halas and Bell saw those audience numbers, and so did Madison Avenue. So, when Bell called CBS, the die was cast. By the winter of '56, he was able to put together the league's first Sunday-afternoon television package. Each team then negotiated its rights-fees deal in its home market. Halas and Marshall and the other teams gladly folded their independent networks and returned to the business of football full-time. Ed Scherick went over to CBS to lend his expertise to the operation.

"I grew up in Hershey, Pennsylvania, where we watched football on a fuzzy picture from WHP, channel 21, a UHF station in Harrisburg," said longtime NFL executive Ernie Accorsi, who ended his career as New York Giants general manager in 2006. "I asked Billy Bidwill, 'Why did I see the Cardinals and Bears when I was a kid?'"

Cardinals' owner Bidwill told him, "George Halas came to Walter Wolfner and formed this network. We didn't get much money, because Halas said, 'Nobody wants to see your games anyway.'"

That same network arced into the Deep South and across the Southwest. "Down in Arkansas, we got the Chicago Bears because they cut out the middle part of the country," Hall of Fame broadcaster Charlie Jones remembered.

Halas's announcer was football's first authentic hero of the Golden Age of Sport in the '20s, Red Grange. The Galloping Ghost gave the network prestige and sold a lot of television sets in the land far beyond the Windy City. Al Ward, who would work in the NFL and

AFL from 1960 on, was a sportswriter with the Waco, Texas, *Tribune-Herald* in 1954 when a friend invited him over to his house to watch the Bears one Sunday. "When I saw that game on his set, I went out and bought my own. I had to see the NFL games on Sunday," Ward said. "It's just a very, very attractive game."

When he formed the Redskins in the '30s, Marshall, an avowed racist who never changed his views, drew the color line and, in league councils, forced his fellow owners, especially Halas and Pittsburgh's Art Rooney, to not hire black players. That lasted through World War II, until Dan Reeves, in need of a stadium lease from the Los Angeles Memorial Coliseum Commission in 1946, bowed to the commission's pressure and signed two prewar UCLA stars and teammates of Jackie Robinson's, halfback Kenny Washington and end Woodrow Strode. Reeves immediately sent scouts out to get more black players.

In the competing league of that era, the All-America Football Conference, Cleveland coach Paul Brown signed two black athletes he knew from his Massillon, Ohio, high school and Ohio State coaching time. They were former Buckeyes prewar all-America guard Bill Willis and fullback Marion Motley, who played for Canton McKinley High, Massillon's biggest rival when Brown coached there.

In 1960, by which time every other team but the Redskins had black players, a reporter asked Marshall if he would integrate his Redskins. He snarled, "We'll start signing Negroes when the Harlem Globetrotters sign whites." Marshall also did not want to let any other franchise gain entry inside the NFL's closed society, but his word in league councils no longer mattered.

Halas, though, not only retained his power but also expanded it after Bell's unexpected death. The Papa Bear decided to abstain from voting for anyone standing for commissioner because he wanted to control the outcome the way he controlled everything else in his league since he led its founding in that Hupmobile showroom in Canton, Ohio, on September 17, 1920. More important, as chairman of the league's expansion committee, he did not want to make any enemies in his mission to finalize his plan to fend off the AFL challenge with his handpicked franchise choices in Dallas and Minneapolis–St. Paul.

America in 1960 was undergoing the first rumblings of a technological, political, social, and cultural transition, all interrelated. These changes would have immediate impact as they consigned what had been the conventional wisdom to the intellectual trash heap much as newfangled concepts such as cheap electricity, clean-burning gas heat, pasteurization, the gasoline-powered automobile driving on paved roads, and the airplane drastically altered life in America and the world at the dawning of the 20th century.

Now, at the six-decade marker of the century, a second wave of change was under way. Jet-powered passenger planes able to connect America's centers of commerce, New York and Chicago, in two hours and to cross the country and four time zones in just six hours were making passenger-railroad travel obsolete as quickly as the airlines were mothballing their smaller, slower, piston-powered fleets.

Even more important were the dynamic changes in communications that already had arrived or were looming on the horizon. Telephones would get smaller, lighter, and, in time, as portable as a pack of cigarettes, a book of matches, and a money clip. Satellites, considered the stuff of Flash Gordon or Buck Rogers space fantasies, were reality by 1958 when the Soviets launched globe-circling *Sputnik*, the first step in putting a man into orbit, and America quickly followed suit, pumping money and resources into its own space program. By 1962, the first major test of television satellite transmission would take place on a summer afternoon and send a portion of a baseball telecast to the universe from Wrigley Field, in Chicago.

Network television in 1960 still was transmitted by telephone landlines that tied the country together on the coaxial cable. The signals moved on a "round-robin" from New York to west of Chicago, with links in Iowa to the West Coast and to a "bottom" half of the robin that hooked up the South. The landline system would still operate well into the '70s before the networks and phone companies decided to place total confidence in "the birds," satellite communication.

Color television programming was rare, and few sets were in use in 1960. Color would phase in through the coming two decades until the early '80s, when black and white was a relic as arcane as an icebox or old-fashioned roller skates cinched up with skate keys. The most-watched programs were so-called adult westerns, namely, "Wagon Train" on NBC, starring John Wayne's best friend, Ward Bond, and "Gunsmoke" and "Have Gun—Will Travel" on CBS. Wayne and "the King," Clark Gable, soon to turn 59, were still turning out movie hits. Gable had just signed to star in Arthur Miller's screenplay *The Misfits*, with Marilyn Monroe, Montgomery Clift, and Eli Wallach.

Television, black-and-white to be sure, barely 14 years old, already had supplanted radio and was about to push aside the print media, newspapers and magazines, as the must-have, must-use, must-control sphere of influence in the realm of public opinion and propaganda. The key areas of coverage were the political news from Washington and a fulminating civil rights movement.

The lid was ready to come off a now tremulous Black America in a year that would feature marches, demonstrations, and a new addition to the lexicon, "sit-ins." The young medium's impact on news, politics, and the culture was evident in the conduct of politics in this election year. Both announced candidates of the major parties were young men, born in the 20th century, tempered by their service as junior naval officers in World War II, and, in their early thirties, career politicians after the war as members of the House before moving up to the Senate.

Richard M. Nixon, the 47-year-old presumed Republican nominee in this final year of Dwight D. Eisenhower's presidency, likely would face 43-year-old Massachusetts Democratic senator John F. Kennedy. Money, big money backed by powerful interests, would fuel both campaigns. And both men would stake their chances on how well they could use television appearances in the news cycle, in live speeches, and, down the stretch, in the first televised head-to-head debates in the history of presidential politics.

Television news organizations still relied on 16-millimeter film coverage. The networks were sending out crews from their key bases in New York, Chicago, and Los Angeles to bring back the news. They would film the story earlier in the day; either drive back or, in certain cases, fly to affiliate stations to process the footage; edit "packages"; and then feed the finished product over telephone lines to the networks' evening newscasts.

By 1960, the key network television news operations were led by NBC, with "The Huntley-Brinkley Report," and CBS News, with anchorman Douglas Edwards. Walter Cronkite was assigned to his early-Sunday-evening documentary program "The Twentieth Century," and a thoroughly disgruntled Edward R. Murrow was preparing for his retirement to join the government if the Democrats won in November. The ABC News operation had been on life support from the beginning of television but had made the decision to devote heavy attention to sports coverage, to catch up to CBS and NBC.

Ed Scherick came to ABC's rescue as he had helped Halas and CBS before, this time with a company he called Sports Programs, Inc. His executive in charge was Chet Simmons. "We made a deal with ABC, which didn't have much of a sports presence, to acquire and produce sports for them. Eventually our company became the ABC Sports Department. That's how all of that started," Simmons said. "That was well before my involvement in professional football. Our involvement then essentially was college football."

The other key player in the new ABC Sports operation in 1960 was a 28-year-old program producer formerly of NBC who had never produced a sports telecast. His name was Roone Arledge. He would become the single most important innovator and catalyst for change in television history.

To this point, television had provided a passive, if not voyeuristic, window to events for the sports fan. Football and baseball games were televised with no more than three cameras, placed high and away from the action, not unlike faraway seats in the stands. Close-ups were few. Producers and directors were not likely to waste shots on close-ups of coaches or managers on the sidelines, since to do so might detract from getting the "big" picture.

It became apparent early that the hardest sports to televise were baseball, because the rhythm is languid and the action often happens in several places at once; hockey, because the puck is small and often gets lost on the ice; and golf, because the small ball and high skies make the shots hard to follow. Basketball was relatively easy, because it takes place in a small, confined area. The best was football, because the action is fast, easy to follow, and exciting, and it's similar to watching war, a skirmish on every play.

Everyone involved with sports in 1960 was paying close attention to the impending Winter Olympics in Squaw Valley, California, and the gamble CBS had undertaken as the first network to televise the games. CBS paid $50,000 for the privilege of airing 15 hours. The games would take place over the last two weeks of February. CBS then anted up $394,000 to televise 20 hours of the Summer Olympics from Rome in the last week of August and first eleven days of September.

Since satellites had not been launched yet, a CBS-hired courier had to transport videotapes of the action by car and get them loaded onto a jetliner outside Rome for the eight-hour flight to Idlewild International Airport, in New York. Then came the fun part. The tapes had to clear customs, and another courier had to drive them through street traffic from Queens to Manhattan to deliver them in time for the evening American audience.

Jim McManus, more familiar to CBS viewers as Jim McKay of "The Verdict Is Yours," would anchor the coverage from a studio in New York. It didn't always work, but McKay created order out of chaos in front of the camera, and when it worked, it caused a cultural revolution. America would have many new heroes, two in particular: a female sprinter from Chicago via Tennessee named Wilma Rudolph, and Cassius Clay, an 18-year-old glib, brash, exceptionally talented light heavyweight boxer from Louisville. Both were black and had come of age after the 1954 *Brown v. Board of Education* case struck down the segregation laws that pervaded so much of American society.

The country also would watch the fortunes of an integrated U.S. Olympic basketball team that meshed the exceptional talents of black athletes Oscar Robertson, Walter Bellamy, and Bob Boozer with white stars Jerry West, Jerry Lucas, Terry Dischinger, and Darrall Imhoff. Their coach was Pete Rozelle's friend and mentor Pete Newell.

Meanwhile in Miami, the National Football League owners were able to conduct their business with little to no media coverage, let alone surveillance. Television news directors were not about to place crews on a costly stakeout that could last for who knew how long. Just a few reporters were on hand. "We were stuck at the Kenilworth Hotel in Bal Harbour, which was Arthur Godfrey's old place," recalled venerable *Miami Herald* sports columnist Edwin Pope. "I think I was the only person who covered it quote-unquote 'end to end.'"

Had Ed Pope been able to get access to the proceedings in the meeting room, he would have witnessed perhaps the closest thing to a papal conclave that secular life in America could provide. Masters of league intrigue thrived in the top-secret atmosphere. Meeting details would be held close for decades among the occupants of that hotel room. "When you go back to get the league minutes of the Rozelle selection, it says, 'The commissioner's election was discussed.' Period. They don't tell you anything," Ernie Accorsi said.

The highly respected Accorsi, who started in pro football in 1970 as public relations director with the Baltimore Colts, worked in the league office from 1975 through '76; rejoined the Colts, where he became general manager; served as Cleveland Browns general manager from 1985 through 1992; and then joined the New York Giants in 1993 as assistant general manager to George Young before his promotion to senior vice president and general manager in 1998. He learned details of the 1960 commissioner's election from his boss in New York, the Giants' late co-owner Wellington Mara.

Those years with the Giants brought Accorsi into daily contact with Mara, who was 9 in 1925 when his father, Tim, founded the team. In 1930, the elder Mara gave his sons, Jack, 18, and Wellington, 14, co-ownership of the team. Well Mara attended every Giants game until his final illness and death from lymphoma in 2005 and never missed a league meeting. Accorsi became a close confidant of the Giants' patriarch. He mailed me a copy of the election ballot, "which was just a scrap of paper," and explained its meaning as Mara saw it during the Miami meeting that stretched into an impossible marathon week of vote after vote.

The candidates were Bert Bell's right-hand man, Austin Gunsel, who served as interim commissioner, and Marshall Leahy, attorney for the San Francisco 49ers, considered the favorite. Nine votes, a three-fourths majority, were needed for election. Gunsel had four solid votes at the outset: Carroll Rosenbloom for Baltimore, Frank McNamee for Philadelphia, Art Rooney for Pittsburgh, and Marshall for Washington. Leahy had a bloc that quickly became designated "the solid seven." Chicago's Papa Bear held the missing twelfth vote. "Halas passed on every ballot," Accorsi said.

"The word is if Leahy doesn't insist on moving the league office to San Francisco, he's got it," Accorsi said. Leahy had league precedent on his side. "You could move the league office to where you wanted."

When the NFL was founded, its first president, Joe Carr, set up shop in Columbus, Ohio, for one good reason. He lived there. His successor, Elmer Layden, took office as the first commissioner in 1941 and set up shop in Chicago, under the watchful eye of Halas. He lived there. That honeymoon had long ended by 1945 when Halas, tired of Layden's lusterless rule, maneuvered the choice of his pal Bert Bell.

"Bell had the commissioner's office in Philly because that's where he lived," Accorsi said. "Even though Rozelle is given credit for moving the office to New York, the league must have known it had to move it there."

After four ballots, with Pittsburgh now in his camp, Leahy was stuck at eight, while Gunsel retained the three votes of Baltimore, Philadelphia, and Washington. League founder George Halas, with the deciding ninth vote, held fast, passing. There was a theory that the two controlling players in the meeting room from the outset were Halas and Accorsi's former boss with the Baltimore Colts, Carroll Rosenbloom. "He had an overwhelming personality, and he liked to get things done," said Carroll Rosenbloom's son Steve in 2006. "He fit right in. He played football at Penn when it was a very good team. Having Bert Bell as his friend and mentor helped. He jumped right in there."

Here's how it evolved. On the fifth ballot, the three Gunsel votes led by Rosenbloom, who had passed earlier in the round, switched to Detroit Lions owner Edwin Anderson, as did Gunsel backers

McNamee of Philadelphia and Marshall in Washington. The other eight held fast for Leahy as Halas passed again.

Then, on the sixth ballot, Rosenbloom's faction switched to his respected general manager, Don Kellett, and Rooney brought Pittsburgh back into the Eastern bloc. "Kellett was basically as close to Rozelle as you could get in personality, class, and PR vision," Accorsi said.

A source familiar with the situation said of Kellett, "Everybody admired him, but people didn't trust Rosenbloom. Half the league thought Rosenbloom was trying to sabotage Kellett because he was jealous of him. The other half thought, 'We better not let Kellett in there, because Rosenbloom's gonna influence the commissioner's position.'"

The Colts' owner finally dropped his Kellett support after the 20th ballot and switched back to Gunsel. "It went on for days. It was stalemated," Mike Brown said. Holding on to that deciding vote, Halas continued to pass.

"The basic problem was the owners could not agree on anybody," respected senior NFL writer Bob Oates said. "There were various factions promoting various people, and they couldn't come close to getting an agreement."

"The job was even offered to my dad," Mike Brown recalled. "He turned it down jocularly. He didn't want to do that if he could."

"My father was a businessman, unlike many of the other owners," Steve Rosenbloom said. "He was a good negotiator and lobbyist, so to speak. At those meetings, like everyplace else, more gets done in the hallway than inside the boardroom." As a businessman, Carroll Rosenbloom hated to waste time. He wanted to push toward a decision. "They were stuck between stupid and somewhere. This could have gone on for a long time," Steve Rosenbloom said.

After a week and 22 rounds of balloting, tempers had frayed. By then, the whole thing was beginning to resemble the chaotic 1924 Democratic Convention, which stretched to 103 ballots before the party turned to compromise candidate John W. Davis, of West Virginia. Davis would lose in November to President Calvin Coolidge.

"My dad, at the end—it really was him—came up with the idea that they ought to pick Pete Rozelle," Brown said.

"He was like a fellow that decides to run for office for the first time: he hadn't offended anybody yet. There was no baggage," Steve Rosenbloom said. "I figured, they said, 'OK, we'll go with this guy.' "

"Pete was considered to be so young, but my dad argued that he would grow into the job. He talked to Wellington, and then they went out and got Dan Reeves. I think they put the inquiry to Pete in the men's room."

"Everybody who knew Rozelle liked him," Oates said. "He got along with everybody. He was 33 when he was named commissioner, but they all liked and respected him."

"It took him by surprise. He was said to have made comments like, 'Maybe in the long run it would be my goal in life.' They pushed it, and they got it through," Brown said. "Dad had a remarkable eye for people. He just had the ability to weigh people's characters and abilities. He saw an exceptional, but young, talent in Pete Rozelle. It certainly proved out that he was every bit of that. It was a marvelous choice. There couldn't have been a better choice."

Before he would accept the offer, Rozelle made a request. "He wanted to go upstairs to talk to his wife and tell her," Mike Brown said. "Today that would be the custom. In those days, that was not the norm. You made the decision without talking to her."

When he returned a few minutes later with Jane's blessing, Paul Brown, Mara, and Reeves sent him to the men's room off the lobby to wait for what they were certain would be his election. They instructed him to wash his hands every time somebody came inside to avoid drawing suspicion. He waited and waited, and waited, and washed and washed, and washed. Thirty-five times in all over the next half hour, by his own recollection.

"Pete won on the 23rd ballot. The 24th and last ballot, after the commissioner was chosen, was for treasurer, and Gunsel got that," Accorsi said. "Rozelle on that last ballot was unanimous except for Halas." The league founder passed on each ballot taken, 23 for commissioner and 1 for treasurer, 24 in all.

Then, according to Michael MacCambridge in his league history, *America's Game*, Carroll Rosenbloom entered the men's room, extended his hand, and said, "Hello, Mr. Commissioner."

"When he came back, he was a little bit flustered and unsure of himself, which is understandable," Mike Brown remembered. "He went from that as the years went along to just being marvelous up there."

The new commissioner took a deep breath to overcome the nerves and then won over the owners when he said after his washroom ordeal, "I can honestly say that I come to you with clean hands."

The meeting was recessed, and Rozelle was whisked to an impromptu press conference attended by a few print journalists, among them Ed Pope, who had spent the entire week waiting for news to break. "It was probably the most boring assignment," he said.

Fortuitously for history and the public record, Louis Effrat, of the *New York Times*, happened to be there. Normally a baseball writer, Effrat, on this day a month before spring training commenced, was pressed into service on this biggest football story in years, a story so important that it rated a page-1 slot under the heading "Ram Official Heads Pro Football League" the following morning, January 27. Next to a picture of the proposed World Trade Center, a $250 million project on 13½ acres of prized land at the bottom of Manhattan, the story ran for four paragraphs before it jumped inside to the sports section on page 37.

In the third paragraph, Effrat wrote that the owners elected "the soft-spoken" Rozelle to a three-year term at an annual $50,000 salary. Next, Effrat reported that the new commissioner said he "eventually" would move his headquarters to New York.

Rozelle displayed an adroit sense of public relations moments later when he dropped an olive branch to the rival, saying the two leagues "will get along if there is a mutual respect of contracts." Then he fired a shot across the American Football League bow when he stressed that he was in favor of the Halas expansion plan to Dallas and Minneapolis–St. Paul and announced that the plan would be the first item on his agenda as commissioner when the meeting resumed after the press conference.

"I would be silly to consider myself anything but a compromise candidate," Rozelle told the reporters. "I hope I will be able to live up to the confidence that has been shown in me."

Away from the National Football League, Rozelle was a virtual unknown. Until this moment, his sphere of influence stretched no farther than the limits of Los Angeles County, and he wasn't that familiar a figure there either. "I didn't know him very well. I had an occasional beer with him," recalled Keith Jackson a half century after they met. But, like so many other West Coast writers and broadcasters, Jackson immediately noticed the young man's awareness and ambition. "He was very active, and he knew who to talk to and who not to talk to."

As Rams beat writer for the *Los Angeles Examiner* before he switched to the *Times*, Bob Oates had closely observed Rozelle since Tex Schramm hired him to replace Tex Maule as the Rams' director of publicity in 1952 at age 26 after he put USF on the athletic map. "No question about it, he was a very bright guy. He always finished what he started as soon as he could. When he was given an assignment, he got the thing in his head and went ahead and did it," Oates said.

As far as Rozelle's selection as commissioner, Oates's evaluation is terse and incisive. "They didn't know they were getting a man as good as this one. He is far and away the best commissioner we've had in America in any sport."

TWO

THE GOLDEN BOY FROM THE GOLDEN STATE

"Pete got straight As and never cracked a book. I don't know how he did it. He had tremendous recall. I don't remember him studying for anything."

—DICK ROZELLE, 2006

*B*y the mid-1920s, the Los Angeles basin had begun to resemble in outline form the megalopolis that Pete Rozelle would know all his life. The first wave of the 20th-century migration was well under way. People flocked to Los Angeles and Southern California by the tens of thousands, especially from the Midwest. An exceptional, year-round sunny climate stimulated the good life, as it provided opportunity. Oil was discovered in L.A. in 1893. By 1926, California was the fourth-largest oil producer in the world, helping to fuel the automotive revolution. Everything literally was coming up roses, or—better yet, in the immortal words of the late Al McGuire—seashells and balloons.

In 1913, an Irish immigrant named William Mulholland, who rose from ditchdigger to superintendent of the Los Angeles Water Company, dedicated the system that would make L.A. the second most populous urban area in America, behind New York. Mulholland's Los Angeles Aqueduct, after much political wrangling and above- and below-board dealing in the California legislature and other governmental areas, would import water overland 150 miles from the Colorado River to support an area whose population by 2007 would surpass twelve million people. Most important, by owning its water, Los Angeles could become a great city to rival New York, Chicago, Philadelphia, Boston, and St. Louis back east, let alone its smaller but influential rival 400 miles to the north, San Francisco.

With water came the largest sustained growth spurt in American history, one that rolled unabated into the 21st century. By 1926, the population of the City of Angels itself had surged from the 1920 census figure, a tidy 576,673, to something approaching a million. By the 1930 census, 1,238,048 persons lived inside the city's 498 square miles among the 2,208,492 residents of Los Angeles County.

"Pete was born March 1, 1926. My birthday was August 12, 1929," said his brother, Dick, in 2006. Alvin Ray Rozelle's arrival into the world on the first day of March midway through the Roaring Twenties was totally appropriate considering his family's roots in the corn country of the Midwest. Well before Hazel Healey and her parents left Mt. Morris, Illinois, a hundred miles west of Chicago, and Raymond Rozelle's French Huguenot forebears made the westward trek from Indiana, cracker-barrel philosophers were quick to remind anyone gathered around the general store's hot stove on snowy winter days that "March roars in like a lion and goes out like a lamb." This boy would not be one to roar, but he would be king of his jungle in adult life as he placed an indelible stamp on a game that became America's richest and most popular sport, football.

"My grandparents came to California in 1894, a pioneer family," Dick Rozelle said. About 75,000 people were scattered through Los Angeles proper in a state that by 1894 had surpassed the one-million mark. "My father was born in Lynwood on a ranch on the Los Angeles River in 1903," Dick said. The Los Angeles River did not become a cemented flood-control sluice until the late '30s when it gained notoriety as moviedom's outdoor set for high-speed car chases.

Speaking of films and Hollywood, just a few hundred people lived in that enclave west of downtown L.A. in the early 20th century. By the time the United States entered World War I, what would become the most glamorous industry yet imagined, motion pictures, would establish permanent roots that would make Hollywood an image, more a state of mind than a place in fact. By then, Los Angeles was the center of the fast-developing aviation industry.

Ray Rozelle enlisted in the navy in World War I and was sent to boot camp at Goat Island, in San Francisco Bay, later renamed Treasure Island. Before he could be shipped out, the war ended. Back in L.A., he settled into a career working in the food markets and groceries. Ray Rozelle and Hazel Healey were married on July 22, 1924. Ray was described as a well-mannered gentleman as well as a gentle man. Hazel, as her granddaughter Anne Marie told Michael Mac-Cambridge, had a dramatic flair and was "an actress without being an actress."

Alvin, their first of two sons, arrived a year and a half later. "We were born in South Gate, just a little southeast of L.A.," Dick Rozelle said, in what "apparently was the only hospital in the area. We went to the local schools in the next town down, Lynwood." Lynwood was one of the first true suburbs in the West, with individually contracted homes, not tract housing. The Rozelles rented a two-bedroom stucco house at 3205 Lynwood Road.

Just how did Alvin become Pete? Early in Alvin's life, an uncle decided that the boy should be called Pete, the name he carried the rest of his life. "There were two different stories. I think I have the accurate one," Dick Rozelle said. One story credited the nicknaming to Ray's brother, their uncle Glenn, a superb athlete at Occidental College, in Malibu. "Actually, it was an uncle on my mom's side, her brother, whose nickname was Fritz. Fritz didn't think Alvin was a good name for him when he was a baby, and he encouraged Mom and Dad to call him Pete," Dick said. "I used to call myself Re-Pete."

About the time Pete was born, Ray opened his own store, Pacific Market, the first grocery in Lynwood. As one of the pioneer residents of the community, the senior Rozelle figured to have a lot of support and plenty of customers. America was swept along in an unprecedented boom, to the point that President Calvin Coolidge proclaimed, "The chief business of the American people is business." His presumed successor, Herbert Hoover, won in 1928 on the slogan "Two chickens in every pot, and a car in every garage."

The great boom went kerflooey when the stock market crashed on October 24, 1929. Nearly everybody was cleaned out. "Dad had friends, customers, who were out of work and didn't have any money," Dick Rozelle said. "He extended credit to a lot of people. Soon they couldn't repay him. Then, he couldn't pay the bills for the groceries to the vendors. The business failed, and he lost the market. I was only a baby. He didn't talk much about it. You can imagine what a terrible blow it was to him."

Life for the Rozelles, as for most other Americans, was a daily struggle in the Depression, but Ray Rozelle had to pay the rent and the other bills and put food on the table. So, he went back to the markets as an hourly worker. He also worked another job for a time, filling orders at an Alcoa plant for 85 cents an hour. Every penny counted for the Rozelles and so many other middle- to lower-middle-class families.

Pete was seven and Dick three and a half when, on the late afternoon of March 10, 1933, an earthquake estimated at 6.3 on the Richter scale rocked through southern Los Angeles County. Since most of the structures there were unsupported masonry, 90 percent of the buildings in the Compton business district had to be razed. "Dad was at work that day in a market in Long Beach. A lot of that stuff came down," Dick Rozelle said. Had it struck during school hours, thousands of children might have been killed. As it was, 102 persons died. Damages ran to the hundreds of millions, and the state changed the building code to upgrade seismic standards in all public structures.

"Dad continued working in the markets during my childhood," Dick Rozelle recalled. "He would be gone in the morning before I got up and come home late. The 12- or 14-hour day was not unusual. Because I never saw him, I did not get to know my dad that well, but he and Pete formed quite a bond. Pete always credited our dad with so much of his character."

The boys did their part as well to help the family. They mowed lawns in the neighborhood as a team. As John Fortunato reported in *Commissioner*, Pete pushed the mower and Dick worked the clippers, doing the weeding and edging. They earned $1.25 a lawn—75 cents for the front yard, half a dollar for the back. When their day was done, they stopped at a local soda fountain and treated themselves to milk shakes.

Lynwood was a hotbed of sports, which from Pete Rozelle's early days dominated his attention. "Two of the greatest stadiums in the world, the Los Angeles Memorial Coliseum, which was built for the 1932 Olympics, and the Rose Bowl, were in our area. We grew up in the shadow of those edifices," Dick Rozelle said. "Pete was influenced by coaches by the time he got to junior high school. They were great role models, and he worshipped them."

Pete found extra time to play games and watch them, especially football, because school for the straight-A student was an absolute snap. "He was so bright in English that in first or second grade they advanced him a grade," Dick recalled. "That was good news, but bad in that Pete was not very well developed physically when he was pushed a grade ahead. He was shorter than his classmates at Lynwood Junior High."

"Pete's uncle Joe Rozelle was my coach in junior high school," said the Brooklyn Dodgers' Hall of Fame center fielder Edwin "Duke" Snider, who went to Lynwood Junior High's rival, Enterprise. "I got to know Pete a little more because of that." They competed against each other in a five-team league and in summer programs.

"We played organized touch football in junior high school," Snider said. "In this one game, I didn't see Pete run over to tell the coach at Lynwood, Bill Schleibaum, who became one of his officials in the NFL, that our side had a 'hideout' play.

"We would send in two substitutions and three would go out, while the other guy stayed on the sidelines. Then I'd throw a pass to the 'hideout,'" Snider said. "When he saw what was happening, Pete told Schleibaum, and they ran over and stopped it."

As much of a gamer as Rozelle was, the scrawny 14-year-old was the shortest boy on the team. Lynwood principal William Jones told the senior Rozelles that Pete was so far ahead in school that he could afford to miss a year to build up his physique, working the earth. So, Ray and Hazel wrote to a relative who owned a ranch in Central California. Pete worked in the fields through the 1940–41 school year and practiced his shot after hours on a hoop attached to the barn. He came home the next fall, filled out, now a muscular six-footer and a deadeye on the basketball court.

When Rozelle enrolled at Compton High in the fall of '41, there to greet him was his junior high basketball rival and pal Snider, now a varsity teammate. To hold down travel costs in spread-out L.A. County with gas rationing during World War II, four area high schools formed the Long Beach–Compton League. They were Compton and three Long Beach schools: Poly, Jordan, and Wilson. Every Friday night, they met in doubleheaders at the Long Beach Municipal Auditorium. The season ended in a championship matchup between Compton, with a lineup of six-footers, and Long Beach Poly, with a monstrous-for-that-era front line that averaged 6'6".

"We worked Pete on a little baseline shot. Pete was making them lights-out in the warm-up," Snider said. "Then we got into the game and he rimmed the first seven shots, and we stopped giving him the ball! We used to kid him about it." Snider laughed at the memory. After the basketball season, Snider turned to his best sport, baseball, and the big-league scouts flocked to watch him play.

When he didn't hold down the first singles and first doubles slots on the tennis team, Rozelle hung around the diamond to watch his pal, the Duke. "He wrote for the school newspaper at Lynwood and then at Compton. Then he wrote high school sports on weekends for the *Long Beach Press-Telegram*," Snider said in 2005.

"He had Duke Snider to write about in school. I think Pete even had his column in junior high and high school," Dick Rozelle said. "He was so into sports. Journalism was the foundation for his career. His goal was to be sports editor of the *L.A. Times.*"

Pete also displayed political acumen from the outset, making friends instead of enemies, avoiding playground fights as he played the role of conciliator. He was so well liked that his classmates at Lynwood Junior High elected him 10th-grade class president for the

1941–42 school year. Because Compton was part of California's junior college system, its school system was set up on a 6-4-4 basis: 6 years of elementary school, 4 years from grades 7 through 10, and 4 more years comprising high school grades 11 and 12 and grades 13 and 14 in college, with two years' credit to finish undergraduate requirements.

At the end of their high school days, Pete graduated with high honors, and Duke got the girl, Beverly Null, a longtime schoolmate and friend of Pete's before she met her husband. Pete and Bev did not date, but they belonged to a group of young people who hung around together. One of their group outings was to the Clearwater ice rink. "Pete was first out on the ice. It was watery, and he hit a rough patch," Bev Snider recalled. "He landed on his face and knocked out his two front teeth. He wouldn't smile, of course, until he got new teeth in. That incident killed the whole party, so everyone came over to my house. He always remembered that when he wrote to me."

By the end of high school, it was obvious that Duke and Bev were a special couple. They married on October 25, 1947, and went on to have four children, two boys and two girls, and 10 grandchildren. "Pete was a wonderful friend. We wrote occasional letters through the years. He wrote his always in small caps. He would sign them 'Alvin,'" Bev Snider said.

Pete Rozelle registered for the draft on his 18th birthday, March 1, 1944. The armed forces in early 1944 were still waiting until school was out before they sent the greetings letter for the induction physical. But there was no escaping service, so Rozelle signed up for the navy to head for boot camp as soon as Compton High's band finished playing "Pomp and Circumstance" for the graduating 12th graders of the class of '44. A year later, so many servicemen had been killed in action in Europe and the Pacific that the armed forces were grabbing boys the day they turned 18, regardless of class standing, as schools granted immediate diplomas.

Pete was inducted into the navy on July 28, 1944. After boot camp in San Diego, Seaman Rozelle, a skilled typist, was assigned to clerical duty aboard the Pacific Fleet oiler USS *Guardoqui*, to write and edit the ship's newsletter. Petty Officer Rozelle served through the duration of the war without seeing combat. He moved up steadily through the ranks, leaving service at the rating yeoman second class.

One of his duties as the only yeoman aboard ship was to assign thirsty and horny sailors who had been at sea for months to one of two liberty sections, port and starboard, when the ship finally made port. In the days leading up to their arrival, he was swarmed by young men begging to get ashore in the first section the minute liberty call was sounded. It was his first taste of power. He told high school friend Max Patterson, "That's the first time in my life I had any power. And I loved it." A few months after the war, the *Guardoqui* made a final cruise that took her through the Panama Canal to Mobile Bay, where the ship was decommissioned and Rozelle received his discharge in May 1946.

"When you turned 18, if you could see thunder and lightning, you got drafted," Duke Snider recalled. "I played one year of pro baseball before I went in. I started in Class B with the Brooklyn organization. I managed to get in a year of baseball before I went into the navy for a year and a half, just like Pete."

Sometime during his period of service, Pete took up the habit that would stick with him the rest of his life. "He didn't smoke in high school," Dick Rozelle recalled. "He started when he was on that ship. When he came back to Compton Junior College, he did smoke, and as the years went by, he smoked more and more heavily."

Before the Surgeon General's Report in 1964 warned against the dangers of tobacco, cigarette smoking was regarded as a rite of passage to adulthood. Before World War I, tobacco users generally smoked pipes or cigars. Few cigarettes were "tailor made," and most who smoked cigarettes rolled their own. The habit was imported into America en masse after World War I when the doughboys returned. By the '20s, most everybody was smoking. The tobacco companies—R. J. Reynolds with Camels, American Tobacco with Lucky Strikes, Liggett and Myers with Chesterfields, and Philip Morris—stepped up mass production and packaging to keep up with demand. They launched all-out advertising campaigns in the newspapers and magazines, on billboards, and on radio, and business took off. Then, during World War II, the tobacco companies locked in their soldier-sailor-airmen customers with free cigarettes in the combat zones and in military hospitals for the wounded men. That further spread the habit to the home front.

Cigarettes were "sophisticated" and "romantic," a symbol of battlefield toughness and friendship. In countless war movies, the last thing a barely breathing soldier would get from a buddy before he died was a couple of drags on a butt. For Pete Rozelle, cigarettes became a three- to four-pack-a-day companion.

"Obviously, it was not healthy, but I think everyone looks at it from the perspective of 2006, where smoking is not allowed and fewer people smoke. Back in those days, everyone, I mean everyone, pretty much smoked, and smoked continuously," his daughter, Anne Marie Rozelle Bratton, said. "You could smoke in restaurants, movies, airplanes, school, and things like that. I don't think anyone then realized how bad it was."

A cigarette filled a conversation hole, as seen on film with a Humphrey Bogart and in real life. For a Rozelle and millions of other decision makers, lighting up gave them a vital moment. "When people would ask him a tough question, he took the opportunity to light up and take a drag as he thought about it, giving him just a few more seconds to sort of think of an answer, make sure he had the right answer, and then deliver," Anne Marie Bratton said. "In so many ways, it was a tension reliever, but an aid in other areas."

The still 19-year-old Snider was discharged on June 26, 1946, in time to resume his baseball career at Class AA Fort Worth in the Texas League. He joined the Dodgers in 1947, was farmed out in June to AAA St. Paul in the American Association, started 1948 at AAA Montreal, and was recalled at midseason with future Hall of Fame catcher Roy Campanella, who came from St. Paul. In 1949, Brooklyn manager Burt Shotton switched center fielder Carl Furillo to right and moved Snider to center field, the springboard to his Hall of Fame career. "He has a picture-perfect swing and legs like steel springs," commented the Mahatma, Brooklyn owner Branch Rickey.

"When I got inducted into the Hall of Fame in 1980, two commissioners attended: the baseball commissioner and football commissioner," Snider said. "Pete brought his uncle Joe and my former football coach Bill Schleibaum to Cooperstown. It made a special time even better." The man beloved in Brooklyn as the Duke of Flatbush offered this touchstone to his friend: "I consider it a privilege to have been on the same path with Pete in those years. He certainly was a dear friend and great supporter of mine."

Less than a month after the Cleveland Rams beat the Washington Redskins 15–14 to win the 1945 NFL title in the bitter cold of Municipal Stadium, owner Dan Reeves pulled up stakes, and the Rams became the first established professional team in any sport to move to the West Coast. Bill John, the Rams' business manager, was one of the few who came west from Cleveland to set up shop at the club's new offices on West Beverly Boulevard. They needed help.

After Rozelle's discharge in May 1946, shipmate Ted Heller invited him to come home to Chicago for a few days before heading west to Los Angeles. In Chicago, Heller and his girlfriend fixed up Pete with a local girl named Jane Coupe. She was a quiet girl. A 1945 graduate of Senn High School on the Far North Side, close to George Halas's home in the Edgewater Apartments, Jane worked in the Loop at Marshall Field's, as did many young women who weren't going on to college.

"They went on a blind date and he was smitten," brother Dick said. "She was a quite pretty blond. Pete then returned home to Lynwood and started back to school at Compton Junior College that fall." At Compton, he sewed up a job as Compton's athletic publicity director. Then, he got his first look at pro football from the inside when he paid a call on Bill John and got hired, along with his friend John Lehman, to work at the team's training camp. Back in Chicago, Jane had fallen for the bright, polite young Californian.

For their first L.A. training camp, Reeves set up shop at Compton JC. The eager Rozelle, helping with publicity, worked so hard that Bill John questioned his hours. "Pay me whatever you want to pay me," Rozelle said. By the end of the summer, John agreed to pay him an extra $50 a game to assemble the Rams' programs.

One afternoon, *Sport* magazine sent a photographer to Compton for a cover shot of returning war hero Tom Harmon for the December 1946 issue. Using a fan-in-the-stands motif, the photographer posed the 1940 Heisman Trophy winner in full football gear holding a helmet in his left hand, with his right hand covering both hands of his wife, starlet Elyse Knox Harmon. Seated directly behind Mrs. Harmon is none other than Pete Rozelle, his face partially obscured by her flowing hair.

The highlight of the summer of '46 for Rozelle was his return to Chicago. John Lehman invited him along for the four-day drive on Route 66 in his battered prewar Dodge to see *Chicago Tribune* Charities' annual football-season kickoff, the College All-Star Game. "They had no tickets [but] Pete had a connection with the Rams and somehow finagled four seats to the game," Dick Rozelle said. "The game turned out to be the least significant thing about that trip back to Chicago. He could see Jane again. They had been writing all summer since they met."

Chicago's 1946 population was 3,600,000, nearly a million more than would live inside the city limits a half century later. Unlike spread-out Los Angeles, Chicago covered half of L.A.'s 500-square-mile area in congested, tightly organized ethnic neighborhoods populated by huge clusters of Irish, Italians, Bohemians, Jews, Germans, Greeks, and Eastern Europeans, including the largest Polish population outside Warsaw.

The fastest-growing group was the blacks (then called Negroes, and later African Americans), who lived in their own racially defined sector on the South Side that ran inside the north-south railroad corridor to a southern border on the edge of the University of Chicago. Chicago was considered the capital of Black America as New York's Harlem was its soul. Jazz was the music of choice, in the clubs and on the radio. Within two decades, the blacks, bursting at the seams of their South Side ghetto, would take over most of the old Jewish and Irish West Side and more of the South Side as longtime white ethnics fled to the suburbs.

To live lean, Rozelle and Lehman stayed that week at the Evanston YMCA, conveniently located in the leafy suburb of large homes mixed with two-flats and four-flats. Everything was close by. It was a five-minute walk to Evanston's downtown business district and an additional quarter hour, tops, to the Northwestern campus, where the all-stars stayed. Dyche Stadium, where the players worked out, was five minutes away to the north on the el, and the Loop, to the south in downtown Chicago, was a half-hour el ride, each trip a nickel.

By day, he watched all-stars coach Alvin "Bo" McMillin drill his 66-man squad on the practice field by Dyche Stadium. This team was loaded with returning GIs, among them, Northwestern's great passer Otto Graham; halfback Elroy Hirsch, of Wisconsin and Michigan; and Hirsch's Wisconsin teammate, fullback Pat Harder. Each man would be part of Rozelle's universe when he became commissioner: Graham as coach of the Washington Redskins, Hirsch as successor to Rozelle in the role of Rams general manager, and Harder as an NFL official. Harder would join the Chicago Cardinals after the game. Graham and Hirsch spurned the National Football League for the new All-America Football Conference, Graham going to the Cleveland Browns and Hirsch to the Chicago Rockets.

Another man Rozelle met that week would become one of his closest confidants over the rest of his career. The Rockets' new equipment manager, Bill Granholm, grew up with Hirsch in Wausau, Wisconsin. Football would be a snap after what "Granny" endured on D-day, June 6, 1944. "He was a GI, landed at Normandy," Ernie Accorsi said. "Granny told me they had 30 tanks, and 29 of them sank in the landing. He lost his unit and found them four or five days later." Granholm would come west with Hirsch when he joined the Rams in 1949 and would go east with Rozelle to New York when he became commissioner.

By night, Pete spent every available hour with Jane, be it at her family's home in Rogers Park on the city's Far North Side 20 minutes south of the Evanston Y, or enjoying the bustling city with her. Jane fixed up Lehman with a girlfriend of hers named Donna. "They double-dated the few days they were there," brother Dick said, "and they went to the All-Star Game." Both couples would marry within two years.

Before Pete and Lehman left for Chicago and the All-Star Game, Dick gave them a scouting report based on a game he had seen the previous December in the Coliseum when Fleet City, led by Buddy

Young, beat El Toro and Elroy Hirsch 48–25 to win the armed services championship. Young was headed back to Illinois for his senior season and would not play. "You gotta watch this guy Hirsch, he's really good," Dick told Pete.

On Friday night, August 23, the two couples and 97,376 other fans watched this tough all-star team manhandle the Rams 16–0 at Soldier Field. Hirsch, nicknamed "Crazylegs" back at Wisconsin for his running style, which, according to *Chicago Daily News* sportswriter Francis J. Powers, resembled someone going six ways at once, was the game's Most Valuable Player.

Hirsch opened the scoring in the first quarter when he took a handoff, tore around the left end, and sprinted 68 yards for a touchdown. Then, in the third quarter, Graham dropped back from the all-stars' 38 and threw downfield to Hirsch, who made the catch in stride and went in for the score, a 62-yard touchdown play. Harder kicked both extra points. The all-stars added 2 more points when Yale's Paul Walker brought down Kenny Washington in the end zone for a safety.

After the game, realizing he had missed his younger brother's 17th birthday nine days earlier on August 12th, Pete stopped by a Western Union office. "Pete, as thoughtful as he was, sent me a telegram as you did in those days," Dick said. "You paid by the word, so it was short. It read, 'Happy Birthday, Dick. You're right. Hirsch is great. Pete.' I got satisfaction. My scouting report impressed my brother."

That was the football game. Then there was the matter of the heart. By the time the game was over, the usually unflappable Rozelle no longer was infatuated. He was madly and irrevocably in love with this striking 19-year-old blond named Jane who was anything but plain. Shortly after he got back home, Pete asked Jane to move to California. "Jane and Donna came west, Jane married Pete, and Donna married John Lehman," Dick said. When they got married in 1948, the Rozelles set up housekeeping in the Noe Valley area of San Francisco while he finished his college education at the University of San Francisco and got his first real hands-on experience running an important sports publicity department, albeit in this case, a one-man shop.

They all were young. Rozelle's friend and ally, basketball coach Pete Newell, turned 33 in 1948. Like so many other men, he had to put his life on hold while he went to war. From 1942 to 1946, he served as a naval officer, getting released in time to launch his college coaching career at USF. "None of us made any money," Newell said. "Pete Rozelle went to school on the GI Bill and was paid $75 a month to be athletic publicist. In later years, we'd go someplace and he'd say, 'Look at that guy there [pointing at Newell]. He paid me only $75 a month!' I would come back, 'Don't forget, you got tuition and books.' "

"We were all close at USF. We had some great people there. Pierre Salinger was another one," Newell said. "He and Pete put out the football book. Then Pierre went to work for the *Chronicle*. Pierre had the great idea of getting arrested in the small towns of California. He got put into seven or eight jails. Then he wrote about it in a weekly series and got a national award."

Newell introduced Rozelle to another man who would play an important role in his development. His name was Ken Macker, and like his younger friend Rozelle, he was developing a career in business in a field called public relations.

The big break for Rozelle and coach Newell came in 1949 when the USF Dons got asked to the National Invitation Tournament in New York's Madison Square Garden. The NIT expanded from eight to twelve teams that year, but the unknown Dons didn't mind. "We were the last team picked," Newell said. The NIT in those days was every bit as prestigious as the NCAA tournament, if not more prestigious. "That was the biggest step he could have made in his life other than being commissioner," Newell said. "He got the chance to meet all those New York writers and the national press. There was no TV to speak of, and writers were the essence. He did a hell of a job and moved among those writers like he knew them all his life."

The tournament itself became a tightrope walk for the Dons. Newell had them ready with his disciplined system featuring tight, hounding, man-to-man defense and precise patterns on offense. "I've always felt that the 1949 NIT was the strongest college tournament ever because the players were service veterans, 25–26 years of age, older than the average NBA rookie," Newell said in a 2004 *American Basketball Quarterly* profile.

After routing Manhattan 68–43, USF sneaked past tough Utah 64–63 and then stifled Bowling Green 49–39 in the semifinals to reach the title game against Loyola of Chicago. It was revealed later in the 1951 gambling-fix scandal that Loyola's path to the championship game was eased, as Adolph Rupp's top three players—Alex Groza, Ralph Beard, and Dale Barnstable—admitted they took $500 each to dump their quarter-final game with the Ramblers, losing 61–56.

In the final, tournament MVP Dan Lofgran led San Francisco to a 48–47 squeaker over Loyola for the title, a delicious irony, since Lofgran was one of the players Newell was scouting when he met Rozelle in that 1948 junior college tournament at Compton. "The New York press was very good to Pete. He got us a lot more ink there than some of the better-known teams," Newell said.

Rozelle and Newell parted company in 1950 when Michigan State athletic director Ralph Young lured Newell with a $12,500 salary and the opportunity to build MSU's nascent program as the school formally entered the Big Ten. Phil Woolpert, Newell's assistant and former college teammate at Loyola of Los Angeles before it became Loyola-Marymount, took over as head coach. Rozelle had plenty on his hands, turning his public relations skills to the school's outstanding but unheralded football team and coach Joe Kuharich. "He was a hell of a nice guy who really loved football," said Gino Marchetti, a tackle at USF who would gain NFL fame with the Colts at defensive end. "Pete did a really good job for the university and for Joe Kuharich. He was easy to get along with."

By 1951, Kuharich's San Francisco Dons were almost literally the best football team nobody ever heard of. This was a machine that overwhelmed nine opponents with an average scoring margin of 33–8 and a lone serious test. "I thought he was great. It wasn't easy playing for Joe, because he really worked your butt off," Marchetti said. "There were a couple of times at our training camp—where it was 115 degrees—that I was ready to go home. If all the running I did for Joe was put into a straight line, I'd have run halfway around the world. He played no favorites, and ballplayers respected that."

Home for the Dons was Kezar Stadium, at the southeast corner of Golden Gate Park, less than a mile down Stanyan Avenue from the USF campus. Eleven men who played for USF in 1950 and '51 made the NFL, nine from that 1951 team. Three of the Dons—running back Ollie Matson, defensive end Gino Marchetti, and offensive tackle Bob St. Clair—are in the Pro Football Hall of Fame. Guards Dick Stanfel and Lou "Red" Stephens were on the cusp of football's highest honor, and quarterback Ed Brown was esteemed by fellow teammates as the best long passer they'd ever seen in his service with the Chicago Bears and Pittsburgh Steelers. Linemen Mike Mergen, Merrill Peacock, and Ralph Thomas joined coach Kuharich with the Chicago Cardinals, where he landed in 1952. Defensive backs Roy Barni and Joe "Scooter" Scudero had fine careers in the NFL.

The game that affected Rozelle's future the most took place at tiny Randall's Island Stadium, in the East River, against still tough Fordham. Before the game, Rozelle took Marchetti and Ed Brown aside. "He told us, 'We're really going to push Ollie Matson for all-America. He has the best chance to make it. I thought you two should know that.' We were fine with that," Marchetti said in 2006. "Ollie had a great day, and he became our all-American."

"Ollie Matson had a big, big day in New York that put him at the top of the draft with the Chicago Cardinals," Pete Newell recalled. "By making sure people knew who Ollie was, Pete had a lot to do with Ollie getting the publicity he got."

"People" in this case included not only Red Smith and Jimmy Cannon but also America's most renowned sportswriter going back to the Golden Age of Sport in the '20s, Grantland Rice, still active and influential at age 72. Rozelle called on Rice at his Manhattan apartment, escorted him personally to the game, and took him back home after USF beat Fordham 32–26.

"The best player on our team never played professional football. He was Burl Toler, a linebacker," Marchetti said. Marchetti, Matson, and Toler were chosen to play in the College All-Star Game in Chicago in the summer of 1952. "Burl looked so good in training camp. Because our linebackers were all Big Ten guys, they put him at defensive end," Marchetti recalled. "He tore his knee up so bad that he was never able to play again." Rozelle never forgot him. When he became commissioner, he hired Toler as the league's first black official.

USF was so good that many teams would not schedule the Dons. At season's end, they could climb no higher than 14th in the polls. There was talk that the Orange Bowl Committee wanted to invite the Dons on the condition that they leave the two blacks on the roster, Matson and Toler, their two best players, at home. USF needed that bowl date to break even, but the school refused to sell out its players. Without the bowl game, the Jesuits who ran the university were left with only one choice. Drop football.

That final act settled it for Rozelle at his alma mater. Approaching 26, he was at the crossroads. Then came the call from the Rams' newly named general manager, Tex Schramm, in Los Angeles, who told Pete that the team's publicist, Hamilton "Tex" Maule, had decided to take a job with the relocated Dallas Texans, who left New York after hemorrhaging money competing against the Giants.

Rozelle would work directly for Rams owner Dan Reeves and Schramm, whom he knew from editing the team's programs before he headed north to USF. Best of all, Reeves and Schramm would give him hands-on experience in other areas besides his public relations duties, especially in the vital area of scouting.

Once again, as Dick Rozelle was fond of saying in regard to his older brother, "It's that old adage. What is success or luck? It's when preparation meets opportunity. Pete was always just sort of there. He didn't pursue them. They came to him."

THREE

GLAMOUR, GLITTER, AND GRIT: THE EDUCATION OF A YOUNG MAN

"Walter O'Malley got a lot of credit for westernizing pro sports in 1952, but Dan Reeves was there a decade before to try out the territory."

—DICK ENBERG, NBC AND CBS SPORTS

"*W*hen Pete Rozelle was the PR guy at the University of San Francisco, if he was making $4,000 a year, it probably was a big year," Bob Fouts recalled. Fouts, the father of Hall of Fame quarterback Dan, called football for Rozelle's University of San Francisco Dons before he began telecasting 49ers games. When the impoverished USF football program folded after its unbeaten, untied, uninvited 1951 season, Rozelle knew it was time to move on.

Many of the athletes and coaches Rozelle plugged and promoted at USF and before that at Compton Junior College were now big stars. Rozelle's pal Duke Snider of the Brooklyn Dodgers by 1952 was baseball's top center fielder, engaged in close competition with a pair of 21-

year-old New York phenoms, the Yankees' Mickey Mantle and, before he left for service early in the '52 season, the Giants' Willie Mays.

Compton College's star running backs during Rozelle's time, Joe Perry and Hugh McElhenny, would be reunited in the 49ers backfield in '52. Perry, the premier fullback in the National Football League, joined the 49ers in 1948. The long-striding McElhenny, who credited his breakaway speed to a childhood fear of running down dark alleys in Compton to reach the safe light at the other end before someone waylaid him, was the team's top draft pick in '52 after earning all-America honors at Washington. "The King" averaged 7.0 yards a carry to win Rookie of the Year and All-Pro honors his first season and establish himself as the most thrilling runner in the game.

Rozelle's former USF basketball coach and early mentor, Pete Newell, was ensconced at Michigan State, where he was bringing the Spartans up to speed as the newest member of the Big Ten. Rozelle's 1951 football Dons were about to invade the National Football League en masse, with future Hall of Famers Gino Marchetti, Bob St. Clair, and Ollie Matson leading the way. Their coach, Joe Kuharich, would be reunited in Chicago with Matson, yet another Compton alum, when he returned home from the Helsinki Olympics to join the Cardinals as their top draft choice.

So, coming home to Los Angeles for Pete Rozelle in early 1952 was euphoric in every sense of that happy word. Owner Dan Reeves jumped his salary to $6,500 and turned him loose to sell the defending league champions. The Rams happened to be the NFL's most innovative and glamorous operation. Reeves and his general manager, Tex Schramm, had pioneered full-fledged college scouting under the direction of Eddie Kotal, who hired 100 "bird dogs" to assemble an incredible talent pool of top players. The Rams were far ahead of the other teams, which generally scouted by cronies, through word of mouth, or, as often as not, from *Street and Smith's* football magazine printed the previous summer.

The Rams had represented the National Conference in the previous three championship games with a high-powered, flashy offense built around quarterbacks Bob Waterfield and Norm Van Brocklin throwing to ends Tom Fears and Elroy Hirsch. Instead of staying in

Chicago in 1949 with the newly reconstituted Hornets of the All-America Football Conference after the Rockets folded, Hirsch, drafted by the Rams in 1945 when he was in the marines, came west and brought along his Wausau buddy, equipment manager Bill Granholm, known as "Granny."

A blond Adonis with a winning smile and personality to match, Hirsch quickly became the franchise's most popular player and, thanks to *Crazylegs, All-American*, the 1953 film biography in which he starred as himself, the Rams' enduring symbol. "Hirsch was one of the two or three best wide receivers who've ever been," said *Los Angeles Times* writer Bob Oates, who started covering football in the '30s. "I think Hutson was the best. I think Hirsch second best. Remember how he caught the ball over his head? Nobody else has been able to do that."

The Rams also had an incredible ground game. In 1950, Reeves and Schramm added the breakaway speed of Army's 1946 Heisman Trophy winner, Glenn "Mr. Outside" Davis, to complement lightning-quick Verna "Vitamin T." Smith and 6'4", 230-pound fullback Dick Hoerner. In 1951, the Rams unveiled their full-power "Bull Elephant Backfield" featuring Hoerner at fullback between two huge, fast halfbacks, both African American—6'2", 225-pound "Deacon" Dan Towler and 6'3", 225-pound former linebacker Paul "Tank" Younger. It was a sight to behold when those three ran a sweep that made the smaller linebackers and defensive backs of that era cringe in fear.

Brilliant as Reeves was in building a team, he was as volatile and impossibly demanding with his head coaches as George Steinbrenner later proved to be with his New York Yankees managers. This personality flaw would stick with Reeves to the end of his life and haunt the franchise. By the time Rozelle arrived in 1952, Reeves was well into a musical chairs game with his coaches, the last three of whom had been closely allied with Chicago Bears owner-coach and league founder George Halas.

Reeves axed the brilliant, eccentric Clark Shaughnessy, Halas's cocreator of the modern T formation, after the Philadelphia Eagles beat the Rams 14–0 in the 1949 title game in near monsoon conditions that turned the Los Angeles Coliseum turf to slop.

Next in line was Joe Stydahar, the future Hall of Fame tackle and the first man Halas chose in the initial 1936 draft. Pat Summerall has described Stydahar, the rough-hewed man he knew as coach of the Chicago Cardinals in 1953, as "the only guy I've ever known to drink whiskey, smoke a cigar, and chew tobacco all at the same time."

To run the offense, Stydahar called on his former Bears teammate Hampton Pool. Pool was smart enough to keep everything the ever-inventive Shaughnessy had dreamed up and then add a couple of his own wrinkles. Behind the one-two passing punch of Waterfield and Van Brocklin, the 1950 Rams ran up a 12-game league-record 466 points, 38.8 per game, losing a 30–28 shootout to the Cleveland Browns on a Lou Groza field goal in the closing seconds before twenty-nine thousand chilled fans in snowy Municipal Stadium.

The next year, 1951, the Stydahar-Pool Rams finally broke through, beating the Browns 24–17 on December 23 in the Coliseum on a fourth-quarter Van Brocklin pass to Fears, who split the defense at midfield and sprinted to the end zone to complete a 73-yard scoring play.

The coaxial cable had connected the entire country earlier that fall. However, in the wake of the 1950 debacle when attendance took a precipitous drop after Reeves put the home games on television, he followed the lead of commissioner Bert Bell and aired only road games to the Los Angeles area. The DuMont Network paid a $75,000 rights fee to air this first national telecast of an NFL championship game, but Reeves and Bell did not relent on the blackout policy for L.A. This NFL telecast beat NBC's New Year's Day first-ever Rose Bowl telecast, called by Mel Allen, when Illinois routed Stanford 40–7.

Off the field, Rozelle's lessons with Reeves paid off. "Dan Reeves was in many ways his mentor," sportscaster Dick Enberg said. "Reeves saw the intersection between television and pro football as a major deal. His influence on Rozelle should not be underestimated. Rozelle and Tex Schramm came through there, and I think it was because of Reeves's ability to pick talent."

"Rozelle got pretty well acquainted with the necessity of theater in selling professional sports. The leaf was just turning at this time," sportscaster Keith Jackson noted. "Pete, by then, understood full well that if you are going to be successful in professional athletics, you had to bring theater to it. Not only be concerned about your box office, but you had to get the word out."

The names Reeves and Rozelle had a theatrical magic, as the younger man complemented his boss in so many ways. "He and Pete both had that droll sense of humor. Both were subtle and would hit you with a literary allusion or a gag in a note," said Jack Teele, who worked in the Rams' front office.

The L.A. to which Pete and Jane Rozelle returned in January 1952 already was the smog-filled, semiconnected smorgasbord of neighborhoods and fast-developing suburban communities in and around downtown that Jack Webb had made famous in his weekly police drama "Dragnet." Under Walter Schumann's compelling, brass-dominated theme, Webb would say over an aerial view of the vast area, "This is the city. Los Angeles, California. My name is Friday. I'm a cop." The music blared. *Dum-de-dum-dum!*

People were moving in by the thousands each year, many, if not most, young men and women from the Midwest. Southern California was a land of abundance in everything from sunshine to food to opportunity and jobs. For operators such as Rozelle and Reeves, this was an incredible, expanding fan base who loved sports back home—football, baseball, basketball—and wanted to identify with the new hometown teams. Rozelle and Reeves could provide that with the Rams.

Before the decade was out, L.A. would get its baseball team, no ordinary ball club either, but the most storied team in the sport besides the New York Yankees and the Brooklyn Dodgers, with their brilliant young announcer Vin Scully. Then, Los Angeles would land the top pro basketball team in the still nascent NBA, the Minneapolis Lakers. Waiting for the Lakers was a transplant from Peoria, Illinois, who knew more than a little bit about the game and could explain it clearly in a voice that chattered as fast as a machine gun. His name: Chick Hearn.

The area was a mass of construction noises, especially on the elaborate network of highways that would define the city, its environs, and Southern California. By 1952, the Hollywood Freeway had been completed for four years. The Pasadena, Santa Ana, and San Bernardino freeways were nearing completion. Construction had begun on the Long Beach and Harbor freeways that would slash through, if not destroy, the pleasant Lynwood-Compton community where Rozelle grew up.

"When he came back to the Rams, we helped him find an apartment, which was just a block away from our place on Olympic Boulevard," Rozelle's old friend from Compton, Al Franken, said. The Rozelles' place was also close to the Rams' offices on Beverly Boulevard near the famed Farmer's Market. "Jane and Pete seemed to have a compatible relationship. We knew her and liked her."

Rozelle joined the Rams too late for the NFL draft held on January 17, 1952. One of the first people he met back in town was University of Southern California's all-America halfback, Frank Gifford, finishing up school that winter. "I remember meeting with him, talking with him. I had brief contact with him," Gifford said. "I was living in L.A., and Dan Reeves had assured me that I was going to be their number one pick."

That likely would have happened had Coach Stydahar been able to pull off a predraft trade with Halas that would have brought the Bears' All-Pro quarterback, Johnny Lujack, to Los Angeles. Aware that Waterfield would play just one more year, Stydahar, as coach of the National Conference all-stars for the Pro Bowl game, also knew from talking to Lujack that he wanted out of Chicago and the clutches of Halas. "When Stydahar found out I wasn't going to get together with Halas," Lujack recounted, "he tried to make a deal for me. Halas wanted four first-team Rams! Silly! So, that didn't come about."

After the Pro Bowl, Lujack, who had played out his contract, left the Bears to join Frank Leahy as Notre Dame's backfield coach. Now the Rams had to find a quarterback. It was their turn to exercise the rotating bonus pick, which the league instituted in 1947 to give each team a chance to get the top college player, to lead off the draft. Eddie Kotal and his scouts rated Billy Wade, Vanderbilt's strong-armed passer and excellent play caller, at the top of the list.

"They took Wade as the bonus pick ahead of me, and I went to the Giants," Gifford said. "I was kind of disappointed. I was making a hell of a lot more money working in films as extras, stuntmen. Then, I thought, New York—why not? We had played there, and we went to *Guys and Dolls.* I had just gotten married. So, I said, we'll go back and spend a year. It turned into a lifetime." And, in less than a decade, Frank Gifford and Pete Rozelle would form a lifelong friendship that would have much to do with the shape of NFL history to come.

Tex Schramm had promised to teach Rozelle other facets of the business. So, Rozelle helped with scouting, the grunt work of the game. His big find came when he drove down to Camp Pendleton Marine Base one day to look over the football team. "There was Pete out there scouting a marine team. He obviously was not a guy who let grass grow under his feet," the writer William Nack said. "He was willing to go out and look at basically a service team, just as a scout, and found Big Daddy. Christ almighty, all you had to do was look at the guy, 6'7", 290 pounds, who moved like a halfback. It was like finding a 42-carat diamond."

Gene "Big Daddy" Lipscomb was just 22 when he got discharged from the Marine Corps in time to join the Rams in 1953. Very little was known about his early years in Detroit. He attended Miller High School and then joined the marines at a time when service ball was big. The Rams' coaches didn't know what to make of the huge man who didn't want to rush the passer, just anchor the line of scrimmage. Finally, Sid Gillman gave up on him. The Baltimore Colts grabbed him in 1956 and installed him at right defensive tackle, where he put the world on notice.

That first 1952 season would give Rozelle a chance to see Reeves's slick television operation. Reeves augmented serious play-by-play calls with a "color" man sidekick, preferably with a show business background. Thus, his play-by-play announcer was rich baritone Bob Kelley, who had started with the Rams in 1937 and came west from Cleveland in 1946. Kelley's sidekick was onetime film and television actor Gil Stratton.

Stratton played bit parts in several films, including Billy Wilder's *Stalag 17*, and then costarred in CBS-TV's "That's My Boy" as the nerdy, sports-hating son of Eddie Mayehoff's "Jarring" Jack Jackson, a loudmouth former all-American football player. In true Hollywood style, Stratton began a two-decade run as a respected sportscaster on the top-rated weeknight KNXT-CBS-TV newscasts.

As the defending champions, the Rams kicked off the '52 season in mid-August with the traditional College All-Star exhibition game in Chicago. They looked sluggish in a 10–7 victory and could not get going throughout the exhibitions, games Bert Bell decreed were now to be called the preseason. "The Rams played their last preseason game against the Giants in the Polo Grounds and then opened the season in Cleveland," Ernie Accorsi said.

The Rams set up shop in Accorsi's hometown of Hershey, Pennsylvania, where the Eagles trained in the summer from 1951 through '67. The future football executive was an avid pro football fan who liked anybody but the local favorites, the Eagles. And these Rams were the game's glamour team. "Bob Waterfield. Even at age 11, I knew that Waterfield was married to Jane Russell," Accorsi said. "These ram's-head helmets [that halfback Fred Gehrke designed in 1948], which I had never seen in color. In black and white, those uniforms looked magical, but to see them live! I told Bill Granholm years later that I saw them in '52 and that gold was almost orange. 'You're right,' Granny said."

"They were practicing on this field where the Eagles practiced," Accorsi continued, "which was my baseball field, where I played Legion and senior baseball. Every day after school, my cousin Gary Ponzoli and I ran over there, and then we would walk back through the park. It was free. We sort of adopted Deacon Dan Towler, and he adopted us. He looked for us every day."

The Rams stayed at the Cocoa Inn for five days before moving on to Cleveland, and Accorsi managed to fill an autograph book with signatures of every player on that team, a book he still has. After the last practice on Friday, Ernie and his cousin Gary walked Towler back to town, as they had all week. When they arrived at the Cocoa Inn, the Deacon told the boys to wait. He went upstairs to get each of them a team picture and then came back with a sad look. "The PR guy won't give me any more team pictures, so you guys will have to share this," Towler said.

"So, my cousin and I shared this picture. He kept it one month, I kept it one month, and so on. Somehow, it got lost. I would love to have that picture," Accorsi said in 2006. "I'll never forget how Deacon Dan griped about 'this PR guy who would only give me one team picture.' It was Alvin Rozelle. Alvin R. Rozelle."

Accorsi added, "You know what burns me up? When Deacon Dan died in 2001, I wrote a letter to the sports editor of the *L.A. Times* remembering the Deacon and how he treated two little kids a half century before. And they didn't even print it!

"Here I was 11 years old, there was Rozelle, and there was Tex Schramm, and they were going to play big parts in my life. Years later, I did talk to Pete about Hershey, but we never brought that up. It's just amazing."

The Browns lay in ambush in Cleveland. They routed the Rams 37–7. After the game, the combustible Reeves decided Stydahar had lost the team. So, he fired him and put Pool in charge, and the team responded. The Rams and Detroit Lions tied for the National Conference regular-season title with 9–3 records, to set up a playoff in Detroit for the right to face the four-time American Conference champion Browns once again.

By 1952, Bert Bell was the senior commissioner in professional sports. When George Halas returned from serving in Admiral Chester Nimitz's wartime Pacific command, he pushed Bell's election in 1945 to counter the aggressive, new All-America Football Conference, which had made serious inroads against the NFL due to the inept regime of Elmer Layden. What Halas got was a take-charge human buzz saw. A short, round man, Bell had a gravelly voice that, to *New York Times* columnist Arthur Daley, sounded like "coal sliding down a chute." Bell's first act was to move the league office from Chicago to his hometown, Philadelphia.

De Benneville Bell had a Main Line pedigree from head to toe, with a name only his banker knew. Nobody, not even his parents, ever called him anything but Bert. He was the football-crazy son of former Pennsylvania attorney general John Cromwell Bell and, despite his short stature, a quarterback on the University of Pennsylvania football team. A somewhat scurrilous member of Penn's class of '19, Bell did not bother to graduate.

Bell loved football, though, and in 1933 at the lowest ebb of the Depression, he and partner Lud Wray scratched up $2,500 to buy the Frankford Yellow Jackets. Bell renamed them the Eagles to honor the blue eagle symbol of President Franklin Roosevelt's National Recovery Act, the NRA. But the team lacked the money and players to compete. So, in 1935, Bell persuaded Halas and George Preston Marshall to start a player draft in reverse order of finish. That, Bell figured, would give the league a semblance of balance and would head the league toward the parity that his successors would strive for, and attain.

In an early test of his character, Bell, who was managing his father's Ritz-Carlton Hotel in Philadelphia, proposed marriage to the woman he had been seeing for well over a year. Florence Upton, a former Ziegfeld Follies showgirl and Broadway actress, was a devout, nondrinking Catholic. She refused, telling Bert she could not marry a man who wasted his life on alcohol. As the story goes, Bell went to a bar across the street, ordered a drink, downed it, went back to tell Florence what he had done, and vowed in her presence never to take another one. They married on January 4, 1934, and he kept all vows.

In his first major test as commissioner, Bell stemmed potential scandal when he suspended two New York Giants players, Frank Filchock and Merle Hapes, on the eve of the 1946 title game with the Bears after they failed to report a gambler's bribe offer. To keep the game on the up-and-up, the realistic Bell hired a crew of former FBI agents to track down rumors, and he opened pipelines to the "illegal" gambling centers. If odds on a game fluctuated, he sicced his bloodhounds on the situation, and he made sure the public knew it.

When Bell started as commissioner, he ran the league from an office in Philadelphia's Center City. By 1952, he had a nominal office abutting the back of a small bank at 1 Bala Place in Bala-Cynwyd on City Line Avenue, Philly's western border, near his home in the Main Line suburb of Narberth. Bell ran up long-distance phone bills upward of $10,000 a year, in the office or at home, where he did most of his work. At home, Bell, his voice raspy from the many cigarettes he smoked each day, washed down by countless cups of coffee, spent long hours at night and on weekends at his dining room table working out the league schedule. He tried to equalize the schedule by pairing the top teams against each other at the outset of the season, and the lesser ones against each other, to create fan interest and not let wide disparities in the standings develop. The process took months as he tinkered away, moving marked dominoes from spot to spot on the "schedule board" until he had it right.

Bell got along with the players better than any owner could, recognizing their right at the beginning of 1957 to form an association to gain a crumb or two's worth of benefits. Bell had no files, though, let alone a record-keeping system, and maintained everything in his head. That's how he ran the NFL.

"We all knew Bert Bell. He was more like an old coach than anything else," recalled Hall of Fame linebacker Sam Huff. "He traveled around to visit every team and talk to the players. He talked to you about staying out of trouble. He'd say, 'Learn another job. This is a stepping-stone to another career.'"

Ernie Accorsi got his first job in athletic administration in the '60s as sports information director at St. Joseph's College, at 54th and City Line Avenue. "I got married in Bala-Cynwyd," Accorsi said. "Our first apartment was 366 Bala, three and a half blocks from 1 Bala Avenue. That is where Pete took over the commissionership. The old-timers like Jerry Izenberg tell me you would call the league office and say, 'Can I speak to Bert Bell, the commissioner?' 'Speaking.' He'd pick up the phone."

"Oh, sure, it was a mom-and-pop operation," lifelong Philadelphian Bill Orr, then a boy who would tag along with his dad, recalled. "I distinctly remember every Sunday night around 9 or 10 when people like Austin Gunsel, Harry Standish, Joe Labrum, Bert Bell, and my father would go to Davis's Drug Store in Narberth dressed in crusty gray sweatshirts. They'd always be looking for the first edition of the *Inquirer* to get the West Coast scores. They'd be saying, 'Yeah, yeah, yeah, the 49ers beat so-and-so.' The game had been over for four hours, but there was no instant communication. They really ran the league out of Bert Bell's shoe."

Wally Orr was especially close to Bell. In 1948, Orr left the N.W. Ayer ad agency in Philadelphia to form three companies: W. Wallace Orr Advertising; the Tel Ad Company, a phone service that carried horse racing results; and a syndicated film production company. "A company called Newsreel Laboratories here in Philadelphia, owned by a guy named Lou Kellman, subcontracted Father to shoot and produce college football games," his son, Bill Orr, recalled. "One of the first schools they worked with was the University of Pennsylvania, with all-Americans Reds Bagnell and Chuck Bednarik." Penn's representative was Castleman D. (C. D.) Chesley, who, years later, produced the weekly Notre Dame syndicated telecast. Lindsay Nelson called the play-by-play in a "live" telecast. To condense the show into a one-hour slot, Nelson cut out dead space with the prerecorded transition "We now move to further action."

Orr's Penn films led to a show called "College Football Highlights." Next came a deal with Bert Bell for a Tel Ra–produced weekly show syndicated to 100 stations called "National Football League Highlights." "My father had an exclusive contract to produce all syndicated television programming for the 12-team National Football League," Bill Orr said. "At that time, television was little DuMonts, RCAs, and Sylvania black and whites."

Tel Ra's pro highlights shows were narrated over the years by Philadelphian Jim Leaming; Chuck Thompson, who would drive up from Baltimore; and three New York–based broadcasters—Harry Wismer, Chris Schenkel, and, after he retired from the Giants, Kyle Rote. "We did the championship games every year as part of the contract. At the end, they became sealed bids when Bert died in '59. When Rozelle came in, in '60, he went to sealed bids."

Bell was well aware that television was important, but he was a prime proponent of the conventional wisdom that fannies in the seats, the gate, would always drive the business. And he had to get the league's house in order by untangling a mess that involved a failing team and another dormant franchise that refused to throw in the towel.

When the National Football League and All-America Football Conference finally ended their war at the close of the 1949 season, the established league agreed to add three AAFC franchises and realign the league. Bringing in the AAFC's top two teams made perfect sense: Paul Brown's Cleveland Browns with an array of superior players were the equal of most NFL teams, and the San Francisco 49ers would give the Rams a West Coast partner.

Halas settled an old score with fellow Chicagoan Benjamin Lindheimer and his actor partner Don Ameche when he made sure that Reeves and the Rams won out in L.A. over their Dons. During that war, Reeves and his original Cleveland partner, Fred Levy, lost piles of money, nearly $300,000, and, to retain control of the club, were forced to take on partners who included oilman Edwin Pauley and entertainer Bob Hope. The partners constantly feuded and were barely on speaking terms.

More of a surprise came when the NFL rebuffed the Buffalo Bills as the 13th franchise, but jaws literally dropped when the 13th franchise turned out to be the AAFC doormat, the original Baltimore Colts. These Colts, founded in 1946 as the Miami Seahawks, were born to lose. Owner Bob Rodenburg moved the team up the Atlantic Coast to Baltimore after a 3–11 inaugural season and, to save money, kept their same gray and green uniforms. The '47 Colts went 2-11-1; they broke even at 7-7 in '48 but resumed their inept ways in 1949, going 1-11. Rodenburg sold the team to trucking baron Abe Watner, who vowed that Baltimore was in the big leagues to stay.

He lasted one season. Operating as the 13th, or swing, team in the NFL, the 1950 Colts produced an identical 1–11 record with a roster that had future Hall of Fame quarterbacks Y. A. Tittle and George Blanda, until George Halas grabbed Blanda off waivers in midseason to bring him back to the Bears, and defensive tackle Art Donovan. At the end of the 1950 season, Watner gave the team and player contracts back to the league for $50,000 and washed his hands of the untidy mess, putting the league back at a manageable dozen teams, six in each conference.

The league staged a dispersal draft of the players who had not already been picked up by other teams, but that did not daunt the diehards in Baltimore. The Colts' marching band and fan club stayed active, and they worked tirelessly to revive the team. They had a tough ally at Baltimore City Hall in Mayor Thomas D'Alessandro Jr., sire of a local political dynasty that included his son Thomas III, who served as mayor of Baltimore from 1967 to '71, and daughter Nancy Pelosi, who became the first woman chosen as Speaker of the House. "Mayor D'Alesandro claimed the demise of the franchise was illegal," Ernie Accorsi said. "William D. MacMillan was this crafty old lawyer. He filed a lawsuit against the National Football League demanding restoration of the Baltimore Colts franchise."

While the lawsuit worked its laborious way through federal court, the league had another problem on its hands. Kate Smith's manager-partner Ted Collins was immersed in debt as he tried to run a competing New York franchise in Yankee Stadium against the Giants. As Halas had kicked the Cardinals out of the West to the American Conference in the East, the Maras had exiled Collins's Yanks to the National Conference out west. At the end of a disastrous 1–9–2 season in 1951, Collins followed Watner's lead and sold the team back to a league that was operating on the edge and barely solvent.

Within two months, Bell found his buyer. He announced that the Yanks would resurface as the Dallas Texans under the ownership of a group headed by young textile millionaire Giles Miller and his brother Connell, with the Yanks' blue and white team colors. One of their first hires was PR director Tex Maule, whose departure from the Rams had opened the door for Rozelle's return to the club the previous winter.

Maule quickly grew disillusioned with the chaotic franchise. The new Texans couldn't draw flies to the cavernous Cotton Bowl, let alone win. Coach Jimmy Phelan had a few good men, namely, rookie defensive end Gino Marchetti, of USF; water bug running back Buddy Young; and defensive tackles Joe Campanella, Don Colo, and the nomadic Art "Fats" Donovan. But that was it. Bert Bell tried to help out the Texans by loading their schedule up front with three home games in the first four weeks of the season.

They opened with back-to-back dates at home and were cuffed around. The New York Giants drew a Texans team-record 17,500 fans as they beat Dallas 24–6. The next week, just 12,581 came out to see the league's most exciting team, the San Francisco 49ers, clobber the Texans 37–14, with quarterback Tittle joining Perry and McElhenny to lead the rout. Two years later, John Henry Johnson came down from Canada to San Francisco to complete the greatest backfield in pro football history. All four men—Tittle, Perry, McElhenny, and Johnson—would be elected to the Hall of Fame.

The Texans hit the road to Chicago to open the Bears' home season and lose 38–20 to one of the worst teams George Halas ever coached. The Texans attracted their largest crowd, 35,429, some 14,000 fewer than the usual Wrigley Field attendance, even in a 5–7 year. The season lurched on. Back home in Dallas, just 14,000 fans came out on October 18 to watch a weak Green Bay Packers team beat the Texans 29–14. After losing 48–21 at San Francisco and 42–20 down the coast in L.A., the Texans returned to the Cotton Bowl for a rematch with the Rams on November 9. "When we were going so bad, the old veterans hid on the bench so our coach, Jimmy Phelan, couldn't find them, so they wouldn't have to go into the game," Gino Marchetti said. "It was hard for a rookie like me to keep self-motivated. We got the hell beat out of us."

The Rams took it easy this time, beating the Texans 27–6 before 10,000 witnesses, including Rams GM Tex Schramm and PR director Pete Rozelle. In four home games, the Texans drew 54,081 customers to the Cotton Bowl, 21,000 less than seating capacity for a single game. They had not come close to winning any of the seven games they played. For Rozelle, seeing this debacle develop before his eyes in a city and state that he knew should have been fertile pro football territory was vital to his education as a difference-making executive.

Sources claim Commissioner Bell wanted to get that team out of Dallas before the Baltimore suit came to trial. "The lawsuit was raging, and the NFL couldn't handle lawsuits. It was short on funds," Ernie Accorsi said. Then, after losing $225,000 in less than two months, Texans owner Giles Miller inadvertently came to the rescue. At first, he begged Bell to advance a bailout loan. When Bell refused, Miller begged him to take the team off his hands. "So, halfway through the season, Bert Bell made the Texans a road team and moved them to Hershey," recalled Accorsi, who was delighted to have the third pro football team that season, after the Eagles and Rams, set up shop in his hometown.

After losing two more scheduled road games in Detroit and Green Bay, the homeless Texans still had to play two home games among the final three. Bell made a deal with the University of Akron to rent the Rubber Bowl for the second game of a Thanksgiving double-header, with a 2:00 P.M. kickoff. As it turned out, most of the good citizens of Akron preferred their turkey at home in the afternoon to a turkey on the field.

"They had a high school game that morning before ours, and they had 20–22,000 fans there. The stadium was packed," Marchetti recalled. "Before we went out on the field, our coach, Jimmy Phelan, said, 'We're not going to introduce you the way they usually do. We're going into the stands and meet each customer individually.' There were probably 2,000 people there."

Bears coach George Halas got into the holiday spirit by starting his second string. He was that confident of victory. Instead, the Texans came alive, hung together, and walked off the field with what would be the only victory of their miserable existence, 27–23 over the winningest team in pro football history. "I remember talking to the guy blocking me," Marchetti said. "Halas walked by and kicked him right in the butt. 'Goddamit! Get in that goddamned clubhouse!' He was so upset."

"That was our first [and only] win that year. The experience was not too good," Marchetti said.

"I knew we could do it," Phelan said after the game.

Afterward, as Accorsi learned years later, "Papa Bear went on the plane, put his arm on everybody's tray, aisle by aisle, and swept all the food onto the deck."

The saga of the vagabond Texans gets even more hilarious, as Accorsi detailed. "John Huzvar, the greatest player ever to come from Hershey, still lives on Maple Avenue in Hershey, a diabetic, both legs amputated. I saw him at a recent talk I gave there. He was playing for the Eagles. This has been verified by Huzvar and Jim Trimble,"

Accorsi said. "Trimble, the head coach, told Huzvar, 'Don't come to practice this week. Spy on the Texans. Write down the plays they're practicing.'

"Huzvar parked his car in the lot, put on his sunglasses, cap over his eyes, and spied on their practices. Huzvar called Trimble the first night. 'What'd they do?' the coach asked.

" 'They played volleyball across the crossbar of the goalpost,' Huzvar said.

" 'What else?'

" 'That's all they did.'

"So, they stayed another night. 'Coach, they're still playing volleyball,' Huzvar said."

"Art Donovan was on that team, and he verified it. Bucko Kilroy was there, and he confirmed it, too," Accorsi recounted.

With nothing to lose, the Texans drove in to Philly and lost to the Eagles 38–21. They ended their brief stay in the National Football League on December 13, 1952, with a 41–6 loss to the Detroit Lions. In the playoff at Briggs Stadium, in Detroit, Bobby Layne ended the Rams' hopes for a fourth straight title appearance as he led the Lions to a 31–21 victory. A week later, Layne again drove the Lions to victory, a 17–7 win over the Browns for the championship.

Now that he had survived that disheartening season, Bert Bell had to find a buyer. He wanted it to be somebody from Baltimore, somebody he knew, somebody he could trust, somebody with old-school ties, somebody from Penn. That description fit Carroll Rosenbloom, who made a fortune supplying the armed forces in World War II with khaki uniforms made at his Blue Ridge Manufacturing Company plant in Roanoke, Virginia.

"Father's good friend and ex–college backfield coach [at Penn] was Bell," Steve Rosenbloom said. Both men had summer places on the Jersey Shore in Margate City, a stone's throw south of Atlantic City. "Bert was at the house often, and he was a terrific guy. He convinced my father in 1953 to stick his neck out."

Accorsi picks up the narrative. "He didn't want any part of this. 'Look,' Bell said, 'just put in $25,000 and get enough other partners to put in enough to raise $50,000, and it's yours. I got a guy who went to Penn, named Don Kellett. He'll run it for you." Bell gave the new owners eight years to pay off the rest of the interest-free $200,000 franchise fee.

"It was a big risk," Steve Rosenbloom said. "The owners in those days were considered civic citizens at that point to underwrite an NFL team in a city. They weren't making any money. They weren't paying the players anything." His father acquiesced.

"Rosenbloom invested his $25,000, and Kellett ran it as president and general manager. The thing turned out to be a lot bigger than Carroll thought it would be," Accorsi said with an admiring chuckle as he recalled those exciting days. "Kellett in time went from president, to vice president and general manager, to just general manager."

So, the reincarnated Baltimore Colts, this time showing the blue and white colors that had been worn in New York and Dallas, were back. "I remember going to the first banquet they had to introduce the new owner," Steve Rosenbloom said. He was eight years old at that time. "They had to sell a certain amount of season tickets. They went way past that, selling more than fifteen thousand tickets. The town was excited, even though they had been through this and had gone belly-up twice."

The banquet emcee was local radio personality Bailey Goss, whose father had been Carroll's boss at the Marlboro Shirt Company, in Baltimore. The elder Goss once sent Rosenbloom to Roanoke to close a plant. Instead, he bought it and made his first fortune. "Bailey Goss said, 'This is Carroll Rosenbloom, new owner of the Colts. It's lucky he's in the shirt business, because he's likely to lose his.' That always stuck with me," Steve Rosenbloom said. "Father had a five-year plan. He talked about that in '53, and people thought he was being overly optimistic. Five years later, we were in the championship game with the Giants."

The Detroit Lions repeated in 1953 when Layne executed a classic championship drive. Trailing 16–10 with four minutes left and the ball at their 20, Layne opened with a 20-yard pass to Jim Doran. He picked his way downfield to the Cleveland 33 and then called time-out. Lions coach Buddy Parker told Layne to throw a screen. Layne, instead, went for the bundle, sending Doran downfield. He caught it in stride and scored, to set up Doak Walker's winning conversion.

Ironically, that title game came at a turning point for pro football. On November 12, 1953, federal judge Allan Grim, of Philadelphia, upheld the league's 75-mile home-game blackout radius. That previous winter, without lifting a hand, Bell and the NFL got the upper hand over the rival they had not been able to beat: college football. In a move that still defies explanation more than a half century later, the NCAA Rules Committee, driven by Michigan's former coach and all-powerful athletic director Herbert O. "Fritz" Crisler, shoved through the rules change that forever put pro football in the driver's seat—junking unlimited substitution.

Crisler conceived the two-platoon concept in 1945 to counter Colonel Earl Blaik's deep West Point powerhouse. By deploying a fresh defensive unit when the Cadets had the ball, he not only gave his offensive team a breather but also was able to keep the game close, holding heavily favored Army to a 28–7 victory. Unlimited substitution after World War II opened the game as never before. Offensive specialists led to wider-open passing games and found places for skilled athletes. Nobody thrived under free substitution more than Blaik at Army, Frank Leahy at Notre Dame, and Biggie Munn at Michigan State, for whom, as Edwin Pope suggested in *Football's Greatest Coaches*, "unlimited substitution meant unlimited victory." The pros copied that success, going to unlimited substitution in 1950.

Crisler, who ran the rules committee as sternly as he and Michigan ran the Big Ten, did not see it quite that way. Instead, he proclaimed, "The committee members were honest and unselfish. They took the best course for the game and the players. Specialization was becoming too pronounced."

Blaik called it a victory for cost-conscious faculties, who could have ordered squad reductions to save money and still retained the crowd-pleasing two-platoon game. He was in the minority. Crisler ally Major General Robert Neyland, Tennessee's powerful coach, taught a simpler, hard-nosed, single-wing offense with little passing. Years later, former Notre Dame coach Ara Parseghian told me the

1953 rules change forced him and all coaches to play their best athletes, that is, best defensive players, instead of potential game-breaking offensive skilled position players. Parseghian's rival at Ohio State, Woody Hayes, abandoned passing for an efficient, non-crowd-pleasing ground attack he called "three yards and a cloud of dust," and won his first national championship in 1954.

For the next decade until the return of unlimited substitution in 1964, the college game was much more dull, by contrast with the pros. By that time, Pete Rozelle's National Football League had overtaken every other sport, even major-league baseball.

FOUR

TO THE OLYMPICS
AND BACK

"The game was built by the players. We owe them everything."

—BERT BELL, 1959

Pete Rozelle had barely unpacked after his arrival in San Francisco in 1948 when Pete Newell introduced him to his 29-year-old friend Ken Macker. Newell and Macker had met in Los Angeles about the time Newell was a child actor in the *Our Gang* film comedies. Macker and Rozelle struck up a fast friendship that transcended sports and endured until Macker's death in 1991.

If Ray Rozelle gave his son Pete his character, if Pete Newell gave Rozelle his start in sports publicity, and Dan Reeves gave him his break to excel and achieve in a premier sports organization, it was Ken Macker whose expertise and mentoring prepared Rozelle to be a businessman who would literally change the sports universe in the way he dealt with owners, athletes, major clients, sponsors, and governments.

Macker was a student of the works and philosophy of public relations pioneer Edward Bernays. In line with Bernays, Macker despised the profession's negative image befouled by glib pitchmen, slick press

agents, and ad hucksters. Macker and the new breed of PR specialists believed they would improve businesses as they connected with
the public by using sound journalistic principles to frame their "messages" tastefully, sincerely, and subtly. In no way did they want to be
known as "flacks," preferring to be called "image consultants" as
they built long-term relationships with their clients.

After World War II, when the Soriano family was able to return to
the Philippines to resume control of the family properties, Macker
joined the Sorianos' Manila-based San Miguel Corporation. He
became the personal secretary and confidant of owner Andres Soriano and handled public relations concerns for the huge brewery and
allied enterprises that, since 1927, had held the first non-American-
owned Coca-Cola distributorship in the world.

The gentlemanly Macker recognized immediately that Rozelle possessed extraordinary qualities that would make him an outstanding
public relations executive. According to Dick Rozelle, Pete was still
at USF when Macker told him that down the line he planned to open
his own public relations firm with Soriano family backing. When that
happened, Macker vowed, he would ask Pete to come aboard as a
partner.

In January 1955, with the backing of the Sorianos, Macker started
his firm, P. K. Macker and Associates, and placed that long-promised
call to his friend in Los Angeles. He offered to pay Rozelle a $9,600
salary, sweeten it with bonus opportunities, and, for the clincher, give
him the option to buy 10 percent of the firm. Aware of Rozelle's love
of track and field, Macker told him he wanted him to manage the
firm's major account, the Victoria Promotion Committee, Australia's
government-sanctioned organizer for the Melbourne Olympics to be
held in November 1956. That meant Pete Rozelle, at age 29, should
he join the Macker team, would manage the official worldwide publicity for the Olympics.

One of Rozelle's fellow Southern California track-and-field enthu-
siasts through the years was future promoter Al Franken. "He was
doing PR for Compton College, and I was doing publicity for another
concern," Franken said of their initial friendship. In due course,
Franken started the Sunkist meet, which he ran for 43 years, and also

managed other meets for such major sponsors as Pepsi, Michelob, and Jack-in-the-Box.

After Rozelle later returned to Los Angeles to join the Rams, he and Franken made time to attend important meets and drive for hours, if necessary, to points as far away as the Bay Area. "When Pete and I went to the state track meet in Berkeley, he bet some guy $5 that Jerome Walters from Compton High School would win the mile. Pete won that bet," Franken said.

Rozelle knew that Macker's offer was the chance of a lifetime with all it entailed. But he loved his job, working for men he admired—Dan Reeves and Tex Schramm—with pro football's cutting-edge team, the Rams. Shortly after Rozelle joined the club in 1952, the astute Reeves and Schramm cleverly pulled off the largest trade for a single player in pro football history. They sent 11 men, in effect a whole team, to the new Dallas Texans for the rights to California all-America linebacker Les Richter, knowing full well that Richter faced a two-year military obligation. Richter, later one of auto racing's most important owners and promoters, returned in 1954 to become arguably the Rams' all-time-greatest linebacker. Most important, none of the 11 men they shipped off to the ill-fated Texans made an impact after leaving the Rams.

The 1954 Rams, despite Richter's arrival, showed signs of slippage following a decade of success. After the team finished a half game behind the champion Lions in the renamed Western Conference in 1953, Norm Van Brocklin led the league in passing, but both Elroy Hirsch and Tom Fears grew old, enduring mediocre seasons as the team fell to a disappointing 6–5–1 fourth-place finish in the Western Conference, behind the champion Lions, resurgent Bears, and 49ers.

Reeves fired Hamp Pool and turned to a college coach from the Midwest who would enter the Pro Football Hall of Fame years later acclaimed as the unquestioned master of the modern passing game. On January 26, 1955, Rozelle handed out a release to the gathered reporters to introduce 42-year-old Sid Gillman.

Gillman, who came from one of the few Jewish families in Minneapolis, left home in 1930 for Ohio State and never returned. After graduation, Gillman played end in the inaugural College All-Star

Game in 1934 on a line anchored by center and future president Gerald Ford. He then entered coaching. After an early tour with the Cleveland Rams, Gillman started at Denison and then moved to West Point as Earl Blaik's line coach to learn the fine points of strategic planning and handling men. In 1944, he left Army to become head coach at Blaik's alma mater, Miami University, where one of his top players was halfback Ara Parseghian. Along the way, he began to develop and refine a unique, sophisticated passing system that would profoundly affect the sport, the West Coast Offense. "No question he was the master of using the field, sideline to sideline," said Al Davis, who got his start with Gillman as a Chargers assistant in 1960.

In 1948, Gillman moved to Miami's hated rival a few miles down the road, the University of Cincinnati. "Sid recruited me to Miami and made me a coach. He went to Cincinnati, and he wanted me to go there, and I did; then I went to the Rams," recalled Jack Faulkner, still associated with the Rams more than a half century after he came to L.A. with Gillman.

Rozelle, like Gillman, believed from the outset that he would make the Rams a winner, but Ken Macker was pressing for an answer. The chance to travel to Australia to work the Olympics at more money than he'd ever made was too good to pass up. With Reeves's blessing, he took the plunge in April, and he and Jane moved up the Pacific Coast to a rental house in Burlingame, on the San Mateo peninsula. That placed him a few miles south of the financial center, in the city, and even closer to the airport, where he met clients at all hours of the day and night, and from where he took off on his many trips around the country and to the Western Pacific and Australia.

Before they left for San Francisco, Pete and Jane Rozelle paid a visit to Al and Shirley Franken at their home near the UCLA campus. "They had a little Buddha doll that some family member, I guess Jane's grandmother, gave her," Al said. "They didn't like it. 'We'll keep it,' I said. 'If Jane's grandmother ever comes back to town, I'll bring it over to her.' We still have the doll. Neither Jane nor Pete ever reclaimed it."

Rozelle made frequent trips to New York, where he met the right people in advertising and the media, all to help his clients. He moved seamlessly into that smoke-filled universe with its business etiquette fueled by liquor and in which success was based on how well you held it and functioned. He discovered a lunchtime or dinnertime drink that he liked and could nurse over conversation and deal with his clients and associates with a reasonably clear head. It was the Rusty Nail, a cocktail his brother introduced to him when he returned home from the navy in 1954: Scotch, Johnnie Walker Red Label preferred, cut with Drambuie, over several ice cubes.

Rozelle spent the better part of the next year escorting Australia's four-minute-miler, John Landy, on an extensive and highly successful American tour. In Landy, the world record holder at 3:58.0, Rozelle had a marvelous client, and an easy sale. As a young graduate student, Landy was an amateur naturalist, a butterfly collector. Rozelle told the writers that Landy's hobby of chasing and collecting butterflies was the secret of his foot speed and endurance.

The big event of their American tour was the Coliseum Relays in May 1956. After Landy met with the writers, several of them badgered Rozelle for one-on-ones. Aware that all the interview requests would interfere with the runner's training, Rozelle moved him to a different L.A. hotel and registered him under an alias, not an uncommon tactic for celebrities. One day when Landy wanted to get away from the crush, Rozelle sneaked him into the hotel garage, told him to lie down on the back floor of his station wagon under a blanket, and whisked him to Lynwood for a welcomed pleasant evening with Ray and Hazel Rozelle and his brother, Dick.

On the morning of the race, Landy loped through a set of practice miles and then arrived at the huge Coliseum for the big race. The promoters assembled a top field, including Landy's fellow Australian Jim Bailey, a University of Oregon junior, and Villanova's Irish import, Ron Delaney. Delaney led at the quarter mile at 60.9, a 4:00-mile pace, but Landy eased through the pack in the second lap to take the lead. On the gun lap, Bailey, who was supposed to be a pacesetter, realized Landy was not running away from him. Bailey caught up on the third turn when he tapped Landy on the rear and said, "Go." Landy did not respond with a kick and turned to look back. With that, Bailey shot past, took a one-yard lead, and held on to win the first sub-four-minute mile on U.S. soil, 3:58.6, a 10th of a second ahead of Landy. "The four-minute mile won't be exclusive anymore," the omniscient Bailey said.

By fall, it was time to go down under for the games. "Pete must have flown back and forth a half dozen times to Australia in '55 and '56," Dick Rozelle said. "I had just started working as a petroleum geologist on an offshore rig when he convinced me to quit and go to the Olympics. He got me on a Qantas flight and gave me the tickets for the events in the main stadium, the Melbourne Cricket Ground. I never regretted it. That was the trip of a lifetime."

Pete Rozelle parlayed Landy's upset defeat in May at the Coliseum into worldwide interest in the 1,500-meter race at the Melbourne Olympics. Landy was about to make his move early on the third lap, when a runner accidentally stepped on the heel of another Aussie, Ron Clarke, just ahead of Landy. Landy leaped over his countryman to avoid a collision and then stopped to see if he was all right. When Clarke got up and continued to run, Landy picked up the pace. He caught up to the leaders and earned a bronze medal behind Delaney and Soviet Vladimir Kuts. Australia's National Centre of History and Education called Landy's act "a spontaneous gesture of sportsmanship" that "has never been forgotten." Soft-spoken, witty, and well read, Landy became governor of Victoria in 2001, serving a five-year term that ended April 6, 2006.

Other Macker clients that Rozelle counseled during his time with the firm included Qantas Airlines; Ampex, which invented videotape and marketed tape and machines to the networks starting in 1956; and the San Miguel Brewing Company. Clearly, the 30-year-old Rozelle was a rising star in the public relations business, but all was not well at home. Pete Newell had returned to the Bay Area from Michigan State in 1954 as basketball coach at California–Berkeley. "Jane was a wonderful lady, a beautiful lady," Newell said. "It was a real good marriage except for her problem when Pete left football and went to Australia." That "problem" was alcohol, and other friends noticed as well.

By 1954, before Rozelle joined Ken Macker, the National Football League had gone on the move. Several teams were televising their games, with the largest network being the one George Halas and his business manager, Rudy Custer, developed and nurtured to carry the Bears' and Cardinals' home games to the hinterlands. To make it easier for the game's new fans, and help the officials, Commissioner Bell created a standard numbering system in 1952. Before then, anybody could wear the number that either he wanted or, more likely, an equipment manager issued.

Bell placed quarterbacks and kickers in single digits and teens, running backs from 20 to 49, centers in the 50s, linebackers generally in the 50s and 60s, guards in the 60s, tackles in the 70s, and ends in the 80s. Other linemen would be assigned numbers in the 90s as the roster limits increased from 1952's 33 to the present-day 53 with 45 active game-day players. Bell allowed a few exceptions, most prominent being Detroit quarterback Bobby Layne, who continued to wear number 22 for the Lions and, after that, in Pittsburgh; end Elroy Hirsch, who stayed at number 40 with the Rams; and Paul Hornung, who wore his Notre Dame number 5 for the Green Bay Packers. Norm Van Brocklin, meanwhile, traded in number 25 for 11, Otto Graham went from 60 to 14, and so forth. Had he been able to play in 1952, the game's most famous early star, Bears halfback Red Grange, might have been forced to give up his number 77, now designated for linemen.

With increased television exposure, the rule makers started taking steps to better protect their players from injury. The Cleveland Browns were playing host to the 49ers, with more than 80,000 in attendance and thousands more watching at home, when Otto Graham got pushed out of bounds in front of the Cleveland bench. Paul Brown detailed the incident in his memoir, *PB: The Paul Brown Story*. "Art Michalik, a 220-pound linebacker, steamed into him and smashed a fist into his face," Brown wrote.

Brown calmed his revenge-seeking players at halftime. While Brown spoke to his team, Dr. Vic Ippolito completed a 15-stitch repair job to the inside of Graham's mouth. Without Novocain. "Before I allowed Otto to play in the second half, I had Morrie Kono attach an inch-thick piece of clear plastic to his helmet to protect his face, and he wore it for several games thereafter," Brown wrote. Wearing that makeshift face guard, Graham returned to the game with a swollen jaw and completed 9 of 10 passes to lead the Browns to a 23–21 victory.

Out of that jury-rigged appliance came the face mask, which, in due course, would be as mandatory as the helmet itself. Experimentation would follow. The players did not like plastic bars because the plastic fogged up and broke in cold weather, and they couldn't adjust them to spit. So, Brown went to Jerry Morgan, of the Riddell Company, the Chicago-based helmet and equipment manufacturer, who devised a light, strong, single plastic bar. Next came the double bar, followed by the current standard-issue face cage all players wear. Until the cage became the norm, Riddell paid Brown a royalty on every single or double face bar made. By 1962, only Steelers quarterback Bobby Layne and Bears punter Bobby Joe Green had waivers to play without face guards.

Graham thrived behind his new facial protection, having his best career years. He announced his retirement on the eve of the 1954 championship game, the Browns' third straight with the Lions. Graham completed 9 of 12 passes for 163 yards and three touchdowns and ran for three more as the Browns routed the Lions 56–10. The following summer, realizing he could not win without Graham because his replacement, George Ratterman, had a torn rotator cuff and could not throw the ball across a room, Brown begged Graham to return. Graham, now 34, led the league in passing and capped off his career in the championship game against the Rams. He passed for 209 yards for a pair of touchdowns and ran for two more to lead the Browns to a 38–14 win. Every year in his decade with Paul Brown was a championship season for Otto Graham. He quarterbacked the Browns to four All-America Conference titles and six National Football League championship games, winning three titles.

These days, every play in the NFL is subject to potential video review. Officials must blow the whistle the instant any part of a ball-carrier's body other than his hands or feet hits the ground. The ball is then spotted, either by sight or by video review from upstairs. Before 1955, a ballcarrier was not declared down until an official ruled he was stopped. A runner could get back up, or crawl, until the whistle stopped play. The rules-changing incident took place at Kezar

Stadium on Halloween 1954 late in the sixth game of the season, between the unbeaten, once-tied 49ers and the Bears.

The 49ers' Hugh McElhenny was on a pace to break the NFL season rushing record and had just gained his 515th yard, an 8.0 average, when he got nailed trying to crawl for an extra yard. He left the game with a season-ending shoulder separation. The Bears won 31–24 on an Ed Brown 66-yard touchdown pass to Harlon Hill in the closing seconds. Without McElhenny, the 49ers' season was shattered, as they finished third in the Western Conference with a 7–4–1 record, behind the Lions and late-surging Bears. The "McElhenny Rule," enacted in 1955, whistled play dead the instant a defender caused a ballcarrier to make ground contact with any part of his body except his hands or feet.

A most significant retirement marked the halfway point in the decade, 1956. That February, saying that at age 61 it was time for him to let a younger man coach his Chicago Bears, NFL founder George Halas, the league's biggest winner with 248 victories, turned over the team to his crony Paddy Driscoll, who actually was 22 days older. That arrangement lasted for two seasons, just enough time for Halas to recharge his batteries.

While Otto Graham was the best among many superb quarterbacks who came of age in the '50s, Paul Brown refused to let him call any plays, save for audibles. Brown was the exception, as, almost to a man, the other players in the league believed it was their game. When it came to calling plays, every other coach—from Halas to Buddy Parker to Browns former assistant Weeb Ewbank in Baltimore to the Giants' offensive coordinator and future Green Bay Packers legend Vince Lombardi—trained his quarterback to run the team on the field.

Accordingly, the quarterbacks met the challenge. In an essay for the 1960 coffee-table book *The Pros*, Tex Maule stated that an ideal quarterback "passes with the instinctive accuracy of a Kentucky rifleman, fakes as coolly as the operator of a carnival shell game, and runs as thoughtfully as a fox before the hounds. He must know all the complexities of a modern pro offense faultlessly and he must be able to command this wide range of information instantly in the 25 seconds between offensive plays."

Maule stressed in that prescient essay that John Unitas, "now early in his career, seems to be the perfect quarterback." Maule placed Unitas directly in the lineage of quarterbacking royalty: "Unitas has evolved out of Sid Luckman and Bob Waterfield and Bobby Layne and Otto Graham and Charlie Conerly and Norm Van Brocklin—or so it seems."

The Unitas story already had become part of NFL folklore. He was the dirt-poor, skin-and-bones Pittsburgh kid that no big school wanted. Forced to learn his craft at the only place that accepted him, the University of Louisville, Unitas was the Steelers' ninth-round draft choice in 1955. He was cut without getting much of a chance and then played sandlot ball that fall in Pittsburgh for $6 a game. In 1956, Baltimore Colts general manager Don Kellett, who checked Unitas out with, of all people, Steelers owner Art Rooney, invited him to training camp in a brief long-distance telephone conversation, the famed 90-cent call.

Unitas starred in the preseason games and made the team as backup to 1955 star rookie George Shaw. When Shaw went down in the fourth game with a season-ending knee injury against the Bears in Chicago, coach Ewbank turned to Unitas. J. C. Caroline intercepted his first regular-season pass and ran it back 59 yards for a Chicago touchdown to start the Bears rolling to a 58–27 victory. Unitas kept throwing, though. Buried deep in that day's game stories and scoring summaries was the cold fact that Unitas threw a late 36-yard scoring pass to end Jim Mutscheller. That was the start of pro football's most enduring record, Johnny U.'s 47-straight-game streak with one or more touchdown passes.

More important to the financial future of pro football, the big networks jumped aboard in 1956. "They didn't have a one-network contract then," former NBC Sports producer Don Ellis said. While Bell could not lock up an exclusive deal for the league, he was able to persuade CBS to air the telecasts of 9 of the 12 teams on Sunday afternoons. Each team involved then had to negotiate its rights payment. As Ellis noted, NBC had contracts with the Steelers and Colts. The Browns had their own Sohio Oil Company network. That confederacy would last through the 1960 season.

In 1955, NBC paid the league a $100,000 rights fee to carry the championship game. "NBC Sports president Tom S. Gallery had a handshake deal with Bell," Ellis said. "In the early part, up through the Giants-Baltimore championship game, they didn't have a formal contract. We did championship games in Cleveland, New York three times, Detroit, Baltimore, Philadelphia, Green Bay, and Chicago."

A galaxy of stars burst into the league in the 1957 draft. Not all made instant impacts, but several would make the Pro Football Hall of Fame. The league split the 30-round draft into two dates, conducting the first 4 rounds on November 27, 1956, before the bowl games, and completing rounds 5 through 30 on January 31, 1957. The Green Bay Packers exercised the bonus pick on Notre Dame's Heisman Trophy winner, Paul Hornung, and for their 1st-round pick, they took Michigan's all-America end and all-America basketball forward, Ron Kramer.

Coach Lisle Blackbourn and his 1958 replacement Ray "Scooter" McLean misused the Golden Boy at three positions the next two seasons, leaving him so dispirited that he was ready to quit. When McLean got fired after the 1958 season, Packers president Dominic Olejniczak and board member Jerry Atkinson called on Paul Brown, who recommended they hire either his longtime assistant and friend Blanton Collier or Giants assistant Vince Lombardi. Not wanting to lose Collier, Brown pushed hard for Green Bay to hire Lombardi. When the new coach and general manager arrived from New York in 1959, he installed Hornung at halfback, where the Golden Boy glittered again to become one of the game's greatest stars.

Because the Browns were in the East and Green Bay was in the West, Lombardi got another break when Paul Brown decided to make him his trading partner. Off the bat, he practically handed Lombardi three defensive linemen who would be linchpins in the Packers' championship dynasty: end Bill Quinlan and two future Hall of Famers— end Willie Davis and tackle Henry Jordan.

The Pittsburgh Steelers, who missed on Unitas, drafted another quarterback. He was Purdue's Lenny Dawson, whom Brown had known about since Dawson's high school days in nearby Alliance, Ohio. Dawson neither made it with Pittsburgh nor succeeded in

Cleveland when Brown finally landed him. "He was a great organizer, but he didn't know anything about quarterbacking. He didn't know that much about the Xs and Os," Dawson said of Brown a half century later, a complaint echoed by controversial defensive back Bernie Parrish.

"Hell, he wouldn't even let us warm up before we started throwing," Dawson added. "We were up there in old League Park. What a nasty place that was to work out. It had two commodes. One of them worked. Maybe two showerheads, no tarp on the field. Every practice, we started a tackling drill, Milt Plum and I: one side tackle; then another side tackle. Then you did your calisthenics. If we wanted to throw, we had to find a way to get out early, the two of us. He never set aside time for quarterbacks to warm up. No, he never gave me a chance." Dawson finally hit the jackpot with his former college position coach, Hank Stram, in the American Football League in Dallas and Kansas City.

The 49ers selected Stanford quarterback John Brodie, who stayed and played quite well in San Francisco for 17 years. The Baltimore Colts picked arguably the best offensive lineman in history, Jim Parker, of Ohio State, and installed him at left tackle as Unitas's protector. When the draft came around to Cleveland and Paul Brown on round 6, the three quarterbacks he sought—Hornung, Brodie, and Dawson—were gone. All that did was force him, albeit reluctantly, to take arguably the greatest single football player who ever lived, if not the greatest athlete in any sport: Jim Brown.

Brown was born in St. Simons, Georgia, on February 17, 1936. After his parents divorced, he moved with his mother to Manhasset, Long Island, where she worked as a housekeeper for wealthy families. An excellent student, Brown earned 13 letters in football, lacrosse, basketball, and track at Manhasset High School. At Syracuse, Brown was all-American in football and considered the greatest lacrosse player in collegiate history.

On New Year's Day 1957, Texas Christian, led by ballyhooed all-America Jim Swink, beat Syracuse 28–27 in the Cotton Bowl despite the incredible afternoon by the Orangemen's Jim Brown, already bound for Cleveland. Six weeks shy of his 21st birthday, Brown scored all 27 Syracuse points on four touchdowns and three extra points!

The strict and demanding Paul Brown knew that Jim Brown was a player he could not intimidate, a man he could not understand. Jim Brown was a revolutionary who changed all sport in the '50s, as an athlete who played with controlled fury, a proud man, the first outspoken "black militant." Paul Brown had prided himself on race relations in the '40s when he signed three future Hall of Famers—guard Bill Willis, fullback Marion Motley, and defensive end Len Ford—plus non–Hall of Fame punter Horace Gillom. Paul Brown, though, was as analytical as he was practical. As he wrote in his autobiography, "We selected Jim Brown strictly because he was the best player available at the time."

In the case of the Browns, the relationship between coach and player abraded and then rubbed raw through the years. Decades after Jim Brown led the players' revolt that resulted in the coach's firing, Paul Brown still was unbending toward a mystery he could only rationalize, never solve. Writing that he felt sorry for Jim Brown and his well-publicized difficult postfootball life, he expressed regrets with reservations concerning "such a great player." He was still galled by Jim Brown's "lackadaisical approach to practice and blocking," an ironic comment seen in the light of the early 21st century, when all running backs put blocking on their skills back burner. Paul Brown had to acknowledge that: "I never faulted his total effort in any game he played for the Browns and never hesitated to compliment him for his outstanding play."

Jim Brown's record provides eloquent testimony to his greatness. He was Rookie of the Year and Most Valuable Player in 1957, the first of four MVP years. He led the league in rushing in 1957 and every year afterward except 1962, eight times in all, for 12,312 yards, a record 5.2 yards per carry. That mark set over four 12-game seasons and five 14-game seasons, compared with the present 16-game schedules, still lasted 18 years, until the late Walter Payton surpassed it in 1984.

Teammates such as defensive back Bernie Parrish, who had his own run-ins with Paul Brown and then with Art Modell, loved Jim Brown as a teammate. "If the hash marks were where they are now, Jim Brown would have gained 20,000 yards, and we would have won five championships as well," Parrish said in 2006.

Out in Los Angeles, the long-running bickering in the Rams' hierarchy had turned to open warfare among Dan Reeves and his partners. After reaching the title game in 1955, the team fell to last in the Western Conference in 1956 with a 4–8 record. The only organizational brightness emanated from general manager Tex Schramm and his scouting staff. In the 1st round of the 1957 draft, Schramm pounced on a local favorite, USC all-America halfback Jon Arnett, and then worked a trade with the league-champion Giants and, with the 11th pick on the 1st round, grabbed Baylor's tall, fast, and gifted pass-catching end Del Shofner. In the 2nd round, Schramm chose Texas A&M linebacker Jack Pardee, followed in round 3 by Arkansas defensive tackle Billy Ray Smith. In the 4th round, he practically stole defensive end Lamar Lundy, of Purdue. All would be mainstays in the league for the next decade and a half. Deep in the pack, in the 25th round, Schramm chose Georgia halfback-end Jimmy Orr, who would play a prominent role with the Baltimore Colts in Super Bowl III, 13 years later.

Schramm had been upset for a long time with the constant feuding among Reeves and his partners. The more quarrelsome it got, the more Reeves turned to drink. Finally, after Schramm locked up one of the great drafts in Rams history, he went to Reeves and told him he was leaving to join CBS in New York as assistant director of sports. Among his duties would be supervision of the NFL telecasts.

When that domino fell, Bert Bell sprang into action. Bell liked and respected Rozelle when he was with the Rams, believed he was a definite comer, and felt he was the only one the bickering partners liked and trusted. So, he called him in San Francisco and told him that Reeves would lose the franchise unless Rozelle came back as general manager. Then, Bell placed a call to Reeves and told him he'd better land his once bright young man if he wanted to hold on to the Rams.

"Reeves called Pete constantly at home in Burlingame, upping the ante with each call," Dick Rozelle recalled. "Pete felt obligated to Macker, but Reeves persisted and finally made him an offer he could not refuse to be the general manager." Macker gave his friend his blessing, and on April 8, 1957, saying he was glad to be back, the 31-year-old Rozelle took over as general manager of the Los Angeles Rams. He calmed the troubled waters everywhere, with the players, persuading the partners to pay them $50 a game in the preseason, raise the per diem from $6 to $9, and pick up half the premiums on each player's health insurance, which had been the player's responsibility prior. He instilled an air of quiet professionalism around the office and started a practice, which he would follow when he became commissioner, of sending each employee a personal Christmas card with handwritten comments praising the person's value to the club.

Rozelle did what he could with the bickering partners. Reeves and Edwin Pauley, especially, would not speak personally to each other, let alone ride the same elevator to the press box. But Rozelle stopped the impasse and got them to at least communicate.

When it came to the PR aspect of the job, he hired David Boss, a superb graphic artist, to produce the team's yearbooks and game programs. Then he hired Larry Kent, a merchandising expert who worked with the highly successful Roy Rogers licensing operation. Kent set up the Rams Store on Beverly Boulevard near the Rams' offices to merchandise everything with Rams logos on them, from T-shirts to highball glasses to earrings, and a new-fangled ceramic helmeted bobble-head doll. It was the forerunner of the merchandising business he would form as commissioner, NFL Properties.

On the field, the Rams went 6–6 that season, finishing a game ahead of the disappointing Bears, who dropped to 5–7 after losing 47–7 to the New York Giants in the 1956 title game. The big feud moved out of the owner's box to the locker room, where the relationship between Gillman and star quarterback Van Brocklin ruptured beyond repair. Tired of splitting time with Billy Wade, whom he considered Gillman's "boy," Van Brocklin vowed to retire, a threat Rozelle took seriously. "Anywhere but Pittsburgh and Philadelphia," the Dutchman snarled.

Rozelle shopped the Dutchman around the league trying to find a taker. Finally, he hooked the Eagles, who gave the Rams defensive back Jimmy Harris, guard Buck Lansford, and 1959's top draft choice, who turned out to be star running back Dick Bass. The irate Van Brocklin still threatened to retire, until Bert Bell told him he would ensure that the Eagles would name him head coach when veteran Buck Shaw retired, which Bell figured would happen within the next three years. Van Brocklin accepted the commissioner's gesture and grabbed the Eagles franchise by the wings and set it on a course toward a title.

On February 16, 1958, George Halas, having recently turned 63, summoned the Chicago sportswriters to his office. "Pro football has changed so much, I thought it would be a good idea if I stepped back in the picture with the things I've learned," he announced. Halas said he would coach for only one season, with this catch: "I don't know what will happen after the year." He stuck around as coach for another decade that included one championship and two Coach of the Year awards.

About that same time, Jane Rozelle told her husband the happy news. She was pregnant with their first and only child. Ann Marie (she would become Anne Marie when she got older) was born, almost fittingly, on opening day, September 28, 1958. The Rams were leading the Browns at halftime when Rozelle left for the hospital to see his little girl. By the time he returned, Cleveland had overcome a 27–14 deficit and won it on a Lou Groza field goal with 16 seconds left, 30–27. "I wasn't able to pass out cigars for a double victory, but I gained a daughter," Rozelle said. It was one of the few happy moments he could share with Jane. Ken Macker became Anne Marie's godfather.

"I have very few memories of her being at home," Anne Marie Rozelle Bratton said in 2006. "They were married for 10 years before I was born, and I think they were hoping that maybe the baby could sort things out. It didn't."

Rozelle and Gillman put an interesting, exciting product on the field in 1958 as the Rams became the biggest moneymaker in the sport. The previous year, on November 10, 1957, the largest-ever crowd in pro football history, 102,366 customers, filled every available square inch of the Coliseum and were treated to a 37–24 victory over the hated 49ers. The turnstiles would click at an even merrier pace in 1958.

On October 19, the Rams blew into Chicago's Wrigley Field and took a 7–0 lead on the first series of the game on a 92-yard scoring pass from Wade to Shofner. That wake-up call was all the Bears needed as they routed the Rams 38–10. The game ended in a fight that saw the Bears' George Blanda ejected. The rematch came two weeks later on November 2. The temperature on the floor of the Coliseum was in the high 90s, and the fans came in droves, not just for the rematch but to yell at Halas, back again after his two-year retirement. Halas had grabbed the headlines the week before at Kezar Stadium, in San Francisco, when a fan jumped out of the stands and went after him. Before the fan could land a punch, several Bears intervened and delivered their licks, and the police took him away. In L.A., Rozelle had predicted another record crowd, but it topped off at 100,470. It was a crowd pleaser all the way, ending in a 41–35 Rams victory.

It was obvious before midseason that the Baltimore Colts had the best team in the Western Conference. Johnny Unitas was not only the best quarterback but also, that year, the league's best player, Jim Brown notwithstanding. On Saturday, December 6, the Colts, conference champions at 9–1, had nothing to play for but pride. The Rams wanted it more that day, winning 30–28 before 100,202 fans.

The next week, the 49ers beat the Colts 21–12 in another meaningless game to everyone but Gino Marchetti. Marchetti had talked about starting a fast-food business specializing in hamburgers with his Colts teammates Alan Ameche and Joe Campanella. "I was from Antioch, California, 40 miles outside San Francisco," he recounted. "One afternoon, I got a call. 'Carroll Rosenbloom wants to see you in his suite.' God almighty, I thought. I got nervous as hell. Here we were going to the championship game, and he wanted to see me. I didn't know if I was going to get traded. So, I walked into his suite, and he took a look at me and said, 'Listen, you dumb hillbilly, what are you going to do with your life?'

"I said, 'What do you mean?'"

Rosenbloom asked sharply, "Yeah, what are you going to do?"

"I don't know," Marchetti told him. He recalled, "I was going back to Antioch, I was bartending, and I was happy as hell."

Rosenbloom replied, "I want you to move you and your family to Baltimore. I want you to go into business in Baltimore. People like you can look for a future there. Plus, I'll help you if you go into business."

"After the game, he told my wife to make the move back to Baltimore. He kept his word. He really helped us get started with Gino's, and it was a big help," Marchetti said. "Anytime we needed any professional advice, whether it was financial advice or going public, he said, 'Come on up.' We'd go to New York and sit with the best minds there. He was a damned good friend and damned good boss to me, and that's why I chose him to present me to the Hall of Fame when I was inducted."

Marchetti concluded, "We worked hard. We ended up selling it to Marriott in 1980 or '81. My life I owe to Carroll. Without him, I would have gone back to Antioch, worked in the fiberboard mill, and probably retired and done a little fishing. Here I do big fishing!" Three weeks after Marchetti was summoned to Rosenbloom's office, the Colts and Giants squared off in "The Greatest Football Game Ever Played."

FIVE

THE GAME
HAS ARRIVED

*"The 1958 championship played between the
Baltimore Colts and New York Giants in Yankee
Stadium was, quite simply, the best football
game ever played."*

—Tex Maule, *The Pros*, 1960

*I*n the George Russell composition
"A Helluva Town," from the late-'50s jazz album *New York, New
York*, vocalist Jon Hendricks's lyrics lovingly embrace the city as a
"somethin'-else town where eight million people live and one million
pass through every day. Some come to visit. Some come to stay," to
reach a rosy conclusion, "New York, New York, a town so nice, they
had to name it twice." But, the song implies, you better be tough!

From the time of its incorporation in 1665, New York has been
America's dominant city. It is the center of commerce as well as the
intellectual and cultural heart and soul. A new concept or product
that gets the New York stamp of approval becomes legitimate.

When it came to opportunity in the '50s, New York was the place
where a hard-edged cynic and a wide-eyed hick could compete as
equals before ability willed out. One hungry outlander who wanted
to make it in the worst way arrived in 1956 from the coal mines of

Appalachia. He was the New York Football Giants' third-round draft choice, a hard-nosed son of a miner, nephew and cousin of many others, a tackle from West Virginia everybody called Sam, whose given name was Robert Lee Huff. Sam Huff would move into the lineup at middle linebacker that season.

"I had to learn my way around New York City and learn that the trains ran underground. The coal cars, you know, were pulled by a coal-powered steam engine. In New York, it was electric. Whoever designed the subway system in New York had to be a genius. It was fantastic," Huff said. "New York just is the greatest city in the world. They had at least two of everything. Look at how many railroads they had—the Pennsylvania and New York Central and the Long Island, all coming into New York City. It's just an amazing city."

Huff arrived at the vortex of a perfect moment in time. New York idolizes its stars, and the Giants had them in abundance. The idol of idols was handsome Frank Gifford, who came of age in 1956 with his teammates as the Giants of Tim Mara and his sons Jack and Wellington bade farewell to their ancient, ramshackle Polo Grounds, the relic of Red Grange's debut and the Sneakers Game, and took up residence across the Harlem River in the home of champions, Yankee Stadium.

"The Yankees were going great at the time. You had Billy Martin, Tony Kubek, Moose Skowron, and all the guys—Whitey Ford, Mickey Mantle. The Dodgers were going great. The Giants, when we came to town—it was just unbelievable," Huff recalled a half century after his arrival. "To be able to play at Yankee Stadium, the stadium you've heard about all your life! And you just know that Joe DiMaggio played here. Babe Ruth played here. Lou Gehrig played here. Every game was like a bowl game to me."

New York and the Giants have been vital to the success of the National Football League since league president Joe Carr persuaded bookmaker Tim Mara to buy a local franchise for $500 in 1925. Mara then named the team the New York Football Giants to avoid confusion with the New York Giants baseball club. On December 6 that year, George Halas brought his Chicago Bears and the game's first great star, Red Grange, to town to make his New York debut.

No one ever was certain how many people jammed into the Polo Grounds that day. Estimates stopped at 70,000 but who knows how many more might have been there? That huge, roaring crowd screamed itself hoarse when Grange scored a touchdown to lead the Bears to a 19–7 victory. The outcome was immaterial to the real story. Pro football would be the next great sport. New York called it legitimate. And it was so.

The Giants through the years have appeared in 17 championship games, more than any other team, and have won six titles. But New York was just one club among a dozen in 1958, still untapped for the assets it could bring to pro football's major league. From the National Football League's beginnings in 1920, the NFL offices were situated elsewhere: Columbus, Ohio, until 1941; Chicago; and, since 1945, Philadelphia. All those years, the NFL danced to tunes called by Halas of Chicago, Lambeau of Green Bay, Marshall of Washington, Rooney of Pittsburgh, Brown of Cleveland, and, to a lesser extent but because of his city's sheer size, Mara of New York. Rosenbloom of Baltimore was knocking on the door and desperately wanted to flex his muscles and considerable ego.

To complete Sam Huff's brilliant rookie year, 1956, the Giants devastated the heavily favored Bears 47–7 for the championship before the largest television audience ever to watch a pro football game. That was all it took for the movers and shakers in New York's media and advertising world to declare the league's legitimacy. The country heard the drumbeat and asked for more football, National Football League style.

At the behest of the networks before the 1957 season, commissioner Bert Bell decreed that all visiting teams must wear white-based jerseys and home teams must wear darker colors. Viewers had complained that they could not tell the teams apart on their black-and-white TV sets in that precolor era. Bell's ruling forced compliance from such teams as the Bears, whose players had worn navy blue jerseys in every game since 1941, and the Browns, who wore white, with a couple of exceptions, since the franchise's founding in 1946.

That decree forced the Los Angeles Rams, who had not worn blue since the '40s, to redesign their uniforms top to bottom. That meant their sunset orange jerseys, which showed up muddy on television, were out. In response, general manager Pete Rozelle, with Dan Reeves's approval, ordered everything to be restyled in a dark blue and white motif, from the contrasting numbers and sleeve trim to the horns on the helmets, which would be white instead of gold on the basic blue background.

That white-jerseys-only policy for visitors would change in 1964 when Commissioner Rozelle decreed that home teams would select the uniform, traditional home or road white, an edict that remains in effect to this day. By then, the NFL would be the hot league in sport, pro and amateur, years removed from its grittiest struggles.

Even in 1958, though, no one, at least in New York, would dare doubt that pro football was shoving aside baseball. Two of the National League's core teams from its early days, the New York Giants and the Brooklyn Dodgers, pulled up stakes after 1957 to go west—the Dodgers to Los Angeles, the Giants to San Francisco. And the Yankees did not thrive at the gate the way they'd hoped, despite another world championship in the Bronx.

As the pro football season wound to its conclusion, the movers and shakers on Madison Avenue took the nation's temperature and sensed a heightened buzz surrounding the coming NFL title game. The five-year-old Baltimore Colts with their blue-collar ethic, led by Cinderella quarterback Johnny Unitas, had a love affair with their city unlike any that professional sports had ever seen. "My father ran his teams as a family. The family is owners, coaches, players, and trainers. Everybody is one big family, everybody has import, and everybody is considered," Steve Rosenbloom said. "It was like going to college. The fans knew every person involved in any way with the team. Part of the Colts family were the fans. Our job was to get out there and reach out to them."

The Colts mystique in Baltimore in the '50s was an underlying thesis of Barry Levinson's classic film *Diner*. Steve Guttenberg's character, Eddie Simmons, refuses to marry his bride-to-be until she passes a stringent Colts' history test—a quiz, incidentally, written for the film by Ernie Accorsi. All is well when she passes, and she marches up the aisle to the Colts' fight song. That may have been fiction. Then there was reality, as Steve Rosenbloom recalls. "In divorces, season tickets were contested. 'The hell with the kids; gimme the damn tickets!'"

The Colts would face the Eastern Conference champions, either the perennially strong Cleveland Browns or the Giants, who were now the league's glamour team. In 1954, the Maras made the tough call when they told coach Steve Owen they were letting him go after 24 years, 155 victories, and two titles. On offense, Owen was known for his unique A formation, in which the quarterback took a direct snap and could hand off or pitch to the halfbacks lined up on each side or to the fullback behind him. He left his imprint on a defensive formation he called the "umbrella": six linemen, a middle linebacker, and four defensive backs as the spokes.

The Maras replaced Owen with former Giants end Jim Lee Howell, who ran the team like a CEO, delegating the detail work to his top assistants, offensive master Vince Lombardi and Tom Landry, while he read newspapers with his feet up on his desk. When Landry took over as player–assistant defensive coach, he modified Owen's umbrella by dropping the ends off the line to form what became the still widely used "4-3," featuring four linemen, three linebackers, and four defensive backs—two on the corner and two safeties. "Tom Landry and Vince Lombardi were the greatest coaches I've ever known," Sam Huff said. "They were great gentlemen. Lombardi swore a lot, but he was a very religious man. Tom Landry didn't swear, and he was a very religious man. He said a lot of 'dadburnit's and things like that, and he would look at you. Lombardi would yell at you. It was so different and unbelievable, and you just knew how great they were."

The Eastern Conference race of 1958 became a classic from midseason on. The Browns opened up with 5 straight wins. The Giants were stuck in second, 2 games behind at 3–2, when they went to Cleveland on November 2 and beat the Browns 21–17. That left them at 4–2 and Cleveland at 5–1. A week later, the defending champion Detroit Lions roared into Cleveland and went home with a 30–10 victory as the Giants beat the Colts 24–21 at Yankee Stadium with George Shaw at quarterback in place of Unitas. Unitas had to miss that game after suffering a punctured lung the week before in a 56–0 rout of Green Bay, when Packers defensive back John Symank landed on his chest with both knees and broke three ribs.

The following week, the Giants got tripped up at Forbes Field, in Pittsburgh, falling 30–10 to the Steelers, while the Browns beat the Washington Redskins 20–10 to take a one-game lead, which they clung to coming into the final Sunday, December 14, at Yankee Stadium. Over the next 60 minutes, a man who was so sick of losing that he nearly quit after the 1957 season would become an all-time Giants hero and parlay that game into one of the most enduring careers in broadcast history.

George "Pat" Summerall, a 1952 graduate of the University of Arkansas, had survived a half dozen forgettable seasons as a defensive end and reasonably good placekicker. He withstood Bobby Layne's rookie hazing in Detroit in 1952 and then moved to the South Side of Chicago, where he played through the 1957 season. He was best known perhaps for a front-page picture in the *Chicago Tribune* sports section showing him receiving a Harlon Hill left hook during an all-hands brawl late in the Cardinals' 10–3 loss to the crosstown Bears at Wrigley Field on December 9, 1956.

Just before the 1958 training camp opened, Summerall picked up his hometown Jacksonville, Florida, newspaper to read that the Cardinals had traded him and defensive back Lindon Crow to the Giants for defensive backs Bobby Joe Conrad and Dick Nolan. Summerall fit in immediately at training camp as a guy who played hard on and off the field.

That Sunday, the Giants knew the task ahead. All they had to do was stop "a freight train masquerading as Jim Brown," as Summerall put it, who would lead the league with a 12-game-record 1,527 yards and run for 17 of his 18 touchdowns. It was cold, the wind was howling, and snow had been falling since morning in Yankee Stadium on a field that grew more treacherous as play proceeded. Late in the game with the score tied 10–10, the Giants lined up for a Summerall field goal to win it. "I missed wide from 31 yards out," he wrote in his autobiography, but linebacker Cliff Livingston gave him a pat on the back and vowed they would get the ball back for another chance.

That chance came with possession somewhere near the Cleveland 45, the exact spot unknown because the snow and wind obliterated the yard markers. Making out the goalposts, located as they were in those days on the goal line, was almost impossible in the swirling storm. Somehow, sure-handed Alex Webster got behind the Browns' defense, and Charlie Conerly hit him alone in the end zone with a perfect pass. He dropped it. A tie would give the Eastern title to the Browns, so Jim Lee Howell walked over to his kicker. "OK, field goal."

"You're kiddin'," Conerly, his holder, said to Summerall when he entered the huddle carrying Howell's instruction. It was no joke. So, they went out and hacked away at the ice and snow with their shoes to get a spot of sorts somewhere around midfield. Then came what Summerall called a good snap and good hold. "All I know to this day is I saw the guy behind the goalposts who shagged placekicks raise his arms. Then I heard the crowd." The kick, officially listed at 49 yards, easily split the uprights for a 13–10 New York win. The Giants forced a playoff on that same Yankee Stadium field a week later, and the new hero in town was the rangy, 6'4" Pat Summerall.

The playoff was almost anticlimactic, but just to be sure, the Giants put the clamps on Jim Brown, holding him to his worst day as a pro, just 8 yards on seven carries, as they advanced to the championship game with the Colts, 10–0. This would be the third straight game for the Giants with the title on the line. "It was a beautiful, beautiful time in sports," Sam Huff recalled. "Hell, none of us made any money. None of us."

NBC, which had the rights to the title game, desperately wanted a thriller. "Had the championship game been a blowout, and a lot of them had been very lopsided, it wouldn't stick," retired NBC producer Don Ellis said. The previous four championship games had been one-sided turnoffs everywhere but for the winning team's home market. "Because the league was smaller, with fewer players, people kind of knew, especially the fans of those teams, all the players—who they were, and so forth," Ellis said. "It wasn't a lot of no-names running around. There were a lot of stars out there: Unitas, Ameche, Gifford. They knew they were seeing something special. That added to it." The Colts were 3½-point favorites at game time.

"It was the greatest game ever played. Played by two great teams," Sam Huff said in 2006. Huff was far from the first to say it, nor will he be the last. By all consensus, *Sports Illustrated*'s Tex Maule is the one who coined the phrase that forever will be associated with that championship game of December 28, 1958, as he noted, "For the first time in football history, the sudden-death ruling went into effect [that] added the final fillip which made it the best ever." The 64,185 fans that did not quite fill Yankee Stadium were the fortunate ones. They were able to see *every* play, something that did not happen for the millions of television viewers around the country.

NBC's announcers were the network's superb staff play-by-play man, Lindsay Nelson, and the Giants' regular-season caller, Chris Schenkel. "No analysts, as they have now," Don Ellis pointed out. He sat with Nelson and Schenkel in the great outdoors. "It was in the overhang box in the baseball outfield. So, you could really get the cold weather. It was no heated press box. If you drank a lot of coffee, you really were in trouble at halftime because you had a long way to go for relief. I was up in the booth, Perry Smith was producer in the truck, and Harry Coyle was directing."

It's almost American folklore now how the Colts broke to a 14–3 halftime lead before the Giants came back in the third quarter for a touchdown and then grabbed a 17–14 lead early in the fourth quarter on Conerly's 15-yard scoring pass to Gifford. The game clock ticked laboriously in the closing minutes. It was third-and-4 at the New York 40 when Gifford took a handoff and went to his right as Gino Marchetti fought off a blocker. "I floated out there in pretty good shape. He cut back, and as he did, I planted and threw my body to the right and made the tackle," Marchetti said. "Big Daddy was chasing the play, and he came on to make sure Gifford didn't make the first down. He landed on top of me and broke my leg. They were saying, 'Gino, goddamit, get up, get up. What the hell are you faking for?' 'Hey, if I could get up, I would,'" Marchetti said.

"Gifford picked up the first down, and the official took the ball and moved it back. We got jobbed on the spot," Sam Huff said. Huff's partisan perspective notwithstanding, Howell had Don Chandler punt, and he left the Colts back at their 1 on Carl Taseff's fair catch with 2:20 left. Unitas was stuck in low gear until he hit Raymond Berry on a 25-yard pass to midfield with 1:04 left. Now the result no longer was a foregone conclusion. "Johnny Unitas was the difference between the two teams," Huff said.

Two passes to Berry, covering first 22 yards and then 15 more, moved the ball to the New York 13. Coach Weeb Ewbank lacked faith in placekicker Steve Myhra, but time was about gone, and he had no other choice. "He moved that ball; then the game was tied," Huff said, as the reality sank in that Myhra had kicked the biggest field goal in pro football history, a 22-yarder with seven seconds left. Don Maynard took Bert Rechichar's kickoff to the Giants' 18 as time ran out. It was 17–17.

"The referee came over to the sideline, and I was thinking, hell, we got half the money, anyway," Huff said. "Then he said, 'All right, we're playing sudden death. We're kicking off in three minutes.' What the hell was he talking about, I thought. Then I remembered the new rule: If it ends in a tie, the first team to score wins the game."

"From a television standpoint, that was the game that foreshadowed something for me that was going to happen later in life," Don Ellis said. A decade later, he would be the producer in the truck in Oakland for the notorious *Heidi* Game. But this game at Yankee Stadium was all that mattered in the cold winter darkness and arc lights of December 28, 1958.

"We had a fellow on the field named Stan Rotkiewicz," Ellis said. "Stan worked for our news department. He was a financial guy, the business manager. He worked on elections because he was a genius with numbers. He did stats on baseball for us, but he worked the sideline in football."

Rotkiewicz, who had played football in college, coordinated the time-outs with the officials, the same sideline job CBS called the "red hat." He would play a key role late in the overtime, a role that may have turned the fortunes of pro football, because he literally saved the telecast.

The Giants won the toss, received, and went three-and-out as Chandler punted to the Baltimore 20. Unitas took charge and led the drive to history. "Yeah, I'll tell you what about Unitas: Every time I played against him, I thought he could read my mind. Every defense I called, he beat. He was a fantastic quarterback," Huff said.

With the clock no longer a factor, Unitas mixed runs with passes as he gave practical application to Tex Maule's definition of a pro quarterback, that "he must know all the complexities of a modern pro offense faultlessly and he must be able to command this wide range of information instantly in the 25 seconds between offensive plays."

It was at that point with first down at the New York 42 that he called a play the Colts dubbed "15 sucker," a trap against hard-charging Giants tackle Dick Modzelewski that opened a hole for fullback Alan Ameche to charge through for 23 yards to the 19. To pull it off, Unitas called a fake audible, and Huff, who had been cheating to his left to stop quick passes, shifted again, leaving Little Mo vulnerable to the trap. Two plays later, Unitas drilled Berry on an 11-yard gain to the Giants 8 as television screens across America turned to snow.

"The fans were so excited about the game that they started climbing out of the bleacher area, and they grabbed ahold of our power cable. When they did, they pulled it apart. It disconnected," NBC's Ellis said. "Nobody knew what happened. Our engineers were running all over the place. In the meantime, I was saying, 'Oh, my God, what's going to happen?' I had to think what we would do if we didn't get the power back."

In those days, the networks could not get to the referee to call a time-out. Without a TV signal, Unitas gave the ball to Ameche, who was tackled at the Giants' 7 for a one-yard gain. They were about to run another play, when all hell broke loose on the field. Someone, apparently a fan who was drunk, staggered out and stopped play. "This guy was running around on the field, and the guards had to go out and get him," Ellis said. "Some people thought that it was our guy Stan out there. The staggering drunk on the field."

As Lindsay Nelson wrote in his memoir, the newspapermen covering the game were not impressed, because the sight of a well-oiled fan stumbling around was not so unusual. But Nelson knew immediately that the "staggering drunk" was NBC's aforementioned Rotkiewicz, who held the security men at bay as the engineers frantically worked to restore the picture. The home audience never knew what happened on the field. "The referee called time-out. Fortunately," Ellis said, "Perry Smith, the producer, had the people in the studio run commercial to stall."

After a delay of nearly three minutes, the engineers signaled that they had reconnected. "There was a lot of tension there until we got that power back," Ellis said. "Then Unitas went to work."

Unitas called another run for Ameche, but, as Tom Callahan reported in *Johnny U.*, Unitas saw New York's left, or strongside, linebacker, Cliff Livingston, take an inside position against right end Jim Mutscheller. He checked off, Mutscheller ran on a slant toward the corner, and Unitas hit him at the sideline, where he slid out of bounds at the 1. On the next play, the Colts opened a huge hole for Ameche, and Alan the Horse plowed through to make it 23–17 for the first championship decided in overtime.

The National Football League suddenly became an incredibly hot national commodity as the Madison Avenue advertising community that drove the media and public opinion jumped aboard. That was confirmed when *Sports Illustrated* came out with its next issue, featuring Tex Maule's cover story titled "The Greatest Game Ever Played."

Before the players went their separate ways after the game, they met the next day in their respective clubhouses to divide the playoff pot. It's human nature that teammates who've worked, toiled, and faced adversity together for months invariably get snarled in jealousies when it's time to split the take. Bitter aftertastes that often last a lifetime ensue.

The Giants' share after the division came to $3,111.33 a man after partial shares were allotted to players who had been with the club for varying times that season. Their dispute arose over how much they should give to quarterback Jack Kemp. Kemp, the future Republican vice presidential candidate who had a brilliant career in the American Football League with San Diego and Buffalo, was an NFL nomad his first three seasons.

Drafted out of Occidental by the Lions in the 17th round in 1957, he got cut by Detroit and was picked up by the Steelers, with whom he saw limited action that season. He was with the Giants in 1958 and '59 and did not play in any regular-season games either year, but he ran the scout team in practice. "We weren't going to give Jack a full cut. He was deactivated for the championship game, and some of the guys didn't want to give him a full share. It wasn't a hell of a lot then, but it meant a lot to us," Frank Gifford said.

"We almost had a fistfight in the locker room. You can't believe who was against him. It was a secret for a lot of years until somebody told him at a dinner party. He still got a big share. It really touched him, because he and Joanne put a down payment on a new home. It really pissed me off," Gifford said. "We didn't like the defensive unit, anyway. They were all guys from the defense who didn't want to cut him in."

"You know, I think maybe Frank was a little bit jealous of us," Sam Huff said. "The offense was not scoring. When the crowd started booing the offense during introductions, they started introducing us, the defense, and we got standing ovations. We were shutting down offenses, kicking ass. People loved us. They started yelling, 'Dee-fense! Dee-fense!' You could hear it, and you could feel it, brother! I was so proud and still am of the way we played."

Two hundred miles down U.S. 1 in Baltimore, the winning Colts received $4,718.77 a man. Then, as Tom Callahan reports, they split an additional $50,000–$75,000 from their broadcast sponsor, the National Brewing Company, and $25,000 from an unnamed "friend of the team" who everybody knew was Carroll Rosenbloom's gambling pal Lou Chesler. When Unitas joked to reporters that he went for the touchdown in overtime to cover the 3½-point spread, the *Baltimore News-American*'s self-appointed conscience, John Steadman, wrote it up. Unitas claimed he didn't even know what the points were or how the spread worked. Commissioner Bell called him onto the carpet in Philadelphia and let him know in no uncertain terms exactly what it meant. Then he said to the star, "You are the best advertisement we ever had."

David Harris made several allegations about Rosenbloom and Chesler's reputed gambling on that game in his 1986 book, *The League: The Rise and Decline of the NFL*. He wrote that Rosenbloom and Chesler made an untold amount of money on it and that people who knew the story claimed Rosenbloom called coach Weeb Ewbank from a press box phone and ordered him to go for the spread-covering touchdown. "There is no evidence of such a phone call on the public record," Harris acknowledged in his narrative.

Steve Rosenbloom told me in 2006 that everyone benefited from the Sudden Death Game. "It catapulted the league into the national TV deal, gave it more legitimacy and more excitement for the gamblers. One of the most talked about things was, how do we settle this bet? Where do we stop? What's the end and where's the point spread? It went on and on, and it was the best thing to push the league to another level. So, that was a very important game."

Rams GM Pete Rozelle made the first dramatic splash of the off-season when he announced on March 23, 1959, that he had traded nine players to the Chicago Cardinals for Ollie Matson, their perennial All-Pro running back. The Cardinals landed two superior linemen in the trade, tackles Ken Panfill and Frank Fuller. The Rams gained a 29-year-old Matson who no longer was the superstar Rozelle had plugged at the University of San Francisco, but he still could run. "We were playing the 49ers when Matson took a little lookie over the middle from Frank Ryan and went 96 yards up the middle," Jack Teele recalled. "He could run like the wind even at that stage of his career. Some guy in the press box said, 'Ninety-six yards, one for every player the Cardinals got for the guy.' "

Matson's best game came in his return to Chicago when he ran for 199 yards as the Rams beat the Bears 28–21 at Wrigley Field on October 11, a defeat that left the Bears in futile pursuit of the Colts all season as they finished a game behind Baltimore for the Western Conference crown. The Rams finished at 2–10, last in the Western Conference. "He was a much better general manager than a PR man," Bob Oates said. "But he wasn't a good enough general manager to compete with Tex Schramm, who had been there in Los Angeles and would be in Dallas."

In August 1959, two wealthy Texans in their late twenties whose fathers struck it rich in oil—Lamar Hunt, of Dallas, and Houston resident K. S. "Bud" Adams Jr., of the Phillips Oil fortune—approached

NFL commissioner Bert Bell. They had this notion about starting up new teams in Dallas and Houston, and they had money to burn. The friendly Bell sent them to Halas in Chicago, who gave them a businesslike no-commitment hearing in his office. Halas was not averse to Hunt and Adams and their resources; he just had no place to put them.

Hunt and Adams had no idea that another pair of Dallas oilmen-entrepreneurs and football fans, Clint Murchison Jr. and Bedford Wynne, had courted Halas for several years. Murchison and Wynne clinched their case in early autumn when they told Halas that Tex Schramm would run the team. "Nobody was more loyal to his people, nor more forgiving after he exploded. He was smart and so creative," recalled Al Ward, who got to know Schramm in Dallas. "Tex'd always say, 'There's gotta be a better way.'"

When Halas rebuffed Hunt and Adams, they rounded up a group of wealthy businessmen around the country. Even as they held out waning hope for NFL slots, on Friday, August 14, 1959, they announced the formation of an American Football League to begin play in 1960 with teams in six cities. "We followed the pattern established by baseball with its American League and National League," Hunt said. "That's why we chose the name American Football League, to resonate with the public."

Hunt would operate the Texans in Dallas while Adams would run the Oilers in Houston. Minor-league baseball owner Bob Howsam had the Denver Broncos franchise. L.A.-based hotel heir Barron Hilton went with the flashy name Chargers. Broadcaster Harry Wismer talked his way into a New York franchise he called the Titans, a word play on the established Giants. A trio of Minneapolis–St. Paul businessmen—H. P. Skoglund, Max Winter, and William Boyer—appropriately called their northernmost team the Vikings. From his experience with Halas, Lamar Hunt knew this was no easy task: "They had an established product and were not in favor of competition."

Everything changed late in the fourth quarter of the Eagles-Steelers game in the end-zone stands at Philadelphia's half-filled Franklin Field on Sunday, October 11, 1959. Bert Bell was watching the game when he collapsed and died from a heart attack. "Chances are he was laughing when the bell rang for him," Red Smith wrote the next morning in his syndicated column, as he noted how Bell had started the Eagles in the Depression and partnered with Art Rooney with the Pittsburgh Steelers during World War II. "They were playing on Franklin Field, where 40 years earlier a little Penn quarterback had played the game that was to become his life. It was almost as though he were allowed to choose time and place."

Three days later, after he eulogized his friend as a "great man and genius," at Bell's funeral in Philadelphia, George Halas made the motion at an emergency league meeting, and his fellow owners agreed, to appoint league treasurer Austin Gunsel interim commissioner. On October 20, at another league meeting in Chicago, Halas, called an "organizing genius" in an unsigned *New York Times* sidebar, ignored the objections of the Cardinals' Walter Wolfner and Marshall and introduced the new would-be Dallas franchise holders, Murchison and Wynne, to the press and league.

Papa Bear added that Houston and its bidder, Craig Cullinan Jr., likely would get a 14th franchise if they could provide a "satisfactory" stadium solution. They couldn't. A few days later, Rice University shot down Cullinan's bid, announcing it would not let the pros use its 70,000-seat stadium.

Even as Halas was announcing expansion plans in Chicago, another coaching legend who learned the intricacies of the T formation from Halas and his favorite player, quarterback Sid Luckman, joined the new league. In Los Angeles, Chargers owner Barron Hilton introduced his new general manager, a reinvigorated Frank Leahy. Leahy had been out of football since his retirement as Notre Dame coach in 1953, burned out at age 45 after winning four national titles and enduring the endless pressure of college football's most demanding job.

By then, Lamar Hunt's American Football League's original six cities had expanded to eight, when Buffalo and Boston joined Dallas, Denver, Houston, Los Angeles, Minneapolis, and New York.

Detroit businessman and Lions season ticket holder Ralph Wilson wanted to put a team in Miami. Mindful of the failure of the Seahawks there in 1946 in the first season of the old All-America Football Conference, Hunt gave Wilson the choice of five other cities: Buffalo, Atlanta, Cincinnati, St. Louis, or Louisville.

When two of Wilson's Detroit friends, Eddie Hayes, sports editor of the *Detroit Times*, and Lions general manger Nick Kerbawy, both said Buffalo was the best choice, Wilson took a look, liked what he saw, and joined up. Then a nine-man Boston syndicate fronted by Billy Sullivan stepped up after a group led by Philadelphia Phillies owner Bob Carpenter decided against getting into football.

Shortly before Bert Bell's death, Denver's Howsam approached Bell with an offer to run the AFL as well. Bell politely turned him down, saying he had enough trouble running one league, let alone two. Years later, Howsam told author Jeff Miller how Bell wrapped up that meeting with a piece of perspicacious advice. "Pool the TV money. We don't have that in our league, but I'm working on it," Bell said. "That is a very important thing."

"They were in a situation where nobody in the American Football League had anything. Also, television wasn't television yet," former NBC announcer Charlie Jones said.

Howsam ran back to Hunt with Bell's advice. "We knew we needed to be on television for the exposure, pure and simple," Hunt later told Jones. "Whatever we got, we'd split among all eight teams." Hunt had Wismer offer the motion at the next league meeting, which passed, as did an agreement to split the gate receipts on a 60/40 home-visitors percentage.

The next order of business for Hunt and his league was to find a commissioner. They quickly settled on two names: Stu Holcomb, an established college football man and athletic administrator; and the most decorated air ace of World War II, Marine Corps Medal of Honor winner Joe Foss.

Once Lamar Hunt knew he was going to start a football team, the first person he hired was Hank Stram, an assistant coach he knew from his days as a lowly scrub at Southern Methodist University, who impressed him with his knowledge and enthusiasm. Stram, a Chicago native, already had amassed a full assistant coaching résumé by age 35. It began at his alma mater, Purdue, where he won seven letters in football and baseball. He then served as head baseball coach at Purdue and backfield coach from 1948 to '55 before making stops at Notre Dame, SMU, and Miami.

One day shortly after he hired Stram, Hunt told his new coach that he was thinking of asking Michigan athletic director Fritz Crisler about his possible candidacy for the commissioner's job. Stram replied that Crisler had no interest in the pros but that Holcomb, his former boss at Purdue, would be an excellent choice. Holcomb had stepped down as football coach at Purdue after the 1955 season to become athletic director at Northwestern. By 1959, he had all the sports on the move—especially football, with his outstanding young coach, Ara Parseghian. Stram quickly arranged to bring Hunt to a meeting with Holcomb at his home in Evanston, Illinois, two blocks from Lake Michigan, near the Northwestern campus. Then he called Billy Sullivan in Boston to go after Foss.

Foss inadvertently had slipped into the search when he visited Los Angeles on a business trip while the AFL owners were meeting at a hotel there. The Minnesota ownership group pushed especially hard for Foss, a former Republican two-term governor of neighboring South Dakota. The other owners liked the prestige the war hero would offer, plus, as Charlie Jones notes, he could help the cash-poor league cut travel expenses "Foss was a general in the Air National Guard. He had a National Guard plane and could fly anywhere in two hours," Jones said.

While Hunt and Stram were talking with Holcomb in Evanston, the phone rang for Hunt. It was Sullivan, who told him Foss had just agreed to a contract. With that, Hunt and Stram took their leave from Holcomb, and the search was over. They would introduce Foss at the Minneapolis draft meeting the weekend of November 21–22.

While the American Football League was conducting its commissioner's search, George Halas was busy working his magic again. As the AFL owners arrived for the meeting, they were sandbagged by a banner headline in the *Minneapolis Star-Tribune*: "Minnesota to Get NFL Franchise."

Papa Bear had convinced Max Winter and the Twin Cities group to join the established league for the 1961 season. That meant the new Vikings had all of 1960 and early '61 to get a new club together —coaches, scouts, players; mount a season ticket campaign; the works. They would play at the newly constructed Metropolitan Stadium, in Bloomington, by the airport. "They told Lamar Hunt they were going to pull out of the AFL," said Charlie Jones, who, in 1960, had just moved from a 250-watt station that he managed in his hometown, Fort Smith, Arkansas, to broadcast the games for Hunt's Dallas Texans for ABC. "Lamar later told me, 'I made the worst mistake of my life. I sent them back their $25,000 franchise fee.'" To his credit, Foss recognized that the Winter group thought they were getting a better deal by going with the established league. So, he told Hunt to let them go.

That meant Hunt and his AFL had to find an eighth team. Finally, in January 1960, the league unveiled a franchise for Oakland, to play, ironically, across the Bay in San Francisco. "The Raiders had 32 owners and were patched together." Jones remembered. "They played their first year in Kezar; then they played at Candlestick. They died until they got to the Coliseum. Al Davis is the one who turned the franchise around." Davis in 1960 had left an assistant's job at USC to join Sid Gillman with Barron Hilton's new Los Angeles Chargers as ends coach and, with his connections, scout. He would arrive in 1963 in Oakland to mold the silver and black in his renegade image.

The National Football League paused to conduct a rematch in Baltimore between the defending champion Colts and the Giants. The Giants were leading 9–7 late in the third quarter on three Summerall field goals when they had a fourth-and-inches chance at the Baltimore 28. "Conerly sent Webster into the line, and he gained not an inch," wrote Tex Maule. The Colts took possession, and the Giants' last hope died.

Unitas blew the game open in the fourth quarter, leading a 24-point outburst to clinch Baltimore's second straight NFL title, 31–16. He threw two touchdown passes, a 60-yard linkup with Lenny Moore and 12-yarder to Jerry Richardson, ran for another, and for the second straight year was named Most Valuable Player of the championship game. "I was married at the time," Sam Huff said. "My wife thought the world of Unitas. 'Don't you hit John,' she told me. I'd like to have hit him, but she thought the world of John Unitas, like everybody did."

Another skirmish in the sniping between the new league and the established NFL came on December 28, the day after the title game, when the unborn Halas-backed Dallas Rangers beat the AFL's Houston Oilers to the punch and signed 35-year-old Tom Landry, for the last six years defensive coach of the Giants, as head coach. At the Landry signing, his new boss with the Rangers, president and general manager Tex Schramm, said he had "no doubts that the National Football League would expand."

For his part, Landry said, "There is no doubt that the long-range future is in the National Football League." Hedging their bets that joining the NFL was now a mere formality, Murchison and Wynne began signing area college stars to personal service contracts. The biggest names were New Mexico fullback Don Perkins and the big prize in the battle for Dallas, SMU quarterback Don Meredith, whom the Bears had taken in the third round in a secret draft with the understanding that he would be traded to the new Rangers.

That flurry as the old year morphed into the new left no doubt that 1960 would be a year of destiny for the National Football League.

SIX

NEW KIDS ON THE BLOCK

"What did Rozelle mean to this game of pro football? He brought theater to it. He was the engineer who put them into show business."

—KEITH JACKSON, 2005

$\mathcal{S}$hortly after 6:00 P.M. on Friday, January 29, 1960, Pete Rozelle, on his third day as National Football League commissioner, stepped out in front of the assembled reporters to announce the admission of the Dallas Rangers as the league's 13th member. The vote became 11–0 when Washington's George Preston Marshall ended his objections to the expansion plans of his longtime ally George Halas and joined the others except for Walter Wolfner, of the Cardinals, who abstained in his one-man protest against what he called Halas's rule over the league.

Dallas owners Clint Murchison Jr. and Bedford Wynne had to ante up a $600,000 chunk, considerable for most people, mere pin money for them. The Dallas entry fee enriched the league's thin treasury by $50,000. The other $550,000 was allocated among the 12 established teams to compensate for the three players each team would lose in an expansion draft. It was Rozelle's first application of equal revenue sharing.

Rozelle also announced that Minneapolis–St. Paul had been granted the league's 14th franchise, to begin play in 1961 as the Minnesota Vikings. Later during his remarks, Rozelle said, "If conditions are practical, two more teams will be added in the next three years." He had no way of knowing at that moment that his timetable would be set back until 1966 due to the increased heavy action on the war front with the American Football League.

Shortly after Rozelle took office, the NFL owners fired another salvo across the American Football League's bow when they reconvened in Dallas, now the front line of the combat zone, as it was Lamar Hunt's hometown and where he had established the AFL offices. Barely arrived in Dallas from his previous job in Fort Smith, Arkansas, Hunt's new broadcaster, Charlie Jones, was invited to attend what the NFL billed as a "major" press conference to introduce the leaders of the new Dallas franchise.

"It was set for one o'clock. Then, we waited and waited and waited," Jones recalled. "Finally, an hour later, a spokesman stepped up and said, 'Rozelle is not starting until Papa Bear finishes his nap.' Talk about power! George Halas had it. At about three o'clock, Papa Bear finished his nap and came down, and the press conference started. That's the reason he lived so long!"

Before he could move into what now would be temporary league headquarters in Philadelphia, Commissioner Rozelle had to return to Los Angeles, settle his business with the Rams, and pack for the move east. At a Los Angeles press conference on Monday, February 8, Rozelle revealed that he and Joe Foss held a private meeting for four hours the previous Saturday during a stopover at Lambert Field, in St. Louis. "We agreed that there should be no tampering with players in the two leagues," Rozelle said, reiterating the gist of Bert Bell's long-standing agreement with the Canadian Football League to honor each other's contracts. Rozelle added that he and Foss would investigate the "double-signings" issue involving Billy Cannon and Johnny Robinson, who backed away from signed NFL deals to go with the AFL on New Year's Day after the Sugar Bowl game, in New Orleans. That issue remained unresolved until later that spring when a federal judge in Los Angeles ruled in favor of the AFL.

Packing up the new commissioner's Los Angeles office was Rozelle's loyal secretary, Thelma Elkjer. "Thelma came from Tex Schramm. She used to work for him," Anne Marie Rozelle Bratton said. "When Dad went to the Rams [as general manager after Schramm quit], she worked for him." Thelma Elkjer stayed with Rozelle for the rest of his life as his personal assistant and confidant. When the Rozelle family and Thelma left Los Angeles, they had to set down in Philadelphia, where she packed away the small amount of business necessities from Bell's old Bala-Cynwyd office.

While Rozelle closed up shop in Philadelphia, the pot still boiled around the league. Operating under the primitive national radar of the time, Wolfner, the Bidwill heirs, and their Cardinals quietly slipped out of Chicago on March 13 to get a fresh start in St. Louis. The mourners basically consisted of that die-hard cadre of South Siders who did their best to support the team after Jimmy Conzelman's brief title and contending era, which featured the Charley Trippi, Elmer Angsman, Pat Harder, and Paul Christman dream backfield of 1947–48.

The last attempt at rejuvenating the franchise failed miserably in 1959 when the Cardinals moved to Soldier Field, on the lakefront, only to average 20,000 fans in the huge arena. Realizing their long run in Chicago was over, Wolfner moved two games to the Twin Cities and still failed to draw. If Wolfner had any hopes of moving the team there, Halas delivered the unkindest cut of all when he engineered the November 20 announcement prior to the Cardinals' transplanted home game with the Giants that the new Minnesota Vikings franchise had jilted the AFL for a 1961 start-up in the NFL.

So, after four decades of crosstown warfare with the other remaining original National Football League franchise, Papa Bear emerged victorious. The city at last was his, and so, at last, was the opportunity to televise his Bears' road games in the second-largest market. Of all the momentous events of recent months, this was the sweetest personal one for the league founder.

On that same day, March 13, 1960, the Dallas Rangers, founded too late to participate in the college draft, selected 36 mostly used-up or never-were veterans from the other 12 teams. Besides knowing that they were in for a shellacking, Tex Schramm and Clint Murchison had a worse problem. Neither of them liked their team's nickname. They felt "Rangers" was confusing because a Dallas Texas League baseball team by that name already existed and was on the verge of failing, and they wanted to be unique. Then, in mid-May, Schramm came up with a moniker that fit Texas like mesquite, slow-cooked barbecue, and the wide-open spaces for which the state was known. "How about Cowboys?" he said. An enthusiastic Murchison loved it. They were the Dallas Cowboys.

Schramm and his new right-hand man, personnel director Gil Brandt, a onetime baby photographer in Milwaukee, knew they had a long way to go to build the football team they wanted. To do it, they would have to go outside the draft, even to the point of finding athletes who never played college football but had the requisite ability and intelligence, especially the smarts, to fit Tom Landry's complex, exacting system. In time, the Cowboys would land gems from the basketball court, men such as Pete Gent, of Michigan State; Cornell Green, of Utah State; and Preston Pearson, of Illinois. Then, after the 1964 Tokyo Olympics, they would land 100-meter gold medalist Bob Hayes, whose incredible speed and the scoring threat he possessed literally changed the game.

Brandt wrote an organizational book in which he charted the specific needs the Cowboys sought to fill. Murchison, who owned a computer company, found a programmer to work with Brandt to set up their "Cowboy" model based on height, weight, 40-yard speed, vertical leaping height, and intelligence. To run those tests and build the playing types they wanted, they hired Bob Ward, the sport's first full-time conditioning coach.

To run Landry's sophisticated offense while young Don Meredith learned the system, Schramm cut a deal with Washington to bring in colorful, 5'7" quarterback Eddie LeBaron, a sleight-of-hand ball handler, excellent leader, and sharp passer. It would be a dreadful season. The Cowboys showed progress, though; while they were winless, they pulled off a 31–31 tie with the Giants at Yankee Stadium in the 11th game of the season.

When Pete Rozelle was elected, he announced his intention to move the league offices to New York. "He had a tremendous feel for public relations and dealing with people. That was probably his biggest strength, getting people together, getting them to agree," said the late Peter Hadhazy before his death in the spring of 2006.

Hadhazy, who would become general manager in New England and Cleveland, and an official in both the NFL and USFL, was a 17-year-old high school junior when he started working in the NFL office in 1961 as a part-timer. "He felt New York was the best place for a professional sports league," Hadhazy said. "That was where all the money was, all the advertisers were, all the television networks were, and it was a big city."

In late spring, Rozelle and Thelma Elkjer moved into space on the seventh floor at 1 Rockefeller Plaza, then called the Time-Life Building. "We, too [like Bell], were a mom-and-pop operation. We had eight people, and I could name every one of them." Hadhazy said. "The entire office in square footage was probably the size of one of our conference rooms at 410 Park Avenue."

"It was very small," recalled Rozelle's daughter, Anne Marie, who still remembered that place in detail 45 years later, even from a little girl's perspective. "It was part of one floor. There was one long hallway you could run up and down. Everyone's offices were off of it. There was a reception desk."

"Soon, we moved to the 27th floor, which had a little more room, and we were up to 18 people," Hadhazy said. Once they were settled in, Rozelle could go about the business of courting the clients who would help the league the best, the television networks and advertisers.

Rozelle had to somehow unravel the television mishmash he inherited from Bell in which CBS held the rights to nine teams, while NBC had the Steelers and Colts, and the Browns had their own Sohio-sponsored network. He had to fit Dallas into the television puzzle as well, in this case with CBS for the 1960 season, the last year of Bell's contracts. He also had to somehow show neutrality when everyone knew about his closeness to new Dallas president Schramm and Schramm's still warm ties to CBS. Yet, Rozelle well understood that he held the trump card, that the money he could find for his bosses far outweighed appearances of neutrality.

Rozelle, though, could not toss every egg into the CBS basket, had he wanted to. Bell had complicated the TV deal when he granted championship-game rights to NBC. That deal started in 1955 with the Browns' 38–14 rout of the Rams in sunny Los Angeles and would last through the Giants-Bears 1963 title game in subarctic Wrigley Field.

So, Rozelle pressed forward in 1960, setting the table for his plan to maximize the money for his owners by unifying the league under a single network. He wanted to get the works, regular season through title games, and that bias, thanks to Schramm, would tilt CBS's way. But he also knew his dream scenario depended on gaining an antitrust exemption when a new Congress and new administration took office in 1961.

Once he arrived in New York, Rozelle joined a more-or-less regular lunch group dominated by media and advertising executives. One of them was Schramm's close friend Bill McPhail, president of CBS Sports. McPhail, a lifelong bachelor, was the younger son of the bombastic, brilliant, alcoholic, innovative, and wildly successful former baseball executive Leland Stanford "Larry" McPhail. Bill's older brother, Lee, would become president of the American League and, like their father, would gain election to the Baseball Hall of Fame, in Cooperstown, New York.

Lee McPhail was not afflicted with his father's alcoholism, but brother Bill was a legendary toper in that era of the three-martini lunch. Most important to Rozelle, he was the overseer of CBS's hot NFL property, and they became fast friends. "McPhail could drink, but he couldn't hold his drinks," said Bert Sugar, who saw Bill McPhail in action during many a liquid lunch. "McPhail would delight in treating everybody to drinks as long as he had one to go along with them. So, every new crowd would get a drink, and he'd get one. He'd be reeling."

Favorite haunts included the legendary Toots Shor's, "21," also known to the group as "the numbers," and Mike Manucci's, a relatively small place with fine Italian food on the 51st Street side of the Americana Hotel before it became the Sheraton-Manhattan. "Mike Manucci was a big friend of Vince Lombardi's," Ernie Accorsi said. "Lombardi and Well Mara always would go there when Vince came to town. The bar was very popular with the NFL gang, especially after banquets or games. Great place. It's gone."

Another important player at those lunch sessions was advertising and marketing whiz Jack Landry, whose acumen turned Marlboro into the world's largest-selling cigarette. Rozelle, the Californian, and Landry, a native of Saratoga Springs, in upstate New York, struck up a lifelong friendship from the start, especially when they realized how much they had in common. Rozelle served in the navy late in World War II. Landry, born in 1924, fought in the Pacific with the marines. Both men loved sports of all sorts.

Landry grew up with horse racing in Saratoga and would become an owner and breeder of racehorses, and promoter of the Marlboro Cup. Rozelle also loved horse racing. Naturally, both men smoked Marlboros to the tune of multiple packs a day. Rozelle showed such brand loyalty that Landry and Marlboro got the prominent center advertising placement in the lineups section of the league-sanctioned game programs.

Jack Landry and Virginia (Jinny) Kavanagh met and fell in love in the summer of 1947. "I went to Saratoga as part of the *New Look*. They had chosen four models and Arnold Newman, the photographer, and a girl from *Life* magazine named Joan Lewine," Jinny Landry said. By the time they got married in 1948, Jack had become advertising director at the Blue Coal Corporation, in Wilkes-Barre, Pennsylvania. In the mid-'50s, he left the mining business for New York, first at *Newsweek*; then he got a call from Philip Morris, one of the big four tobacco manufacturers.

First concerns were rumbling by then, in that time prior to the Surgeon General's Report in 1964, of a definite link between cigarette smoking and lung cancer. Smokers switched almost en masse to filters. Philip Morris did not make filter tips then, but it marketed a milder brand earmarked for women, called Marlboro. So, the company decided to relaunch Marlboro as a filtered alternative smoke. Because they still were considered a "feminine" cigarette, soft and sissified, they didn't sell. Philip Morris then called on the Leo Burnett advertising agency in Chicago to make it go.

Burnett and Marlboro's new brand manager, Jack Landry, took charge of the campaign. Aware that they needed a rugged symbol to turn the image around, they were stumped until one of Burnett's copywriters said, "How about cowboys?" They knew they had a winner. The craggy cowboy was joined by a rugged-looking man with a mysterious tattoo on his hand. Someone in the agency came up with the slogan, "You get a lot to like with a Marlboro." Sales soared when they hired sultry Julie London to put a tune to the slogan. As a man's hand reached out to light her cigarette with her gentle guidance, London then exhaled and sang in her exquisite breathiness, "Filter. Flavor. Flip-top box."

The idea of a Marlboro Man translated to another rugged outdoor pursuit: the game of football. Jack Landry soon hired a built-in cast up at Yankee Stadium. "You saw pictures of people like Jim Patton, Jack Stroud, and others endorsing, what else, Marlboro cigarettes," Bert Sugar said.

"Charlie Conerly was one of the original Marlboro Men," Pat Summerall said. "It started the association with the NFL." Other Marlboro Men included defensive tackle Dick Modzelewski, kicker Don Chandler, and middle linebacker Sam Huff.

"I spoke and promoted Marlboro cigarettes to stores, back in West Virginia, colleges, everything else, and I never smoked. I never smoked," Sam Huff said. "You know what I did? I said, 'Here, do you smoke?' If they said yes, I said, 'Sample these. You know, you're better off not smoking, but if you're going to smoke, smoke Marlboros.' "

While Rozelle was getting acquainted with his chosen network and preferred sponsor, Lamar Hunt and the AFL did not let the grass grow under their feet. Ed Scherick, the man who helped George Halas with his Falstaff/Bears network in the early '50s, lost a power struggle with Bill McPhail to run CBS Sports. So, in 1959, he formed his own outfit, which he called Sports Programs, Inc.

Scherick's first hire was a tough-minded, knowledgeable programmer named Chet Simmons. Their breakthrough came when he made a deal with ABC to produce sports programs. To produce their events, they hired a 28-year-old NBC show producer named Roone Arledge. Arledge overflowed with plans and concepts for new television programs. His NBC claim to fame had been a kids' show for puppeteer-ventriloquist Shari Lewis that brought him the first of what would be scores of Emmy Awards.

Scherick and Simmons started by outbidding NBC for the NCAA football package. They hired accomplished veteran Curt Gowdy for play-by-play and landed the quick-witted Paul Christman, the former Missouri and Chicago Cardinals quarterback, as television's first pure football analyst. In Christman, they found a man who knew the game as a player, was telegenic, talked in plain language that fans could understand, kept it short and sweet, never outshone his partner, and was funny. He was at his wry best years later in a telecast with Ray Scott on CBS. Observing a tight first-down measurement, when the referee showed the "inches to go" sign, upraised index fingers, Christman said: "Coat of paint."

Scherick and Simmons wanted more. Aware that CBS had locked up the NFL, the AFL hired the MCA agency to go shopping for a television deal. In early spring, Simmons took a call from MCA's Jay Michaels. "Jay was Al Michaels's dad," Simmons said. "Jay and I spent an awful lot of time together. We talked to them about our willingness to talk about the American Football League. It gave us the opportunity to get involved with professional football, which was a crapshoot. Even then, in retrospect, the NFL was a very strong professional sports league with a very close tie to CBS. We thought this might be a way for us to get involved with professional football. Jay Michaels got us there."

Thanks to Michaels, the league signed a five-year contract with ABC Sports for $2,125,000 a year. Each of the eight teams received $100,000 from the pot, enough to pay at least a dozen salaries and, more important, give the league the prestige of a network television contract. "The Boston Patriots didn't want to play at home on Sunday because they didn't want to go against the Giants on television," Charlie Jones said. "All of their home games for the first couple of years were on Friday or Saturday night. Their road games would be fine because they could put them on later in the afternoon."

Boston, New York, Buffalo, and—to split Texas into two rival divisions—Houston composed the East. Denver, Dallas (later Kansas City in 1963), Oakland, and Los Angeles (which moved to San Diego in 1961) were the Western Division teams. The NFL did not telecast doubleheaders then. That would come down the road. But, in 1960, you had the doubleheader effect on two networks.

"The AFL games [on ABC, and starting in 1964 on NBC] started at four o'clock in the afternoon in the East," Jones said. "The NFL was all in the East except for L.A. and San Francisco. Most people who watched the AFL were kids in the late afternoon, and the games were high scoring, like 48–45."

Observers and followers such as the *Chicago Tribune*'s Bill Jauss who were hardened from covering Woody Hayes and his "three yards and a cloud of dust" attack at Ohio State and Halas in the NFL called the AFL's shootouts "basketball in cleats."

ABC Sports and its new senior producer Roone Arledge knew they could not let the viewers back home see acres of emptiness. "My solution," Arledge wrote, "was to provide the *appearance* of a reasonably full house by bunching everyone near the 50-yard line and censoring any shot that tracked the long flight of the ball on a kickoff or punt, because to do so would reveal endless rows of empty seats."

That bit of stage managing was something that became known in the trade, especially by Rozelle, who kept a close eye on the competition, as "AFL coverage."

The AFL, though, offered ideas the NFL either chose to ignore or had not thought of first. Bill Veeck in 1960 was the first owner in any sport to put the players' names on the back of their uniforms when he introduced the concept with his defending American League champion Chicago White Sox. The AFL liked it and followed suit.

The league also adopted college football's popular 2-point conversion option. "The AFL lost the 2-pointer in the merger because the coaches didn't want to make the decisions. That would make them think," Charlie Jones recalled. "Later, the NFL brought it back."

Because they were handling the NCAA package, Gowdy and Christman would not become the lead announcing team on AFL telecasts until 1962. "Jack Buck and George Ratterman were the lead team, at first," Jones said. "Les Keiter and Bullet Bill Dudley were another team, and I was the other announcer with whoever we could get as an analyst. I was thrilled to be involved."

Jones's involvement came when Chet Simmons called him to join the team. "Bill Mercer did the radio games with me—a neat guy. We did minor-league baseball together," Jones said. "When Chet called, I went to Lamar about ABC. 'I think that's a great idea,' he said. 'It's good for the league, it's good for the Texans, and I know that's what you want to do. We'll have Mercer do the play-by-play for the radio, find us a good color man, and go do it.' "

Jones was assigned to call play-by-play for the American Football League's first game on Saturday night, September 10, 1960, in Los Angeles, between Hunt's Dallas Texans and Barron Hilton's Chargers. The latter team was quarterbacked by Frank Gifford's good friend Jack Kemp, the Giants' castoff. "I was scared to death. I had never done television. And I was not about to tell anybody," Jones said. The producer was Roone Arledge. "In my whole life I'd never met anyone named Roone, let alone Arledge, and I couldn't remember his name. I had to write it down and carry it around with me."

"We did the game with three cameras, like everybody did, which they always put on the 50-yard line," Jones recalled. "But Roone put one on the right 20, one on the left 20, and one on the 50 in the booth with us so we could come on camera and do that. To my knowledge, that's the first time all the cameras weren't on the 50. We didn't have replays because they hadn't been invented yet. The lower thirds' superimposed titles were rudimentary [had to be shot with another camera]. We had a good telecast; it was a pretty good game. If I remember, the Texans lost to the Chargers 21–20."

Only 17,724 fans attended, leaving the vast Coliseum nearly empty. "You couldn't see 'em. You'd hear this crowd . . . *Heyyyyy.* There's somebody out there. They didn't shoot crowd shots. There wasn't any crowd you could find. And the crowd they did have was on our side, the camera side," Jones said. Then came the clincher.

"After it was over, Roone said some real nice things, and I said, 'I really appreciate it, because it's the first television game I ever broadcast.' "

"Thank God you didn't tell me," Arledge said.

"Why?" Jones asked.

"It's the first television game I ever produced!"

Jones further recalled, "After the 1988 Seoul Olympics, I got a letter from Roone. It's the only letter I ever got from him, and I have it framed. He congratulated me on the calls I made in the Olympics, and he wrote, 'and you've come a long way since that game in Los Angeles!' He obviously remembered that one too."

Lamar Hunt and his fellow AFL owners had considered revenue sharing since Bert Bell planted the seed with Bob Howsam in 1959, but the concept violated the securities laws. Both pooling of funds and monopolies were illegal.

"Everybody gives Rozelle credit for sharing and everybody having smaller TV territories. Rozelle divided them up differently," Jones said, with the reminder that Hunt and the AFL had their own ace in the hole: the AFL's commissioner. "Joe Foss went to Congress and made the deal. He had political buddies from his time as South Dakota's governor and congressman. Foss is the one who got the revenue sharing through first." Rozelle would launch his own campaign in 1961 in Congress.

As the AFL viewed the situation, it was the scrappy underdog doing battle with the well-financed, slick, media-savvy established NFL. "CBS, plus Tex Maule, the pro writer for *Sports Illustrated*, and Rozelle were the New York City triumvirate that tried to destroy the AFL," Charlie Jones charged. "With Maule, every week in *SI* was something about how great the NFL was and how shitty the AFL was."

Bill Wallace, who started covering pro football for the late *New York Herald-Tribune* in 1959 before he joined the *Times* in 1964, had a different perspective. Wallace credited Maule's "magnificent essays in the still-young [six years old in 1960] but already quite influential *Sports Illustrated*" as a significant aid to Rozelle in his early years as commissioner. "Most beat writers on papers were either jealous or contemptuous of Maule and *SI*," Wallace wrote in our correspondence. "Maule knew more football than I, and I was admiring to the point of aping his techniques. Maule was high in his praise of Rozelle for many good reasons. Tex was a delightful character. We were good friends. I enjoyed his company."

Rozelle executed his first significant publicity coup for the league thanks to his friendship with Bill McPhail. In early summer, he and the league granted CBS News permission to be the first broadcast outlet to put a wireless mike on a player. The show was Walter Cronkite's popular "Twentieth Century." The player, Sam Huff.

"I asked, 'Do I get paid for this?'" Huff said.

"'You don't get paid for it,' CBS said, 'but in training camp, we'll rent a car for you.'"

"In training camp at Winooski, Vermont, I got a car, and everybody borrowed it. There were no cars in training camp. So, that was worth a lot of money," Huff said. "Even Frank Gifford borrowed my car. The CBS guys were great. They wired me up and put that one-pound battery pack on my back and microphone on my chest and ran the antenna down my leg. Then I realized how much one pound is. It's dead weight! 'What's all this about?' I asked.

"'Just be yourself. Don't worry about it.'

"'There may be some swearing.'

"'Don't worry about it. We're going to edit all that out.'

"I was just myself, and what took place was really the true thing in a preseason game that we played up in Toronto against the Bears."

The Giants won that August 15 exhibition 17–16. The most memorable moments of the piece, titled "The Violent World of Sam Huff," came when Huff got into it with Mike Ditka's predecessor as the Bears' tight end: number 88, Willard Dewveall. "He hit me right in the face. They always called the Bears 'the dirty Bears.' They threw more punches and more elbows than anybody in the history of the game," Huff said. "I was getting off a pile, and he hit me.

"'What the hell are you doing?' I asked the kid.

"'Sam,' Dewveall said, 'I'm just trying to get on TV.' And he never hit anybody with a fair shot!"

"The Violent World of Sam Huff" gave the NFL more than just a wonderful forum on a prestigious network. It moved the league into the mainstream as it lured women to the game, popularized the sights and sounds of pro football as had not been seen or heard before, and humanized the athletes behind the helmets and armor.

Rozelle also took a step on November 9 that happily resonated throughout his league when he expelled the hapless Harry Wismer, owner of the AFL New York Titans, for violating the NFL's conflict-of-interest bylaws. He gave Wismer 30 days to dispose of his 25 percent interest in the Washington Redskins. Rozelle charged that Wismer torpedoed any case he might have had when he skipped an August hearing on the matter. That, Rozelle said, proved that Wismer did not make a conscious effort to "divest himself of the dual interest."

Claiming that Redskins principal owner George Preston Marshall had blocked other efforts to sell his stock, Wismer countered that he had a buyer, one William McDonald of Miami, who would buy his stock for $350,000. On that one, Wismer called Marshall's bluff, forcing Marshall to buy him out. On December 2, 1960, he received a $350,000 check for his 200 shares of stock from Milton W. King, the Redskins' vice president and general counsel. Wismer then made himself and his Titans the laughingstock of the AFL for the next three years before he was forced to sell out.

Washed in booze, Wismer's life fell precipitously from fame to footnote. His 24-year-old son, naval aviator Ensign Henry Richards Wismer, was killed in a collision on a training flight over the King Ranch, in Texas, in the fall of 1965. Wismer got drunk at a New York restaurant on December 2, 1967, fell down a flight of stairs, and died the next morning from a skull fracture. He was just 54.

David "Sonny" Werblin and his partners, who bought out Wismer in 1963, moved the team to the brand-new Shea Stadium for the 1964 season, renamed them the Jets to play off the baseball Mets, and made history in 1969 when they won Super Bowl III.

SEVEN

THE TORCH IS PASSED

*"Let the word go forth from this time and place,
to friend and foe alike, that the torch has been
passed to a new generation of Americans."*

—PRESIDENT JOHN F. KENNEDY, INAUGURAL ADDRESS, 1961

*T*he country was undergoing transition by November 1960, a dynamic change that would profoundly alter the conventional wisdom as it affected politics, society, culture, and sport. The men of the old order, born late in the 19th century, who led the country out of the Great Depression to victory in World War II and stood fast in the cold war against an implacable monolith, Soviet Communism, either had exited the public stage or were about to through death or retirement.

Few other Americans have enjoyed a bipartisan expression of genuine affection as did outgoing president Dwight Eisenhower in 1960. Regarded as the hero of World War II in Europe, General of the Army Eisenhower swept to landslide victories in 1952 and '56 over the former governor of Illinois, Adlai Stevenson. Now 70, and the oldest man to date to occupy the Oval Office, Ike was crafting a no-nonsense farewell address in which he would warn the country to beware of the "military-industrial complex" that he was positive would seize control of the federal budget and policy agenda.

A new order of confident, young progressives who called themselves the New Frontier was about to take office in Washington under the leadership of the youngest man ever elected president, 43-year-old John F. Kennedy. JFK, who edged Ike's vice president, Richard Nixon, in the closest-ever election to that time by 118,574 votes, had prominent NFL backers, including Green Bay Packers coach Vince Lombardi and Baltimore Colts owner Carroll Rosenbloom, a business and personal friend of patriarch Joseph P. Kennedy. "My father raised money, and they became friendly. When Jack and Bobby were killed, it was hard on Father. That was when Democrats were Democrats," Steve Rosenbloom said.

While Ike was an enthusiastic golfer, JFK, a scratch handicapper, downplayed his golfing skills. Ike played football at West Point in 1912 before he injured a knee. He was an enthusiastic fan of Army football. Kennedy let the word go forth that a hard-nosed version of touch football was the game he and his brothers Bobby and Teddy, along with their wives, Jackie, Ethel, and Joan, and their aides and associates, played on fall weekends. After the games, everyone moved inside and kicked off their sneakers to settle down in front of the television set on Sundays to watch the National Football League at the family compound in Hyannisport, Massachusetts.

America in 1960 was deeply enthralled by television. Pete Rozelle knew full well what a hot commodity he had in the National Football League, and he knew that more people were getting their information from the evening newscasts, especially on NBC and CBS, than from newspapers. Rozelle also knew that Kennedy's use of television was the model to emulate and that the way Kennedy outmaneuvered Nixon in the debates won the election for him.

The network newscasts were going so well that long-range planners at CBS and NBC were thinking about increasing their reports from the long-held 15-minute standard to a half hour, and there was more than enough material to fill expanded time slots.

Americans were stunned to wake up on Sunday, November 6, to learn that Ward Bond, the star of NBC's top-rated "Wagon Train," died unexpectedly of a heart attack the day before in a Dallas motel room where he was preparing to appear at halftime of the Cowboys-Rams game at the Cotton Bowl. Bond, just 57, paid his dues in two hundred films, playing such character parts as priests, cops, and cowboys, many of them with John Wayne, his best friend going back to the '20s when they were teammates on the USC football team.

Bond's death was prelude, though, to the most significant Hollywood passing in decades when film's most popular actor, Clark Gable, the "King," died from a heart ailment 10 days later. The 59-year-old Gable had just completed filming in the Nevada desert on *The Misfits* with costars Marilyn Monroe and Montgomery Clift. That ill-fated film was also the final screen appearance for both Clift and Monroe.

From its position of strength as the established league, playing most of its schedule on the dominant network, the NFL flourished in its war with the AFL. Few fans outside the AFL's markets—and, judging by attendance that year, few in those cities—cared much that the entertaining Houston Oilers, led by former Bears quarterback George Blanda, and the Los Angeles Chargers, quarterbacked by Giants castoff Jack Kemp, were on a collision course for the first AFL title game, on New Year's Day 1961, which the Oilers won 24–16 before 32,163 fans and a relatively small ABC television audience. Blanda and Billy Cannon, the Heisman Trophy winner who broke the contract he signed with the Rams and GM Pete Rozelle to go with Houston, teamed up on an 88-yard scoring pass to put the game away.

Commissioner Rozelle had a barn burner going in his National Football League. In the Western Conference, a brutal, physical battle took place on November 13 in Chicago between the two favorites, the defending champion Colts and the Bears. Don Ellis produced NBC's telecast back to Baltimore. "Unitas got clobbered by several Bears. Some monsters! He went to the sidelines at the end, where they shoved cotton up his nostrils. His face was a mess, but he came back."

With 17 seconds left, on fourth-and-10 from the Chicago 39, Unitas disdained a frantic pass rush and hit Lenny Moore in the far corner of Wrigley Field's north end zone to give Baltimore a 24–20 victory. The game devastated both teams and opened the race.

The Eastern Conference boiled down to a pair of back-to-back games between the Giants and improbable Philadelphia Eagles. The Eagles had been losers in recent seasons until they acquired premier quarterback Norm Van Brocklin in 1957 for a number one draft choice in a trade engineered by Los Angeles Rams general manager Pete Rozelle. And the title game would be played for the first time since 1948 in William Penn's City of Brotherly Love.

The Philadelphia of 1960 had become the center of popular music, thanks to young disc jockey Dick Clark, who, in 1957, persuaded ABC to put his local WFIL-TV afternoon record hop on the program-starved network. That show, "American Bandstand," became a cultural phenomenon as it made superstars and teen idols of South Philly kids Frankie Avalon, Fabian, and Bobby Rydell. In the summer of 1960, Clark touched off a national dance mania when he gave another South Philadelphian, 19-year-old Ernest Evans, the stage name Chubby Checker—who gained instant fame with his number one hit, "The Twist."

The long-suffering Philadelphia citizenry, jaded by perennial baseball and football losers, fell in love with the 1960 Eagles. Philly fans were passionate about their teams—tough, demanding, and knowledgeable—and would boo their own as loudly when things went wrong, which was often, as they cheered them joyously when things went well. Reflecting their fandom, local writers were tough, perceptive, acerbic critics. The Eagles' broadcasters were first-rate. Bill Campbell called play-by-play on radio for WCAU, the CBS station. Jack Whitaker handled the play-by-play over WCAU-TV, flagship of the Eagles' mostly Pennsylvania-based network of CBS affiliates. John Facenda, who would gain fame later in the decade as "the Voice of God" for NFL Films, was not a sportscaster, but since television's start-up in 1948, he was the anchor of the top-rated newscasts on WCAU-TV and WCAU radio's afternoon drive-time newscast.

"All of our so-called beat writers figured we would end up at the bottom of the division in 1960," steady team leader Pete Retzlaff recalled. "It started that way in Cleveland when the Browns beat us handily. Then, all of a sudden, we won nine straight and ended up in the championship game. It was a great year."

The Baron, as Eagles cornerback Tom Brookshier tagged Retzlaff, played wide receiver in 1960. He later would move to tight end and become an elite player with Mike Ditka and John Mackey. "We had two Hall of Fame quarterbacks on that team, Jurgensen and Van

Brocklin," Retzlaff said. Van Brocklin, a coach on the field, was the odds-on favorite to succeed Lawrence "Buck" Shaw, who had announced this was his last season and hoped to go out in style.

"Van Brocklin had the authority to kick a player off the field and get somebody else in there if he thought the guy was not getting the job done and it was needed. The coach had given him all that authority as the team leader, but that was not that unusual then," Retzlaff said. "Other quarterbacks like Bobby Layne and Johnny Unitas had that same authority."

The Eagles' favorite son was captain Chuck Bednarik, who, in his 12th year after an all-America career at Penn, thrived as the NFL's last iron man. Since the fifth game when linebacker Bob Pellegrini was forced out with a broken leg, the 35-year-old, onetime B-24 Army Air Force waist gunner went both ways: He snapped and blocked ahead of Van Brocklin on offense. On defense, he returned to his old outside linebacker position as he smashed through enemy offenses and smacked down ballcarriers. During possession changes, he stood alone, hands on hips, as he took a couple of deep breaths and redirected his thoughts. He took quick sideline breathers only during kickoffs.

"Concrete Charlie" seemed to gain energy with each game, never more so than on November 20 at Yankee Stadium when he leveled Giants star Frank Gifford on a jarring tackle that knocked him out of football for the rest of that season and all of 1961. "The rule of thumb was never run a receiver under us, 'cause we're gonna hit you and we're gonna hurt you. Frank came underneath of Bednarik," Sam Huff said. "When I went by him, his eyes were in the back of his head, and he was shaking and everything else. I told Dick Modzelewski, 'He's dead. He's dead.' The game wasn't over. There was a couple of minutes to go. Frank fumbled the ball, and the Eagles recovered it, and we had to finish out the two minutes."

When the game ended, the Giants went up the ramp into the clubhouse they shared with the Yankees. "I shared the locker with Mickey Mantle," Huff said. "Out came the security guys, and there was a gurney with a body on it under a sheet by the showers. I thought it was Frank. I turned to Mo and said, 'I was right. He's dead.' They wheeled the body out. It wasn't Frank. A security guard got so excited that he died of a heart attack, and they had him in the back. Frank already was on his way to the hospital in an ambulance. Seeing that body was a scary moment." Bednarik played his college ball for Penn at Franklin Field. He would play perhaps his most memorable, if not greatest, game on this same turf in the title game.

Because Christmas fell on a Sunday in 1960 and athletic events in those days were never played on Christmas Day, millions of workers from coast to coast would observe the holiday on Monday and spend the afternoon watching the Eastern Conference champion Eagles square off with the Green Bay Packers. The Packers had seized the Western Conference title when the twice-defending-champion Baltimore Colts lost their last four regular-season games.

The resurgent Packers, the league's last link to its small-town roots, Green Bay, Wisconsin, nearly went belly-up twice in the previous decade, first in 1949 and again in 1956. That's when archrival George Halas, owner-coach of the hated Chicago Bears, led a successful bond drive to build a new stadium that would be renamed in 1965 after Packers founder Earl "Curly" Lambeau. When the 1958 Packers fell to a single victory against 10 losses and a tie, the management of the league's only publicly owned franchise turned east for a savior.

He was the New York Giants' offensive assistant, 45-year-old New York native Vince Lombardi, granted authority to run the club without interference as coach and general manager. Lombardi operated under the principles and system he learned at West Point from his mentor Earl Blaik. Lombardi's system wasn't slick or tricky. He kept it simple; he stressed correct blocking and tackling fundamentals, and repetition in practice. They ran each of his few basic plays—the power sweeps, quick openers, and precise passes—over and over again until the plays became rote. Then they ran them some more. He demanded execution and, with that execution, the only thing that counted: victory.

Lombardi found his quarterback early in the 1959 season in young Bart Starr, the son of a career soldier and the 17th-round draft choice out of Alabama in 1956. Then, he took the shackles off Notre Dame's 1956 Heisman Trophy winner, Paul Hornung, a brilliant cutback runner, receiver, option passer, kicker, and clutch performer who had been stifled since his arrival as 1957's bonus pick. Under Lombardi, Hornung set a league scoring record in 1960: 176 points, on 15 touchdowns, 15 field goals, and 41 conversions. That record lasted until 2006, when San Diego's LaDainian Tomlinson scored 31 touchdowns for 186 points.

Pro football was dominated by white men in the front office, on the sideline, and on the field. Both rosters reflected that condition. Nine Packers would make the Hall of Fame: Hornung, Starr, Taylor, Forrest Gregg, Ray Nitschke, Henry Jordan, and three of the four black members of the team—Willie Davis, Willie Wood, and Emlen Tunnell. Tunnell was in the twilight of his career in 1960, imported from the Giants by Lombardi for his veteran know-how. The other black member of the Green Bay roster was halfback–special teamer Paul Winslow, who would not play another NFL game. The Eagles had three black players. All were running backs: rookies Ted Dean and Tim Brown and injured veteran Clarence Peaks. The three future Hall of Fame Eagles were Van Brocklin, Bednarik, and receiver Tommy McDonald.

Philadelphia's weather had been changing and unpredictable for days. A fast-moving snowstorm snarled the city the previous Tuesday, overwhelming the grounds crew at Franklin Field. By Christmas Day when the Packers arrived for a workout, temperatures had edged upward. Snow had been cleared to the sidelines, where it lay in piles by the running track.

When Pete Rozelle woke up Monday morning at his hotel in Center City, a bright winter sun cast long shadows throughout the buildings of Benjamin Franklin's ancient Penn campus. The sun turned the sideline snow piles into an icy slush that left a moat of sorts surrounding a tundralike field, muddy on top and frozen underneath, making the footing treacherous.

The players treated it like another game. "We didn't go to a downtown hotel the night before the championship game," Tom Brookshier said. "I, myself, stayed in a hotel, the Walnut Park Plaza, where six or seven Eagles and our wives lived."

Every inch of available space in Franklin Field was occupied. The announced attendance was 67,235 paying customers, with many others who found a way to get inside. One of them was Bo Ryan, from nearby Chester, who turned 13 on December 20 and whose dad, Butch, had vowed to get him inside Franklin Field. Bo Ryan, who became the University of Wisconsin's renowned basketball coach decades later, could recall every detail of that game on and off the playing field. "They were scalping tickets for 20 bucks. The price on the ticket stub, which I still have, was $8. My dad did not have $40 to get us in. He was hoping to get 'em for $10 apiece," Ryan said. "So, we found another way in."

Father-and-son pairings were common throughout the ancient stadium that offered perhaps the best sight lines in America. To reach those marvelous seats in the upper stand that Red Smith called "Thrombosis Terrace" required extraordinary effort, especially when making the perilous climb in heavy winter clothing. That promised land came only after a forced march through a jammed crowd, step by step without ramps in a tight, confined space, with much huffing and puffing. One of those father-son pairs, who sat in the lower north stands behind the Packers bench while their Tel Ra crew filmed the game for the NFL, was Wally Orr and 16-year-old Bill Orr. On the other side of the field, 18-year-old Steve Sabol watched the game with his dad, Ed, after they scaled the south upper stand.

"In 1960, I had just started this little production company in Philadelphia and was trying to keep it going. I wanted to make documentaries," Ed Sabol said. He recently had sold the family business, which manufactured men's topcoats and overcoats. "I was 45 and just retired. I hated the family business. It was like going to the dentist every morning. I just decided I wasn't going to go out and get a job just to support my family and pay bills. I was going to do something, but I had to be damned sure I'd like it. I'd been a jock all my life, and it would have to do something with sports and photography."

NBC's telecast, called by voluble Lindsay Nelson and the Packers' terse TV announcer, Ray Scott, whose descriptions augmented the on-screen picture, was blacked out in Philadelphia. WRCV, the local NBC/Westinghouse station, announced it would show the game that night on videotaped replay, but that sop offered no solace to the many fans who could not get tickets. Those fans wanted to see it live, so they scurried to places that could pull in a television signal. One of the closer outlets outside the blackout area was WHP, channel 21, a

UHF station in Harrisburg, the state capital, 115 miles outside Philadelphia and some 15 miles west of Ernie Accorsi's blacked-out hometown, Hershey, which depended on Philadelphia for TV. Getting a UHF signal from Harrisburg was a difficult proposition considering the mountains, even at that short a distance. "I went to our neighbor and close friend's second-floor apartment with rabbit ears, trying to see it through the snow," Accorsi, who was 19 then, said. "I gave up at the half and came home to listen to Bill Campbell on the radio."

The Eagles ducked a quick takeout when Lombardi's Packers failed to convert early opportunities that might have blown the game open. Instead, Green Bay had to settle for a pair of Hornung field goals that left the Eagles with a 10–6 halftime lead on a short Bobby Walston field goal and Van Brocklin's 35-yard touchdown pass in the second quarter to McDonald.

"That was a crazy game. Lombardi was so good, but he always had to do everything his way," Tom Brookshier recalled. We had a defensive coach named Jerry Williams who didn't get any credit. We were all slow. He had us ready." And the Eagles rolled their coverage to nullify the power sweep.

"Lombardi was furious, storming up and down. They would go from 20 to 20, and that's the way it was," Brookshier said. "One time, I hit Jimmy Taylor right in the face with a forearm right in front of the Green Bay bench. You know what? Taylor looked up at me and grinned like hell. So, I got up and started grinning back. This is how tough that little bastard was."

Midway through the third quarter, Hornung started a sweep to the right and cut back, where Bednarik, who slipped Fuzzy Thurston's block, throttled him. Hornung was left on the ground with a pinched nerve in his right shoulder. When he reached the Packers' bench, he tried to grip a football and couldn't hold it. Then, he tried to throw a few minutes later and felt numbness in his arm. "My right side was so bad, I couldn't play," he said.

"We knew every time they started a play where they were going," Brookshier said. "Because Lombardi did it his way, they would keep doing it until the cows came home. The only time we got into trouble was when my safetyman Don Burroughs, the Blade, number 45, got knocked out by Taylor. They took him out for one play and put in a rookie [Bobby Jackson]."

Bart Starr did what any veteran NFL quarterback would do. He picked on the rookie and called Max McGee's number. McGee made the catch that gave the Packers a 13–10 lead with nine minutes left. "He got mixed up a little on the coverage. Otherwise, McGee wouldn't have caught that touchdown, because he was supposed to be picked up on a quick hitch by the safetyman," Brookshier said. "Blade came back after that touchdown and everything was shut down back there."

Hornung, who still could kick despite his pinched nerve, booted to Ted Dean at the Eagles' 2. Dean, the hometown rookie from nearby Radnor, broke to the near sideline, following Tim Brown, and took it 59 yards to the Green Bay 39, where Willie Wood ran him out of bounds in front of the Eagles' bench.

On the seventh play after the return, Dean swept left from the Green Bay 4 behind pulling guard Gerry Huth and slogged four yards through the mud for the touchdown to make it 17–13 Philadelphia and set up a wild finish that saw Starr lead the Packers back down the field. With eight seconds left and the ball at the Philadelphia 22, Starr's downfield receivers were covered. So, he dumped off to Taylor, who brought the crowd to its feet in a roar. Red Smith captured the moment unlike any other writer: "That wonderful runner ducked his head like a charging bull, bolted like an enraged beer truck into Philadelphia's congested secondary, twisted, staggered, bucked, and wrestled on, a step at a time, to go down at last in a sprawling pile-up nine yards from victory."

Bednarik held Taylor down until he heard the final gun and then let him get up. "We tried to get the goalposts afterward," Bo Ryan said. "Frank Rizzo was the police chief, and he wasn't about to let the fans on the field." Rizzo's force, decked out in their woolen, navy blue, ankle-length coats with brass buttons glistening in the low late-afternoon sun, circled the goalposts. "The goalposts were made from boxwood, not round wooden poles," Ryan said.

When the police didn't budge, a barrage of well-aimed snowballs flew down from the upper stand amid a chorus of full-throated Philly-style boos. "Unfortunately, some of the fans made ice balls fashioned around broken glass—Seagram's 7 bottles, as I recall—and threw them at the police," Ryan said. "Some of the police were cut. Rizzo then called back his men, and the goalposts crashed in an instant."

Norm Van Brocklin was the league's Most Valuable Player that year, deservedly so, but nobody since in this era of the specialist has come close to Chuck Bednarik's epic performance. At every change of possession, he stood tall in the center of the field, hands on hips, catching a breath as his teammates either left the field or returned from the bench, seemingly gaining energy as every minute counted down toward the finish. Bednarik stayed on that field for 58 minutes and every play from scrimmage, leaving only for placekicks, as he willed his Eagles to victory.

After the game, Brookshier and Bednarik appeared on a local radio show and then went to the Warwick Hotel, in Center City, for the victory dinner. "A couple of guys came from out of town. Lou Groza, from Cleveland, was one," Brookshier said. "He gave us this little timid wave from across the room. Out of all this, Rozelle entered the room, our new commissioner. Everybody gave him a salute. Our owner had gotten drunk, a little excited during the game, and they carried him out around seven thirty."

As the revelry proceeded, a hotel employee came into the room to inform Brookshier that he had a long-distance call in the cloakroom. "It was a reporter named Bob Bowie from the *Denver Post*. I was living in Colorado then, where I went to college."

"Hey, Brookie, how're ya doin'?" Bowie asked. "We're getting ready to run a story, and I thought I'd better call and check with you."

"Fine, what is it? Was this a good game, eh?" Brookshier answered, still focused on the events of the day at Franklin Field and believing Bowie had called to pass along his congratulations.

"The story we're gonna run is that Bart Starr was paid off and bought off in the football game when you beat the Packers today," Bowie said.

"*What?*"

"Yeah. I didn't think it was fair not to call," Bowie said.

"God," Brookshier interrupted as he thought out loud, "why in the world would Bart Starr, of all people, the straightest guy I've ever known, do that?"

"Well, Berry called a gambler this morning and said Starr was on the take and had accepted the cash," Bowie said.

Brookshier explained 46 years later, "I was thinking Raymond Berry." He asked Bowie, "Why would Ray Berry do that?"

"No, no. Not Raymond Berry," Bowie said. "A guy named Arley Berry, here in Denver."

Brookshier recounted, "So, this guy Arley Berry, who I had gone to Colorado with and was always on the edge of getting into trouble, had started this story. I understand he got pistol-whipped because he crossed the wrong guys on the bet." At the moment, though, all he knew was that a disaster was pending. " 'Hold it,' I said to Bowie, and I ran out to get the commissioner."

He told Rozelle, "Commissioner, the *Denver Post* is getting ready to break a story that Bart Starr was paid off."

According to Brookshier: " 'My God!' Rozelle said, and he ran in there. The first thing he said to Bowie on the phone was, 'You've got 12 lawsuits as soon as you run that, and the personal lawsuits will follow with all the people that you're going to destroy. The *Denver Post* will never run again.' "

Brookshier took back the phone from the commissioner. By then, he had figured it out. He said to the reporter, "You know what, Bob? It's Arley Berry, that rat from the University of Colorado."

He concluded, "Then, we put two and two together, and they didn't run the story. Thanks to Rozelle. Rozelle looked at me like, 'Is this what my life is going to be?' "

EIGHT

BUILDING A MODERN NFL

"Bert Bell laid the foundation and Pete Rozelle built a skyscraper."

—JACK WHITAKER, 2006

*F*rom the onset in 1960 of Pete Rozelle's long run as commissioner, the pace Rozelle set and extracted from his staff was relentless. He took Bert Bell's folksy, mom-and-pop National Football League operation in Philly and blew into New York with a round-the-clock three-ring circus. It was remarkable, with the high-energy workload he carried and the things that were happening everywhere surrounding the NFL.

The ability to understand and anticipate that his highly visible and popular product needed retooling and modernizing, and then to do something about it before it grew stale and atrophied, always set Rozelle apart from the crowd, be it in sports or in business. Taking charge when adversity struck unexpectedly and turning it into a positive made him the model sports commissioner while he still was in his middle thirties.

"So many people today are reactive, and whatever fire ends up in their lap, they put out," Rozelle's daughter, Anne Marie Bratton, said. "He was thinking, what do I have to deal with now? Reacting to it, but then also looking at the long-term picture: What do I want to do down the road? What do we need to have done down the road?"

Rozelle settled seamlessly into the New York groove, meeting regularly with media movers and shakers such as Bill McPhail and Jack Landry. That sent a signal that his league would be a leader in the go-go-go universe of Kennedy's New Frontier, with its stress on physical fitness such as 50-mile hikes that set the mood and style of the country. When it came to the inner workings of pro football, Rozelle changed the league's way of doing business, a contrast to George Halas, in Chicago, who operated as a one-man band, hiring the players, running the practices, drawing up the game plans, selling the tickets, making the payrolls, writing the press releases, and visiting the city newsrooms to beg editors for a mention, any mention at all, in the papers.

Unlike so many other young leaders, he did not ignore the lessons of his forebears. He used and applied them to better the product. Dave Anderson, writing for the *New York Journal-American* before its demise in the last debilitating New York newspaper strike and his 1966 move to the prestigious survivor, the *New York Times*, caught on quickly to what Rozelle was doing. "Bert Bell did virtually everything himself. He had a PR guy [Joe Labrum], but nobody knew who he was or what he did," Anderson recalled. "Rozelle was the guy who got the guy who did this. He knew as a PR guy that you have to spread the word." That guy was Jim Kensil.

"Rozelle came from a PR and media background. If you take the triumvirate of Rozelle, Kensil, and Don Weiss, all three had media backgrounds," said Chuck Day, Weiss's close friend and coauthor of *The Making of the Super Bowl*. Another key man in PR-think whom Rozelle consulted was the innovative Tex Schramm, Rozelle's confidant and mentor going back to the Rams.

Don Weiss had been a rabid Bears fan from childhood. After graduating in 1943 from East Aurora High School, 35 miles west of Chicago, he earned a degree from the University of Missouri School of Journalism in 1949. He and his wife, Charlene, then moved to Huntington, West Virginia, where his first job was writing news for AP Radio. In 1951, Weiss moved up to the AP Radio sports desk at 50

Rockefeller Plaza, in New York, where he would spend the next 14 years mostly inside, occasionally getting out so he could cover basketball and golf. The senior writers at the Associated Press drew the prime beats, especially baseball, with the game's glamour teams—the Yankees, Giants, and Brooklyn Dodgers—right there in town, and, in the fall, college football. Only the best of those writers garnered the elite assignments, heavyweight boxing title bouts and the Olympics. "NFL games were assigned to the least experienced, and least talented writers," Weiss wrote in his memoir. But Weiss believed in the game going back to his youth in suburban Chicago.

Weiss found his sporting kinsman in 1956 when he met another young AP writer, Jim Kensil, who agreed with him that pro football was the emerging sport. On Sundays before they were scheduled to report at the office for their night shifts, they went unassigned on their own time to Yankee Stadium to cover the Giants when the team was at home. They made contacts, placed phone calls, did the legwork, and wrote profiles and features for the wire service desperately in need of non-game-day stories. It was the type of material that would become a staple of the NFL-controlled *Game Day* printed programs years later.

Even after the Colts beat the Giants in 1958's "Sudden Death" title game, the AP and its veteran sports editor Ted Smits still could not care less about pro football. That all changed by 1961 as Smits read the attendance figures and heard the buzz from his reporters and fans on the street. Most important, he could see how he was getting scooped by the national magazines, not just Luce's *Sports Illustrated* but also other Luce publications such as *Time* and *Life*, and their competitors, *Newsweek*, *Look*, *Collier's*, and *Saturday Evening Post*, on the hot game, pro football.

Smits, though, was too late to prevent his rising young star Kensil from jumping ship. "Don Weiss was covering an owners' meeting in New York when he met Pete," Chuck Day said. "Don was talking with Art Rooney Sr., and Rozelle emerged from the meeting and approached the group, asking, 'Is anybody here from AP?'"

"Yes, I am," Weiss said.

"Do you know this guy Kensil?" Rozelle asked.

"Kensil was writing an early column on TV sports for the AP called 'The Sports Dial,' " Day recalled.

"I've been watching his columns about TV," Rozelle said.

"Rozelle told Don that he wanted Kensil to call," Day said. Weiss passed on the commissioner's not-too-subtle request, and Kensil set up a meeting with Rozelle.

"Jim told me about that when I worked for him in the NFL office," Ernie Accorsi said. "He was the Associated Press radio-TV columnist and went to interview Pete in Rockefeller Plaza. Pete laid out this TV-rights plan. 'You're not pulling this off,' Kensil told Pete. Kensil was a real blunt guy, the antithesis of Pete, and that's why they were the perfect combination."

Accorsi added, "I think he wrote the story, but Pete did call him to say, 'I want you to come over and talk about working for me.' Pete later told me, 'I loved Jim's spunk. I knew he was going to give me an honest answer.' Pete also confirmed that he considered hiring John Steadman, at that time, the Colts PR man. Steadman then left the Colts and returned to the *Baltimore News-American*."

"Kensil was the guy who really gave the NFL some PR personality," Dave Anderson said. "He sent out releases. There were no releases then. There were no league statistics to speak of until the Elias Sports Bureau got there. Kensil developed the liaison with Elias."

"He probably was the person who called the most on the phone when I was little. I remember him calling 10 to 12 times a night," Anne Marie Bratton said. "Dad and Jim Kensil, especially in the early years, were in constant communication, bouncing ideas off each other and constantly working on NFL things."

It would take a little more time, a couple of years tops, for Rozelle and Kensil to standardize the way teams handled press releases and published standardized game programs, the aforementioned *Game Day*. That was for the fans. Kensil's most important and most vital media publication was the "Game Capsules," still used today. The league still sends them out to the writers. They feature every important piece of information. "The capsules made it easy for the writers to write," Accorsi said. "All those old writers, from Bob Oates to Dave Anderson to Normie Miller, all talked about Kensil's capsules."

"Rozelle may have been the rocket and Kensil the fuel when it took off. They operated as a tandem," Peter Hadhazy said in late 2005. Hadhazy's 45-year football career, which included service as Cleveland Browns general manager, New England Patriots assistant GM, and executive positions in the NFL and USFL, started in 1961. He was 17 and still in high school in Brooklyn when Rozelle and Kensil hired him. He went in after school every day following tennis practice for a couple of hours and also worked during weekends, summer, and holiday vacations. That continued when he went to college at Iona, in New Rochelle. "I ran errands, made copies, and performed what was known in the trade as an office boy, now called an administrative assistant. It was like a big family, not a business. We got a lot done. Everybody got along very well, thanks to the guy whose lead we followed, the commissioner."

Kensil wanted Hadhazy to build a clip file as extensive as any major newspaper's. "Kensil ordered the newspapers from every league city," Hadhazy said. "My main job was to clip all the articles of interest that referred to the league, league office, other professional sports, football, or television that I thought would be of interest to the staff, who really was Kensil, Rozelle, and Aus Gunsel, our treasurer. Then I filed them."

The work hardly qualified as glamorous. "I would paste them up on these 8½ × 11 sheets with rubber paste, put a name to it, and file it, so we always had a reference point at the time. That was our filing system," Hadhazy recalled. "When a topic came up, we would just take that file out. We had a roomful of filing cabinets that contained from *A* to *Z* every topic of any interest that pertained to professional football. We had player files and team files. It was terrific. Kensil set the whole thing up, and it was used extensively."

This all was done in a time before personal computers and the first true modern copiers, staples of American business, came into vogue. "I hate to date myself: We needed to make a copy, two pages. Remember the old Ditto machines? That's the way we and other businesses in the early '60s had to operate," Hadhazy said.

"One page had film on it, the treated page. The other had no film on it. If you wanted to copy an article, you had to put the clip on the treated page, put the other page on top of it, and run it through a wet copier; it would come out, and then you had to wait a minute, minute and a half, for it to dry. Then you had to separate the thing, and there was your copy." The ink usually was a shade of purple, and as Hadhazy remembered from sad experience four and a half decades later, "You ruined many a white dress shirt!"

While Kensil's part-timers were building the NFL file system, Kensil was staying in close, almost daily, contact with his pal Weiss over at AP. One day in June 1965, Kensil called Weiss with a note of urgency in his voice. He let him know that the NFL intended to expand its PR operation and asked if he could recommend anyone. Weiss had a ready answer: "I might be interested myself."

"Kensil became the new executive director of the league, and Weiss became Kensil's successor as PR guy," Dave Anderson said. Then Weiss, the PR man, added a collateral duty just over a year later. "He was put in charge of the Super Bowl. It lasted for more than 30 years and was his main assignment. All this started with Rozelle. Until then, it might as well have been in a hut in Montana." Weiss became executive director in 1977 when Kensil left to become president of the Jets.

"He went in on Saturdays most of the time, and I would go with him," Anne Marie Bratton said of her father's work habits. "I'd go work the Xerox machines and the paper clips. It was fun. It helped him be prepared for what was coming."

"New York was where all the networks and agencies were. It was a great move, and Pete built on what Bert Bell had laid down, and built so very well on it. We were lucky at CBS in those days. We had the package," Jack Whitaker said.

"Rozelle saw the television market in the regional idea. Another thing was his ability to convince people," Chuck Day said. Rozelle knew the league could not continue with a few thoroughbreds lording it over a ragtag bunch of mutts. Bill McPhail exerted the most pressure when he told Rozelle that CBS wanted all the teams in one package because NBC was getting two teams in Baltimore and Pittsburgh and was paying a lot less than CBS did for nine teams, while NBC got all the benefits of the arrangement.

Rozelle had to persuade the strongest franchises, and then the others would fall into place. That meant going to Wellington and Jack

Mara, of the New York Giants; Dan Reeves, of the Los Angeles Rams; and Papa Bear George Halas, of the Chicago Bears. "It amazed me, because he was so much better at negotiation than anyone else I ever saw. And I saw some pretty good ones—Louis Nizer and others," said Rozelle's close friend Herb Siegel, a megadeal maker in his own right. "He handled everything so well. He had to get them all to agree they would split the television money. Those guys really understood it from the bottom up. They not only loved the game, but all three came aboard, and the rest stepped into line."

As Rozelle told David Harris years later for *The League*, "We were able to do it because the owners thought league." That meant, according to Rozelle, that "all of the franchises have remained viable and have the means to compete with the rest of the league." Rozelle added, "That's what I think sports should be."

That was part of the perfect storm for Rozelle. Yes, he got the league to agree that absolute revenue sharing would make it possible for a Green Bay to survive. But so much of that depended on the arrival of arguably the game's greatest coach, Vince Lombardi, who would drive the Green Bay Packers to five titles in seven years, starting with his two greatest teams in 1961 and '62, to form a dynasty as he created a "Titletown" mystique for small-town America. It saved the franchise for its loyal fans, isolating it from the likelihood of incredible pressure to force a move to a much larger city.

Rozelle also knew his tidy, socialistic revenue-sharing plan was illegal. So, he hit the road for Washington and the halls of Congress to secure a limited exemption to the Sherman Antitrust Act. When a federal court nixed that plan, Rozelle went to work lobbying House Judiciary Committee chairman Emanuel Celler. He had done his homework. Aware that Celler, who would represent his Brooklyn constituency from 1923 to 1973, despised baseball's antitrust exemption and was still furious at Walter O'Malley for moving the Dodgers from Brooklyn to Los Angeles in 1958, Rozelle treaded carefully and won him over. Then he went to the Senate.

Accompanying Rozelle to Washington was the new owner of the Cleveland Browns, 36-year-old Art Modell, an advertising and television executive in New York before he formed a syndicate to buy the team. "The only exemption we could get was through a collective bargaining agreement. When you negotiate something with a union, that takes precedence over everything else," Modell said.

Rozelle and Modell found a sympathetic ear in Rhode Island's senior Democrat, Senator John Pastore, chairman of the Senate Subcommittee on Communications. "He realized it was good for everybody if we pooled our resources, especially when it was divided up equally," Modell said. "We were off to the races."

For assurance, Rozelle had presidential press secretary Pierre Salinger, his longtime friend from the University of San Francisco, enlist the help of America's number one football fan, President John F. Kennedy. All that effort paid off when, on September 30, 1961, Congress passed the Sports Antitrust Broadcast Act. In essence, the act let any league sell its games as a "package" to television on one or more networks. President Kennedy immediately signed the legislation.

Because the 1961 season was already under way, Rozelle and the league had to live a while longer with the deal Bell had negotiated before his death. As for the near-term future, since CBS already had the broadcast rights to nine clubs through the 1963 season, Rozelle bargained only with that network. He came away with a two-year deal that paid the league $4,650,000 a year for both 1962 and '63. Each of the clubs would get $332,000 a year, found money, worth about $9,000 a player for a 36-man roster, and enough to nearly meet if not exceed most payrolls of that era. That meant every team started the 1962 season, and has played every season thereafter, with the assurance it would earn a profit.

"Rozelle certainly had a vision of what television could do for the National Football League," Chuck Day observed. "He could see, 'For us to get from number three on the sports spectrum, we need to cultivate the media to get higher.'" While Kensil and Weiss built the structure with the releases and files they sent out, Day said, "it was Rozelle's vision that 'if we could help the writers, that will help get us the exposure in the papers we need.'"

A key component in Rozelle's scheme was his intention to use former players on his telecasts, not just for their names, but to make them big television stars. Rozelle believed that would better bring the game to the fans. "Pete Rozelle always had an affinity for players that came before, and I always thought he was respectful that way," Tom Brookshier said. "Pat [Summerall] and I would be doing games at the Meadowlands, and we'd get a suite and stay in the same room. We'd get a phone call from Pete and his bride, and they'd be watching the game: 'Have a good game, you guys.' I thought it was nice the commissioner took the time to do that."

"Jock" sportscasters did not suddenly materialize when Rozelle became commissioner. He just made them stars. The first big-name football announcer was the biggest name of all in football's early era, Red Grange, who started calling games in 1940 on radio and moved to television in 1947 when Halas first aired Bears games in Chicago. When NBC held the NCAA package in the '50s, Grange handled the color-storyteller-and-occasional-analyst role alongside play-by-play man Lindsay Nelson. Wherever he was on Saturdays, he got back to Chicago to handle play-by-play for Halas for the home games of the Bears or Cardinals on those telecasts, seen in much of the nation except for blacked-out Chicago.

When Rozelle inherited the Bell-negotiated contracts, the NFL telecasts were still regional affairs. The telecasts were directed and produced by a single crew with dual audio feeds, the "partisan" call to each team's home market. So, if the Bears were playing the Green Bay Packers, fans in the Bears' territory would hear Grange and his color man, ex-Bears star George Connor, while the Packers backers heard play-by-play man Ray Scott and sidekick Tony Canadeo. And so it went throughout the league. Former players were featured with the likes of Warren Lahr in Cleveland, Gordie Soltau in San Francisco, and Don Paul in Los Angeles.

The two ex-players who benefited the most and lasted the longest once Rozelle befriended them were two retired New York Giants, Frank Gifford and Pat Summerall. "He was very close to Gifford," Summerall said in 2006. "When I stopped playing and took over as the analyst on Giants broadcasts with Chris Schenkel, Bill McPhail, who then was the boss of CBS Sports, said to me, 'You need to meet Pete Rozelle.' I went to lunch with McPhail and Rozelle. We became very good friends. I think it was as close as it could be."

Summerall grew to appreciate the delicate spot Rozelle was in as the close friend of a couple of players, albeit retired ones. "You're not working for the players; you're working for the owners. You have those big egos to satisfy," Summerall said. "His relationship with the players was OK. I could remember a lot of times when we'd be down on the field before a game, a Super Bowl, and people would come over to shake his hand. Pete was always congenial. It was close to fear that the players had, but certainly a lot of respect."

Gifford first got serious about broadcasting in 1961 when he had to sit out that year to recover from the concussion he incurred on Chuck Bednarik's big hit late in 1960. Thanks to a developing friendship with the commissioner, Gifford landed the five-minute dinner-hour program "World Wide Sports" on the CBS radio network to gain exposure, experience, and a foot in the door. "I talked to Pete almost every day, through a very difficult time in my life," he said.

By 1961, Summerall had begun his second year reading sportscasts for CBS in New York, a job that had been destined for another teammate. "I happened to be rooming with Charlie Conerly in 1960 and was in bed watching TV. We had played a preseason game over in Newark, and we had three or four days before we had to be back at Bear Mountain, where we were training at the time. The telephone rang, and a voice said, 'Can I speak to Charlie?'"

"He's in the shower; he can't come right now," Pat said. "I'll be glad to give him a message."

"Remind him that he's supposed to be at CBS this afternoon to read an audition script for a five-minute sportscast," the CBS man said.

"I'll be glad to tell him."

Summerall recounted, "I was about an inch from hanging up when I heard him say something, so I put the phone back up to my ear. 'What are you doing this afternoon?' the guy said."

Summerall answered, "I'm going to go somewhere and drink beer with the boys, go to a movie, something to see what New York's all about."

That voice at the other end turned out to be Jimmy Dolan, the head of CBS Radio at the time. "Why don't you come with Charlie?"

Dolan said to Summerall. "Kyle Rote, Alex Webster, Charlie, and you will read from the same script." He accepted the offer.

"We all went to CBS at four o'clock to read that same script. CBS said they liked the way I sounded, and that's the way I got into the broadcasting businesses. Right time, right place." And, by 1962, Summerall just had retired from the Giants when his career took another leap. Johnny Lujack had been Chris Schenkel's color man on Giants telecasts, but Kyle Rote learned that Lujack had to quit because his wife's family owned a prominent Chevy dealership in the Quad Cities, where he lived, and Ford had just signed on as a major NFL sponsor. Rote, who worked for NBC by then, called Summerall and urged him to call CBS Sports immediately.

Summerall thus became Schenkel's color man on Giants' telecasts, with one admonition. "He stressed that television was a visual medium, and that I didn't need to tell people what they already could see. It was basic, but useful advice that I applied throughout my broadcasting career," Summerall wrote in his autobiography. By 1964, he had become the morning man on WCBS, 88 on the radio dial, coincidentally the number he wore with the Giants.

Years later, long after his apprenticeship with Schenkel was over and he had become a successful game analyst with several Super Bowls to his credit, Summerall turned to play-by-play, where he became the top voice at CBS and then at Fox when that network took the NFL rights from CBS for the 1994 season.

His first color man was former Philadelphia Eagles defensive back Tom Brookshier, whose playing career ended on November 5, 1961, at Franklin Field in a game against the Bears. "Brookie" got his legs tangled with receiver John Farrington, who was blocking on a reverse, when ballcarrier Willie Galimore was knocked into both men. "My leg was broken right in front of the Bears' bench. My bone came through the sock in the mud," Brookshier said. "Billy Wade, Bill George, and Coach Halas sort of moved out. Halas looked down and said, 'Tough break, kid.' That's all I needed to hear. Years later, I was doing a game at Soldier Field. We'd go to the Saturday practice. 'How're you doing, kid?' Halas said."

Brookshier replied, "Mr. Halas, I'm 50 years old now." Halas answered, "That's good news, kid."

"I was still a kid. Won't I ever get to be a grown-up? He was just a funny, funny guy. Tough old dude," Brookshier said.

Brookshier joined WCAU in Philadelphia shortly after his injury, where he handled color on the radio broadcasts for two years and read the nightly television sportscasts. Then, in 1965, he joined the CBS network full-time.

Brookshier's career-ending broken leg halted any repeat hopes that the 1960 champion Eagles might have entertained. Sonny Jurgensen launched his own Hall of Fame career into orbit as a superb replacement for retired quarterback Norm Van Brocklin. "Norm was told in 1958 that if he came here as a player when Buck Shaw retired, he would replace him as head coach," said all-time Eagles receiver Pete Retzlaff. "Van Brocklin knew that 1960 was his last as a player. Coach Shaw had said it was his last year as a coach, whether we won or not. We went on to win the title. Both Buck Shaw retired as a coach and Van Brocklin retired as a player. The Dutchman should have taken over as Eagles coach."

Pete Rozelle, who, as the Rams' general manager, had been forced to trade the quarterback to Philadelphia in 1958, knew as well as any man would ever know that Norm Van Brocklin's life was a matter of unfinished business. As long as he was around football, it was constitutionally impossible for that brilliant, flawed, troubled, hot-tempered man to savor whatever success he achieved, and he accomplished plenty. He left hard feelings wherever he traveled, but he was so uniquely gifted that someone else always was willing to take a chance on him.

"He didn't get the job as coach because something happened," Retzlaff said. "He indicated publicly he would make some changes as coach. The Eagles backtracked on their commitment, and that's when he became coach of the Vikings."

Naturally, Van Brocklin's introduction to the good citizens of the North Country was almost as rancorous as his departure from Philly had been. "One of the writers asked him about it, and he said, 'The way they stocked this franchise, they just gave me a bunch of stiffs,' " Retzlaff recalled. "Not a good way to start out with your club, I suppose. He was very frank about it."

Yet, Van Brocklin got the Vikings off to a rousing start in their franchise opener the following September when he unleashed rookie scrambling quarterback Fran Tarkenton. Tarkenton ran and passed his way through the Bears' defense in a 37–13 Minnesota victory that left NFL founding father Halas sputtering and ranting on the team's flight back to Chicago.

The famed Halas furnace was stoked to a raging fury throughout those years. Frustrated at his inability to beat Lombardi's Packers from the 1960 rematch through 1961–62, Halas drew the close scrutiny of the commissioner. It had nothing to do with the Green Bay rivalry, but it had everything to do with the way the Old Man disdained league rules when he didn't want to be bothered with them. Rozelle had known for a long time that he needed to rein in the patriarch, but he needed to find the right opportunity to seize the moment.

As Don Weiss told Chuck Day for *The Making of the Super Bowl*, Weiss had taped a photograph of Halas below his desk to the backside kick plate. Little Anne Marie Rozelle, then a preschooler, came to work on most Saturdays. Peter Hadhazy's collateral duty was to keep her occupied in games of hide-and-go-seek. One of little Annie's favorite hiding places was that niche under Weiss's desk. One day, while hiding, she poked her head up to ask Weiss, who was at work that day, "Why is that man's picture there?"

Weiss delicately explained that the picture was there because Mr. Halas was a special man and that was a special spot reserved for him. Weiss did not tell the child that the Bears had ignored Rozelle's protocols concerning media relations, proper press releases, and timely and accurate weekly injury reports. In short, Halas could not care less about media needs, let alone wants.

Halas's longtime public relations man, Dan Desmond, worked only in season for the Bears, spending the rest of his time working for Arthur Wirtz at Chicago Stadium on hockey, basketball, and ice shows. In football season, when he was in the Bears' offices, he might send out a statistics sheet once or twice a season and did little if anything else to help out on other public relations matters, which Halas performed anyway through other people, namely, business manager Rudy Custer, who handled media credentials.

As I wrote in *Papa Bear*, Rozelle found his opportunity when he decided to challenge Halas's longtime control over the officials, under which Halas had his favorite referees game after game, men such as Bill Downes and Ron Gibbs. "Pete created an officials' department, a well-developed one in New York, where the assignments were made on merit," Weiss told me in 2003.

That big showdown came when Halas sharply criticized the officiating after the Bears' only loss in 1963, at San Francisco. Early the next week, Rozelle called Chicago. "He told George that he wanted him to visit New York and have a chat," Weiss said. "George said he would meet him at O'Hare. 'No,' Pete said, 'get on a plane and come to New York. I want you in my office.'"

"Mark Duncan was the supervisor of officials," Peter Hadhazy recalled. "Halas blasted the officials, and he blasted Mark Duncan and wanted Bill Downes, who was an ex-official and was Chicago's commissioner of aviation, to come in and run it. When Rozelle took the stand, that was part of the metamorphosis of Pete Rozelle from a commissioner to a leader. He fined the Holy Grail."

"They left that meeting with a great deal of mutual respect," Weiss said. "George realized there was a guy who was going to be fair and firm, as well. Rozelle didn't settle for something less, but he made you feel you got part of what you wanted. That's persuasion."

With that bit of "persuasion," Pete Rozelle had tamed the last and only person who could give him trouble on his mission to mold the National Football League to his design. Halas became Rozelle's greatest champion, and the commissioner honored him in the twilight of his 63-year career, naming him, after the merger, president of the National Football Conference.

It was a far different story in Cleveland, though, as disagreement and jealousy turned into open warfare in 1961 between Paul Brown, the founding coach whose name was the team's, and new owner Art Modell. "Art was in the TV business in New York. I was executive vice president and general manager from '76 to '81," Peter Hadhazy said. "He used to tell me he produced the first daytime serial, which was a soap opera. He said in the '70s and '80s that he still had an archive from the beginning of television in the '40s and '50s. He still gets asked for them and leases them to the networks."

According to Hadhazy, "Art was always a football fan. A friend told him the Browns were for sale. He borrowed $50,000 from a guy named Bob Gries, who was his partner." Hadhazy noted, "That loan backed by the Union Commerce Bank, in Cleveland, covered the rest of Modell's share of the $4 million purchase price. Bitterness later ensued in that partnership, which involved several other investors. "Art and Gries's son had a falling out after I left," Hadhazy said. "I told Gries that I would not testify against Art. Art and I left on very, very good terms, excellent terms."

Modell and Brown, however, could not get along. Brown, the football man whom no owner had ever dared to cross, resented what he called Modell's "lack of background in the football world." He felt Modell was eroding his position as coach by cozying up to certain players and creating factions that undermined the morale of the team. Late in the 1961 season, Brown saw an opening that he believed would guarantee an immediate title for the Browns. Aware that Rozelle had ordered Washington's Marshall to integrate his Redskins, Brown made a deal that benefited both sides. In the draft held December 4, Brown picked Leroy Jackson, a black halfback from Western Illinois, and told Marshall to select the first black Heisman Trophy winner, Ernie Davis, from Syracuse, which he did.

When the season ended a week later, Brown dropped the other shoe, announcing that he was sending the rights to Jackson and his star black running back, Bobby Mitchell, to the Redskins for the rights to Davis. Davis would be paired in the same backfield with his fellow Syracuse all-American, Jim Brown. "If Davis plays to his potential, you've got it made next season," said Vince Lombardi to Brown in a conversation Brown repeated for his autobiography, *PB.*

In his book, Brown wrote that he told Modell that the Browns did not give no-cut contracts, especially in the war with the AFL. Modell ignored him when he not only granted Davis a no-cut deal but also announced that he would pay Davis $80,000, far more than Buffalo, of the AFL, would offer. Worse, according to Brown, that was more money than Jim Brown was making. Tragically, Davis was at the College All-Star training camp the following summer when doctors at Evanston Hospital discovered he had acute leukemia. He died on May 18, 1963, and the Browns retired the number 45 that he never wore in a game.

While George Preston Marshall did make the trade for Mitchell to satisfy Rozelle, he remained a racist at heart when, in the team's introductory luncheon to the fans in 1962, he ordered the dignified Mitchell to stand at attention and at least mouth the words to "Dixie." But Bobby Mitchell, of Hot Springs, Arkansas, and the University of Illinois, had the last word on Marshall with his feats as a Redskins lifer. He played his way into the Pro Football Hall of Fame as the most dangerous pass catcher of the '60s and then remained with the Redskins long after Marshall's passing, to serve the team for decades as personnel director.

The Brown-Modell relationship ruptured over Jim Brown, who by then answered only to the owner, not the coach. Other players got involved, including cornerback and defensive leader Bernie Parrish: "Paul Brown was the epitome of organization. I don't understand why he didn't keep up with the game. He did not understand defense."

Parrish maintains to this day that Modell orchestrated Brown's firing. "We thought we pulled off the revolt, but we really didn't. Paul was a part owner of the team. We knew he wasn't going anywhere. We simply said, 'We can't do this.' We went to him and asked to take over part of the coaching or whatever. Everybody was asking to get traded before the following season."

It got no better for the Browns in 1962 when the Giants sewed up their second-straight Eastern Conference title behind the All-Pro passing of Y. A. Tittle, who had come to New York a year earlier in a trade with the 49ers. "We were coming back from San Francisco when Ken Coleman came to me," Parrish recalled. 'Bernie,' he said, 'if you guys are planning to go and confront Paul, don't do it. Art's already taken care of it.' That struck me as odd that Ken Coleman, the announcer, was the insider.

"I was vice president of the Players' Association, and I wanted to replace Pete Rozelle with Paul Brown," Parrish continued. "That made Modell mad. He called me into his office. 'Bernie, those guys you're representing don't give a shit about you. They don't give a damn about that crap. If you just resign as vice president of the Players' Association, I'll give you lifetime security from the Browns. You'll be with the organization forever.'

"I told him to stick it and that I was going to finish the fight with the Players' Association. Modell's only comment to Terry Pluto [the writer] was I had a bad attitude."

Brown, though, stood up for Modell in his book. "Parrish embarrassed Modell when he called for Rozelle to step down because, he claimed, Pete was not protecting the players' interests—and then proposed that I be named the new commissioner. That was some switch! Obviously, Pete and I paid no attention to it."

Modell then turned to Brown's friend and loyal assistant Blanton Collier, who had the support of the players, especially Jim Brown and the offense. Collier had met Paul Brown in the navy, served on his staff at Great Lakes, followed him to Cleveland, and stayed until 1954 when he replaced Paul "Bear" Bryant as coach at Kentucky. He and Brown remained close through those years, to the point that he was one of the two people Brown recommended to Green Bay along with Vince Lombardi when the Packers were looking for a coach in 1959. When Collier was fired at Kentucky after the 1960 season, Brown immediately brought him back. But the friendship turned icy when Modell fired Brown and Collier accepted Modell's offer to become the team's second head coach.

Brown took the first real vacation of his life and then moved to LaJolla, in the San Diego area, where he played a lot of golf and thought about ways to get back into pro football. After all, Pete Rozelle owed him one.

The American Football League was not about to go away either. On May 24, 1962, federal judge Roszel Thompson in the Baltimore District Court ruled in favor of the NFL in the AFL's two-and-a-half-year-old antitrust suit. The new league had charged the NFL with monopoly and conspiracy when it came to expansion, television, and player signings.

In somewhat of an interesting sidebar to that case, in the National Football League draft held on December 28, 1960, George Halas and the Bears had made University of Pittsburgh all-American end Mike Ditka their first selection. Bears assistant coach and personnel director George Allen then tracked down Ditka after the Hula Bowl in Honolulu, took a plane with him from San Francisco back to Pittsburgh, and signed him. Halas announced that Ditka, who'd played linebacker at Pitt as well as end, would play a new position for the Bears that the coach had designed with Ditka in mind called "tight end."

On January 14, 1961, Willard Dewveall, who had lined up at end or slotback in his two seasons with the Bears, announced he had played out his option in Chicago and had signed with his hometown Houston Oilers. Dewveall, the opponent Sam Huff singled out in CBS's 1960 "Violent World" special with the warning, "Watch yourself, number 88," was the first player to deliberately move from one league to the other. Halas didn't mind his departure. He knew Dewveall had diabetes. And he had the player he really wanted, Mike Ditka.

Three other NFL developments of interest in 1962 included the signing of a two-year contract giving television and radio rights to NBC for the championship game for $615,000 a year. The league announced it would set aside $300,000 of that fee to be paid directly into the NFL Player Benefit Plan.

Also, on April 27, commissioner Pete Rozelle awarded the new Pro Football Hall of Fame to Canton, Ohio, where the league had been founded in an auto showroom on September 17, 1920. Construction began immediately, with dedication set for early September 1963.

Finally, the commissioner awarded a contract to Philadelphia-based Blair Motion Pictures to write, produce, and film the 1962 league championship game.

NINE

NFL FILMS

"Did he tell you how he got the deal with the NFL? He made the deal for Blair Motion Pictures, named for his daughter and the school."

—HERB SIEGEL, BROTHER-IN-LAW OF ED SABOL, 2006

*O*f all Pete Rozelle's many accomplishments, the ones many people consider his most significant were (1) revenue sharing through television, (2) the Super Bowl out of the merger with the AFL, and (3) NFL Films. The latter especially was a natural for someone who spent most his formative years in and around the world of motion pictures and the pomp and pageantry that is the state of mind called Hollywood.

Rozelle was immersed in film well before he became commissioner, understood its potential, and firmly believed it was the forum that his product, the National Football League, needed to give it class, image, style, and the power to deliver and control his message. He found his willing and able producers in the Sabol family, of Philadelphia.

"We were a bunch of young people who loved to make movies, loved pro football, and wanted to convey our love of the game to our audience," said Steve Sabol, the creative and artistic force behind NFL Films since 1965. "We have the largest sports film library in the world. The only other 16-millimeter library that is more thoroughly documented is World War II. We'll pass them in two or three years.

We have a hundred million feet of film. We do 50 hours of programming a week, and a lot of it is out[takes]."

NFL Films has filmed every play of every game and archived them since Rozelle and the league bought the Sabols' production company, Blair Motion Pictures, in 1965, named it NFL Films, and hired the Sabols to run it, with total backing and artistic freedom. NFL Films has won scores of awards that include 92 Emmys, 34 of them to Steve Sabol for his innovative productions. It is possible in 21st-century America to turn on the television any day of the year and find at least one program, usually many more, produced by NFL Films, especially on ESPN. And that does not include the fast-growing NFL Network, an entity that relies on NFL Films for its footage and video packages.

NFL Films was the creation of one man, Ed Sabol, Steve's father. It took Rozelle's recognition of its potential value to make it work. "Pete was a listener. A lot of people call a meeting to tell others what to do. Pete called a meeting to gather information," Steve Sabol said. "I read once about the difference between MacArthur and Eisenhower: Eisenhower always had conferences and listened, while MacArthur gathered his generals and told them, 'This is the decision.'"

"*Sports Illustrated* once wrote that the league has had the best public relations tool of any corporation in the world—NFL Films," a proud Ed Sabol said in October 2005. Envious detractors have called it the greatest propaganda tool any business ever conceived. Truly, "Films" is a powerful entity, a vital linchpin of the NFL.

The story of NFL Films, how it began and how and why Pete Rozelle bought into it in 1962 and made it a foundation piece of the National Football League's fabulous wealth and power, is, for certain, an American business epic. That the living participants tell it in their own words as they remember it makes the story all the better.

Because of where and when it was born, mostly in Philadelphia and the city's Main Line suburbs to the west in the early '60s, this is a Philadelphia story, but one that in no way resembles the classic film that starred Katharine Hepburn, Jimmy Stewart, and Cary Grant. The *NFL's Philadelphia Story* features a cast with names such as Ed, Steve, and Blair Sabol, and Herb Siegel, all of the same family; Wally and Billy Orr, and Dan Endy, the Orrs' onetime lead producer at NFL Films' predecessor, Tel Ra; the ever-resonant John Facenda and his magnificent narrations; and, of course, Pete Rozelle himself.

"I went to a school called Blair Academy, in Blairstown, New Jersey, near Princeton," Ed Sabol said. "I spent two years at the school. I was on the swimming team there and set a world scholastic record for the 100-yard freestyle. It was one of those times in our life when it was so beautiful. I went to Ohio State for a couple of years. They had a great swimming team." In the course of our interview, Sabol who is Jewish, neglected to say that he was chosen for the U.S. Olympic swim team in 1936, at age 20, but refused to go to Berlin because, as he remarked years later, he would not swim in a pool built by Adolph Hitler. "Then, I tried the theater for a while, and that didn't last."

"Ed was at Ohio State with the great coach Mike Pepe," said Sabol's brother-in-law Herb Siegel. Sabol's main competition at Ohio State and in all of America was Peter Fick. "Ohio State had this pool where you could see the swimmers underwater through the portholes. So, Pepe filmed Ed both above and under water and then told Peter Fick to learn Ed's style."

Despite filmed evidence that he touched well ahead of the silver medalist at Berlin, Fick, the world-record holder in 1936, finished fifth in the 100-meter race. Besides Sabol, another great Jewish athlete who stayed home that summer because of Nazi anti-Semitism was track sprinter Marty Glickman, a competitor in the same events as respective gold and silver medalists Jesse Owens and Ralph Metcalfe, who were black. As did Glickman, who became a network sportscaster in New York, Sabol made his mark in another field, film, a field he didn't enter until he was 45, after World War II military service and his time in the clothing business.

Before 1960, the man his friends and associates admiringly call Big Ed ran the Jacob Siegel Coat Company, a firm his father-in-law's family founded in Baltimore. The Siegel family patriarch, an immigrant from Russia who had been a tailor by trade, made raincoats in his basement. "He would get on the train, go up to New York, sell the raincoats, buy more material, and go back to make more," said Dan

Endy, Big Ed's early associate in the film business. "It's a great American success story. The Jacob Siegel Company was sold for anywhere from $8 million to $12 million in 1960. I don't know all the details. I know Ed had enough money to retire and live in comfort."

Sabol, though, had a different goal. "I was going to do something, but I had to be damned sure I'd like it. I'd been a jock all my life, and it would have to do something with sports and photography."

While he was running the coat company, a business he loathed, Sabol took a passionate interest in motion pictures. It began with a Bell and Howell movie camera received as a wedding present when he married Audrey Siegel on October 4, 1941. "I had a bug for photography. I made a lot of home movies with the little camera, and I got a kick out of that," Sabol said.

When Steve started playing football in fourth grade, his father went along to film his games. By the time Steve reached high school, Ed had an architecturally adventurous 25-foot tower built above the field at Haverford School to provide a vantage point from which to film the games, and from where he kept rolling even on days when the rickety wooden tower swayed in the wind. "To me, football was the greatest sport to film," Ed Sabol said. "Even a football film is the shape of a movie screen. You had this progression: a play; then you'd stop. Play and stop—unlike basketball, where it just keeps going back and forth."

"My dad was a dreamer and big thinker, and the thing he decided he had the most experience in was filming football, filming me," Steve Sabol said. Ed's films of his son's grade school games were of such high quality that the coaches would come back to the Sabol house in Villanova after the films were processed to rehash the games and "scout" the players.

The rights holder in 1962, as he had been since 1948, was Bell's friend W. Wallace "Wally" Orr. Orr owned Tel Ra Productions and the W. Wallace Orr Advertising Agency. "Tel Ra struggled until 1958, with *The Greatest Game Ever Played*," Bill Orr, Wally's son, said. "From then until 1962, Tel Ra Productions really did very well." In 1960, Tel Ra also secured the syndication rights to the new American Football League.

After Bell's death in 1959, the dynamic of the NFL changed dramatically with the election of Pete Rozelle and the move from the relative quiet of Philadelphia to frenetic New York. "Rozelle went to sealed bids in '60," said Bill Orr, who was 16 that year.

That move alone should have been a signal to the Orrs that the landscape was shifting below their feet. "My father had been tangling with Rozelle because we were part of the old guard. Then, my father, at age 57, had an unexpected embolism and dropped dead on June 5, 1962. He left Tel Ra Productions in a voting trust. I was 17 going on 18."

Dan Endy was just 20 when he joined Tel Ra in 1949, his first job after college. He had known the Orrs all his life as neighbors in the closest-in Main Line suburb, Merion Park. Young Dan got the sports bug when Wally Orr took him to Phillies and A's games in the summer. "I used to babysit for Billy, mow Wally's lawn, and wash his car," Endy said. Regarding his Tel Ra tenure, he stated, "He was very, very good to me. I could never say anything bad about Wally Orr, except I didn't think he paid me enough. I thought if I were paid a little more, I would never have thought of leaving."

Leaving the employ of a man who had been a mentor was a gut-wrenching decision in 1959 for Endy. "Wally was a prince of a guy. Sometimes I look back and say, did I stab him in the back? When I left, he was still there. When I went to resign, Wally said, 'When are you leaving?' "

"Is it that obvious?" Endy asked.

"Yes," Wally Orr said.

Endy formed a company that he called Cine-Sports, Inc. His main client was the Miller Brewing Company, a former Tel Ra sponsor that he took with him. "In 1962, a mutual friend named Bob Levy introduced me to Ed Sabol. Bob's father owned the Atlantic City Racetrack, a whole bunch of waterfront property, a wealthy family."

Bob Levy's father, Dr. Leon Levy, was a business associate of Wally Orr's who handled advertising for the Atlantic City Racetrack. Leon Levy and his brother Ike founded WCAU in Philadelphia in the '20s and then brought in a local cigar maker named William S. Paley and helped arrange his purchase of the fledgling Columbia network, CBS, in 1928. Ike Levy's daughter Ann was married to Herb Siegel until her death in 2005.

"I wanted to see if I had it or not. I wanted to get it out of my system," Ed Sabol said. Acting on that desire, he formed his own company, Blair Motion Pictures, named after his school and younger child, his daughter. "As I was messing around with other projects, I settled on pro football as the best situation to go after," he said.

"From 1958 to '62, Ed Sabol visited Newsreel Laboratories, where we put our shows together. He came into the studio just to watch," Bill Orr recalled.

"So, I watched it and found out how it worked, how they shot games, what they were," Ed Sabol said. "Then came the time when I decided to make a bid on the championship game. It was 1962 at Yankee Stadium."

At this point, the story arrives at a five-way intersection. All versions will converge at the same end point at the moment Pete Rozelle awarded Ed Sabol the rights to film, produce, and market the 1962 championship game, but the roads the principals traveled were varied and intriguing. The initial money involved in the birth of NFL Films, which grew into a massive film-production operation that would entail industrial-size revenues to the tune of hundreds of million dollars, was comparative small change.

"Dad found out in 1961 that the film rights to the NFL championship sold to the highest bidder for $1,500," Steve Sabol said. That was equivalent to a year's tuition at a top private university on the level of a Penn, Northwestern, or University of Chicago. "My dad's theory in life and in business is, if you like or need something, you always double it. He would do that with medical prescriptions. The doctor would prescribe two pills: he would take four. If he wanted to get a car, he'd buy two Mercedes in case one broke. He'd say, 'With the medicine, they're always conservative. They say take two: take four. If it's take three, take six.' Following that philosophy, he overbid and got the '62 championship."

"I think I wrote a letter or made a call to someone in the league office and asked 'em, 'How do you go about trying to film that game?'" Ed Sabol recalled. "He said, 'You just hand in a bid, and

they will be opened in November in the league office in New York.' "
According to Ed Sabol, the stakes were higher than Steve's stated
$1,500, but he held fast to his bidding principle. "I found out the pre-
vious bid the year before by Tel Ra was for $2,500. I decided, if I'm
gonna get this, I'm not gonna pussyfoot around; I'm gonna double it.
And I did," Ed Sabol said. "So, I made out a check for $5,000 [note
that amount, the going price of a '62 Cadillac] and took a train to
New York and went to the league office. They had a meeting of about
three, four, or five independent producers, one of which was, of
course, Tel Ra."

Sabol continued, "As a matter of fact, when Rozelle opened my
envelope, he waited a few seconds before he said, 'Blair Motion Pictures has the deal,' because he never heard of me and didn't know if
I could produce a film. And I think he was a little taken aback from
going from $2,500 to $5,000."

Dan Endy offered a different take in 2006, asserting that more
than twice as much money was involved. Endy got to know Sabol
earlier in 1962. "Ed and Bob Levy at some point were considering
buying my company, Cine-Sports," Endy said. "I told them quite honestly that I had a lot of eggs in one basket, namely, Miller; if something went sideways, there wasn't a lot left there."

As Endy recalled, his conversation with Sabol took a different tack
after Endy said he was not ready to sell. "What would you do if you
really wanted to grow the business?" Sabol asked.

"The first thing I would do would be to go after the NFL," Endy told
him. When Sabol asked why, Endy replied, "Tel Ra has the rights."

"Yeah?" Ed said. "Well, how would you get started?"

"One thing I would do would be bid on the rights to the NFL
championship game," Endy said.

"How would you do that?" Sabol asked.

"I'd set up an appointment with Pete Rozelle," Endy answered.
Endy had directed and produced two Miller-sponsored films on the
Pro Bowl. Both did well on the service club circuit, the venue those
days for sports highlight films and related programming that fell
under the heading "industrial" films before television became the
major client for such businesses.

"We used Chris Schenkel as the narrator on those films. I worked with Chris while I was at Tel Ra, and he was a good personal friend," Endy said. "So, I asked Chris if he would arrange a meeting with Pete Rozelle, and he did that. At that meeting were Schenkel, Sabol, Rozelle, and me." This meeting took place in the late summer of 1962.

"I took along the two Pro Bowl films I had done. They were played out in the Los Angeles Coliseum, and we had bright, sunny days. The stage and the venue were right. The films turned out nicely," Endy recalled. "We showed one film to Rozelle, and he was absolutely awestruck."

"I don't have to watch the other one. I like this one," Rozelle said.

"We were granted permission to bid on the film rights to the 1962 championship game," Endy said. "It was an unusual position. I knew what Tel Ra previously paid for rights. That was $5,000 [not $1,500, nor $2,500]." They went back to New York in November for the formal bid. "We said that we would pay $10,000."

While they walked on Broadway, Sabol told Endy that he had a feeling that $10,000 was not enough. "Ed upped the ante," Endy recalled. "Ed said, 'We'll go to $12,000.'" In a *Sports Illustrated* story, "C. B. DeMille of the Pros" (November 20, 1967), Tom C. Brody writes that Sabol told Endy, "We'll try $12,500." Endy stands by the $12,000 figure as the winning number.

Regarding that late decision to up the bid, Endy recalled, "That was easy for Ed to say in light of the fact that he was retired. I was 33 years old with a mortgage; the oldest child was about nine, but I did have the money. The good news is we got the film rights. The bad news is we got the film rights. For the $12,000 we paid for the rights, $6,000 of that I put up, and $6,000 Ed Sabol put up. It was a joint production between Blair and my Cine-Sports. The film was both an artistic and financial success."

Thus, Ed Sabol was technically correct when he told people that *he* paid $5,000 (or $6,000—what's another grand or so in a bidding situation?), because it was a joint production; however, only the name Blair Motion Pictures was on the credits.

Bill Orr corroborates Endy's account. Since he still was a minor and Tel Ra was managed by a voting trust, Bill did not attend that meeting, but he did know about the money involved. Brody wrote that the runner-up bid was $10,000. "Tel Ra bid $6,500 on the 1962 championship game," Orr said, "and we were the runner-up."

They all agree on what happened after the commissioner opened the envelope and announced that Blair Motion Pictures had won the bid. The deal was not final. "Pete Rozelle opened the envelope and was very impressed that someone would double the bid over the previous year," Steve Sabol said. "But Pete was somewhat concerned that on my dad's résumé, it said he was experienced filming football, 'of my 14-year-old son.'"

"Pete said, 'I'll make my decision and let you know at the end of business tomorrow,'" Ed Sabol said. "So, I went back to Philadelphia, sat by my phone, and awaited the call. The biggest thing was the increase in the rights fee. They were interested in money. I didn't even get into detail of what I had in mind. I thought, if he opens the envelope and they're supposed to give it to the highest bidder, we had enough to do it. Obviously, it was."

To pay the bills for production and cover their bid, somebody had to sell the product. "That was Ed's sport, as far as I was concerned," Dan Endy said. "He had a brother-in-law named Herb Siegel who was very successful and helped Ed a lot in contacts."

"Ed used to have a trick," Herb Siegel said. A dozen years younger than Sabol, Siegel was a teenager when Ed started running the family business after the war. "Ed's married to my sister. He would test my wife, Ann, when he came to New York. He'd call around five and say, 'Darlin', I'm in New York. What're you havin' for dinner?' He wanted to see if she could handle an unexpected dinner guest. He used to do this once a month. One night he called and asked the usual, 'What're we havin' for dinner tonight?'"

"I'm sorry. I've gotta meet Herb," Ann Siegel answered. "We're going to the Four Seasons. It's for business." Herb, just 34 in 1962, was running a large talent agency and handling such clients as Perry Como and Jackie Gleason. He had not yet met Rozelle.

"Ah, jeez, I've gotta talk to him," Ed said.

"Well, come along. I'm sure it won't make any difference," Ann said.

"Ed came along, and I was having dinner with Al Hollander, of Grey Advertising," Siegel said. "Ed said before Al came that he paid $5,000 for the rights."

"Christ, I don't know what to do with it. What am I gonna do? Nobody wants to buy it," Sabol lamented to his brother-in-law.

"During the dinner," Siegel recalled, "I was talking to Hollander about television, and my wife said, 'Al, Ed here is doing television motion pictures of football.' "

"Yeah? What?" Hollander asked.

"The NFL," Sabol answered.

"*You* got the NFL?" Hollander roared.

"Yeah."

"That's interesting."

"Yeah. What'll I do?" Ed asked.

"Could you turn out these films fast enough so I could have a 'Monday-Morning Quarterback' thing we could run in different cities?" Hollander asked. It was supposed to be shown in six or seven cities. "We have a luncheon on, like, Tuesdays. It will be like a Monday-morning thing. We could run it in places like Cleveland and these towns. I got a sponsor who would do it."

"Who?"

"I think Lorillard would do this, because they bring in all the distributors. We represent them. Let's talk about this," Hollander said.

Sabol explained what developed next. "Grey Advertising sent it around to clubs, groups, organizations, like Rotary. In those days, you could advertise cigarettes, and they got Old Gold to sponsor it," he said. "They used Del Shofner, an end for the Giants. He and I traveled around a lot to these clubs and groups. I answered questions about the production, and he would give out pictures of himself and autograph them and talk about the game. That's what we did."

"Ed left there and got enough money committed to deliver the films, the highlights," Herb Siegel said. "Ed always said that my wife, Ann, made the deal that saved Blair Motion Pictures and led to NFL Films. What they did was unbelievable."

"That really was the bedrock of NFL Films," Dan Endy said. "This was Ed's first foray into it. Ed was very flamboyant, compulsive, and an interesting guy. He did a good job. He was, probably still is, a man with a lot of chutzpah, a lot of charisma, and had a lot of things going for him." More important for the Sabols, Ed had no other partner in Blair Motion Pictures. His deal with Dan Endy did not include equity, just sharing the profits in a joint production after they covered the overhead.

While Ed Sabol and Blair Motion Pictures were putting together the NFL title-game film deal, son Steve was busy out west at Colorado College partying with his Kappa Sigma fraternity brothers when he wasn't playing football. By 1962, he had become a legend among his peers. "He said he was from Possum Trot, PA. Then he called himself the Fearless Tot from Possum Trot," Bill Orr said. "It made *Sports Illustrated* [November 22, 1965] and was a very good thing. A classic. He and Ed made a great combination. They were PR animals."

"After a three-martini lunch, my dad convinced Pete to let him do the film," Steve Sabol said. "We had just played Idaho State, the second-to-last game of the season, and my dad said, 'I can tell by your grades that all you've been doing is going to the movies and playing football. That makes you uniquely qualified to come back and help me with this film.'

"So, I came back over that Christmas vacation and applied the limited knowledge I had about football to the film, and we did the '62 championship. There wasn't anything really different about the ones that had been shot before, except we shot it in color, and instead of using four cameramen, we used eight. The doubling theory." Steve Sabol did not return to school. He was hooked on the film business, eager to shoot, write, and edit.

"Since it was my first time in the big leagues, I used ten cameras, which was too many, but I didn't want to take any chances of missing anything," Ed Sabol said. "So, I loaded up with cameras. Since then, we can shoot a Super Bowl with four cameras. The techniques get better; the cameras get better. In those days, you didn't know if a camera was going to break down. Now it's a lot different."

The 1962 title game was a rematch between New York and Green Bay. The Packers had routed the Giants 37–0 in 1961 in the bitter cold of then Green Bay City Stadium for Vince Lombardi's first championship. For the film, Blair Motion Pictures shot a scripted opening with quarterback Bart Starr and a comment from Coach Lombardi, who extolled the virtues of little Green Bay as a big-time football town. At Yankee Stadium, the crew filmed opening remarks from future television star Frank Gifford, back with the Giants in 1962 after missing 1961 as a result of the Chuck Bednarik–inflicted concussion.

Conditions for the game were elemental. Cutting cold and a raw, biting wind that swirled through Yankee Stadium affected everyone—players, fans, strategists, and camera crews. "It was terrible. I titled that film *Pro Football's Longest Day*, because it was like D-day," Ed Sabol, the codirector with Endy, said. "That's where I got the idea. The movie Darryl Zanuck called *The Longest Day* came out that year. That was my longest day."

The Packers beat the Giants 16–7 for their second straight championship, thanks to the unrelenting defense led by middle linebacker Ray Nitschke and the determined runs of fullback Jim Taylor, who engaged in a memorable duel with New York's Sam Huff. "I hit him so hard, I dented my helmet. I got accused of hitting late," Huff said. "You didn't have to hit Jim Taylor. He was going to run over you. You didn't have to go after him, because here he came. He liked to say, 'I like to run over guys. I like to sting 'em.'"

So, Huff yelled back to Taylor, "Come on, you want to get stung? I'll show you who in the hell is gonna sting you."

Huff commented, "Then you hit him, and he'd say, 'You hit me late!'"

"You asked for it!" Huff screamed back that day.

"Jimmy and I now are pretty good friends," Huff said. "We let that go. We were competitors. There's no doubt about that."

The Blair team, practically frozen from its ordeal, packed roll after roll of shot film for the 90-mile trip back to Philadelphia, where the film would be processed and edited. Two cameramen had shot from upstairs, one at the standard 24 frames per second, the other in slow motion, using more film at 36 to 48 frames per second. They filmed tight shots focused on the runner and the ball, an effect that humanizes the players as it takes the fan onto the field. The slow-motion shots let the viewer see the subtleties of play and the energy the players expend. More cameras worked at ground level, shooting game action as well as cutaways of the fans in the stands and the shivering players on their benches—one shot in particular with flickering flames burning in an oil drum to lend a semblance of warmth. They used freeze-frames to stop action. One showed precisely what happened—specifically, the Giants' only touchdown—after a blocked kick and recovery at the goal line by Jim Collier.

"I remember after that '62 championship game, Ed gave a speech that we shot so much film that it would stretch to the moon," Dan Endy said. "I told him, 'Ed, that's not factually correct.' "

"Well, nobody's gonna check that out!" Sabol roared. "You gotta romance 'em."

Steve Sabol had been one of the cameramen. Back in Philadelphia, Steve assisted editor John Hentz, who assembled the finished product. As assistant editor, Steve did the grunt work—setups and splicing. "I taught Steve how to splice film," Endy said. "I remember going through that process where you have to wet your lips to find out which side of the emulsion sticks to your lips, so you know where you have to scrape the emulsion off and glue it to make the splice." Turning out a finished product ready for distribution and showing took three weeks.

"That's the way you did it," Ed Sabol said. "They didn't have any cable; you couldn't get it on television. There were only three networks."

First, before it hit the service club circuit, came a "world premiere" of *Pro Football's Longest Day* at Toots Shor's, in New York. In his review, football writer Hugh Brown, of the *Philadelphia Evening Bulletin*, called it a visual delight and, quoting the words of Commissioner Rozelle, the "best ever" NFL title film.

That was the start of something big. Blair Motion Pictures had improved the way football was shot. The pictures, in color, were better; use of slow motion and cutaways added impact; and the story line had advanced. The music, though, still was the standard marching-band sound that had pervaded sports highlight productions since the start of television and, before that, in the movie newsreels. It sounded ponderous.

Tel Ra made a final stab in 1963 at regaining rights to the NFL championship game. The voting trust, acting for 19-year-old Billy Orr, negotiated for several months with Ed Sabol through his lawyer Sylvan Cohen. "Sabol had a vision: he believed in slow-motion, tight-lens filmography and music," Orr said in 2006. "Not the 'John Philip Sousa music,' as he called it."

The Orr family told Ed they wanted him to come in and take over Tel Ra Productions as president with 49 percent of the company. At the last minute, he demurred, saying he had to have at least 51 percent, and the negotiations collapsed. Orr never forgot their parting words. "Bill, you'll have to learn in life," Sabol said.

The Sabols continued their march toward NFL Films and winning the confidence of Pete Rozelle. "After we got it going the first year, and after the second when he saw what a good film we made, it was much easier," Ed Sabol said. "I didn't have to double the rights fee, but I had to increase it. The other bidders didn't go any higher, so I got it again." According to *Sports Illustrated* (November 20, 1967), Sabol paid $17,000 for the 1963 film, but he still did not enjoy exclusive rights, and Tel Ra did not go quietly into the night.

Dan Endy returned to Tel Ra in 1963, where, under the sponsorship of Miller High Life, he wrote and produced the season highlight package for the Chicago Bears, which turned out to be propitious when they reached the championship game at Wrigley Field against the Giants. Tel Ra filmed that title game, blending ground shots, as well as sideline and crowd cutaways, with the standard high shots. Endy's black-and-white package runs some 34 minutes, 6 minutes longer than the usual season package, due to the championship-game highlight section.

Ed Sabol, as director and executive producer, titled his '63 championship film *Deadline to Glory*. "I wanted it to be more like a Hollywood film with the big music, the good narration, and close-ups," he said. "I began using more of that in the football stuff, and I think people began to notice that." Using more natural sound than he and Endy had employed the year before, Sabol's film featured tight shots, ground level action shots, a camera from Wrigley Field's left-field bleachers behind the north end zone, and a memorable overhead close-up of George Halas at the final gun to signal his sixth coaching title and the Bears' eighth overall championship. But the music still had a "carnival midway" sound.

Ed Sabol brought Endy back to work with Blair Motion Pictures in 1964 to direct and edit *Anatomy of a Championship*. Scriptwriter Tex Maule, of *Sports Illustrated*, received top billing over narrator Chris Schenkel. The production was more memorable than the game, a 27–0 Cleveland rout over Baltimore. "At the end of the third year, I made a decision that sooner or later some big outfit was going to come in and triple the bid, and I'd be gone," Ed Sabol said.

With costs going up, a small production company such as Blair Motion Pictures could not compete with the Hollywood titans. "Twentieth Century-Fox and Warner Brothers were thinking of bidding against us," Steve Sabol said. "There was no way this little family company would ever have been able to bid against those giants."

"I figured that I'd better talk to Pete. By this time, we'd become very friendly. Our office was in New York, and I was commuting from Philadelphia to New York, so we had lunch almost every day," Ed Sabol said. "He had an idea that these films could go into people's homes, and they could see them all-year-round. So, with these highlight films of each team, they could be seen in the off-season." And on television.

Sabol pushed Rozelle hard on the concept of the season highlight films, one for each team. "He understood it. That's why I liked him so much. A lot of owners did not like the idea. A lot of them thought we were a nuisance. 'Keep them off the field! Don't let them go near the sidelines.' They were very tough." And in 1964, the owners did not accept the idea of NFL Films. The league did not buy it.

In the beginning, George Halas and Vince Lombardi were Sabol's toughest critics. "Halas! Halas was miserable. And the language Halas used would scare anybody," Sabol said. "He'd make a marine sergeant sound like a choirboy. Like the rest of them, he gradually came around and began to like it. When we finally made a film just on him, he couldn't have been more cooperative. Lombardi just said,

'Sabol, you stay the hell out of here!' In the end, he just couldn't get enough. He even made me take pictures of him in the steam room."

A classic moment for fans of NFL Films is the marvelous scene in which Lombardi, in green Packer ball cap, stands at the chalkboard and draws and describes his bread and butter play—the power sweep. As he shows the key blocks and the runner's intended path, he states the play's intentions as the teacher he was. "What we try to get is a seal here." He draws a vertical line. Then, as he draws another vertical line to the left, he precisely states, "and a seal here." As he cuts a path between those lines, he declares, "And run the play *up the alley!*"

Sabol knew what his next step should be. "It was simple," he said. He went to Rozelle in early 1965 and said the magic words: "You just buy my little company out." Sabol's price, as he recalled, was a nominal $20,000 from each of the 14 teams, $280,000 in all, to be used as seed money. "I just had some equipment and let the National Football League own it." The owners accepted the offer, and from that point on, each of the league teams, 32 in 2007, became an equal partner in the ownership of NFL Films. The Sabols have no ownership whatsoever.

Sabol cinched the deal when he told Rozelle that by owning its own film production company, the league could control its product and the content. "Nobody can come in and take those films and turn them into porno or something," Sabol told Rozelle. "It's not censorship, but you keep an eye on it so every Tom, Dick, and Harry can't take those football films and turn them into something that shouldn't be."

In turn, Rozelle gave the Sabols a deal with incentives that included artistic freedom, within the framework of the NFL constitution, and each team anted in. "It worked out well. I could say I should have made more money, the old story. I loved it so much, I would have done it for nothing," Ed Sabol said. "Without Pete Rozelle's support, we would not have an NFL Films today."

"I still get calls from people who think we own it, who want to negotiate," Steve Sabol said. "I say, 'That's not the case at all.' People say, 'I can't believe it. If you had only 1 percent of what it is, imagine how many millions of dollars that would be.' I always say, in lieu of money, my dad and I got a life and a profession that we love. I would never change. We definitely made the right decision."

Another was Ed Sabol's decision to put Steve in charge of production. This was no matter of nepotism. "Steve has a great imagination, and he was just born for that job. It's the only job he's ever had in his life," his father said. "I very seldom make suggestions. We've always agreed and had our eye on the same results."

"When you think of football, the only other sport where music is as integral a part is bullfighting," Steve Sabol said. "Football always had the bands, the drums. I felt our films should have our own musical style. As a kid, I grew up watching 'Victory at Sea,' with the Richard Rodgers music. When we started NFL Films, that was one thing both my father and I believed: we need our own musical style, our own cinematic style."

In 1964, Ed Sabol met a composer named Mahlon Merrick, whose work had been showcased on film and Broadway. He agreed to compose some music for the Sabols. The key man, though, was Merrick's assistant Sam Spence. "He came here that summer and convinced my dad and me to come up with our own style of music," Steve Sabol said. "As a kid, I went to summer camp in the Poconos. Every Friday night, we sat around the campfire and sang, 'What're you gonna do with a drunken sailor!' I thought that we needed catchable, hummable melodies. And, with that, I wanted a rich sound filled with cellos, French horns, and the like. Sam took that and developed the Sam Spence style of music, which is basically the foundation for all the music we've used since then."

NFL Films viewers through the years have heard the "drunken sailor" musical quotes, along with many passages from Spence's eclectic mix that include such classical composers as Mozart, Chopin, and Beethoven, to name a few, combined with contemporary popular. The touch of spice that endured came with a man called "the Voice of God."

Where a Chris Schenkel and every other announcer to that time recited a standard play-by-play narration over game action, Steve Sabol wanted visual qualities and a story line to dominate his pieces, which consisted of original film often blended with historic footage, natural sound, perhaps a coach or player on a wireless mike, a taut script for the narrator, and the timely, contemporary-sounding original music composed by people such as Spence. No sportscaster filled that bill. "With less script, I felt the voice that read that script had to be arresting and compelling, and that's the way we ended up with Facenda."

John Facenda was a Philadelphia institution, the city's first television anchor when WCAU-TV, then a CBS-owned station, took the air in 1948. He dominated the ratings from the start, especially after sportscaster Jack Whitaker arrived in 1950. They worked together until Whitaker moved to the CBS network in 1961 when Tom Brookshier joined WCAU after a broken leg ended his career. Not only did Facenda possess a lyrical bass-baritone voice perhaps unequaled in local television news anywhere, but also he was a beloved and endearing personage whose neighborly opening line, "Hello, there," invited a viewer to watch. "I was just struck by his voice. It was like hearing a new musical instrument you never heard before," Ed Sabol recalled.

"How many great narrators are there? There's Orson Welles, Richard Basehart, Westbrook Van Voorhis, and Facenda," Steve Sabol said. "His voice was like an instrument. If music is the passageway to your soul, his voice was the passageway to your heart. He was warm, sincere, really cared about pronunciation. He had a great concern about the weight and tone of words and the balance of sentences."

"I wanted to get away from the normal sportscaster voice," Ed Sabol said. His fledgling NFL Films still had not moved across the Delaware into tax-friendly New Jersey when he met Facenda, a regular customer at a small Italian restaurant near his shop in Center City. "Every night I went in there, I'd see Facenda at the bar. We got to say, 'Hello,' and he sat down. The first thing he started talking about was pro football. Pro football. I began to think. 'John, you're really into this game.'"

"Ed, I love it. I really love pro football," the great voice said.

"I got an idea: how would you like to narrate a film?" Sabol responded. "By then," Sabol noted, "he knew who I was. He said, 'By God, Ed, I'll do it for nothing.'"

"You got a deal! Right now," Sabol told him.

"We finished dinner," Sabol recounted, "and walked across the street, where we were making highlight films then. That's about all we did. I got ahold of a script, put him in a sound booth, told him to read a few pages, and that was it. As soon as I heard that voice, I said, 'John, you gotta do these films.' "

"There's nothing I'd like to do better," Facenda said.

"That started it, and every film I could get him to do, he did. Not only did he have the great voice, but what a nice man," Sabol said. "He never argued about, 'Hey, I want more money,' or, 'I should be getting this,' or, 'I should be getting that.' People started wanting to use his services, and he'd come to me and say, 'Ed, do you think I should do such and such?' He was just so honest, and so loyal, and had just what I had been looking for. Here was a guy who came from news who had this great profundo, this great bass voice, and his love of the game."

"I developed a style that fit perfectly to his voice, as in 'It starts with a whistle and ends in a gun.' Or 'Lombardi—a certain magic still lingers in the very name,' " Steve Sabol said. "I would read those words aloud knowing he had never seen the film. The tempo of his voice timed in such a way that I could write a script and know exactly where it fit. We found that when he looked at films, it distracted him; we'd have to do a lot of retakes."

Incidentally, John Facenda never delivered the phrase "the frozen tundra of Lambeau Field." That is the creation of ESPN's Chris Berman, paying homage to NFL Films' great voice.

So, Steve would hand him a sheet of paper, go over it to discuss emphases, and talk it through. "John had that oaken, compelling delivery that was perfect. For the style of filmmaking we developed, he was the perfect voice," Steve Sabol said.

With all the elements in place—the techniques, the music, and the narrator—Steve Sabol went to work in 1965 on the project that set the course for NFL Films, *They Call It Pro Football*. It opens with a ticking clock over shots of a football field in an empty stadium. The sight and sound of a foot kicking the ball is followed by close-ups of the airborne ball intercut with the gridiron. It cuts to silent-era footage with a sepia tint. Players, some wearing leather helmets, others bareheaded, start play at the snap.

After a brief clarinet fanfare, Facenda speaks his first words for NFL Films: "It was a game a handful of spectators came to see." In a cut to a long-ago bench scene, the first recognizable face is young Red Grange of the New York Yankees. Seated next to a man in a fedora and overcoat, Grange is holding a cane due to a knee injury he suffered in a 1927 game against his once and future Chicago Bears. The pictures cut to a scrum and sloppy action. "A tug-of-war. Twenty-two nameless men grappling in the mud. They called it pro football."

The film proceeded to cover the history of the game to 1965 in a variety of shots, sounds, and colors never before seen in a single, cohesive package that combined the nuts and bolts the average fan demanded with the balletic violence of the game. The style became the NFL Films look. "The script was written in our style; we changed the music; it was the first time we miked a coach; it was the first time we ever showed Follies," Steve Sabol said. Four decades later, that film remains a work of art.

"After Pete saw *They Call It Pro Football*, he called my dad and said, 'I want you and Steve to come up to my office, and we'll talk about it.' I think they were at 410 Park Avenue then, only one floor. He sat us down at his desk and pulled out a sheet of paper. It was the Nielsen ratings. Baseball was first, college football was second, and the NFL was third. 'In order to succeed on television, we need to create an image for the game, a mystique,' Pete said. 'The film that I just saw is the image I want.' Pete Rozelle saw it as a very sincere, authentic, romanticized version of the game, which he felt would be great to promote."

"To me as a 22-year-old filmmaker, that was a mission statement, even though we didn't use those terms then," Steve Sabol said. "We didn't have demographics. We didn't have survey groups. We didn't have focus groups. The films were made about the way we felt about the game. Pete saw it in a much bigger picture, not only as a film, but a marketing tool."

When a few owners saw the film and complained about Facenda, saying he didn't know the game like a familiar Schenkel, Ed Sabol stood up for his man. "Facenda doesn't need to know anything about the game," he said. "Steve is writing it for him. He's reading a script."

"The greatest thing any young artist can have is freedom—freedom to come up with your own ideas and freedom from interference," Steve Sabol said. "Pete Rozelle always gave my dad and me that double-edged freedom. 'Steve, Ed, do what you think is right, and I'll make sure nobody from up here gets in your way or bugs you,' Pete said."

"Facenda over the years drank more, smoked more, and his voice got deeper, deeper, and deeper," Bill Orr said. "At the end, he could not read a script without at least a couple of cups of coffee and a couple of cigarettes before he could wind up."

Cigarettes eventually killed John Thomas Ralph Augustine James Facenda. He died of lung cancer on September 16, 1984, at age 71. Jeff Kay, Facenda's successor as chief narrator at NFL Films, had to stop work due to throat cancer. The current narrators are longtime Philadelphia sportscaster Harry Kalas and Rob Webb.

"Pete always protected NFL Films," Ed Sabol said. "Any problems I had, he'd just go to work and help me with them. He was a real good friend, too, besides the business part of it. We developed an extraordinary friendship. He was a unique guy. He didn't want the glory. We had a helluva time collecting film on him. He never asked us to get film of him. For a documentary on him, we only had a few minutes of film. He never wanted to sit down in front of a camera and be interviewed. We could have done it, but he was uncomfortable doing that."

Ed Sabol stepped down as president of NFL Films in 1987 and turned it over to Steve. Ed is now in his nineties, and he and wife Audrey spend most of their year in Scottsdale, Arizona. Steve has more than enough to keep him going at Mt. Laurel, NFL Films' New Jersey production facility. "Twenty-five percent of our staff has been with me since 1970. Another 25 percent has been with us for five years or less," Steve said.

NFL Films is so busy these days that it no longer does the United Way public service announcements that highlight NFL players' involvement in the organization's programs. "The new NFL Network keeps us so busy that we don't have time. We do one or two things for the History Channel, because I believe you gotta give a filmmaker a break from football. One of our guys is working on a history of the Spanish-American War for the History Channel." NFL Films also has produced memorable, emotion-filled football histories for Notre Dame, Army, and Navy, in that same enthusiastic style that began with *They Call It Pro Football*.

Dan Endy stayed with NFL Films until 1970 and then moved to the Twin Cities, where he produced sports films and hired on with the Vikings to work game days. "They put me on the stats crew there, and I still do it to this day. I've been around the Vikings longer than any other employee," Endy said.

Bill Orr had one more go-round with the NFL. It came in 1969 three years after the NFL-AFL war ended, and a year after Orr broke the Tel Ra voting trust and took control of the company. The company had lost $4.5 million since Wally Orr's death in 1962, but Tel Ra still held the rights to AFL highlights. Orr had just negotiated a deal with AFL president Milt Woodard and was about to sign the contract. Woodard, however, reported to Rozelle, now commissioner of both the merged NFL and AFL.

"At the last minute, the owners' committee members said, 'Come on up. We'd like you to meet Commissioner Rozelle,'" Orr said. "So, I met Rozelle. He was very nice and charming, and he said, 'We're not going to sign this deal because we have NFL Films, and that's too bad.'"

"I then secured the services of a New York law firm," Orr said. "I could prove something nobody else could prove: I could show that we actually lost $2.5 million in a defined time when Rozelle negated the deal with Woodard. We filed a $5 million suit, with the possibility of treble damages. We went down that road."

After six months, Orr and his lawyer met with Chiefs owner Lamar Hunt; Phil Iselin, of the Jets; and Wayne Valley, with Oakland, in a New York restaurant. "Bill, we appreciate your position. You're a businessman. We're all businessmen," the three owners said.

That was another way of telling the 25-year-old Orr to drop the suit. "Basically, we settled at 10 cents on the dollar. It was a very amicable settlement," Orr said. "I was trying to get out of hock with all the losses I took after my father died. So, I took the money and ran and had no regrets. NFL Films was established and should have had it, and should have been there. There was no reason for me to be in there."

Bill Orr carried on at Tel Ra. When times were tough, he had to sell the Tel Ra library. Former Eagles star Pete Retzlaff bought it and, being a smart businessman, sold it at a nice profit. "He got rid of the NFL stuff to NFL Films immediately," Orr said. That move gave NFL Films historic coverage from 1948 through 1964.

Bill Orr has endured and was thriving again by the 21st century. Now in his early sixties, he markets and packages events for several clients, among them the National Football Foundation, and produces the season highlights for several universities, including Notre Dame and Penn State. "Ed and Steve Sabol are the legends of NFL Films and are the emulation of every single league," Orr said recently. "None has been able to emulate the success of NFL Films. I hold them in great regard."

One final name must be mentioned. Despite the protests of Blair Academy, Blair Sabol has no doubt that her father did name Blair Motion Pictures for her, not the school he attended. Blair became a writer of considerable note, especially in the fashion trade, and is every bit the colorful character to equal her famous father, brother, and uncle Herb. "Blair Motion Pictures was for 10 minutes," the lady said. "The reason I get down on my hands and knees for Pete Rozelle is, 'Thank God it's the way those chips fell.' Pete gave my father that break, and brother Steve his."

"Who knew what was in Pete's head?" Blair said. "That really opened the door for my father, then my uncle Herb Siegel, who became very close to Pete. I think it was almost a rivalry between my father and Herb as to who was closer. I think nobody. He kept everybody so charmed."

TEN

THE CRUCIBLE

"His first real test came when he had to suspend Hornung and Karras. 'You gotta do what you gotta do,' said Lombardi to Rozelle. That showed he was the commissioner."

—Dave Anderson, 2006

*R*umors began to circulate in early 1962 that the National Football League had a major gambling problem and that much of that problem was rooted in the Midwest. It burst into the open on Friday, January 4, 1963, when United Press International broke a banner-headline-producing story with two words that terrify a sports commissioner unlike any others: "Scandal Rumors."

Speaking from Hollywood Beach two days before the National Football League's Playoff Bowl in Miami's Orange Bowl, which paired conference also-rans Pittsburgh and Detroit, commissioner Pete Rozelle told both UPI and the Associated Press that he had "been investigating rumors concerning the Chicago Bears and three or four other teams."

The AP reported that Rozelle's staff of 16 former FBI agents "constantly investigate such rumors" and that the agents told the commissioner that a number of players had "associated with undesirable types." Yes, there was smoke, all right, but, the commissioner stressed, "we haven't found any fire"; his agents had "not been able to find anything of a criminal nature."

The next morning, January 5, a Saturday, usually the sleepiest news day of the week, the first name surfaced. In a story in the early edition of *Chicago's American*, below the 48-point banner headline "I Passed Lie Test—Bear Star," Rick Casares, Chicago's veteran fullback, admitted to reporter Norman Glubok that he had taken two lie detector tests in which he was asked if he ever shaved points or had thrown games. "I volunteered for the tests," he said, "and they told me I passed them both." Casares also said he took the tests at the request of Bears owner-coach George Halas and Commissioner Rozelle. The tests were administered by two private Chicago laboratories. After learning the results, Halas, who had long feared gambling as a severe threat to the league, now considered Casares's name cleared.

The commissioner's comments did not ease fears that a scandal was imminent. Respected *American* sports columnist Bill Gleason called on Rozelle to act. "This is no time for hope on his part. It is time for swift action," Gleason wrote, adding that Rozelle "must save professional football. Nobody can help him."

Late in that column, Gleason wrote, "There can be no doubt that some of Rozelle's problems were inherited from Bell's administration." There certainly was no doubt among those in the know. Bert Bell had told reporters for years that he hired investigators to watch the betting lines and, moreover, had his own network of illegal bookmakers whom he frequently called to check on odds fluctuations and unusual betting patterns on games.

Rozelle was well aware of gambling's sinister implications. Yet, while he knew full well that millions of people bet on football, he also knew that those sports bettors included some of his bosses, the owners. Thus, he had to tread carefully through this minefield. "Carroll Rosenbloom, [Charlie, Sr.] Bidwill, and [Art] Rooney were all supposed to be big bettors," said Joe Schmidt, Detroit Lions Hall of Fame linebacker of the '50s and early '60s. "I don't think they bet against their teams; they had confidence in them and put a few bucks down."

In short order, bigger names than Casares, two of the NFL's biggest, would surface. They were the Golden Boy of the Green Bay Packers, superstar halfback Paul Hornung, and the league's finest defensive tackle, Alex Karras, of the Detroit Lions. By January 1963, Hornung had become an NFL poster boy and Vince Lombardi's biggest star for a Packers team many experts were calling the best ever assembled.

The Green Bay dynasty emerged in 1960 when Hornung scored 176 points in a dozen games to lead the Packers to the championship game in Philadelphia. That scoring record stood until 2006 when the San Diego Chargers' LaDainian Tomlinson broke it in his 13th game. Hornung was the key man again in Green Bay's superbly drilled title seasons of 1961 and '62. The only offensive players close to Hornung in performance were Cleveland's Jim Brown and Baltimore's Johnny Unitas.

When it came to sports gambling, a convenient source of easy money for the Outfit dons could be found in the colleges. On campuses, the quick and easy choice for bettors who lacked the experience, sophistication, and bankrolls to be serious players was the parlay cards. The parlay card was a small-time bet. Added up, though, the cards meant truckloads of easy bucks for the guys with manicured fingernails and pinky rings, who wore fedoras and big dark overcoats with bulges below their left pockets.

The "boys" would land a contact, usually a football or basketball player, who, in turn, hired his own runners to distribute cards at the start of the week. The cards typically found their way to fraternity houses or men's dorms, where they sat on end tables or piano tops. The contact's real value to the guys who passed out his cards was information—inside information such as injuries or personnel problems that the gamblers could put to profitable use.

The parlay card game was simple, similar to today's lottery, a pick-'em setup, only the odds of winning big were even longer. To cash in, a player had to make a number of correct picks against the spread. The investment usually was a couple of bucks, beer money for college boys. To win big, a player had to beat the point spreads in say, 10 games, college and pro football or basketball. As veteran Chicago sportswriter Bill Jauss said, "Nobody ever knew anyone who got the big payoff. Guys said anyone who could pick all 10 games won the universe. If you picked 9 out of 10, you won the earth."

In other words, forget it. But the suckers played and they paid. A miniscandal of sorts erupted at the University of Michigan in early 1960 when police arrested two close friends and athletes who graduated from St. Philip High School, on Chicago's West Side, before they matriculated at Michigan. It was alleged that Tony Rio, the 1959 football captain and Most Valuable Player, and Jack Lewis, the star basketball guard and captain, were running the parlay card operation on the Ann Arbor campus. That ended their athletic careers on the spot. Nothing more was heard from them as that story made a fast fade.

Troubles had built to a rolling boil for most of the '50s in Detroit. Until the Baltimore Colts came of age in 1958, the hard-bitten Lions dominated the tough Western Conference. Their leader since 1950 was a towhead from Texas named Bobby Layne, whom George Halas traded away, to his eternal dismay, in 1949 to pay off a major obligation to the estate of late Cardinals owner Charlie Bidwill. Layne, one of the true elite quarterbacks, may have been the hardest-drinking, wildest player in league history.

"Bobby Layne was quite a guy, a bulldog, not the type of leader you envision," Lions Hall of Fame linebacker Joe Schmidt said in 2005. "His idea was to keep the guys together by going out as a group after practice. He enjoyed taking rookies out to get them drunk and roam around with him at all hours."

Layne and the Lions were seizing control of NFL championships as Schmidt arrived in 1952 after an all-American career at the University of Pittsburgh. "When I was a rookie, I used to hide from him," Schmidt said. "I went to the bathroom and stood on the commode while he came in and looked around for rookies. He couldn't see me. He'd find a couple of guys and then leave. That's the kind of stuff he liked. He liked guys who played hard on and off the field." And, Schmidt stressed, Layne despised anyone who wouldn't party with him.

Layne was surrounded by a team that knew how to win, especially when the game was on the line. "They never got panicky when we got behind," Schmidt said. "Layne would orchestrate it himself. He'd say, 'I guarantee you, if we do this, we will win.' He would fulfill his promise and we would win."

Layne led Detroit to titles over Cleveland in 1952 and '53. One day during the '54 training camp, the Lions' quirky coach, Raymond "Buddy" Parker, buttonholed Schmidt after breakfast. "He was walking down the hall smoking a cigarette. He always smoked," Schmidt said. "He always addressed everybody by their full name. 'Joseph,' he said. 'Yes, coach?' 'Joseph, I want to make you captain for this year.' He just looked at me. I was startled. He never looked at me that much, let alone talk to me."

"That's OK?" Parker asked.

"I said, 'Yessir.' And he just kept walking," Schmidt said. "That was it. No reason why or anything else."

Layne led the Lions to their third straight championship game in 1954, only to be ambushed in a blizzard of eight touchdowns as Otto Graham, who announced his retirement before the game, passed and ran the Browns to a 56–10 rout. Late in Cleveland's 1955 training camp, a desperate Paul Brown begged Graham to return for one more season. He did, and the Browns won their third NFL championship when they beat the Rams 38–14 in Los Angeles. The Lions fell to 3–9 in '55 when Layne hurt his shoulder and barely could throw.

Led by a healthy Layne, the Lions came within a half game of beating the Bears for the Western title in 1956. They were leading 7–3 in the second quarter at Wrigley Field when Chicago's Ed Meadows slugged Layne from behind and sidelined him with a concussion. That opened the gates to a 38–21 Chicago rout. Two weeks later, though, the Giants smashed the Bears 47–7 at Yankee Stadium for the championship.

The Lions were revved up for another push in 1957. Parker, the architect of Detroit domination, took out an insurance policy of sorts when he picked up premier quarterback Tobin Rote in a trade with Green Bay. Before the season opener, the team held its annual "Meet the Lions" banquet downtown in the Book-Cadillac Hotel, where the team's partners, many of them auto industry heavyweights, had gathered.

"They asked Parker to come up and say hello to some of the customers before the banquet," Schmidt said. "He saw several of the guys having drinks. I wasn't one of them. Then we get on the podium. They introduced him, and he got up and said, 'I quit! I can't handle this team anymore.' Then he walked off. He didn't have any trouble with our team; most of the guys were scared of him."

Longtime assistant George Wilson took over and got the team rolling late in the season. When Layne suffered a broken leg late that year, Rote met the challenge. In a playoff at San Francisco, the 49ers built a 27–7 lead early in the third quarter. Rote took over the game and led the Lions back to a 31–27 victory. A week later, they gained revenge at Tiger Stadium for 1954 when they beat the Browns 59–14 for the title.

In 1958, rookie and top draft choice Alex Karras got a one-on-one initiation that summer from Layne, who made him his personal training-camp caddy and drinking buddy. Karras's days consisted of double workouts under a blazing sun followed by nonstop evenings with Layne, who ordered Karras to match him Cutty Sark and water for Cutty Sark and water until the rooster crowed the next morning, when they'd return to the dorm to grab a few winks before starting over.

As defending champions, the Lions were 4-point favorites in the second game of the season on October 5 at Green Bay against the moribund Packers in that last, long season before Vince Lombardi's arrival. The two principals who would cross swords with the commissioner in 1963 played that day: Karras, the Detroit rookie defensive tackle, and halfback Paul Hornung, of Green Bay, two years removed from his 1956 Heisman Trophy season with a 2–8 team, the worst in Notre Dame history.

With the score tied 13–13 late, Layne marched the Lions to the Packers' 11. On fourth down, Layne, always the absolute boss on the field, waved off the field goal team to go for the touchdown. His pass fell incomplete in the end zone, and the Packers ran out the clock for the tie. "On Monday, he got traded to Pittsburgh! The very next fuckin' Monday, he was gone!" Paul Hornung said in our 2003 interview for *Papa Bear*. "Do you know, there was not a thing written about it!"

"I remember they say he was drunk," I said.

"Drunk? Bullshit, he was drunk! He was betting 15 or 20 thousand. He told me! He gave 4 or 5 points, and he had to cover. He didn't give a shit. When Bobby made a bet, it made the rest of the guys who bet look like paupers."

"He was the biggest hitter in the league, wasn't he?"

"Sure," Hornung replied.

"When it came to throwing money around?"

"Absolutely!"

The coach who greeted Layne with open arms in Pittsburgh was none other than Buddy Parker, his fellow Texan, whom Art Rooney had hired in the off-season, not only to keep him company at the track and over drinks but also to win football games for the Steelers. Joe Schmidt was shocked that Layne suddenly ended up in Pittsburgh. "If you sit and think about all these things, maybe Layne's departure was orchestrated," Schmidt said. "If you see who was involved and how things developed, it leaves questions, but there's no proof to back that up."

When Paul Hornung was starring at quarterback for Louisville's Flaget High School in the early '50s before he moved on to Notre Dame, no one doubted that he was destined for stardom. As good as he was on the football field at Notre Dame, he was more advanced away from the gridiron. Hornung was incredibly popular with women and was a popular figure at stag gatherings with older gentlemen long out of college. In his first two years at Notre Dame, Hornung played basketball in the winter as sixth man. As the season wore on during his sophomore year, he became a favorite drinking partner of basketball coach Johnny Jordan. Naturally, his studies came second behind the game of life and action.

When he got home to Louisville to be pampered by his beloved mother, he spent many an afternoon at Churchill Downs to play the horses. He spent most of his free time, though, in Chicago, where he found some of the fastest action anywhere in the company of some of the most dangerous and notorious rogues in America. "Sure. I was on the street almost every night," Hornung told me. "Hell, you'd run into all kinds of people on Rush Street. They usually went to the 10 or 12 spots that I went to. I knew a lot of people."

Did he ever! The "people" Hornung knew merely included the upper echelon of the Chicago Outfit! Hornung, in his book *Golden Boy*, discusses his introduction to the Chicago bright lights in the summer of 1955 while he was enrolled in summer school at Notre Dame before his junior season. A South Bend trucking executive named Julius Tucker escorted the Golden Boy to Chicago, where he met a high roller named Abe Samuels. Samuels, in Hornung's words a half century later, "took me downtown and had four or five suits made for me."

Samuels also introduced the athlete to gangster Mandel "Manny" Skar, who ran the Outfit-owned Sahara Inn, on the notorious Mannheim Road "strip," which ran along the eastern edge of O'Hare Airport. By midsummer, Hornung was a man on the go, covering great chunks of turf on Rush Street, on the North Side, and out on Skar's strip, and always in the company of a gorgeous woman. Hornung became a regular at places on the Near North Side such as the Pump Room and mob-owned Chez Paree, and he met such show business celebrities as Tony Bennett, Phil Silvers, Sammy Davis Jr., and Dean Martin.

During that summer of '55, Hornung also got acquainted with Sam "Momo" Giancana, who ran Outfit operations for the don, Tony "the Big Tuna" Accardo. "I knew Sam as a guy in the clubs, not the boss of the Chicago mob," Hornung wrote. "I didn't really wise up about some of these characters until Manny was killed in a garage, shot 20 times."

Skar paid the price for messing with his bosses in June 1965 when they learned he was about to tell the Feds all about the Outfit. Gambler Gil Beckley, a non-Chicagoan, was another Outfit-connected gambler Hornung knew, from the racetracks and action spots such as heavyweight title fights. "I don't know what happened to Gil. He just vanished one day, and nobody ever found him, as far as I know," Hornung said.

Bernie Parrish described Beckley as "the league's conduit to organized crime. He was the guy Rozelle checked with constantly in case there was some fluctuation in the point spread indicating there was a problem in a game." Hornung did not know that Rozelle knew Beckley.

Sam Giancana is still mentioned in connection with President Kennedy's assassination after four and a half decades, but nothing ever was proved. In 1975, Giancana was subpoenaed to testify before a Senate committee about CIA and Mafia links to an assassination plot against Fidel Castro. Fearing he would spill mob secrets, several senior Outfit veterans visited Giancana at his Oak Park home on the night of June 19, 1975, long after Hornung's retirement.

Special undercover Chicago police detective Howard McBride, assigned to cover Giancana night and day, was on a stakeout outside Giancana's house when he got a call from a downtown dispatcher. The dispatcher, with an urgent tone in his voice, ordered McBride to go immediately to Tony Accardo's home in nearby River Forest. When McBride arrived, the detective at Accardo's told him nothing was wrong. Fearing the worst, McBride sped back to Giancana's.

Noting that the other cars were now gone, McBride ran over to look into a basement window, where he saw Giancana lying on the floor in a pool of blood near a stove on which he had been cooking a late-night snack of sausage and peppers. Once inside, McBride could tell that Giancana had been silenced with a single shot to the back of the head and six more for good measure into the jaw, seven shots in all, most likely by the Outfit's execution weapon of choice, a .22 caliber pistol.

Hornung in his book claimed to know nothing about Skar and Giancana's true affiliation until sometime after he had served his suspension and was restored to the active list in "good" standing. Rozelle, though, began his investigation of Hornung in January 1963 even as he tightened the screws on Karras.

In 1963, Alex Karras at age 27 was regarded as the top defensive tackle after five NFL seasons. Karras grew up in the rough steel city of Gary, Indiana, a competitive, hard-bitten melting pot of 140,000 tough people. It was the biggest city in Lake County, the Calumet

Region, on the southern rim of Lake Michigan, abutting the southeast side of Chicago and neighboring suburbs in Illinois 15 miles to the west.

The Region, as the locals call it, was the industrial heart of America through most of the 20th century. The air could be foul and nearly impossible to breathe, especially when the wind wafted off the lake. The skies burned red at night from the glow of the open-hearth blast furnaces that forged the girders and beams that became the framework for scores of mighty skyscrapers, stadiums and arenas, and bridges, along with plates and sheets for the auto and railroad industries.

The series of company names painted on the soot-covered walls and roofs of the huge mills provided a litany of American industrial might. In Chicago, it was the U.S. Steel South Works, Republic Steel, Interlake, and Wisconsin Steel. In East Chicago, Indiana, it was Inland Steel, which grew out of Ryerson Steel, and Youngstown Sheet and Tube. Whiting was built around the massive Standard Oil refinery. Next came Gary, with the biggest mill in the world, U.S. Steel. U.S. Steel's massive complex stretched for miles along the lakefront all the way to Bethlehem's huge mill in Burns Harbor.

Judge Elbert H. Gary and the other industrial moguls of the Region made fortunes on the toil of their workers, men who worked hard and played harder, whether knocking back boilermakers after their shifts or competing in men's games such as baseball, basketball, and, the defining game of manhood, football. Their sons followed suit in perhaps the toughest high-school sports area in the country. A Region coach knew better than to cut a boy for smoking or having a beer. The fool who tried that couldn't field a team.

Before Lou, Teddy, and Alex Karras came along, Gary's great athletic names were middleweight boxing champion Tony Zale and an incredible all-around athlete from Horace Mann High School who would gain fame and the 1940 Heisman Trophy at the University of Michigan, Old Number 98, Tommy Harmon. One Horace Mann athletic wannabe in Harmon's time was a steelworker's son named Charlie Finley. Finley would make a fortune in insurance, buy a ball club in Kansas City, and move his A's to Oakland to win three straight world championships in the '70s, and unwittingly become the catalyst to baseball players' gaining free agency.

Tony Roberts, the longtime sportscaster who called Notre Dame football on Saturdays and NFL games on Sundays for more than a quarter century, got his start in radio calling high school games at WWCA, Gary. "You had Slovaks, Serbs, Croatians, Poles in Gary; Hispanics in East Chicago; African Americans in both cities—an ethnic melting pot," Roberts recalled. "You had Thursday-night football games at Gilroy Stadium through the weekend; then, starting on Tuesday in winter, basketball every night. No better place anywhere than Gary War Memorial Auditorium on a Saturday night. Talk about rockin'."

Alex Karras, of proud Greek ancestry, was the third and most gifted football-playing son of Dr. George Karras, who died when his youngest son was 13. The Karras brothers all were linemen, and all starred at Emerson High, in college, and in the NFL. Lou, 7 years older than Teddy, went to Purdue and then played 3 years for the Redskins. Teddy, a year older than Alex, went to Indiana and then played 9 years in the NFL, winning a championship ring with the 1963 Bears. Alex, a year younger than Teddy, was the best athlete, a 6′2″, 245-pounder, All-State in basketball and four times All-State in football at defensive tackle and offensive end. The quick-witted Alex used his reflexes and graceful moves to become the best defensive tackle of his time.

"I knew there would be people on the field bigger than me, stronger than me, faster than me," Karras said. "I had to figure out whether I would play offense or defense all the time. The leverage would be the same, whether I would grunt or groan—or they would. I made sure that would happen, so they wouldn't be bashing me. That's the game that I played. Call it chicken, but that's the way I played. I didn't get hurt much. I was really fortunate."

Karras was twice an All-American tackle at Iowa and was the Lions' number one draft choice for 1958 after he won the Outland Trophy as college football's top lineman. At Iowa, Karras was constantly at war with his coach, Forest Evashevski. Karras wanted to carry a "real" academic workload. Evashevski made him enroll in the easier, "jock" courses. Karras hated Evashevski so much that he told the coach never to speak to him away from the football field. When he got to Detroit, he found teammates he liked and a city like Gary, on a larger scale, where plenty was happening after dark.

Karras spent most of his time while in Detroit at a restaurant called the Grecian Gardens and at a nearby bar, the Lindell AC, owned by two fellow Greeks, brothers Jimmy and Johnny Butsicaris. The Lindell was a popular spot and for decades was a beer and hamburger hangout for Detroit professional athletes and their out-of-town opponents in all sports, from hockey's Red Wings and baseball's Tigers, to the Lions. "The original Lindell AC was down the street from the old WWJ studios," said Sonny Eliot, a popular Detroit radio and television weatherman personality since 1946. "I had an office above the Lindell. It was home to me."

"John Butsicaris and Sonny Eliot were best friends," said longtime *Detroit News* sports columnist Jerry Green. "They flew together. Sonny got shot down over Germany in World War II. He took his dog tags and threw them away so they would not identify him as Jewish."

In 1961 when the Butsicaris brothers decided to build a new Lindell AC, they asked Karras to become a partner. He invested $40,000 with them and tended bar when he was around the place. Matters took a dark turn in the summer of 1962. "We were playing a preseason doubleheader in Cleveland," Joe Schmidt said. "We played the New York Giants in the second game after Baltimore played Cleveland in the opener. The guys from Greektown had a bus down there, a mobile home."

"Tony Giacalone bought the bus from the City of Detroit, one of those old buses," Eliot said. "Tony—no—Billy Jack, Tony's brother, painted it on the outside with the [silver and Hawaiian blue] colors of the Lions." They completed the rehab with an engine tune-up and installed several easy chairs and tables.

These were hard-bitten men. The late Anthony Giacalone, better known as "Tony Jack," and fellow mafioso Tony "Tony Pro" Provenzano were supposed to meet former Teamsters president Jimmy Hoffa for "lunch" more than a decade later on July 31, 1975. That was the day Hoffa disappeared and likely was murdered, a still unsolved crime. "The Giacalones supposedly stomped Denny McLain's foot in the '67 season as well," Jerry Green said.

"We all got on that bus in Detroit and drove it to Cleveland," Eliot said. "We played cards and had some drinks. Tony Jack drove it."

"I got caught in that too," Schmidt said. "We had the next day off, so coach George Wilson gave Karras, John Gordy, Wayne Walker, Sam Williams, and me permission to ride back with them to Detroit. The state troopers had been watching those guys in the mobile home. They stopped them earlier. They got stopped at the Ohio-Michigan border, and the cops took names. Nothing happened out of that."

When the cops told Lions general manager Edwin Anderson about the incident, he called Karras to his office and ordered him to stay out of the bar business. "Those people are gangsters and hoodlums, guys you have to stay away from," Anderson yelled. Karras exploded and threatened to sue if Anderson could not prove what he said.

"During the fall, Alex made some bets," Schmidt said. "Rozelle's guys had been following him." In any other season, against any other team than Lombardi's 1962 machine, the Lions likely would have won the championship. They had destiny in hand in the fourth game, at Green Bay, when they held a 7–6 lead and the ball at the Green Bay 49 with 1:45 left. As Karras wrote in *Even Big Guys Cry*, coach George Wilson told quarterback Milt Plum to control the ball, meaning, run it to use up time. Yale Lary, the NFL's best punter, then would pin the Packers back near their goal line.

On third-and-8, instead of calling a run to bleed the clock, quarterback Milt Plum, for reasons he could not or would not explain to his teammates, defiantly threw a down-and-out pass. Herb Adderley intercepted it and ran it back to the Lions' 18. Three plays later, Hornung kicked his third field goal, to give the Packers a 9–7 victory those Lions still talk about after four and a half decades.

All hell broke loose in Detroit's locker room. "The defense jumped all over Plum, and Karras threw his helmet at him," Jerry Green said. "I wasn't there, and I don't think anybody in the press, as we were called then, saw it, but we heard about it. When I was on the beat, I asked Alex about it. I covered him from 1965 through 1971. 'Yeah, I threw it,' Alex said. 'I missed him by about this much!' His hands were 8 to 10 inches apart. He came up with the line, 'That's about how much Plum missed the pass.' "

Green added, "Schmidt, who also was irate about that, told me that Plum got a bad rap because Terry Barr slipped on the play. It was a play that pretty much has defined the Lions since their last championship." As it was, Detroit was the only team that beat Green Bay in 1962, when the Lions destroyed the Packers on Thanksgiving Day at Tiger Stadium. The enraged front four—Karras, Roger Brown, Darris McCord, and Sam Williams—sacked Bart Starr 11 times, for 110 yards in losses, before they coasted to a 26–14 victory. As they headed into the final game against the Bears at Wrigley Field, the Lions were 11–2, a game behind Green Bay in the West.

"The Lions were so sure they were going to win, they told Jimmy Butsicaris they would put everything on the line," Eliot said. "So, Jimmy and I each put $100 on the Lions. None of them bet on it—Joe Schmidt and all the guys. They lost 3–0 that day. They had been so sure they were going to win."

Pete Rozelle started the Playoff Bowl in 1960 as a second-place game and television showcase to give the NFL more postseason exposure and divert attention from the fledgling AFL. That game, no longer relevant after the merger and birth of the Super Bowl, lasted through 1969. It always was played in the Orange Bowl, in Miami, the week after the league championship game. Officially, it was called the Bert Bell Playoff Bowl, but because it was a game for also-rans, the Bell name on the label could not supplant the likes of Lombardi's "Hinky-Dink Bowl," or Schmidt's "Bathroom Bowl." The Lions were going for a three-peat against the Pittsburgh Steelers in this game that the players detested in every way except the paycheck.

On December 31, 1962, the day of the NFL championship in blustery New York, several Lions in Miami for the Playoff Bowl took time off from practice to visit the Florida home of Karras's friend Archie Long, who worked at a Detroit racetrack. "We went over, a bunch of us. Night Train [Lane] was there too, to watch the game," Schmidt said. "Archie was on the phone putting a bet down. 'You guys want to get down on the game?' Archie asked. "So, I said, 'Give me a hundred on Green Bay.' So, we all bet a hundred bucks, watched the game, and off we go."

The next day in Miami, Rozelle called Karras and ordered him up to his hotel room, where, as Karras wrote, a league attorney and a stenographer were present. Rozelle, described in Karras's book as furious, named the Detroit names in question and asked Karras if he rode on the bus and if he ever bet on any NFL games. After silence, Karras admitted he placed a bet on the previous day's championship game. "You could be in a lot of trouble," Rozelle said as he informed Karras that an investigation was under way. Karras told the commissioner he had not thrown any games, he never bet against his team, nor did he have any ties with criminals. At Rozelle's request, Karras signed an affidavit.

A week later on January, 6, 1963, the Lions beat the Steelers 17–10 in the Playoff Bowl before 36,284 fans, less than half the capacity of the Orange Bowl. Bobby Layne played the final 8:30 in relief of Steelers starter Ed Brown. The next day, Steelers coach Buddy Parker, speaking to reporters, referred to Layne as "the greatest quarterback I have ever seen" but said that it was time for him to retire. Layne, the last position player who refused to wear a face mask, told reporters he would think it over.

The next shoe dropped on Monday, January 7. Lions GM Edwin Anderson told a *Detroit News* reporter that he "would try to pressure Karras to get rid of his share in the Lindell AC." Karras, who was in Los Angeles for the Pro Bowl, to be played the following Sunday, snapped back. Calling Anderson's comments ridiculous, Karras said he would sue the team if it tried to make him sell, adding, "I might have to quit to protect my interests."

Karras and Schmidt roomed together at the Biltmore Hotel in downtown Los Angeles. "People were calling the room, tracking him down," Schmidt said. " 'Huntley-Brinkley' wanted to talk. After the game, Jimmy David, our old teammate, now with the Rams, and I went to the hotel bar for a beer. Alex said he was going up to the room. 'Just don't say a goddamn thing that can get you into trouble. Don't say anything,' I said."

"All right," Karras said.

"So, he went up there," Schmidt said.

"Alex would never have been suspended had he kept his mouth shut," Paul Hornung said. "He was just being a smart-ass, saying, 'What the hell is the difference? Everybody is betting those little [parlay] cards!' "

"We were all upset with what happened to Alex, because we could tell by the way the ["Huntley-Brinkley" NBC News] piece was aired," Eliot said. "They asked him if he bet, and he said, 'Yeah, we bet candy bars, cigars, and stuff. Like, I'll bet you this pair of shoes against that pair.' They edited that like we knew they would. When they asked the question, 'Did you bet?' and he answered, 'Yes', they cut it right there—not, *for candy bars*. I happen to know that he bet—everybody did—but he never bet on the Lions to lose. He said, 'Don't ever bet on the Lions, 'cause I'm in trouble.' "

"When he admitted that, he put himself in the category," Hornung said. "I am sure—I am just guessing—that Pete didn't want to suspend Karras, but he was questioned because of his affiliation with that bar in Detroit where he hung out."

"Jimmy David and I had a couple of beers. He was going to leave to go home in Detroit. I was leaving the next day," Schmidt said. "They were asking Alex about the gambling thing. When I got home, a guy from the *Detroit News* called me Monday night and said the story was going to break on the wires."

"You know what Alex said to the 'Huntley-Brinkley' guy?" asked the reporter.

"They questioned him about gambling," Schmidt told the reporter. "He said he gambled on games, not to throw games, but he bet on games. Then Alex said, 'All the players and owners on all the teams gamble.' "

"You better get ahold of George Wilson," the reporter told Schmidt.

Schmidt recalled, "George stayed over in Florida for a while to be with his family. I tried to get ahold of him and finally reached an assistant coach. 'Holy shit,' he said.

"That broke it open. Rozelle got the guys involved with Archie Long," Schmidt said. "They knew we were there. They sent an undercover guy out here. They interviewed each one of us in a room at a place by the airport. They accused each one of us of gambling all the time. 'You're crazy!' I said. I told him what happened. The guy said, 'I don't know what the outcome of this will be.' Another 10 days—two weeks—passed, and the guy came back. I went in, and the guy said he was going to give me a lie detector test. 'No, you're not!' I said. 'I'm telling the truth.' That went away." The next day, Rozelle ordered Karras and teammate Wayne Walker to fly to New York, where they took lie detector tests.

On January 8, 1963, Paul Hornung, who had been injured and did not play in the Pro Bowl, was having dinner with Bart Starr, Jim Taylor, Jerry Kramer, and their wives when he got a message to call Commissioner Rozelle at his home in New York. When the commissioner asked Hornung when he could come to New York, the Golden Boy jumped on the red-eye and arrived the next morning. "At first I denied gambling on anything," Hornung wrote. "But I knew he had me when he told me the league had been conducting a secret investigation for ten months and had tapped into my phone in Green Bay." So, Hornung confessed, admitting he had bet on many games. When the commissioner pressed for names, Hornung dug in his heels. "The FBI wanted me to take a lie detector test, and I told them I wasn't going to answer any questions about anybody else but myself, and I'd answer them truthfully," Hornung said.

Hornung long has stated that he could have brought down the world of pro football had he named names, places, and events. "I mentioned to Rozelle at the time, 'You know, Pete, I'm going to tell you the truth. You know I'm not gonna answer any questions about anybody else. If you don't know who gambled, that's your problem. It's not mine. I'll tell you one thing, if we go to Washington under a probe or something, like there had been in the past, and they ask me questions under oath, I'm gonna have to tell the truth. So, you better keep my ass out of Washington.' So, I believe that was his focus after that, to make sure we didn't have to go to Washington and be embarrassed."

On Tuesday morning, April 16, 1963, Peter Hadhazy arrived at work at the NFL office to find Pete Rozelle waiting for him. Rozelle asked, "What are you doing this afternoon?"

"I'm working. Nothing special," Hadhazy said.

"I want you to take a trip to Washington this afternoon," Rozelle said. "There are some papers I want you to deliver to Robert Kennedy at the Justice Department." Hadhazy knew that Rozelle had been keeping the attorney general apprised of the gambling probe. "He gave me a manila envelope that contained the release on Hornung and Karras being suspended. I took the shuttle from LaGuardia down to Washington."

That shuttle, Hadhazy's first time on an airplane, cost $12.50. He took a cab to the Justice Department. "The commissioner had told me, 'I want you to hand this personally to the attorney general.' There was no security, and I asked someone in the main lobby where the attorney general's office was. 'You take the elevator to the seventh floor.' So, I got off and walked down the hall and walked into the office. There was a little alcove, where a lady was sitting. 'I'm Peter Hadhazy; I'm here from the NFL.'

" 'Oh,' she said, 'the attorney general is expecting you. Take a seat.' "

"There was no place to sit, and she ushered me into his office, not a huge office," Hadhazy recalled. "I sat in his office waiting for him. He had a picture of his brother, the president, and a couple of other pictures, and a couple of pens. She knew my name, but she didn't ask for an ID or anything like that. I sat there for 20 minutes; then she came in and said, 'Mr. Kennedy is going to be delayed. I'll take your material.' "

"I was instructed to give it to him, personally," Hadhazy said. Besides, he wanted to meet Kennedy.

"Finally, after another 5 or 10 minutes, she came in again and said, 'He's really tied up.' So, I gave the envelope to her," Hadhazy said. "While I was sitting there, I could have taken a pen or a picture, which I didn't. So, I took the next shuttle back to New York. That's the way things were done in those days."

While Peter Hadhazy was getting the official word to the attorney general, the commissioner called Karras at home in suburban Detroit. He told Karras that he, as commissioner, had the power to fine and suspend any player who accepted a bribe or bet on a game. "I am now invoking that rule. You are hereby suspended indefinitely," Rozelle said.

At least Karras got the courtesy of a phone call. "I walked into a restaurant where I had part ownership," Schmidt said. "It broke. Rozelle fined five of us [John Gordy, Gary Lowe, Wayne Walker, Sam Williams, and himself] 2,000 bucks and suspended Paul and Alex, not us. I was pissed." Night Train Lane was not mentioned. "I told Rozelle, 'The least you could do was give me the courtesy to tell me I was getting fined.' He said, 'We didn't have enough time. People had information, and we were afraid it would come out in the papers. We wanted to release it ourselves.'"

"There is no evidence that any NFL player has given less than his best in any game," Rozelle said in his statement announcing the suspensions of Hornung and Karras. He stated that no evidence had been found that a player had bet against his own team, nor that any player sold information to gamblers. He also fined the Lions another $2,000 for lack of supervision. Late in the statement, Rozelle said, "Karras bet $100 on his own team [in 1962] when it played at Green Bay."

"That thing with Alex and Paul was a matter of procedure" Schmidt said. "They never found a thing that anybody was throwing games. I don't know of anybody who did. It makes good reading, and people look at it."

"I made more money when I wasn't playing," Hornung said. "Jantzen stuck with me. I had more commercials during those years than any other athlete in football."

Karras earned his keep at the Lindell AC during 1963, tending bar and talking with customers. He got into a well-publicized brawl in the bar with pro wrestler and former NFL tackle Dick "the Bruiser" Afflis. That set up a "wrestling match" on April 27 at the Detroit Olympia. "The Bruiser pinned me with a 'choke hold' after I threw him out of the ring a few times," Karras wrote. "I collected my money and quit the game forever."

That June, the new Lindell AC opened at Cass and Michigan. Many friends and teammates, fearing NFL reprisal, stayed away. Teammates John Gordy and Wayne Walker came in, ordered drinks, and toasted their buddy's good health.

In early 1964, Karras was commiserating one night in the bar with a Detroit lawyer named Joe Louisell. Much of his business in that tough town came from defending Mafia operatives. Louisell checked out the Lindell liquor license and found that the place and its owners were clean. He told Karras he had a good case for reinstatement because the NFL was in violation of restraint-of-trade laws. He agreed to represent Karras pro bono. In early March, they met with Rozelle in New York. "I didn't know him as a person," Karras told me 42 years later. "They looked at each other. My lawyer said to him, 'Let's hope we can get this through. If we don't this time, I'm going to have to do something else, and I don't want to.' He changed the color of the room. And that was it."

"Vince set the law down," Hornung said, for his part. It also happened in early 1964.

"I don't want to hear of you going to the races," Lombardi told him. "You're not to be in Vegas. You're not to be on any gambling boats or any of that shit. Come next year, if you keep your nose clean, I'm going to try to get you reinstated."

"And he's the man who did it, of course," Hornung said. "He stood up for me. Rozelle would do anything Vince wanted because he really respected him."

Years later, Rozelle told Ernie Accorsi, then working in the league office, what happened next. "After he talked with Pete, Lombardi said, 'Let's go get a drink.' They sat around, had cocktails, and relaxed at the end of a hard day," Accorsi said. "Pete was the best of all worlds."

On March 16, 1964, the league issued a statement under Rozelle's name. "The suspensions of Paul Hornung of the Green Bay Packers and Alex Karras of the Detroit Lions have been reviewed separately and both players are reinstated immediately."

The commissioner did not stand in front of reporters to take questions. He wasn't even in New York, thanks to the advice of his executive director, Jim Kensil. "Jim was the greatest PR director and executive officer of all time, in my opinion," said Ernie Accorsi, who was a PR director for the Colts in the early '70s before he went to finishing school at league headquarters with Kensil and Rozelle; he later became general manager for the Colts, Browns, and Giants. "You might issue a release on a controversial subject the way you want it written. If they question you, they will write it the way they want. So, Kensil put Pete on a plane at Kennedy [then Idlewild] and sent him to the West Coast. Once the plane was in the air, they announced the suspensions of Hornung and Karras. Seven hours later, Pete landed in L.A. after the deadlines were gone and then came back east. Kensil sent him out there and back. So, every news story had to be written the way Kensil had written it for the release. That's one of the great PR stories of all time."

Hornung resumed his career in Green Bay and played at a high level through 1965. He was hurt during most of 1966 and watched Super Bowl I from the sideline, was taken by New Orleans in the expansion draft in 1967, and retired. He had a brief, but indifferent, television career with WBBM-TV, the CBS station in Chicago, until Brent Musburger joined the station in 1969 and began his meteoric rise to network stardom. Hornung moved back to Louisville, where he made a substantial fortune in real estate. He was elected to the Pro Football Hall of Fame, class of '86, a year after Pete Rozelle was chosen.

New Lions owner William Clay Ford rewarded Karras in 1964 with a two-year contract and a healthy raise to $25,000 a year. Karras was still an outstanding player, but he could not shake his bitter experience. On Thanksgiving Day that year, when the Bears beat the Lions 27–24, Karras had an angry postgame shouting match in the Lions dressing room with Brent Musburger, at that time still a sportswriter with *Chicago's American*. "Musburger asked Karras a question about his Bears line opponent," Jerry Green recalled. "Karras blew up and went all over Musburger. Yelled at him, 'Get the hell out of here,' and all that stuff. He wasn't always beautiful to the media."

Joe Schmidt retired in 1965 and became the Lions' head coach in 1967. In 1969, he was named the "greatest-ever Lion" in a fan poll, and his number 56 was retired. Then, on the eve of the 1971 season, he made the toughest decision of his coaching career. He cut a less mobile, 36-year-old Karras. "Late in his career, the *Detroit News* picked its own all-pro team," Jerry Green said. "Karras came up to me and said, 'Put me on your all-pro team, will ya?' He and Schmidt had a falling out at the time he got cut."

Karras dusted himself off and dug into a new career as an actor and broadcaster, in which he thrived for the next three decades. He gained early acting fame in Mel Brooks's classic *Blazing Saddles* when Mongo, his character, walked out of a saloon and knocked out a horse with one punch. Karras worked on ABC's "Monday Night Football" telecasts for three seasons and then had a long run on ABC as costar of the sitcom "Webster" with his second wife, Susan Clark. He retired from acting in 2000 when he turned 65. "It was much like the athletic part of it, which is: I've done enough; I've seen enough; I've heard enough; I've had it," Karras told me. "They were great moments for me—don't get me wrong."

"Karras is no tragic figure. He has done very well," Jerry Green said. "George Plimpton came out in '03 for the 40th reunion of the book's [*Paper Lion*] publication. I got invited to a party where Alex was. He didn't even look the same. You see a guy who could age! I did a double take. He sure looked more polished than the Alex Karras of Gary, Indiana, I knew then."

The one great moment Karras has been denied is election to the Pro Football Hall of Fame. "A couple of years ago, Karras's name came up," Green said. Green represents Detroit in the Hall votes, but he could not attend the meeting to speak for Karras. "It's a difficult selection process for the old-timers. It was one of my years off. Alex lost in the five-man vote, three to two. Had I been there, I think the vote would have been reversed."

Joe Schmidt has been a manufacturer's rep in Detroit for the auto industry since he quit coaching in 1973, but he still thinks about those days and his teammates. "Karras should be in the Hall of Fame," Schmidt said. "I try to keep contact with the guys. Alex had bypass surgery a while ago, and John Gordy was in the room when I called."

Those who covered the commissioner agree that the 1963 investigations and suspensions set the course for his term and standing with the owners and the public. "That was probably the most important thing he did in his early years," said Dave Anderson, of the *New York Times*. "He was commissioner for almost 30 years. That's when he put himself on the map."

"Gambling was serious in the public eye. It's always serious," said *Los Angeles Times* football writer Bob Oates. "When the public perceived something was wrong, he stepped in and acted on that decisively and correctly."

"There was a different morality of sorts. Don't forget, those guys just got a year's suspension," Anderson commented. "In baseball, they would have been out forever. Of course, there was no evidence that either Karras or Hornung was dumping any games. This was nothing like what the Black Sox did that created the baseball rule."

"He did the right thing with me," Paul Hornung said. "I never had any animosity toward him, and I think he understood that. We kind of joked about it. I caught him at the racetrack one day down at Del Mar when we both were retired. So, I walked over and said, 'Commissioner, is it OK if I bet the horses now?' He got a big kick out of that."

Alex Karras didn't like Rozelle then, and he still doesn't more than a decade after his adversary's death. When he and his first wife had a son during his suspension, he made sure everyone knew the boy's name. Alvin. Rozelle's given name. The perceived underhandedness of the way he was treated still sticks in his craw.

"It's embarrassing how they did it," Karras said. "They paid me off. They gave me my money; let's get real here. Six million—I mean six thousand; excuse me! Isn't that the truth, though? They paid me off. They wanted to get a quick scapegoat, pay him off—$6,000, which they gave me, and life went on. That's God Bless America."

"Like a good Jesuit student," Dave Anderson observed, "Rozelle discovered the difference, distinguished between betting on the games and dumping them."

Rozelle did not go after Bobby Layne, the tragic figure in this case and the man who should have been the real focus of the investigation. Rozelle's FBI agents had to have told him all about Layne's activities, but the commissioner knew that Layne was at the end of his career, and he needed to make an example of current stars to make his point and make it stick.

Layne never played another game after that Playoff Bowl. He quietly announced his retirement on May 6, 1963, in a four-paragraph wire service story buried deep in the *New York Times* sports section. Layne was elected to the Hall of Fame in 1967. He was well invested and had plenty of money, but he never stopped drinking. He died on December 1, 1986, just 18 days short of his 60th birthday.

Joe Schmidt offered an appropriate eulogy to a troubled teammate and friend, in an interview for this book. "When [former Detroit defensive back] Jack Christiansen died, I went out to Palo Alto, and Bobby Layne was there," Schmidt said. "His stomach was distended because his liver was so huge, must have been like a basketball. I saw him drinking. 'What the hell are you doing drinking?' I said. 'You shouldn't be drinking.'

" 'That only goes for when I'm within a 250-mile radius of Lubbock. I'm outside the limit,' Layne said. In all his accomplishments, there was some sadness within him. I cannot say what in his life made him that way, sad. He kept looking for that high all the time."

ELEVEN

THE DIFFERENCE MAKERS

"Christ almighty, all you had to do was look at the guy, 6'7", 290 pounds, who moved like a halfback. It was like finding a 42-carat diamond."

—WILLIAM NACK, ON BIG DADDY LIPSCOMB, 2005

In the late '50s and early '60s, two extraordinary black athletes with the improbable nicknames "Big Daddy" and "Overdrive" burst into the National Football League and did things nobody had ever seen before. By the end of the 1964 season, both were gone from the scene, one a tragic victim, the other because he knew it was time to move into the business world. While these flamboyant personalities were around, though, they truly made a difference.

In 1953, early in his stint as Rams public relations director, Pete Rozelle took a short scouting trip down the Pacific Coast to Camp Pendleton Marine Base and came back with the prize discovery of his life: a 21-year-old defensive tackle, crude, with virtually no technique, but oozing talent. You can't coach size and speed, and Rozelle knew that this youngster had to be the biggest man in the entire Marine Corps, rock hard, not an ounce of fat on his 6'7", 290-pound frame. He could run like a halfback but preferred to hold down the line of scrimmage and swat aside anyone who dared venture into his territory.

Rozelle quickly learned that his name was Eugene Lipscomb, that he never knew his father, that his mother's boyfriend stabbed her 47 times and left her body on the street in the Detroit ghetto when Gene was 11, that he had to work to pay his grandparents room and board, that he suffered from insomnia and often burst into tears in fear of the dark, and that he had played football for Miller High School for three years and then dropped out to join the Corps in 1949.

Lipscomb joined the Rams when he got discharged in '53 and started to pick up the rudiments of the game. Oh, yes, his nickname was "Big Daddy." The logic there was simple: he got that name because he called smaller teammates whose names he forgot "Little Daddy."

He drove Rams coach Sid Gillman nearly crazy with his antics on and off the field, never more so than during a 1955 game in the Coliseum against the Bears when he dreamed up a novel defensive maneuver. As William Nack wrote, "George Blanda lined up to kick a field goal. Suddenly behind the Rams' defensive line loomed Lipscomb with safety Don Burroughs sitting on his shoulders like a boy astride his father. The 6'4" Burroughs had his hands above his head to block the field goal."

The 10-foot-tall Lipscomb-Burroughs tower so rattled Blanda that he hooked the ball short of the goalposts. A Rams defensive back picked it up and took off. As everybody broke to set up for the run, here was Lipscomb still carrying Burroughs on his shoulders, until Bears guard Herman Clark chopped down the "tower" with a cut block. When Bears owner-coach George Halas had a fit about the matter, his pal commissioner Bert Bell quickly made any such future piggyback routines illegal. By no means was this the last time some inventive player would conjure up a rules-stretching maneuver.

In the summer of 1956, the Rams cut Lipscomb, and the Baltimore Colts picked him up off the junk heap for the $100 waiver price. In Baltimore, the rough-hewn Big Daddy of L.A. became a superstar as the line-of-scrimmage anchor while line mates Don Joyce, Art Donovan, and Gino Marchetti pursued quarterbacks and runners. His cunning and strength were legendary.

A player facing him across the line of scrimmage was a prime target. At the snap, Big Daddy whacked the helmet ear hole of his opponent with his cupped, pawlike hand, like a cat swatting a ball of yarn. That blow, literally a bell ringer, would reverberate through the man's mind and body. It was the forerunner of the lethal head slap perfected by Rams defensive end Deacon Jones, which the league finally outlawed. After the initial helmet pop, Lipscomb held the line like a steel beam. If a runner came his way, Big Daddy favored a novel response. "I grab a whole armful of guys with the other-color jersey," he would say. "Then I peel 'em off until I find the one with the ball." Having sorted through the "armful" and brought down the ballcarrier, Lipscomb as often as not helped the player to his feet, not unlike an overgrown man-child picking up a rag doll.

Lipscomb played for the Colts from 1956 to 1960. He made All-Pro twice, and was twice named best lineman in the Pro Bowl, and became a larger-than-life legend. George Plimpton related one of the best Big Daddy stories as told to him for *Paper Lion*. "They say Big Daddy used to get into these horrible fights, close to kill these guys during the training season, really beat up on them," Plimpton wrote. "Everybody'd say, 'Boy, Big Daddy's got a mean temper this year.' Then the coaches look around and find that cooler than hell he'd been beating on the guys trying for his position so that finally there wasn't anybody at his position but Big Daddy."

"I really liked Big Daddy," Steve Rosenbloom said. "He was a pretty glib, funny guy and actually a lot brighter than anybody thought, for someone who went no further than Miller High School. He knew all the Jewish holidays. He was always kidding us about them. I remember, as a water boy, Big Daddy sitting nude on the bench after a postworkout shower. His *schwantz* was about touching the floor."

Lipscomb was traded to Pittsburgh in 1961 and made All-Pro again in 1962 for the Steelers. But his off-field problems were escalating, problems that included his daily intake of about a quart of VO Canadian whiskey, three marriages with attendant alimony and child-support issues, and, toward the end of his life, a fiancée, along with scores of lovers and quickies, especially with hotel maids on the road. "Big Daddy drank, screwed, and dominated football games," his Steelers teammate Brady Keys said. In Pittsburgh, when he wasn't partaking in carnal pleasure, Lipscomb downed his daily liquid ration with Bobby Layne's revelers, including the Texan's longtime drinking chum who came with him from Detroit, fullback Tom "the Bomb" Tracy.

In the off-season, Big Daddy continued to live in Baltimore, where his closest friends on the team were his absolute opposites, the great running back Lenny Moore and defensive back Milton Davis. "Milt was very well educated," Ernie Accorsi said. "He roomed with Lipscomb at home, where he was studying for his doctorate in education."

The future Dr. Davis got a practical education keeping an eye on the company Big Daddy kept. "I'd be sitting there studying, and it was like a waiting room in a dentist's office," Davis told Accorsi. "The women would come in, go to the bedroom, and come out."

Lipscomb's contemporary, R. C. "Overdrive" Owens, joined the San Francisco 49ers in 1957 from the College of Idaho, in the NAIA (National Association of Intercollegiate Athletics) conference, after being drafted in the 14th round in 1956 as a future. Owens liked football well enough, commenting, "I led the nation as a junior in a category of pass catching," but basketball was his game. A forward, Owens stood 6′3″ and weighed 190 pounds, a little smallish for basketball, but he could leap out of the gym, run fast, and kick into an extra gear—hence the nickname "Overdrive." He also had big, strong hands. "I led the nation in scoring one year, with a 27.6 scoring average," Owens said. "I had over 2,000 rebounds in the same period."

One of his teammates at COI in 1954–55 was Elgin Baylor, who transferred to Seattle University after COI's coach was fired and who led Seattle to the 1958 NCAA final against champion Kentucky. After his junior year of eligibility, Baylor joined the Lakers in their last season in Minneapolis before they moved to Los Angeles, where he became an all-time NBA standout and Basketball Hall of Famer.

With Baylor gone, Owens skipped football in 1956 to play for the prominent AAU (Amateur Athletic Union) Buchan Bakers team, of Seattle. He was trying out for an amateur tour of Europe when the San Francisco 49ers took a stab and drafted him as a future. He was an immediate hit in training camp and made the 1957 roster.

After the Niners lost the opener to the Chicago Cardinals, they next had to play the Los Angeles Rams at Kezar Stadium. In practice that week, the offense was showing the defense the Rams' attack, but 49ers quarterbacks Y. A. Tittle and John Brodie refused to throw any passes. "Coach Frankie Albert was on this scaffold looking down, and Red Hickey was on the field," Owens recalled. "Hickey came unglued. 'How are we going to get any practice without throwing the ball?'"

"Coach," one of the quarterbacks said, "how can we throw the ball when they have two men on them? Why throw the ball? They'll knock it down." Hickey ordered them to throw.

"So, they threw," Owens said. "One guy was on me; I made the catch. Two guys were on me; I made the catch. Coming back to the huddle, Hickey said, 'Every time we throw it down there, the defense is trying to knock down the ball, and they can't knock it down.'"

"He could really jump," said longtime 49ers announcer Bob Fouts. "The first time came in practice when Tittle accidentally threw a pass that became the 'alley-oop.' Tittle was a perfectionist. He didn't like it because he didn't think it looked good—that dying duck. Owens could outjump the two or three guys who tried to guard him."

Finally, seeing what happened when he threw that high lob to Owens, Tittle went to coach Red Hickey. "Why don't we put it in?" Tittle suggested.

"Out of that came the words *alley-oop*," Owens said. "That's how it was coined in practice at Redwood City, as a play actually called 'alley-oop.' I caught two alley-oops, one in the last minute of play, and we beat the Rams." The following week, the 49ers went to Wrigley Field, in Chicago, and Owens bedeviled the Bears in a 21–17 San Francisco victory. "I caught a backward alley-oop, with my back to cornerback Erich Barnes, for a touchdown," Owens said. "Then, I caught the winning pass on my knees in a play we called the 'alley-down.'"

The 49ers' rematch with the Bears took place two weeks later on October 27 at Kezar Stadium. Chicago held a 17–7 halftime lead when word came from the press box that original owner Tony Morabito had suffered a heart attack while watching the game there and died late in the second quarter. "When Morabito passed away, we were told at halftime, and that stimulated us," Owens said. "We came out and beat the Bears 21–17 on a long pass to Billy Wilson."

That victory left the 49ers at 5–1 halfway through the regular season. They lost three games in the season's second half, to finish at 8–4 in a tie with the Detroit Lions. The league and CBS treated the Western Conference playoff game at Kezar Stadium like a normal, regular-season game: no special pregame show; just sign on at the top of the hour, set the scene, and start the game. The winner played host to the Eastern Conference champion Cleveland Browns for the title.

Owens opened the scoring when he caught Tittle's 34-yard alley-oop for a touchdown. Tittle threw touchdown passes to Hugh McElhenny and Billy Wilson, and a Gordie Soltau field goal gave San Francisco a 24–7 halftime lead, and team officials in the press box started flashing tickets for the championship game the following week at Kezar. That game never took place. Tobin Rote took charge in the second half to lead Detroit to three touchdowns and a field goal for a 31–27 win. A week later at Tiger Stadium, the Lions routed Cleveland 59–14 for their third championship of the decade and fourth in team history.

R. C. Owens became one of the NFL's premier receivers at the right time, 1961, as the American Football League showed that it was not about to fold its tent and disappear. This was the year when new 49ers head coach Red Hickey unleashed his direct-snap shotgun offense on the league. With Tittle traded to the Giants, Hickey alternated three quarterbacks on every play. John Brodie was the pure passer; Billy Kilmer, a single-wing tailback at UCLA, was a running threat; and Bob Waters was a double threat, run or pass. The 49ers rolled to a 4–1 record in their first five games in a series of lopsided routs, climaxed by a pair of shutouts, 49–0 over the Rams and 35–0 over the Lions.

Then they came to Wrigley Field, where Bears Hall of Fame middle linebacker Bill George clogged the shotgun and forced Hickey to junk it when he moved into the line over center Frank Morze and simply ran around him to harass the quarterbacks in a 31–0 Chicago clobbering. Owens that season caught 55 passes for 1,032 yards, an average of 18.76 yards a reception, and scored six touchdowns.

Earlier in his career, when he was upset with his San Francisco contract, Owens threatened to rejoin Elgin Baylor and play pro basketball with the Lakers. After he had an excellent season for that era, in 1960, with 37 receptions for 532 yards and six touchdowns, Owens came up with another plan when the team came up short with its offer. He played out his option.

Until R. C. Owens, no player ever had invoked the option clause, which had been part of the standard player's contract for as long as anyone could recall. If a player wished to test his value on the open market, he would not sign a contract, but would tell his owner that he would play for 90 percent of the value of his last contract and then, after the season, would make himself available on the open market.

"I did not sign a contract with the 49ers in 1961," Owens said. "At the end of the year, my stand was, I must play football; then we can talk at the end of the season." He took the mandatory 10 percent pay cut for the option year and waited to see what would happen. "The AFL was calling, and Canada was calling too, because they knew I was leaving the team. People said, 'You can't do it; you'll get blackballed.' There were other teams in the league that approached me besides the Colts. I said, 'I will play where I want to play.'"

Bert Bell had always told players that the option rule was the one thing that set them apart from the other professional sports. "There was no rule in 1961, because there was no Rozelle Rule," Owens said. "So, for one year in '62, it was the R. C. Owens rule, because I was the first guy to play out my option and sign back in the league. I got to Baltimore with no compensation between the Colts and 49ers. It was movement without a rule."

Owens chose the Colts because owner Carroll Rosenbloom had a reputation for paying his players well and helping them in business. "They had great players and a great team with Unitas, Parker, Moore, Berry," Owens said. "I never regretted it one bit. I was treated very well. I never made a splash about the movement. I didn't want to talk about it."

Commissioner Rozelle acted immediately to close that loophole. "In '63, the Rozelle Rule took effect," Owens said. "That gave players a chance to move either by trade, money, or draft choices as compensation." Until the Rozelle Rule was struck down in 1975 by a federal judge in Minneapolis, no player other than Owens was able to play out his option and move to another NFL team, because nobody could work out a compensation agreement when it was tried.

Owens also was responsible for another rules change that, had it not been instituted, might have seen teams sign tall, athletic basketball players à la a 7'1" Wilt Chamberlain for special teams instead of that 1955 Lipscomb-Burroughs teammate-on-shoulders goaltending ploy. "I'm the only guy in NFL history to block a field goal at the goalposts. I did it as a member of the Colts in '62, the year after I played out my option, in a game we won 34–21," Owens said. "Bob Khayat, of Washington, was the kicker. It was a 40-yarder, and I blocked it at the crossbar. Consequently, again, they changed the rule. I guess I'm the only guy in the NFL that caused them to change two rules." The new rule, as longtime NFL supervisor of officials Art McNally explained, made it illegal for a player to leap and bat away a field goal in an attempt to prevent a score.

Baltimore was also the dateline of the shocking news that broke early on the morning of May 10, 1963, three weeks after Pete Rozelle announced the gambling suspensions of Paul Hornung and Alex Karras. Gene "Big Daddy" Lipscomb, 31 years old, was dead. Police called it a heroin overdose, a violent end for a man who stretched every known limit of a "normal" lifestyle. Nothing that Big Daddy ever did fell under the definition of normal. Not even in death. Especially in death, in fact, because everyone who ever knew him swore up and down that he was deathly afraid of needles, and under no circumstances whatsoever would he choose to shoot himself up, let alone allow someone else to stick a syringe full of dope into one of his veins. The mysterious death of Big Daddy Lipscomb is the ultimate cold case in the history of sport.

The unquestioned leader of the Colts' defense in that era was Hall of Fame end Gino Marchetti, who knew and liked Lipscomb and still kept in touch with him after he was traded. "He had just gotten a big advance from the Pittsburgh Steelers," Marchetti said. "I don't know how much money he had. He hung around with this guy Black. Black was a drug dealer, and he had a record. They were out partying, and Big Daddy overdosed."

"He had some money on him, and they wanted to get it off him," said veteran writer William Nack. His January 11, 1999, *Sports Illustrated* piece, "The Ballad of Big Daddy," is the classic profile of that tragic athlete and his mysterious death. "Apparently, they gave him heroin to get it off him, but I don't know. Maybe he was hooked up with people who were unpleasant."

At least, that's the story the Baltimore police settled on. Timothy Black first told police that he and Lipscomb had been partying with a couple of girls. Black said he went out alone to grab breakfast at an all-night diner, returned to his apartment, and found Lipscomb's body slumped over the kitchen table. Black then changed his story. He said Lipscomb paid for a $12 bag of heroin sometime in the early hours of May 10. Black claimed that he was not at home when Lipscomb somehow administered himself a lethal dose of heroin. Now, this is the same man his friends said feared needles and whose drug of choice always, without fail, was VO.

"Lenny Moore did not think Big Daddy did that," said William Nack. "As much time as he spent with Big Daddy, there was no indication, Lenny said. There were no needle tracks on his arm. He did not act dopey. 'I just don't believe it. He was deathly afraid of needles.' Lenny never bought into police reports that it was a self-administered dose of heroin."

"They both swear, Lenny and Milton [Davis], there's no way that Lipscomb would have died from an overdose," Ernie Accorsi said. "He would not even take a needle. They are convinced he was done in and people stuck all kinds of stuff in his wrist. He was a devout coward when it came to that stuff."

"You can ask anybody on our team: we don't think he was using drugs," Marchetti said adamantly. "He was absolutely afraid of the needle. At training camp, Fatso [Art Donovan] and I would have to get him out of his room and sit there when they took blood tests from him. He wasn't faking. They put a towel around his eyes, and he'd be sweating from fear. I don't see a guy who's scared of the needle shooting himself up."

Steve Rosenbloom agreed, recalling how Lipscomb behaved in training camp concerning inoculations. "They had to sneak up on him as part of the incoming annual physical, to give him a shot. He literally would hide," Rosenbloom said. Coach "John Sandusky would have to go get him. He was scared to death of a needle. He was a giant in those days and would be good-sized today with all these huge guys. I try to think who would handle him if he got out of hand."

"Lenny Moore did not believe that Big Daddy administered heroin to himself, much like a lot of friends of Sonny Liston, who died of a suspicious overdose, thought about his mysterious death," Bill Nack said. "Lenny felt that somebody got him drunk. Dr. Rudiger Breite-necker, who did the autopsy, said his liver was shot from a quart of booze a day. He said if he hadn't died of this, he would have died of cirrhosis. I don't care if you're 6'7" like he was, all livers are about the same. The booze will get you."

"Buddy Young and some of those guys knew him pretty well," Rosenbloom said. "You see, he died of an overdose. Anybody who knew him at all knew that was impossible because of the needle. What I heard was somebody gave him something to calm him down, and it was too much. I just can't fathom Big Daddy shooting himself."

In the aftermath of Big Daddy Lipscomb's death that 1963 spring, R. C. Owens was preparing for his second season in Baltimore. Owens and his wife and two small children were driving east in their Pontiac Grand Prix from their California home to the Colts' training camp in Westminster, Maryland, when they got caught in a midsummer tornado near Durango, Colorado. "That twister sent us up in the air and dropped my car like a pancake," Owens said. "I was out for four days. I lost a young daughter in the accident. My wife broke her neck. My son was injured, and I eventually lost him four years later. I was in Presbyterian Hospital in Denver for a long time. Sonny Liston came to my bedside." R. C. and his wife later had two more children, a son and a daughter.

Owens recovered well enough to make spot appearances in the last three games of the season, but it no longer was the same. In the off-season, the Colts traded Owens and veteran defensive back Andy Nelson to the New York Giants for lineman Lou Kirouac, a draft choice, and the highly talented, but impossible, running back Joe Don

Looney, who tangled with every coach he ever played for, from Bud Wilkinson at Oklahoma to Allie Sherman in New York and, finally, Don Shula in Baltimore. Owens caught just four passes for 45 yards in 11 games in 1964 for a Giants team that suddenly got old after chasing titles for nearly a decade. He reported to training camp in 1965, realized it was over, and retired.

"I had been training in the off-season with the J. C. Penney Company," Owens said. "So, I called them and went to work. It was fabulous." Owens spent the next 15 years traveling the nation as a motivational speaker for J. C. Penney. He estimated that he spoke to 1,300,000 young people, promoting the company as he urged kids to stay in school and get an education.

"After the J. C. Penney years, I worked 22 years as an administrator with the 49ers, the last 5 as a consultant," Owens said. "Bill Walsh, John McVay, and George Seifert gave me great background that helped me with the 49ers' alumni. When I started in 1979, we had six alumni. Bill wanted their support, and he told me to go at it. Today the alumni guys understand how I worked with them. We had a reunion in Las Vegas with the Super Bowl teams. It was outstanding. [San Francisco owner] Mr. DeBartolo set it up, and it was wonderful."

Owens spent 9 of those traveling years undergoing kidney dialysis treatments without telling anybody about it. "I got a kidney transplant a year ago. The focus is on the team and should be that way," he said. Owens retired to Northern California and still enjoys keeping up with the fortunes of his beloved 49ers.

Through the years, Bill Nack covered hundreds of events and individuals, including horse racing's Triple Crown, football, baseball, and boxing, and he met more than a few seamy characters on the fringes. One story that he could not shake, nor could the great majority of us who came of age in the '50s and '60s, was the mysterious death of Gene Lipscomb, a death that pulses in the undercurrent of cover-up. "I became kind of obsessed with finding this guy Black who was with Big Daddy when he died," Bill Nack said. "I found out through networking and reporting that he was still alive."

Big Daddy was too big, too imposing, too unforgettable, to be tossed away and forgotten. And that's what led Nack to act on his reporter's instinct, his obsession, to turn the clock back three and a half decades and pursue what became "The Ballad of Big Daddy." Nack was able to find and sort through police records with the help of *Sports Illustrated* investigator Marty Dardis, who served for 40 years with the Broward County sheriff's office, in Florida. "He knew cops, their language. All he had to do was say, 'I'm Marty Dardis with *Sports Illustrated.* I'm a retired sheriff's deputy from Broward County; you speak my language.' Cops talked to him all the time. Right away, they trusted him."

Their efforts, however, yielded only more frustration. "Dardis came in and looked at some documents," Nack said. "I remember him saying to me this was all very fishy, that the cops didn't want to talk about it. It did not have a pleasant odor to it." Dardis died from leukemia in the spring of 2006 before he could be interviewed for this book.

For Bill Nack, actually landing the key witness, Timothy Black, turned out to be another search through a hall of mirrors. "I found Timothy Black's address. He was still alive. I had already interviewed Lenny Moore. I told Lenny he could be the key that we're looking for. 'Do you want to go with me to this guy's house? It's up to you.' 'Sure,' Lenny said. So, Lenny and I went over to the house where Timothy Black was living."

Nack explained, "He was a man in '63; he had to be old now. And having Lenny Moore along, who was an icon in Baltimore, could be very persuasive. He still is. That would help get a guy to talk. Plus, I was a white guy, and I had read that Timothy Black was black, and of course, Lenny was. You know, black folks sometimes are afraid to talk to white folks. That's the way it is. I thought that if Lenny, a friend of Big Daddy's, was as interested as I was in this, it would be helpful to have him along, especially if Black had anything to say."

The moment arrived. "We knocked on the door, and of course, they recognized Moore," Nack said. "He introduced himself. 'I'm Lenny Moore, a former Baltimore Colt, and this is Bill Nack, from *Sports Illustrated.*' They invited us in. We said we were looking for

Timothy Black and we wanted to get some light shed on Big Daddy Lipscomb. They all kind of looked at one another, and the woman said, 'Timothy just passed away.'

"We missed him by a week. I think it was cancer. The key was gone. He had just died. I was kicking myself: 'Damn it, if I had done it a month ago.' When we left there, I said to Lenny, 'Christ, we were late by a week. I'm sorry.' I haven't talked to Lenny since."

I made several calls to Lenny Moore's home; I talked several times with his wife, but he apparently chose not to return those calls, nor did he answer when I called at appointed times.

The late Baltimore running back Buddy Young had told Bill Nack that the key was a substantial amount of cash that Lipscomb was carrying. Young's widow, Geraldine, told Nack that Lipscomb started out with $700 before he went out with Timothy Black; police found $73 in his pocket. That tip amounted to another dead end.

"I'm very suspicious that he was killed for just $73," Bill Nack said. "He was deathly afraid of needles, much like Sonny Liston, who died the same way a few years after Big Daddy. Both died of very suspiciously administered drug overdoses. I think that Big Daddy had some money in his pocket, someone wanted to get it, stuck a needle in his arm, not necessarily wanting to kill him, but they did kill him. It was a tragic thing."

Lipscomb was one of the most beloved of all the Colts in a city that adored its team and players. More than 20,000 people filed past his open coffin in the cramped quarters of the Charles Law funeral home that hot May weekend to pay their respects. The body was then flown to Detroit for burial in Lincoln Memorial Park, near Mt. Clemens. It became clear that Baltimore police did not wish to pursue the matter, preferring to let it die as memories of the bigger-than-life Big Daddy faded away. There is no record that Pete Rozelle commented on the death. As for the case: "I don't know how hard it has been looked into. It would be in the league's interest to bury it as soon as possible," Steve Rosenbloom said. Buried it is and has been since May 1963.

"Big Daddy Lipscomb belongs in the Hall of Fame," Nack said. "I had a half dozen people tell me that when I was reporting the story—

most prominently, Gino Marchetti, Raymond Berry, a bunch of them. The late John Steadman kept him out of there. Steadman told me he wanted Jim Mutscheller, a slow white end, in the Hall of Fame. Sorry. Jim was a fine end, but he was not in Big Daddy's league in terms of the impact that he had on the field. Jim was a good player. Big Daddy was a great player—a Hall of Fame player."

"It was a shame," Marchetti told me, "I think he's another one of the Colts who should be in the Hall of Fame. No question in my mind."

THE IRRECONCILABLE DECISION: NOVEMBER 22, 1963

But O heart! heart! heart!
O the bleeding drops of red,
Where on the deck my Captain lies,
Fallen cold and dead.

—WALT WHITMAN, "O CAPTAIN! MY CAPTAIN!" 1865

*P*ete Rozelle was operating in high gear as the 1963 season opener approached. In the wake of the Hornung-Karras gambling suspensions, he and the league enjoyed high public esteem, and, most important for his own cause, he had the approval of the owners. Now he would unveil his game's answer to the National Baseball Hall of Fame in Cooperstown, New York: the Pro Football Hall of Fame in Canton, Ohio. By dedication day, September 7, the last floor had been swept of sawdust and the last coat of paint had been applied to the glistening new shrine.

Rozelle knew from the outset of his term that to knock baseball out of the catbird seat as the preeminent sport, he had to outdo it in every manner to gain public acceptance. He had seen how Walt Disney had made his Disneyland project in Southern California a destination that contributed to the immense growth of that area. He didn't have such a grandiose scheme in mind for a Pro Football Hall of Fame, but he wanted it to be a modern, visitor-friendly place that showcased the history of the game and its heroes who had captured the public fancy before and during the television age. The idea originated during Bert Bell's early years as commissioner. Latrobe, Pennsylvania, where the first acknowledged pro game was played in 1895, was the initial town suggested, but support never blossomed, and the idea died before the Korean War.

Then, in 1956, a young reporter for the *Canton Repository* named Germane Swanson happened to bring up the subject of a football Hall one summer afternoon in a postpractice chat with Paul Brown at the Cleveland Browns' training camp in Hiram. Brown had an enduring reverence for the game's history and, as an unmitigated Ohio jingoist, was well aware, as was Swanson, that Jim Thorpe, George Halas, and several other men had met in a Canton auto dealership in September 1920 to form the association that became the National Football League. Over the course of several discussions, Brown and Swanson decided that Canton was the right place for a shrine. Swanson took the idea to his editors, it gained steam, and the paper got the backing of local executives, businesses, and industrial powerhouses in that era of smokestack prosperity in Canton led by the Timken Company, maker of industrial roller bearings; Hoover, the vacuum cleaner manufacturer; and Republic Steel.

The city fathers offered 14 acres of undeveloped land in North Canton adjacent to the large McKinley High School with its outstanding and sizable high school stadium located just minutes from downtown Canton. Unlike hard-to-reach Latrobe, nestled in the Alleghenies some 40 miles east of Pittsburgh and approachable only by two-lane roads, Canton had location. Just an hour south of Cleveland, Canton was the center of such bustling, football-crazy small cities as Akron, Massillon, Youngstown, Warren, and Barberton. Easy access to Canton would be enabled by a new expressway in the nascent interstate highway network, which would be cut through the hills and run adjacent to the new Hall. That location along an interstate highway would make Canton and the Hall of Fame a convenient stopover for vacationers en route to their destinations. To cap it off, the interstate would be designated I-77, the uniform number of football's greatest early star, Harold "Red" Grange, offering a constant reminder of the Hall for football fans and potential visitors.

Commissioner Rozelle liked the plan so much that he brought the owners aboard at a league meeting on April 27, 1961. Former Washington Redskins official Dick McCann was named the Hall's first executive director. Baseball's shrine in Cooperstown memorializes its inductees in bronze plaques featuring their likenesses with thumbnail biographies. Instead of plaques, Rozelle had a sculptor cast two bronze busts of each inductee, one for permanent display in the Hall and another as a personal keepsake.

Seventeen men were named as original inductees: George Halas, Red Grange, and Bronko Nagurski, of the charter Chicago Bears; Jim Thorpe and Wilbur "Pete" Henry, of the charter Canton Bulldogs; Joe Carr, the league's first president; former commissioner Bert Bell; Earl "Curly" Lambeau, Johnny "Blood" McNally, and Don Hutson, of the Green Bay Packers; Earl "Dutch" Clark, of the Detroit Lions; Ernie Nevers, of the Duluth Eskimos and Chicago Cardinals; George Preston Marshall and Sammy Baugh, of the Washington Redskins; and Tim Mara, Mel Hein, and Cal Hubbard, of the New York Giants. Hubbard, who also played for the Packers and a single season for Pittsburgh, also served 15 seasons as an American League umpire. He is the only member of both the Pro Football and Baseball Halls.

The induction was the beginning of a remarkable year for Halas, still active as owner-coach of the Bears. Halas's brilliant young personnel director and defensive coordinator, George Allen, had assembled the best Bears team in years. After they ran off victories in their first three games at Green Bay, Minnesota, and Detroit, the Bears opened at home on October 6 against the Baltimore Colts and their 34-year-old rookie coach, Don Shula. "Here it was, my rookie year, and I was looking across Wrigley Field seeing George Halas on the other side," Shula recalled in late 2005. "The guy on the other side had the most coaching victories of any guy in the history of the league, and I was coaching against him and someday would have the opportunity to break his record. It left me in awe."

Shula set aside his feelings of wonderment well enough to have his well-prepared Colts frustrate the Bears and take a 3–0 lead into the fourth quarter. That's when Chicago's backup quarterback Rudy Bukich, in relief of Billy Wade, hit Ronnie Bull coming out of the backfield. Bull took off, was sprung by a crushing open-field block when Mike Ditka left his feet and flattened Bobby Boyd, and went in standing up to complete a 44-yard scoring play. The Bears later added a field goal to win 10–3. They won the rematch a month later in Baltimore 17–7. It was the last time Halas would hold the edge on the younger man, who would surpass his 324 victories and end up first with 347 wins over a 33-year career.

Shula's rise to that premier coaching job began a year before in 1962 when he met the young commissioner. "I was a young assistant coach with Detroit, and we were playing a preseason game in New Haven the day after the doubleheader in Cleveland," Shula recalled. "George Wilson sent me to scout the doubleheader. After the second game, I caught my flight, and Pete Rozelle was on the same plane. When we got to Newark, he asked, 'How are you getting to the hotel?' "

"I'll call a cab," Shula said.

"No, no. I have a limo driver. I'll drop you off," Rozelle said.

"Here I was, a young assistant coach, and he was kind enough to do that," Shula said. "That's something I'll never forget—the chance to meet and spend some time with him. Later on in the competition committee, I got to realize how knowledgeable he was about the game."

Whether that was a stardust moment for Shula is pure speculation, but his very real opportunity with the Colts emanated from a game on November 25, 1962, when he was hundreds of miles away in Detroit savoring the Lions' 26–14 Thanksgiving Day rout of the Packers. Halas's Bears could do no wrong that Sunday as they smothered Weeb Ewbank's Colts 57–0 in Memorial Stadium, Chicago's largest victory margin since the 73–0 championship win at Washington in 1940.

Shula's former Baltimore teammate Gino Marchetti got a call the next morning from Carroll Rosenbloom's secretary, who said the boss wanted to see Gino in the Baltimore Sheraton at 11:00 A.M. "I was driving in from Towson; it takes about 35 minutes, and I was sweating blood," Marchetti recalled. "I sat down, and he was wearing a white T-shirt and had a smile on his face. 'Gino, why the sad look on your face?'"

Marchetti responded, "Carroll, we got the shit beat out of us. Number two, you called me in here at 11 o'clock in the morning, and I'm kinda concerned."

"Ah, nothing to worry about," Rosenbloom said. "I've got my excuse now."

"What do you mean?"

"I have my excuse to fire Weeb."

"You're going to fire him?"

"Yeah."

"What do you want from me?"

"I want you to recommend somebody."

"If I were you, owner of this team, there's no question in my mind I'd hire Don Shula."

Marchetti related in 2006, "We were going to play Detroit the following week. Don't you know, he hired Shula. I kept it quiet, because I didn't want people to think that I was happy Weeb was going. I wasn't. But I was happy Shula was coming. Shula was like a coach in 1953 when we went to Baltimore. He taught the defensive coaches everything. We knew he would coach. He wasn't fast or agile, but his brain enabled him to play for seven or eight years. He was the smartest guy I ever played with on my side of the ball. John Unitas, of course, was on the other side. He had to call 180 plays without help."

"Shula turned out to be the right fella following Weeb," Steve Rosenbloom recalled. "When Shula came in, he was still young, and there were guys on the team that he had played with. It is difficult to teach people that you played with. Initially, it was hard, and he worked his way through all that and became successful."

The American Football League had reached the point of no return by late 1962. The Dallas Texans, Oakland Raiders, and New York Titans had hit dead ends and needed to make positive changes or go out of business. Of the three, the Texans were in the best shape, backed by Lamar Hunt's fortune, but Hunt knew that he could not keep losing money in his hometown of Dallas, where the Cowboys had solid Murchison backing and the still dominant NFL cachet behind them.

On the field, the Texans, led by Hank Stram's solid, innovative coaching and quarterback Lenny Dawson's passing and generalship, halted the Houston Oilers in their attempt at a three-peat in one of the zaniest championships ever, even by AFL standards. When the game ended in regulation tied 17–17, Stram issued specific orders to his Texans captain, Abner Haynes. He told Haynes if he won the coin toss to take a strong wind blowing toward the scoreboard. Instead, when Haynes won the flip, he told the referee, "We'll kick to the clock." Thus, by taking the kick option, Haynes forfeited the right to take field position. So, Houston took the wind and the ball!

Haynes was vindicated when the teams changed sides after a scoreless first overtime. Early in the second overtime, Tommy Brookins kicked a short field goal to win the AFL's third title game, 20–17, and give Dallas its first AFL title.

On May 22, 1963, Lamar Hunt solved his problem in Dallas and ensured instant prosperity for his team and his rival Cowboys when he announced that the franchise would move to gung-ho Kansas City and take the name Chiefs. "It has been a great association for our family for 43 years," said Hunt in an interview for this book in May 2006, six months before his death. "I couldn't be prouder of what the organization has accomplished in Kansas City. That has been very important to the process. Dallas [the Cowboys] has done extremely well." Acknowledging that his team performed well as the Dallas Texans, Hunt remarked, "We needed more than artistic success." And, in Kansas City, they got it.

After two seasons as nomads across the Bay in San Francisco, the Oakland Raiders finally set up shop in their home city in 1962 in a temporary venue, 22,000-seat Frank Youell Field, named for a local undertaker. It was built to house the Raiders until their permanent home, the all-purpose, 53,000-seat Oakland Coliseum, was completed. After three money-hemorrhaging seasons and last-place finishes in the AFL West, Raiders managing partners Wayne Valley and Ed McGah made a franchise-defining decision that reverberates to this day.

To run their operation as coach and general manager, they hired 33-year-old Al Davis, an assistant with the Chargers in Los Angeles and San Diego, who learned the fine points of sophisticated offense from Sid Gillman. Armed with total control, the savvy Davis came to Oakland and redesigned the uniform—jerseys in silver and black with silver pants, and silver helmets with the one-eyed-pirate logo on the sides. He brought fire to the organization with slogans—"pride and poise," and "commitment to excellence"—and he signed winning players, with immediate results: a 10–4 record in 1963 that earned him AFL Coach of the Year honors. It was only the beginning.

In New York, the burlesque that had been the Titans lurched to an end on March 28 when a group led by show business agent David "Sonny" Werblin bought the team from the league for $1 million. "Werblin's taking over the New York franchise was a major reason for the league's success," said longtime *San Diego Union-Tribune* sports columnist Jerry Magee, who started covering pro football when the Chargers moved from Los Angeles to San Diego in 1961.

The AFL had taken over the team the previous November when founder Harry Wismer failed to make the payroll. "He was a joke," Magee said. "I remember watching games in the Polo Grounds with crowds of nothing. Wismer greeted me like he greeted everybody. He'd always say, 'Congratulations!' He figured that you had done something to merit his congratulations." With Sonny Werblin in charge in New York, the joke no longer was on the AFL.

As far as the NFL was concerned, everything was clicking on all cylinders. It had been a glorious autumn all over the East and Midwest, featuring weekend after weekend of sunny, high skies and temperatures in the 60s and 70s—shorts weather—into early November. The Steelers were giving the Giants a hard push in the East, while the Bears-Packers rivalry was the big story in the NFL West as the teams marched in lockstep into week 10 and their rematch at Wrigley Field with 9–1 records. Although Paul Hornung was sidelined in the gambling suspension, the Packers didn't miss a beat. Hornung's replacement, Tom Moore, gave Vince Lombardi a superb season as he averaged 5 yards a carry, good for 658 yards. The Bears answered with an inspired 26–7 victory that left them atop the Western Conference at 10–1 and coach Halas that much closer to winning his sixth and the Bears' eighth championship.

America and the world stood still at 12:30 P.M. central standard time on Friday, November 22, on yet another sunny day, this time in Dealey Plaza, in Dallas. A grinning President John F. Kennedy was riding with First Lady Jacqueline Kennedy and the Connellys in the presidential limousine at the head of a motorcade through cheering throngs along the Dallas streets. The reception in every Texas stop on this political fence-mending trip had exceeded expectations, and the president planned to complete it with a major policy address at the Dallas Trade Mart. As the limousine turned toward the Triple Underpass, a number of gunshots, at least three, rang out and reverberated through the plaza. Seeing a scramble ahead, UPI White House correspondent Merriman Smith, riding in the press pool car, was first to grab a mobile telephone. He called the UPI office in Dallas and scooped the world on the biggest story in history. "Three shots have been fired at the presidential motorcade," Smith screamed over the noise of sirens and revving engines speeding away from the scene. Within seconds, the news broke on the wires, and broadcast networks interrupted the soap operas and other programs with the bulletin.

Moments later, after racing behind the presidential limo to Parkland Memorial Hospital, Smith jumped out of the press pool car to see Mrs. Kennedy cradling the president's bloody head in her lap. He spoke with her assigned Secret Service agent, Clint Hill. "How badly was he hit, Clint?" Smith asked. "He's dead," Hill replied curtly. The flash moved on the UPI wire at 12:39 P.M. "Kennedy seriously wounded. Perhaps fatally, by assassin's bullet." Within an hour, it was official.

"Everybody remembers exactly where they were when they heard the news," Sam Huff said 43 years later. "We had finished practicing. Don Chandler and I were on the Triboro Bridge coming back to Long Island after practice. I helped John Kennedy win West Virginia when he ran over there. That was one of the greatest things I ever did, and he was one of the greatest people I ever met. He was phenomenal. He had so much class. It was unbelievable. He was wonderful."

News operations across the country went to general quarters. "I was in the newsroom, and I felt someone had just hit me," recalled Herb Klein, then editor in chief of the *San Diego Union-Tribune*. "I had to stop feeling that way and get reporters on the story." Klein, who served Richard Nixon as press secretary from 1946 to 1961, and again as White House director of communications, had liked John F. Kennedy, from the time they met in 1946 when Kennedy and Nixon served in the House through Kennedy's victorious 1960 presidential campaign. His was a typical reaction across America.

As the Chicago Bears finished their Friday workout, the news from Dallas spread through the clubhouse at Wrigley Field that the youthful, vital leader was dead. "We were so shocked," cocaptain Mike Ditka said. "We didn't know if there would be a game or not. Everything was put on hold."

"We were flying out to Los Angeles and were just about to Kansas City when the pilot announced to all of us that the president had been shot," Colts Hall of Fame defensive end Gino Marchetti recalled. Marchetti had stood alongside Kennedy during 1960 campaign appearances in Maryland. "He's the one guy I met that when I looked him straight in the face, I thought the guy came from heaven. I met a lot of guys in my day, but for some reason, when I shook his hand, he looked me in the face, and something, a spirit, came over me."

"Boy, I'll never forget," said Tom Brookshier, by 1963 a sportscaster with WCAU-TV in Philadelphia and the analyst on Eagles radio broadcasts. "I was sitting there at the station that Friday night. We didn't do sports that night. John Facenda closed the show reciting 'O Captain! My Captain!'. When he finished, everybody in the studio was crying. We all were crying like babies. I'm telling you, boy, that was as tough a time as I can remember."

"I covered a high school football game that night in North Carolina," said Ernie Accorsi, then a young sportswriter with the *Charlotte News*, fresh off the campus of Wake Forest. "It was one of those things where the impact grew. I guess they made a decision rather quickly. Then the NBA went dark, and Broadway went dark. I had it out with the athletic director and then the president of Davidson. Davidson was supposed to play Wofford the next day. All these games were being cancelled, and I called over, and they said, 'The game is still on.'

" 'What are you talking about?' I, the reporter, said. 'Army-Navy is canceled, and you're playing Davidson-Wofford.' Here I was, a reporter, and I got into a screaming match, until the university president finally calmed me down. It probably got away from them. You knew Salinger was going to say, 'Jack Kennedy would have wanted us to play, because he was a sportsman.' It just got out of control."

Most of Saturday's college games were postponed. Twenty-one games were canceled outright, most prominent among them Notre Dame's finale with Iowa and Boston U. versus Boston College. By nightfall, the Davidson-and-Wofford game was cancelled as well. Eleven games were played, all in the South or border states. Oklahoma coach and athletic director Bud Wilkinson had served since 1961 as consultant to President Kennedy's Council on National Fitness and had been a significant promoter of Kennedy's 50-mile hikes. When the news came, Wilkinson acted. He called Bob Devaney, his counterpart at Nebraska, and told him he thought Kennedy—his friend—would want them to play. The next day, Nebraska beat the Sooners 29–20 in Lincoln before a then-record crowd, 38,362, at Memorial Stadium. At the end, Nebraska students pelted the field with oranges, signifying a New Year's date in the Orange Bowl.

Also that day, Florida beat Miami 27–21, and Auburn beat Florida State 21–15. Five other Saturday games coincidentally all ended in shutouts: Tennessee 19–0 over Kentucky; LSU 20, Tulane 0; Vanderbilt 31, George Washington 0; Ohio U. 17, Marshall 0; and Northeast Oklahoma 13, Southeast Missouri 0. In a Friday-night game played within hours of the assassination, North Carolina blanked Wake Forest 49–0.

In Chicago, Ward Quaal, vice president and general manager of radio giant WGN, had to make quick decisions. The station was scheduled to air Saturday's battle for the Big Ten title and Rose Bowl bid between Illinois and Michigan State at East Lansing. A fast-moving rainstorm cancelled flights to Michigan, forcing the WGN crew announcers Jack Brickhouse and Jack Quinlan and producer Jack Rosenberg to take the train. "It was so quiet on that train, it was eerie," Rosenberg recalled four decades later. Rosenberg and Brickhouse were supposed to go on to Pittsburgh for Sunday's game between the Bears and the Steelers after the Illinois–Michigan State showdown.

"Kennedy really did mean a whole lot to us," said Pittsburgh Steelers owner Dan Rooney, in 1963 vice president to his father, Art, the team's founder. "I called Pete almost immediately and said, 'Pete I don't think we should play the games.' "

"We have a whole lot of problems if we don't play the games," Rozelle told Rooney. "We got problems with television and all those things. I'm going to call Pierre Salinger and find out what the administration thinks and what he thinks."

The American Football League acted immediately and shut down its Sunday schedule. Through the ensuing years, AFL commissioner Joe Foss was highly praised for the decision. But, as writer Jerry Magee said in our interview for this book, Foss had nothing to do with it.

"Remember when the AFL made probably its most fortuitous decision that it would not play on the weekend that President Kennedy was assassinated? It wasn't Foss," said Magee. "He was up in South Dakota, probably following his dogs around. It was Milt Woodard [the deputy commissioner] who made the call. They couldn't get hold of Foss, so Milt made that decision."

With Sunday fast approaching, the AFL's decision to cancel increased the pressure on Pete Rozelle, who understood that whatever he did, it would be controversial. Rozelle had been friendly with the Kennedy administration since the beginning. The help he got from attorney general Robert F. Kennedy was invaluable in gaining the revenue-sharing exemption through pooling television revenues. The commissioner then placed a call through the White House switchboard to track down his friend from their days together at the University of San Francisco, the presidential press secretary. Pierre Salinger and most of the cabinet, led by secretary of state Dean Rusk, had been en route to Japan on a government jetliner for a trade conference when they got the news.

"Pete was caught in a terrible conflict emotionally," Art Modell said. "I begged him not to play the games. Tex Schramm said play it. Then we got hold of Salinger, his old buddy, and he said, 'Jack would have wanted you to play the games.' That, plus Bud Wilkinson, also a friend of Pete's and a friend of the Kennedys'—his Oklahoma team had played the day before. So, we went ahead. I had the ironic situation of playing the Dallas Cowboys in Cleveland. We were terrified about that."

"I remember one night years later when Pierre was in San Diego and we had dinner at Gene Klein's house," said Herb Klein, now the retired publisher of the *San Diego Union-Tribune*. It was Pete, Pierre, Gene, and myself. We might have been opposites, but we were friends. Ted Sorensen is another. We were recounting what happened after the assassination, and that was the agreed-upon story of what happened then."

After Rozelle spoke with Salinger, he and Jim Kensil huddled and then consulted with CBS Sports president Bill McPhail; then, the commissioner announced his decision. The National Football League would play its seven scheduled games on Sunday, but, out of respect to the Kennedy family and the citizens of America, the games would not be televised.

"They said, 'You should play, because it will give the people something to think about other than this.' I remember saying this publicly," Dan Rooney recalled. "It was written. I may not have agreed with him, but once Pete made the decision, I was all behind him."

Bill Jauss, then writing for the *Chicago Daily News*, recalled that the Illinois–Michigan State game was still on for Saturday morning when he arrived at Spartan Stadium. "The governor of Michigan, George Romney, told Michigan State athletic director Biggie Munn not to play," Jauss said. "I swear that [Illinois linebacker] Dick Butkus would have torn apart somebody in charge had they decided to play. He was that upset about Kennedy's death."

Romney also asked Michigan to postpone its game in Ann Arbor with Ohio State. Finally, on Saturday morning, the four schools agreed with Romney. A special Grand Trunk Railroad train carrying Illinois football fans from Chicago to Lansing stopped at Battle Creek, turned around, and returned to Chicago. The reporters went home and then came back to cover the game on Thanksgiving morning as Illinois shut out Michigan State 13–0 to earn its first Rose Bowl trip since the 1951 season.

That same Saturday morning, Big Ten commissioner Bill Reed told Rosenberg at his hotel in East Lansing that the game was postponed until Thanksgiving. The storm front had moved east, allowing the three WGN men to catch the 45-minute flight back to Chicago in time to board the Bears' charter to Pittsburgh. When they landed, Rosenberg called Quaal. "We won't broadcast," the general manager said. "This is no time for a football game."

"It's the only time in all those years that we did not air a scheduled Bears broadcast," Rosenberg said.

It was a throwback to the pioneer days of the league. No radio. No television. But the NFL games went forward on Sunday, November 24. "I wanted to play that day," cocaptain Mike Pyle recalled. "I didn't feel the world had come to a stop. For a period of time on Friday, yes. But sitting home all weekend, I wouldn't have been as happy as doing what I felt my job was."

"Our job as football players was to do what they told us," Ditka said. "Rozelle made the decision, and to this day some people say he regretted it. I don't know if he did or not, and I don't know if he should have."

"I know there was tremendous pressure on the commissioner," Pyle said. "I was glad, believe me, that he decided to play."

"I don't know what Jack Kennedy would have said, but he probably would have said, 'Go ahead and play,'" Ditka said emphatically. "That's what I felt."

The Bears, coming off their huge 26–7 rout of their closest rivals, the Green Bay Packers, were desperate to play as much for themselves as for the memory of President Kennedy.

Out in Los Angeles, the Baltimore Colts, whose owner, Carroll Rosenbloom, was extremely close to the Kennedys, wrestled with the decision to play or not to play. "It was a shocker. It was a controversy," Gino Marchetti said. "Should we play? Should we not play? They asked us, and I said, 'I think we ought to play. It would give the fans a break.' "

Former New York Giants teammates and fellow Hall of Famers Sam Huff and Frank Gifford retain strong, conflicting feelings about playing that weekend. "We shouldn't have played," Huff said. "That was a mistake Rozelle made. We played the St. Louis Cardinals at Yankee Stadium."

"Pete has gotten a bad rap on the Kennedy assassination," Gifford said. "When we got there that Sunday, the whole country was in a malaise. All the TV channels were playing classical music. The country was in a mess. He could have said, 'Let's don't play.' How long would we have gone on doing that?"

"It was the worst game I ever played," Huff said. "You can't play pro football without emotion. I was emotional about John Kennedy, not about the football game."

"I have three little Kennedy grandchildren. My daughter [Victoria] was married to Michael Kennedy," Gifford said. "They don't think that way. They are competitors who get up and fight back. I played enough touch football with them to know they didn't want to sit around on their thumbs. It was a tough decision for him to make."

"I don't even remember the score. I don't remember the game," Huff said. "It was just awful. It was awful."

"Some people said nobody would go to the games," Gifford recalled. "We got to Yankee Stadium, which was sold out with season tickets. Thousands of people were outside trying to get into the game because they thought there were people who would not show up. Everyone showed up!"

"It was terrible, and Rozelle should have called it off," Huff said. "We did not want to play, but we did."

"Still you get these flaming-ass crazies who want to knock Pete. It drives me up a wall," Gifford said. "It was the strangest crowd. We played the Cardinals. They were almost polite. It was not a raucous crowd, typical Yankee Stadium. It was almost reverential. What the hell was wrong about playing a football game? The Kennedy family loved football." The Cardinals, incidentally, beat the Giants 24–17, New York's last loss of the regular season.

"I think he had to make the right call, and he had to do it in a hurry," said veteran writer Frank Deford. "The jingoists and professional patriots could easily look to Joe Foss and say, 'He knew what to do.' It was perfectly possible to criticize him [Rozelle], but it was a tough call. A lot of people said, 'We need this for the country.' "

"In Cleveland, I beefed up the security, hired extra police," Art Modell said. "We even had snipers on the roof of the stadium to protect Clint Murchison and his party from any harm. It was a very, very tough ordeal emotionally. On Sunday morning, the day of the game, Tex Schramm, Murchison, and Bedford Wynne came into my office. Someone rushed in, and there it was on live TV: Ruby shooting Oswald. It was a very tough time. I instructed our PA announcer never to say 'Dallas,' just 'Cowboys.' Keep the name of the city out. We had to try to cool things."

"I had this little portable radio, two inches by two inches, a transistor," Dan Rooney recalled. "I used to stand on the roof [of Forbes Field], following the plays, looking straight down on the players. I was listening to this radio; then I heard this Ruby shooting Oswald, wondering what kind of country we had. We went on and played the game."

The Steelers overcame a 14–0 deficit to take a fourth-quarter 17–14 lead. It was third down and 20 with the ball at the Chicago 20 when quarterback Bill Wade called a pass for an exhausted Mike Ditka. The future Hall of Fame tight end, playing on adrenaline, said "throw me a hook about 10 yards out and I'll try to get free to get the first down."

Lining up at tight end left, Ditka broke to the 30, caught Wade's pass, tucked it away, and started running. He broke tackle after tackle, finally going down at the Pittsburgh 15, a 65-yard gain to set up Roger LeClerc's field goal for a 17–17 tie to save the season.

Hearts were heavy to the east in Philadelphia. "We didn't televise on Sunday," Tom Brookshier said. "They still played the game with the Redskins. I was on the Ben Franklin Bridge heading for the stadium from New Jersey when Oswald got shot. Everybody lurched around in traffic. That night, we went out. A bunch of the Eagles were now Redskins—Billy Ray Barnes. Everybody was so nervous. Fights broke out everywhere. It was awful. I don't know how our country came through that. It was a tough moment. I look at that now. The riderless horse."

"So much had been talked about it for the last couple of days, and it would give the fans a break," Gino Marchetti said. "So, we played, and we had a real good crowd out there, I guess." The underdog Rams beat the Colts 17–16 before slightly more than 48,000 fans in the half-filled Coliseum.

By the time the fans got into their cars and hit the Los Angeles freeways to end that most difficult day for the NFL, football definitely was a small concern for most Americans. A major critic of Pete Rozelle's decision, who swung hard and cut deep, was America's leading sports columnist, Red Smith. "John Kennedy enjoyed games as a participant and spectator, and sports had his hearty official support as President," Smith wrote in his November 24, 1963, column. As he discussed the day's scheduled big game in New York between the Giants and Cardinals and the Bears-Steelers game in Pittsburgh, Smith snarled through his typewriter, "There's a race to be finished and there's money invested. Money."

For the rest of his life, Smith said he liked Rozelle but could never forgive the commissioner for going ahead with the games. As he told his biographer, Ira Berkow, years later, "It was the public display of indifference that bothered me."

"It was just terrible," Art Modell said. "I liked Red very much, but he was off base and tried to destroy Pete." It must be noted that Rozelle was among the mourners at Red Smith's funeral service at St. Patrick's Cathedral on January 20, 1982.

The controversy has not abated after all these decades. "Pete was upset that he did it," Rozelle's close friend Herb Siegel said. "He told me and said it publicly that was the one thing he regretted."

"How did he view his handling of the Kennedy death weekend? He regretted it forever, as he stated several times afterward," former *New York Times* football writer Bill Wallace recalled. "I never heard an explicit explanation of his thinking."

"He did what the Kennedy camp wanted and took the flak for it," Anne Marie Rozelle Bratton said in 2006.

"In retrospect, Pete probably always felt, if that's the way people want to treat it, fine," Frank Gifford said. "He would not openly defend himself. He let the chips fall where they may, and through the years, the chips have fallen into the wrong stack."

The tots of World War II, now senior citizens, still feel the searing events from that November weekend. They were the children of the '50s who grew up during the cold war. They endured the civil defense drills when they had to crawl under their school desks and cover their heads against the fear of a nuclear attack. Their older brothers and sisters loved swing, Sinatra, Harry James, and young Nat "King" Cole. They grabbed on to rock and roll, be it Bill Haley and the Comets, Elvis Presley, Fats Domino, or someone more edgy, such as Chuck Berry. They obeyed the law, especially when it came to registering for the draft, and, by all means, listened to their parents and, more often than not, heeded their admonitions.

They were close to kindergarten age when FDR died and the war ended, in grade school when Harry Truman drew the line against the Soviets, in junior high or high school when Ike got elected, and completing high school or starting college when JFK and the New Frontier blazed into Washington for their 1,037-day run. They had high hopes. Then, after the gunfire in Dallas, the wonderful innocence of fun and games was over, and the dark, wild days with drugs and rebellion broke loose. "I think the '50s ended November 22," said Ernie Accorsi. Ask anyone from that era and he or she will agree.

THIRTEEN

SPORTSMAN OF THE YEAR

"He knew that responsibility for stopping the scandal was his alone."

—KENNETH RUDEEN, *SPORTS ILLUSTRATED*, JANUARY 4, 1964

*A*s the National Football League's 1963 schedule moved forward toward the December 15 regular-season conclusion, it seemed that nobody wanted to take control of the Western Conference. On the morning of Saturday, December 14, the Chicago Bears, at 10–1–2, held a half-game lead over the Green Bay Packers, who stood at 10–2–1. The Packers applied the heat to Chicago that afternoon when they beat the 49ers 21–17 in Kezar Stadium.

Needing a victory to gain the title game, the Bears got a break when, sadly, Lions star defensive back Dick "Night Train" Lane had to miss the game after awaking Saturday morning at home in Detroit to discover that his wife, the famed jazz singer Dinah Washington, had died in her sleep. On Sunday afternoon at Wrigley Field, Johnny Morris caught eight Billy Wade passes for 171 yards and a touchdown against a Lions team led by Lane's replacement, Tom Hall. The Bears won 24–14 as Davey Whitsell ensured the victory with a 39-yard interception return for the clinching touchdown in the closing seconds. In New York, Frank Gifford's reaching, one-handed catch of a Y. A. Tittle pass sparked the Giants to a 33–17 victory over the Pittsburgh Steelers to win the Eastern Conference. They would meet the Bears at Wrigley Field on December 29.

After the weekend hiatus following the Kennedy assassination, the American Football League resumed play on Thanksgiving Day, and red-hot Oakland beat Houston 26–10. Sid Gillman's San Diego Chargers had the league's most explosive offense, led by veteran quarterback Tobin Rote and his talented young backup, John Hadl, and including running backs Paul Lowe and Keith Lincoln, as well as the best young receiver in football. That difference maker was Lance Alworth, a running back at Arkansas whom Gillman's top assistant at the time, Al Davis, lured away from the NFL's San Francisco 49ers in 1962, calling him "one of the three players in my lifetime who had 'it.' You could see right from the start," Davis said, "that he was going to be a superstar." The graceful Alworth, appropriately nicknamed "Bambi," would be the first AFL-drafted player to be elected to the Pro Football Hall of Fame.

Now, a year later in 1963, Gillman's protégé, Davis, the 34-year-old coach and general manager of the heretofore moribund Raiders, was making noise and winning games in bunches in Oakland. "He came, and all of a sudden we had a direction," said Tom Flores, Oakland's quarterback in '63 and later Davis's two-time-winning Super Bowl coach. "With Al, we had a purpose, a guy who knew how to play the game. Then he started making some personnel moves that showed us he wanted to improve the team."

The Raiders opened the '63 season with two wins, lost the next four games, and won their last eight, including two significant victories over Gillman's Chargers, 34–33 at San Diego and 41–27 in Oakland's "little wooden bleachers, Frank Youell Field," as Flores called it. "We didn't have a real stadium until 1966," he noted. But they had the league's Most Valuable Player and leading rusher in Clemon Daniels, who gained an AFL-record 1,099 yards. Davis was named Coach of the Year, destined for greater success and years of notorious showdowns with the high-riding commissioner of the National Football League.

The Buffalo Bills, now led by quarterback Jack Kemp, were locked into a battle for the AFL East with the Boston Patriots. Kemp had led the Chargers to the 1960 and '61 title games. He broke a finger on his throwing hand early in 1962, starting a series of events that led to his moving to Buffalo. "I didn't want to leave San Diego," Kemp said. When Gillman placed him on waivers to move him to the injured reserve list, several teams claimed him for the $100 price. "The Raiders tried to trade for me two or three weeks earlier, and he wouldn't trade. So, it's quite evident that it was a mistake. I was picked up by Denver and a couple of other AFL teams. The commissioner [Joe Foss] thought the Bills needed a quarterback. So, they gave me to Buffalo, and it turned it to be a blessing in disguise. It was pretty well disguised for some time."

The Patriots squeaked by Kemp and the Bills with two victories, 20–14 on the last day of the regular season and 26–8 in an Eastern Conference playoff on Saturday, December 28, a game that flew under the radar because national interest was focused on the NFL championship the next day in Chicago, between George Halas's Bears and their ancient Eastern rivals, the New York Giants.

This would be the sixth time the two would meet for the crown. Each game was a classic, dating back to the first NFL title game, played at Wrigley Field in 1933, when the Bears edged the Giants 23–21. The Bears held a 3–2 series lead, with its other wins in 1941, 37–9; and 1946, 24–14. New York's two came on frozen fields when the Giants twice outfoxed Halas and Chicago by donning basketball shoes to gain solid footing. In the famed 1934 Sneakers Game, clubhouse attendant Abe Cohen took a hasty subway trip to Manhattan College before the second half and returned with basketball shoes, and the Giants scored 27 points in the fourth quarter to win 30–13. In 1956, Andy Robustelli outfitted each of his teammates with basketball shoes from his Stamford, Connecticut, sporting goods store, and the sure-footed Giants ran over the unsteady Bears 47–7.

Before this 1963 title game, the league conducted its third punt, pass, and kick competition. The favorite in the nine-year-olds class was a young quarterback from Southern California named Gary Carter, who won the first competition as a seven-year-old in 1961 and, as an adult, would make the Baseball Hall of Fame as a catcher, for his stellar play with the Montreal Expos and New York Mets. "They honored us at the 1961 title game at Lambeau Field [City Stadium], in Green Bay," Carter recalled. "They did not hold the competition that day, and it's just as well, because it was so cold. It was an incredible thrill to meet Commissioner Rozelle, who gave us our awards."

This time, young Carter and his fellow competitors put on their show before the kickoff of the Bears-Giants championship game. "Was it ever cold. Felt like 25 below, awfully tough on a California kid," Carter said. Actually, the chill factor was −4 on the frozen and slippery field. "I was ahead after the kick and punt competitions. But, on my pass attempt, I slipped as I stepped up, and the ball went only 15 yards. So, I was runner-up that year. That was my first visit to Wrigley Field, where I would have some wonderful baseball memories years later."

"Pete Rozelle was so classy, and he left a lasting impression long after I became a major-league ballplayer," Carter said in 2005. "He made me and everyone else feel great with his personal touch. When I was a boy, I loved football as much as baseball, and I got a football scholarship. Then I hurt a knee, and that ended football, and I turned to baseball. I know it turned out fine, making the Hall of Fame."

Ten future Hall of Famers took the field that icy afternoon. Both teams this time wore sneakers on the frozen field. For Sam Huff, this game meant going nose to nose with his pal from their college days, Chicago fullback Joe Marconi. "He's the best friend I ever had in my life," Huff said. "Joe was my roommate for four years at West Virginia. We were great friends. He was drafted number one by the Los Angeles Rams; then he went to the Bears. When he was with the Rams, we played a game in Los Angeles. He had that high-pitched voice. He took a little flat pass, and I came across the field and knocked him clear over the Rams' bench. 'Hey!' he yelled in that high-pitched voice. 'What'd you hit me like that for?' "

"Joe, you got the ball."

"You didn't have to hit me like that," Marconi complained to his buddy.

"Joe, when you got the ball, I gotta hit ya," Huff answered.

"It's another thing on the football field. I loved him," Huff said. "We were the greatest friends. When he got leukemia, I went to Chicago to visit with him, went to the hospital. It was just a tough time for me. He knew he was gone. I went to his funeral in Chicago. I hate funerals."

The two great friends battled to the end. The Bears took the lead after left defensive end Ed O'Bradovich intercepted Y. A. Tittle's screen to set up a short drive. Wade hit Ditka on a look-in pass to the Giants' 1. Then Wade scored on the quarterback sneak to make it 14–10. The Bears ended the game on a Rich Petibon interception in the end zone to give the franchise its eighth league-championship title, Halas's sixth as coach, to tie him with Packers rival Curly Lambeau, a shared record that still stands. Pete Rozelle made his way to the cramped, steamy confines of the Chicago clubhouse to honor Papa Bear, but he didn't have control over the content captured by the NBC television cameras, especially when the defensive unit saluted their coordinator, George Allen, with this ditty, sung to him and the nation at the top of their lungs: "Hooray for George, hooray at last. Hooray for George; he's a horse's ass!"

On Sunday, January 5, the Chargers put on a superb offensive show at the right time in a league noted for its high-scoring games as they routed the Boston Patriots 51–10 for the AFL title. Gillman's offense rolled up 610 yards as quarterbacks Rote and Hadl each passed for more than 100 yards while Lincoln gained 205 yards on just 13 carries. After the game, Gillman challenged his former Rams boss Pete Rozelle to broker a true pro football championship game with the Bears. The commissioner laughed it off.

Rozelle had just been honored with the most significant accolade of his career when *Sports Illustrated*, the magazine that had done more to promote pro football and the National Football League than any other publication, named him Sportsman of the Year. Frank Deford was a young *SI* writer then, just a year and a half removed from the Princeton campus, where he had been chairman of the *Daily Princetonian*. Deford, who later would profile Rozelle for *SI* in 1980 to observe his 20th year on the job and then write another piece about the commissioners of the four major pro sports—football, baseball, basketball, and hockey—was a reporter-researcher for the lead article in the Sportsman issue. As Al Davis knew at first sight that Lance Alworth had "it," everyone at *Sports Illustrated* knew from the moment Frank Deford strode into the Time-Life Building, in Rockefeller Center, that he was "the one" and would remain so, at his choosing, as he did into the 21st century.

Benjamin Franklin Deford III was born in 1938 of a Baltimore family that once abounded in money, but his grandfather and namesake had lost his lucrative tanning business and fortune after World War I. The Deford family, though, retained an "old money" social standing that far exceeded material wealth. Frank's father joined New York Bell in White Plains after graduating from Princeton in 1926. He then moved to Richmond, Virginia, where he met and fell in love with banker's daughter Louise McAdams in 1934.

The family experienced a financial rebirth to a lesser extent when Frank's maternal grandfather took over a Baltimore bank in 1936. Frank was born two years later. He enjoyed the advantages of private schooling, though was culturally sensitive and no snob, and had an innate love for sports and the people who play them. Most important for a writer, he loved the characters who make the games fun and give them their soul.

He entered Princeton in 1957 as a member of the class of '61. He was midway through his January-January one-year term as *Daily Princetonian* chairman when he got caught with a woman in his dormitory room and was tossed out of school. As Deford explained to Michael MacCambridge for *The Franchise: A History of Sports Illustrated Magazine*, "It sounds a lot more exciting than it actually was."

Jose M. Ferrer III, a nephew of actor Mel Ferrer, finished Deford's term at the *Daily Princetonian*, and then Deford's close friend and fellow journalist Lester Munson took the helm in January 1961. While Deford was out of school, he made the most of his time. He served six months in the army and came back, after a year away, more mature and focused. Standing a lean, Clark Gable–like 6'5" (the moustache would come later), the movie-star-handsome Deford returned to the *Daily Princetonian* as a columnist and film reviewer and "did whatever he felt like doing," according to Munson.

They went their separate ways in 1962, but they stayed close. After Princeton's commencement, Munson joined the *Chicago Daily News* as a reporter, where he remained until he got his law degree from the University of Chicago in 1967. Then, in 1990, he walked away from his successful law practice in Chicago to rejoin Deford, now the editor of the short-lived but well-written sports newspaper *The National*, as its legal and investigative correspondent. When *The National* folded, they again joined forces at *SI*, where Munson held an associate managing editor title as the magazine's top investigative reporter until 2007.

Deford's 1962 graduation from Princeton came at a propitious time for the Luce empire's sporting publication. Deford, who wanted only to work for *Sports Illustrated*, landed an interview with the magazine before commencement. Before he spoke to his future boss, managing editor Andre Laguerre, a demanding perfectionist known to leave his writers with heartburn and stomachaches, Deford had to run the corporate gauntlet during the interview process. He told the people at *Time*, *Life*, and *FYI*, the house organ, he didn't want to work for them. By the time he arrived at Laguerre's office after a lunch with *SI* writers Jeremiah Tax and Ray Cave, the building was abuzz with word about the kid who blew off everyone for *SI*. After a short interview, Laguerre hired Deford on the spot as a reporter-researcher. He skipped graduation to start work immediately.

Not only did Laguerre hire Deford in 1962, but he also brought aboard Dan Jenkins and John Underwood, acquiring three men who combined the three qualities famed senior editor Roy Terrell told Michael MacCambridge that a *Sports Illustrated* writer must have: "talent, a thorough knowledge of the sport being covered, and hard work." They were, in Terrell's words "three guys you could almost build a magazine around."

Deford developed a working relationship with Rozelle that would provide much of the gist for the January 4, 1964, Sportsman of the Year cover story, written by Kenneth Rudeen. "Rozelle was relaxed," Deford said. "He had such a wonderful sense of what the press wanted. 'This guy wants Xs and Os.' 'This guy is an investigator.' That was his brilliance. He instinctively understood what the press wanted."

Rozelle drew blistering negative comments around the country, especially so in New York, for going ahead with the games the Sunday after John F. Kennedy was assassinated. At *SI*, Laguerre's decision to keep a Dan Jenkins cover story on Roger Staubach and, while he lauded Rozelle's decision to play, to bury that commentary in the Scorecard section, triggered an outpouring of angry mail from readers who believed the magazine had underplayed the assassination and its significance. When Laguerre made his decision to make Pete Rozelle the Sportsman of the Year, many of his own writers, Jenkins included, were incredulous. When the smoke cleared after the article was published, Rozelle could say that he had gained credibility with the old guard of owners: "Suddenly I was no longer a 33-year-old kid commissioner."

Deford unraveled Laguerre's reasoning when I interviewed him for this book. "You have to go back to the year before," Deford said. "Laguerre—the managing editor, a brilliant guy, the Pete Rozelle of editors—sees how important the NFL has become to the rest of the country and *Sports Illustrated*. He is bound and determined to pick a pro football player as Sportsman of the Year for '62. Green Bay is riding high that year, and Laguerre decides to pick Bart Starr. Starr is the field general with no flies on him whatsoever, even as Hornung is the 'Golden Boy.' So, the football writer was Tex Maule, who also was one of Laguerre's closest friends. Maule says, 'They can't lose. They're so much better than anybody else, they can't lose.'

Laguerre, though, did not share Maule's supreme confidence in Lombardi's Packers. "Laguerre's afraid. Sportsman of the Year is going to come out December 26 or 27, and the championship game would have been right before or immediately after," Deford said. "If Green Bay gets beaten, here we are with Bart Starr, Sportsman of the Year, on the cover, and he's a loser.

" 'They can't lose,' Maule tells Laguerre. 'Don't worry. It's a lock.'

" 'OK,' Laguerre says, and they start to do the Bart Starr story."

"I know all this because I was a kid reporter, and they sent me down to Alabama to talk to his father, Master Sergeant Ben Starr," Deford recalled. "The Thanksgiving Day game was the only loss: Green Bay at Detroit, and Detroit killed them—absolutely wiped them out. Just one of those things. Laguerre gets cold feet. He tells Maule, 'I thought you told me it was a lock.'

" 'Don't worry,' Maule still says. 'They'll win in the end.'

" 'I can't do it,' Laguerre says.

"They make a U-turn and pick Terry Baker: the all-American boy from Oregon, quarterback and also a basketball star," Deford said. "They do this rush job and make Terry Baker the Sportsman of the Year."

In *Sports Illustrated*'s previous nine years of existence, its yearly honorees had all been athletes: three trackmen, Roger Bannister, Bobby Morrow, and Rafer Johnson; baseball players Johnny Podres and Stan Musial; boxer Ingemar Johansson; golfer Arnold Palmer; basketball player Jerry Lucas; and Baker. "So, the next year, Laguerre still doesn't have his white whale," Deford said. "So, he thinks to himself, I won't get in the same position picking a player; I'll pick Pete Rozelle. That's how Rozelle got the award. Because Laguerre couldn't pick Bart Starr the year before and then, of course, gamble on a winner, he picks Rozelle, just says, 'Look what he's done for the league.'

"Then, of course, November 22 comes, and Laguerre says, 'The hell with it; I'm staying with Rozelle.' Of course, had that happened the year before, who knows what Laguerre would have done, because the magazine took a lot of crap for that. Rozelle's choice was very controversial because he wasn't a player, not because of the Kennedy assassination and decision to play. So, that's how Pete Rozelle became Sportsman of the Year for 1963. That's the reason. Players lose."

Kenneth Rudeen interlaced his story of the handling of the Hornung-Karras affair with poignant quotes in a paean to pro football's 37-year-old CEO. In many ways, the story could have been dictated by Rozelle's brilliant PR man, Jim Kensil. " 'Pete Rozelle's handling of the investigations,' says Texas Schramm, the general manager of the Dallas Cowboys, 'was the thing that made everybody accept him as commissioner and no longer a boy playing the part. He gained once and for all everybody's complete respect.' To Art Rooney," Rudeen wrote, " 'he is a gift from the hand of Providence.' "

That assessment was fitting, Rudeen wrote, because "excellence among administrators was scarce in 1963." The other major sports baseball, basketball, hockey, and horse racing were stuck in ruts and, by and large, struggling, as were boxing and amateur sports. "Alone," Rudeen wrote, "professional football grasped the opportunities afforded it, and Pete Rozelle, who demonstrated his insistence upon high integrity by firing Paul Hornung and Alex Karras, did much more."

Much more, Rudeen concluded, as Rozelle created a television policy that provided more money. (Much more money would be coming beginning the following season, with a new contract.) Rudeen praised Rozelle for the league's expansion into Dallas and Minnesota, the Cardinals' move to St. Louis from Chicago, and the fact that "he shaped a player pension plan." The pension issue involving players of that era remains unsettled and contentious.

The key, though, was Rozelle's response immediately following the Kennedy assassination when he ordered the games played but not televised. "It is a tribute to the prominence of professional football that only the NFL's decision was widely discussed," Rudeen wrote, noting that by Sunday, Pittsburgh's Art Rooney "concluded that Rozelle's decision was 'the right one.' "

Most interesting were the conclusions Rudeen reached, some of which would be acted on within a few years, others decades later, as he opened with an inadvertent reference to a word never mentioned in the article, *merger*. "Most fans," Rudeen wrote, "want to see the AFL prosper and many want it to play the NFL champion in a pro football World Series game. Rozelle's stock comment is, 'We have no plans for such a game.' "

In fairness to Rudeen, nobody on January 4, 1964, had any notion whatsoever that, three years from that date, the National Football League and its *new* American Football League partner would be gearing up for the first championship game of the merger, between the Green Bay Packers and Kansas City, a game that would become known as the Super Bowl.

Rudeen also discussed Rozelle's plans for such futuristic notions as bigger and better stadiums; further expansion to at least two more warm-weather cities, among Atlanta, New Orleans, Miami, and Houston; and overseas games, which began with exhibitions in the

1980s. One concept that failed was big-screen televising of home games before a paying theatrical audience. It worked in Chicago for the Bears-Giants championship game but never was tried again. It died completely when Congress ended the home-game blackout policy in 1973.

All told, Kenneth Rudeen and *Sports Illustrated* captured the essence of young commissioner Rozelle in this straight-A report card as matters stood at the outset of 1964. "The men of the NFL have one plan of their own, which can be stated in two words: 'Keep Pete.' No man was more valuable to sport in 1963. No sport is in more competent hands for the years to come."

"That's like the dark ages compared to today," Deford observed. "You have to go through agents. The players' union would have limits on what you do. Rozelle had to punish those guys, for sure, but it also shows you the latitude he had. He was essentially Judge Landis; in 40 years, it had not changed. Landis told the Black Sox, 'You guys haven't essentially fixed the World Series. I can't prove it. You're out anyway!'

"That's essentially what Rozelle did," Deford concluded. "Yes, he did operate beautifully, but, yes, he really did have the benefit of the right time and place, and he used it successfully."

FOURTEEN

LICENSES TO PRINT MONEY: NFL PROPERTIES AND TV

"The NFL is America's clothier."

—DAVE ANDERSON, 2006

*O*nce upon a time, the only way anyone could find an authentic ball cap, made to major-league specifications—wool, sized to fit, with a malleable visor, eight equally spaced rows of seams, sewn-on embossed logo, and exact team colors—was if the person knew someone on a ball club who had a key to the equipment room.

You might come close if your dad took you to a ball game and bought you a 75-cent hat from a ballpark vendor. Logos, though, usually were glued onto cotton fabric, the colors were slightly off, and the hats didn't fit just so, nor look quite right. Authentic jerseys were out of the question. They did not exist, nor did anything else official such as T-shirts, sweatshirts, sweatpants, pens, drinking glasses, or playing cards, to name a few items with logos. Kitchen magnets had not been invented.

The concept started where so many of pro football's other marketing ideas originated, with the Los Angeles Rams, where a man named Larry Kent, who got his start working with the remarkable Roy Rogers licensing operation, which licensed everything from cowboy hats, boots, and chaps to lunch boxes, joined Pete Rozelle in 1957. Once there, Kent set up the Rams Store and began licensing and marketing team-related gear to the public. "All of a sudden, out of nowhere, all these insignias were on the helmets," Ernie Accorsi recalled.

Well before Rozelle joined the club, Fred Gehrke, a Rams running back in the late '40s and early '50s and a professional commercial artist, sat down at home one night and, on a whim, drew up the now familiar ram's-horn logo. Sometime in 1948, in that era before the hard-shell plastic helmet took over the game, Gehrke painted that same insignia on each teammate's blue leather helmet, or "hat," as the players called them. That was the start of something big. Some whim!

NFL Properties did not exist until Rozelle created it in 1963. "The idea of NFL Properties was so simplistic when you think about it," Accorsi said. "I remember the bobble-head dolls, which now are worth a fortune. Then it was putting logos on the helmets. After the Rams, the Eagles were next. They wore solid helmets until the mid-'50s; then came that eagle's wing. The Colts wore horseshoes on the back of their helmets when they came into the league in '53 and moved them to the sides in '56. Dallas had the lone star from the outset in 1960. The Bears wore nothing until that C in '61. The Packers went to the G in '61. The Giants came in with the lowercase *ny* that year."

Accorsi continued, "I asked Mr. Mara until the day he died who thought of the lowercase *ny* and why. It's one of the great logos in sports. I brought it back. Some New Jersey legislator took a shot at me in the papers: 'Why don't you worry more about medical care for seniors instead of worrying about a logo on a helmet?' I wrote back: Did this man think that if eight miles to the east, the greatest city in the world wasn't there, he'd have a football team here?

"They [the Maras] think an equipment guy named Sid Moret did it. If you look at the Giants from 1959 or '60 in a picture of one of our trainers taking Charlie Conerly off the field, we had the New York Yankees logo," Accorsi said. "Exactly. There were no rights then that they protected, and nobody complained about it. Our jacket for the trainer was the Yankees' *NY*. If you see pictures of Lombardi and Landry in those days, you see them in jackets with the Yankees' *NY*. Whatever happened, it disappeared, and in 1961 came this lowercase logo, and it was phenomenal."

The other teams followed suit, with one and a half exceptions. Paul Brown tried a *CB* on the helmet, but it didn't look right to him or anybody else. So, the Browns did not create a logo. "They became known by never having one," Accorsi said. "The Steelers put it [the U.S. Steel logo] on one side [the right]. Can you imagine that?

"You could see the different logos springing up, and that all was by design. That's what they started to market first," Accorsi said. "The Redskins kept changing it. The feather in the back was first. Lombardi put the *R* in the circle that kind of looked like Green Bay's *G*, with the Indian head. They were bouncing all over the place. It's amazing how this started. Then they brought it all in-house as NFL Properties. That was the forerunner of all this stuff, the NBA and the others. This was all Pete and Larry Kent.

"That whole marketing concept was so simplistic, but they had so much fun with it," Accorsi said. "The NFL of the '50s had a sandlot nature about it. The fields were dirt, playing in baseball parks, and they didn't sod the infields or scrape down the mounds. All of a sudden, they got these logos: the Giants moved to Yankee Stadium, the Eagles to Franklin Field, and it made it seem big league. They had prestige to it. As a kid, you don't know quite why. One of the reasons was Rozelle."

"With NFL Properties, Pete had a promotional arm of the league and made sure the funds went to charity," Cincinnati Bengals owner Mike Brown said. "It was not operated to maximize income. Norman Braman came into the league with the Eagles, and he wanted to change that. He enlisted supporters, Jerry Jones being one. Today we have something different from what it was originally. I think Pete was right on that. It was better for the league when it wasn't looked upon as a money machine. It was looked upon as a promotional arm, not a moneymaking device."

"For many years, everything Properties brought in was going to NFL Charities," retired NFL commissioner Paul Tagliabue said. "Initially, the concept from Pete's standpoint was quality control, and a lot of it was developing a consistency to license the same high-quality products. As sports sponsorships and naming rights started to become greater opportunities, Properties was growing."

As it grew, though, Pete Rozelle understood that he had two problems with licensing. First, players and newer owners wanted to make money off their images and jerseys and the like, and not devote all the money to charities. Second, as Tagliabue saw it, "Properties was not really integrated with the TV advertisers. It was not integrated with what he thought was really important."

Rozelle did understand the value of charity to the league's image and how it related to the way teams and players got involved in their communities. When Ernie Accorsi worked at the league office in the mid-'70s, one of his assignments was NFL Charities, which Rozelle also started in 1963. "I was the secretary, and Val Pinchbeck the treasurer, of NFL Charities," Accorsi said. "The board was Ethel Kennedy, Lowell Perry, Jack Kemp, and the Marlboro guy, Jack Landry. The honorary presidents were Lamar Hunt and George Halas. It was my job as secretary to take all these applicants and try to get it by the board. Ethel Kennedy used to give me the business all the time because I didn't have enough Native Americans. I kept looking. We weren't given a lot of money initially. We gave a lot to the Lombardi Comprehensive Cancer Center and the Piccolo Cancer Research Fund project. That's where I got to know Mr. Halas. Every time he came to town, we went over to Sloan-Kettering. I'd ride in the car with him and [his son-in-law] Ed McCaskey."

Through television, the National Football League became closely identified with the nation's largest charitable organization, United Way. It started in Denver in 1887 when religious groups there brought 22 fund-raising groups under a unified Charity Organizations Society. That name gave way to Community Chest, which began in Cleveland in 1913. By 1948, more than one thousand communities had set up what became known as United Way.

Rozelle by 1973 found a fit for the NFL as a pillar of United Way's circle of basic programs—to help children and young people succeed, strengthen and support families, improve access to health care, and promote self-sufficiency. So, in 1974, he worked with the networks and through NFL Films created the "Great Moments" series, one-minute public service announcements tailored to each team's market as they humanized the men behind the helmets. Players, owners, and coaches appeared in the spots, while teams supported local United Ways in personal appearances, special programs, and board service.

"Those ads are something that stick in our minds," said Mike Brown. "I think those ads are good for the NFL too. The thing about it that was different with Pete was he did not operate the league to generate the most money possible." Times changed, dramatically.

How much money is generated by NFL Properties? "It's not as big as people think," said Art Modell. "*Profit* is a dirty word in sports particularly, even though you want to sustain your business and make a profit to make sure you are doing all right. Then the players got into the act, and they were claiming part of this and part of that, and it became an adversarial position with the players. We worked it out, and the licensing was a very important ingredient for the control of the quality of our products, which we decided was more important than the money it brought in. Having 24 or 28 units going off in different directions with, say, a soft drink was not the way to go. We wanted to consolidate our efforts."

Modell dramatically understated the money involved in both the potential and reality of current-day licensing and marketing. In the early days of the NFL Players' Association, the owners would not share a cent with the players. Past NFLPA president Mike Pyle, a former captain of the Chicago Bears, recalled, "George Halas got up at our 1965 meeting and said, 'The money that comes in is ours, because we deserve it for all we put in to start this league and keep it going from the beginning.'"

Twenty-nine years later, in 1994, in the wake of the 1987 strike, decertification, and the union's revival in 1992, the NFLPA formed Players, Inc., the first for-profit licensing and marketing subsidiary of a professional sports union. Today, Players, Inc., works with more than 90 licensees and sponsors and claims to generate more than $100 million a year for all 1,800 active players and the 3,500 retirees who pay a $100 union membership dues fee. NFL Ventures, Inc., oversees the league's various business properties and marketing operations. Commissioner Roger Goodell also is NFL Ventures' president and CEO.

The problem that has forced many of the retirees to sue their union has evolved from a catch-22-like statement by NFLPA president Gene Upshaw in 2006. Upshaw said the union does not represent the retirees who continue to pay dues, because labor law forbids a union from representing retired players. Some retirees have benefited; most have not. Litigation and court challenges are likely. The result is not known as of this writing. For the retirees, survival on a small union pension, Social Security, and Medicare mirrors the problems that many other people face in early-21st-century America.

New York Times columnist Dave Anderson, who's been covering the National Football League since 1956, sees money where Art Modell sees quality control. "NFL Properties is a billion-dollar business," Anderson said. "I've written this many times: the NFL is America's clothier. Walk down the street, and all you see are guys with jerseys on, hats, or jackets, whatever it is." Anderson could have included Europe and Asia as well. That adds up, one believes, to a substantial cut for the league, exactly how much few people other than league insiders know. "They're the ones that license it," Anderson said. "It adds up and adds up fast."

Pro football came into its first big money in 1964 when the two league television contracts came up for renewal. The National Football League was coming off Pete Rozelle's cobbled-together $4.65 million breakthrough deal with CBS, which took his league through 1962 and the tumultuous 1963 season and concluded with just under a million from NBC for the Bears-Giants championship-game rights in Chicago. This time, the commissioner offered a unified package of regular-season and championship games. Most important, he opened the bidding to all three networks.

"It was a strange business for a lot of people in the league," said Modell, Rozelle's league ally and TV point man. "We achieved results early in the game that were startling. The money was much bigger than anybody thought."

How they got to that point was a tribute to Rozelle's creativity. NBC had televised the league championship games since 1955, Pittsburgh Steelers and Baltimore Colts games in 1960 and '61, and, in conjunction with Los Angeles Newspaper Charities, the Pro Bowl following the 1951 and '52 seasons, and again from 1957 to '64. At that time, NBC Sports was a division of NBC News, not a separate operating entity within the company as CBS Sports was. NBC let Rozelle know that it wanted to take the NFL away from CBS and had the money to make it worthwhile. Leading the NBC charge was the network's new vice president of sports, the brilliant and well-regarded Carl Lindemann Jr.

Carl Lindemann, an army officer in World War II, came back from the New Guinea jungles in 1945 to finish his schooling at MIT and then joined NBC as a broadcast engineer. Leadership came naturally to Lindemann, who led a NABET (National Association of Broadcast Employees and Technicians) union strike against the company in the early days of live television over wages and working conditions. He served as lead cameraman for Sid Caesar's "Your Show of Shows" and then joined the singer Kate Smith and worked as general manager of "The Kate Smith Evening Hour."

When the "Today Show" took the air in 1952, Lindemann became its manager and later ran daytime programming for the network. On the side, he was NBC's liaison with the government in case of a national disaster. As Lindemann's widow, Cissie, said, "His job was to get the president on the air from a secret place so he could talk to the nation."

In those days, when television networks relieved executives before the end of their contracts, they gave them small, well-hidden offices with a secretary and nothing to do, along with the impressive, but empty, title "vice president, special projects." When Lindemann was named vice president for special projects for NBC in 1961, his title, however, meant precisely what it stated, and it had teeth. He supervised the "Today Show" and coverage of space shots for NBC News.

In 1963, as the company geared up to grab the NFL, veteran announcer Lindsay Nelson left as the voice of NBC Sports to join the New York Mets full-time as the team's lead broadcaster. Also, Nelson's former boss, the division's longtime president, Tom S. Gallery, in ill health and soon to die, retired. NBC president Robert Kintner had to put someone in charge in time to negotiate with Rozelle. "Bob, I don't know a lot about sports," Lindemann told Kintner when they discussed the job.

"I'm not asking you to suit up; I'm asking you to run the department!" Kintner replied. And he did. Able to spend upward of $40 million to make it work, Lindemann went to Rozelle early in 1964 to see if he could pry the league away from CBS.

"Rozelle was a quiet manipulator behind the scenes," said Charlie Jones, who was still with ABC in 1963–64. "The CBS guys in the '60s had the inside track to the NFL. They were the NFL—guys like Gifford and Summerall." CBS Sports, with division president Bill McPhail's close relationship to Rozelle, knew it must pony up considerably more than the just-expired deal, $4.65 million a year.

Unlike NBC, ABC had never televised the NFL as a full network. Newly minted ABC Sports president Roone Arledge decided not to renew with the AFL. He wanted the more prestigious NFL. When Arledge studied the fine print in the league's bidding specifications, he thought he found the difference maker. In his memoir *Roone*, Arledge wrote, "I thought I spotted something that would permit us to televise *two* games every Sunday."

Positive that nobody at CBS or NBC had read the doubleheader clause, Arledge got the ABC board to authorize a two-year package worth $26.4 million—$13.2 million each year. Unfortunately, as Arledge explained, ABC had a lawyer call Rozelle's office to see if the doubleheader clause was true. When that call was made, Arledge wrote, he was certain his little secret was no longer his alone, and he feared that at least one of the other networks—namely, CBS—was likely to hear about it and bid accordingly.

"The owners as a group went on a vacation at Spanish Cay, [Clint] Murchison's island in the Bahamas," Modell recalled. "On this one trip, I decided to stay back in Florida to await the results of the silent bidding from the networks. Pete was in his office and called me up somewhat excited and said, '$14.1 million a year; for two years, $28 million, two.' I thought it was a staggering figure for the league.

"I quickly got on a private plane and flew over to Spanish Cay," Modell said. "All the owners were waiting on the porch of the hacienda, just lounging around, trying to show indifference to what I was saying. Actually, they were ready to climb the walls. 'Gentlemen,' I said, '14 million and one.'

"They faked the enthusiasm that they were happy," Modell remembered. "Then I said, 'Per year.' They started high-fiving each other like we had scored three touchdowns. We were off to the races. That was the first big contract, $28 million, two." That was for regular-season telecasts. CBS also paid $3.6 million for the 1964 and 1965 championship games—$1.8 million a year.

Arledge was furious when he learned that he and ABC fell short of McPhail and CBS by just $900,000 a year. "I don't like being snookered," Arledge wrote. "I couldn't prove it, then or later, and Pete Rozelle has vociferously denied it, but I was sure he had 'leaked' my doubleheader discovery to Bill McPhail, a longtime crony of his with whom he shared a Long Island summer house and who just happened to be the president of CBS Sports."

After he vented his frustration at losing the NFL bid, Arledge, always a player for the long haul, realized he could cultivate Rozelle, which he did to his advantage with the "Monday Night" deal in 1970. To fulfill an immediate need, and spend that allocated money he got for the NFL bid, Arledge grabbed the NCAA's college football series from NBC for 1965. Almost immediately, it became a blue-ribbon ABC property, as did another former NBC staple, the U.S. Open golf tournament. Arledge then grabbed the rights to NBA basketball and the properties that made him famous, the Olympics, starting with the 1968 Winter and Summer Games.

That new CBS deal brought tears to the eyes of league founder George Halas, who years later told his protégé Jerry Vainisi that until then, he had to borrow money every off-season. Never again. "That says it all," a delighted Modell recalled. "That brought immediate prosperity to the NFL and its players."

Indeed it did, putting a million dollars in each club's pocket before the season, ensuring that each team could make its payroll before it sold a single ticket, let alone hot dog or bag of peanuts. That largesse bumped the average pay of 40 players and a typical five-man coaching staff to $22,222.22. Obviously, that was a skewed figure, since stars and head coaches got more money than others. For instance, when Gale Sayers signed his headline-making $100,000 deal with the Bears in 1965, the deal ran for four years at $25,000 a year. No bonus.

Rozelle got CBS to nationalize its broadcasts. From the beginning of the NFL Sunday telecasts in 1956, each game had split audio feeds: one for the home team, the other for the visitors. For the 1964 season, Rozelle moved each team's second, or color, announcer to the field to cover "his" team's bench area. In the booth, the home team's announcer would call the first half, and the visitors' announcer would call the second half. It was a two-sided coin. It gave wider exposure to announcers, but the fans, accustomed to their "home" calls, did not like it when the "other guys" called the action. Rozelle had CBS return to a split audio feed in 1965. "I started with Jack Whitaker," Frank Gifford recalled. Nineteen sixty-five was his first year in the booth as a full-time NFL analyst, working Giants games. "We were heard only in the New York area. The other announce team was heard in its home area. In 1968, Pete had CBS cut the announce teams in half, and we covered all teams, not the old home club. That's the way it's done now."

While the new CBS deal pumped megadollars into the established NFL, that same deal could have buried the younger AFL. With ABC opting out of the AFL package, the league was in danger of going under. Then, along came the Peacock. "The AFL was saved by NBC and Carl Lindemann," Charlie Jones said. "NBC was sitting there with $36 million. In any major company, if your division has $36 million, you will find something to spend it on. It's lost if it goes back into the general fund."

Lindemann needed a deal, so he found an outlet for that "found" money. Unlike Arledge, the supreme self-promoter, Lindemann was a master at working behind the scenes and bringing people together. Enter AFL commissioner Joe Foss and David "Sonny" Werblin, since late 1963, the managing owner of the New York Jets. Werblin for years before had been vice president of the powerful, Hollywood-based superagency MCA, the Music Corporation of America. MCA's Jay Michaels had acted as the American Football League's bargaining agent for television contracts from the league's start-up. When Werblin and his partners bought the Jets, Werblin had to leave MCA, but he did not have to stop talking to his friends there. A man who knew the networks and show business inside and out, Werblin could smell the NBC money waiting to be spent. Acting on behalf of the Jets, he took Carl Lindemann for a ride into history in his limousine. "They made that deal in the backseat of Sonny Werblin's limo with a binding handshake," Cissie Lindemann said. "In those days, a handshake deal was done in good faith." Especially with a signed contract in hand.

How they got to that handshake is testimony to the way Lindemann put together deals in that freewheeling time. The negotiating game started in late January and continued into the first week of February. In *Going Long*, Jeff Miller's history of the AFL, former commissioner Joe Foss is quoted as saying, "I was holding out for $36 million. Some of the owners wanted to settle for $32 million, which was what NBC was offering."

The numbers had been moving fast. Before Foss and Werblin got to $32 million, Buffalo Bills owner Ralph Wilson, who was at the Innsbruck Winter Olympics with Lamar Hunt, took a call from Boston's Billy Sullivan, who was ecstatic about the NBC offer that would bring each team between $600,000 and $700,000, nearly $28 million over five years, well more than the $100,000 each team got from ABC. "Billy, we can't compete," Wilson said to a stunned Sullivan. "What do you mean?" Sullivan asked. "We need more," Wilson said. Wilson relayed that conversation to Hunt.

Foss held out for more, and with Werblin's work, they got Lindemann and NBC to up the ante to $34 million. Werblin, eager to make a deal and being Kintner's close friend, told Foss that NBC had maxed out. Then, Foss went over to NBC alone and haggled with Kintner, Lindemann, a lawyer, and one other man. Finally, a day or so later, Foss and Lindemann agreed to a face-saving deal in a phone conversation. NBC would pay the AFL the previously deadlocked $34 million for the existing eight teams and another $2 million for the two planned expansion teams that would become Miami and Cincinnati, to bring it up to $36 million. At $850,000 per team, that deal brought the AFL close enough to the CBS-NFL money to make it work. After Lindemann read the contract to Foss over the telephone, he offered to meet the commissioner at Toots Shor's legendary saloon at 51 West 52nd Street to close the deal.

Foss arrived at Shor's to find the entire ABC executive team there. After a quick wave-off, the famed World War II marine flying ace returned to the front door in time to intercept Lindemann. Foss spotted a phone booth down the street, and somehow he and Lindemann, two big men, wedged themselves into the booth to review the contract. As passersby did double takes at the sight of two large men holding a business conversation in a phone booth, Foss read the document and then signed it, as did Lindemann. Lindemann then invited Foss to "21" just down the street for celebratory drinks and dinner.

They walked inside to see none other than Sonny Werblin sitting at table one, and they pulled out the signed contract. As much as Foss took credit for the deal, Lamar Hunt gave full credit to the owner of the Jets. "Sonny Werblin was the key negotiator," the AFL founder told Jeff Miller. "NBC made a substantial offer that put us on the map."

A good share of that money was earmarked to outbid the National Football League and sign players. Werblin, himself, made good on that vow, grabbing Ohio State all-American fullback Matt Snell away from the crosstown Giants for the 1964 season, especially after the Giants told Snell he would back up their number one draft choice, Joe Don Looney, of Oklahoma. The eccentric Looney, however, refused to sign and forced a trade to the Baltimore Colts, where he lasted a single year in his first of many stops that took him to Washington, Detroit, and New Orleans before his career ended in 1969. Years later, Looney took up company with a guru in India. Snell would play a key role in the emergence of the Jets. That deal gave the AFL money and prestige in the New York advertising and television world that Rozelle had made his personal playground.

After NBC and the AFL signed the deal, Lindemann needed to get a nuts-and-bolts guy to run the department. "Now, Carl didn't know anything about the AFL, pro football, or anything else at all in sports," Charlie Jones said. "The man who did was Chet Simmons."

In late 1963, Simmons had been entangled in what turned out to be a losing corporate fight to the finish with Roone Arledge at Sports

Programs, Inc., the company that ran ABC Sports. "Roone was the best corporate game player in the world, a man with talent and ambition," Jones said. "Chet was falling back to a number three position behind Arledge and Ed Scherick. Then Lindemann offered Chet the number two position at NBC, primarily because they now had AFL football. So, Carl signed him; he moved over and took us with him. Chet took everybody."

"We went bag and baggage to NBC in 1964," Simmons said in late 2005. Top director-producers Harry Coyle and Ted Nathanson already were there with NBC's superior engineering. From ABC, Simmons brought Charlie Jones, Jim Simpson, and the network's top pair, Curt Gowdy and Paul Christman. "Gowdy and Christman ended up being our main announcing team. Paul, a lovely, lovely man, died in 1970," Simmons said.

"Lou Kusserow was the main producer, the Columbia man who scored the winning touchdown to beat Army [21–20 in 1947]," Jones said. "Kusserow was the best producer that I ever worked with my entire life, and he knew absolutely nothing. All he did was tell everybody how great they were. Thus, everybody had to be at their absolute best because of my buddy Kusserow, as in, 'My buddy Kusserow's producing, and we're gonna kick ass.' "

Jones cited an example: "I did an on-camera opening at a football game that he was producing, and I must have blown four different takes. It was the worst opening in television history—just terrible. We went to a commercial, and I was sitting and about to die, when Kusserow got in my ear. 'That's the best fucking opening I ever heard.' "

"Lou, are you crazy?" Jones replied.

"No. You captured the moment," Kusserow assured him. "You made it so real. And you were so involved the way that you said it. Boy, are we going to have a great game today!"

Jones related, "I was 10 feet tall. I didn't figure out what he told me until Wednesday."

Money was not a problem at either network. CBS Sports could count on major funding from Jack Landry's Marlboro cigarette account and the largesse of the Ford Motor Company, whose number three man, William Clay Ford, happened to own the Detroit

Lions. Plenty of well-heeled spot sales accounts were ready to go. "At that time, Chrysler sponsored half of everything on NBC Sports, with the exception of the Bob Hope Classic," Charlie Jones recalled, "and they sponsored *all* of that. The plum as an announcer was the Bob Hope Classic. That meant you were accepted by Chrysler, and no matter what anybody said, you had to be accepted by Chrysler."

"It just happened to be the right timing," Simmons said. "At the same time, not forgetting our college roots, the Orange Bowl moved from ABC to NBC in the same year. Those two things, getting the American Football League and the Orange Bowl for NBC, always stuck out in my mind." And, NBC moved the Orange Bowl to New Year's night after its Rose Bowl telecast, locking up the audience for the biggest bowl games.

The NBC-AFL deal had another major ramification for sports and television in general. RCA, the parent of NBC and manufacturer of television sets, sat in the driver's seat for the color revolution. The government made RCA color technology the television standard in 1953, and it would remain that way until 2007, when all transmissions were to become digital. By 1963, NBC programming was all color. Because few people had color sets, CBS and ABC had lagged. But when NBC got the AFL to begin in 1965, that meant NBC would have superior pictures to CBS. That forced CBS to make the conversion to color in 1965. ABC followed suit a year later. All that from one pro football television-rights package signed in a New York City phone booth crowded by two large men.

So, the great pro football war had moved on to full-front combat in living color, and with it would come the hired guns whose presence would alter sports forever, the agents. For the first time, the players would earn some real money, and it would only get bigger and bigger.

FIFTEEN

THE HOME FRONT

"He was like being with James Bond."

—Anne Marie Rozelle Bratton, 2006

*B*efitting his position as commissioner of the National Football League, the long black limousine reserved for Pete Rozelle and his wife, Carrie, was positioned near the head of the cortege. It was just before noon on Thursday, November 3, 1983, in front of St. Ita's Church, in the Edgewater neighborhood of Chicago's Far North Side, when the doors opened and the worshippers filed out.

Family, friends, players, reporters, and fans had packed the parish church to overflowing an hour earlier for the funeral mass for George Halas, the 88-year-old patriarch of the league and of arguably its most renowned team, the Chicago Bears. In his 40 seasons as coach, his Bears won a record 324 games and six of the team's nine titles. As owner, Halas carried the league on his back through its 1920 founding, its pioneer days, the Great Depression, World War II, and two major football wars. He lived to see his dream become reality as professional football became the most popular sport of all.

No man had done more during the past 23 years to fulfill and implement George Halas's dream and carry his league to its position of preeminence and wealth than the 57-year-old commissioner, who brought his lovely wife with him from New York to pay their respects. No man had done more to earn Pete Rozelle's respect than George Halas. No man had done more to earn the patriarch's respect than Pete Rozelle.

In character to the end, George Halas remained basic. He spent his final days at home in the familiarity of his apartment overlooking Lake Michigan, to battle the pancreatic cancer that left him no rally room, rather than breathe his last in a large, impersonal downtown hospital. It was fitting that he ordered his heirs to conduct his funeral mass in the parish church he had attended faithfully since he, his late wife, Min, and their two children, George and Virginia, moved into their secure building some 42 years before.

The night before the funeral mass, every head in Birren and Sons, the cozy neighborhood funeral home where Halas lay in repose, turned as one when the commissioner and his wife appeared mid-evening to pay their respects to the patriarch's survivors, the McCaskeys. The Rozelles—he, tall and elegant in a dark suit and glistening shoes; she, tall and magnificent, her thick chestnut hair resting on her shoulders over a long mink coat—looked like royalty, movie stars.

As they departed the church the next morning for the limousine, they donned sunglasses against a sharp midautumn sun whose rays filtered through the gathering clouds of an approaching cold front. Once they were settled in the plush bench seat, he lit a cigarette and surveyed the scene as the driver started off.

The cars fell into line in the longest funeral procession Chicago had seen since the death of Mayor Richard J. Daley in 1976. It began its journey slowly up Broadway to Ridge Avenue, a block away, where the lead car made a 45-degree turn to the northwest and accelerated, and the others followed suit, like the military on the move. The procession would end at St. Adalbert's Cemetery 10 miles to the west.

The cortege gained speed as it proceeded up gently sloping Ridge toward the crest and made another half turn onto Peterson at the Y-junction west of Clark Street, headed for the cemetery. The scenery outside Rozelle's window was familiar, views he had not discerned in the darkness the night before, ones he had not seen in daylight for a good 35 years. Although he had not set foot in this neighborhood in all that time, he knew exactly where he was as the big car glided past the huge masonry building to the right, where Ardmore Avenue meets Ridge—Senn High School. Her school. Not Carrie's, but Jane's.

Memories of Jane and their long-ago dashed hopes washed through his mind as he took a deep drag and exhaled slowly. Jane Coupe Rozelle was not merely his first love. She was his heartbreak and his despair, their marriage the only failure he ever experienced. But the union produced the true love of his life, the daughter he cherished more than anything else, a delightful young woman named Anne Marie, who never failed to please him as he happily led her from childhood to maturity. That's why the mother of a man's child could retain a niche in his heart and soul, no matter what transpired between them. And plenty did.

They met in this Chicago neighborhood in the late spring of 1946. Twenty-year-old Pete Rozelle came to town to spend a few days with shipmate Ted Heller to celebrate their discharge from the navy before he caught a train home to Los Angeles. Ted's girlfriend fixed Pete up with Jane, her friend from Senn. The moment he saw her, he was gone, heart struck, madly in love. The feeling was mutual.

Nineteen-year-old Jane was an eye-catching, lens-friendly blonde, confirmed by her senior portrait in the 1945 *Forum*, her high school yearbook. She wore her shoulder-length hair in the classic pageboy bob that so many girls preferred during the war years. She may have been quiet, if not outright shy, but her classmates at Senn elected her to the post of room president as a freshman and again as a junior after she served as room secretary her sophomore year. Jane participated in a normal schedule of after-school activities, which included memberships in the Senn Girls' Athletic Association and the Pitman club, where young women who planned to join the workforce instead of go on to college honed typing and clerical skills.

After school let out, she and her friends more likely than not retreated to the little soda shop across Ridge Avenue to catch up on daily doings and smoke a cigarette or two. That's the way it was on the home front in World War II. Smoking was a rite of passage, and these young men and women grew up fast watching neighbors and older school chums leave for war, especially after the D-day invasion of Europe in 1944, where so many teenage soldiers died on the beaches of Normandy or elsewhere. After Jane graduated in June 1945, she found work at Marshall Field's department store in the Loop and was still living at home when Pete entered her life.

Pete and Jane came from similar urban backgrounds. As he came of age in Lynwood-Compton, between Los Angeles and Long Beach, Jane grew up with her parents, Charles and Isobel, and her sister in a brick two-flat in Halas's St. Ita's parish, which was in the Edgewater neighborhood due south of Rogers Park (about nine miles and a 25-minute el ride to the Loop). The densely populated area was heavily Catholic, a friendly place where people knew their neighbors' comings and goings as they watched the kids grow up. They stuck together.

Unlike Rozelle's Lynwood-Compton area, which decades ago morphed into L.A.'s Watts–South Central ghetto, 21st-century Edgewater and Rogers Park look much as they did in the postwar years, their mixed population befitting the changing dynamics of Chicago. Most of the two- and three-story apartment-building clusters endure in their settings among nicely kept brick and stucco houses on block after block of tree-lined streets to the east and west of small shopping and business districts on the "main drags," Clark Street and Sheridan Road by the lake.

The aptly named Ridge Avenue, a natural watershed and the highest land on the Far North Side, is a major artery. Trucks are not allowed to travel the four-lane street where traffic peaks at the morning and evening rush hours, much of that traffic leading to and from Evanston and the North Shore suburbs as it zips past Senn to its end at Bryn Mawr, where it merges into Lake Shore Drive three blocks later, hard by Halas's old Edgewater Beach Apartments.

"Pete met Jane's mother and father on the first visit," Dick Rozelle recalled. Jane's father, Charles, emigrated to Chicago from St. Helen, on England's Isle of Wight, and was a stone mason. Charles, an alcoholic, had stopped drinking by the time Pete met Jane.

"He went through AA and had endured that chapter in his life. He was a stately, gentle man. Pete liked him a lot," Dick said.

But, as Pete sadly would discover in coming years, Jane would follow her father's earlier drinking pattern and could not stop or change, adding pills to the volatile mix. In 1946, especially after a second trip to Chicago when he shared driving expenses with friend John Lehman, Jane was the focus of Pete's life. If she had a drinking problem, the somewhat naive, 20-year-old beau, whose parents in L.A. were not drinkers, didn't recognize it.

Shortly after Pete and John Lehman returned home, Pete sent for Jane, and she came out to California to get married, but they had to wait. "My mother was Catholic, and he had to go to what is called 'marriage Catholic,' " their daughter, Anne Marie Rozelle Bratton, said. Pete was required to complete a course of instruction in Catholicism and agree to raise their children in the Church, which he did. "He was not a practicing Catholic," Anne Marie said. "He was Methodist, and he wasn't practicing that either." They got married in 1948 and settled into an apartment in San Francisco while he finished school and handled sports publicity at USF.

His job entailed travel, not just in and near San Francisco. Pete was on the road a lot during football and basketball season. That included two weeklong cross-country trips to New York in those years. "Being left alone was bad," Dick Rozelle said. "Jane was beautiful but not a social person. I'm sure she did her best to support Pete, but she could not handle the partnership part of it."

The cold beers they likely enjoyed in that sun-kissed Chicago summer of '46 when they got acquainted at local college taverns by Loyola or on Howard Street near Northwestern became troublesome predinner cocktails for Jane whether or not Pete was with her at home. "He always was very clearheaded when he had a drink," Dick said. Jane, unfortunately, started drinking in off-hours as she lolled around the empty apartment or, worse, passed the time in nearby bars.

By then, Pete was well aware she had a drinking problem. He had quit his publicity job with the Rams to join Ken Macker's public relations firm for the 1956 Melbourne Olympics project. When Dick Rozelle was in school at Berkeley, he occasionally visited his brother and sister-in-law at their Burlingame home, on the San Mateo peninsula. "There was something going on by that time with Jane," Dick said. "Pete had to go out and pick up people at the airport, deal with clients, take them around, go to dinners. Pete never took on a job he didn't do 110 percent. He was dedicated to it with Ken Macker. A lot didn't involve Jane, and she sat around at home alone a lot. The drinking got horrendous."

The senior Rozelles were flummoxed. Dick related, "My mother was stressed about it and could not understand Jane's problem: 'Why does she drink? She should eat chocolates.' "

Pete kept these woes to himself. "I don't think anyone ever knew Pete had a problem about anything," said close friend Frank Gifford. "He just didn't share things. He was very private. He had a small group of friends, a handful he would discuss anything with. Even then, he was cautious about that."

"He was very inward and did not talk about his personal problems," Dick said. "If he went to the dentist, it was just a 'root canal,' nothing else. No details."

The couple returned to Los Angeles in 1957 after commissioner Bert Bell personally asked Pete to replace his friend Tex Schramm, who had fled the turmoil with the Rams to join CBS in New York. As general manager, Pete had to persuade the team's wealthy partners to end the fight that was devastating the franchise. Enter Thelma.

When Schramm left for CBS, Thelma Elkjer stayed behind in Los Angeles to work for his replacement, the 31-year-old Rozelle. Thelma meant far more to Pete and Anne Marie Rozelle than any title could portray. As Dave Anderson recalled in his *New York Times* obituary-tribute to Elkjer after her death in February 2000 at age 77, she still came to the office after Rozelle's death on December 6, 1996. Without exception, she answered the phone, "Mis-ter Rozelle's off-ice," the same way she did when he was alive, when she ruled the roost as his gatekeeper and confidant through the years at NFL headquarters.

In no way was this a romantic situation. Thelma, who never married, maintained a menagerie of mostly cats, with a few dogs, and a mission named Rozelle. "She was with him for 40 years," Anne Marie Bratton said. "She had an incredible relationship with him. Think of her as Miss Moneypenny with James Bond, but more so. She was completely and totally his right hand in everything—guard dog, protector—and she filled in not only for business, but personal."

They worked as one, but when it came to politics, they diverged in a good-natured way. Thelma was not one to keep her mouth shut. "She was an extreme Democrat. He was very conservative, and she was very liberal," Anne Marie said. "They had a lot of fun at each other's expense over that."

In early 1958, Jane told her husband that they were going to have a child. Anne Marie was born on September 28, the same day the Rams were playing the Cleveland Browns. Pete hurried to the hospital from the Coliseum and arrived at halftime to see his wife and their newborn daughter. He immediately hurried back to the Coliseum in time to see Lou Groza kick the winning field goal for Cleveland to defeat the Rams 30–27. For a while, Anne Marie's presence helped the situation. Pete spent as much time with her as his busy schedule allowed, but Jane's drinking remained a constant.

Anne Marie was 16 months old in late January 1960 when her father and mother dropped her off with the senior Rozelles in Lynwood and flew to Miami for the league meetings. As Michael Mac-Cambridge reported in *America's Game*, John Lehman was convinced that his friend Pete was ready to return to journalism because the Rams job, like the one with Macker, had put a "major strain on his marriage." The couple made plans to escape to Jamaica for a week-long vacation after the meetings were over.

They never took that trip, for at lunchtime on January 26, 10 days after the meetings began, Paul Brown, Dan Reeves, and the Mara brothers, Wellington and Jack, buttonholed Rozelle after the morning session. They said they wanted to back him as a compromise candidate to break the logjam to elect a commissioner after 22 ballots. When he went to Jane in their room to discuss the offer, she was one step ahead of him. "They want you, Alvin Ray Rozelle," she said. He nodded. And so, she gave it her blessing.

After the election, when asked what it was like to be the wife of the new czar of the NFL, the rarely quoted Jane quipped, "What does that make me? A czarina?" The couple started a new life, he as commissioner, she as the wife and mother. Being the 110-percenter that he was, Rozelle put down the hammer as he unleashed a flurry of energy. He zoomed back to Los Angeles to wrap up his job as the

Rams' general manager while he took charge of league affairs. After a brief stay in Philadelphia to close up Bert Bell's old office, the new Rozelle wave roared into New York that spring, all four of them: Pete, Jane, Anne Marie, and Thelma Elkjer.

The family settled into a marvelous apartment at 16 Sutton Place, on the East Side, near the 59th Street Bridge. They lived there until Rozelle's second marriage, to Carrie, in 1974. Anne Marie Bratton retained fond but distant memories of the wonderful place in the great city, the first home she knew from childhood. Then, many years and several moves later, everything came back in a single reminder.

"Somebody e-mailed me and said, 'Is this anywhere near where you lived?' " she recalled. "I looked at it online. Not only was it near where I lived, it was the exact same building and exact same apartment, and it was for sale." The apartment was an 11-block walk across town to the new league offices in Rockefeller Center, even closer when headquarters relocated to 410 Park Avenue.

Being commissioner entailed day after day of early-morning wake-ups, arriving at the office at 7:00 A.M., and meetings with colleagues, phone calls, and lunches with television and advertising executives and other deal makers at restaurants or in the office. "He had terrible eating habits. It was amazing," Anne Marie said. "He loved a hamburger patty with chili on it and onion and cheese, or creamed chipped beef on a baked potato. If he had lunch at the office, it was *always* a baloney sandwich with mayonnaise on white bread and a vanilla milk shake. Always, always, always."

Almost from the time they arrived in New York in 1960, Jane Rozelle's disease dominated their personal existence. As is the case with so many other people in Jane's plight, the bottle, its contents, and pills came first in her life. "I have very few memories of her being at home," Anne Marie said. "She wasn't there. He totally raised me. He had to work the career and be a mother and father. Thelma certainly helped, I can give you that."

"Thelma was the secretary; she was the mother who took care of Anne; she did all the work that Pete really needed," Blair Sabol said. "I loved Thelma because I knew the placement of that character. That was a true guardian lion."

"He did an absolutely marvelous job of raising Anne Marie," said broadcaster Pat Summerall, a close friend of Rozelle's from his early days in New York. "There is no way you can adequately describe the hell he went through with Jane and how devoted he was to Anne and Thelma."

Pete Newell, Rozelle's early mentor at USF, had known Jane since she and Pete were newlyweds in San Francisco. Newell realized early that she could not handle liquor. "She was a nice gal, but she was an alcoholic," Newell said flatly. The situation only deteriorated in New York. The commissioner had to make excuses for her frequent absences at social events. He did not feel comfortable having visitors at the apartment.

"He tried to do everything he could to help his wife," Newell said. "It happened. It was a shame. He couldn't take her anywhere. She'd get drunk and do just about anything." Everything came to a head in 1963. She was hospitalized for a few days in January and again in June. She then suffered a major setback in September, forcing Rozelle to institutionalize her at an alcoholic treatment center. "He tried to get help, and it didn't work," Newell said. "It made it extremely hard for him."

Coach Newell made a trip to New York in his capacity as athletic director at California, and Rozelle invited him to a Giants game at Yankee Stadium with Joe Kuharich, then in the NFL office, and CBS Sports president Bill McPhail. Afterward, they planned to come home to dinner with Jane. "She cooked this big roast, and when we got back, she was bombed," Newell recalled wistfully. "She had dropped the roast about five times on the kitchen floor. Poor Pete was mortified. We were his friends, and he was so concerned about the bad impression. It was a terrible situation. She was just gone."

"I have to admit that whenever there were bad situations with my mother, the first thing I would do was run downstairs, get a cab, and go over to Thelma's apartment," Anne Marie said, as she invoked the memories of a little girl, five, six, or seven years of age, sadly experienced beyond her years. "Thelma was a savior. She was everything. I had it worked out where I would call her, the doorman would get me a cab, and she would be at the other end and pay for it."

Pete cleared his schedule as much as possible to be with Anne Marie and get her out of the apartment and, unfortunately, away from her mother. "He protected his little girl, Anne Marie," the late Peter Hadhazy recalled. "He probably was as good a father as anybody, considering the circumstances."

"Lacking a mother figure, Thelma was always there to do ballet, the museum, shopping for school clothes," Anne Marie recalled. "He did a lot of that as well, obviously, but she was there. On weekdays, a lot of times I would come over to the office after work or school. He went in on Saturdays most of the time, and I would go with him. On a lot of weekends, Thelma would take me shopping or to a museum, many things."

Hadhazy was still in high school when he started at the office. By 1962, he had enrolled at Iona, in New Rochelle, where he played on the tennis team. After sessions on the court, he put in time in the office to work on Jim Kensil's newspaper files. "I used to babysit for her on Saturdays in the office," Hadhazy recalled. "I had to keep her busy, so I'd tell her, 'Let's play hide-and-go-seek. And you go hide.' About an hour later, she'd say, 'You haven't found me.' She grew up to be such a terrific young lady. She is great."

"Dad was more than business," Anne Marie said. "He knew everyone's children's names, where they went to school, what their relationships were. He was at weddings, graduations, and funerals. You name it, he was there."

"I was home on leave from the Marine Corps in 1965, and I went over to see Annie and Jane at 16 Sutton Place because Pete was in Hawaii at a meeting," Peter Hadhazy said. "He called three or four times, talking to Annie and talking to Jane. He never forgot his priorities, as tough as they were. He never talked about it with anybody."

"He'd return to the apartment at the end of the day, and here would be Anne crying, and her mother was stumbling and falling-down drunk." Dick Rozelle said. "That's what it was."

The bottom fell out of Pete's relationship with Jane in a series of incidents in 1965, the year her father, Charles, died. (One can conjecture that his death triggered the outbursts at that time.) Two stand out. The first came when Jane threatened six-year-old Anne Marie and her teenage sitter with a knife. Then, a short time later, Thelma Elkjer took a phone call from Jane, who asked Pete to come to a midtown bar and take her home. He arrived to see Anne Marie seated at a bar stool next to her mother. "When she took Anne Marie with her to the bars for the afternoon, that was the turning point. He loved that girl," Pete Newell said.

"Pete wanted to do the best for Anne," brother Dick said. "He had to get her away from that. He was as tolerant as he could be, but he was fighting an enemy in her drinking that he could not defeat. He exhausted every possibility. Pete had a heart of gold."

"The media was good on that," Newell said. "They knew, but they treated him as well as anyone could ever expect, because they liked him so much. They had a story about her if they wanted to use it, but they never did."

Pete Rozelle filed for divorce and stayed in the Sutton Place apartment with Anne Marie while Jane moved into her own place. It was an extremely difficult time for Rozelle. He had to assume more and more of his parental obligation, even as the pressure of the pro football war and merger discussions intensified. He got home from the office most evenings as soon as possible, changed into a bathrobe, and dined with Anne Marie in front of the TV. After dinner, he helped her with homework as he engaged in his reading, which included newspapers, magazines, and books, especially novels.

As renowned as he was, his fame did not affect his daughter at school. "As the job grew, obviously his position grew," Anne Marie Bratton recalled. "I went to a Catholic girls' school. It wasn't quite as big a deal there as it might have been elsewhere."

As he watched over Anne Marie, the phone rang constantly in the evenings. As bustling as the office was when Rozelle was there, at home he was as busy as a captain on an aircraft carrier during night-flight operations, taking calls from his sea cabin on just about any imaginable issue or problem. Most of the calls came from people such as Bill McPhail, Jack Landry, and consigliere Jim Kensil. Rozelle and Kensil spoke as often as a dozen times a night. "Dad and Jim Kensil were bouncing ideas off each other and constantly working on NFL things together," Anne Marie recalled "When I was very young, I would say his best friends were Bill McPhail, Jack Landry, and Ed Sabol. As time went on, Ed Sabol moved away, and Dad met Ed's brother-in-law Herb Siegel, who came into the picture. Frank Gifford has always been there consistently from the beginning."

One of the highlights of her childhood was summertime at the Long Island beach house the Rozelles shared with McPhail and Pat Summerall. "Dad was very close to Pat Summerall," Anne Marie recalled. "We had nicknames for everyone at the beach house—Pat Summerbum, and Bill McFlunk."

Winter in New York was every bit a delight spending it with her father. "We all have memories of childhood," she said. "I remember going sleigh riding in Central Park. Snowball fights. Going to the horse show, the circus, hockey games."

Finally, in 1967, a New York court awarded Pete Rozelle custody of Anne Marie, who was then nine. "I think that drove a nail through Jane's heart," Pete's brother said. "She couldn't forgive Pete for that. Alcoholics rationalize. She took that as the final straw, and she ended up absolutely hating Pete. She didn't consider herself an unfit mother."

Pete became mother and father to Anne Marie and did his best to make sure that Daddy's girl got to experience his world and pal around with his notable friends, especially on Sundays in the fall. "He loved movies," Anne Marie recalled. "He had a lot of friends in show business, film and entertainment people: Johnny Carson, Bob Newhart, Jack Lemmon, Burt Bacharach. It was very James Bond-esque."

Yet, according to Anne Marie, Pete "James Bond" Rozelle was as much of a fan of his show business friends as they were fans of football. "It's funny," she said, "but even though he knew a lot of celebrities and would be with them a lot, he always looked up to them." One was "Tonight Show" host Johnny Carson. "He was a big football fan and was there on Sundays," she recalled. "Bob Newhart was one of his all-time-favorite comedians, a friend as well. There was never a time when Dad would fail to get a charge by listening to the Bob Newhart [*Button-Down Mind*] album—driving school, and all."

He took her wherever he went on football weekends, in New York and on the road. "In the very beginning, if you see pictures at games, only men were allowed in the press box," Anne Marie said. "They were not luxury seats as they are now. They were places with work being done, smoking, press people getting out stories. He was generally up there because that's where they had the TV and the news and the microphones and anything else going on. I would sit out in the stands. Most women wore matching coats and hats, and jackets, and skirts. It was cold. I don't remember any indoor stadiums at that point."

As Anne Marie got older, and especially after the merger, when his position became more secure, he spent more time in the stands with her and less time in the press box. "There would be a seat next to me in the stands, and he would run back up to the press box and see different people he had to talk to," she said.

"I never went with a babysitter. It was generally understood that there would be plenty of people I knew there, like owners' wives, or whoever," Anne Marie said. "It was like going to a huge family reunion and somebody would watch over me and take care of me. A few times, everyone thought somebody was taking care of me when nobody was, and I'd get badly sunburned. That was probably the worst thing that happened."

For Anne Marie, life with her father was Christmas, New Year's Eve, the Fourth of July, Halloween, and the Super Bowl rolled into what became a fabulous childhood. "It really was fun," she said. "Here, I lived in New York, and we'd go to Hawaii every year and Florida. It was a schedule, and everything worked. It was an incredible way to grow up."

By 1971, Jane realized she could not regain custody of Anne Marie. She moved as far away from New York as she could and still be in the continental United States—to San Clemente, California where her mother had lived since the senior Coupes moved west in the late '40s. As part of the separation agreement, she got Anne Marie for a month. They had to split Christmas. Anne Marie discussed the difficulty: "How do you split that? Do you wake up really, really early in the morning and do the first bit of Christmas with her, get on the airplane, and spend the last part of Christmas with him? She was very unstable in many different ways, so it was kind of scary going out there. When things were going great, they were great, but you were always waiting, even in great times, waiting for something bad to happen. There were rare times when she actually was good. She did teach me how to drive. She took me horseback riding and things like that. Miraculously, there were periods of normalcy, when things were good."

The final divorce decree ending the 24-year marriage of Jane and Pete Rozelle was issued in 1972. Their daughter was 13 years old. "I don't know a man of today who could pull that off with what's going on with kids and divorces," Blair Sabol said. "He really was magical on that front. Anne was the island in his life, this little girl, who turned out to be terrific. She looks like him. The kids look like him. He did what he had to do as a father. She must have been the woman in his life."

"He was a handsome, charismatic man that seemed to be capable of doing anything, was very well liked, and seemed just like James Bond," said a loving Anne Marie Rozelle Bratton of the father who did everything possible for her. "I can't think of anyone who was more likely to be cast in that role in real life. He was just so exciting, so invincible, so cutting edge, suave, debonair."

Jane Rozelle died on December 3, 2004, in San Clemente. She was 77. "Anne wrote me a note, and I wrote back to her expressing how sad it was for her mother's life," her uncle Dick said. "It was one of those chronic things."

SIXTEEN

WHO DO YOU TRUST? OR, LET'S MAKE A DEAL

"Rozelle adapted and ran that merger softly and smartly. Lamar Hunt was a player, too."

—KEITH JACKSON, 2005

*P*ro football, like so much else in 1964 America, seemed to be in limbo. The shockwaves from the John F. Kennedy assassination still reverberated throughout the land and shook the body politic. In a near manic election-year push, hard-nosed, clear-eyed president Lyndon Johnson picked up the pieces and cajoled his Democrat-dominated Congress to unblock the logjam that had stymied Kennedy's proposals and write them into law. LBJ also enacted a lot more of his own bills, getting everything he wanted.

In a tumultuous July convention in San Francisco, the Republicans rejected Eastern Establishment mainstay Nelson Rockefeller, governor of New York, and turned to the most different candidate they'd ever nominated, Arizona's conservative junior senator, Barry Goldwater. Goldwater sealed his fate when he declared in his acceptance speech that moderation was "no virtue" and extremism was "no vice." When Goldwater said he would arm field commanders with tactical nuclear weapons, the electorate rejected him in a landslide. The voters did that even as LBJ turned a minor incident involving a couple of small, armed North Vietnamese boats in the Gulf of Tonkin, that may have been provoked, into a virtual act of war and persuaded Congress to give him a virtual blank check to wage war on that Communist regime.

Major antidraft rallies had not started yet. They would begin a year later, when Vietnam no longer was a "volunteer" war, as would riots in several urban ghettos, most prominently in the Watts district of South Central Los Angeles, close by Lynwood and Compton, where Pete Rozelle came of age. Smokers, and a majority of college-age Americans and their elders were smokers, by and large still went for tobacco, not grass. People took pills to alleviate pain, not get high. That transformation would be full blown by late 1967 when draft-age citizens marched on the Pentagon to protest the war. And heavyweight champion Muhammad Ali, the former Cassius Clay, now a follower of Black Muslim leader Elijah Muhammad, declared, "I ain't got no quarrel with those Viet Congs."

Led by four guys whose hair fell over their ears and down to their collars, the all-white pop-music invasion from Great Britain had become a tidal wave. They were the Beatles, and everything they did turned to gold, as in records. The Fab Four caused a storm when they appeared on "The Ed Sullivan Show" in February. Two months later, the Great Stone Face played host to another young English group, named the Rolling Stones. The Stones, led by singer Mick Jagger and guitarist Keith Richards, took their name from Chicago blues legend Muddy Waters and their sound from other black musicians, especially the edgy Chuck Berry. Young men started wearing long hair, some growing moustaches. Athletes would not follow suit until the beginning of the next decade.

In pro basketball, the Boston Celtics were halfway through their run of 11 NBA championships in 13 years. Coach Johnny Wooden at UCLA took a team with no starter taller than 6'5" to the school's first NCAA title, as the players ran and zone-pressed their way to a 30–0 season, routing Duke 98–83 in the finals. As did Boston in the pros, Wooden and UCLA would become a dynasty, going on to win 10 collegiate championships over a dozen seasons.

In late September, the Philadelphia Phillies collapsed with a dozen games left in the season, losing 10 straight and blowing a 6-and-a-half-game lead to finish in a tie for second with the Cincinnati Reds behind the St. Louis Cardinals. The Cardinals kept rolling, beating the New York Yankees in the seventh game of the World Series to end that long dynasty. The Yankees, now owned by CBS, hit the skids. They would finish last in 1966 for the first time in their distinguished history and would not win another pennant until 1976.

The banished Alex Karras was reinstated in Detroit, as was his partner-in-suspension, Paul Hornung, in Green Bay. The Golden Boy was rusty after his year in exile and injured his right knee, and the Packers stumbled to an 8–5–1 tie for second with Minnesota in the Western Conference. The talk of the league was the 12–2 Baltimore Colts, led by their second-year coach, 35-year-old Don Shula, who kept out of Johnny Unitas's way in a blistering run to the title game at Cleveland. The Eastern Conference champion Browns took charge from the outset and shut out the heavily favored Colts 27–0 on a dank, overcast afternoon on the shores of Lake Erie.

In the American Football League, Jack Kemp led the Buffalo Bills to their first of back-to-back championship-game victories over the San Diego Chargers. Pete Rozelle was general manager of the Los Angeles Rams when Kemp graduated from nearby Occidental, but they didn't know each other. "I met Pete when I became president of the American Football League Players' Union in '64," Kemp said.

The most stunning news in the NFL came from off the field in the 1963–64 off-season when the New York Giants shipped longtime All-Pro middle linebacker Sam Huff to the Washington Redskins for two journeymen. "When I was traded, I lived in Flushing," Huff said. Returning home from a trip to Cleveland, Huff found a commotion on the street. "There were cars lined up with media in front of my house. Unbelievable. Even the ticker tape for Wall Street stopped when I was traded. Finally, after all of them left, there was a knock at my door. It was a chauffeur."

"Are you Sam Huff?" the chauffeur asked.

"Yes."

"I have Mr. Werblin in the car, and he wants to know if it's OK if he comes in to talk to you."

"Of course," Huff replied.

David "Sonny" Werblin, the Jets' owner, entered and talked with the now ex-Giants star. "You know something, Sam? They're playing right into my hands," Werblin said. "We're going to have a merger, and we're going to take this thing."

"I don't want to leave New York," a stunned Huff said. "Can I play for you?"

"No. That would stop the merger," Werblin said. "I can't break contracts. What are you doing tomorrow? I'm going to the racetrack, my wife and I. Why don't you come into Manhattan, and we'll go to Monmouth Park and talk more about this."

Huff agreed, and they went to the Monmouth Park racetrack, in New Jersey, where Huff sat in Werblin's box. "We will be friends," the Jets owner said. "I can't do what you'd like me to do for you. This is too big a deal. Go ahead and go to Washington, and play there. You will do well there."

"He was a friend of mine until the day he died," Huff said wistfully. Huff's wife did not want to uproot the kids and move. Frank Gifford didn't want Sam to go. Nevertheless, to Huff's credit, he made the move to Washington without regrets, and thrived there. Yet, to this day, he still looks back with fondness at his first great loves, the city of New York and the Giants. "Allie Sherman traded me for two guys he thought would help him, a defensive end and an offensive back: Dick James and Andy Stynchula. Stynchula was the first guy in history to play out his option with the Giants. Dickie James never amounted to a thing."

When the smoke cleared after the 1964 season, several conclusions were evident. After five seasons, which is the normal player-development time in football, the American Football League no longer was a minor league, if, indeed, it ever had been one. Most important, the AFL's existence forced rival league owners to spend more to stay ahead in attendance and TV ratings despite their advantages in marketing, with more large-city teams and the NFL's well-honed, Pete Rozelle–crafted image. "We fortunately had Milt Woodard, and [public relations director] Jack Horrigan, and of course, Al Davis, plus Lamar Hunt," said Ron Wolf, who served as

Davis's personnel director in Oakland. "The league survived because the people wanted to survive."

Now that the resourceful Werblin was calling the shots as owner of the New York Jets and had converted his long relationship with NBC into megabucks, his AFL could play hard in the arms-and-legs race. "It gave some of us who didn't have money a chance to compete with others," Wolf said. "Al did a fabulous job at that." The price to play was only going up.

Since 1960, one team had grabbed the spotlight: Vince Lombardi's Green Bay Packers. The others were not that far behind. As 1965 approached, Lombardi had everything in place to dominate as the Packers had done in 1961 and '62. Lombardi had trimmed older, worn-down players and replaced them, through either trades or smart drafting, with equally able and hungrier young players. He had stockpiled futures as they completed their college eligibility.

Another key, subtle change had evolved. This Packers team and the ones in coming seasons would rely more on Bart Starr's passing and savvy play-calling than it did in the early years. Yet, Lombardi would not depart from his tried-and-true superior ground game. Jim Taylor and the rejuvenated, 30-year-old Hornung, who had shaken off the rust that bogged him down in 1964, came to summer camp in top condition. That fall, 50,000 Packers season ticket holders would enter Lambeau Field for the first time.

That is not to say the other teams didn't have a chance. In the West, the Baltimore Colts were defending conference champions, and Shula still had Unitas at the top of his game. In Chicago, George Halas's defensive coordinator and personnel director, George Allen, stole the draft, grabbing Illinois's nasty linebacker, Dick Butkus, on the third choice after a trade with Pittsburgh, and Kansas's superbly elusive running back, Gale Sayers, on the next selection. Forced to make good on those selections, the tightfisted Halas had to pay more for each rookie than he'd ever paid for any single player in the long history of pro football's winningest franchise.

The intrigue, the cloak-and-dagger maneuvers behind Halas's signings of Butkus and Sayers and the ways other teams bagged their prime choices, was the true story of the draft. As the master manipulator of the intrigue, Halas was at the vortex of this spy drama and film noir, with a few O. Henry twists thrown in as well. He put team executives, scouts, and friends of the teams to work as "babysitters." Even before a player was drafted, he was pounced upon by one or two babysitters (premier stars required more help), taken to hideaways, and given a high-priced, third-degree pitch. Depending on the athlete—not with all, by any means—that pitch was fueled by booze, babes, and, when all else failed, cash. When the babysitter deemed the time was right, he brought his charge into the team office, where the top negotiator, usually an owner, closed the deal.

Butkus chose Chicago over the AFL—first Denver and then the Jets—because he was not sure about the money in the newer league, and he wanted to play in his hometown before his people for the team he had followed all his life. To play it safe, though, Butkus hired shrewd Chicago attorney Arthur Morse to negotiate with Halas. Morse squeezed more out of Halas than any other player had ever received: a solid, no-strings-attached, no-incentives $200,000 for five years. Once signed, Butkus returned to the Illinois campus, where he finished his courses and graduated on time at the May commencement.

Sayers chose Chicago and Halas for $100,000, spread over four years at $25,000 a season. Lamar Hunt and Kansas City offered Sayers slightly more, $27,500. Because he wanted to play against his hero Jim Brown, of Cleveland, Sayers chose the Bears instead of Hank Stram and the Chiefs.

In Butkus and Sayers, the Bears and the NFL landed young men who would become two of the game's most legendary figures, still ranked on the all-time lists as the best who ever played their positions. But neither won a championship.

That was reserved for the single biggest star of that draft, a gimpy-kneed, black-haired, sleepy-eyed, sassy, insolent, fun-loving pool shark of a party animal. His name was Joe Namath, of Beaver Falls, Pennsylvania, and the University of Alabama, a surefire major-league baseball prospect, a slick ball handler and excellent shooter on the basketball court, who on a football field was a natural athlete, born leader, and superb play caller with an impossibly quick release and deadeye accuracy at any distance. Desperate for a star for his league's sake and his battle with the NFL Giants in New York, Sonny Werblin, the superagent who knew a star when he saw one, was certain Namath had the show business flair to go with the ability. He traded the rights to Tulsa quarterback Jerry Rhome to Houston for the rights to Namath. All he had to do was sign him.

Namath couldn't say when he smoked his first cigarette or took his first drink, nonconditioning qualities that got him kicked off the 'Bama squad in 1963, his junior season. But Paul "Bear" Bryant, his coach, whose tastes included unfiltered Chesterfield regulars and bourbon to Namath's Salems and Johnnie Walker Red Label Scotch, didn't hesitate to bring him back in '64. Calling him the greatest athlete he ever coached, Bryant marveled at Namath's ability to visualize situations. "He would sit down and hear some football concept for the first time, and snap-snap, he'd have a mental picture of every phase of it," Bryant wrote.

Alabama was crowned national champions on November 30 after going unbeaten in the 1964 regular season. The Crimson Tide's opponent in the first Orange Bowl played at night would be number five Texas. Since the St. Louis Cardinals held Namath's rights, Werblin put on the heat to sign him. As Mark Kriegel wrote in *Namath*, the kid from Beaver Falls was no slouch when it came to cutting a business deal. "He wanted to set money aside, and he wanted to know about the tax implications of doing so," Kriegel wrote. "He was already thinking long term."

Namath and Werblin also suspected early in the bargaining game that the Cardinals were acting as silent spear-carriers for the Giants, who, they knew, desperately needed a quarterback to replace the soon-to-retire Y. A. Tittle. Only, Wellington Mara was not showing his hand, nor would he ever admit to wanting Namath. By December 30, two days before the bowl game in Miami, the deal finally reached the famous numbers, $427,000, if he hit the incentives. The Cardinals officially dropped out. Away in the shadows, the Giants also folded. For good measure, Werblin added a green Lincoln Continental like the one Namath originally demanded from the Cardinals just to talk.

The only hitch was Namath's right knee. It gave out as he executed a handoff in practice four days before the game. Ever the competitor, he wanted to play, but Coach Bryant did not want to jeopardize his future. So, Steve Sloane, also playing on a bad knee, got the start, and Texas opened up a 14–0 lead. With just under 10 minutes to go in the first half, Namath limped onto the field, with the ball at the Alabama 13, and started passing. Texas blitzed but couldn't get to him. His release was that quick, his accuracy that superb. All told that night, Namath went 18 for 37, for 255 yards and two touchdowns, and was stopped at the goal line short of the winning touchdown.

Alabama lost 21–17, but Namath, the AFL, the Jets, NBC, and Werblin came out the big winners. "He signed Joe under the goalposts after the game," said former NBC Sports executive Chet Simmons. "That was typical Werblin. He was a showman to the nth degree, and he knew he had to bring show business to the league to make them viable, make them more accessible, and make people more interested in them."

The next day, Namath and Werblin reenacted the signing before the media. "Sonny invited me personally to the press conference," said Simmons, himself an Alabama alum, class of '50. "I met him in the parking lot of the Diplomat in Miami Beach and walked into the hotel with Sonny and Joe. The press conference went on from there when he announced that signing. Joe was his first move. He knew he had a genuine star. The question was how he was going to get Joe to become the New York star. The best man in the world to do that at that point was Sonny Werblin, or, as Howard [Cosell] called him, 'Sonny, as in money, Werblin.' "

New York Daily News curmudgeon Dick Young, normally a naysayer on anything and everything, wrote such a glowing column that an outsider might have thought he was Namath's press agent. "I'm convinced the Jets aren't paying him enough. He's a steal at the alleged $400,000," Young wrote, adding that Werblin should throw in a Playboy Club membership because "Joe is said to have a wholesome interest in bunnies."

On January 25, 1965, Dr. James Nicholas cut into Namath's badly damaged right knee and did his best to repair it so the young man could continue his career. An hour and 13 minutes later, after he removed the medial meniscus, cut out a cyst, and tightened and sutured a damaged ligament, Dr. Nicholas pronounced the surgery as successful as it could be for someone who "has the knees of a 70-year-old man." The legend of Broadway Joe was under way.

The Buffalo Bills repeated their success in 1965, handcuffing San Diego 23–0 for the American Football League title. The NFL Eastern Conference turned out to be a cakewalk for the defending champion Cleveland Browns, who went 11–3. Two 7–7 teams going in opposite directions tied for second: the fast-rising, newly confident Dallas Cowboys and the fading New York Giants. The race in the NFL West went to the wire among Green Bay, Baltimore, and late-charging Chicago, which, after opening the season with 3 straight losses, went on a 9–1 tear behind rookie stars Sayers and Butkus. The Bears lost their finale, 24–17 to Minnesota, to end up at 9–5 as 70-year-old Halas was named Coach of the Year for the second time in three seasons.

Green Bay tied Baltimore on December 12 with a week left in the season. Hornung, who stayed out all Saturday night, stepped lively on Sunday as he scored five touchdowns in fog-shrouded Memorial Stadium to key a 42–27 Packers victory. That superb performance was overshadowed by Sayers's monumental effort that same afternoon in Chicago as the Bears routed the San Francisco 49ers 61–20 in the mud of rainy, windy Wrigley Field. On just 14 touches, the 22-year-old rookie gained 336 all-purpose yards that included 89 yards on two pass receptions for one touchdown, sandwiched around four scoring runs of varying distances among his nine carries for 109 yards, and 134 yards on three punt returns. His final punt return was for 85 yards for his sixth and final touchdown, tying the mark set years before by Ernie Nevers, of the Chicago Cardinals, and Dub Jones, of the Browns, in games played against the Bears.

Baltimore and Green Bay won the following week to finish 10–3–1 and set up a playoff for the right to meet the Browns. Playing at home, the Packers were heavy favorites against the Colts, who were down to their third quarterback. He was running back Tom Matte, the only man on the roster with experience at the game's glamour position. John Unitas had been sidelined with a season-ending knee injury on December 5 in a 13–0 loss to the Bears. His backup Gary

Cuozzo suffered a dislocated shoulder the next week in that afore-mentioned defeat against Green Bay.

In perhaps the most resourceful coaching job of his life, Don Shula literally worked night and day with Matte, tutoring him in a crash course in pro quarterbacking. It helped somewhat that Matte had played under center at Ohio State, but Woody Hayes's quarterbacks ran when they didn't hand off, and they seldom threw. Aware that Matte had never dropped back into a pocket to throw a pass, Shula drilled him on a short list to play to his ability. The list included a couple of rollout passes to keep the defense honest. Shula wrote the plays on a plastic wristband Matte would wear in the games, now on display in the Pro Football Hall of Fame.

Matte previously led the Colts to a 20–17 victory over the Rams in the Coliseum to set up the December 26 playoff and now had the Colts holding on to a 10–7 lead late in the fourth quarter at Lambeau Field, in Green Bay. With 1:58 left in regulation, Don Chandler came in for a 22-yard field goal with Starr holding. On a still-disputed play, Chandler's kick went up and sailed either over the right upright or just outside it.

Was that kick good? "Bart said it was," Bill Curry, Green Bay's center that day, recalled. "I was at the bottom of the pile, with everyone on top of me. With a rookie snapper, you know they knocked the stuffing out of me. Don Chandler, who was good about keeping his head down, looked up. When he did, the ball was definitely outside the uprights. What caused the uproar was he kicked the ground, like he missed."

"When Chandler kicked the ground, by his actions, he knew he had missed it," said Baltimore coach Don Shula. "That's when the goalposts were only half as high as they are now."

"Bart said it was clearly over the upright, and in those days, it was always good," Curry said. "The official was standing underneath the posts."

"One official would stand in the middle under the goalposts and move from side to side, depending on where the ball was kicked," said Shula, for years an influential member of the NFL Competition Committee. "After that, they stationed two officials there, one under each upright, so they didn't have to move and they'd have a better position to see whether the ball was in or out."

"Don said it was no good. Bart said it was. I've always trusted Bart," Curry asserted.

"After that, they doubled the length [of the uprights]," Shula said. "So, I think a few people think that call was blown. If Curry thinks it's right, a few people think otherwise. All I can say is, why did they change everything? They call those the Baltimore extensions."

The controversial field goal tied the game at 10–10. At 13:39 of overtime, Chandler drilled a 25-yard field goal down the middle for the 13–10 victory to put the Packers in the championship game for the first time in three seasons, against the defending champion Cleveland Browns, again at Lambeau Field, on January 2, 1966. It was the first time the league would play its title game in the next calendar year, and it happened in Green Bay, not Baltimore.

"A few years later," Curry said, "I showed up in Baltimore, and Tom Matte, my new teammate, walked up and said, 'You've got my ring on.' I showed him my ring and said, 'Well, let's look at it and see what it says here. Is your name C-U-R-R-Y?' We've laughed about that for 40 years."

Pete Rozelle had experienced half-decent weather in just one title game, his first, in Philadelphia in 1960, before three straight bone-numbing contests in zero-degree-windchill cold. Then came the gloomy 1964 championship staged in the dank overcast of Cleveland Municipal Stadium. This time, in Green Bay, the weather changed three times before kickoff. No sooner did the Lambeau Field grounds crew shovel off a four-inch overnight snowfall than the temperature rose to 33 degrees, and it started sleeting. Then, as the two teams lined up for the kickoff, freezing rain began to fall.

Within a few first-quarter plays, the field became a sea of mud and goo, nullifying the power and breakaway speed of Jim Brown. The weather favored the Packers' power game. Jim Taylor crunched out 96 yards, and Hornung, playing on gimpy knees, gained 105 more yards and scored the clinching touchdown on a 13-yard power sweep to his left as Green Bay won Lombardi's third title in five years, 23–12.

After another winter's heavy spending on untried rookies, it became obvious to the owners in both leagues that something had to be done. AFL founder and Kansas City Chiefs owner Lamar Hunt met Rozelle almost in passing a couple of years before. Neither Rozelle nor his NFL owners had any reason then to sit down and talk. "They had an established product and were not in favor of competition at that point," Hunt recalled.

But a growing number of people in his league were ready to end the arms race. "Going all the way back to the start of the league, there were people who felt the leagues should get together," Hunt said in a 2006 interview. "There were friends on both sides." As Jeff Miller reported in *Going Long*, Buffalo's Ralph Wilson had as many as eight meetings in South Florida at the winter home of Baltimore owner Carroll Rosenbloom.

"Some of them had experienced the idea of the competition between the old All-America Football Conference and the NFL years before," Hunt said. "People had friends who thought there might be a solution."

That was 1965, but, as Miller noted, the NFL wanted the AFL to pay to get in. Wilson had another Florida meeting—with Rozelle and the Cowboys' powerful president, the late Tex Schramm—which ended abruptly when Wilson asked the NFL commissioner to name a price, and Rozelle said, "$50 million." Wilson told him to forget it. The AFL owners who were dead set against a merger and wanted to fight were Werblin, of New York, who knew it was coming but didn't want it, and Oakland's Wayne Valley, who had the absolute backing of his coach, Al Davis.

By 1966, the prices for bonuses and salaries had escalated sharply. Up in Green Bay, Vince Lombardi cashed in a parlay. He signed his number one future from the year before, halfback and left-footed punter Donny Anderson, of Texas Tech. Before the 1966 draft, Lombardi came to terms with Illinois fullback Jim Grabowski and his agent, the same Arthur Morse who represented Dick Butkus the year before when he signed with George Halas and the Bears. "What I didn't realize was that Green Bay had a lot of cash, because when they were founded and formed a corporation, there were no dividends,"

Portrait used for *Sports Illustrated*'s 1963 Sportsman of the Year cover.

The once and future commish: already all business.
COURTESY: DICK ROZELLE

(L–R) Dick, mother Hazel Rozelle, and Pete at home, 3205 Lynwood Road, Lynwood, California.
COURTESY: DICK ROZELLE

Pete, age 14, wore number 8 on Lynwood's eighth-grade basketball team, 1940.
COURTESY: DICK ROZELLE

(L–R) Dick, Pete the sailor, Hazel, and Ray Rozelle. Home from the Navy for a short visit, 1944.
COURTESY: DICK ROZELLE

(L–R) Dick, Hazel, Pete, and Ray Rozelle in front of their new home in Lynwood, 1950s.
COURTESY: DICK ROZELLE

A rare tranquil moment with Jane and daughter Anne Marie, New York, 1962.

Rozelle returns home from the Melbourne Olympics, December 1956, soon to become general manager of the Los Angeles Rams.

The new commissioner on his first day on the job, January 26, 1960.

(L–R) Philadelphia Eagles General Manager Vince McNally, Rozelle, and New York Giants co-owner Wellington Mara. Mara doesn't seem to like the result of Rozelle's coin toss.
UPI Photo, December 14, 1961, Chicago

(L–R) Bill McPhail, Rozelle, Susan Reeves, Jack Landry, and Pat Summerall, New York, 1963.

Rozelle with Chiefs owner Lamar Hunt and House Majority Leader Hale Boggs (D-LA), who, with Senator Russell Long (D-LA), delivered votes in Congress for the merger approval and received the Saints franchise for New Orleans in return, 1966.

Bill McPhail (CBS Sports) and Rozelle announce the 1962 deal with the NFL. Note the black-and-white TV set with "rabbit ears."

(L–R) Mayor Ivan Allen of Atlanta; Carl Sanders, governor of the state of Georgia; Rozelle; and Falcons owner Rankin Smith at the opening game for the Atlanta Falcons, Fulton County Stadium, September 11, 1966.

With Jim Kensil behind him, Rozelle presents the first Super Bowl trophy to Vince Lombardi after the Green Bay Packers beat the Kansas City Chiefs 35–10, January 15, 1967.

New York Jets owner Phil Iselin, Rozelle, Toots Shor, and NBA Commissioner Walter Kennedy, circa 1970.

Rozelle with *New York Times* football writer William N. Wallace before the Jets beat the Colts 16–7 in Super Bowl III, Miami, 1969.

(L–R) Chiefs General Manager John Steadman, Rozelle, Frank Gifford, and Lamar Hunt prior to Super Bowl IV, Tulane Stadium, New Orleans, January 11, 1970.

Rozelle presents the Vince Lombardi Trophy to Oakland Raiders owner Al Davis, as head coach Tom Flores and NBC reporter Bryant Gumbel watch, in the locker room at the Louisiana Superdome following Super Bowl XV, where the Raiders defeated the Philadelphia Eagles 27–10 on January 25, 1981.

Captain Rozelle at the helm of the *Triple Eagle*, 1970s.

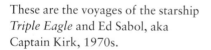

These are the voyages of the starship *Triple Eagle* and Ed Sabol, aka Captain Kirk, 1970s.

Rozelle and Tex Schramm relax on the fantail of the *Triple Eagle*, 1975.

(L–R) Three pals:
Rozelle, Herb Siegel,
and John DeLorean,
mid-'70s.
PHOTO BY HAROLD
MECHLER

(L–R) Karen Lerner,
Rozelle, and Pierre
Salinger, circa 1982.

(L–R) Gene and Joyce Klein (San Diego Chargers), Carrie and Pete
Rozelle, and Patty and Art Modell (Cleveland Browns), at Rancho
Santa Fe, California, 1981.

(L–R) Bebe Rebozo, Rozelle, and President Richard Nixon, circa 1972, when Rozelle took an unexpected trip to Key Biscayne, Florida, after a visit to the White House.

(L–R) Congressman Jack Kemp (R-NY), Joanne Kemp, President George H. W. Bush, and Rozelle.

(L–R) Rozelle, Chicago Bears owner and NFL founder George Halas, and league attorney Paul Tagliabue testify before a U.S. Senate committee in 1982.

Rozelle congratulates NFL attorney Frank Rothman outside the federal courthouse in New York after the NFL victory in the USFL antitrust trial, July 29, 1986.

Future Hall of Famer Walter Payton, wearing the "ROZELLE" headband made famous by Chicago Bears teammate Jim McMahon, with a delighted commissioner who loved the publicity it generated during the week of Super Bowl XX, New Orleans, January 1986.

Pete and Carrie Rozelle, the "beautiful couple," at Wimbledon, circa 1980.

Rozelle delivers his Hall of Fame acceptance speech, Canton, Ohio, August 3, 1985. Roger Staubach is sitting to the left of the commissioner.
Photo by David F. Austin

The Brattons in front of a mural portrait of the commissioner: (L–R) Doug, Miles, Anne Marie, and Alexandra.

The major commissioners with Anne Marie Bratton at the sporting luncheon for Sportsman of the Century, December 14, 1999: (L–R) Paul Tagliabue (National Football League), David Stern (National Basketball Association), Anne Marie, Gary Bettman (National Hockey League), and Bud Selig (Major League Baseball).

Schramm told Jeff Miller. Green Bay, by its charter, had to reinvest its profits in the team. Schramm reasoned, "If that can happen to us, it can happen to anyone."

Things got moving at the start of April. "I was in Kansas City when Tex called," Hunt said in our interview. "He said he had something that might be important to discuss and asked when I might be available. Of course, I lived in Dallas, not very far from where Tex lived at that time. I told him I was on my way to Houston the next day for an AFL meeting and I would be happy to stop off at Dallas's Love Field to see him. He seemed to have an urgency about him.

"I met Tex the next day at the Texas Ranger statue out at Love Field," Hunt said. "We sat in Tex's car and talked about the general concept. Tex felt the climate was right, and he wanted to see if I felt there would be interest. We didn't get into a lot of details. I said we would be interested in hearing the ideas. He said he would be back to me in a few weeks, and indeed, that's where it got started."

Joe Foss could read the tea leaves. Dead set against any merger, but aware that several of his owners wanted it, that Hunt was listening, and that only Valley and Werblin were in his camp, Foss had no choice. "We needed more of a hands-on person," Hunt said. "It was at the meeting in Houston a day or so later that Joe Foss resigned and Al Davis was named commissioner."

"Al didn't campaign for the job as commissioner," Ron Wolf said. "It took three ballots. And he got it." If any AFL owners did not know this was no Mr. Nice Guy they had chosen, Davis set them straight. Taking charge, he moved the league offices to New York to go head-to-head with Rozelle and the NFL. Next, he brought aboard Wolf, his young personnel wizard, as talent coordinator for the league and New York Giants Hall of Fame center Mel Hein as supervisor of officials. Then, he hired three skilled publicity agents: Mickey Herskowitz, of the *Houston Post*; Val Pinchbeck, from Syracuse University; and Irv Kaze, from the California Angels. He wanted to sign as many top NFL stars as he legally could.

"When Davis came in, Rozelle was itching for a fight," said Don Weiss's collaboraor, Chuck Day, who had Weiss's files concerning all facets of his long working relationship with the NFL. "Word on the street was the AFL could not keep going even though they had the TV contract with NBC. The NFL felt they could outlast them and pick up the pieces and expand on their own." But Rozelle did not stand in the way of Schramm's approaches to Hunt concerning a merger.

"I was not involved with Pete. All my conversations were with Schramm," Lamar Hunt told me. "There was a point where we got on the phone with Pete. Tex authenticated the process; he said it was something that he and Pete devised."

"Pete told me pretty early that there was merger talk," said Pittsburgh Steelers owner Dan Rooney. " 'We gotta look at it,' Pete said. 'Some of our teams are in trouble. Now, don't say anything to anybody.' He knew I wouldn't. I don't think the AFL would have made it, because some of their teams were in serious financial trouble."

"I outlined it," Schramm said. "It involved the moving of teams—the Jets to Memphis and the Raiders to Portland." Well aware that Werblin and Valley would balk at any such talk, Schramm had placed himself and Hunt in the forefront of any merger talks and movement.

"I didn't inform our people at that point because it was all so vague," Hunt said. "But, some four or five weeks later, there was another meeting with Tex, where he actually read from a prepared sheet of paper, and I took notes. At that point, I felt it was appropriate to talk to the AFL people."

The merger talks were moving toward a resolution. "I was interested in the best interests of the league," Hunt said. "What they presented had merit, and we moved right along. People were tired of spending money. These are supposed to be businesses, and they were at that time also. That was a prime consideration."

"Davis didn't get involved in the negotiations at all. He didn't even know they were going on," longtime Bay Area football writer Glenn Dickey said. "His idea was they were going to win. That's always been his philosophy. He was going forward with his plan to sign NFL stars. Meanwhile, Lamar Hunt was meeting with Tex Schramm, working out the deal."

While the deal makers toiled in Dallas, the New York Giants wooed a placekicker from the other league. Cornell-educated Buffalo

Bills soccer-style placekicker Pete Gogolak, whose family fled to America from Hungary in 1956, played out his option in 1965 after making just $9,900 for the AFL champions. Gogolak's agent, Fred Corcoran, was a fellow member at Winged Foot Golf Club, in Westchester County, with Giants owner Wellington Mara. When Gogolak became a free agent on May 1, Corcoran told his friend Mara that his client was available. Later that month, they worked out a four-year deal at $35,000 a year, and the walls nearly came crumbling down when Mara announced the signing at the NFL spring meeting in Washington, D.C.

"To Al Davis, just named [AFL] commissioner, that was like a punch in the nose," Ron Wolf recalled. "I was in the process of moving my family from Oakland back to New York City. I got on the airplane and opened up the *San Francisco Chronicle*, and there it was in headlines that morning: 'Giants Sign Pete Gogolak.' Oh, my God, I thought. Do these guys know just what they did? That was a declaration right there, and out of that came the merger."

"The [NFL] owners could see the handwriting on the wall, and they said this was holy hell," Chuck Day recalled. The owners knew that Schramm and Hunt were moving toward a deal and recessed the meeting, but Rozelle was not dismayed by Mara's announcement. At that point, Rozelle let it be known that he was not in favor of a merger. Schramm huddled with several owners and then met with Rozelle at a hotel in D.C.

"The majority of the owners in the league want to merge," Schramm told him. "We are going to merge, and we want you, Pete, to lead the merger." Then Schramm drew the line in the sand: "If you don't want the merger, we're going on without you."

"Schramm recounted all this in a letter to Weiss," Chuck Day said. "Don had a copy of the letter, and we used it in our book [*The Making of the Super Bowl*]. Pete said he had to excuse himself to the men's room and let loose. Then he came back and said, 'OK. Let's go.' At that point, Rozelle got involved, and a few weeks later, the merger was announced. I think that's significant."

Art Modell agreed that Rozelle was not enthusiastic about the merger, but he liked his job. "He did not like the idea of surrendering, or at least a perceived surrender, to the American Football League," the Browns' owner said. "The day the Giants signed Gogolak was the shots fired at Fort Sumter."

"It was at that point that people in our league felt they had been misleading us," Hunt said. "When the Giants signed Gogolak, that almost caused the thing to fall apart in the days of late May and early June. We held it together. At that point, Al Davis initiated his plan. Of course, he didn't want the merger. He wanted a war. If there was a merger, he was a general without a war to fight."

So, Davis focused his attention on the biggest stars on any team, the quarterbacks. All they had to do was play out their NFL options and they were fair game. "He caused it because he evolved that strategy of going after the quarterbacks," said Glenn Dickey. "That became very costly to keep the quarterbacks."

"I believe that Al's strategy of signing NFL quarterbacks was kind of a nuclear time bomb," Jack Kemp said. And those were the shots that would end the war.

"It made a lot of sense," Ron Wolf said. "It was a matter of finding out who would become free agents, and you went to talk to them. A lot of guys went over and came back."

"That was a hopeless situation that would have ended up in total chaos," Modell said. "Hell, they went after some of my players, my quarterback Ninowski." Using the NBC money as lucrative bait, Davis got such players as Rams quarterback Roman Gabriel, Bears tight end Mike Ditka, and 49ers quarterback John Brodie, all of whom were playing out their options and would be free agents in 1967, to sign with the AFL. John David Crow, of the Cardinals, agreed to terms. All would be making six-figure salaries.

The Brodie go-round was like so many other deals in that time, much of it smoke and mirrors. This time, the deal benefited one man, John Brodie. Houston owner K. S. "Bud" Adams wanted the 49ers star in the worst way. He already had signed Ditka to the Oilers and given him a $50,000 bonus check. Then came his move on Brodie, who traveled to Houston with his agent, Kenny Marx, after Oilers general manager Don Klosterman told him the team was prepared to pay him so well that he'd never have to worry again about anything, let alone go to work.

Brodie, Marx, Klosterman, and Adams met in a hotel room, where Adams offered the then unprecedented sum of $500,000 over three years, more than the Namath contract. While Brodie nearly swooned at the offer, Marx calmly raised it to a million. After some haggling, the two sides orally agreed to $750,000. Then they went to dinner.

"Brodie and his agent were talking to Adams at dinner in some restaurant," Glenn Dickey recalled. "Adams didn't have any paper, and he wrote the offer on a napkin. Brodie put it in his pants pocket, went home, and sent out the pants to the cleaners. He lost it. He had no record of it. But Marx, his agent, bluffed Adams, and they had to pay him." By then, other AFL owners were making frantic calls to Adams telling him that the Brodie deal would ruin the now serious merger talks in Dallas between Hunt and Schramm and the interested third party, Pete Rozelle.

Roman Gabriel went to the Rams' offices in Los Angeles to meet with new coach George Allen to explain the Oakland Raiders' offer of $100,000 a year and a $100,000 bonus check, one the Rams could not meet. Allen had gained plenty of recent experience with contracts and their meaning when George Halas took him to court after Allen, his protégé, tired of waiting for Papa Bear to retire, jumped ship, and signed on with the Rams. Now Allen listened to Gabriel, who told him he had been sitting on the $100,000 bonus check for weeks. "Don't cash it," Allen pleaded, telling Gabriel he would get owner Dan Reeves to raise his salary from $22,500 to $32,000 and would have a $100,000 retirement clause inserted into his contract. Gabriel accepted and stayed.

As far as Brodie was concerned, "The 49ers got him back, but they had to pay him half of what Houston agreed to as a bonus," Glenn Dickey said. Details of all those transactions had to be placed in side letters to the forthcoming merger.

Everything moved quickly after Memorial Day. At a Washington meeting, final details were worked out that included the AFL's paying a $20 million indemnity to the NFL, as well as the franchise shifts of the Jets to Memphis and the Raiders to Portland. Then Wellington Mara, who, along with the 49ers had never favored a merger, stood up. "We're going to get sued. It's going to be a terrible mess," he said.

"So, everybody started thinking, and we gave the Giants $10 million and the 49ers $8 million," Schramm said. And the Jets and Raiders remained in place. Thanks to their New York location, the Giants were a league anchor. Three thousand miles across the continent in San Francisco, the 49ers had to scrape by. The founding Morabito family had little money. They owned a lumberyard and put all their trust in longtime employee Lou Spadia, who started with the club in 1946 and functioned as a one-man front office in the early days. "Spadia was hired out of the navy, and he did everything," Glenn Dickey said. "He was selling tickets, putting out press releases. It was not a big-money operation until Eddie DeBartolo bought the team. They were trying to keep expenses down, and that's why the Brodie thing was such a blow to them. They didn't have the type of money to fund that. Lou was worried about the competition from the Raiders, and that's why he got that concession in the merger to get some money."

The announcement came on June 8 at the Warwick Hotel in New York. Al Davis, who had been kept out of the loop, had no idea it was coming. "We didn't know. We didn't know," Ron Wolf said. "Al was in Oakland, and we were up there on Madison Avenue, south of Grand Central." He added, "We weren't there very long."

"Of course, there was no history of this, but I must say that the NFL was more cognizant of the legal aspects of it, and they crafted their side of it to make sure it would meet the legal tests of antitrust," Lamar Hunt said. "The AFL didn't have quite those concerns there. We were more interested in the economics and the conditions that it would take to make it work."

To make it work, the first term of the joint statement of the National and American Football Leagues concerned Rozelle. He would be commissioner. "That was the proposal from the NFL side," Hunt said. "I felt that it was reasonable, and I recommended it to the AFL heads. The AFL had nine teams at that point. That was one of the conditions. The majority felt that Pete as commissioner was the logical thing to happen."

Hunt, ever the practical man, explained, "I thought that Rozelle had excellent public relations sense. Nobody is perfect, but he certainly had led the NFL forward as a young man. He had been in the job only five and a half years himself. We felt he had leadership qualities, and it was obvious to us that under this consolidation structure we could not have two commissioners. Again, it followed the baseball pattern of one commissioner.

"The two leagues would play a championship game that year," Hunt said of a game that would be known as the Super Bowl by 1969, its fourth year. It was to be called the AFL-NFL championship. That was what the public wanted. That was what the media wanted. That was the most newsworthy. Second, there would be a common draft after the season was over."

The merger would evolve over the next three and a half years. That would allow current television contracts to expire and give time to properly set up everything. The new league would retain all existing franchises without movement. The league would add two franchises by 1968 to balance the league and augment the new NFL Atlanta Falcons and AFL Miami Dolphins that started in 1965. Interleague preseason play would begin in 1967. A single schedule would start in 1970 with interleague play. Two-network television coverage, on CBS and NBC, would continue. "That was a key consideration. Because we could not make a unilateral deal the networks would find acceptable, we agreed to operate as separate leagues for the duration of the TV contract," Hunt said. "That was why the first Super Bowl was televised by two networks."

"I knew it was going to be the salvation of the league and was going to save my franchise," Modell said. "I had everything tied up in the Cleveland Browns, and then some. In order to stay alive and do business, we had to have peace."

"They announced it, and Davis was stunned by it," Dickey said. "Then Davis thought he could be commissioner of the combined league, and Wayne Valley told him, 'You won't even get the votes of the owners in this [AFL] league.'"

"Of course, Pete and Al just could not get along, and I liked them both," Jack Kemp said. "Al didn't like it because I was a friend of Pete's."

"So, he came back to the Raiders," Dickey said. "He didn't have anything in the club at the time the deal was made. Valley brought him back. Valley wanted him to coach, but Davis didn't want to coach anymore—too physical, and things go wrong."

"Al had the opportunity to go back to Oakland, and he took me back with him," Wolf said. "We got back there after training camp."

"He came back as general manager and managing general partner, and Valley allowed him to buy 10 percent of the club," Dickey said. "At that time [1966], the book value of the club was $185,000. So, he bought 10 percent of the Raiders for $18,500."

While Al Davis picked up the pieces of his brief term as commissioner and went back to Oakland with a check from the league to fulfill his five-year contract, Pete Rozelle had to return to Washington to get the merger through Congress with some kind of antitrust protection. Powerful Brooklyn congressman Emanuel Celler had worked with the young commissioner to gain the antitrust exemption that paved the way for the revenue-sharing TV contract of 1962. "Naturally, Rozelle went back to Celler and said, 'I need your help again,' " Chuck Day said. "When Rozelle made that request, Celler said, 'Drop dead. I'm not doing it.' "

That's when Rozelle made a smooth and almost seamless transition to rival any move Fred Astaire ever pulled on a dance floor. "That thing was dead on arrival," Day recalled. "Rozelle kept working behind the scenes. It was becoming public the thing was in trouble. They had public hearings, and Rozelle was very smooth, never got hot, nothing. He was still a young guy."

"He explained it to members of Congress," Jack Kemp said. "His understanding of the legislation and its antitrust roots, and his integrity, gave him communications skills that were very sincere. He wasn't a phony. He believed and understood what he was promoting."

"Somehow, Senator Russell Long, of Louisiana, and Senator Everett McKinley Dirksen, of Illinois, found their opening in an investment tax credit bill that LBJ said pass or else. They attached a provision involving four preseason games for charity." The charity games involved were the College All-Star Game and the Armed Forces Game, both in Chicago; the Midwest Shrine Game, in Green Bay; and *Los Angeles Times* Charity Game, in L.A.

"They passed the merger as a rider," Day said. "One version had already passed the House. A different version had passed the Senate. It was now in conference committee for the differences to be reconciled."

The trick in the conference meeting was getting around Representative Celler's roadblock. "Celler knew that by keeping the legislation bottled up, the leagues would have held their separate drafts around Thanksgiving, the merger would be off, and he would have won," Day said. "Somehow, Rozelle was able to work the Senate side of Capitol Hill to get it through. It was so masterful that Celler had to acknowledge the political artistry." Rozelle did it by promising Senator Long that New Orleans would land the next NFL expansion team, which in 1967 became the Saints.

"They caught me bathing and stole my clothes," said the outwitted Celler. That paved the way for the merger.

"The ultimate beneficiary of the merger was a more prosperous game, not only for the owners, but for the players and the fans," Kemp said.

"I think the fans of America were the winners," Lamar Hunt said. "The merger was the first step in building a great sport. Out of that grew the Super Bowl, "Monday Night Football," and all that's gone with it. The greatest sports league in the world came out of it. It has turned out well for the investors in the teams."

"We did not breathe a sigh of relief," Pittsburgh's Dan Rooney said. "We were still at war after the merger." The merger was a year old, and the combined leagues had 25 teams, 16 in the NFL with the newly minted Saints, and 9 in the AFL, when Paul Brown came forward in 1967 to apply for a franchise. Out of football since Art Modell sacked him in 1962, the founder and namesake of the Cleveland franchise had grown tired of playing golf and gazing at the beauty of Pacific sunsets at his La Jolla, California, home. He was ready, refreshed, and prepared to battle.

"We were awarded the franchise in September 1967 to play in '68," Mike Brown said. "I think Pete looked favorably on my father. I think he respected my father." Rozelle wanted Paul Brown to establish a franchise in Seattle, but Brown, first and always a dedicated Ohioan, was bound and determined to get a franchise for Cincinnati at the other end of the state from Cleveland. "It was a two-pronged effort on our part: a stadium effort and a franchise effort," Mike Brown said. "We played at Nippert Stadium in '68 and '69. The first year in Riverfront Stadium was 1970, two years after we started."

The deal almost hit a snag when Brown balked at joining the American Football League. "Father thought of himself as an NFL guy because he got into the league from the old All-America Football Conference," Mike Brown said. "By 1967, we were thinking of ourselves as NFL people."

Paul Brown's resistance came to a head at a meeting in New York. "Pete came up to my father's hotel room," Mike Brown said. " 'Paul,' Pete said, 'you've got to make the commitment to go forward with this, or we're going to have to withdraw the franchise from you and give it to somebody else.'

"Pete left, and I leaned on my father as hard as I could to accept it," Mike Brown said. "It was one of those times when you give in, one of those times when people's faces are flushed and things like that. It was hard for him to swallow that, but he did."

Then came the touchy matter of league realignment that transpired at a league meeting at the Waldorf Astoria, in New York, in 1969, to cross the t's and dot the i's of the merger, now a year away. "Rozelle called in Booz, Allen, and Hamilton, a blue-ribbon outside group, to provide consulting help with the merger," Day said. "That's the way Pete Rozelle was, first class all the way." The first item agenda, pushed by Senator Hiram Fong, of Hawaii, was perhaps the easiest issue ever agreed upon by the owners. Moving the league's winter meeting and Pro Bowl to Honolulu passed with virtually no discussion. Then came the fight.

"The merger proposal was to keep the leagues separate," Day said. "Originally, the suggestion was to keep the NFL as a 16-team league, with the AFL 10. Any planned expansion would come through the AFL side of the new umbrella organization."

"We were arguing to keep the two leagues the same," said Pittsburgh's Dan Rooney. "It would have been 16–10. The AFL, rightly so, would not go for that. 'We can't be a second-class conference or league,' they said."

Paul Brown led the AFL in its opposition. "We maintained that the league should be evenly balanced and that our franchise agreement represented that it would be," Mike Brown said.

Next, according to Don Weiss's meeting notes, Brown took the floor, spoke for most of the AFL, Al Davis not included, and turned the meeting around. "I agreed to come back into the National Football League, and that's where I'm going to play," Brown declared adamantly. Other AFL owners agreed that this was not the merger they had been led to believe.

"Edward Bennett Williams [Redskins' owner] told the group, the AFL guys and NFL guys, that indeed was what the franchise agreement said and that any court would hold for us against the league," Mike Brown said.

Thus, "16–10" was scrapped, and Rozelle had to find a solution. One of them involved three NFL teams agreeing to go into the AFL and be indemnified at $3 million each. "There was some concern about which three teams would move from the NFL to the AFL to form the AFC to balance the league," said *Detroit News* pro football writer Jerry Green, who covered the meeting. "I asked Pete one day there, 'What about the Lions? Could they be one of the teams that go?' He looked me and said, 'This is not for attribution, but the Ford Motor Company sponsors our telecasts. In other words, you can safely write that the Detroit Lions will not be one of the teams that move to the new AFC.'"

The three that eventually agreed to go were Baltimore, Cleveland, and Pittsburgh. As much as anyone, the chief engineer in that maneuver was Cleveland's Art Modell. "I went to dinner with Pete, [Atlanta owner] Rankin Smith, and Tex Schramm," Modell said. "When we got settled, I said, 'I have an announcement: the Browns are moving to the American Football Conference.' They didn't believe me. Sure enough, I did."

Modell took ill and was hospitalized at Doctor's Hospital in New York with intestinal bleeding. He asked the Rooneys and Wellington Mara to come to his room, where he told them his plans. "I have an obligation to each of you. I want your blessings, or tell me not to do it: I want to move the Browns to the American Football Conference to give that league parity of teams," Modell told them.

"So, I said to Art Rooney and his son, Dan, who now runs the Pittsburgh Steelers, 'Art, can I make the move and have you come along with me, so I would not leave you alone?' We were his meal ticket, with our rivalry, with crowds in Pittsburgh and Cleveland."

According to Modell, the senior Rooney chomped on his cigar, and before he could answer, Dan said, "The Pittsburgh Steelers will never, never move into the American Football Conference. End of discussion. We're not moving."

"The old man chomped on his cigar again," Modell said, a smile in his voice as he recalled the words of the beloved Art Rooney.

"Son," the elder Rooney said, "you can stay where you are, because I'm moving with Art Modell."

Dan Rooney acknowledges that he was "extremely adamant" about his resistance to moving, but he denies that his father made such a threat. "That's not true. People love to say that. That is definitely not true," Dan Rooney said. "I was definitely pushing that we not go. My father was very strong that we should go, but he *never* said, 'I am going without you.' He never said that. That was a fun story. That did not happen, but what did occur, my father, Well Mara, and I went out to dinner.

"When we came back from dinner, we went to Pete's office," Dan Rooney recalled. "He handed me a piece of paper that was an inch by two inches. What was written on there was 'Cleveland, Cincinnati, Houston, and Pittsburgh.' I looked at it, and my father said, 'What's that?' I handed it to him. 'That's your new division,' Pete said." Once they did that, I knew it was all over. We agreed to go, and it was and has been a great division. Three teams really would be old National Football League, and Houston was the backbone of the old American Football League. Houston had the Astrodome. It was a good thing."

"We were very pleased with that because it put us in with the Browns and Steelers, which we thought were our natural rivals, and Houston," Mike Brown said. "Klosterman was the general manager down there. He called Bud Adams and encouraged his boss to get out of the AFC West because they thought they could win in our division. They didn't win our division for 20 years. I shouldn't say much, because we've had our dry spells too."

"To complete the triangle, I got Baltimore in the back door. Carroll did it on his own," Modell said. "Cincinnati came in later. It was a tremendous success. Pittsburgh, us, and Baltimore in the AFL was a hit." Now that the former leagues were realigned, the divisions had to be reconfigured. The American Conference setup was easy, with Baltimore joining New York, New England, Miami, and Buffalo in the East, to go with Oakland, Kansas City, San Diego, and Denver in the West, and the new Pittsburgh, Cleveland, Houston, and Cincinnati Central.

The true test of division realignment would come in the new National Football Conference, where nobody could agree. "I was there when all the fights were on," Dan Rooney said. "It was all from the Central Division of the NFL, where you had Minnesota, Green Bay, the Bears, and Detroit. Minnesota wanted to go to the West Coast. The Bears, Detroit, and Green Bay wanted Minnesota to stay with them. The majority of the people wanted them to stay, but you had to get them to agree. The people on the West Coast were trying to take them too."

It was mid-January, and the league had to button down schedules—and television. "Monday Night Football" was starting, and Rozelle was antsy. Chuck Day recalled Don Weiss's recollection of that moment: " 'There are five plans you guys have agreed to,' Rozelle said as he wheeled in a chalkboard. 'Here are the five. You guys can't make a decision; I'm going to make a decision.' He put five pieces of paper into a fishbowl, each piece representing one of the plans. He brought in Thelma Elkjer, his secretary. Thelma reached into the bowl, pulled out a plan, and that's how the NFC realigned."

It came out with the NFL's version of the "new geography." Dallas stayed in the East, with its natural rivalries with Washington and the Giants; Philadelphia was an Eastern pillar. The Bears, Packers, Lions, and Minnesota formed a natural Central rivalry that took on the nickname "Black and Blue Division." The West in its own way reflected the changing America, with longtime rivals San Francisco and L.A. holding the coast against Southern newcomers New Orleans and Atlanta, which wanted to be together. It worked.

Whenever the realignment issue arose, Rozelle had a stock answer: "I'm not going through that again, not in my lifetime." And he didn't.

"The NFL envisioned a 32-team league, which it became today and is logically finished," Chuck Day said. "I don't know that there's any interest in expanding that. That's why L.A. sitting out there without a team makes people nervous. It will come from somewhere, probably an existing city."

"Rozelle was a big-time planner," Charlie Jones said. "The sad thing is he died in 1996 and did not live to see where his league has gone. He set it up to be a 32-team league, 16 and 16, four divisions of 4. The math makes it perfect."

"At the end of the merger talks, Al Davis raised the issue that Rozelle took away his league," *New York Times* sports columnist Dave Anderson said. "Al Davis has never forgiven him to this day. Rozelle never forgave Davis."

SEVENTEEN

EVERYTHING'S COMING UP SUPER!

"To me it's the greatest game ever played, under those conditions. It is the résumé of what Lombardi's Packers stood for."

—STEVE SABOL, ON THE ICE BOWL, 2005

*F*or better or for worse, the merged leagues and their season-ending extravaganza had arrived and were here to stay. There was no turning back. The future was now. The first AFL-NFL World Championship Game, its official title then, would be played Sunday, January 15, 1967, in the Los Angeles Memorial Coliseum and televised to the nation on CBS and NBC.

Pete Rozelle and his staff had to create a template for the massive enterprise as they entered previously unexplored territory. They had just two and a half months to pull it off once Congress approved the merger agreement late the previous October. Before then, they didn't even have a place to stage the game, let alone a finished plan of action.

As chair of a six-man Joint Committee of owners formed the previous June, Rozelle issued his criteria for a Super Bowl. It must be played in a warm-weather site on a neutral field before as large a crowd as possible.

The Joint Committee's first choice was the Rose Bowl, in Pasadena. When the two sides met, the Tournament of Roses Committee demanded its usual 15 percent rental and added 15 percent of the television and radio rights. That fee would have run as high as $480,000. According to Don Weiss in his memoir, "That left the Joint Committee thinking it would be appropriate for the Rose Bowl directors to appear at meetings wearing black masks and toting loaded pistols." Weiss added that Big Ten commissioner Bill Reed and Pac-10 Commissioner Tom Hamilton suggested in a joint letter to Rozelle that "pro football had no business traipsing across what was the exclusive grand stage of college football."

All that Pasadena posturing left Rozelle to pursue the logical choice, one he knew well through the years: the L.A. Coliseum. When Coliseum general manager Bill Nicholas told Rams owner Dan Reeves, a Joint Committee member, that his rental fee would not exceed $50,000, the bargain was sealed. The deal was concluded on November 9, 1966, just 67 days before kickoff the following January 15.

Purists who felt a football season should end within the confines of its calendar year hated the idea of staging a championship game this deep into a new year. For Rozelle, though, this was the stage he wanted, the first step in making pro football a game for all seasons, making all other sports olio acts and trailers. Coliseum ticket prices were scaled from what was considered an exorbitant $12 top, to $10, and $6.

Each 30-second commercial on both CBS and NBC cost $42,500. Forty years later, in 2007, 30 seconds would go for $2.6 million; ticket prices started at $550 before the now legal scalpers set their scales into the thousands of dollars. Ray Scott, Jack Whitaker, and Frank Gifford were the designated announcers in the booth for CBS, with Pat Summerall on the sidelines. Curt Gowdy and Paul Christman would call the game for NBC, and Charlie Jones was on the field.

The pregame and halftime shows were staged by the University of Michigan and University of Arizona marching bands. The Grambling Marching Band would join the other two for the national anthem. Special musical guest star was trumpeter Al Hirt. The referee was Norm Schacter, who led a 12-man crew of regular and alternate officials, 6 from each league.

Lamar Hunt's Kansas City Chiefs represented the American Football League. The Chiefs had roared through the AFL with an 11–1–2 record and then mashed the Buffalo Bills 31–7 in their league championship game. Coach Hank Stram's offense, quarterbacked by NFL castoff Lenny Dawson, led the AFL in scoring with 448 points and led in rushing. The Chiefs' superb defense featured future Hall of Famers Buck Buchanan and Bobby Bell and All-AFL safeties Bobby Hunt and Johnny Robinson. "That was a really good team. They had players," said Ron Wolf, then personnel director for Al Davis in Oakland. "Johnny Robinson, defensive back from LSU, is another guy who belongs in the Hall of Fame."

Appropriately, the NFL's representative would be the Green Bay Packers, winners of their fourth title in six years. With a squad that would boast 10 Hall of Famers, nine players plus coach Vince Lombardi, the Packers beat the Dallas Cowboys 34–27 in the Cotton Bowl to win their 10th NFL championship. That afternoon in Dallas, as Jerry Green, of the *Detroit News*, headed toward the field, he missed the Packers' go-ahead touchdown. "I saw Pete squatting down by Green Bay's 2-yard line; it was muddy, so he couldn't kneel," said Green, who would cover every Super Bowl through XLI in 2007. "I joined him. There was no security to move me away. Here was Don Meredith driving the Cowboys to the touchdown that would have sent the game into overtime.

"Pete looked over and said, 'This is something, isn't it!' He was friendly. Al Davis would have called the cops. We both saw Meredith get the ball to the 2-yard line. Dallas had a guard named Jim Boeke, who then got whistled for illegal procedure. That set them back to the 7. Meredith then rolled right and, hounded by Dave Robinson, threw the pass that Tom Brown intercepted in the end zone. 'Shit!' we heard Meredith say."

Years later, former Cowboys receiver Peter Gent, author of *North Dallas Forty*, told me that pass failed because coach Tom Landry mistakenly inserted speed receiver Bob Hayes at flanker into the goal-line offense instead of Frank Clarke, a tight end who played flanker at the goal line. "Clarke would have held up Robinson to prevent Brown from forcing toward the line. Then Clarke would have slipped free in the end zone, and Meredith would have made the play in front of Brown, the safety," Gent said. "Bobby Hayes, who never played at the goal line and never blocked, was the wrong man in the game on the most important play to that point in franchise history."

So, it was off to Los Angeles for the first Super Bowl, as the media already started calling it. "Super Bowl" came from a casual remark after the merger by Lamar Hunt, who said his kids enjoyed playing with the Super Ball, a toy made by Wham-O that could bounce over a three-story house. "Why not call it the Super Bowl," Hunt said over the mild protest of the commissioner, who thought the name had a "carnival" connotation. When Tex Maule matter-of-factly used the words *Super Bowl* in his John Facenda–narrated script for NFL Films' *The Spectacle of a Sport*, the term stuck and became part of the lexicon.

Vince Lombardi, unhappy with the hoopla surrounding the instant classic, wanted to stash the team in Palo Alto, some 400 miles to the north. Jim Kensil and Don Weiss, who knew how much Rozelle wanted to garner publicity, persuaded Lombardi to house the Packers in Santa Barbara, 80 miles away from the Coliseum. To accommodate the anticipated press horde, Kensil and Weiss chartered a bus to Santa Barbara, but only Weiss and AP writer Jack Hand made the bus trip. The other writers drove there instead. The Chiefs encamped in Laguna Beach, down in Orange County, and the league handled its media day the same way.

The battle of the networks had started before the season, when a Super Bowl became reality. "We struggled over the first championship game, now called the Super Bowl: how it was going to be televised and who would handle it," former NBC Sports vice president Chet Simmons recalled.

"When the time came for Rozelle to award the Super Bowl telecast, he gave it to his friends at CBS," former NBC sportscaster Charlie Jones said. Simmons's boss at NBC, Carl Lindemann, who engineered that television deal with the AFL back in 1964, was not about to get shut out of the big one. "Lindemann called Rozelle and said, 'Hold it! Wait a minute. You don't have an AFL-NFL championship game without us. We saved the AFL! We want to be part of this, and what are you going to do?'

"Rozelle made the only move he could," Jones said. "NBC would get a clean feed, video, and background audio. This was the first time it had ever been done on a cross-network basis. Rozelle did it again, a masterfully compromised decision."

When the CBS and NBC crews gathered at the Coliseum early in game week, hostilities broke out anew. "Our two engineering groups got into a fistfight during the setup of the game, and we had to erect a chain-link fence between the two operations," Simmons said. "Who knows with engineers? They work like hell when they're working and play like hell when they're playing, and God knows how those two things came together and started that."

The fight more likely than not concerned the sensitive area of union jurisdiction and where you are allowed to work. For decades, CBS engineers have belonged to the IBEW, the International Brotherhood of Electrical Workers. NBC and ABC engineers, on the other hand, have always been members of NABET, the National Association of Broadcast Employees and Technicians.

Management saw it all differently. "There wasn't a time that the sports guys at the networks—McPhail at CBS, myself and Carl Lindemann—didn't get along," Simmons said. "We'd go drink together. We'd go to dinner together. We spent time together. We just wanted to do the best job we could under the constraints we had. We were friends."

Not so on the front lines. "We had meetings at the Wilshire with the CBS people," Charlie Jones said. "Then we'd go back to the Sheraton and have meetings with everybody that was there and discuss how we were going to fuck CBS. Hell, they were holding meetings to discuss 'How are we going to fuck NBC?' This was the first time for the Super Bowl, and there we were playing the screw-the-other-guy game."

Making their telecast look different caused considerable difficulties for NBC. CBS cameras covered the game and stadium atmosphere, while NBC took CBS's feed with a couple of modifications. "We had one camera for our on-air talent," Simmons said. "We just had to take their feed and be satisfied with it."

"We also embellished the video as we saw fit and used our own audio," said Don Ellis, the associate producer on the telecast. "We had a good chief technical guy, who came up with the idea of putting a camera inside one of our trailers with a zoom lens on it. We would zoom in on plays inside the picture we were getting from CBS off the monitor so we could have an extreme close-up on shots. We thought at the time that we probably had the best announce team: we had Gowdy and Christman on color. Paul was so great."

A crisis hit the NBC Sports camp in midweek. Lou Kusserow, the telecast producer, had some drinks at dinner and totaled his car, but he escaped unhurt. Feeling he had embarrassed NBC, let alone himself, the producer made his way to LAX and caught a flight to New York. Chet Simmons found out about it and alerted Carl Lindemann back in New York. Lindemann met Kusserow's plane at JFK, bought him a cup of coffee, and sent him back to L.A. on the next flight to pick up where he left off.

Charlie Jones's own pregame crisis came when he was assigned to interview Coach Lombardi. "Oh, Lombardi. Lombardi was a very difficult human being to deal with no matter who you were," Chet Simmons recalled. "Charlie was recording a stand-up with Lombardi, who wanted to get it over with so he could devote his concentration to the game."

"It was at the end of the Monday-morning practice at 11:30," Jones said, picking up the story. "A luncheon was to follow a media-day thing, and he was supposed to speak. The only time he would do the interview was right after practice. I had to ask specific questions that he approved for the pregame show. It was not free-form; I had questions on a cue card. I told the cameraman to start rolling when Lombardi started walking over."

"They did one take, and it wasn't good," Simmons said. "They did another take, and it wasn't good. Lombardi looked at Charlie or the producer and said, 'If that little red [recording] light doesn't come on right now, I am out of here!' He said it in a mean way: 'If that little red light doesn't come on now, I'm out of here!' "

"Lombardi's gonna kill me," Jones said, rolling back four decades in the window of his mind. "He gave me that stare. We did it. It was the worst interview I ever did in my life."

"Charlie had to sweat through that," a still grateful Simmons said. "He got it done under great pressure."

Something else was off-kilter all week. For all the media attention the upcoming game got, more than any other football game ever had, ticket sales never took off. As game day approached, the league couldn't even give seats away. "The Super Bowl was not that big a deal to the owners," Chuck Day noted. "The thinking went, 'Who can stay with the Packers?' The Packers, Colts, Rams, and Cowboys were top-tier NFL teams then. The conventional wisdom was there's no way an AFL team could stick with them. There was interest, but the game was not the driving force."

Then along came the Hammer to fill the publicity void, and did he ever. He was Kansas City's big cornerback, Fred Williamson, who made himself the pregame center of attention when he told anyone who listened that he would take out Green Bay's two top receivers, Carroll Dale and Boyd Dowler, with karate chops to the side of the head, a move he called "the hammer."

Williamson, who played his high school football at Froebel High School, in Gary, Indiana, was a college freshman when Ara Parseghian arrived at Northwestern after the 1955 season. In that single-platoon era, he started at end in 1956 and '57 and was joined at the other end in 1958 by Elbert Kimbrough. He lettered as a shot-putter and discus thrower on the track team with Irv Cross, a high school rival from Hammond High. The quiet, efficient Cross, respected by every member of the team and elected cocaptain as a junior, beat out Williamson in the '58 season and never looked back. Cross enjoyed a 10-year career as a defensive back with the Philadelphia Eagles before he became a key member of CBS's "NFL Today" team in the '70s. Kimbrough played seven years as a defensive back with the San Francisco 49ers.

Williamson, the second-stringer, who boasted that he had a degree in architecture from Northwestern, was an art major. The university did not have an architectural program. He played for the Pittsburgh Steelers in 1960, got cut, and then joined the Oakland Raiders, where he stayed until 1965 before he moved to Kansas City. The glib, handsome Williamson stood 6'3", weighed 220 pounds, and became a menacing villain in Super Bowl week. Befitting his future film-acting career, Williamson was, in the words of veteran Chicago sportswriter

Bill Jauss, "a guy who thrived in the spotlight, flashy, a natural self-promoter."

Whether or not Williamson sold any tickets, the prize money was incentive enough to gain the players' interest. The winning share was $15,000, more than double most salaries at that time. And the loser's share was $7,500, nothing to overlook either.

Game day was sunny, pleasant, and warm enough to remind the folks back east that they were stuck in winter's gloominess. Jack Whitaker shared play-by-play with Ray Scott for CBS on the telecast. "That first Super Bowl, we kind of looked down our noses at that other league. We didn't know much about them," Whitaker said.

Charlie Jones roamed the sidelines for NBC, and Pat Summerall did the same for CBS. Before the game, Jones had a chat with his CBS counterpart. "I knew Summerall a little bit in college at Arkansas, and we had a lot of the same friends," Jones said. "I went down and said, 'You know Green Bay, and I know Kansas City, and they don't know in the truck. We find out, share it, and go on at the same time, and nobody back home will know who got it first.'" And to this day, nobody does but Jones and Summerall. No videotape of that game is known to exist. Bean counters at both networks looking for shelf space ordered the broadcast tapes tossed or, worse, erased, much as NBC did with Johnny Carson's early "Tonight Show" tapes.

The Packers opened the scoring in the first quarter when Max McGee, now a backup playing in his final game, without sleep, reached back with one hand to pull in Bart Starr's pass for the touchdown. "Boyd Dowler got hurt, and McGee, who had a hangover, came in and was the star," Jones said. "He had been out all night partying with Paul Hornung. He should have been the MVP, not Bart Starr, but they always give it to quarterbacks. That one-handed catch made the ball game. If he didn't make that catch, Kansas City could have won that ball game—not would have: could have."

Jones related, "When Dowler left the game and was just sitting there on the bench, I went over to Pat and said, 'Find out what's wrong with Boyd Dowler.'

"'I can't do that. The game's going on,' Summerall said. I swear to God, he said that.

"I told him to go ask the trainer," Jones said. "Pat came back and said, 'He has a separated shoulder, and he's out for the game.' This was a huge story. Pat told CBS, and I told NBC. I don't know when CBS used it, but I do know Gowdy never liked to use anything I got on the sideline. At an all-star game in Houston a couple of years before this, they kept going to the sidelines, and I was interviewing all these people. Gowdy finally told a producer, 'Who the fuck's doing this ball game: me up here or Charlie on the sideline?' So, they stopped coming to me. I know that NBC did use the Dowler story, about 10 or 15 minutes after CBS. That was the key to the whole ball game."

The Chiefs bounced back with the tying touchdown. After Jim Taylor scored the last touchdown of his Packers career on a 14-yard power sweep, Mike Mercer answered with a field goal to leave Kansas City down at halftime, 14–10. "It didn't take long for us to realize that we were all in it together now," Jack Whitaker recalled. The Packers broke the game open when Willie Wood intercepted a Len Dawson pass in the third quarter and ran 50 yards to the Chiefs' 5 to set up Elijah Pitts's touchdown blast. Green Bay added scores by McGee and Pitts again, to win 35–10. As for the Hammer, Williamson had to leave the game in the fourth quarter when Donny Anderson's knee accidentally knocked him out on an attempted tackle. "You know who got it?" Willie Wood said on the sidelines. "The Hammer," a teammate answered as the Packers enjoyed a hearty laugh.

"This was when the loser's locker room did not have that cachet," Jones said. "Now they say the biggest and best stories are the loser's locker room. The networks did not think in those terms then." Jones languished in Kansas City's empty locker room, and Summerall enjoyed the hullabaloo of the winning Green Bay locker room.

"I got Lamar Hunt when he came in," Jones recalled. "We were sitting on the edge of the platform. He had on a short-sleeve white shirt, open necked, tie pulled down, and looked like he had been hit by a tornado. Here was the guy who started the American Football League, involved in the merger, creation of the Super Bowl, the man they all laughed at, the rich man's son. What was he feeling at this moment? It was losing, and it also was winning? The CBS guy, Bob Dailey, was the producer. He wouldn't come to me with Lamar. 'Agh, he's a loser. Who cares?' Dailey growled."

Jones added, "Today Dailey says the same thing. Every year around Super Bowl time, they call him up, and he says, 'Who cares?' and they call me, and I say, 'He really screwed up.' Then he says something nasty about me, and I say something nasty about him, and we go on to the next Super Bowl. I don't even remember what he looked like."

Attendance was a disappointing 61,946, two-thirds of stadium capacity, evident in the official NFL Films production, in which a viewer can see vast areas of empty seats, especially by the peristyle at the east end. Pete Rozelle could take solace in the television ratings: the game drew sixty-five million viewers, the largest sports audience ever, and netted $3 million, a $500,000 profit over the $2.5 million the networks guaranteed. CBS, with the larger NFL markets, did a 22.6 rating and 43 share. NBC, with an 18.5 rating, drew a 36 share. Thus, together, more than 41 percent of the television sets in America were tuned to a game watched by 79 percent of the viewers. That means about 2 percent of America watched the game telecasts.

Rozelle knew, though, that he had to fill the place to make it work, not just for the box office but also for the image conveyed to the viewers at home. "Pete, Jim Kensil, and Don Weiss, on the plane ride back to New York, hashed it out," Chuck Day said. "Rozelle never got over the fact that the first Super Bowl was not a sellout. On that plane ride back east, he said, 'I don't ever want to see another championship game that is not a sellout.' He never did. A few weeks later, he put Don Weiss in charge of the game, and that's what changed Don's life. Don took that statement: it was not a sell-out-this-stadium-or-you're-fired order; it was a statement of conviction that this game should be a sellout at all times."

"The first game is monumental," Chet Simmons said. "It's in all of us who are still alive."

After Green Bay's 35–10 victory, Rozelle presented Lombardi with the first AFL-NFL Trophy, designed by Tiffany's Oscar Riedener, the silver football on a tapered three-sided pedestal, in elegant simplicity.

"Afterward, they were badgering Lombardi to talk about the American Football League and the Kansas City Chiefs and to compare it to the NFL," Chiefs Hall of Fame quarterback Len Dawson said. "He finally said, 'Yeah, they're a good team, but there're a lot of teams in our league and our division that can beat them or anybody else.' That was not a real pleasant way of putting it, from our point of view. We remembered it."

Interleague preseason play began the next summer. The most noteworthy game was played on the hot night of August 23 at Kansas City Municipal Stadium when coach Hank Stram and the Chiefs played host to Stram's childhood idol from his hometown of Chicago, NFL founder George Halas, and the Bears. The resulting 66–24 Chiefs runaway, in which Kansas City unleashed everything in its well-drilled arsenal, could have borrowed the title from the deliciously cynical screenplay *A Slight Case of Murder*. The white horse that circled the field after Kansas City touchdowns was so lathered up that some in the crowd worried that he might collapse and die on the spot. "Hell, we had the first team in there at the end of the game," Dawson recalled. "Nobody wanted to come out!"

Dawson noted, "A lot of us in that game came from Purdue. Abe Gibron, who was one of the Papa Bear's assistants, went to Purdue, where he and Hank were close. Tom Bettis and Pete Brewster, who both went to Purdue, were on our staff. I remember Abie came in before the game to see Hank."

"Hell, this is just another scrimmage," Gibron remarked. "It doesn't mean a thing. We're not going to throw a lot at you."

"Us, too," Stram said. "No big deal."

"Abe didn't know that, during the week, Hank showed us the highlight film of Super Bowl I a couple of times," Dawson said. The Chiefs were convinced that Tex Maule's script taunted them and their league. "One phrase that stuck was John Facenda calling us 'the soft underbelly of professional football.' Our guys were fired up for that game, I'm telling you. After the first quarter, there were guys who wanted to put a hundred points on the board. We scored 66! The fans got into it; everybody was into it. That was the first chance we had after losing the Super Bowl."

After the Super Bowl, Vince Lombardi lost his two Hall of Fame running backs. Following a protracted battle over money when Taylor thought he should be paid better than rookies Donnie Anderson and Jim Grabowski, Lombardi traded his disgruntled star fullback to the expansion New Orleans Saints for their top draft choice in 1968, linebacker Fred Carr, from UTEP. Carr played 10 years in Green Bay. Then, Lombardi reluctantly put his pet, Paul Hornung, into the expansion pool, and the Saints grabbed him. Hornung, who had not seen action in the Super Bowl, never played another game. The pinched nerve in his shoulder, going back to Chuck Bednarik's hit that knocked him out of the 1960 title game at Philadelphia, forced his retirement.

Their replacements, Elijah Pitts and fullback Grabowski, both were lost for the year in midseason with leg injuries. Anderson, the rookie, replaced Pitts, and Lombardi turned to former Ram Ben Wilson to take over at fullback. That left third-string rookie Travis Williams as the only available running back. Desperate for help, Lombardi placed a call to New York to Wellington Mara, his college friend at Fordham and former boss with the Giants, to check out a player that coach Allie Sherman had cut earlier that season. It's a case study in the money infusion of the pro football war and how a smart operator always trumps a lesser one.

Chuck Mercein, an All–Ivy League star at Yale before he joined the Giants in 1965, was no stranger to the Midwest. "My dad was quite a radio personality back in Milwaukee and Chicago in earlier days," he said.

In 1955, Tom Mercein moved his wife and four young children from Milwaukee to Chicago, where he was a staff announcer at NBC when network president Sylvester "Pat" Weaver started "Monitor" in an attempt to rekindle the magic of live network radio. The programming's 40-hour-long weekend format was a huge success in the late '50s, featuring the likes of Steve Allen, Gene Rayburn, and Bob and Ray and, at nights, remotes from jazz spots around the country. Chicago's jazz host on "Monitor" was Tom Mercein, who started bringing Chuck along on Saturday nights in 1957 when he was a 14-year-old freshman at New Trier High School, in Winnetka. "We went to places like the London House and the Blue Note," Chuck recalled. "We met so many great people: Count Basie, Joe Williams, Stan Kenton, the great Oscar Peterson."

The Merceins' neighbors at the other end of the block on Scott Avenue were the Pyles. Their oldest son, Palmer, was a star lineman for Duffy Daugherty at Michigan State in 1955. Middle son, Mike, four years older than Chuck Mercein, was the big noise of Winnetka when Chuck was in junior high school. Mike Pyle was All-State center in football and was Illinois high school record holder in the shot put and discus. "I tried to be like Mike, and I emulated him," Mercein said. "I saw him make All-State. That was my goal: to make All-State in Illinois. I did make All-State at fullback and linebacker. When the All-State team came out, they put the little one-inch pictures in the paper, the *Daily News*. I was upset. 'What's the matter?' my mom asked. 'I didn't see my picture.' "

"Chuck, you didn't look hard enough. Look in the upper-left corner," Mrs. Mercein said.

"The state of Illinois was silhouetted," Mercein explained, "and there was a picture of me in one spot. The other fullback in there was a pretty good fullback-linebacker. Guess who that was: Dick Butkus." For good measure, Mercein broke Pyle's Illinois shot put record in the state track meet.

More than 50 schools came after Mercein, now a rock-hard, 6'2", 225-pounder. Within the Big Ten, he was chased hard by the Elliott brothers—Bump, at Michigan, and Pete, at Illinois, who wanted to team Chuck with his prized recruit, Butkus. Stanford, however, had the inside track—until Pyle came home at Christmas 1960 after an all-American season as captain of Yale's unbeaten Ivy League champions and draft choice of the hometown Bears. "He said I could do what he was going to do, play professional football," Mercein said. "I felt if Mike Pyle could do this, I could. I wanted the best education I could get, and Mike sold me on that, too."

When Chuck left for Yale in fall 1961, his family moved with him. The best days of "Monitor" were over, and jazz popularity was waning, so Tom Mercein quit NBC to find work at WNEW, in New York. "He worked the 'Milkman's Matinee,' a late-night show [jazz from

2:00 to 7:00 A.M.]. His career didn't take off here as it did in Chicago, but my parents saw me play all my games at Yale and with the Giants," Chuck Mercein recalled.

The Giants retain a warm spot in Mercein's heart. In New York he is considered a Giant, as in Wisconsin he is considered a Packer. He loves everything about the Giants except the experience with his coach.

"Sherman and I couldn't get along," Mercein said in 2007. "It was like oil and water." Their clash raged on many fronts and began with the 1965 NFL draft at the peak of the pro football war, when the Giants made Auburn fullback Tucker Frederickson the first pick of the draft, ahead of future Hall of Famers Gale Sayers, Dick Butkus, Roger Staubach, and Joe Namath.

"Several picks later, the phone rang, and it was Bill Ford for the Detroit Lions," Mercein recalled. "He asked me if I'd be interested in coming out to play for them. Nick Pietrosante was retiring. I was thrilled to be that high a pick. He asked me if I had been in contact with the AFL. I told him the Buffalo Bills had picked me number one in a secret draft. They wanted me to replace Cookie Gilchrist."

"Have you negotiated?" Ford asked.

"Yes, sir." Mercein said. "I'm at three years, no cut, at $100,000."

"I can't compete with that," Ford said.

"Excuse me. Save yourself the trouble," Mercein said. Detroit chose another fullback, Tom Nowatzke, of Indiana. "The whole first round went by, and I didn't get picked." The Giants came up for their second pick. Wellington Mara called and went through the same spiel Ford had used, and Mercein repeated the Buffalo no-cut deal and money offer to Mara.

"That's OK. We'll compete with that," Mara said.

"Why would you want me?" Mercein asked.

"Allie Sherman tells me you'll play fullback; Tucker will play halfback. We'll have a brand-new backfield," Mara informed him.

Mercein signed a no-cut deal with the Giants for three years and a guaranteed $115,000. Otto Graham invited him to the College All-Star camp in early summer, where he played a fine game as he caught a John Huarte touchdown pass and kicked a field goal and an extra point in the all-stars' 24–16 loss to the Cleveland Browns. Tucker Frederickson saw little action. "When I got to the Giants, they lined us up: him at fullback, me in back of him," Mercein said. "I'd been lied to, and that set me and Allie off on the wrong track. Tucker played our first year and got hurt. I played the second year and got hurt."

Moreover, Mercein said, Sherman never got off his case about, of all things, where Mercein went to college. "He couldn't get over that I went to Yale, not one of the bigger colleges," Mercein said. "He kept needling me, got under my skin."

Three days before the 1967 opener, Sherman signed a linebacker and, with a now filled roster, put Mercein on waivers. "He was able to get me through waivers because nobody was going to pick me up a couple of days before the first game with a guaranteed contract at $25,000-plus for the year."

To stay in football shape, Mercein played a couple of games with the Giants' Westchester semipro affiliate. Then Sherman called him back to the active roster when somebody got hurt. "I had a groin pull, and I knew I couldn't kick," Mercein said. "He warned me, 'If you miss one, you go back down again.' Sure enough, I missed a kick, and I did go down. I gave up on the Giants. I called Otto Graham and said, 'I'm a free agent.'

"Graham wanted to sign me but said he couldn't use me that week, but he wanted to hire me and told me to come in Monday," Mercein said.

That Sunday night, Wellington Mara called Mercein at home. He had just got off the phone with Vince Lombardi in Green Bay. "He's had two serious injuries in his backfield," Mara told Mercein. "He wants to know if you'd like to play for him, but he wants to be sure you haven't signed with the 'Skins."

"Mr. Mara, I haven't signed," Mercein told him.

"The next call you get will be from Vince Lombardi," Mara stated.

"It was like the voice of God. I was halfway scared, halfway elated," Mercein recalled. " 'Young man,' Coach Lombardi said, 'you can help us win another NFL championship and a world title.' What a lift."

The Packers sliced through the new four-team Central Division as much on their experience and know-how as on their talent, to reach the postseason one last time under Lombardi. This was the first year for the two-tiered playoff system, and, as it happened, a team that should have been a division champion was cut out of the playoffs. While the Packers coasted through a top-heavy Central Division schedule against relatively weak Minnesota, Chicago, and Detroit and clinched their playoff spot with two games to go, and basically took the last two weeks off, the Baltimore Colts and Los Angeles Rams in the new Coastal Division had to claw every inch of the way.

Baltimore had the best record in the league after 13 games, 11–0–2. One of those ties came in the fifth game, in Baltimore against the Rams, a 10–1–2 team. George Allen had inspired his Rams to beat the Packers in the Coliseum in a nationally televised game on Saturday, December 9. NFL Films persuaded Lombardi to wear a wireless mike that afternoon, and he gave the audience an earful, as in, "What the hell is going on around here?" and, on sloppy tackling, "Grab, grab, grab. Is that all you can do?" The game didn't matter to Green Bay, but it meant everything to the Rams, who pulled out a 27–24 win. The following week, in the showdown with Baltimore, the Rams played their finest game in more than a decade to beat the Colts 34–10 and ensure a return engagement with the Packers.

After all those years with George Halas and now two on his own as head coach, Allen thought he knew everything he ever had to know about handling Lombardi. But, as was the case with everyone else who tried, he could not outwit the hard-driving master. Home field rotated every year in the playoffs. This time, despite an inferior, 9–4–1 record, Lombardi and Green Bay owned the edge.

Because Lombardi had become a league icon, not even the commissioner would challenge him over the home schedule. From the league's early days, the Packers divided their home games between Green Bay and Milwaukee. The only sure Green Bay–played game year in and year out was the hated Chicago Bears. Too much tradition. This time, in 1967, instead of bringing the Rams to Green Bay, Lombardi turned on the con. He took them to a place where Allen never had coached a regular-season game: the Packers' second home, Milwaukee County Stadium.

In effect, he was telling his fans from Milwaukee who couldn't get into Lambeau Field that this was their chance to see the greatest team in history in case they couldn't get tickets for the following week in Green Bay. And he was letting his Green Bay ticket holders know they need not worry: they would get to see the title game as they had in 1961 and '65, on the "hallowed turf," as the Packers call Lambeau. By that maneuver, he sent Allen and the Rams a message in 72-point boldface type that they didn't have a chance.

That became evident on a gray, 18-degree day, pleasant by Packers standards, cutting for the Rams, when Green Bay took charge in the second quarter and romped to a 28–7 victory. In Dallas, the next day, the Cowboys, peaking at the right time, routed the Cleveland Browns 52–14 to set up the title-game rematch at Lambeau Field on New Year's Eve, pairing Jim Lee Howell's former Giants assistants, Lombardi and Tom Landry, one more time.

Now that he was commissioner of both the National and American leagues, and had seen enough wintry games in Green Bay to last a lifetime, Pete Rozelle winged away that weekend to the land of avowed enemy Al Davis to see the Raiders and Houston Oilers. When he arrived on Saturday, December 30, in Oakland, where it was sunny and in the 50s, Rozelle checked in with Jim Kensil and Don Weiss, who had the Green Bay duty, where it was cold by any standard. The next day's forecast called for temperatures near zero and an Arctic front descending from Canada, with temperatures well below zero, to arrive in late afternoon. "Better you than me," Rozelle said to Weiss after the game.

"I don't think they considered postponing the game, because the weather forecast for Monday was worse than Sunday's," Chuck Day said. Besides, Vince Lombardi had installed a well-publicized, never-before-used heating grid buried six inches below the Lambeau Field surface. It was an electric blanket of sorts, guaranteed to keep the field from freezing. He bought the $80,000 electric heating system, ironically, from George J. Halas, nephew of Papa Bear. The Lambeau grounds crew placed a tarpaulin on the field after the two teams took brief workouts on Saturday. The Arctic front, moving faster than predicted, arrived that night.

"We had about eight or nine cameras," Steve Sabol, of NFL Films, recalled. "I stayed at the Northland Hotel with my dad. He was such a worrywart, you know. There wasn't the winterizing of the equipment we have now. We feared the film would snap. Dad had a rule: if a game started at one o'clock, he wanted all of us in place by nine. The wake-up call came at five o'clock. The phone rang, and I picked it up. 'Good morning, Mr. Sabol. It's minus 16 degrees. Have a nice day.'"

"Dad, you're not going to believe what I just heard!" Steve said. He repeated the current temperature.

"Oh, that can't be true. They won't play the game if it's that cold!" Ed said.

When the players came out for the warm-ups, everyone knew it would be a test of character, human endurance, and pure will—all those qualities within that trump talent alone. Never had any championship game been played under more brutal conditions.

A slashing wind between 20 and 30 miles per hour roared out of Canada through the north end of the 50,000-seat stadium. The field was frozen hard. As Ed Gruver reported in *Ice Bowl*, grounds crew chief Joe Proski told Lombardi that he had to turn off the underground heating system before it exploded and blew up the field. The system was designed for temperatures around 15 to 20 above zero, not 15 to 20 below. When condensation formed on the underside of the tarp, the field froze soon after the cover was removed. "The field was solid like an ice rink, like the Hubbard Woods Park field we flooded as kids for skating," Mercein said. "The ground was like stucco. It was like landing on concrete, and it was scratchy."

"We only had one sound camera, but we didn't get much sound," Steve Sabol said. "We had a soundman up in the scoreboard with a flask. He passed out and nearly froze to death. We had to take him to the hospital. A lot of us came from the East and did not realize that kind of temperature. I was wearing cowboy boots."

Some of the Dallas Cowboys tried wrapping their feet and legs in Saran Wrap. The musicians couldn't play their instruments because the mouthpieces were so cold that they would tear away the skin on their lips. The Packers got a sporting goods store to open up and provide gloves, thermal underwear, and earmuffs for the officials. But, when referee Norm Schacter blew his whistle after the first play, he tore open his lip. Also, the pea in the whistle froze, and the sound that emanated resembled a peep. So, the officials yelled and stepped in at play stoppages.

Tom Brookshier told NFL Films years later that Frank Gifford set down a cup of hot coffee in the CBS broadcast booth, only to pick it up a minute later to find it had frozen solid. The late Jack Buck, who called the game with Gifford and the late Ray Scott, asked Gifford if he was having a drink of coffee. Gifford replied, "No—a bite of coffee."

The temperature at kickoff was 13 below zero. Perhaps the first time the term *windchill* was used for a general audience was when Ray Scott told the world that the windchill factor, a measurement used by U.S. Air Force personnel in the Arctic, was 45 below zero!

That area of Wisconsin and Michigan's Upper Peninsula, near Green Bay, is far and away the largest consumer of brandy in the United States. Plenty was downed that day. "Green Bay is a different place," Brookshier said. "You know those people came to that stadium. Some of them had kids with them. It was 18 or 20 below zero, and nobody left."

The Packers, more acclimated to the conditions than the Cowboys, opened a 14–0 lead on a pair of Starr touchdown passes to Boyd Dowler, the latter a 43-yarder. The game turned with 4:30 left in the second quarter when the Dallas defensive ends sandwiched Starr. Willie Townes forced a fumble that George Andrie picked up on the 8 and carried into the end zone. Danny Villaneuva booted in a 21-yard field goal just before the half to cut the deficit to 14–10. Dallas had taken charge.

After a scoreless third quarter, Landry opened the fourth quarter with a play that had been a Lombardi favorite going back to New

York: the halfback option. Lombardi had two Hall of Famers to make it work: Frank Gifford with the Giants, and Paul Hornung for the Packers. Dallas had running back Dan Reeves, a converted quarterback from South Carolina. Reeves was not related to the Rams' owner of the same name. Meredith sent a pitchout to Reeves moving to his left. As free safety Willie Wood and right cornerback Bobby Jeter forced toward the line of scrimmage to defend the run, Lance Rentzel broke past them all alone. Upstairs, Scott made the call on CBS. "Meredith pitch to Reeves—the halfback option—Rentzel—touchdown—Dallas." Rentzel, virtually skating, had somehow come to a stop without falling as Reeves threw into the wind. He made the catch, turned, and outraced Tom Brown coming from the other side of the field to the end zone. It was 17–14 Cowboys.

Five possessions later, with 4:54 left, the Packers took over at their own 32. The scene was set to close the deal. The NFL Films crew members who still had working gear moved into position for the finish. The sportswriters left the press box to head for the clubhouses, and the players and coaches got ready for a final push or last stand. The temperature had fallen to somewhere near 20 below, with a corresponding drop in the windchill.

"My camera focus-wheel froze in the fourth quarter," said NFL Films' Steve Sabol. "In that final drive, I picked up the camera and moved it to a point about 30 yards away as they started moving down the field. There weren't that many people on the field, so you could get set up."

On the camera deck upstairs, cameraman Charlie Boyle, of NBC in Chicago, who was shooting the game for the network's Sunday newscast, threaded a 400-foot roll of film through his camera housing, shut the door of the fully loaded camera, and started shooting when Bart Starr called signals. Because it was so cold and cameras were jamming or film was breaking, Boyle kept his camera rolling, hoping the film would last until the game ended. It did.

The writers left the press box, with Don Weiss leading them downstairs. "Don said he was so cold that 'I almost couldn't do my job,'" Chuck Day said. "They had to go through the stands in Green Bay then. He would get quotes and go back up to the press box and deliver them to writers who had to hit their stories. He said somebody broke out the Jim Beam and passed it around. That was something not ordinarily done, but this was the absolute exception. And Rozelle was out in Oakland."

On the third play of the drive, Starr passed to Dowler on a slant over the middle for 13 yards and a first down at the Cowboys' 42. Dowler was knocked out when his head bounced on the frozen field after Cornell Green's clean tackle. When Donny Anderson was nailed for a 9-yard loss, Landry made a defensive adjustment. "He stationed the backs deep to prevent a long gain by the wide receivers," Pete Gent recalled. "That left the underneath open for the running backs, and Starr chipped away."

Coming out of the 2:00 warning, Starr hit Donny Anderson underneath, and he carried to the Dallas 30. "I never did this before, but I told Bart in the huddle, 'I'm open over in the flat if you need me,'" Mercein recalled. "He looked at me on the very next play. I was so open because Dave Edwards [the right-side linebacker] took a straight drop. Bart kind of guided the ball. When you do that, you don't get enough mustard on it, and it started to float to my outside shoulder. I had to make the pivot and catch it with my hands. I got around him and couldn't make the cut back into the field and went down the sidelines. I got 19 yards."

After a time-out, Starr called Mercein's number again on a rarely called run that the Packers dubbed "brown right, give 65." "Bart Starr calls 'give 65' the best play he ever called in his career," Mercein said. "On a sweep from the 'brown' formation, where the fullback lined up behind the quarterback, the fullback has to block where the guard left, in effect to replace him. [Dallas's defensive tackle] Bob Lilly, being the great All-Pro he was, read the play and followed the guard [Gale Gillingham] down the line of scrimmage. I would have had to clip him. Bart could see that if Lilly took what we call the influence, I could get the ball and run through the vacated place. Bob Skoronski had to make a good seal block, which he did, and I had to run over the middle linebacker, which I did. I was bigger than Leroy Jordan. You couldn't cut." Mercein's burst carried him to the Dallas 3 for first and goal.

After Anderson slipped short of the end zone on two running plays, Starr called Green Bay's last time-out with the ball at the 1, with 00:16 left, and ran over to the sideline to consult with Lombardi. Lombardi called "31-wedge," nominally a fullback plunge between the center and right guard. Starr, who had the coach's trust, said it was too slippery to make a handoff and told the coach he would carry it. To Starr's delight, Lombardi answered, "Run it, and let's get the hell out of here."

"The drama of getting it there and having Donny miss twice and the QB wedge made it so great," Mercein said.

"We had seven or eight cameramen, and everybody was shooting that," Steve Sabol said. "There wasn't a doubt we would get it. The end-zone cameraman was there to get it." From the field, Pat Summerall told CBS director Tony Verna to look for Starr to roll out right and throw to Dowler. But the cameraman in the end zone could not swivel his camera; it was frozen and set directly behind Jethro Pugh, in front of Jerry Kramer. Kramer, who might have beaten the snap by a fraction, but no one called a penalty, hit Pugh low with help from center Ken Bowman on his left and Gregg's seal block on Willie Townes to his right. Starr followed, as the Packers secured their third straight NFL title and fifth in seven years, 21–17.

"To me it's the greatest game ever played, under those conditions," Steve Sabol said. "It is the résumé of what Lombardi's Packers stood for—a 68-yard drive against the Doomsday Defense across a frozen field."

CBS showed the replay in the clubhouse celebration so many times that Jerry Kramer and his collaborator, Dick Schaap, had an easy title for their classic memoir of that season and game: *Instant Replay* is still bought and read four decades later. Kramer, for his part, shed a new light on his coach, calling Lombardi "one beautiful man."

A moment of tension came when Tom Brookshier, handling the interviews in the Packers' locker room, buttonholed middle linebacker Ray Nitschke. "I turned around and said, 'Here comes the madman of the Green Bay Packers,' and his face was all screwed up," Brookshier recalled. "Bob Dailey in my headset said, 'If he hits Brookie, let's go to the commercial.' Nitschke was ready to punch me on live

TV in the locker room. He was gonna drill me. Then later, he said, 'Hey, Brookie, you made me famous calling me the madman.' "

Unlike the earlier case with Charlie Jones, who couldn't persuade director Dailey to come to him in the losing Kansas City locker room after Super Bowl I for an interview with Lamar Hunt, Dailey agreed to put Frank Gifford on the air with Cowboys quarterback Don Meredith. What makes the spot memorable isn't what Meredith said to Gifford—"Dadgummit, we didn't lose anything" was the gist of their session—it's the way they clicked on the air. One important man was watching in New York. In three years, that man, Roone Arledge, would team Gifford, Meredith, and Howard Cosell to form their memorable "Monday Night Football" triad for ABC Sports.

One final Ice Bowl memory must be recounted. After they took a few moments to thaw out in the Packers' locker room, the CBS crew went their separate ways. Ray Scott headed home for Minneapolis, and Pat Summerall headed out at game's end to catch a flight to New York. Frank Gifford, Tom Brookshier, and Jack Buck chartered a four-seat Piper to make the 200-mile hop to O'Hare, in Chicago, about an hour-and-a-half flight. "Buck was going to St. Louis, Brookie was going to Philadelphia, and I was going to New York," Gifford said.

The plane was operated by an experienced local pilot, who, among his many flying skills, did some crop dusting in northern Wisconsin near Green Bay. "Buck was in the back with me. Gifford was in front riding shotgun with the pilot," Brookshier said. Gifford, Mr. USC, sat on the damned seat belt and didn't put it over his body. We were up about 500 feet, and all of a sudden, the damned door on Gifford's right, which hadn't been secured properly, opened, and he went halfway out. I reached out and grabbed him by the nape of the neck by his overcoat. I held on to keep him from going out the door."

"The door kind of popped open, and I pulled it as tight as I could, but it was 20 below zero, just getting dark," Gifford said. "I pulled the door so hard, I broke a strut on the plane. I couldn't really hold the door completely closed. I turned around, and there was frost all over Brookie and Buck's faces."

"Buck was drinking a little Jack Daniel's straight," Brookshier said. " 'Let him go!' Buck screamed over the roar of the engine. 'We'll do the commercial he's doing.' Buck thought it was a joke. It was no joke. Frank wasn't tied down."

"We were lucky we had a pilot who had been a crop duster," Gifford recalled. "The pilot said, 'Hold on. I'm going to get this thing on the ground.' We landed in a landing strip he knew that was about a quarter mile long. It happened shortly after takeoff, and we had barely gotten up to five hundred feet. Had we been up much higher, the controls would have frozen up, because they already started to. We were coming in for the landing, and he was pumping the steering wheel back and forth because he was starting to freeze up."

Once they landed, the pilot fixed the door strut and then rechecked and secured the passenger door, and they started up and took off for O'Hare and made their connections. "We laughed so hard," Brookshier said. " 'Frank,' I said, 'I had you right there, buddy. The only time I could have dumped you, and I could have let you go.' "

"It was a nightmare at the time, but we were lucky to have this guy as the pilot," Gifford said. At O'Hare before they caught their flights, Gifford and Brookshier said good-bye to Buck and then sat down for a drink. "The whole bottle! It was New Year's Eve!" Gifford said.

"We did a high-five at O'Hare, and I got on a plane to Philly and he caught one to New York," Brookshier said. "We always were competitive with each other. He was such a great player, and we had great mutual respect."

"That story just kills me," I said to Gifford in our interview.

"It almost killed me!"

Vince Lombardi was weary after driving himself and his teams so hard to gain the successes he achieved in just eight storied years in Green Bay. They still had a Super Bowl to play down in Miami against the American Football League champion Oakland Raiders, who routed the Houston Oilers 40–7. "It was a solemn week because we knew he was quitting," Chuck Mercein said. "It was almost like being at a wake. It was very anticlimactic. You couldn't take away from the Ice Bowl. You couldn't take away from the way we came back from a year that looked like it was going out of control."

CBS telecast Super Bowl II with Ray Scott handling play-by-play and Summerall and Jack Kemp providing analysis. "The Super Bowl that year was like playing an exhibition game," Mercein said. "I didn't play much. I was banged up. Lombardi was a hunch player, and he went with a hot-weather player who hadn't played in weeks, Ben Wilson." Mercein was out of football after the 1970 season.

After taking a 16–7 halftime lead, the Packers finished in style, winning 33–14. At the final gun, the Packers carried the victorious Lombardi off the field to the locker room, where a beaming Pete Rozelle awarded him his second Tiffany trophy, averting such a moment with Al Davis. Those moments would come three times over the next 16 years, but this day, January 14, 1968, belonged to Vince Lombardi, his Packers, all the denizens of "Titletown, U.S.A.," and the good citizens of Wisconsin.

"That was our third championship in a row," Mercein said. "I have a Super Bowl ring: it has three diamonds, signifying three straight NFL titles." No other team can make that claim.

The sun would set on the Packers empire 17 days later when Lombardi announced he was stepping down as coach and would remain as general manager. The Pack would not be back in the big game until Mike Holmgren led them to victory in Super Bowl XXXI in 1997. After an uneasy year as general manager watching the team fall to 6–8 under his successor and former defensive coordinator, Phil Bengtson, Lombardi announced his comeback as coach and general manager of the Washington Redskins with "equity," the block of stock he could not own in Green Bay because the team is publicly owned, by charter.

By September 1970, the indomitable Lombardi would be dead; a virulent form of intestinal cancer killed him within three months of its diagnosis. By Super Bowl V the following January, Pete Rozelle would give the silver football championship award to the victorious Baltimore Colts. It had been renamed the Vince Lombardi Trophy.

EIGHTEEN

THE *HEIDI* GAME

"Parents and kids were waiting for Heidi, *and the football fans wanted to see the end of the game. It blew out the switchboard at NBC!"*

—CHET SIMMONS, VP, NBC SPORTS PROGRAMMING, 2005

"*H*e wasn't really a yeller or a screamer," Pete Rozelle's daughter, Anne Marie Bratton, said of her father. If ever an individual truly possessed grace under pressure, those who knew him say Rozelle was that man. But, those closest to him also knew that fires raged under the commissioner's cool facade. He vented by smoking cigarette after cigarette. "Clenched teeth would be his way of expressing anger," Ann Marie recalled, "talking between clenched teeth and a tensed-up face."

"The part of Rozelle that people did not know was how tough he could be," said Ernie Accorsi, who served on Rozelle's NFL staff in the mid-1970s. The "broken pencil" story is one that's been passed along so many times that it has become NFL insider's folklore. Accorsi heard it repeated often by those who were there. The blowup came in a tense and testy meeting of the old National Football League members in 1968 after the merger. In the merger, both leagues agreed to end the practice of drafting players who had not completed their college eligibility and holding on to their rights until they had, but the issue had not been settled on the NFL side—yet. Those players were called "futures," and Vince Lombardi had mastered the art of finding burgeoning prospects, letting them ripen for one more year on the campuses, and then reaping the harvest.

Lombardi had just quit as Green Bay coach after Super Bowl II but still served the Packers as general manager. "The league was upset because Lombardi was winning championships and stocking up with future stars like Donny Anderson," Accorsi said. "Pete would not call the question in those days until he had the votes. On this day, he had the votes to defeat the thing."

When Rozelle put the issue on the table, Lombardi staged a filibuster. "He was getting up, making speeches, going on rants," Accorsi said. "Pete listened, and listened some more, through the diatribes."

Finally, he said, "We've heard from everybody." He turned to Kensil. "Jim, call the roll." Up went Lombardi, and he started in again. Tex Schramm, who was there, told Accorsi what happened next. "Pete held this pencil in both hands," Schramm said. "I could see the veins in his head starting to pop."

"Thank you, Coach," Rozelle said. When Lombardi got up one more time, Rozelle interrupted. "We have heard all we're going to hear from Green Bay!" Rozelle exclaimed as he broke the pencil. "That was like a gunshot," Tex said. "You could hear a pin drop as everyone heard that pencil break." Lombardi sat down, the vote was held, and they defeated it. Basically, they all said they had never seen anything like that. Lombardi kept his mouth shut.

That meeting serves as a prelude to perhaps the wildest-ever pro football game in the television era. On Sunday morning, November 17, 1968, *Heidi* was the name of a sweet little Swiss girl and the title of a made-for-television movie to be broadcast at 7:00 P.M. EST. With darkness descending across America well before 6:00 P.M. at this time of year, the network expected a huge audience that would continue through the evening in that preremote era when viewers tended to turn their sets to one station and leave them on through prime-time hours.

NBC had promoted the movie for days on the air and in the newspapers. Millions of children across America, especially little girls, could not wait to see it.

By nightfall, though, the very word *Heidi* would elicit curses by millions of football-fanatical fans.

Broadcast operations control, called BOC by television engineers, producers, and management, is the network nerve center. Every station has a BOC. All those switches and backup systems that BOC comprises are necessary for the network to stay on the air. NBC had major BOC operations from west to east, in Los Angeles (Burbank), Chicago, and—the number one BOC, at 30 Rockefeller Plaza—New York.

"As the BOC supervisor doing sports, I was supposed to print out a set of conditions each week describing what the network was going to do before, during, and after a live broadcast," Dick Cline, NBC broadcast operations control supervisor, said.

As he did every weekend at BOC in New York, Cline went about his routine assignment to keep the network running seamlessly. "I would sit down each week with the salespeople and the telephone people," Cline said nearly four decades later. "The salespeople would tell me what their commitments were after the game was over, if there were any. On this particular week, they had *Heidi* behind it, which was being sponsored by Timex."

Single sponsors still controlled the programming slots in those days. Timex bought NBC airtime from 7:00 P.M., straight up, eastern standard time, to 9:00. "From the sales point of view, we had to start *Heidi* at seven o'clock, because that was the agreement that they had made [with Timex]," Cline said. It was not deemed a big problem, because we never had gone beyond seven. Never."

For the telephone company, over whose coaxial cable lines the network transmitted its programs, Cline detailed the exact words to signal an engineer sitting at a switching station in the Midwest to switch from the live remote, the football game in Oakland, to the full network. "Here is your word cue, to run at (6)58:20," Cline wrote in his operation order. "This is the NBC Television Network. Stay tuned for *Heidi*." At that exact moment, the engineer out there in the Midwest would make his switch.

"There was only one way we could get the game out of Oakland to the network," Cline explained, regarding the presatellite transmission days of long lines and coaxial cables. "They fed it to our studio in Burbank, which inserted the commercials and fed the network. To feed the network, we bought a line from Burbank that tapped into the network round-robin along the Illinois-Iowa border west of Chicago. That tap fed the bottom [southern portion] of the round-robin, then came back into New York. New York saw it incoming, then fed it back. That way, Burbank was in control of the network." This sequence would be vital to the fate of the football game late that Sunday afternoon.

This was no ordinary game NBC was carrying that afternoon at four. The defending AFL champion Oakland Raiders, with a 7–2 record, trailed the Kansas City Chiefs by a half game in the hotly contested AFL West. The visiting team, Joe Namath and the New York Jets, also had a 7–2 record. The Jets were off to the best start in their history and had the best mark in the AFL East. A New York victory at the Oakland Coliseum would clinch the division.

The Raiders headed into the game with two prominent injuries. Quarterback Daryle Lamonica was doubtful with a knee injury. His backup, 41-year-old George Blanda, Oakland's placekicker, who'd been a pro since 1949, was ready and able, if needed. Oakland's top cornerback, Kent McCloughan, definitely was out. He had a severe knee injury that would never improve and, in time, would end his career. That meant rookie George Atkinson had to defend against the best receiver in the league, the Jets' Don Maynard, and the lethal accuracy of Namath at the top of his game.

The big pregame interest, though, focused on facial hair. Even Dave Anderson in the *New York Times* paid special attention to the red handlebar moustache of Oakland's larger-than-life defensive end, Ben Davidson, versus Namath's stylish Fu Manchu 'stache, the hip personification of his public identity, Broadway Joe.

Televised games still ran well under three hours in 1968, closer to two and a half. "There were fewer commercials and no overtimes, then," Cline said. All he knew was: "At seven, we gotta go. My main concern was what do we do if the game ends before seven: What do we fill with? Do we stay at the field? Do we have something to run?"

Everything had been worked out in midweek as it always had been. So, Cline published his orders and distributed them throughout the company as he always did so every department knew what it had to know. "Again, nobody called after the orders were sent out to say, 'Gee, what should I do if we go long?'

"I had the answer," Cline said. "We go away anyway. At seven o'clock, we go to *Heidi.* That was cut-and-dried."

To help you follow the action behind the scenes, here's a capsule of NBC's eight-man front line:

Dick Cline—BOC supervisor (New York)
Scotty Connal—executive producer (Connecticut)
Don Ellis—producer (Oakland)
Julian Goodman—network president (New York)
John Kimmelson—associate director (Oakland)
Carl Lindemann—president of NBC Sports (New York)
Ted Nathanson—director (Oakland)
Chet Simmons—VP, Sports Programming (New York)

Chet Simmons came from ABC in 1965 to serve as NBC's vice president of Sports Programming. Known as a tough boss ("My door is always ajar," was the pithy way he put it to many a cowed announcer and producer), Simmons was regarded by his loyal staff as a consummate pro who had your back. None was truer than executive producer Alan (Scotty) Connal, who served with Simmons at NBC and later rejoined him in the early days of ESPN.

"Scotty and I would alternate Sundays on who would handle problems if they came up," Simmons said in late 2005. "This particular weekend, our family was moving within the same apartment building in Manhattan. So, Scotty would give full-time attention at home to the games and be available if there was a problem. But I had the TV set on, and I was watching and kind of listening."

NBC Sports assigned its crack announce team of Curt Gowdy and Paul Christman to the broadcast and its top production team, led by director Ted Nathanson and producer Don Ellis. "Before we started, Scotty called me," Ellis said.

"We gotta get your game going early," Connal told his producer. "No guys talking for five minutes. Get to the game and get it going. The conditions demand we get out. We have the *Heidi* movie for kids at 7:00 P.M."

"I've worked at NBC for years, and it's part of my grounding that we cannot switch out of a game," Ellis answered.

"The salespeople have made the contract that this show—for kids with school the next day, and we can't keep them up—must run as scheduled," an adamant Connal stated. "It's gotta start on time! And that's the way it's gonna be, Don!"

Both Lamonica, who did start and played the entire game, and Namath threw plenty of passes that day. Lamonica threw 34 times, Namath 37. "Scotty called me at halftime, and we just talked about the fact that the first half seemed to run a little long," BOC supervisor Dick Cline said. "Nothing tragic. Nothing alarming. Just a reminder that we had to get off on time. Scotty, in turn, also dealt with Carl Lindemann, who was Chet's boss. Of course, Carl was at home, and Scotty was at home as well."

"They kept promoting *Heidi*, kept promoting *Heidi*. I kept looking at my watch, and I said to myself, there's no way to me that *Heidi* is going to make this at seven o'clock," Chet Simmons said. "Julian Goodman, the president of the company, told us going into the weekend that *Heidi* had to start on time. It was highly sponsored, well promoted, and could not start off the clock after seven."

"You get involved in the game," Don Ellis said. By that time, the action was going back and forth. It was the best game NBC had televised all season, and the roughest. The Raiders were penalized for 93 yards; the Jets, 146. Namath passed for 387 yards as Maynard burned Atkinson, the rookie, for 10 catches and 228 yards, still a Jets team record.

"Scotty was sitting at home with his wife and eight kids. I think some of the kids were waiting to see *Heidi*. At some point in our conversation, he said, 'Put up the score graphic.' It was important to him, so I put it up again," Ellis said.

"Teddy, put up the score," said Ellis to director Ted Nathanson.

"So, Teddy put up the score. Back in Connecticut, Scotty, who was showing off for the kids, said, 'See, Dad has control over everything.'"

Chet Simmons remembered, "I looked at my watch, looked at another table clock, looked at the game, and thought, no way is this going to happen."

Connal, who had been enjoying the telecast, also sensed the urgency, according to Dick Cline. "At about quarter of seven, Scotty called me, and I said, 'It looks like we might have a problem here, and I got to go away at seven o'clock,'" Cline recalled.

"I'm gonna call Lindemann and see if he can't get hold of the president of the company and see if we can get permission to stay on," Connal told Cline. "I'll get back to you."

As Lindemann tried to reach Julian Goodman, the tension heightened at Connal's home and in BOC, New York, while the game clock ticked ever so slowly way out west in the Oakland Coliseum. "Scotty called me," Ellis said. "He called me more than once during the game. This time, he called me in the latter part of the game. 'Don, it looks like this game is gonna run long.'"

Ellis answered, "Yeah, Scotty, we've got Namath and Lamonica throwing incomplete passes and stuff." The "stuff" included 19 penalties and each team using its allotted time-outs, a dozen in all, let alone postscore commercial interruptions.

"Yep," Scotty said. "I'm going to talk to Lindemann [whom Connal had called after speaking earlier with Cline]. We're gonna have to run over."

"So, Connal called Lindemann again, who was still trying to reach Julian Goodman," Ellis said. "They were trying to get this sorted out."

In the middle of this frantic activity, Connal's second phone line rang while he was on another call. Chet Simmons explained, "I picked up the phone and called Scotty. Now, we had the most glorious relationship until the day he died. He told me, 'Get the fuck off the phone,' and I knew something was going on."

While the minutes counted down to seven o'clock, Connal was trying to get everything "sorted out" with NBC Sports president

Carl Lindemann, who still was trying to get hold of the big boss, Julian Goodman, the only man who could avert the impending train wreck.

"It got to be 10 minutes before seven, and I hadn't heard anything," Dick Cline said. "I knew Scotty had two different phone lines in his home. I called the one line, and it was busy. So, I called the other line, and it was busy. They were both busy. I waited as long as I could, and I tried one last time," Cline said. "They were still busy. I had to go with what I had last known."

"Scotty was trying to find a way to bring this really good football game to conclusion and figure out what was he going to do with *Heidi* on both sides of the story," Simmons said.

At last, a desperate Connal got the call directly from Goodman granting permission to finish the game and "slide the network," that is, start *Heidi* as soon as Curt Gowdy signed off at game's end.

Out in Oakland, the call Don Ellis had been awaiting for the last quarter hour came at last. "Scotty called back and said, 'I've got permission from Julian Goodman; he gave us permission to run over. Pass the word.' I told John Kimmelson, who was our associate director, to pass the word along that we would stay with the game. He told Burbank, and presumably in my mind when I heard him over the PL [private cable line] explaining what happened, we were OK."

Connal then called BOC in Burbank, which had control of the entire network. "The operations director in Burbank would not listen to him because he didn't know who he was," Simmons said.

"These are Mr. Goodman's orders," Connal said.

"I have to talk to Mr. Goodman," the stand-on-ceremony Burbank operations director maintained.

"All hell had broken loose," Simmons said. "Parents and kids were waiting for *Heidi*, and the football fans wanted to see the end of the game. It blew out the switchboard at NBC!" One of those eager kids was the commissioner's 10-year-old daughter, Anne Marie, who let her household know where she stood: "I was obviously voting for *Heidi*."

"What had happened was, from a quarter of seven on, people called to find out if *Heidi* was going to start on time," Dick Cline said. "It started to overload the circuit. Then, at seven o'clock, more people called in, outraged, saying, 'Where's the football game?' So, fuses continued to blow, and I couldn't talk to a soul."

Connal, trying to reach Cline at BOC, was stymied by the busy signals. Nobody could get through because the huge switchboard was jammed beyond hope with all those irate callers, which neither man knew. Thus, lacking a countermanding order from Connal, who was the man in authority that afternoon, Cline had no choice but to follow his operation order. The switch had to be made.

After six lead changes, the Jets went ahead 32–29 on Jim Turner's 26-yard field goal with 1:05 left. Now the Raiders had the ball as the clock ticked toward its doomsday destiny, 6:58:20 P.M., eastern standard time. It was 6:57:30 and counting.

"I was in communication on a private cable line, not telephone land line, with the mobile unit," Dick Cline said. "I was on with the AD [John Kimmelson] and said, "At 58:20, we have to hit the NI—network identification. You got to give the word cue."

"No," Kimmelson said, "we're not gonna do that. We want to stay on."

"Now, I'd heard that a million times," Cline recounted. "Everybody wants to stay on."

"No, you aren't," he said to the AD.

Raiders quarterback Daryle Lamonica had just taken the snap and was in his drop-back before he flung a pass to his left for Charlie Smith, who caught it underneath the Jets' deep coverage, when Ellis's headset crackled again. "I heard yelling from Scotty's end," Ellis said.

"Why are you playing the closing theme?" Connal screamed.

"I'm not playing the closing theme," Ellis replied. He recalled, "I turned around and yelled back at our audio guy, 'Are you playing the closing theme?'"

"No. I'm not playing the closing theme," the audio man answered.

"Kimmelson, our AD, yelled at Burbank, 'Are you playing the closing theme? What do you mean we're going off the air?' And, for all of the country except the West Coast, it ended."

Remember the context of Dick Cline's operational instructions: The engineer in that cornfield near the Illinois-Iowa border had to listen for the word cue at 6:58:20, "This is the NBC Television Network. Stay tuned for *Heidi*."

"At the appropriate time, I said, 'That's it. You gotta go to the NI.' So, they went to the NI," Cline related. "The guy sitting out in the cornfield somewhere heard it, made the switch as he was supposed to, and the network doubled up to New York. That was it. I didn't see anything from the game after that. I could not physically see or hear anything more from the truck [from Oakland, via Burbank]."

"I told the crew to keep going and take it to the finish," Don Ellis recalled. "I didn't know where we were. We had switched to the network. There was only one line going from east to west. The telephone company had to make the switches to make it work. They heard the station ID cue to pull the plug and switch the switches, and they did it. That was it, and we couldn't get it back. There was no way they could switch back to us. The rest of the game was very exciting." At least the West Coast got to see it.

It turned out to be perhaps the most frantic windup in NFL history, and, because of that finish and the circumstances leading up it, the game still is regarded as the best regular-season contest ever played. Oakland's Charlie Smith had just caught Lamonica's pass and was running when *Heidi* came up across most of America's screens tuned to NBC. A Jets tackler grabbed Smith by the face mask and downed him at the New York 43, tacking on an additional 15 yards with the penalty. Lamonica then threw down the right side to Smith, who caught the ball in stride and outraced the Jets' defenders to the end zone to give the Raiders a 36–32 lead. "What a game!" Curt Gowdy yelled as Smith scored.

On the ensuing kickoff, New York returner Earl Christy collided with a teammate and fumbled. Oakland's Preston Ridlehuber picked up the loose ball at the 2 and went in for the score. In just nine seconds, the Jets had gone from division-clinching victory to 43–32 defeat.

When he got the final score from Ellis in the truck at Oakland, Cline ordered a technician in New York to flash it. The screams of irate football fans were then joined by equally enraged *Heidi*-ites across America. "The flash-caster graphic came up over the crippled child in the Alps as she was trying to walk for the first time," Cline said. "Just as she's going up the mountain singing the song, up came this huge crawl across the picture," Simmons recalled. "Is that the Peter Principle or what?" Well, it was certainly Murphy's Law.

Dick Cline had a long evening ahead back in New York answering questions about a situation not of his making and writing a report of the proceedings. "We went into the station break, and *Heidi* came up on time," Cline said. During the station break, Cline's phone rang. It was the president of the company. BOC had a private number that only he knew, and it was *not* a CIrcle 7 (247) number, NBC's switchboard exchange. That's the only way he got through. "This is Julian Goodman. Go back to the game," the president of NBC said.

"I didn't have a prayer, but like a very intelligent person, I told Mr. Goodman, 'I'll do the best I can,' " Cline recalled. "Now, I knew there was no way on earth I could do that. The guy who was out in a cornfield somewhere heard the word cue, made the switch, got in his car, and drove home. That was it. I was dead in the water, but nobody called. I got no phone calls, just as I didn't hear from Scotty."

He couldn't. NBC's old-fashioned switchboard crashed, and so did the company's exchange, CIrcle 7. "The whole exchange blew," Cline said. "They would put in a new fuse, and it would blow, and so on. They blew 26 fuses in an hour!"

Dick Cline could not reach Scotty Connal because both of Connal's lines at home were busy. Connal, already in conversation with the truck in Oakland, could not get through on his other phone to Cline in BOC because the switchboard was out. One key order that was missed or omitted during all that bedlam might have saved the game. "Scotty told the mobile unit in Oakland to tell me that I should stay with the game—and tell me that Julian Goodman had said so, that it was OK," Cline said. "The AD didn't do that. Fortunately for me, there were people in the postgame show studio who were on the circuit and vouched for the fact that such a conversation never occurred. Ellis told the AD that Scotty said Goodman told him to stay with the game." That imprimatur was not effectively communicated to Cline.

Cline was writing his BOC report when President Goodman called back to find out what happened. "I told him about the operational conditions," Cline said.

"Who did you send them to?" Goodman asked.

"As a matter of fact, you got a copy [along with the other executives on that long distribution list]," Cline told Goodman.

"Please make sure there's a copy on my desk before you leave there tonight," Goodman said.

"So, I sent a copy up to him—the original conditions with the distribution list," Cline said. "I had to write a BOC report, but no special report. I did get called into a meeting with my bosses the following morning. I was told that if I had done anything differently, I would have been fired because Timex would have killed us. If I hadn't made the switch, I would have gotten fired. Exactly one month later, I was promoted! I became an AD on remotes and never went back to BOC."

Back in Oakland, a furious coach Weeb Ewbank stormed into the Jets' locker room, where a clubhouse attendant told him he had a phone call. It was his wife back in New York. "Congratulations on the great win!" Mrs. Ewbank exulted.

"What are you talking about?" Ewbank screamed.

"Well, honey, you were ahead, and there was only a minute left, and we lost the feed."

"We lost the goddamned game! ———— it all."

The postmortems already were under way at NBC in New York. Ninety minutes after the switch, company president Julian Goodman issued a statement calling the incident a "forgivable error by humans" and adding, "I missed the end of the game as much as anyone did."

The *New York Times* ran the story on page 1 the next morning. Under the headline "Jets Cut for 'Heidi'; TV Fans Complain," Thomas Rogers wrote: "Fans of Heidi, the diminutive Swiss orphan girl in the story by Johanna Spyri, were happy, but professional football fans were irate last night when the National Broadcasting Company terminated its telecast of the New York Jets–Oakland Raiders game with one minute left to play and the outcome still to be decided."

The *Times*'s award-winning television critic, Jack Gould, couldn't resist a setup this juicy. "When it comes to doing the wrong thing at the wrong moment, NBC should receive a headless Emmy for last night's fiasco," he wrote.

NBC's Chet Simmons, though, understood the importance of that story placement in the country's most prestigious newspaper. "We made the front page of the *New York Times* the next morning. The American Football League made the front page of the *New York Times*. It really brought the AFL, the Jets, and Namath right to the forefront."

On Monday evening, David Brinkley concluded NBC's "Huntley-Brinkley Report" with the final minute of the wild finish at Oakland that nobody east of the Sierras saw live.

And, NBC called in the telephone company to make one last-minute adjustment. "To make a long story short," Cline said, "they put in a phone, which was known forever as the 'Heidi phone,' and it was on a different exchange so that could not happen ever again. It's still there."

NBC turned what should have been disaster into a huge success, making fun of the moment and winning new viewers. "They put an ad in the paper, which, as I recall, showed a shot of Namath with Heidi sitting on his shoulders to promo the next week's game," Cline recalled. Another print ad showed a drawing of Heidi with testimonials from the critics. At the bottom of her picture was this quote: " 'I didn't get a chance to see it, but I hear it was very good.'—Joe Namath."

"That was the season the Jets went all the way and won Super Bowl III," Cline said. "I think that *Heidi* Game had to have an effect on Rozelle and the NFL crowd, when they realized how passionate the AFL fans were about that ending. 'Hey, we have something here!' "

The following January, NBC publicist Ed Weisman, whose son Michael later would become executive producer for NBC Sports, created big blue-on-white buttons that read "Heidi loves the Super Bowl."

"We all wore those buttons," Don Ellis said. "We handed them out and gave them to people. It got everything going. All that publicity made fans for NBC and the AFL. So, we can credit Ed Weisman for that."

The *Heidi* game did change the rules of televised games: you must finish them to conclusion. Pete Rozelle himself did not issue a public comment, preferring to let AFL president Milt Woodard, who came to New York in the merger, handle the inquiries.

There was no need for the commissioner to say a word.

"Oh, yes. It was a crazy finish," Dick Cline said. "The perfect storm where everything came together at the wrong time."

NINETEEN

JOE WILLIE GUARANTEES VICTORY—AND TROUBLE

"I guarantee it."

—JOE NAMATH, JANUARY 9, 1969

*C*ontrary to the description offered by legendary college basketball coach Al McGuire, life for Pete Rozelle as 1968 morphed into the new year was not "seashells and balloons." His professional universe was pockmarked with nagging troubles.

For starters, Rozelle faced a new political culture after working with the Kennedy and Johnson administrations. Fellow Southern Californian and Republican Richard Nixon got elected president 12 days before the *Heidi* disaster/bonanza. The Nixon victory came at a heavy cost for America and a personal loss for Rozelle when close friend Senator Robert F. Kennedy was assassinated the previous June in Los Angeles just two months after civil rights icon Dr. Martin Luther King Jr. was cut down by a sniper in Memphis. On the upside, Rozelle knew this White House would be friendly, as Nixon was a rabid football fan, more so than any of his presidential predecessors.

At this same time, Rozelle's own National Football League lost its biggest star for the season. On November 10, the most electric runner ever, Gale Sayers, of the Chicago Bears, was carried out of Wrigley Field by several teammates after a diving hit by San Francisco's Kermit Alexander tore all the ligaments in his right leg. Sayers would return after months of strenuous rehabilitation to lead the league in rushing in 1969, but never again could he display the physics-defying moves, still shown repeatedly by NFL Films, that befuddled and dazzled defenders through the first 50 games of a spectacular career that would last just 68 games.

Meanwhile, the Baltimore Colts continued their rampage through the National Football League campaign that started in the last regular-season game of 1966. From that time through their surprisingly easy 34–0 rout of the Browns in the 1968 NFL championship game in Cleveland, the Colts won 26 games, losing just once, with three ties. That sole loss, 1967's final game, in the Los Angeles Coliseum against the Rams, knocked Baltimore out of the playoffs because the Rams outscored them 58–34 in their home-and-home series.

So, despite the 1968 league title-game victory, the Colts still had nothing to show for all that excellence except what had become a secondary league title and stepping-stone to the only game that mattered, the Super Bowl. As for the likelihood of their finally reaching the pinnacle, the so-called experts were convinced that Baltimore was the strongest NFL team in years, including Green Bay's championship run, and would easily handle the AFL New York Jets on January 12, 1969.

Rozelle did not relish the presence of Baltimore owner Carroll Rosenbloom on the Super Bowl's large stage. In the beginning, the Colts' owner had been a Rozelle partisan, first to congratulate him on his election as commissioner in 1960. Now, however, they barely spoke.

Their breach opened wide in 1963 over gambling. Steve Rosenbloom admitted in our interview for this book that his father bet on college games. He was not as certain about the pros, but he could not rule it out. "There was an incident," he said. "One of these hoodlums went to the league and said, 'Carroll is betting on these games.' He was trying to blow the whistle."

That was the outgrowth of a federal suit filed in 1960 by one Mike McLaney. Carroll Rosenbloom and crony Lou Chesler backed McLaney in a Havana casino before Fidel Castro's regime took over. McLaney charged in a deposition that Rosenbloom cheated him out of a finder's fee. Then he alleged that he and the Colts' owner had partnered in a football betting operation. In the course of that deposition, McLaney claimed that Rosenbloom placed a $55,000 bet against the Colts.

Steve Rosenbloom addressed his father's 1963 crucible in our interview, stating, "As long as I can remember, and we were pretty intertwined for a long time, I never knew him to bet on a professional game."

Carroll Rosenbloom denied all charges, but the case lingered in Rozelle's office through the spring of '63 after the commissioner suspended Paul Hornung and Alex Karras. Rozelle explained to Rosenbloom that he had to investigate him or else admit to a double standard.

Rosenbloom, a man who took orders from no one, did not like what he was hearing. "This incident really upset my father with Rozelle," Steve Rosenbloom said. "My father felt that Rozelle didn't stick up for him, in a sense. That pissed him off because, first of all, the commissioner works for the owners. Sometimes they forget that, but that's how it works. One of the reasons the NFL's so strong is the owners, starting with George Halas, granted strong powers to the office of commissioner to protect the league against themselves. They didn't want individuals running around creating havoc, and it paid dividends, actually."

The case went to trial in the summer of '63. "I knew the fellow [McLaney] who brought him into the situation," Steve Rosenbloom said. "He came to the house several times. He swore in court that Carroll bet on those games. He picked a year and said, this team, this team, this team. It turns out that the Colts did not play half those teams that he named for a particular year. And that's why that case went down the toilet."

Sayers's injury left Pete Rozelle with just one truly bankable superstar: Joe Namath. And he was trouble. Not only was Namath in the other league under Rozelle's domain, but also he was under J. Edgar Hoover's FBI microscope, dossier and all, with everything that entailed, from facts to semitruths to rumors to total fabrications. The Namath dossier dated from 1967 when Hoover's minions called in accounts of Broadway Joe's hangouts and predilections. The gleanings featured an Outfit-tinged joint called the Pussycat Bar, owned by a member of the Lucchese mob family; numerous sexual escapades that included a possible abortion; plenty of long nights in New York bars in the company of one beautiful woman after another; and whispered rumors that he had "thrown" several games. Truth be damned: the dossier, with all its innuendos, was bound to stir up trouble for its subject.

Since the FBI kept the commissioner's office up-to-date on the comings and goings of players, Rozelle was apprised of the contents of the Broadway Joe file. He and his security people paid close attention to the activities at a bar-lounge in which Namath had an interest, a place called Bachelor's III that he owned with restaurateur Bobby Van and ex-Alabama teammate Ray Abruzzese.

The way things transpired that star-crossed year of 1968, Rozelle could have wondered if he was undergoing payback for knowing and saying nothing back in 1966 when both the Oakland Raiders and New York Jets were endangered species. In the original draft of the merger agreement submitted by Tex Schramm and Lamar Hunt, the two owners proposed moving the Raiders to Portland to preserve the Bay Area for the 49ers and sending the Jets to Memphis to give free rein to the Giants in the Big Apple. Only Wellington Mara's about-face in recognition of the legal implications of such a scheme stifled the deal before it became public knowledge at the time.

Ever since the merger, Rozelle had been forced to cope with Raiders major domo Al Davis. "The Genius," as his associates called him, made the commissioner his avowed enemy. Rozelle couldn't abide him. The Jets had become less of a problem for Rozelle these days since the AFL's other difficult owner, David "Sonny" Werblin, sold his interest in the team at the outset of 1968 to his partners Phil Iselin and oilman Leon Hess.

Still, both teams, the Raiders and Jets, continued to take up too much of Rozelle's time, especially in the aftermath of the wild *Heidi* Game on November 17. After that penalty-filled brawl, Rozelle lowered the boom on the Jets. He fined safety Jim Hudson $200 for being ejected and giving the Oakland crowd the finger as he left the field. He fined assistant coach Walt Michaels $50 for berating the officials. John Elliott was fined $50 for his ejection compounded by slugging Raiders Hall of Fame center Jim Otto. Similar offenses in the present big-money era would incur five- or six-figure fines.

Finally, the commissioner fined the team $2,000 for "extreme bad manners." That resulted when Jets physician Dr. James Nicholas stormed the officials' locker room after seeing one of the Raiders work over Namath. Coach Weeb Ewbank exacerbated the situation when he showed game film of the incident to the press. "Whenever coaches made comments at press conferences [or to the press], I would remind them that 'Commissioner Rozelle will follow the constitution [forbidding criticism of officials] to the letter, and it's very possible that you will have repercussions coming from it,' " former NFL supervisor of officials Art McNally said.

As Paul Zimmerman, then a *New York Post* beat writer, recounted it to Mark Kriegel in *Namath*, Ewbank's game film showed Oakland tackle Dan Birdwell firing a bolo punch at Namath well after he'd thrown a pass. "Birdwell hit Namath as hard as he could," Zimmerman said, "right in the balls."

A few weeks later, a major officiating gaffe in Rozelle's original NFL made headlines in the wake of the Bears' 17–16 victory over the Rams in the Los Angeles Coliseum on December 8. It was a game Chicago had to win to stay alive in its chase for the NFL Central title with the Minnesota Vikings. "I was there. This was my first year off the field as an observer," Art McNally said. "I'd sit in the press box, take notes of what I had seen in the game, but nothing in detail."

In the final minute, Roman Gabriel threw a first-down pass that was batted down near the goal line. One of the officials on the far side of the field called holding. The officials penalized the Rams 10 yards, which moved the ball back toward midfield, out of field goal range. It should still have been first down, but then came a sequence that eluded everybody on the field and upstairs. "We didn't know at the time that this still was first down," McNally said. "The box man [downs marker operator] with the chains on the Rams' side flipped the one over to the two. In those years, we didn't have a box man or chains on both sides. He was up close by the Rams' bench area, and everyone was standing up close to the sideline. So, no one picked this up, including the officials. They believed it was second down."

Gabriel threw three more incomplete passes. The Bears took over, ran out the clock, and went home with a 17–16 victory. "When the game was over, I went downstairs to the dressing room," McNally said. "Shortly thereafter, there was a knock on the door. It was Elroy Hirsch, general manager of the Rams, and he said, 'Art, can I talk to you?'"

"Sure," McNally said. "What do you got, Roy?"

"They tell me upstairs that we only got three downs in that last series."

A disbelieving McNally replied, "You what?"

"We only got three downs in that last series," Hirsch said firmly.

"I don't recall," McNally said. "Come on into the dressing room."

"I'm not supposed to go in," Hirsch said.

"Elroy, come into the dressing room," McNally said. "Talk to the crew."

Once inside, McNally spoke first to the crew: "Elroy Hirsch here indicated there was only three downs instead of four on the Rams' last series."

"Wait a minute," the officials said as they recapitulated the sequence. "Nah, everything's fine."

"I hope everything's going to be OK," Hirsch said. Then he left.

McNally was scheduled to catch the 10:30 P.M. red-eye for New York. He went to dinner with referee Norm Schacter, whose day job was principal at the famed Hollywood High School, which many of filmdom's biggest stars attended when they were young. Hollywood High was the model for television's Walt Whitman High depicted in the ABC series "Room 222," which ran from 1969 to 1974.

After dinner, McNally called his boss, Mark Duncan, in New York to fill him in. "Look, instead of taking the red-eye, stay overnight," Duncan said. "Tomorrow morning about eight o'clock, go down to the Rams' office. You can look at the film, and then you'll know."

McNally rose the next morning at 6:30 and called Duncan back east, where it was 9:30 A.M., to let him know he was heading to the Rams' offices. "You won't have to," Duncan said. "They missed a down."

Duncan had called the game's film cameraman, a man named Walter Poret, who verified that the Rams got only three downs. So, McNally went to LAX and flew to New York. When he landed, he called the office and spoke to his assistant, who told him, "The commissioner made a decision. He's going to suspend the entire crew."

That meant referee Schacter, umpire Joe Connell, head linesman Burl Toler, line judge Jack Fette, back judge Adrian Burk, and field judge George Ellis got no assignments for the rest of the season and playoffs. They all returned in good standing in 1969. Schacter, who had refereed Super Bowl I and the Ice Bowl in Green Bay in 1967, came back to referee Super Bowl V and Super Bowl X.

In today's NFL, with the layers of officials checking and cross-checking replay video, that lapse would not have transpired. Even had it slipped through that screening process, the victimized coach would fling a red flag to stop play to force a review and discussion until it was corrected. "The commissioner knew it was so serious that he had to take the very serious step of suspending them," McNally said. "We knew we could not let that happen again, and it never has."

The Jets got their chance at redemption against the Raiders in the AFL title game on December 29, 1968, at Shea Stadium, a week after Oakland clobbered the Kansas City Chiefs 41–6 in an AFL West playoff. It was another bare-knuckled brawl, especially after Namath got nailed in a pincer between Ike Lassiter and Ben Davidson's knee-to-the-head. Obviously groggy, Namath got up and played the rest of the game with a concussion.

The score was 20–16, Jets, in the fourth quarter when Oakland's George Atkinson intercepted a wayward Namath pass meant for Don Maynard. Namath ran down Atkinson and put his shoulder to the rookie, knocking him out of bounds at the 5. When Atkinson got up and threatened to kill him, Namath countered with an expletive. After the officials broke it up, Oakland's Pete Banaszak drove in for the go-ahead touchdown to make it 23–20, Raiders. Then Namath showed his mettle. When he saw the Oakland corners press his wide receivers, he sent George Sauer and tight end Pete Lammons to the left to clear the field. Maynard, playing despite a balky hamstring, had enough left for one last major effort. He broke downfield past Atkinson, and as he arrived for the long pass, the gusty wind grabbed it. Maynard skewed around to make a circus catch at the 6 for a 52-yard gain. On the next play, Namath checked off his primary and secondary receivers, Sauer and fullback Bill Mathis, saw that tight end Lammons was covered, and, after he slipped, found Maynard in the back of the end zone. The drive took just over a minute, giving the Jets a 27–23 lead with 7:47 left. Namath had passed for 266 yards and three touchdowns.

Daryle Lamonica, who passed for 401 yards, led Oakland to the New York 12. With two minutes left, Lamonica, under a heavy rush, threw wildly behind running back Charlie Smith. Ralph Baker recovered the lateral for the Jets, who iced their AFL title and trip to Miami.

In the clubhouse, when reporters asked Namath about the Colts, he said he hadn't seen enough of them to comment. That would change. That night at Bachelor's III, Namath poured champagne over Johnny Carson. "First time I ever knew you to waste the stuff," the king of late-night television cracked. The party went until dawn.

The Jets arrived in the Miami area on Friday, January 3, 1969. From that point on, all eyes, ears, cameras, and tape recorders were directed to Joseph William Namath, of Beaver Falls, Pennsylvania; Tuscaloosa, Alabama; and New York, New York. For the next week, a man called Broadway Joe would deliver a bravura one-man, off-Broadway performance the likes of which had not been seen in those parts since 1964. That's when 22-year-old, 7-to-1 underdog Cassius Clay taunted, provoked, hustled, and outboxed "that ugly bear" Charles "Sonny" Liston for the heavyweight title in this same sub-tropical city, Miami, and then announced to the world that he had a new name, Muhammad Ali.

Another notorious self-promoter, the oddsmaker Jimmy "the Greek" Snyder, despised by the rest of his fraternity, proclaimed that Baltimore was a 17-point favorite. And that was the low end. One bookie made the Colts a 7-to-1 favorite, the same prefight number the smart guys called before the first Clay-Liston fight. Odds favoring the NFL titleholders kept shifting upward, from 18 to as high as 23 points.

Actually, many predictions tilted much more toward Baltimore. "I picked the Colts to win that game 42–7. I believe they were 17- to 18-point favorites," *Miami Herald* columnist Edwin Pope said. "Namath hung around Miami a lot and had good times. He was conscious of what the *Miami Herald* wrote about the game. He didn't speak to me for 30 years after that game because of that pick. I saw him at a celebrity golf tournament a month later. He was teeing off, and he said, 'Forty-two to seven!' and he spit on the grass. Namath was the perfect guy to do that. No other quarterback had the charisma to do that."

"Growing up as I did in Chicago and covering the Bears forever, I was caught *up* in the NFL euphoria," Bill Jauss admitted. Jauss was still working at the old *Chicago Daily News* in 1969 when his editor asked him to make a prediction on the score. "There was only one answer that made sense. If Baltimore was the greatest team since the days of Halas's Monsters of the Midway, I had to go with 73–0. So, I did!" Jauss roared at the memory.

The huge point spread and the supreme confidence that NFL partisans displayed in the Colts seemed all the more reasonable considering how Baltimore tore apart the league without any help from the team's formidable leader, quarterback Johnny Unitas. In the final exhibition game back in September, against Dallas at the Cotton Bowl, the great quarterback felt something snap in his right elbow as he threw a long touchdown pass to John Mackey. "The two tendons that hold the upper and lower bones together were snapped off at the bone," Unitas said. In today's world, with the "Tommy John" elbow-tendon replacement surgery becoming almost routine for athletes, some wizard of an orthopedic surgeon could have fixed Unitas posthaste. Instead, as Tom Callahan wrote in *Johnny U.*, "the tendons just lay in there while he compensated as best he could." By the end of his life, his right arm, still unrepaired, was virtually useless.

The Colts' front office immediately went shopping for a quarterback. Coach Don Shula knew Earl Morrall from his time as an assistant in Detroit, when the former Michigan State all-American quarterbacked the Lions. Detroit was one of six NFL stops for Morrall, an NFL vagabond starting his 13th season in 1968 in what would be a 21-year career. Top draft choice of the San Francisco 49ers in 1956, the crew-cut Spartan became expendable when the Niners grabbed local product John Brodie, of Stanford, as their top pick the next year.

The 49ers shipped Morrall and guard Mike Sandusky to Pittsburgh in 1957 for guard Marv Matuszak and two first-round draft picks. He started ahead of Lenny Dawson that year and for the first two games in 1958, until the Steelers swapped him to Detroit for the legendary Bobby Layne. Happy to be "home," a little more than an hour away from his college triumphs, Morrall started most of the next seven seasons for the Lions. He enhanced his personal celebrity and income by delivering sports on the newscasts at the CBS affiliate WJBK-TV. The usually affable Morrall was plenty tough, reputed as the best fistfighter, if pushed, on a team renowned for brawlers. After Morrall hurt his shoulder in 1964 against the Bears, the Lions shipped him to the Giants in the off-season. He started the next two seasons, but it was back to the eyeshade and clipboard in 1967 when Fran Tarkenton arrived in New York from Minnesota. Then Shula called.

All Morrall did at age 34 was attain that bright, shining moment that every professional craves. While Unitas tried to get healed, Morrall became the league's Most Valuable Player as he threw 26 touchdown passes on a 93.2 quarterback rating, both NFL bests. Instead of creating factions and being jealous, Morrall and Unitas became close friends—and remained so until Unitas died from a heart attack during a workout on September 11, 2002. While Unitas saw tune-up action in five games at the end of the season, completing 11 of 32 passes for a pair of touchdowns, this was Earl Morrall's hour, and he would start the Super Bowl, and likely finish. But John Unitas was ready, just in case.

When the Jets settled into the New York Yankees' spring training facility at Fort Lauderdale, Namath, propitiously, was assigned Mickey Mantle's locker. The team encamped at the old Galt Ocean Mile, a seaside resort on A1A, the South Florida Seaside Highway, that housed the Green Bay Packers the year before. Namath and Jim Hudson stayed in suite 534, the Governor's Suite, the same one Vince Lombardi had occupied. Inside, instead of doing what people had come to expect of America's party animal, the young man studied films of Baltimore and took careful notes as he stored away the "edge" information that would make the difference on Sunday.

"Namath swore that they stopped looking at the film of the Colts five days before the game, because they didn't want to become over-confident," Charlie Jones said. Namath told him, "We knew we were better than them."

Broadway Joe was feeling his oats in his week in America's fun-and-sun capital. Before the AFL championship game, he had shaved off his Fu Manchu whiskers for a Schick commercial and $10,000 fee. Then, on the flight to Florida, the savvy Namath opened the war of words in comments to Dave Anderson, of the *New York Times*. He called Oakland's Daryle Lamonica a better passer than Earl Morrall and, to make certain that nobody missed his point, said, "I mean it."

On that flight, Namath made it clear to Anderson that his league had it all over the established, old-line NFL. "We've got better quarterbacks in our league—John Hadl, Lamonica, myself, and Bob Griese," Namath declared. For good measure, he tossed in the name of his backup, Vito "Babe" Parilli. "You put Babe with Baltimore, and they might have been better. Babe throws better than Morrall."

By the time the Colts arrived on the morning of Sunday, January 5, Namath had them sputtering like Daffy Duck. That evening, the first person Baltimore's Lou Michaels saw when he entered Jimmy Fazio's House of Prime Rib, in Fort Lauderdale, was none other than his fellow western Pennsylvanian, Joe Willie Namath. Namath had quit smoking nearly two years before, but he was not about to give up the hooch.

Mark Kriegel wrote in *Namath* that the quarterback was wearing his fur coat and sipping a tumbler of Red Label as he eyeballed the scene near the waitress station. Lou Michaels was the younger brother of Jets assistant Walt Michaels and had been a college team-mate of Joe's older brother Frank at Kentucky. Somehow, the two got into an argument over who was the better Catholic. Finally, as Namath told Jeff Miller in *Going Long*, Michaels said, "We're gonna kick your butt!"

Broadway Joe's retort lit up Michaels: "Hey, Lou. What are you talking about? You're just a goddamned kicker!"

Michaels admonished that Joe's hero John Unitas would never act that way, to which Namath snapped, "Unitas is an old man. He's over the hill." With that, Michaels got set to take care of the wise guy, when Hudson, of the Jets, and offensive guard Dan Sullivan, of the Colts, intervened. The quick-thinking Namath then pulled out a hundred-dollar bill. He bought a round for the bunch and also paid for their dinners. Afterward, he gave Michaels and Sullivan a lift to their hotel. The con was in full swing.

The next day, the Colts' king-size and agile defensive end Charles "Bubba" Smith said that while he respected Namath's ability, "a football player who's real good doesn't have to talk." Smith still held fast to the post–World War II all-America credo, flouted by Ali and Namath, that champions were solemn, dignified, and humble. "This gives us a little more incentive to get him—understand, not try to hurt him, but to get to him like any other quarterback," the intimidating Smith said.

Smith's former Michigan State roommate, Jets defensive tackle Jeff Richardson, warned that Bubba, a great player in college, "now has learned to play like Superman."

The Jets, though, had other thoughts about the Colts, especially after studying their game films and seeing how they played. On offense, Baltimore always ran to the strong side, never the weak, and the Jets felt they had a shaky passing game. On defense, they relied on the safety blitz and did not cover the vacated area. They employed a zone, which played into the hands of Namath and his receivers, who attacked zones like a pack of starving jackals going after raw meat. When it to came to handling a blitz, Namath and his receivers had studied the Colts' tendencies so well that the quarterback didn't have to call an audible. The receivers went to the vacant area, and he got them the ball before he got hit.

On Thursday afternoon, after a team barbecue, Namath swapped his cup of beer for a cup of Red Label on the rocks; then he showered and dressed for an evening at the Miami Springs Villas, where the Miami Touchdown Club honored him as Pro Football Player of the Year. One speaker after another gave him a good-natured ribbing. When Namath finally took the mike, he proceeded to deliver the usual perfunctory remarks.

As he thanked his family, teammates, coaches, and the Jets ownership, a heckler tried to shout him down. Namath, his eyes no longer sleepy, cracked back, "We're gonna win the game." Every reporter there but Luther Evans, of the *Miami Herald*, missed the story. The Herald ran a banner over an Evans article that now is on display in the Pro Football Hall of Fame. That "guarantee" could have buried Namath, but instead, because of his performance, it ensured his lasting fame.

On Friday, both coaches announced they would enforce 11:00 P.M. curfews. Commissioner Rozelle also made some announcements, beginning with the news that Sunday's Super Bowl would be the next-to-last one pairing the champions of the National and American Football leagues. Rozelle said new divisions would be formed into a single league. He did not detail the intricacies of the realignment, which did transpire later in the year when Cleveland, Pittsburgh, and Baltimore agreed to join the intact 10 AFL teams to form a 13-team American Football Conference, leaving behind a 13-team National Football Conference and creating a balanced overall league. In addition, Rozelle stated that NBC and CBS had the first rights of refusal on a new television package to start with the 1970 season.

For the Super Bowl telecast, NBC charged $55,000 for a 30-second spot and sold out easily. Tickets in the Orange Bowl still were scaled at $12, $8, and $6, and all 75,389 seats were sold.

To this point in the merger, Rozelle had looked at NBC with a skeptical eye. CBS had been the favored network from the time he took office. Rozelle became close personal friends with many people there, from Bill McPhail to Frank Gifford and Pat Summerall. In general, he felt at ease in the company of the men from Black Rock, be it over drinks, lunch, vacations, or proven performance. In Rozelle's eyes, NBC had to atone for the Super Bowl I second-half kickoff fiasco when referee Schacter, realizing that NBC had not returned to the air from its lead-in commercial after halftime, had to blow the whistle to stop play and then restage the kickoff. The *Heidi* turmoil only enhanced the tension in the pregame scenario.

Rozelle was still bothered as well by the nomenclature *Super Bowl* for his special game. He considered *super* a slang word, and he had no use for slang. As Don Weiss wrote, the commissioner really wanted to call the game the "Pro Bowl," but that name had long been used for the league's postseason all-star game. He even staged a naming contest in 1968 among sportswriters, dangling an all-expenses-paid trip to the 1970 NFL meetings to announce the winner. Sobriquets such as "Ultimate Bowl" and "Premier Bowl" turned out to be the best of the mediocre entries. So, at his Friday pregame press conference, he threw in the towel. "We're pretty well stuck with it," he acknowledged.

For all of Pete Rozelle's worries, the NBC Sports operation was in excellent hands. When it came time to produce Super Bowl III at the Orange Bowl, Chet Simmons had his team ready to show the world who they were and how well they would stage football's show of shows. "It was a huge amount of fun because we felt, even though we were under the guise of the NFL, that we were the underdog," Simmons said. "We were the AFL guys. We took it very seriously. We were very, very creative on how we put the original AFL teams into markets where we thought we had a better shot at a better number than CBS because we had better games, better matchups, high-scoring games."

Ted Nathanson was NBC's lead football director, so capable that he was the only director at any network who also was given credit as his own producer, although he did not handle the producer's many tasks during a telecast. "Teddy was, perhaps, among the top one or two football directors during the time I was involved," Simmons said. "I think Teddy never got the recognition he deserved because Harry Coyle got so much for baseball. Football was Teddy's piece of cake."

NBC's lead announcer for every big event from 1964 through 1979 was the late Curt Gowdy. "The best word I could find about Curt," Simmons said, choosing precisely, "was *irascible*." The Gowdy temper was legendary. He did not want to share airtime with fellow announcers. He was sparing with credit. *Cheap* is the first word that producers who last worked with him nearly four decades ago still invoke when they tell how he went out of his way to avoid sharing a tab at dinner or over a drink. Picking up a check was out of the question.

Yet, in the category of professional ability, no one gets higher marks from peers. "Talentwise, there was no one better," Simmons said. "There are periods in our lives when we are at the top of what we are doing. When Curt was at the top of his game, you could not touch the man for his versatility and ability. When it came to calling baseball, football, basketball, the top three sports in our country, there was no way to touch him. He played basketball [at Wyoming], he served for years with the Yankees and Red Sox, and was a top football announcer."

But Gowdy "had his own way of doing things, his own way of wanting things done," Simmons said. "He could be a very difficult guy to work with. He hated athletes in the booth. He hated it, but he loved Paul Christman, and he loved Tony Kubek."

Christman did not partner with Gowdy on the Super Bowl III telecast. He had joined CBS in 1968 to work with Ray Scott, a position that allowed him to cover the Midwest and be closer to his home outside Chicago. Ex-Giants Kyle Rote and Al DeRogatis joined Gowdy for a three-man booth, a year and a half ahead of Roone Arledge's creation at ABC.

Jim Simpson, who worked the game of secondary importance in all sports during Gowdy's reign, handled the sidelines. Simpson put everybody at ease, including coworkers, athlete-experts, and, most important, the audience. "Jim had patience. He had kindness. He had talent," Simmons said. "That's the difference between people. You could throw Jim at arm wrestling with gators, and he'd do a good job."

Simmons's MVP—most versatile player—was Charlie Jones, who would call the radio play-by-play on Super Bowl III, with CBS mainstay and fellow Arkansan Pat Summerall and ex–Notre Damer George Ratterman handling the analysis. "Charlie was another one of these extraordinarily dependable talents," Simmons asserted. "I guess if you asked him, football was his favorite sport. He did a lot of great work with track-and-field. He could do them all. He was an Olympic kind of announcer; give him any venue, and he could do it. He was a sweet, good guy to work with."

Television had not yet turned Super Sunday into a daylong event. The program opening featured a panorama shot from the end zone as Gowdy set the scene: "NBC Sports presents the third AFL-NFL World Championship Game. The Super Bowl. The American Football League champions, the New York Jets, versus the National Football League champions, the Baltimore Colts. From the Orange Bowl in Miami, Florida."

Appearing on camera over a chroma-key background of the stadium below, Gowdy noted that they could have sold 150,000 tickets had there been room. Whether it was Namath, the Colts, or both, for sure the game had drawn America's interest.

Baltimore opened strong as expected, running for big chunks of yardage. Then, the Jets held and forced a Lou Michaels 28-yard field goal attempt. The left-footed kicker pulled the ball wide right. Namath came back and shook the Colts with a 55-yard pass for an open Maynard that the receiver just missed and, had he not had a sore leg, would have caught in stride. So, Baltimore adjusted and dropped into deeper zone coverage. Namath started working underneath, connecting with George Sauer and tight end Pete Lammons.

Baltimore got the ball back with 18 seconds left in the first quarter when Sauer caught a Namath pass and fumbled at his own 11 after Lenny Lyles's hit. On the second play of the second quarter, Morrall fired a quick pass to the end zone. Jets middle linebacker Al Atkinson got a finger on the ball, which deflected off the shoulder pads of wide-open Tom Mitchell, and Randy Beverly pulled it in for the touchback. New York had turned back Baltimore twice in scoring territory. "Right from the opening kickoff it was a football game within a 'this can't be happening' aura," Don Weiss wrote in his memoir.

Namath led the Jets back with an 11-play, 80-yard drive, mixing short passes to Sauer and releases to Matt Snell before he called Snell on a sweep around left end for the touchdown. The Jets led 7–0. New York stop number three came when Johnny Sample stepped in front of Willie Richardson to intercept Morrall's pass at the New York 2.

But the key play of the game came at the end of the half. With time for one play, Shula called a flea-flicker. Morrall handed to Matte, who rolled right and lateraled back to the quarterback. As wide-open Jimmy Orr waved futilely at the New York 10, Morrall, who did not have a strong arm, threw instead for receiver Jerry Hill, and Hudson intercepted to end the half. NBC's cameras did not catch Orr in the open either live or on replay. NFL Films, fortunately, had an isolated camera follow Orr and intercut that sequence into the Super Bowl film with a master shot of Morrall lining up to throw.

Everything was going wrong, and Baltimore's Bubba Smith knew it. "He was wide open, the primary receiver, and Morrall said he didn't see him," Smith said in 2006. "How can you not see your primary receiver? Tom Matte broke loose, and nobody was close to him when the guy got up off the ground and caught him. Unitas was supposed to start the second half, but the game was still too close [7–0]." Because he didn't start, Unitas believed to the end of his life that Shula had lied to him; he was certain he could have led the Colts to victory had he opened the second half. Smith and his line mates, meanwhile, were getting beaten off the ball all day by the well-drilled Jets.

"We had a lot of opportunities in the first half that we didn't take advantage of," coach Don Shula said, in his evaluation of the game for this book. "In the second half, they just dominated us. They had the ball, and we couldn't get the ball. They had ball control and kept putting points on the board." While the Colts made no first downs in the third quarter, Jim Turner's three short field goals gave the Jets a 16–0 lead.

Finally, at the start of the fourth quarter, Shula sent in Unitas. "I worked on the radio with George Ratterman and Pat Summerall," Charlie Jones said, "and the thing I remember is the moment Johnny Unitas came in. He's the man. He's still the man. After three plays, you knew he didn't have it. The arm wasn't there." That became evident with just over 11 minutes left, when Unitas executed his precise drop-back and then took aim on a down-and-in pass for Jimmy Orr in the end zone, a signature feat that had terrorized the NFL for 13 seasons. The ball hung up as Beverly stopped in front of Orr to make the Jets' fourth interception of the afternoon.

"For whatever reason, you could feel it," Jones said. "That's when we knew the AFL was going to win." Playing on guts alone, Unitas led the Colts downfield on their next possession in an agonizing drive that the Jets contested every inch of the way. Jerry Hill plunged over from inches out with 3:29 left to cut the margin to 16–7. Then Tom Mitchell kept it alive when he fell onto an onside kick at the New York 44. Unitas ate up 25 yards on three pass completions; then, no more. His last of three straight incompletions badly missed Orr, and it was over.

The enduring image of Super Bowl III is that shot of Namath captured by NFL Films as he runs off the field waving his index finger, the first time most people had ever seen an athlete use that now hackneyed gesture. The Jets had pulled off the greatest upset in pro football history, 16–7.

Pat Summerall was on duty all day, working for NBC radio during the game and doing the television pre- and postgame shows. Along with so many other NFL stalwarts, he went into the game confident in a Colts victory. "I went down out of the radio booth with about two minutes to go right after Unitas came in and led them to their only touchdown," Summerall said. "Bob Cochran, the league's broadcast liaison, came up to me and said, 'You got a minute?' "

Summerall answered, "Yeah, I got about a minute. I have to do a postgame show in a strange locker room." The Jets were about to win.

"The commissioner is back under the stands," Cochran said. "He wants to talk to you."

"I went back, and Pete was standing there smoking a cigarette as only he could smoke a cigarette," Summerall recalled. "He could get one done in about two drags. He was nervous. 'What do you know about Weeb Ewbank?' he asked. He had to present the trophy to Weeb, and he was not prepared. 'Tell me everything you know about Joe Namath.' He was totally unprepared to make the presentation. He did not know Weeb at all." After their brief huddle, Rozelle took one last drag, tossed the butt, entered the Jets' locker room, and handled it flawlessly.

When the commissioner finished his presentation, Summerall went to the Colts' locker room. "There was only one person who would speak. 'Let me take a shower first, and then I'll talk to you.' That was Johnny Unitas."

Years later, Bubba Smith claimed in his autobiography that the game was fixed, a charge that he repeated to me but that never has come close to being proved. Danny Sheridan, who has made his living for decades publishing betting odds, could not be more adamant in his disagreement with Smith's allegation. "Let me tell you why it wasn't fixed," Sheridan said. "When an inordinate amount of money shows up on a sporting event, and that money is ripe, something suspicious is going on. In Super Bowl III, there was no inordinate money bet. Period. The Jets upset the Colts. The bookmakers didn't care about that. They got equal betting on both sides."

"The thing that really sticks out most in my mind about that game—forget the winning; the losing; the telecast, which was good; and the great shots, which were good—after the game, we went back to the league part of the hotel to see people," Chet Simmons recalled. "The greeting that we got was anything but cordial. It was as if we, the NBC television guys, had won the game. We were treated so coolly, it was almost like, 'What are you doing here?' "

Then Simmons had a confrontation with Rozelle's second in charge, Jim Kensil, a powerful executive and physically imposing man. NFL all the way, Kensil was upset by the AFL upstarts' victory. "He started giving us a lot of hell about certain people using their credentials in the wrong part of the stadium after the game," Simmons said. "I took a line of hell from him for God knows it felt like a long time. The game was over. We won. The American Football League won. It was a great game. If anybody didn't know how good that would be for professional football, they were asleep. And this guy was so frustrated that he was banging my head about credentials."

After that set-to, Simmons rejoined his group and their party while Kensil stepped aside, went back to his people, lit a cigarette, and then came to his senses. He realized he had committed the cardinal sin in Rozelle's universe by losing his poise. "Jim Kensil was with the league for 16 years. He was the anchor of the league office," Joe Browne said. "After the game, we were all upset that the other league, especially Namath, beat us. Kensil took a puff of his cigarette and said, 'This is the best thing that happened to us.' And I think if Pete didn't say it, he certainly realized it."

"Pete was fine with it," Simmons said. "Pete was smarter than those guys. He knew what this was going to do for the NFL with the merger. He did all the right things. I'm sure it wasn't great for him to stand there and give the trophy to Phil Iselin, but it was better than it turned out to be when he had to give it to Al Davis years later."

For Charlie Jones, Super Bowl III was a life-changing experience. "At some time during the Vietnam War, I had mentioned a personal desire in a casual conversation with Rozelle," Jones said. "He smiled and nodded, the kind of reaction you figure is, 'That's dead in the water.' The Wednesday after Super Bowl III, the phone rang here at the house. It was Pete Rozelle. 'Charlie,' he said, 'I'd like you to go on the NFL-USO tour of the hospitals in the Far East: you, Joe Namath and Jim Otto, [tight end] Marv Fleming, and Steve Wright. Can you go?'

" 'You bet,' I said. I was absolutely thrilled. That was my personal desire. We were gone for 21 days. It was the best 21 days I ever spent in my life, because I got up in the morning and knew I was doing the right thing, helping people. It's the only time I ever felt that way. I knew I was wanted and needed, that I was there. It was fulfilling. It was very special, hard to describe—the young men that I met. I did Super Bowl III on the radio. One kid ran up to me: 'I gotta shake your hand. I gotta shake your hand. You saved my life.' "

Jones asked, "How did I save your life?"

"I was in the guard post, and we had the radio there," the soldier said. "It was four in the morning, and we couldn't get reception. I took the radio across the street and set it on a big rock and got the reception perfectly. As soon as you came on the air, incoming [fire] came in and blew the shit out of that shack I was in."

Well before Pete Rozelle had to deal with Al Davis in a victorious Raiders' locker room, his next order of business concerned Joe Namath, who remained the big story during the off-season when the commissioner came down on his part ownership in Bachelor's III.

Paul Tagliabue was 29 in 1969 and had just joined the Washington office of Covington and Burling, the firm that handled major legal work for the NFL, after serving three years in the Defense Department as a nuclear weapons planner. He was assigned to senior partner Hamilton Carothers, who acted as the NFL counsel. "Ham asked me to do something about the Joe Namath ownership of Bachelor's III," Tagliabue said. "I met Pete later that summer in connection with the Bachelor's III hearing."

All spring, several law enforcement agencies—the NYPD, Manhattan district attorney, and feds—were looking into activities at Bachelor's. Namath was not an active owner, but the notion that he might drop by the bar was enough to bring in revenue. Unfortunately, as Paul Zimmerman recalled, much was happening. "Everything was going on there," Zimmerman recalled. "Gambling, narcotics, prostitution. They had a bank of 20 phones downstairs."

According to raconteur Bert Sugar, "Bookies frequented the place, and they used those phones, which the authorities traced." Commissioner Rozelle wanted Namath to get out of there because the appearances were damning to himself and the league, but Namath was as true to his friends as he was to his teammates. Weeping openly before the New York television news cameras, Namath announced that Rozelle delivered an ultimatum to sell his interest or face banishment. So, Namath told the world he was quitting football.

"I was beat man on the Jets [for the *New York Post*] when the Bachelor's III stuff with Namath broke," Paul Zimmerman related. "Receiver George Sauer said, 'I'll dig ditches before I go back to play football,' to which Jets defensive tackle Gerry Philbin said, 'There's a guy who never dug a ditch.' They were calling Pete a fascist and all that. So, I went up to his office. 'You can't write this story,' Rozelle said. 'The FBI tipped me that they're going to bust this place.'"

When Rozelle made Namath aware of the economic consequences of his stubbornness, he decided to sell out rather than flush away several million dollars in endorsements and playing contracts. His partners agreed to buy his share, and, presto, he was back in football. "I had to get him out of there before they moved in," Rozelle told Zimmerman. "He wouldn't go on his own, so I ordered him out.

"Two days later, a guy from FBI called me," Rozelle continued. " 'What the hell did you do? You ruined our whole operation. None of those guys are hanging around there.'

"Gosh, I'm terribly sorry," he said to the agent. "Then," Rozelle told Zimmerman, "I just breathed a sigh of relief. I got him out of there."

A seriocomic scene ensued when Namath went to the commissioner's apartment to iron out the details. "Rozelle told Anne Marie to stay in her room," Sugar said. "Joe was her hero and the biggest heartthrob of every teenage girl at that time. She said the meeting was almost deep-sixed when she ran out and asked for his autograph."

Realignment was set by the time the old National and American Football Leagues kicked off their final seasons in 1969. For the NFL, this was season 50, and the players wore a commemorative league patch. The AFL, now a decade old, had its own patch. It was fitting that an expansion team, the Minnesota Vikings, won the last original NFL title. Jim Finks, a Pittsburgh Steelers quarterback in the early '50s before he became a successful executive in the Canadian Football League, was named general manager of the Vikings in 1964. In 1967, he traded quarterback Fran Tarkenton to the New York Giants. Then he imported two key men from Canada. One was coach Bud Grant, who replaced Minnesota's first coach, Norm Van Brocklin. The other was quarterback Joe Kapp, a tequila-drinking, hard-nosed, gung-ho leader who preached "40 for 60," meaning all players play all out for each other every minute of the game.

In 1968, Kapp, whose fluttery flings somehow found receivers, led the Vikings to their first of 11 division titles over the next 15 seasons. Then, in 1969, they smashed through the NFL regular season with a 12–2 record, allowing just 133 points over the 14-game schedule. Enjoying home field advantage in the bracing Minnesota air, the Vikings eked out a 23–20 victory over the Rams in the division playoffs. Then they hacked their way to a 27–7 victory over the Cleveland Browns in the final NFL title game.

To help ensure that AFL teams would stay even with their NFL brethren and not lose their edge in the Super Bowl, Oakland's Al

Davis came up with an idea in 1966 that revolutionized the game. "He's responsible for the extra games in the playoffs. He thought that up with the wild card game," Ron Wolf recalled. Instead of divisional champions meeting for the league title in the game following the regular season, the "wild card," like a wild card in card games, gave a second-place team a chance at redemption and possibly winning the championship in the postseason playoffs.

"Al introduced that in AFL meetings and it got passed," Wolf said. "The old National Football League never had that." Naturally, Weiss in his book gave the NFL credit for the wild-card playoff concept.

The wild card Kansas City Chiefs had to beat the defending champion Jets and the Raiders to reach the Super Bowl. The Raiders beat the Chiefs twice in the regular season to win the AFL West by a game. In the regular season finale at Oakland, Hank Stram ordered quarterback Lenny Dawson to call running plays in a vanilla game plan that showed nothing of value to Al Davis and his rookie coach John Madden in a game the Raiders won 10–6.

In the AFL division playoffs on December 21, the Raiders dispatched the Houston Oilers 40–7, while the Chiefs went into the icy, swirling winds of Shea Stadium in New York to face the Jets. With Kansas City leading 6–3 early in the fourth quarter, the Jets had first and goal at the one, and the Chiefs held, forcing a Jim Turner field goal for a 6–6 tie. The Chiefs took the lead for good, going 70 yards on two plays. First came Dawson's 51-yard strike to Otis Taylor, followed by his scoring pass to Gloster Richardson for a 13–6 victory.

When the Chiefs and Raiders met two weeks later, again at Oakland, in the final game of the old American Football League, the Chiefs' defense keynoted a 17–7 victory to become the league's first two-time Super Bowl representative and its first wild-card champion.

Progressive Hank Stram loved to talk about his "offense of the '70s," with shifting backs, plenty of motion, moving pockets, reverses, and the like. And Stram had assembled a huge, mobile team on both sides of the ball. Most important, Stram was a trendsetter. Realizing that many able black athletes were being overlooked by the NFL, Stram gave his astute personnel man Lloyd Wells carte blanche to find and bring back talent from the lesser-known black schools.

Wells returned with players such as future Hall of Famers Buck Buchanan and Willie Lanier; defensive backs Jim Marsalis, Emmitt Thomas, and Jim Kearney; and Willie Mitchell, to name a few who would augment such veterans as Minnesota's all-American Bobby Bell and Jerry Mays. Eight of the 11 starters on the Kansas City defense were black. In time, every team would mirror that trend.

Lenny Dawson has been a regular sportscaster at KMBC, in Kansas City, since 1967. In 1968, he would run from practice to the station, to go on the air at six; edit stories and prepare scripts after dinner; and go back on the air at ten. Then he went home to see his wife, Jackie, and say hi to the kids. By day, Dawson was Stram's quarterback, a player the coach grabbed off the NFL scrap heap when Cleveland's Paul Brown gave up on him in 1961. From that point forward, Dawson enhanced his all-America credentials from Purdue to become a member of the Pro Football Hall of Fame.

By game week in New Orleans, though, Lenny Dawson was a marked man. NBC's "Huntley-Brinkley Report" ran a story on January 6, 1970, naming the Chiefs' quarterback in a federal investigation out of Detroit focused on gambler Donald "Dice" Dawson. They were not related, but for that week at least, their names became almost interchangeable and, for the 34-year-old quarterback, a colossal burden. "Sure is, when you can't defend yourself," Len Dawson said in 2006. "There was no truth to it. I couldn't defend myself, and I was the center of attention. It not only affected me, but it affected my family, probably more so; I had the outlet of practicing football and getting away from it for a few hours each day."

By the time the story broke, Dawson already had spoken with Rozelle. "He called me before the Oakland championship game," Dawson recalled. "That's kind of strange, I thought. Why would the commissioner call me on the eve of a championship game? He called to wish me luck and probably had other reasons to do that. It couldn't have been just that."

Then he heard that NBC was going to break the story. "My name was just one of the names that came up," Dawson said. NBC correspondent Bill Matney, from the Chicago bureau, covered the story at the federal building in Detroit. Donald Dawson was a Detroit restaurateur who ran a book and gambled, his specialty being dice games. Names tossed about included Hall of Fame baseball pitcher Dizzy Dean, Lions quarterbacks Bill Munson and Karl Sweetan, and Len Dawson.

"In New Orleans, they came rapping on my door," Dawson said. "There wasn't security like they have today. There is no way today in the Super Bowl hotel that people can just walk on the floors where the players are staying; you have security all over the place. That wasn't the case back then. They were knocking on my door. 'I want you to answer this now,' the reporter said.

"Everybody congregated," Dawson went on. "When I talk about everybody, I mean Stram, Lamar Hunt, and Jack Steadman, the general manager, who brought somebody in to discuss how to handle the PR situation. Eventually, I said, 'Tell them the truth. I've met the guy, Donald Dawson, and I haven't seen him in years.'"

Dawson added, "He did call me the previous November when my father died in Alliance, Ohio, to offer his condolences. If they had a record of his phone calls, that's how my name popped up. Frank Gifford was interviewing me after the game, and he said, 'Hey, all of us on the Giants knew that guy.'

"They put me through enough tests," Dawson said. "The head of security came up and grilled me. I forget who that was, but he said, 'I've grilled a lot of guys—murderers, rapists, and others—but I never had anybody fall asleep on me while I interviewed them.' I had a cold." At midweek, Rozelle announced that Lenny Dawson had passed all tests. He was cleared on all counts. Dawson remarked, "I knew if I could handle that, I could handle anything."

Despite the success of the Jets in Super Bowl III, NFL bias still prevailed in pregame speculation as conventional wisdom favored the Vikings by at least 13 points. "That was an incredible game," Dawson said. "I think we surprised a heck of a lot of people. Propaganda was for the National Football League. They tried to kill the American Football League before it got started by offering Minneapolis an expansion team if they dropped out of the American Football League deal. How embarrassing was that when the [AFL] owners were up there to have a meeting to discuss scheduling and the draft, and the headlines are 'They Back Out'? That's when the Raiders came in."

For this Super Bowl, Ed Sabol, of NFL Films, knew he wanted to put a wireless microphone on a coach. Of the two candidates, the choice was obvious. Minnesota's Bud Grant wasn't known as the "Great Stone Face" for nothing. That moniker, which he shared with Ed Sullivan, derived from the fact that he truly never showed emotion on the sidelines. Hank Stram, on the other hand, was a nonstop, roving chatterbox, as colorful as he was competent. He was even better in the cut version of the NFL Films production. In that priceless study, keyed to the theme "Everything Is Up-to-Date in Kansas City," with the song from Rodgers and Hammerstein's *Oklahoma* playing underneath John Facenda's narration, Stram grabbed the spotlight and never let go.

The game quickly turned into a romp for the Chiefs, as the defense stymied Joe Kapp and the Vikings, and Dawson and the offense meticulously had their way. Stram's running narration was a classic. "They can't cover you in a million years. . . . That's like stealing. . . . Kassulke's running 'round like it was a Chinese fire drill! . . . Just keep matriculatin' that ball down the field, boys."

By this time, Dawson and the Chiefs, who did not know Stram was wired, figured their coach was up to something. As talkative as he always was on the sideline, he'd never been so voluble. Then, late in the first half with the ball on the Minnesota 4, he called Gloster Richardson to his side and issued an order on perhaps the most famous play call in pro football history. "Tell Lenny to run '65 toss power trap,'" Stram declared. Twice. Then, as Richardson relayed the call to Dawson in the huddle, Stram told everybody within earshot to "look for '65 toss power trap.'" It ran to perfection as Mike Garrett shot between the left guard and tackle for the touchdown, and a gleeful Stram chortled again and again, " 'Sixty-five toss power trap.' Yes!"

It was great television for NFL Films and Kansas City fans. While not so hot for Minnesota followers, it lives on as the cap on an outstanding performance. "We snuck up on the Vikings in that game,"

Dawson said. "They had beaten up the National Football League, and they had a heck of a defense. Not nearly as good as ours. We pulled in our horns after Otis Taylor scored. I can still remember looking up at that clock when Hank took me out of the game with about a minute to go or so and saying, 'Wow. We did it.'"

Dawson added, "After the game, President Nixon called to talk to Hank first, then me. At first, I said, 'President of what?' I never would have guessed the United States. Then he told me."

Len Dawson was inducted into the Pro Football Hall of Fame in 1987. "I played in that stadium in Canton when I played for Alliance," he said. "I remember going back home visiting my relatives in '63 when they built it. They had one building at the time. Now it's really something. I figured, the only way I'll get in here is pay the admission charge. Little did I know that I would be there."

So, the great Pro Football War officially had ended. The new, two-conference, 26-team National Football League would carry on and enhance the tradition, but, of course, it would not be the same. In the coming decade, the new AFC would win 8 of the 10 Super Bowls, with Dallas winning the NFC's pair. But 5 of those AFC titles would belong to former NFL stalwarts, with 1 to Baltimore and Pittsburgh taking the other 4.

This was the product of one man's ingenuity, blood, and sweat. "Rozelle was a heck of a guy," Len Dawson said. "It wasn't easy, but it is amazing that he got people to work out the details of what he proposed."

TWENTY

TURN ON THE LIGHTS, THE PARTY'S STARTED

"'Monday Night Football' was not *Arledge's baby; it was Rozelle's, and anything to the contrary is bullshit."*

—CHUCK DAY, 2005

By 1970, Pete Rozelle was 44, and his leadership style was fully developed. "He was a passive, but firm, type of commissioner who had a good vision, good outlook," said Ed Sabol, founder of NFL Films and Rozelle's close friend for most of his time in office. "Pete was not a blustering sort of guy. He was not a General Patton. He was more of a General Bradley."

A decade into the job, Rozelle knew who he was, knew where he was going, and still entertained greater ambitions for his now fully merged National Football League. As calm as he appeared, that internal motor still raced at a high rev with the habit he could not break. "Too bad he smoked so much," Sabol said. "He smoked two or three packs a day. Chain-lit them. Marlboro was his brand."

The first thing people noticed about Rozelle was his impressive bearing. He stood tall and always looked elegant in his clothes, correct whatever the occasion. The gentleman's mode was an acquired look for the California native, thanks in large part to Ed Sabol. "I went to prep school," Sabol said, "and we had to wear jackets and a certain tie at every meal. I think people look better when they dress like that."

To complete his friend's success persona, Sabol, who spent his early life in the clothing business, became Rozelle's style mentor. "When I first met him, he was wearing cheap suits and wingtip shoes. 'Pete,' I told him, 'those clothes gotta go! We got to get a little more style here.' " So, Sabol called a Philadelphia tailor he knew from his overcoat business and had him visit Rozelle in his office. "He measured Pete, then came back and tried the fittings. Pete began to like the way he looked." Soon he had a closet full of custom-made suits with all the trimmings for every occasion.

Sabol finished his sartorial tutelage with lessons in the fine points of neckwear. "He had a tie where the knot was about the size of your fingernail, and he'd keep sliding it up and down," Sabol said. " 'Pete,' I told him, 'you gotta stop with that ugly little knot. Now, I'm gonna show you how to tie your tie.' Then he learned how to tie his tie."

That polished style made his appearances before any group a special event, especially those directly involved with the league. "Rozelle after the merger, after everything was settled, became almost like a mystical person," former NBC sportscaster Charlie Jones said. The big event for the NBC Sports football operation each summer was the annual preseason meeting in New York, and the highlight was the commissioner's visit. To the announcers and producers, it was a chance to see the great man in person. To the brass, it was D-day.

"The whispers began on the morning of his arrival at 30 Rockefeller Plaza," Jones said. " 'Rozelle will be here at 11:45. He will speak to us at noon, and he's going to talk for 15 minutes, and we won't ask any questions.' Now, this was all set up in advance. We'd take a five-minute break and cover items, then be set for the commissioner. At 11:15, the NFL guys that were there started to get reports: 'He's now left the building.' Then, 'He's in traffic in a limousine.' Then, 'He's arrived downstairs.' As soon as he came up the elevator, the world stopped! He had this great tan. He was always upbeat, immaculately tailored, full of life."

"It was like the trumpets of royalty," said Merlin Olsen, the Rams Hall of Famer who worked for years alongside Dick Enberg on NBC telecasts. "You literally had that feeling. It was gracious royalty. Pete was always there with a smile and good, positive information for us."

"His talk would go along the lines of the NFL is fully sold and how exciting a year it will be," Jones said. "And then he disappeared. I think that part of his power was the mystique that he built."

Having assumed the role of overall czar of the combined National Football League, Rozelle decided at an early-1966 postmerger meeting to unveil a plan to free the league from its Sunday confines. "He asked the owners for support to look for prime-time football as part of the regular season," said Chuck Day. "In the notation in the minutes [which Day's writing partner, Don Weiss, retained in his files], the owners were in accord that 'if he thought such games were necessary, it was his call.'" Rozelle asked the owners to agree that when he went to CBS, and then to NBC, and finally, as a last resort, to ABC, he would have their support, "and if I come back with a package, you will approve it." He got it.

Rozelle had taken a couple of stabs at prime time in the premerger days. He floated a Friday-night trial balloon in 1964 that got punctured before liftoff when critics screamed that such a move would destroy high school football. That same season, the first in years that Green Bay and Detroit would not play on Thanksgiving, Rozelle scheduled the Packers and Lions on Monday night, September 28. The game was not televised, but it packed Tiger Stadium with 59,203 fans, the largest Detroit crowd ever in the old ballpark.

Rozelle finally persuaded CBS to undergo a prime-time trial on Monday night, October 31, 1966. The Halloween special matched the league's charter teams, the visiting Chicago Bears in St. Louis against their former crosstown rivals, the Cardinals. "Busch Stadium was equipped with the type of lights that color television required," Chuck Day said. The network treated it like a playoff game, splitting the play-by-play call between the Bears' regular announcer, Lindsay Nelson, and the Cardinals' Jack Drees, a native Chicagoan. Bears Hall of Famer George Connor handled the color as the Big Red prevailed 24–17. The matchup was interesting but no ratings success.

"You knew he had 'Monday Night' in mind," Dave Anderson mused. "Rozelle had to be thinking, do you think this will go?'"

The experiment continued through 1969 under the premerger contracts. NBC slated two Monday-night AFL games in both 1968 and '69. CBS returned with a Packers-Cardinals game in 1967, again in St. Louis, and two more Monday-nighters in '68 and '69. "I did a Monday-night football game at CBS in Dallas between the Giants and Cowboys," Jack Whitaker said. The 'Boys, now an elite team, toyed with New York in a 25–3 victory.

Before Rozelle made a television move in those days, he called in his network liaison, Bob Cochran. "Bob had been a salesman at CBS," Pat Summerall said. "He used that salesman's approach: let's keep the clients happy, let's keep the image perfect, and let's not let anything interfere with what we're trying to paint here. He was terrific."

Speaking of that relationship, Chet Simmons recalled, "He had a small coterie of really close pals that included Summerall, Bill McPhail, Gifford, and Bob Cochran, who became his television liaison guy with us for many years. If you walked into Manucci's, where they had lunch several times a week, you were always welcomed into their group. I always enjoyed being in Pete's company. Cochran did all the television legwork for him. Bob built great relationships with the networks. He was that kind of a guy. I was extremely close to him. I felt my relationship with Cochran made my relationship with Pete a little bit deeper."

"Bob was a Harvard football player, a man's man," Ernie Accorsi said. "He went to school with Bobby Kennedy but knew Jack well. He campaigned with Jack Kennedy—used to ride in the car with him. He knew Jack way back when he was a representative. He was a bald-headed, strong-looking guy, not an ounce of fat on him. We used to call him Cocky. He, Pete, and Kent Flower, who was executive head of NFL Films' New York office, would go out and have their cocktails."

Bob Cochran was just 46 when he died unexpectedly in 1979. "He had a heart attack. He lived a hard life," Pat Summerall said wistfully about a man who had set the table for the NFL's incredible journey into prime time.

"We joked that if you could only put football into prime time, you could make more money," Pete Rozelle's close friend Herb Siegel said. "Then he did it."

Rozelle possessed the supersalesman's knack for making the customer or client feel that a sale was his idea, not the salesman's. Rozelle knew going in, before the convincing began, that the people he went after were willing buyers. That certainly held true with Roone Arledge and ABC Sports. " 'Monday Night Football' was *not* Arledge's baby; it was Rozelle's, and anything to the contrary is bullshit," Chuck Day said.

Arledge was back in the hunt for an NFL deal by 1969. Crushed in 1964 when his bid to grab the entire NFL package fell short, the ABC boss zeroed in on a prime-time package. "Football has the potential for drama and heroics," Arledge wrote decades later in *Roone*, his memoir. Sensing that the game could reach more people than it currently did in 1969, Arledge admitted, "I was thinking about women. That other half of the viewing audience."

Arledge had become the unquestioned star executive at ABC. His run to the top began in 1960 when he first tested his production theories on the college football package that he'd deftly swept away from the sleepyheads then in charge at NBC. He picked up speed in 1961 with the success of his weekend anthology series, "ABC's Wide World of Sports," and kicked into high gear by 1965 when he grabbed prestige sports franchises one by one.

By 1969, ABC owned the rights to NCAA football, golf's U.S. and British Opens, and the NBA and had televised at least one set of Olympic Games since 1964, to the point where ABC's production trucks bore the slogan "Network of the Olympics."

Yet, in both news and prime-time programming, ABC still was regarded as the poor relation among the three networks, a klutzy kid to be kept out of sight when company comes. Arledge used ABC's prime-time schedule as the punch line to a joke: "How do you end the Vietnam War? Put it on ABC. It will be canceled after 13 weeks!"

In conversations with his key executives and producers after his experiences and production innovations with the AFL and college football, Arledge knew CBS and NBC had done everything wrong in their experiments with prime-time games. "Their idea was to plant cameras at the fifty-yard line and call it a day," he wrote. To Arledge, that old-school approach may have fit noncompeting hometown Sunday-afternoon telecasts, but prime time, he believed, required multiple cameras and interesting varieties of shots, stirred in with pageantry, hoopla, and promotion to form a thoroughly entertaining package. A prime-time game, in his view, had to be special and compelling, and he intended to make it happen.

So, Arledge began his courtship of Pete Rozelle. "It took many lunches over the next eight months to persuade Mr. Rozelle that we weren't as bad as it seemed," Arledge wrote. At the same time, Arledge had developed a friendship with Rozelle's longtime chum Frank Gifford. The ex-Giant and the ABC executive got to know each other at Winged Foot Golf Club, where they were both members, and then became close when they commiserated over Scotch at P. J. Clarke's as they were undergoing divorces. Gifford's contract with CBS ran until 1971, at which time Arledge intended to bring him aboard, not only because he was camera friendly and a personal friend, but also because surveys showed he was believable and extremely popular with men and women alike across America.

"When he was planning to negotiate 'Monday Night Football,' Roone came to me," Gifford said. "He knew that I knew Pete well. They had met, but he didn't really know Pete well. I was at CBS, and I had no plans to go to 'Monday Night Football,' but Roone was a good friend running 'Wide World' at ABC. We had long talks before their meeting. It was interesting to me."

Soon Rozelle was joining Arledge and Gifford at Arledge's bachelor pad for drinks, conversation, and friendly pool games. They clicked. "Roone was the same kind of guy as Pete," Gifford said, "very bright and a great negotiator."

Before Arledge could get serious about a deal with Rozelle, he still had to clear the hurdle at home base. His ABC bosses remained unconvinced that he could deliver women, the key element to prime-time success with football or any other program. As Arledge remembered it, ABC's new president, Elton Rule, "did not want football intruding on our prime-time schedule, no matter how dismal the ratings."

Intrusion threatened from the outside as well. For several years, Howard Hughes, in all his mysterious aura, had been looming over the ABC network. Long an ABC suitor, the reclusive billionaire bought the independent Sports Network in the early '60s. Hughes Sports Network, HSN, a confederation of a hundred or so independent stations, had done well televising college basketball when interest was small. Starting in the Midwest with the Big Ten, HSN eventually gained the rights to the NCAA Final Four when it paid $140,000 in 1963 for a five-year package to telecast the championship weekend, then played on Friday and Saturday nights. That contract covered the tournaments from 1964 through 1968, when NBC got the rights starting in 1969 for $500,000.

In August 1969, Bob Cochran dropped by Arledge's office to inform him that the NFL was listening to HSN's blandishments. "You've got to be kidding," Arledge told Cochran. "That's not even a network."

Cochran then dropped the other shoe when he said that as many as one hundred ABC affiliates were ready to jump ship and go with Hughes on Monday nights. That included ABC's top affiliate, WFIL-TV, in Philadelphia. "ABC was doing test-pattern ratings," Gifford said. "So, Roone convinced his people, including chairman Leonard Goldenson, to take it."

Gifford, who was still at CBS then, related, "When they got around to negotiating 'Monday Night Football,' it started with lunch at Toots Shor's. I joined them for lunch, then went back to do the local news. I got a phone call just after the local news, and they wanted to know if I would have dinner with them at '21'! They were still together, and both of them were really good drinkers. I've often thought about how both were just charming and great listeners. It's amazing anything happened. They came away from it with a deal."

Out of that long day of liquid negotiations, Arledge and Rozelle came to agreement on a three-year, $25.2 million deal. When they started to draw up a contract, however, the commissioner extended his palm in the classic "wait a minute" gesture. He told Arledge that because CBS and NBC had been NFL contractors for so many years, they still had first rights of refusal. Arledge boiled inside at the unfairness of that, but he had no choice as Rozelle shopped the package one more time to ABC's competitors.

"I remember being on the boat [Rozelle's *Triple Eagle*] with Bill McPhail, Pete, and Bob Wood, the head of CBS at the time, when he begged CBS to take 'Monday Night Football,'" Pat Summerall said. "He didn't want NBC included or ABC either. NBC was covering the AFL games then. He wanted CBS to have 'Monday Night' because of his close friendship with McPhail." According to Summerall, Rozelle beseeched Bob Wood, "Please take 'Monday Night Football.'"

CBS had a powerful Monday lineup with the likes of "Gunsmoke," "Lucy," "Mayberry R.F.D.," and "The Carol Burnett Show." As Summerall recalled it, "Wood called Bill Paley from Pete's boat. 'No!' Paley said. 'We're pretty happy with our schedule on Monday night. I don't want to mess with what we have, because we're number one!'"

With CBS out of the picture, Rozelle had to go to NBC. The network executives told him to forget it because "Tonight Show" star Johnny Carson threatened to walk if his late-night extravaganza and rating champion would be forced to start well after midnight in the East on Mondays, when the audience had gone to bed.

"Now, Rozelle realized that ABC might be a player," Keith Jackson said. "Roone had signed, and ABC had carried, the old AFL. The production ideas already were alive at that level, so ABC was a player, in Pete's mind. Roone walked in and dropped the package on them, and the rest is history. Tagliabue did the same thing in 2006 to NBC; he walked in and handed it to 'em. I guess if you're tolerant and keep your mouth shut, good things will happen."

Rozelle called Arledge with the news. "I guess you owe a thank-you note to Johnny Carson," the commissioner said. "It's your show, Roone."

Now that he had prime-time football in hand, Arledge had to figure out who would broadcast the games. That led to an exchange that has been reported through the years, most prominently by Arledge himself. "What would you think if I put Howard in the booth?" Arledge asked the commissioner.

"Cosell?" Rozelle shouted. "Why don't you just dig up Attila the Hun?"

Howard Cosell, née Cohen, a native of Brooklyn and an attorney of repute, started his broadcasting career at age 38 in 1956 on a late-night radio show on WABC. The pay was lousy, and the hours were worse, but he had the drive to do it, and his wife, Emmy, said, "Go ahead." And he did. He went everywhere, covered the games in season, asked the tough questions, and made a name for himself, whether or not anybody liked it or him. "There was a pest who used to hang around the locker rooms with a tape recorder, named Howard Cosell," Pat Summerall said, as he resurrected those days in the late '50s when the Giants reigned at Yankee Stadium every fall. "He'd interview us from time to time, anybody who'd talk to him, but we viewed him very much as a pest at the time."

He got widespread radio exposure with his daily shows and signature open, "This—is—Howard Cosell—speaking of sports!" And he gained notoriety on the Floyd Patterson–Ingemar Johansson heavyweight championship bouts as Les Keiter's color man and interviewer in that nasally Brooklynese, as in, "Floyd! Floyd! Tell me what happened, Floyd!"

From there, he moved on to champion the fortunes of Cassius Clay's career, starting with the first Sonny Liston fight in 1964 and continuing on television when Clay changed his name to Muhammad Ali. He had handled the color in 1959 when ABC carried a series of Saturday-night preseason games and never again was seen on television football. Until 1970.

"I think prior to the time I got there, the league exercised a great deal more control over broadcasters and the networks, but the maverick in this deal was ABC when they put their Monday-night package together," Merlin Olsen said. "I don't know that Rozelle enjoyed Cosell's flamboyance, but it was hard to argue with his success. Rozelle was smart enough to understand that some of what Howard was doing was distasteful because Howard was busy aggrandizing Howard, but Rozelle realized this was a whole new window and whole new audience for the NFL. More than anything else, he had a wonderful grasp of the big picture. He wasn't so busy in the minutia of his responsibilities that he couldn't look at something and say, maybe this is a little unpleasant at the moment, but ultimately it's going to be good for us."

And good it was. Arledge wanted Gifford immediately and knew he could extract him from his CBS commitment, which had a year to run, but Gifford chose to honor his contract to its finish in 1970. As they shook hands, Gifford left his pal Roone with one recommendation that paid off immediately. Frank's friend Don Meredith retired after the Dallas Cowboys lost their 1968 playoff to the Cleveland Browns. Since then, he had done nothing. Gifford told Arledge that Meredith would be terrific on television, something Arledge knew from watching the two of them interact in their postgame interview for CBS on December 31, 1967, in the dreary Dallas locker room after that crushing loss to the Packers in the Ice Bowl at Green Bay.

Arledge told Gifford to have Meredith call. Then Arledge left Meredith dangling as he displayed the notorious trait that infuriated everyone who ever tried to deal with him. He didn't return the Texan's calls. Finally, after Meredith left four unanswered messages in as many days, he left one more, informing Arledge that he was going to negotiate with CBS. That one brought a response. With Gifford acting as the intermediary, Meredith agreed to meet the ABC maestro for lunch at Toots Shor's. Meredith entered the famed saloon with an insult: "I only came to tell you to your face what a horse's ass you are."

"That is the kind of candor I want in an expert commentator," Arledge replied. After several hours and a gaggle of giggles and outright horse laughs, the two agreed on a deal. Where CBS had offered Meredith $20,000 for his wisecracks, Arledge finally agreed to $30,000. "This lunch cost me $10,000," Arledge said as they shook hands.

"It'll be the best $10,000 you ever spent," the former Cowboy answered.

After the Meredith deal broke, Arledge ducked Cosell for several days. He found him as he was downing his third silver bullet at Jimmy Weston's and brought him into the fold. Arledge was convinced that Cosell was a key ingredient. Now, with Meredith, he had an expert, an eccentric one to be sure, and with Cosell, he had his gadfly, one audiences loved or hated, down the middle, no neutrality whatsoever.

Without his first choice to do play-by-play, Gifford, and with the opening kickoff just a couple of months away, Arledge had to move quickly. Curt Gowdy, long the star of ABC's "American Sportsman" outdoor series, was a logical choice, but he now was well into his glory years at NBC and was unavailable. Chris Schenkel earned his early television fame calling pro football on DuMont's "Saturday Night" series in the '50s and Giants games on Sundays for CBS. Since 1965, he had been the voice of ABC's "NCAA Football" package, and those in charge weren't about to let him go. Vin Scully, another possibility, did not want to compete for airtime with Cosell.

So, Arledge turned to a 42-year-old Georgia native via the U.S. Marine Corps, Washington State, Seattle, and Los Angeles who could broadcast anything ever dreamed up, smartly and skillfully. His name was Keith Jackson.

Jackson cut his sportscasting eyeteeth during the '50s in Seattle, where he did radio play-by-play for Seattle University basketball in the Elgin Baylor days. He also called football games for his alma mater, Washington State, and then joined ABC in Los Angeles.

The opener on September 21, 1970, paired two Rozelle favorites, Joe Namath and the New York Jets against Art Modell's Cleveland Browns, playing before a record Municipal Stadium crowd, 85,703. "It is a hot . . . sultry . . . almost windless night here at Municipal Stadium," said the hard, nasal voice that would be the most famous presence in television for the next decade and a half. Howard Cosell was off and running, with his sidekick and foil, "Dandy Don" Meredith, riding shotgun and with interlocutor Keith Jackson at the wheel, doing his best to drive this madcap bus through the bright lights of prime-time TV.

Newsweek's Pete Axthelm loved the show, saying, "It had more imagination and fewer clichés than any football telecast in memory." Browns owner Art Modell, who sat in the press box with the commissioner that night, said they both were "ecstatic" when the ratings came in the next morning. Much of the success had to do with the crack production team, led by director Chet Forte and young producer Don Ohlmeyer. Arledge gave Forte 11 cameras and the top video equipment, manned by the best technicians in the company culled from ABC's New York, Chicago, and Los Angeles stations.

As the crew members would come to learn, they had a long haul ahead of them in an NFL prime-time journey that began anew year after year. They would say good-bye to their families in late July and hit the road across America, going from stadium to stadium in city after city, until the end of December. Each time, they had to set up, pulling hundreds of miles of cable in all weather and checking everything out to make certain the pictures and sound were perfect. As soon as a game ended, they tore it all down, packed it up, and drove as far as they had to go to reach the next city on the schedule. They usually arrived on Wednesdays or Thursdays. They did it because they were paid well and, most of all, because they loved it.

Howard Cosell, in contrast, was the type of man who could not be happy doing what he did. From the outset, he was a target. After the initial broadcast in Cleveland, a neighbor and fellow commuter from Pound Ridge, New York, *New York Times* television critic Jack Gould, proclaimed that Cosell's sport was boxing, definitely not football. The viewing public, though, was split down the middle. In letters to ABC, people either loved Howard or detested him. In television, that type of response translates into a ratings driver so powerful that even sponsor Henry Ford II, who called chairman Leonard Goldenson and demanded Cosell's removal from the telecast, was not able to get his way. To make sure, Arledge put his foot down and refused to buckle.

Don Meredith also sparked viewer interest and reaction, but for other reasons entirely. Everybody talked about the excitement Meredith brought to the proceedings. "Ah . . . there were times. He had his moments, good and bad," Keith Jackson said. "I was with him when he mixed up the two linebackers in the Pittsburgh-Cincinnati game. That was the first time he really got some mail." Jackson could not stifle a laugh. "He was a character. That was why he was hired. He was hired as a character, not as an expert, because he was Don Meredith, and you never knew where he was coming from."

With Cosell and Meredith around, Jackson, a superior career professional who would gain fame for his college football calls through the 2006 Rose Bowl, got so frustrated with his role that he went to the boss. "I told Roone, 'You've made me the world's highest-paid public address announcer,'" Jackson said. "Fundamentally, that is all I did: just keep the river running, and don't interfere with whatever the other two guys were doing, and let them do it."

Jackson's true value to that first season of "Monday Night Football" was his ability to get along with the difficult Cosell. "I was young and limber," Jackson explained. "The linchpin for that series was Howard Cosell—even when he got drunk in Philadelphia. I was there. That was the night he threw up on Meredith's brand-new boots."

It was the night of November 23, by which point "Monday Night Football" had become the biggest event on television and in those cities where the traveling circus alighted each week. Before getting into the booth that evening, Cosell got into the martinis at a party thrown by Eagles owner Leonard Tose. "He was whipping them down, and he went outside, and it was 24 degrees," Jackson recalled. "You know what that does to someone who's full of booze. When he introduced me on the air, he couldn't even say 'Philadelphia.' He never could finish. His parting shot was throwing up on Meredith's boots and taking a cab home to Pound Ridge."

The cab ride cost ABC $300 and got plenty of ink. The PR mill, working overtime, went with Cosell's account that he had the flu and had a reaction to medication. His colleagues did not say that the medication was an 80 proof fluid better known as vodka. Cosell survived to thrive for years. Why? "He was the essential ingredient—the baking powder. He was the sourdough," Jackson declared. "We did 11 years of baseball together and a lot other things. I'd say we probably worked together for 18 years. Never had a bit of trouble with him."

More than any other man who ever worked the same broadcast with Cosell (no one ever "shared" a mike with the Mouth That Roared), Keith Jackson understood and appreciated his talents. Speaking of Cosell reminded Jackson of the legendary play-by-play broadcaster Ted Husing, whom Jackson met when he was a young broadcaster in Seattle. "Husing laid a line on me that I never forgot and never will," Jackson said. "'Never be afraid to turn a phrase. And if they don't know what it means, let 'em look it up.' Howard operated on that line, too. He relished dropping some of that hyperbolic bullshit on people and let them wonder what it was. Howard could do a nine-minute obit on a guy he never heard of."

But Keith Jackson, a purist who placed the game first and could never play it any other way, could not settle into his broadcasting rhythm in the whirlwind environment that was the "Monday Night" booth. "It was not my thing," Jackson said. "My thing is Middle America. I can talk to folks who work for a living. It used to piss Roone off because I used to say the most important guy is the one who spent $600 for a color television set and put it in his house, not the martini sippers at Manucci's. He used to get mad as hell."

At the end of the season, the ax fell on Jackson. "It was all right," the broadcaster said. "The idea was new enough, and the promise of what it could become was new enough. I wasn't a fool; I knew what was going on. I was filling in until Gifford got loose from his CBS contract. Roone was a hero worshiper. Gifford was a hero. So, I didn't have any foolish ideas. I did the best I could. Nobody could foresee the public reaction. It was huge. That's the old domino effect."

"Keith Jackson I handled miserably," wrote Arledge. In his book, the memory of how he mistreated Jackson still stung many years later. "He stormed into my office, furious. I did a mea culpa and apologized profusely." Then he told Jackson he was making him the lead college football announcer, an assignment that made him a broadcast legend. "But, the personal rupture between us was permanent, and all my doing."

"The only thing I ever heard Pete say about it, and he said it to me and me only: 'It was poorly handled.' And it's true," Jackson said. "There's one thing about the business: I always treated it like a business. I never got all that buddy-buddy with anybody." But Jackson did establish an enduring friendship with the audience during his glorious run as ABC's voice of college football.

If any man made "Monday Night Football" an institution, it was Howard Cosell. "I liked Howard. Everybody who knew him well liked him, except Red Smith and Dick Young," *Miami Herald* columnist Edwin Pope said. "He was larger than life. Cosell brought a lot of attention to the NFL, whether people liked him or not. He came across as the most popular or most unpopular man in television. He had such a huge ego and had to be the whole show. When his wife was alive, he could handle almost anything. Cosell made 'Monday Night Football'!"

For years, Cosell endured and somehow prevailed despite the obvious braggadocio and his cynicism with the media, including the hand that fed him, television, sports, and former athletes in the booth, whom he called the "jockocracy." In time, he estranged himself from his colleagues, whom he considered intellectual inferiors: Gifford, whom he called "Faultless Frank"; "Dandy Don," or the "Danderoo"; Fred Williamson, who didn't last out the 1974 preseason; Alex Karras; and O. J. Simpson. Then, America grew sick of How-ahd Cosell. He had become more than insufferable. He became impossible.

Arledge fired Cosell from "Monday Night Football" after the 1983 season when one remark in particular sealed his fate. It came in the opener in Dallas on September 5 when Alvin Garrett, a diminutive African American wide receiver for the Washington Redskins, made an excellent play and Cosell burst out with, "Look at that little monkey run!" Once he was out, Cosell railed at the world, starting with Arledge and ending with Rozelle. After Emmy's death in 1990, Cosell withdrew to his apartment. He died a recluse in 1995.

Much has been written and millions of words have been spoken about the impact of ABC's "Monday Night Football" during and after Cosell's tenure. It was not the same after he left, and nowhere near as interesting. Nobody after him championed the underdog with the zeal that Cosell displayed all his life. A triad of Gifford, O. J. Simpson, and Joe Namath lasted through 1985. That's when Arledge, who by then was phasing out his sports duties because ABC News had been dominating his time and energy, went to a two-man booth with the superbly versatile Al Michaels and Gifford as analyst. Gifford lasted in that role through 1998, a 27-year run, second only in television to Johnny Carson's longevity on the "Tonight Show."

They tried other three-man combinations, but at the end, it was Michaels and John Madden, in his fourth network stop since he started in 1979 at CBS, who finished the series. When Michaels and Madden joined NBC's new Sunday-night telecast in 2006, ESPN's new Monday-night announcers in the booth were Mike Tirico, Joe Theismann, and Tony Kornheiser.

For the record, Hank Williams Jr. was the final presence seen and heard on ABC's "Monday Night Football." For many years, his "Are you ready for some football?" introduction was the signal to prime-time fun from September through the wildcard playoffs. In the early years, when Don Meredith crooned "Turn out the lights, the party's over," that was the signal to sleepy folks across the land that the weekly issue was settled. This last night, Williams sang that song in its entirety over the closing credits. And for ABC Sports, it also was lights out. ESPN took over all its functions just a little more than four years after Roone Arledge's death on December 5, 2002, at age 71.

For better or for worse, when they turned on the lights in Cleveland that long-ago Monday night at a long-gone stadium, and ABC television exposed America to pro football as it had never been seen, everything changed. The National Football League in 10 years had gone from a dozen mom-and-pop operations to a full-blown entertainment colossus. Rozelle had found the elixir in television money, which in reality was a prescription drug that kept the league viable over the long term. It became a free pass for owners to profit before a single ticket was sold. And Rozelle was able to hold television in thrall to his allurement as he always asked for more money, and got it with little to no resistance.

For certain, Pete Rozelle was a man of vision, but matters in his professional and personal life were about to undergo transformations that not even he could foresee.

TWENTY-ONE

CARROLL AND CARRIE

"Rosenbloom felt betrayed because it was his hometown."

—ERNIE ACCORSI, 2005

*I*n the beginning, Carroll Rosenbloom was Pete Rozelle's strongest backer. By January 17, 1971, though, when Rozelle presented Rosenbloom the Vince Lombardi Trophy after his Baltimore Colts defeated the Dallas Cowboys 16–13 in Super Bowl V, the first official Roman-numeral-designated title game, the bloom was long off the rose.

Rosenbloom and Rozelle were on the outs, and there was no turning back in a league filled with self-made men and cutthroats who had clawed their way to the top. "It was like a lion act, with Pete the guy with the whip in the middle of the stage with 14 lions on the chairs, making sure they didn't jump him when his back was turned," said businessman Herb Siegel, Rozelle's close friend. "You had Carroll Rosenbloom and some of those real rough guys. He was a tough guy, a liar, and a cheat."

"At one time, they were very, very close. It was rough," Ernie Accorsi said. Accorsi, a top NFL executive for 37 years, worked for each man and liked them both immensely. Rosenbloom gave Accorsi his first NFL job when he hired him as Baltimore publicity director before the 1970 Super Bowl season. Accorsi declared, "I loved Rosenbloom. If you worked for him for one year, you worked for him for life, and I worked for him for three years."

Accorsi was an assistant sports information director at Penn State, handling publicity for coach Joe Paterno, in 1970 when the Colts called to interview him for the job as director of publicity. Don Klosterman, in his first year with the Colts as general manager, conducted the interview. "He was flamboyant, and I was totally unnerved," Accorsi said. "Here was this guy who wore flashy jackets, green plaid and all, and I walked in the offices in a row house across from the Greyhound bus station. He had just come from Houston and had pictures of the astronauts all over his office. I went running to Steve Rosenbloom, I was so scared of Klosterman: 'Am I working for you and your dad, or him?'"

"You will be working for me and my dad," Steve Rosenbloom assured him.

"That's the only reason I took the job," Accorsi said. "Later, I grew to love Klosterman. He was the antithesis of what I had experienced or stood for." A case in point came in Chicago in 1971 before the College All-Star Game when Accorsi went to a Chicago restaurant with several Baltimore writers and Klosterman. "'Waiter, get me a phone,' Klosterman said before he turned to the writers. 'Who do you want to talk to? Mickey Mantle? Bobby Layne?' I found out later that the Kennedys, Bobby Layne, and all the others really were his friends," Accorsi said.

"The most remarkable thing was he knew everybody, and everybody loved him," former NBC sportscaster Charlie Jones echoed. "When he was general manager of Houston," Jones said, "we were doing a preseason game there in the Astrodome, and we couldn't get out, so we went over to his house. He just invited everybody out. It was hotter than hell; he had a bunch of swimming suits, so we all sat around the swimming pool. His life was like an open house. That's the best way I can describe it."

Don Klosterman was born on January 18, 1930, in Le Mars, Iowa, the 12th of 15 children. His parents, like so many other Iowa farmers, got caught in the vortex of the Depression, pulled up stakes, and moved to California. They settled in Compton, where Don, whom everybody called Duke, became close friends with Dick Rozelle and, after World War II, Dick's older brother, Pete. A marvelous natural athlete, Klosterman led the nation in passing in 1951 at Loyola-Marymount and was drafted third by the Cleveland Browns. He got cut and finished the 1952 season as the Rams' third quarterback behind Norm Van Brocklin and Bob Waterfield. He then went to Canada, where he starred at Calgary.

In a sense, Klosterman was a walking miracle. He almost lost his life on a ski slope near Banff, Alberta, on St. Patrick's Day 1957. "He was going like a bat out of hell," Charlie Jones said. "He skied into a tree. He tried to avoid hitting somebody; he might have killed him."

The accident so severely damaged Klosterman's spinal cord that doctors told him he'd never walk again. He underwent eight operations, regained partial feeling in his legs, and walked with the aid of a cane within a year. "He fought back to shoot golf in the 70s," Accorsi said.

"He should never have been able to walk," Jones said. "He learned how to do it just by balance. One time, I came up to him and put my arm around him. 'No, Charlie, don't do that.' I looked at him, unable to figure out what he meant. 'It's my balance.' Any little thing like that could have knocked him off balance, and he would have fallen."

He progressed over the years and was in full command by the time Accorsi made his acquaintance. "Company cars were not that widespread then," Accorsi said. "The head coach got one, the general manager got one, and the PR guy got one. The only reason the PR guy got one was because of punt, pass, and kick. Klosterman got an LTD. I had just gotten the job and had a little Fairlane. Klosterman opened his blinds to a parking lot behind."

"See that Ford?" Klosterman practically spat out the words as he pointed to the LTD. "You want it?"

Accorsi nodded. "I'd love to have it."

" 'I'm not driving a Ford.' He had a Chrysler Imperial delivered later that day," Accorsi recalled. "That was Klosterman!"

One of the enduring myths of pro football contends that you win by filling your weaknesses. Another myth counters that you should draft the best available athlete whether or not that "great" athlete can help your team. "Klosterman's whole thing was to fill your weak-nesses and fill them so you don't have weaknesses," Jones said. "From that standpoint, he was ahead of his time."

"We used to have this blowout after the draft and get drunk at Uni-tas's restaurant," Accorsi related. "One night, he was giving me this baloney about Texas having better football players than Pennsylva-nia." Accorsi proposed, "Why don't we just start with this, Duke: Why don't we just start with Unitas, Namath, Lujack, George Blanda. Do you want me to stop yet?"

Klosterman warned, "You're on your way to getting your ass fired."

As Accorsi explained, he wasn't worried: " 'We have more quarter-backs than you have players,' I retorted. "You could do that with the Duke. He's the guy who took the chance on me. The Rosenblooms didn't know me. Somehow, [director of the NFL PR program] Jim Heffernan recommended me to him, and he's the guy who hired me. I might not have gotten hired in this league. I don't forget that stuff.

"Klosterman was never accepted in town even though he put together the two trades that got us to the Super Bowl," Accorsi con-tinued. "Baltimore wanted no part of that style." But Carroll Rosen-bloom did, and his was the only vote in Baltimore that counted. "He was as good a judge of talent as there was, and that includes George Young. The two best talent evaluators I ever worked with were [Colts GM] Joe Thomas and Klosterman."

The troubles definitely began between the Colts and Baltimore when Rosenbloom decided that he needed a modern facility. Memo-rial Stadium, located on 33rd Street in a pleasant residential neigh-borhood several miles north of downtown, was a sizable, poorly designed, cobbled-together chunk of steel and concrete, ill suited for both football and baseball.

After World War II, the City of Baltimore tore down the original ballpark on the site and rebuilt a horseshoe-shaped facility to attract major-league football and baseball franchises. The old single-deck stadium could seat 31,000. To lure the NFL, the city added an unroofed upper deck to increase capacity to something near 54,000. The cranes and cement mixers were still in place when the Colts started play in 1953. Baseball's St. Louis Browns arrived as the reborn Baltimore Orioles the following spring. Both teams had rabid fan bases, none in any sport the equal of the Colts, who, by 1959, their second championship season, began to fill the place every game with standing-room-only crowds of just over 57,000 screaming partisans.

Going to a game there was an adventure. Parking was virtually nonexistent. The football field was laid out so that the upper deck extended 60 yards, from the end zone of the horseshoe, past the 50-yard line, to the 40-yard line, where it ended on both sides. Not only were quality seats missing, but also, along with the obstructed seating behind huge cement pillars that buttressed the upper deck, the seats at midfield actually took fans away from the field. Moreover, Carroll Rosenbloom complained for years to his landlords, the Park District, that the ballpark was "filthy." The stadium had one advantage. "It was loud. They called it the loudest outdoor insane asylum in America," Steve Rosenbloom said.

Still, as the elder Rosenbloom would carp endlessly from 1971 on, the place was hopelessly antiquated. "He didn't start off complaining about it," Steve Rosenbloom said. "But after we won a couple of championship games, I remember going to those meetings with him. In Baltimore in those days, you went to the Park Board. He tried for years, but there was always some gadfly on one of those boards who was a problem. They also figured out that we were not going anywhere. Our league teams didn't move. So, he tried for years to do something and even mentioned the Camden Yards as a potential site."

Carroll Rosenbloom, who could outbluster just about anybody, met his match in the city controller of Baltimore. Hyman Pressman was a tough politician and every bit the autocrat in the mold of New York City's master planner Robert Moses. "He was not going to let Rosenbloom get a new stadium," Accorsi said.

"Finally, it reached the breaking point," according to Steve Rosenbloom, as the Colts' stadium saga became *the* ongoing issue in Baltimore's media. "The *Record-American*'s John Steadman was instrumental," he said. "He wrote that all we've done is win here. Steadman barraged my father on a daily basis. It was bad. It was continual. That finally got Father to say, 'I'm getting too old for this.'"

After the merger, AFC teams introduced a policy of making exhibition games part of season ticket packages. NFC teams soon followed suit. Rosenbloom, one of the last holdouts, strongly believed that loyal fans deserved to see the best product, one they never saw in the preseason, when coaches would test their rookies and play veterans for only a series or two to limber up. In fact, until 1971, he scheduled all six exhibitions on the road.

"We had this big powwow after the '70 championship season," Accorsi said. "Of course, as the PR guy, I was urging them not to put those games on the season ticket package at full regular-season prices. We were going to play the Cowboys; the Chiefs, who had been Super Bowl champions the year before; and the Bears, who were always an attraction. Those were our three exhibition games at home. We drew 17,000, 19,000, and 21,000, and my rear end was in trouble."

Accorsi continued the story: " 'So, you have all the answers, huh?' Carroll roared. "Believe me, he was looking for somebody, and I was in his sights. When he floated the idea, Steadman annihilated him on a regular basis. So, he backed off and never put them on the season ticket package. When Robert Irsay took over the Colts in '72, his general manager, Joe Thomas, put the exhibitions on the package."

"It was an accumulation. It was never one incident," Accorsi said. "In every one of these cases, Robert Moses and O'Malley in Brooklyn, or Irsay later in Baltimore, there was a point when some politician called somebody's bluff. In Rosenbloom's case it was the city controller of Baltimore. They kept changing mayors, but the guy who held the power was the controller, Hyman Pressman. He was not going to let Rosenbloom get a new stadium. Rosenbloom felt betrayed because it was his hometown. He couldn't get anywhere. He threatened to move the team to Tampa. We actually practiced in Tampa for the championship game in Miami. There were thousands at the airport. They were welcoming us because he was trying to move the team there. So, he was flirting."

Baltimore did not want to lose the Colts to Tampa or any other city, but Rosenbloom was fed up with the situation. Then Los Angeles opened up. There was some history on that front. One day in the late '50s when the Colts played the Rams, the Rosenblooms, father and son, were talking with L.A. owner Dan Reeves as the players came out to warm up. "I was young," Steve Rosenbloom said, "but I remember Danny Reeves saying, 'Carroll, if something happens to me, I would like you to have this team. This would be a great slot for you.'"

Steve Rosenbloom, just 27 in 1972, did not know that Reeves had been ailing for years with Hodgkin's disease, but his father did. Reeves died in April 1971, which placed his estate into probate and the team, the major estate asset, in limbo. Carroll Rosenbloom was ready to make his move. Tampa remained his first choice, but now the executors of the Reeves estate wanted to make a deal, and the Rams were as attractive a franchise as any in pro football.

"Rosenbloom had placed us in Tampa for the entire summer at training camp, and we played three preseason games there in '72," Ernie Accorsi said. "Then word came down that he had been told, 'You're not moving the Colts.'"

That was confirmed by William N. Wallace on July 14, 1972, in the *New York Times* when he wrote that Rosenbloom had sought permission to move to a new stadium planned for Columbia, Maryland, or to Tampa. "Reaction was so strong against him, from Commissioner Rozelle and other NFL owners, that he turned instead to Los Angeles, where the Reeves executors had out a for-sale sign."

"So, that instigated the whole thing with L.A.," Accorsi said. "In my opinion, it broke his heart to leave. He was never the same."

Presented with an opportunity to get away from what had become a hopeless situation in Baltimore, Rosenbloom went shopping for a willing buyer. That buyer turned out to be Robert Irsay, a 49-year-old businessman from Chicago who made a fortune as an industrial contractor before he sold out to Zurn Industries in a nine-figure deal. As Bill Wallace wrote, Irsay, a dedicated football fan, was an "avid admirer of John Unitas, the Colts' quarterback." Furthermore, Irsay had money to burn.

Irsay had made a halfhearted stab at buying the Bears from George Halas. "He tried to portray he was Halas's friend, but I don't think Mr. Halas cared for him," Ernie Accorsi said. Then the Colts came onto Irsay's screen. The deal, while unprecedented in professional sports, was relatively simple. Irsay had the money and in Joe Thomas, a superb judge of talent who had just been fired after building Miami's Super Bowl team, he had a football man to run his team and spend his money well.

"It's taught in law school because of what my father understood," Steve Rosenbloom said. "First we had to find somebody to buy the Colts. Joe Thomas found him. Joe wanted a piece of something. So, he was Irsay's first general manager. The object here was to buy the Rams. You couldn't sell the Colts, which were worth probably $20 million at the time, because of the capital-gains tax penalty. When Modell came into the league, he paid between $4 and $5 million, and that was, you know, 'Is this guy crazy?'"

After Rosenbloom established a price for the Rams with the Reeves executors, Irsay stepped in, wrote a $19 million check, and, just like that, became owner of the Rams. It was the highest price ever paid to that point for a professional sports franchise. "It was all predetermined," Steve Rosenbloom said. "Irsay was buying the Rams in name only. He knew that he was actually buying the Colts. It was not as though he would go in and buy the Rams and change his mind; it was all worked out in advance. They were able to swap properties. It really was a simple thing, and it was ingenious, really. One reason it had not been done in sports before [was that] owners weren't changing teams. I don't know of any owner who had a team and then showed up in another city with another team."

By trading the Colts for the Rams without a cent changing hands, Rosenbloom avoided a $4.4 million bill from the IRS for capital gain taxes. His personal investment in the Colts over the years from the time he put down $250,000 did not exceed $1.2 million. "I am a 100 percent owner of the Rams," Rosenbloom said. "That's the only way I operate."

The players and coaches did not move, but Rosenbloom took along Pete Rozelle's pal Don Klosterman, his brilliant general manager in Baltimore, to run the Rams organization. A year later, Rosenbloom replaced coach Tommy Prothro with Chuck Knox, who took the Rams to NFC West titles for six straight years, but no Super Bowls.

Robert Irsay attended the University of Illinois until 1942, when he joined the Marine Corps during World War II and lasted for six months. In 1986, *Sports Illustrated* debunked his claim that he was on the roster of Illinois's 1946 Rose Bowl team. In fact, there was no record that he ever played football for the Fighting Illini.

He joined his father's heating and ventilation business in 1946 and then set out on his own in 1951 when he founded the Robert Irsay Company. In time, the Irsay Company became one of the world's largest industrial heating, ventilation, and air-conditioning construction firms. Its most prominent projects were two of the world's largest skyscrapers, both located in Chicago, the 100-story John Hancock Center and 103-story Sears Tower.

Irsay owned a high-end men's clothing store, London Corner, Ltd., in Wilmette, on Chicago's North Shore. Having one of the early outlets for designer Ralph Lauren, he outfitted his Colts in Lauren clothing, and Lauren in turn featured Colts quarterback Bert Jones in magazine ads during the '70s. Irsay used the store for after-hours poker games and was notorious after a few drinks for tantalizing his sales crew by going as far as selling them the business, and then reneging on the deals the day after.

He spent little to no time in Baltimore, preferring to operate out of his Chicago office in the Hancock Center. People who knew Irsay after he bought the Colts warned others who wanted to do business with him to reach him in the morning, before he went to a local bistro for his customary long lunches that featured multiple martinis and lingered over the course of many an afternoon.

That held true for football business as well. Irsay was a chronic coach baiter who, when he wasn't firing one of them, would have an aide deliver a message from his seat in the owner's box to an assistant coach ordering the head coach to run a specific play. Worse, he would take friends down to the field and walk through the bench area to introduce them to his coach.

When the late Peter Hadhazy served as Art Modell's general manager in Cleveland, he had a memorable postgame conversation with Irsay—in their native language, Hungarian! "Dick Szymanski was Irsay's general manager," Hadhazy said. "Cleveland played Baltimore—in fact, we beat them—and Irsay, Dick, Ernie Accorsi, and I had a drink after the game. While Ernie and Dick sat at the table and talked, Irsay was telling me in Hungarian, 'Dick Szymanski is a piece of shit. Ernie Accorsi is a good guy. I've got an idiot working for me and a good guy.'"

As to John Unitas, his hero, Irsay said nothing when his first general manager, Joe Thomas, humiliated the great star and then benched him halfway into the 1972 season. Unitas, who was furious, finished his great career in San Diego in 1973 with a dismal team and sorrier surroundings before he abruptly retired and went home to spend the rest of his life in Baltimore.

After taking over the Colts, Irsay promised the Baltimore city fathers that he intended to stay. However, it didn't take long for him to realize why Rosenbloom got out. Irsay wanted skyboxes for Memorial Stadium; when he didn't get that perk, he demanded a new stadium with luxury boxes and all the trimmings. When he didn't get that either, he went shopping for a new city. Indianapolis dangled the most attractive package, including an indoor stadium and training facilities. Negotiations with Baltimore officials collapsed in March 1984, and the Maryland legislature enacted a law granting Baltimore the right of eminent domain to seize the team.

Irsay's attorney, Michael Chernoff, advised him that such a maneuver, taking his property, violated the search and seizure provisions in the Fourth Amendment to the U.S. Constitution. Thus, the Maryland legislature played into Irsay's hands. To play it safe, Irsay called in the Mayflower moving vans in the middle of the night on March 28, 1984, and ran off to the Hoosier state capital, signed a 20-year lease with the Hoosier Dome, and set up shop.

The old Colts, led by Unitas, told Irsay that they and their legacy belonged to Baltimore, and Baltimore alone. And that included their records. They have refused to associate themselves with the Irsay-Indianapolis version of their heritage.

Late in life, Robert Irsay divorced his wife Harriett, remarried, and moved from Chicago to Indianapolis and devoted his life to charitable fund-raising. In 1996, he turned the team over to his son Jim, who hired professional football people to run it and turn it into a model franchise. Robert Irsay died on January 14, 1997. A decade later, quarterback Peyton Manning, who idolized Unitas, led the Indianapolis Colts to a 29–19 victory over the Chicago Bears in Super Bowl XLI.

"It takes a team moving for things to change," Steve Rosenbloom said. "It's ironic. Look at what Baltimore did, and Cleveland, too."

In 1975, Ernie Accorsi jumped off the Irsay merry-go-round and left the Colts, the team he loved, to join Rozelle in the NFL office as assistant to the NFC president—at that time, league founder and Chicago Bears owner George Halas. "I always envisioned this is what it must have been like with the New Frontier," Accorsi said of his time with Rozelle. "This is the way it must have been with Kennedy when Pete would go to Washington in 1961. He had a charisma; he had a morality to him. It was understated, soft-spoken; never insulted anybody; went through a tough thing in his family. He just was fair and honest."

Herb Klein, Richard Nixon's longtime director of communications, contributed some personal observations on that subject. "If you are commissioner of football, you can deal with both parties easily," Klein said. "He had to work the White House; that was part of the job. He was very friendly with the Kennedy people. One time, I invited him to an event at the White House. The president was going to leave this cocktail party for a trip to Key Biscayne, but he was so intrigued with talking to Pete that he invited him to fly down there with him. So, Pete got on Air Force One and flew down there with him."

Asked what one trait sticks out, Accorsi replied, "It's hard to pick between humility and integrity. He had both to a point, and—I don't give a damn what anybody says—humility is tougher when you're a star. Frank Gifford and Rozelle are the two biggest stars I have ever been around who had that much humility. They were very similar in that respect and, ironically, were great friends. Rozelle made you feel important every day you were around him."

Reminiscent of that Kitty Kallen oldie "Little Things Mean a Lot," Rozelle always let his employees know their importance to the good of the operation. "The ironic thing about Rozelle's first marriage, I went through something similar," Accorsi said. "In '75, my wife had as serious a postpartum breakdown as you can have. I was making $20,000 a year. I had no money, and I had a huge bill to pay to the hospital. She was in the hospital for 11 months. Medical insurance was vague then."

He continued, "Jim Kensil called me and said, 'Pete wants you.' Pete offered me the job, and I said I couldn't take it. 'Why?' Pete said. I hadn't explained my situation. 'I can't leave Baltimore and go to New York. I can't afford it.'"

"You take this job. We'll figure it out," Rozelle said.

"He gave me more money than he had offered originally," Accorsi said. "He hiked the salary up so I could handle the payments better. As it turned out, I didn't need a loan, but he offered it. He would have done anything I needed. I did not know how personal it was to him. Now when I read all of this—I knew some of it—I realize how much he went through, and it lasted longer. I'll never forget that."

Nor would Accorsi forget what happened at Christmastime in 1976, when the championship game was played in Minnesota on December 26. "I was gone Christmas week," Accorsi said. "On Christmas Eve, he called my house and talked to each child, who were seven, six, and three. 'It's my fault your father's not home,' he said. And he wrote me a note saying the same thing."

Pete Rozelle led an active social life in the late '60s and early '70s, all the while tending to the well-being of his daughter as she entered her teens. "He had a life," Anne Marie Bratton said. "He dated and had friends, went out, and traveled. A lot of trips I went along—Marcus Island, Acapulco. He loved fishing." A favorite fishing partner was Tex Schramm. She emphasized, "He was not a golfer; golf requires a long commitment. Fishing and tennis are quick. When he was single, living in New York, he played all the time at the East Side Tennis Club."

Blair Sabol also offered insight on Rozelle's recreational proclivities." We shared a birthday within a few days," she said. "He was March 1, and I'm the 6th. We always had a party in Acapulco. This one year [circa 1970], we were in Acapulco, and pot was starting to be demotic. Pete sat there one night and asked, 'What is it?'"

"You want to try it?" Blair asked.

It took some cajoling and entreating, but he eventually yielded. "You know what? Let me try it," Rozelle said.

"Pete really was a diplomat, not a schmuck. He was very smooth, but he was smart," Blair said. "He was cool, not hip. He was a smart guy. He knew at every minute what he was doing. So, we rolled him a joint—I'll never forget this. It was strong stuff. Pete took about three hits. We showed him how to hold it—the lung, all that. I gotta tell you nothing happened! He was exactly the same, and my brother and I were hysterically laughing. He said, 'I feel nothing,' got up, had a chat, was perfectly normal, went to bed. The next day, we asked, 'How do you feel?' 'Nothing.' You know what? I believe it."

She added, "Pete was that cool, that centered, and that held in that present. He found me later that next day. 'Now I get it,' he said. 'I'd rather drink booze.' "

The fast lane held no appeal for Pete Rozelle. But he loved anything that ran fast, from world-class sprinters to Thoroughbred horses. His fondness for horse racing was enhanced by his friendship with Jack Landry, who persuaded the Philip Morris Company to sponsor the Marlboro Cup Invitational Handicap to showcase the great Secretariat. On June 9, 1973, the commissioner joined Landry at Belmont Park to see if Secretariat could make history in the Belmont Stakes and become the first Triple Crown winner in 25 years. "The horse was on the cover of three national news magazines in one week—*Time*, *Newsweek*, and *Sports Illustrated*, said Bill Nack, *SI*'s famed turf writer for decades. "Jack Nicklaus was down in Boca Raton by himself in the family den. He knew nothing about horse racing. As Secretariat turned for home, 20 lengths in front and widening, Nicklaus found himself on the floor of his den, pounding on the rug, tears rolling down his cheeks. He said to Heywood Hale Broun later, 'Woody, you were at that race, weren't you?' "

"Yah, I was," Broun answered.

"Why was I kneeling down and crying? I know nothing about horse racing."

"Jack," Woody said, "your whole life has been spent in the pursuit of perfection. That day, you saw it for the first time."

"Back at Belmont," Nack recalled, "there was a guy in the grandstand screaming as Secretariat widened, 'He's going too fast.'

"Pete Rozelle was standing in the dining room at Belmont Park. 'As the horse rounded the far turn and started home, I felt somebody grab me around the ankles,' Rozelle said. 'I thought somebody had collapsed. And I looked down and found the guy standing next to me had grabbed my ankles. I was standing on the dining room table. I have no idea how I got there.' I thought, after all these years, Rozelle is an all-right guy," Nack said.

"He loved people. He loved being around people," Anne Marie Bratton said. "He had a strong moral fiber. I was the child who was picked up the earliest from every party, that had the earliest curfew. He was, by far, the strictest parent. He was always teaching values and morals and what you should do to people and the right thing to do. I couldn't have a two-door car, 'cause that would be selfish; I had to have a four-door car. I had to understand the value of money. It wasn't something I had as a sophomore in high school, but as a junior in college, I had to earn the money and understand how important it was."

Rozelle also loved being on the water and spent as much free time as possible through the years on his powerboats, the *Double Eagle* and its larger successor, the *Triple Eagle*, which Chris-Craft gave him, courtesy of chairman Herb Siegel. "He could get out on that water and forget everybody," said Herb's niece Blair Sabol. "It was always docked in the Hamptons or the 72nd Street basin. It was never like he was out there on the high seas. All those guys—Carson—got into that. Jerry Lewis got into that. The water is a real metaphor for Pete to lose his brains and get out there."

"But a lot of deals were made on the *Triple Eagle*," Anne Marie pointed out. "That's a great way to do business—not e-mail and telephones—personal lunches, personal fishing trips, personal time spent together. There were a lot more handshake deals and things worked out. The personal deals and longevity made in those deals just don't happen now. How else do you negotiate with those owners and players' unions, without people skills and trying to reason together? That can't work with an e-mail."

In summer, at the end of spring term at the small Catholic girls' school Anne Marie attended, she and her father packed up for some fun in the sun and on the water at a Long Island beach house they shared with the commissioner's CBS pals Bill McPhail and Pat Summerall and Kathy, Pat's first wife. "To share a beach house with three different people, McPhail and the Summeralls, you had to be very close," Ann Marie noted.

One of Rozelle's favorite boating stops out in the Hamptons was the summer home of the late baseball commissioner Bowie Kuhn. Commenting on his relationship with Rozelle, Kuhn remarked, "He was a very sociable man, a very congenial man. He loved socializing and having a glass of a strong drink every now and then. He was a very good, pleasant man. We frequently got together, the various commissioners, to discuss common interests. In the course of those, there really got to be storytelling. The congenial lubrication made the stories better. We had a lot of fun, and there was more laughter than anything else. Whether it advanced the cause of sanity in the commissioners' ranks is quite debatable, but we had a good time and enjoyed each other's company, particularly in the days when Walter Kennedy was in the NBA and Clarence Campbell was in hockey. It very much continued with Larry O'Brien in the NBA. We had a great time."

By no means, however, was Rozelle's life out of the office focused on socializing with deal makers or those in the sporting life. Anne Marie always came first. "We had that great fishing trip, Pete, Dad, Anne Marie, and I," Jack Landry Jr. said. "Dad and Pete got fly-fishing rods and caught nothing on those great fishing lakes in Canada 150 miles north of Montreal."

"Even with a fishing guide!" added Jin Landry, still adamant that Virginia Slims cigarettes—the brand her husband launched for Philip Morris—were not named for her. "They named it after Virginia tobacco, not me. That is really a silly notion."

"That was the only time I spent family time on a vacation with Dad and Pete," Jack Jr. said, wistfully recalling those days and his father's friendship with the most powerful figure in sports, still a kid at heart. He shared a telling comment from Rozelle: "Dad and Pete were in the limousine at the Super Bowl one year, and Pete said, 'Not too bad for a couple of kids from Lynwood, California, and Saratoga Springs.'"

In the years after the divorce from Jane, the kid from Lynwood was seen around New York with many women. One frequent partner was actress Caroline Williams, whose credits include several popular television programs, among them "The Guiding Light," "Benson," "Murphy Brown," and "Judging Amy." She lived in New York when they were dating and shared the good times at the beach house and on the boat. Although that relationship was temporary, Anne Marie remains close to her. "I cherish the years we spent together," she said. "She also makes the best lasagna in the world."

"She was a nice gal, a professional actress," Blair Sabol said. "She fell for him, and many women did. I think Pete was a master at keeping people comfortable yet was aloof. He kept people far, far away, but you didn't feel it."

He could also stir people up on occasion. One evening, Pete and Caroline went to the Landrys' for dinner in their Nyack home on the west bank of the Hudson about 19 miles upriver from Manhattan. "They both enjoyed not eating," Jack Jr. said. "Now, Dad was looking over at Pete and wondering, where was all this food going? Both were bird eaters. All of a sudden, Caroline let out this yelp. Pete had been moving whatever he was having, chicken, into the claw of a lobster Caroline was eating!"

"I think he did go home alone half the time with this gal," Blair Sabol said. "God knows if they even had a sexual relationship; they must have—I don't know. She never went to his apartment. He had Anne at home. He was a fabulous father. And I thank God she was there, because I don't think Pete was that interested."

Another woman did capture Pete Rozelle's interest at long last. "Carrie came along at a time when Pete had to have a companion," Blair Sabol said. "That was clear. He needed to get out."

On January 14, 1973, Don Shula's Miami Dolphins beat George Allen's Washington Redskins 14–7 in Super Bowl VII at the Los Angeles Coliseum to become the only unbeaten team in NFL history, winning all 17 games. One afternoon in the days before that historic game, Pete Rozelle fell madly, irrevocably in love. It happened in the lounge at the Bel-Air Hotel, where he was sipping a Rusty Nail in the company of friends. He looked up and saw a chestnut-maned vision in white stroll across the room as if she owned it. From that moment on, Carrie Cooke owned Pete Rozelle, heart and soul.

"Don Klosterman introduced Pete to Carrie," Jack Kemp said.

"I thought Klosterman had a lot to do with it, because I remember the stories when they met," Anne Marie Bratton recalled.

Both were wrong, according to Pat Summerall. Klosterman was not there that day. "Pete, Jack Landry, and I were sitting at the bar of the Bel-Air Hotel," Summerall said. "There was a piano in the middle of the bar. This woman who was dressed all in white came up to the piano bar to make a request. Pete said to me, 'Who is that?'"

"I don't have any idea," Summerall responded.

"Well, find out who she is," Rozelle said. "I want to meet her."

"I don't know how to do that," Summerall answered, "but I'll ask the bartender. Maybe he knows her."

He recounted, "I went up to the bartender, who was a friend of mine because we always stayed there, and his answer was, 'You don't want to know.'"

Summerall, naturally, asked, "Why don't I?"

"I know who you're with, and I know you," the bartender said. "That's Jack Kent Cooke's daughter-in-law."

Summerall went back to the table where Rozelle and Landry were sipping their drinks and reported, "You don't want to know who that is."

"Yes, I do. I want to meet her," Rozelle said.

"I told him who she was," Summerall said. "He took a drag off his cigarette as only he could and said, 'I still want to meet her. Can you get her to come over here?'

"So, I went over to her table," Summerall said. "She was sitting with a couple of other women, and I told her who I was."

"I know who you are," Carrie Cooke said.

"I'm sitting with the commissioner of the National Football League, Pete Rozelle, who would like very much to make your acquaintance," he told her.

"To my surprise, she said, 'I would like to meet him.' So, the two of us walked across the dance floor to where Landry and Pete were sitting, and that's how they met.

"That's as much as I thought was going to happen," Summerall said. "She was married to Ralph Kent Cooke, whose father owned the Redskins."

"Carrie was after him at that point," Herb Siegel said. "Her marriage was in a divorce. I think she thought she married Jack Kent Cooke, not the son, and was disappointed because there wasn't enough money."

It was a messy situation. Jack Kenneth Cooke was born in Hamilton, Ontario, in 1912. He was a high school dropout and supersalesman, running a band, pushing soap door-to-door and then encyclopedias, before he found his niche and reinvented himself, down to his name. By 1941, when his first son, John Peter Cooke, was born, Jack Kent Cooke was making his first of many millions, as he began a media empire of radio stations, newspapers, and magazines. When Ralph, his second son, was born, Jack, who had a fondness for the royal-sounding name "Kent," gave him that middle name and prevailed upon his older son to rename himself John Kent Cooke.

He bought his first sports team in 1951, the Toronto Maple Leafs, an AAA minor-league baseball team. In 1952, he was named *Sporting News* Minor League Executive of the Year for his Bill Veeck–like promotions. When Cooke lost a bid to gain Canada's first private television license, he came to the United States, worked through Congress, and gained instant citizenship. Then, he started buying teams. Cooke was the one who bought Harry Wismer's piece of the Washington Redskins in 1960 when Pete Rozelle forced him to dispose of it because he owned the AFL New York Titans.

Then, in 1965, Cooke bought the National Basketball Association Los Angeles Lakers; two years later, he started the National Hockey League expansion Los Angeles Kings. He kept acquiring properties, among them the Chrysler Building in New York, a huge ranch in the Sierra Nevada, and as many franchises as he could obtain in the fledgling cable television business. In 1974, Cooke became copartner of the Redskins with a man he hated, famed attorney Edward Bennett Williams.

"Jack Kent Cooke was the last boss of the world; at least, he thought he was," said Pete Newell, Rozelle's early mentor and close friend, who got caught in the middle of the budding romance. "It was tough. I was Cooke's general manager. She'd call me up to tell me something to tell Pete. Pete would call me to tell her something. The divorce was acrimonious. She was a nice lady, and Pete was Pete. She was separating from her husband. He's dead now. He went out at nights to various places, a nightclub guy, in the Beverly Hills area. Jack never forgave her; he blamed the divorce on her, where it was the son who ran on her. Cooke didn't like Pete, but there was nothing he could do. It was a tense situation. The kid she married had a lot of Jack Kent Cooke in him. He was no good."

"Carrie was so very young, so very beautiful, and captivating," said Anne Marie Rozelle Bratton, who was turning 15 when the romance heated up. "She was the type of woman who walked into a room and everybody noticed. She had unbelievable presence."

"We went to Tres Vidas, down in Acapulco, where Pete got a house," Herb Siegel said. "We all were going down together. He said, 'Tomorrow, this girl I met in California is coming down. She really is something else.' That was the start of it. He really was gone."

"About six weeks later, I was doing the morning show over at CBS radio. I was the morning disc jockey," Summerall said. "I got a phone call from Rozelle: 'What are you doing this weekend?'"

"I have to do the ABA all-star game," Summerall said.

"Don't you have some vacation time?" Rozelle asked.

"Yeah. I do, but I can't walk away from the ABA all-star game. It's in Charlotte."

"I want you and your wife to meet me in Acapulco. Carrie is going to meet me there with some of her Canadian friends," Rozelle said. "I want to see what you think of her. Let's have a closer look."

"So, I got some time off, and my wife and I flew to Acapulco," Summerall recalled. "Pete met us at the airport. As it happened, a guy named Alan Miller, who had been with the Raiders and head of the players' association before Ed Garvey, had a house there. He and Pete were big buddies, so he let us use his house. Pete, my wife and me, and Don Klosterman went to this house. Carrie and some Canadian friends of hers were staying at another house. So, we partied at our house; then we went to their house. She was in the process of getting a divorce at this time. So, they got into the process of getting romantic.

"We were at their house one afternoon, and I was in the pool just swimming," Summerall continued. "Pete and Carrie were sitting on deck chairs. All of a sudden, I looked up, and there were five guys around me, Canadian guys. 'We want to talk to you,' they said."

Feeling badly outnumbered, Summerall asked, "What is it you want?"

"This guy Rozelli," one man said, and he pointed toward the commissioner.

"You mean Rozelle?" Summerall said.

"Yeah, Rozelli. Is he a wop?"

"No," Summerall said, "he's Dutch."

"Oh, OK," the man said. "Do you think he's good enough for our Carrie?"

"The question here is, is she good enough for him?" Summerall exclaimed. "That seemed to satisfy them, and they left us alone. That was their way of questioning his merits. 'This guy Rozelli,' indeed!"

"They got married in December 1974 at Herb Siegel's apartment," Anne Marie Bratton said.

"I was Pete's best man. They were married in my apartment," Herb Siegel said.

"Herb Siegel's. Peter Duchin on the piano. I was there. There were, like, eight couples," Summerall said.

"The honeymoon was at John DeLorean's house," Anne Marie said. "It all seems so funny now. We moved out to Westchester, I think right before."

They needed the room, for Pete Rozelle now was head of an extended family, starting with Anne Marie, 16; and including Jeannie Kent Cooke, 13; Jack Kent Cooke II, 11; Ralph Kent Cooke II, 7; and Philip Kent Cooke, 5.

He seemed to adapt with no real problem. After all, he was a people person. "I don't think a week went by that we didn't have lunch— Summerall, Giff, David Mahoney of Norton Simon, Inc., and that crowd," Herb Siegel said. "There were about five of us twice a week. Then, Pete went on my board, Chris-Craft. It was the only board he was on. We were going after Piper Aircraft, and there was a big lawsuit that went all the way up to the Supreme Court. Everybody was saying to Pete, 'You gotta get off that board; it's too controversial.' He stuck. He was a great friend under fire. Between us, he was my closest friend."

Cooke's divorce settlement with his wife Jean in 1979 was the largest in history. As part of the settlement, he sold his Los Angeles teams and their arena, the Fabulous Forum, and bought out Williams, who then became sole owner of the Baltimore Orioles. Cooke got married four more times. By 1979, his former daughter-in-law Carrie had been married to Pete Rozelle for nearly five years. As Bill Wallace noted in correspondence, "Jack Kent Cooke, like Rosenbloom, attacked Rozelle from dark corners, jealous of his power, influence, and popularity."

TWENTY-TWO

MR. GARVEY'S RESTLESS WORKERS

"The real battle began in 1971 when we filed the Mackey case."

—ED GARVEY, 2006

"*R*ozelle was not a phony. He was a man in the gray flannel suit, a man to whom marketing and control were everything, and look what he created," said William Nack, former senior writer for *Sports Illustrated* and no admirer of the commissioner. "You can't knock what he created. He did exactly what he set out to do. If you consider somebody a success who accomplished what he set out to accomplish, he was an enormous, unbelievable success."

By January 14, 1973, when the National Football League returned the Super Bowl to its birthplace, the Los Angeles Memorial Coliseum, for its seventh staging, the game itself had become a lesser adjunct to a colossal midwinter marketing pageant. Ticket demand was overwhelming. For those without tickets, the broadcast was easily the most watched television show every year. "The NFL is always summed up best by its halftime show," Bill Nack said. "Tits and ass; a flyover of Blue Angels jets; run up the flag; everybody have a hot dog, sit in your seats, and behave yourself, or else we break your kneecaps. I was a reporter in those situations, and we were like little pawns on this huge board, that they moved around."

Nack, that rare sportswriter who couldn't care less if he landed another credential to one more pro football game, truly enjoyed the whole experience. "When I was there covering it, I went to the Super Bowl parties. Was there anything ever more extravagant than a Super Bowl press party? Nothing. Absolutely nothing. I remember writing about the thousands and thousands of dollars they would spend on this party. There would be eight tons of shrimp, 7,500 pounds of lobster. It was always fun to write down how much food they bought to seduce the press."

The commissioner turned his personal-appearance tours through various Super Bowl parties into an art form. Blair Sabol, the writer of the filmmaking family, went along with Rozelle on one of those occasions for the *Village Voice*. While Rozelle's driver, Wayne Rosen, waited in the car, the boss put on a show of his own. "I went to one party after another with Pete," Sabol said. "The title of my piece was 'Pit Stops with Pete Rozelle.' He had it down to a science: He would walk in, no topcoat like Jack Kennedy, go to the right people, have a chat that was meaningful, out the kitchen, in the limo in record time—at the most, 15 minutes—and off to the next one. It wasn't cursory. It wasn't rude. He didn't have someone whispering instructions and directions into his ears to greet somebody. Pete just had radar."

"He would have itineraries," daughter Anne Marie Rozelle Bratton said. "Each party was called a 'walk-through.' You would walk through the front door, say hello to everyone, never pick up a drink or have food, never sit down, shake hands, talk to people, quick hellos, walk out to the kitchen, where a driver would pick him up, and go on to the next one. He called each one of them a 'pit stop,' a 15-minute pit stop."

It wasn't just his moves that impressed Blair Sabol. "His patter was the best I've ever heard in my life," she remarked. "It wasn't bootlicking or brownnosing. He knew enough about who he was talking with. He spoke really softly; people had a hard time hearing him. You had to lean in to hear Pete, which made it more intimate with him.

He really pulled you towards him. I think it actually was a technique Pete used so he didn't have to project anything, but you would really have to lean in to him and really listen hard."

Pacing was key to his party-hopping mastery. "He would save the one with either the most friends or the most relaxing," Anne Marie said. "Finally, he would actually sit down and really have something to eat and something to drink."

"He was safely in bed by 11," Blair Sabol said. "He lived a very measured life."

The Super Bowl parties were among the few remaining functions in which the commissioner could at least put on the appearance of enjoying his post. By 1973, success had translated into restlessness among the troops. The NFL Players' Association had an executive director who was deadly serious about his business. He was a young labor lawyer from Burlington, Wisconsin, named Ed Garvey. Educated at the University of Wisconsin in Madison, he was a disciple of progressive icon Fightin' Bob LaFollette.

Garvey was a child when the first meeting of the future NFLPA was held in 1956 at the Waldorf-Astoria, in New York, on the eve of the NFL title game between the Giants and the Chicago Bears, the only team that refused to join up. Among representatives from the 11 teams that participated, Los Angeles Rams quarterback Norm Van Brocklin presided over a session attended by two future Hall of Famers, 49ers quarterback Y. A. Tittle and Lions linebacker Joe Schmidt. The players sought a modest list of benefits that included a pension.

Commissioner Bert Bell did not stand in the way, after his friend and ally Carroll Rosenbloom, the Baltimore Colts' owner, told his team's player rep, Bill Pellington, that he did not mind the players' organizing. "In 1959–60, the league offered to form a pension plan, but there was no money in it," said former NFLPA president Pete Retzlaff. "I first met Rozelle when I became president of the Players' Association and he had been named commissioner to replace Bert Bell. That was 1961–62."

Retzlaff noted, "Van Brocklin always felt that his involvement as a founder and player rep when he was with the Rams was one of the reasons he was traded to Philadelphia." Incidentally, the man who traded the Dutchman was young general manager Pete Rozelle. "When he got to Philadelphia," Retzlaff said, "and I became player rep for the team, he gave me some advice: 'When you go to the meetings, sit in the back of the room, never raise your hand, and keep your mouth shut.' Unfortunately, I didn't heed his advice and became president of the whole damned association for two years."

The players still had not gained recognition from the league. So, Retzlaff's first order of business in 1961 was to get things moving with Commissioner Rozelle. He used Rozelle's own words to gain access. "He kept saying that not only was he commissioner of the National Football League, but that title included the owners and the players," Retzlaff recalled. "He continually said he was the players' commissioner, so we kept saying, 'If that's the case, you should hear us out and acknowledge that we exist as an association.'"

The impasse broke in south Florida. The players had convened at the Hollywood Beach Hotel. The owners were encamped at the Fontainebleau in Miami Beach. "We discussed at our meeting if it would be possible to meet with the commissioner, since he was in the area, so I called him," Retzlaff said.

"What time would you like to come down?" Rozelle asked.

"We would come down, but we would prefer to have you come up," Retzlaff replied. "The reason is, we have some players on our committee who are wagering that you will not come to our turf because that would be tantamount to recognizing that the association exists."

"What time do you want me to be there?" Rozelle asked.

"In a short time, a limousine pulled up to the hotel. All the player reps were out on the steps, and he came in, and we had a meeting," Retzlaff said. "That was the first visible acknowledgment of the Players' Association. That was a moral victory, even though it was a struggle afterward." And recognition from the commissioner was all they got.

Retzlaff's next order of business, one that would make or break his organization, was to land the Chicago Bears, the only team that had not joined the association. "I had received several phone calls—

one from Green Bay; the Cardinals, I believe; Detroit," Retzlaff said. "Upwards of five teams indicated to me through their player reps that if the Bears weren't going to be in the Players' Association, then they didn't want to be. Either we were all together, or forget it."

That meant a young football player who doubled as would-be union leader had to confront the living symbol of the National Football League, its founder and winningest coach. "So, that's when I called George Halas, and I don't know to this day how I did it," Retzlaff said of the hard-nosed, jut-jawed Bohemian who had broken the wills of many a tough bruiser on the football field and across the desk negotiating contracts. Papa Bear was a formidable man. "Here I was, asking him if I could talk to his team and try to get them to become members of the Players' Association. 'Come on in,' he said, to my great surprise."

Retzlaff continued, "I met with them and talked with them. Halas had told his players he would provide benefits for them later in life, because every year, he invested in oil stocks from the proceeds the Bears took in at the gate. When they turned 65, Halas promised, they would be allowed to tap into that fund for supplemental income. They wouldn't need a league with a pension plan or to be part of it."

Retzlaff put his finger on the weakness in their position. "If he told you that, I'm sure that's true," he said to the team. "But you better have it in writing, because when you're 65, he'll be 120-something, and I'm not sure who will be owning this franchise then." In practical terms, most of the players who lived to 65 would have had to wait until the turn of the 21st century to draw funds.

"So, they voted," Retzlaff said. "I suggested to them they should have a majority rule, then make it unanimous so they wouldn't be split on and off the field. They agreed to that. The vote was 21 to 19. Then they closed ranks. Stan Jones told me that he was called in by Halas sometime later and told that both he and Bill George were being relieved as cocaptains because Halas believed they should have held the squad together better than they did."

In our interview, Retzlaff commented, "I don't know why Coach Halas should have thought that Stan Jones should have taken a management position. What happened to Bill George is a mystery to me.

Later, Stan called me and said publicly even though he lost his captain's job, it was the best decision he ever made. That was part of it."

It did not end there. Retzlaff was recovering from a broken arm and therefore did not have to rush back to Philadelphia to rejoin the Eagles. So, after the vote and his chat with Jones, Halas asked him to dinner that night. They went to the coach's lair, the Tavern Club, atop the 333 North Michigan Building. "I'd like to invite some of our beat writers who cover the Bears," Halas said. "You can tell your side of the story about this Players' Association, and then I'll tell my side, and we can kind of go from there."

Papa Bear invited several scribes from his legion of newspaper loyalists. They included George Strickler, his number one cheerleader at the *Tribune*; *Herald-American* sports editor Leo Fischer; Bruce Morrison, the Bears writer for the *Sun-Times*; and Howie Roberts, of the *Daily News*, who wrote a noncritical biography of the Old Man after the glory years of the '40s.

"I tried to do the best to explain who we were and what we wanted," Retzlaff said. "At the time, there were only three things we felt strongly about. First, we wanted an injury clause written into the standard contract so that if a guy got hurt, he was not going to be released, and the team was obligated to pay him until he got healthy again. We also wanted, which should have been no big deal, some preseason pay. We were not asking that the contracts should be paid during the preseason, but we wanted some sort of economic supplement. The third thing we wanted, which we thought would be the most difficult part of it, was the pension plan. I'm happy to say that it took some time, but they were all put together."

Halas and his writers tried and failed to dissuade Retzlaff. Typical of converts to a cause, the Bears became enthusiastic members of the Players' Association. Cocaptain and center Mike Pyle was elected NFLPA president in 1967.

A year later, the NFLPA elected Detroit Lions tackle John Gordy president, and the Teamsters pushed both Gordy and the league hard for control of the players' union. The Teamsters' brilliant organizer Harold Gibbons, of St. Louis, who steered clear of Jimmy Hoffa and counted Bill Veeck and Edward Bennett Williams among his close friends, was aided by former Cleveland Browns defensive back Bernie

Parrish. "I knew I had problems because of the Teamsters' association," Parrish said.

"Bernie," Gibbons said to Parrish, "we've got loans out to probably half the owners in the NFL."

"The guy in Philadelphia, Leonard Tose, who had the trucking company, was in bed with Hoffa," Parrish said. "They didn't want that coming out."

Everybody knew and many feared what a difference the Teamsters could have made had they landed the players under their banner. The players almost jumped after listening to Gibbons. "We got better than 80 percent of the players to sign the cards. We had a majority of the teams," Parrish said. "I had all the cards I needed to win the election."

The Players' Association officers argued that the public would not be happy if the Teamsters had the players. "We told the players, 'All right, go ahead, but we're coming back,'" Parrish said. "I held that over Rozelle's head for years after that election. That was 1968. The players didn't even know that. The players were asking for different things; I would call Rozelle and tell him, 'You'd better give it to them, because you know I still have the cards.' Rozelle always wanted the cards. He wanted to know who had signed them, which I certainly never gave him. I used that for years when the players were bitching. I still have the cards." The Teamsters soon disappeared from the NFL universe.

It took some help from baseball for the pro football players to gain traction with their situation. On October 7, 1969, the St. Louis Cardinals traded star center fielder Curt Flood, catcher Tim McCarver, reliever Joe Hoerner, and outfielder Byron Browne to the moribund Philadelphia Phillies for first baseman Dick Allen, second baseman Cookie Rojas, and pitcher Jerry Johnson.

Flood refused to report and sued Major League Baseball and commissioner Bowie Kuhn for violating the antitrust laws and asked for $4.1 million in damages. Citing his status as a 12-year veteran, Flood stated in his brief, "I do not feel that I am a piece of property to be bought and sold irrespective of my wishes."

Rozelle testified in a New York federal court, with the NFL's young attorney Paul Tagliabue acting as counsel. "I think that both sides wanted him to testify," Tagliabue said in 2006. "They were drawing comparisons between the reserve clauses of both sports. The players' association wanted Rozelle to show there was a less restrictive situation in the NFL. The baseball people wanted Rozelle to explain that while there was a restrictive rule in football, there was relatively little movement of players from team to team."

After five years of testimony and appeals, the U.S. Supreme Court in a 5-to-3 vote refused to strike down the 1922 ruling that upheld baseball's reserve clause. But the genie was out of the bottle.

By the time of the merger, Pete Rozelle had formed an enduring friendship with Buffalo Bills quarterback Jack Kemp, who would finish his playing career in 1969 to enter electoral politics. Kemp was a cofounder of the American Football League Players' Association in 1964 with Boston's Tom Addison. "We had the first collective bargaining agreement, signed in '65, premerger," Kemp said.

Kemp, in no way a trade union advocate, served five terms as AFLPA president and, with NFLPA president Jim Bakken, of the St. Louis Cardinals, helped lead the merger of the two associations. "I helped elect John Mackey, who was the first African American head of the players," Kemp said. "We are good friends, and, tragically, John has dementia. However, I am pleased that I got all of the AFL player reps to support John. John had a pro-business, pro-labor attitude and would supply a bridge for racial reconciliation and reconciliation with the problems between labor and management."

As soon as Kemp wrapped up the details of the merger of the players' associations, he retired from football and ran for Congress as a Republican in New York's old 39th District. He represented the area around Buffalo and western New York until 1989. "Pete Rozelle went to my kickoff dinner when I had Frank Leahy, Nick Buonoconti, Ernie Ladd, Herb Klein, and my teammates," Kemp said. "Pete came in with Joe Foss. I always thought Pete would have made a great U.S. senator from New York." Had Rozelle ever chosen to run, his Democratic opponent conceivably could have been Howard Cosell. Neither man took that step.

Rozelle had enough problems trying to cope with the new militancy of the merged NFLPA. Confrontation was never his style, while

confrontation at a business and personal level was the only way Ed
Garvey played the negotiating game. He viewed union politics in two
phases: before the players could take on the owners, Garvey believed,
they had to become a true union, instead of what he had seen in the
early years as "company fronts."

In John Mackey, the Baltimore Colts' great tight end, the players
had a leader who enjoyed their utmost respect. "The two associations
met to merge, and a deal was made whereby the AFLPA would vote
for John Mackey as president with the understanding that he would
hire Alan Miller as counsel [from AFL days]," Garvey said. "The balance was four from the old NFLPA, three from the old AFLPA."

Mackey did not want anybody dictating the person he should hire
as counsel. So, he talked to a pair of player reps he knew as opponents and responsible union men: Ken Bowman, of Green Bay, and
Pat Richter, of Washington. "You guys are both in law school,"
Mackey said. "We need a labor attorney. Who should we hire?"

"Mackey urged them to check with their law professors at Wisconsin, where they went in the off-season," Garvey said. "They went
to Nate Feinsinger, who had strongly pushed me to go to the
Lindquist and Vennum firm, in Minneapolis, where Walter Mondale
was a partner." In short order, the NFLPA hired Garvey as counsel.

Before Garvey got installed, the owners called Mackey and Vikings
player rep Alan Page. Page, a future lawyer, would become a justice
on the Minnesota Supreme Court in 1993. They wanted Mackey and
Page to go to Hawaii where the owners were meeting to start bargaining "on a friendly basis." Nothing developed, and they agreed to
meet in New York without lawyers. According to Garvey, Rozelle had
argued that "lawyers complicate matters."

"They met in New York at the NFL offices," Garvey said. "Rozelle
told Mackey, 'I would like you to meet with Ted Kheel.'" Kheel was
a noted labor mediator.

"If we're not having lawyers, how come you have one?" Mackey
asked.

"He's not here as our lawyer," Rozelle said. "He's here to explain
the recognition agreement."

"He looks like a lawyer to me," Mackey said.

"Kheel presented a recognition agreement to the players, and John called us in Minneapolis to say it was unacceptable," Garvey said.

"Tell him you are not going to sign it," Garvey told Mackey. "We'll work on it and file a petition with the National Labor Relations Board to have them certify you as a union."

Garvey did just that. "The owners continued to refuse," Garvey said. "We filed a petition and were the first group of athletes to be certified as a union. The Players' Association became a union. We were the only one recognized as a union by the National Labor Relations Board, Marvin Miller and his Major League Baseball Players Association notwithstanding."

In short order, Garvey realized he was dealing with football players, not miners, teamsters, steelworkers, or any other trade unionists. They were disorganized, had no idea how to contact fellow players in the off-season, and had not established a bargaining strategy. What passed for negotiations that first time took place at the Plaza Hotel. "Pete Rozelle was the chairperson. Al Davis was carping at him to speak up, and so on, and they wouldn't allow me in the room," Garvey said.

All player caucuses with Garvey took place in the hall. "It is fair to say that the agreement was hardly a groundbreaking deal. It bought some peace and some time," Garvey said. "That's when Mackey asked me if I would set up the union as a real organization with a real staff. We had a meeting in January and decided to relocate the offices from Michigan, where Gordy had established them, to Washington, D.C. I agreed to become the first executive director."

The owners, led by Tex Schramm and with help from counsel Kheel, did their best to undercut Garvey with the players, which Garvey learned from a surprising, sub-rosa ally. "Coach George Allen became a friend," he said. "He would call me and say, 'You can't believe the stuff they say about you.' Incredibly, George represented Jack Kent Cooke at an NBA meeting when they were looking for a new commissioner, and he nominated me. 'Ed, you would not believe what happened,' Allen said. 'People went completely crazy.'"

Garvey emphasized, "The real battle began in 1972 when we filed the Mackey case. It was focused on the Rozelle Rule. He wanted to call it the player compensation rule, or whatever. We kept hammering it in our newsletter, calling it the 'Rozelle Rule,' which drove him crazy. We continually called it the 'Rozelle Rule' because we needed to explain to people what the problem was." Rozelle had instituted the "Rozelle Rule" in 1962, making himself the arbitrator to decide compensation when a team lost a free agent. Compensation was prohibitive, usually involving at least a first-round draft choice.

"The first wave of serious hostilities between the owners and the Players' Association had started," Ernie Accorsi said. Still a Baltimore employee until 1975 before he joined the league office, Accorsi worked for the negotiators when collective bargaining negotiations began in earnest in 1974, the year of the freedom issue. As Garvey targeted Pete Rozelle, the owners made the players' leader the object of their disaffection.

"It was a personal vendetta for Garvey to weaken Rozelle," Accorsi said. "He did not want Rozelle to be the personal arbitrator. He did not want the Rozelle Rule. He wanted Rozelle to be commissioner of the owners. He wanted to be commissioner of the players. That's essentially what he wanted. Not one time did I hear Pete make the appeal 'Save my power.' Everybody did it automatically. You had this devotion to the guy, and everybody had it, except for Al Davis—from Curt Mosher, who was the PR director of the Cowboys, all the way to Tex Schramm, for obvious reasons, and, in those times before relations got strained, Carroll Rosenbloom."

"We were at a player rep meeting out in San Francisco," Garvey said. "We always heard this stuff about Rozelle being neutral, and so forth. So, I came up with the idea, 'Let's fire him!' Everybody laughed. 'Of course, we can't fire him.'"

Garvey wasn't joking. "Let's hold a news conference and fire him. Let the NFL tell us we can't fire him," he urged the reps.

"So, we did," Garvey said. "We held a news conference and said, 'We are terminating Mr. Rozelle from his position as commissioner.' Mara and others fell right in and said, 'The players have no right to fire him. We hired him.' We said, 'Thank you very much, Wellington. You made our point.'"

"I think that we made his office such an issue, and I feel we were right. If the commissioner issued a ruling on a player, and a player appealed, guess where it went?" said Bill Curry, who served as NFLPA president in 1974. "When we pointed it out and just said, 'How can we have a system like that?' I guess that was the reason he felt like he better stay either above or beyond the fray. I really don't know."

"Fortunately, Red Smith was alive, because he was about the only one who consistently supported us nationally," Garvey said. "We had to somehow deal with the myth of neutrality, that only the commissioner was walking between the players and owners on behalf of the fans—all that nonsense. We did that by talking about the Rozelle Rule, how his role was to hold wages down, stop free agency, and how he was the one the owners selected to keep order in the house. Anyone who confused him with being neutral was too dumb to listen to the next thought."

Bill Curry started his career in Green Bay under the devoutly anti-union Vince Lombardi, moved to Baltimore, and then played in Houston in 1973. In that off-season, he found his way to Los Angeles. "I ended up with the Rams because of Carroll Rosenbloom. If you ever played for him, he backed you," Curry said.

It was in that spirit, confident he had the support of Rosenbloom, the single owner whom the players around the league truly liked, that Curry became union president. "I went to New York in 1974 to meet with the commissioner with the executive committee," Curry said. "We sat and talked for a half hour or so about the situation, what we could do. He was very cordial, but nothing got done; the differences were too vast. Plus, we had the Mackey suit in progress, and since it was being litigated, I couldn't say anything. I didn't say anything that put us at risk. I've often wondered if that was the purpose of the meeting, but maybe it was paranoia. The bottom line is, I can't remember Pete being involved."

Rozelle, according to David Harris, in *The League*, called Garvey "a prototypical early-sixties radical, a militant ideologue who is unable to see any good, any justice, in any action of management. He is unable to see in any shades of gray, no in-betweens. He has no ability to get close to the center of an issue."

Joe Browne, who joined Rozelle soon after he came to New York and has served in recent years as the NFL's executive vice president of communications and public affairs, seethes at the mention of the name Ed Garvey to this day. "Garvey was a smart-ass pain in the ass, probably still is to some of the people in Wisconsin." Browne alluded to the fact that voters in the state rejected Garvey in runs for state attorney general and the U.S. Senate. He added, "He was not a reasonable person."

Reasonable or not, Garvey set down a 57-point list of demands. They included elimination of the Rozelle Rule, total free agency, a union shop provision for all players, elimination of the commissioner's authority to discipline players, and an extended roster of freedom issues, such as the right of veteran players to veto any trade, putting an end to psychological testing, and forbidding teams from cutting or trading elected player reps or NFLPA officers without their consent.

The owners rejected everything on the table. Negotiations at the Hyatt-O'Hare, in Chicago, in the presence of the federal mediator, broke down on July 3, 1974, before the veterans were scheduled to report to their training camps. They went on strike and wore T-shirts with the slogan "No freedom. No football."

"Bill Usery, with federal mediation, was at the meeting," Ernie Accorsi said. "I was sitting in the suite with Wellington, Jim Finks, [Miami Dolphins owner] Joe Robbie, Art Modell, Rankin Smith, Mugs Halas, and John Thompson. Usery, a seasoned politician, said, 'Gentlemen, you got a problem with your players.'

"Of course, Usery wanted someone to cave. His job as mediator was to get an agreement. So, he was looking for the weakest spot he could find," Accorsi said. The owners remained steadfast.

"No freedom. No football. Yes, the strike shut down the College All-Star Game in '74," Accorsi recalled. The list of union demands, already unwieldy at 57, kept growing, finally reaching a staggering 93, impossible for anyone but a savant to name.

The exhibitions were scheduled to start the first weekend in August. Rookies and free agents played the first exhibition games, and few fans bothered to show up. Picket lines were manned by small cadres of unenthusiastic players. There were no negotiations at that time as the owners worked hard to break the union.

"All the clubs were offering the players a 10 percent bonus if they crossed the picket line," Garvey said. "We decided that this would ultimately defeat us as more and more players went into camp. They were saving their jobs. We had miscalculated, and the better way to go was to simply call off the strike and go back to work without a contract."

When Garvey called Usery on August 10 to say he was calling off the strike, the mediator countered with a face-saving offer. "Why don't you do it under my auspices as a cooling-off period?" Usery suggested. "OK," Garvey said. The cooling-off period started August 13. The strike officially ended August 29. The owners had won the battle, but the war continued, and Garvey was in it for the long run.

The players had gained a single concession. They could wear moustaches. "That turned our focus to the litigation, the Mackey case," Garvey said. To make sure they were in control, the owners stopped collecting dues, the payroll checkoff. "We had to get the players to write checks, so I visited all the teams and asked them to bring their checkbooks. I told them the good news was we raised the dues. And they paid. We had 100 percent on teams where we had good leadership. So, management kept expecting us to collapse, and Rozelle continued the drumbeat."

Dues payments did fall off on many teams. Fewer than half the players paid dues in 1975, the year after the strike. The owners, confident they would win in the courts, didn't bargain with Garvey and the players after 1974.

"The league created the management council in '73 to keep Pete in the neutral position," Accorsi said. "Garvey wanted Pete to get his hands dirty. He was trying to drag Pete into a fight. Pete was smart enough to stay out of it. The management council was the negotiating arm. The battle cry from the league office was, 'Tell them to get the hell out of Washington.' Kensil and Pete would call down and say, 'Tell them to get the hell out of Washington.' "

Garvey now realized he and his union had to go back and tackle the bread-and-butter issues they should have put first. He explained the background: "In 1970, we were meeting in a small hotel in New York; we moved out of the Plaza after I said, 'How can we afford to be here?' Alex Karras came in and said, 'Ed, until you negotiate wages, this union will never have any strength.' That was the first time the thought had really come to me to take a different approach, that free agency itself was not the answer. The question was how to get a decent wage for everybody."

"What they did, and I don't know if it was a conscious thing, but they forced us to go to the one place that we actually had a chance: the courts," Bill Curry said. "And that's where the NFL system took big hits, like the Mackey decision, the Kermit Alexander decision, all those cases. Had we been able to sit down and negotiate our way through those issues, the litigation would not have been necessary."

Enter, once again, Carroll Rosenbloom. Rosenbloom long had defied the commissioner whenever circumstances might benefit him or his teams, especially when it came to free agency. Back in 1962, it was his signing of free agent R. C. Owens that brought the Rozelle Rule into play.

As NFLPA president John Mackey wrote in his memoir *Blazing Trails*, "No teams were willing to pay the price to sign free agents. [The Rozelle Rule] rendered free agency meaningless." Mackey asked a federal court in 1972 to dissolve the Rozelle Rule and grant free agency to the players. From the time the case went to trial in 1973, it would take three years for the suit to wend its way through the courts.

"I was in on the last implementation of the Rozelle Rule," Ernie Accorsi said. In 1974 as the NFLPA strike failed, talented wide receiver Ron Jessie played out his option with the Detroit Lions. Carroll Rosenbloom immediately signed him to a Rams contract.

Accorsi had just joined the league in 1975, when he got assigned to the Jessie case. "Rozelle put me, as conference coordinator, and Nick Skorich, a former coach, on it to figure out what was fair compensation. We looked at tape, studied statistics, went over the Rams' roster. They had Larry McCutcheon at running back. We came back and said, 'Jessie's worth more than a number one, Pete.' We recommended Cullen Bryant, a backup running back with potential, and a number one, as fair.

" 'Do you think you are not being affected by Rosenbloom, or by the fact that he signed Jessie?' Rozelle asked. 'No,' I said. Pete was being advised by the management council not to do it, that the Rams were going to challenge the ruling.

" 'If it's right, we're going to do it,' Rozelle said.

"I have never seen more courage or more integrity in a leader," Accorsi said. "We implemented it. Rosenbloom got a temporary restraining order against him. The union, of course, supported Rosenbloom/Jessie. It spelled the end of the Rozelle Rule. The fact of the matter is, he knew it was going to be attacked, and he knew he was going to be vulnerable, but he felt it was the right thing to do.

"He could have said, 'Let's not move a body. Let's put in a three here, not Bryant.' He didn't say that. We felt the Lions ought to get a player because they were losing a better player. We argued that, and he went with it. If he was in any way politically inclined, as sharp as he was, he would have said, 'I don't want to move a player; that's going to cause trouble.' He knew that the player was more valuable."

The Rozelle Rule was struck down by a federal appeals court in Minneapolis in 1976. Both Ron Jessie and the compensatory player, Cullen Bryant, stayed with the Rams. The Rams did not give up a draft pick of any kind to the Lions. The free agent issue reverted to collective bargaining and was not settled until after Rozelle left office, with the Freeman McNeil decision in 1992.

"As we moved forward in the litigation, we thought about other ways to skin the cat," Garvey recalled. "When we won the Mackey case at the court of appeals level, suddenly the NFL wanted to negotiate. Through all this time, Rozelle did nothing to ever try to bring the parties together to bring about a negotiated settlement."

Garvey never did realize that Rozelle truly was powerless because he had turned over negotiating strategy and tactics to the management council. That concession, in fact, served to hamstring the commissioner for the rest of his time in office. "We played without a contract from '74, '75, and '76," Accorsi said. "Got a contract in '77." Accorsi, by then, was assistant general manager of the Baltimore Colts.

While the league was haggling with its disaffected players, it had another battle on its hands, another challenge from a new league in 1974. The World Football League emerged from the fertile imagination of Gary Davidson, who had also started up the World Hockey

Association and American Basketball Association. Davidson had managed to place a few franchises in the National Hockey League and National Basketball Association. That was his long-range goal with the WFL.

The league made headlines when teams signed several big NFL stars to future contracts to start in 1975. The biggest names to sign up among 60 NFLers to whom the WFL laid claim were Miami Dolphins stars Paul Warfield, Larry Csonka, and Jim Kiick; Oakland Raiders quarterbacks Kenny Stabler and Daryle Lamonica; and two Dallas Cowboys, running back Calvin Hill and quarterback Craig Morton.

The league opened play in the summer with 13 teams, a cobbled-together independent television deal, and a lot of papered houses. By September, two franchises had relocated: one from New York to Charlotte as the Hornets, and the other from Houston to northwest Louisiana as the Shreveport Steamer. Most of the other teams went broke. The Birmingham Americans beat the Florida Blazers 22–21 on November 29 in the only World Bowl. After the game, sheriff's deputies confiscated the Birmingham uniforms, and it was revealed that the Blazers had not been paid for weeks. Because nobody could guarantee a check, the players literally divided cash lying on a guarded table on the sidelines at Legion Field.

The WFL tried to make a go of it again in 1975 but folded a dozen games into the season. The man who benefited most from the experience was Florida's first-year coach, Jack Pardee. New Chicago general manager/operational boss Jim Finks was so impressed by Pardee's ability to hold his payless players together that he hired him to coach the Bears in 1975. Two former WFL franchises, Memphis and Birmingham, tried to join the NFL and were refused. Memphis even sued to get into the league as an expansion team, but it lost its case in court. The NFL, which added Tampa Bay and Seattle in 1976, was able to prove to the courts that expansion plans had been in the works for several years before the WFL experiment went down the drain.

History had marched on toward new horizons from the time Rozelle took office in 1960. America was a far different country after the events of the '60s at home and abroad. While the negotiating impasse continued, Ed Garvey made significant strides in an area that would affect more and more players, eventually 80 percent of the league—its black players. "The NFL was a whites-only club until Buddy Young [and a couple of others out west—Kenny Washington, Woodrow Strode, Tank Younger; Marion Motley, Bill Willis, and Horace Gillom on the Browns in the AAFC] broke the color barrier," Garvey said. "When I was executive director, it was clear that there were no black head coaches, no general managers, no front-office people."

In many ways, the NFLPA was the most active quasi civil rights organization anywhere, although that was not its declared purpose. "Blacks were very much involved in the operation of the union," Garvey said. "Whites felt the same way, that there shouldn't be a racial barrier. Everybody knew there was an informal rule to keep the teams one-third black. Hank Stram was the first to go to a majority. We had a meeting with Rozelle which I think summed up his role—Ernie Wright, Brig Owens, and myself, the three of us. Rozelle said, 'If there were qualified blacks, we would hire them.'

"It finally helped break through and force the NFL to hire black coaches and to let them play center, guard, linebacker, and quarterback," Garvey said. "As a joke, in our newsletter, we said black colleges must have just a scrum, because they couldn't have a quarterback, and how do they score all those points?"

It was a problem then and continued into the 21st century. A milestone was reached on February 4, 2007, when, for the first time ever, the Super Bowl pitted two African American head coaches against each other: Tony Dungy, of the Indianapolis Colts, and Lovie Smith, of the charter Chicago Bears.

The league had seven black head coaches in 2006 and would have six to start the 2007 season, with a net loss of one. Dennis Green, in Arizona, and Art Shell, for the second time in Oakland, were fired after the '06 season. Pittsburgh hired Minnesota defensive coordinator Mike Tomlin to replace longtime coach Bill Cowher, who resigned. Despite those black successes in coaching and management, race remains an unsettled issue in the league.

Major-league baseball players, meanwhile, gained their freedom in 1976 when arbitrator Peter Seitz ruled in favor of Andy Messersmith and Dave McNally, who played out their options and knocked out the reserve clause. Commissioner Bowie Kuhn couldn't do a thing about it. "So, that spread in one way or another to the other sports and drove up salaries all around," Kuhn told me in the summer of 2006, a year before his passing.

Kuhn admitted that he was taken by surprise at the way the tap opened and the money began to pour out into the hands of players and their now powerful agents. "You could see it was coming," Kuhn said. "The system needed a little bit more flexibility than it had, but to rise to the extent that it has was quite astonishing. The only limit is rationality, and rationality doesn't seem to play a large role across the board."

Ernie Accorsi still was working for Rozelle as the NFC coordinator in 1977 when the Pro Bowl rolled around. "We couldn't draw for that game," Accorsi said. "Players wouldn't play. The only way we could get people to attend the game was to put it on the season ticket package in Seattle. There was no way we could have taken the players to Seattle to practice. So, we practiced in San Diego.

"I had the NFC team," Accorsi continued. "Pete came into town, and I took him to practice. We walked on the field, and here were all these superstars—Staubach and all these people. I stepped aside. I knew my place. I stepped back, and he grabbed me and said, 'No, no, stay with me.' He didn't know the players very well. Times weren't good, and Garvey had planted the seeds of bitterness among the players. Still, when they saw Pete, they responded to him. I'll always remember how shy he was. I wanted to get out of his way, and he wanted me standing beside him."

Ed Garvey remained an unrepentant foe of Pete Rozelle more than a decade after the commissioner's death. "Rozelle played no positive role in labor relations. He forced Joe Kapp out of the game. He did nothing to come to grips with racism," Garvey said. "One thing I loved about Pete was he had this big desk, and there was nothing on it. He had no artwork in his office. It was like, here was a guy who did not have a lot of deep thoughts. He would say, 'I don't have any authority.' Of course, if you don't have any authority, then why don't you just announce that?"

For the owners, how was Garvey as an adversary? "Tough! Tough! Ed knew what he was talking about," said Art Modell, the former Browns and Baltimore Ravens owner and Rozelle's close friend for 35 years. "He was up to speed as far as his knowledge of the game and the nuances of our contacts and relationships."

"Art Modell during the Mackey trial was on the witness stand," Garvey said. "We asked him about Rozelle and how he could be neutral when it came to compensation. 'We pay him to be neutral,' Art said. I thought that was one of those comments that stay with you the rest of your life. '*We* pay him to be neutral.'"

TWENTY-THREE

THE NFL TODAY AND GEORGIA TAKES OVER

"My take was, he'd have to change the habits of a lifetime to have gone in the water that I saw."

—STEVE ROSENBLOOM, ON HIS FATHER'S FATAL SWIM,
APRIL 2, 1979

*B*ecause he always knows more than anyone else in his dealings, Robert Wussler is the consummate manager in a universe where flash and glitz define success. Since graduating from Seton Hall University in 1957 and launching his career in the CBS mailroom in New York, Bob Wussler quickly advanced up the ranks and has been a man to watch, a man who fixes failing network franchises, a man who gets things done, still making deals in his seventies.

At CBS in the late '60s and early '70s, he directed the special-unit coverage of Walter Cronkite–anchored space shots and election returns. Then, in 1972, he moved on to rescue WBBM-TV in Chicago, a company jewel that had become moribund. In a 19-month period, he literally remade the industry standard. He junked news film coverage, with its processing and handling problems, and replaced it with small, easy-to-handle, portable electronics packages—minicams, transmitting live and often by satellite, with feeds from the scene of breaking news, along with the latest in electronic editing. To make the viewer a part of the process, he converted a studio into the newsroom and aired the broadcasts from there, complete with real reporters and producers scurrying in the background.

All those Wussler-promoted innovations sped production from what often was a languid, day-after news format to constant, almost instant, deadlines and live events—the 24-hour news cycle. In so doing, he made WBBM-TV the top-rated news shop in Chicago and the model everywhere for local broadcast news as it became the most honored television station in America. For good measure, he made certain the newspaper television critics were well fed with inside stories, wined and dined away from their desks, and flattered with personal, individual treatment.

Through the winter and spring of 1974, back in New York, the CBS brass were growing increasingly concerned about the slippage in the sports division. Roone Arledge at ABC and the Carl Lindemann–Chet Simmons operation at NBC clearly were outpacing Bill McPhail and CBS. McPhail, a popular, hail-fellow-well-met charmer who would buy the first and last rounds and several in between, could no longer rely on Pete Rozelle to bail him out. He had lost control of matters.

So, on July 7, after weeks of farewell luncheons from just about every service club and entertainment organization in Chicago, Bob Wussler returned to New York and "Black Rock," at 51 West 52nd Street, to get CBS Sports back on track. On weekends in the beginning, followed by a permanent move a year later, Wussler brought with him a 35-year-old hard-charger named Brent Musburger, who'd been on a fast track since he left Billings, Montana, in 1957 for Evanston, Illinois, and the Medill School of Journalism at Northwestern University.

After spending his high school years pent up in the tightly disciplined Shattuck Military School, in Faribault, Minnesota, Musburger was ready to spread his wings. He loved Northwestern, with its unique diversity of students and its proximity to Chicago, a city acclaimed for its great newspapers with colorful writers and traditions, as well as worldly broadcasters. The personable Musburger made new friends on a dorm floor that housed budding engineers, actors, doctors, lawyers, accountants, and athletes, one of them a black football player and trackman from Hammond, Indiana, named Irv Cross.

By the end of the fall term, Musburger, along with a few friends who likewise had better things to do than go to class, had to cram for finals and, if lucky, earn gentlemen's Cs. Those who knew him recalled a young man who was an extremely quick study, had an almost photographic memory for sports facts and trivia, and regularly listened to Jack Brickhouse, Bob Elson, or Jack Quinlan call ball games in Chicago or, late at night, tuned in faraway stations to hear men such as Harry Caray in St. Louis or Bob Prince in Pittsburgh. He had more than overwhelming curiosity; he wanted to be somebody.

Musburger first attracted notice from students and faculty at Medill when, at barely 20 years of age, he dropped out of college for a couple of quarters, enrolled in an umpiring school, worked in a lower minor league, and came back richer for the experience, if not in cash. When he returned to school in 1960, he became an assistant editor for *Dimension*, a campus magazine, and contributed photographs to the 1961 yearbook, the *Syllabus*.

Before the first kickoff of 1960, at the urging of Medill professors Fred Whiting and Ben Baldwin, who kept watch on wayward young men with potential, Musburger called on Ed Wheeler, the owner-manager of local Evanston radio station WEAW. Wheeler hired him as his spotter on the station's Northwestern football and basketball broadcasts.

In those days, the big Chicago stations frequently offered competing broadcasts of the same college football game. When Northwestern games were carried on WGN, Musburger was able to meet and spend time with Jack Brickhouse, Jack Quinlan, Vince Lloyd, and sports editor Jack Rosenberg. He also got to know the sportswriters and the bigwigs, including Big Ten commissioner Bill Reed. From them, he picked up pointers and potential leads. From hanging around the teams, he became acquainted with the players and coaches. And, on a personal note, he found love and marriage with fellow student Arlene Sander, from Chicago's Northwest Side.

Brent Musburger was all of 22 when he landed a big-time sports-writing job, covering the White Sox for *Chicago's American*, a blue-collar paper heavy on crime and heavier on sports. He also worked nights laying out the next day's first edition. When beat writer Ed Stone antagonized Bears owner-coach George Halas one too many times, Luke Carroll, the paper's editor, cravenly relieved him of his duty during the 1963 championship season. Stone told his friend Musburger to go for the open slot. Musburger got the beat and more kudos. Then, when columnist Bill Gleason jumped to the rival *Sun-Times* in 1966, Musburger, at age 27, took over the column, his newspaper's plum forum.

On May 27, 1968, the hustling journalist bagged the local scoop of the previous half century. Early in the morning, he overheard a colleague's side of a phone conversation with a Chicago Bears official, got confirmation, and reported exclusively that Halas would announce his retirement that day after 40 seasons as coach.

When Musburger covered the 1968 Mexico City Olympics for the *American*, he moonlighted with CBS's all-news WBBM radio station and sent back as many as a dozen pieces a day concerning the most turbulent summer games in history. With a strong, clear voice and excellent diction, he conveyed that sense of urgency and insider's knowledge that sell audiences. When Musburger returned from the Olympics, the WBBM-TV management signed him to contribute commentaries to inject life into Paul Hornung's shaky, ill-prepared sportscasts. Next, they split airtime. Soon, it was all Musburger.

When Wussler arrived in the fall of 1972, WBBM-TV's ratings had dipped far below those of the city's other network-owned-and-operated stations, known as "O&Os," at NBC and ABC and, on many nights, even trailed Chicago Tribune–owned WGN-TV. He wasn't sure what to expect. "When I made my first appearance in the newsroom at WBBM, normally the general manager or news director is the greeter," Wussler said. "In that particular instance, it was Musburger. He was the leader."

When Wussler then headed back to New York to run CBS Sports, he knew he wanted Brent Musburger on his team. What he would do with him was yet to be determined. Wussler had an open mind and was not afraid to remake the long-established template.

One man in particular wanted to get out of a rut. Pat Summerall had been cast as an analyst from the time he started at CBS as Chris

Schenkel's color man. "Pat came to me after about three weeks, maybe four weeks, of the '74 season," Wussler said.

"I've always wanted to do play-by-play," Summerall said. "You know, I do morning radio."

"I'm a great listener of yours," Wussler said. "OK. Start this Sunday. Who are you going to use as color?"

"Oh, Tommy, of course—Brookshier," Summerall said. His good pal on the mike and in pub-crawling expeditions was a natural choice.

"They lasted a long time," Wussler said. "When John Madden arrived, he was a secondary play-by-play guy. What made Madden—I was long gone at this point—they had a Friday-afternoon luncheon in Los Angeles, and they had three or four of the analysts. Madden entertained everybody. One of the guys at CBS, Herbie Gross, said, 'We're using this guy the wrong way.' Last year, he probably made a couple hundred million dollars of his own."

Musburger was still the main sportscaster during the week at WBBM-TV in 1974–75, getting his network feet wet on small-market, play-by-play assignments. Wussler, though, knew he had a budding star; all he needed to do was plug him into the proper situation. "During the '74 season, we were using a couple of different guys, Jack Buck and Lee Leonard," Wussler said. "They were splitting the half-assed version of what we called 'The NFL Today.' Jack had to go to a confirmation ceremony on a Sunday and asked me if he could have the day off. 'Sure,' I said.

"I said to a couple of my guys, 'Let's bring in Musburger. I think he can do this well.' He came in and did the whole Sunday. In those days, we didn't have the magnificent technology they have today. We did everything live. We were on the air from 12:30 until the wrap-up after the second game. Late in the day, Musburger said on the air, 'Folks, I'm like a kid in the candy store. I've got all these games on little television sets in front of me. I've never been so enthralled in my whole life.' I turned to my assistant and said, 'Next year, we use Musburger as the host of this thing.' "

One day the following winter, Wussler was walking with his long-time liege Clarence Cross to a New York Television Academy event, where he was scheduled to make a speech. En route, he spotted 1972 Miss America Phyllis George, who had just started working at CBS. She was heading in the same direction. "You know, pairing her with Mus-burger might be pretty good," Wussler told Cross. "We'd have to set it up so she didn't make any obvious errors." No sooner said than done.

"So, I announced at the speech that Phyllis, who was sitting out in the 14th row, was going to cohost 'The NFL Today' with Brent Mus-burger," Wussler said. "About a month or two later," he added, "one of our lead producers, still a big-time producer with Fox, came to me and said, 'I have an analyst guy named Irv Cross. He'd be terrific in the studio.'

" 'Get him in here,' I said. 'Get him here to New York.' None of those guys lived in New York in those days. He lived in Philly," Wus-sler said. "Irv came in two or three weeks later, and we talked. I sent him away and talked to a couple of people in the office and said, 'The team now is Brent, Phyllis, and Irv.' " That meant Cross, a star end and cocaptain for Ara Parseghian at Northwestern before starting a 10-year NFL career as a defensive back, mostly with the Eagles, was reunited with Musburger, his friend from the freshman dorm.

The final addition to the broadcast team was self-styled gambling expert and full-time self-promoter Jimmy "the Greek" Snyder. "Our lawyers didn't want anything to do with the Greek," Wussler said. "We established some ground rules. He couldn't come out and say, 'Dallas is a three-and-a-half-point favorite.' We found ways to get around that. He would say things like, 'If my friends in Vegas were here today, they'd say, out there, Dallas is a three-and-a-half-point favorite.' "

Naturally, Wussler's job entailed up-close and personal dealing with the well-seasoned commissioner. "Pete was Mr. Cool," Wussler said. "He didn't get on your back. He didn't yell and scream if he saw something wrong on a Sunday. I remember I brought a Redskins-Cincinnati game into New York instead of more of an NFC battle. He called me the next day and said, 'Hey, it's time for you and I to have a drink.' So, I met him at his favorite watering hole down the way on 56th Street in the Laurent Hotel."

"You know, I don't get into the networks here," Rozelle said. "Did you have to bring the Redskins and Cincinnati into New York for that one o'clock game?"

"No. I had choices," Wussler replied.

"Well, you made the wrong choice," Rozelle said.

"He did it that way, even in his negotiations," Wussler recalled. "In 1976, we were up against a big negotiation. We were paying like $50 million a year, and we knew we were going to pay a lot more. I went over to see him for coffee at his office, 410 Park Avenue. We chatted about nonsports stuff, other sports stuff. He wanted to know what I thought about the NBA: Would they ever compete with the NFL? At the end of it, he said, 'Well, Bob, we're scheduled to negotiate. Let me write down the number.'

"He took out a little three-by-five card and wrote out the number," Wussler said. "I still have that card here someplace. 'When you get back to the office, take a look at the card,' he said. 'You'll probably have to talk to Mr. Paley and others. Why don't I come over to see you in a week or so?'

"Of course, the number on the card was like four times what we had been paying," Wussler said. "I don't remember the figure. I think it went up from $50 million to $200 million. Pete loved four-year deals. You lost a lot of money in the first year. You lost a fair amount of money in the second year. You broke even in the third year, and you made a penny or two in the fourth year. That's the way he conducted his negotiations. Of course, networks were not eager to give up the NFL. They figured, if we can make some money in the fourth year, maybe we can do better, maybe we can get our losses back, and we'll set ourselves up for the new deal."

Pete Rozelle knew that the networks needed the NFL for the prestige factor, and each time a network has let it go, ratings have collapsed. "It's the promotional value of the NFL, as CBS discovered seven years ago when they got back in after giving it up," Wussler said. "Look what it does for '60 Minutes'—all of those things. You can't just look at what the games themselves do. You have to look at the overall picture, which CBS did when it got it back.

"For instance, one of the reasons the CBS evening news is third in the ratings is in Detroit, where the CBS station is a UHF that cannot get what old WJBK, now a Fox station, got," Wussler said. "At that time, 1993, Lawrence Tisch, who was born with blinders on, said,

'Gee, I can save all that money. I don't have to pay that NFL money.' He was a shortsighted guy."

While "Mr. Cool" fared well with relative newcomer Bob Wussler at CBS, the heat was turned up in his relationships with two owners, Carroll Rosenbloom and Al Davis. On the eve of Super Bowl XI, scheduled for January 9, 1977, at the Rose Bowl, in Pasadena, Rosenbloom told Oakland Raiders owner Davis that the commissioner was "up to his neck" in Super Bowl ticket scalping. The ticket allocation had been made on March 16, 1976, in a league meeting in San Diego. As David Harris wrote in *The League*, that allocation "was, in Al Davis's eyes, 'unique' and 'unheard of.' " That claim would be disproved years later in a New York court.

In a unanimous vote, the owners agreed that the 26 nonparticipating teams would get 1,000 tickets apiece; each of the two Super Bowl teams would get 15,000 tickets; the commissioner's office got 10,000 tickets; and 8,000 tickets were offered for public sale. The "unique" clause Al Davis found was an allocation of 30,000 tickets to the host franchise, Carroll Rosenbloom's Los Angeles Rams. As Harris wrote, "Just a day after charging him with 'stealing from his partners,' the league gave C. R. enough tickets to make it Carroll's Super Bowl, whether his team got there or not."

In the L.A. Coliseum's antitrust suit against the National Football League a few years later, Davis testified that the commissioner claimed he needed his large bloc of tickets for Congress and sponsors and for league reasons. "Then," Davis said, "I began to see that the people who were getting all the tickets were the host team and commissioner's office." Davis alleged that the competing teams got only enough of an allotment "to keep them in place."

The other issue Davis raised concerned ticket prices. By 1977, the Super Bowl had become the hottest sports ticket in America. Rozelle, though, kept scale at $20, well below the price he might have charged. Other owners, Lamar Hunt included, thought the list price easily could have been $50. Davis quoted the commissioner as always saying he didn't want to "gouge the public."

After Oakland beat Pittsburgh 24–7 to reach the Super Bowl, the ticket demand by Raiders fans was so great that Davis went to the commissioner to try to supplement his quota. Rozelle said that his allotment was gone but that he could "loan" 200 seats to Davis, which he took. Then, Davis learned for the first time what Rosenbloom was doing with those 30,000 seats of his, and he got a lesson in brokering from the master.

According to David Harris, Rosenbloom asked Davis what he was going to charge for his tickets. "Face value," the Raiders managing partner replied. Rosenbloom called Davis a "fool" and said he had a man named Harold Guiver who owned a ticket agency and knew how to market tickets. "He could make us a fortune," Rosenbloom asserted. He then told Davis that Rozelle was "in this up to his neck." He added, "This is where he makes his big killing." Davis never forgot that.

After the Raiders beat Minnesota 32–14 in Super Bowl XI, Rosenbloom called Davis again. Davis said that Rosenbloom told him that he and Guiver "made a killing" on their scalped tickets.

Rosenbloom was long dead when those scalping allegations arose four years later in Davis's lawsuits against the league to move the Raiders to Los Angeles. They arose again five years after that, in the USFL-versus-NFL trial.

Already harboring anger toward Rozelle, Rosenbloom was driven to fury by a scheduling conflict early in the 1977 season. He raged at the league, meaning the commissioner, for scheduling a 4:00 P.M. kickoff for the Rams-Dolphins game in Miami on October 3, the eve of one of Judaism's high holy days, Rosh Hashanah. Because of the late start, the game would end after sunset, which meant he had to leave the stadium for temple to begin his observance while the game was still in progress. Well after Rosenbloom's early departure, his Rams overcame a two-touchdown deficit to beat the Dolphins 31–28 on a late Tom Dempsey field goal.

The estrangement between the two former close friends worsened. Word got out that Rosenbloom tried to get Rozelle fired. "Don Weiss would tell you a case where Rosenbloom really ripped him: 'I'm gonna have your job,' and words like that," Chuck Day said. "Don said Pete remained calm, and when Rosenbloom got done, Pete said, 'Anything else?' No one answered. 'Let's break for lunch.'"

As was the case in his last days in Baltimore, Carroll Rosenbloom had been seething for years because he was forced to operate in an inadequate venue with many problems. The Coliseum was run down and lurked on the edge of the South Central ghetto, a place white fans feared. The vast arena had just 28,000 seats between the goal lines. Washroom facilities were sparse and dirty. In early 1978, Rosenbloom told the Coliseum Commission that he wanted immediate improvements, including luxury boxes, or he intended to get out. He hoped to cut a deal with the Dodgers, but Walter O'Malley wasn't about to share the baseball palace that he built and owned with any football team. So, Rosenbloom turned to California Angels owner Gene Autry and the city of Anaheim.

After much negotiating, Rosenbloom got Autry's blessing and Anaheim's OK to increase seating capacity of Anaheim Stadium to 68,000. On July 25, 1978, he announced that the Rams would move to the Big "A" for the 1980 season. Bill Robertson, a former labor leader who was running the Los Angeles Memorial Coliseum Commission, tried to get Rosenbloom to change his mind. He failed.

Since the early merger days, Rozelle had been pushing hard for newer and better stadiums and, as much as possible, for new football-dedicated arenas. He passed a rule in the late '60s setting minimum seating capacity at 50,000 by the end of the 1970 season. Thus, in 1970, the Chicago Bears ended their 50-year association with the Cubs and Wrigley Field and moved to dumpy, 65,000-seat Soldier Field, on the shores of Lake Michigan. The powers that be could never make the place right. Finally, in 2002, the Bears worked out a deal with the city and state to raze everything within the outer walls of Soldier Field and rebuild it from scratch. They moved into their space-age facility on Monday night, September 29, 2003.

Throughout Rozelle's reign, one team after another moved into updated facilities. The 49ers left Kezar Stadium in 1971 to share Candlestick Park with the baseball Giants. The Dallas Cowboys left the Cotton Bowl in 1971 for 65,000-seat Texas Stadium, with its unique hole-in-the-roof design, left open because the stadium could not support the weight of an enclosed roof. The New York Football Giants cut a deal with the New Jersey Sports Authority to build a new, 80,000-seat Giants Stadium in the huge Meadowlands, a former garbage dump. They moved over from New York in 1976 and took in the Jets as cotenants in 1984 when the team's lease ran out at Shea.

The Kansas City Chiefs moved into their own facility, 79,000-seat Arrowhead Stadium, in 1972.

Some teams would build again in the early 21st century. The only city that did not build a new stadium or at least, as with Chicago and Green Bay, improve what it had was Los Angeles, home of the Coliseum. For 15 years, Al Davis hitched his star to Los Angeles and the eternal and unfulfilled hope of gaining a modern, luxury facility with all the trimmings, bells, whistles, and whatevers.

Three weeks after Rosenbloom's announcement, in a letter to Coliseum Commission head Bill Robertson and L.A. County supervisor Kenneth Hahn on August 15, 1978, Rozelle doused the Coliseum's hopes of luring another NFL franchise to Los Angeles to replace the Rams. Rozelle, who noted that he grew up watching football in the Coliseum, wrote, "As NFL commissioner, I cannot in good conscience encourage any existing franchise to leave its present metropolitan market without professional football."

To make sure there was no mistaking his intentions or desires, the commissioner stated, "The Rams' proposed move to Anaheim should not, in my view, be considered a metropolitan area departure." As a clincher, he informed the two men that the league did not foresee additional expansion in the near future, nor could he assure Los Angeles preferential treatment if it did.

Infuriated, Robertson initiated his overtures to Davis in Oakland, whose lease with the Oakland Coliseum, conveniently, was expiring at the end of the 1979 season. "I told them my lease would be up shortly," Davis recalled for David Harris. "I told them I may want to move. I told them I don't think I need a vote to move."

Carroll Rosenbloom turned 72 on March 5, 1979. On April 2, 1979, he was dead. The Rams, caught in a firestorm surrounding their imminent departure from their longtime Coliseum home to share Anaheim Stadium with the baseball Angels, became convulsed in a one-sided estate battle engineered by Rosenbloom's widow, Georgia, against his oldest son, Steve, whom his father had wanted as his successor.

"He put that in the will," Steve Rosenbloom said. But there was a major catch. "He couldn't put strings on how he divided up the team, because if he did, he would forgo the tax benefits. He was trying to pass this on the right way without the government making it impossible for anybody to keep the team."

Carroll and Georgia Hayes met in the late '50s in Palm Beach. She claimed that Joseph P. Kennedy, father of the future president, introduced them, and Rosenbloom, who was 21 years older than the gorgeous blonde singer-dancer, flipped. She was his mistress for as long as a decade before he divorced Velma, his first wife and the mother of their four children, in 1966. He then married Georgia, who had been married five times. They already had a two-year-old son, Chip. Rosenbloom underwent a triple heart bypass in 1976 and quickly recovered to resume his active life.

At the end of March 1979, the couple went to their south Florida home in Golden Beach for a spring vacation. "When I get back, I want to talk to everybody about exactly what I'm thinking about so that everybody understands it," the boss said to his son Steve. He never got that chance.

On the morning of April 2, 1979, Carroll Rosenbloom went down to the beach. The surf was unusually high that day for a swim. "He went down to the beach, disappeared, and washed up in short order. It was clear that this did not appear to me to be an error on his part. It seemed to me like he was done in by somebody," Steve Rosenbloom said. The case, as he mentioned, became notorious four years later in the premiere of "Frontline," PBS's investigative series. He added, "One of the fellows came down here to interview me."

During his life, Carroll Rosenbloom was known to spend much time in the ocean, treading the waters off the New Jersey Shore as well as Los Angeles and Florida coasts. "He could swim, but because he wasn't the greatest swimmer, he knew about tides, undercurrents, and those things," Steve Rosenbloom stated. "He would never have gone into the water the way it was. I went down the next day, and it was unusual for Florida to be that rough. I know that when he went in the water, he usually went in with somebody. He just wouldn't have gone in that day. My take was, he'd have to change the habits of a lifetime to have gone in the water that I saw."

When Rosenbloom was pronounced dead, his widow got down to business. "She had him cremated," Steve said. "She was going to do it very quickly, but I said, 'Georgia, we're coming down there. My brother and I will be coming down there; and before that happens, we want to see him.' She wasn't happy with that—but I turned my head after I saw him, and he was cremated."

"They did do an autopsy," he acknowledged. "But what are you looking for in this autopsy? A quick cause of death." Implications abounded that Rosenbloom was a victim of foul play, but freelance investigative journalist Dan Moldea, who saw the autopsy photos and pored over the report, wrote in his book *Interference* that "the evidence appears to be clear that Rosenbloom died in a tragic accident and was not murdered." When Moldea was accused in a *New York Times* book review of making the exact opposite allegation, he sued the paper for libel, citing that same quote, which appears on page 360 of the book. He published the details of that tortuous litigation on his website, Moldea.com.

The memory of Carroll Rosenbloom's memorial service has left deep scars with his son. "Father's brothers and sister at the time were either in Florida and coming or coming down," Steve said. "He was one of the younger ones, and they were in their eighties at this time. Georgia was an hour and a half late. These were his brothers, and they were sitting around. It was unbelievable. It's sickening."

The entire atmosphere of the service, held at the Rosenbloom estate in Belair, further estranged the son from his father's widow. "I went over there, and she was building a goddamned stage, and it was going to be a real party, completely different from anything he wanted," Steve Rosenbloom said. "It was a coming-out party for Georgia. It was a celebration. It was disgusting."

In the aftermath, Steve Rosenbloom, who had trained all his life to carry on his father's legacy, found himself squared off against Georgia and her advisers, attorney Ed Hookstratten and Carroll's longtime friend and executor Hugh Culverhouse, owner of the Tampa Bay Buccaneers. "She called me up to her house one day, and she had some lawyer there, and he was doing all the talking," Steve said. "He was saying, 'We'd like to give you the opportunity to resign.' Rosenbloom refused to comply and finally forced Georgia to fire him, which she did in August. He joined the New Orleans Saints as vice president and general manager on December 20, 1979, resigned 13 months later, and has been out of pro football ever since.

"I had 2 or 3 percent of the Rams at the time I was working for the Saints," he said. Pete Rozelle told him he had to divest his Rams stock because he was in conflict of interest. He responded that he just wanted a reasonable price, not a fire sale.

"That's what Culverhouse and Hookstratten are trying to do," he told Rozelle. "They're not executors; they're executioners." He added, "This is all about Georgia, and they are actually trying to steal this [team] from the kids—the little bit that they have. I know what a minority partner is, and they don't have many rights. They can get run over in the process."

Los Angeles Lakers owner Jerry Buss came through with what Rosenbloom called a decent offer. "That made them nervous," Steve said. "Jerry Buss just wanted to get his foot in the door. He figured that he could do something with Georgia down the pike." After talking it over with Hookstratten and Culverhouse, Georgia met Steve's price. Within months, Dominic Frontiere, described as Georgia's personal lyricist, moved into the Belair mansion.

They got married in Florida on July 21, 1980. He was her seventh husband. In 1986, Dominic Frontiere was convicted of income tax evasion for not reporting thousands of dollars he made scalping some 16,000 Super Bowl XIV tickets he obtained from Georgia's allotment. The Pittsburgh Steelers won their fourth Super Bowl title of the decade in that game as they beat the Rams 31–19 at the Rose Bowl. In 1988 after Frontiere got out of prison, Georgia divorced him.

TWENTY-FOUR

COMMITMENT TO EXCELLENCE

"Davis beat him [Rozelle] on two fronts. First, he's the guy who won the battle and forced the merger. And second, he got inside the tent and changed all the furniture around."

—FRANK DEFORD, 2005

Pete Rozelle spent most of his life cultivating an erudite, polished, classy, born-to-the-manor image. Al Davis has spent most his of life cultivating a tough-guy image, one step away from the gutter. In each case, the image was the opposite of the reality.

Glenn Dickey, a Bay Area journalist who has covered the Raiders' comings and goings for more than four decades, always has seen through Davis's facade and his clash with Rozelle. "Mel Durslag, who championed Davis in bringing him down to L.A., said it was ironic that people portrayed it as Davis, the street fighter, against Rozelle, the patrician," Dickey said. "Rozelle actually came up from humble beginnings, and Davis came from a middle-class family. He wasn't a street fighter at all in that sense. Rozelle became a member of the establishment, which Davis never has been." Dickey added, "He resented Rozelle, because he thought he really had a chance to be the commissioner at the time of the merger."

Until his death, Carroll Rosenbloom was Rozelle's chief rival, not Davis. The Genius, as Davis liked to be called, was regarded by the NFL camp back east as more of a pest, albeit a successful one, stuck far across the country in remote Oakland, that city on the east side of San Francisco Bay that the writer Gertrude Stein characterized as a place where "there is no there, there." Stein is famous for another succinct quote that has direct application to Davis, who came to Oakland years after her death. Asked by a friend what it was that writers most wanted, she replied, "Praise, praise, praise."

Praise, praise, praise—self-administered or poured on by his loyalists—has been a constant for Al Davis. During the triumphal "genius" years climaxed by two Super Bowl titles in his first Oakland go-round, it was all praise, praise, praise.

By then, Davis had fashioned an Orwellian style, down to Big Brother–like slogans. In Oakland, the living motto was "Pride and Poise." Huge rectangular signs with the words printed in white block letters on a black background were plastered around the playing field edges, in camera view, so that no one in the stadium or watching at home could miss the message.

In Los Angeles, the achievement slogan "Commitment to Excellence" became the operative bromide. As the string played out, however, the braggadocio of "Just win, baby!" after Super Bowl XVIII, like the printed slogans, became quaint reminders of the ever-fading triumphs.

When the Los Angeles Raiders did not sustain the "excellence" part of their self-styled "commitment to excellence," the huzzahs muted to "praise, praise." Davis's 13-year stay in the city became more of a showdown than a triumph as time went by. And yet, despite the disorganized mess that Davis has fostered since the 1995 return to Oakland, he still draws his modicum of "praise" while holding fast to his "pride," if not "poise."

During the early days of *Star Wars* mania, after the troubles between NFL commissioner Rozelle and Raiders owner Davis evolved into open warfare, it became fashionable in certain sportswriting circles to characterize the Oakland/Los Angeles AFC major domo as a Darth Vader, for his dark ways, his preference for black in personal dress and dominant team color, and a tunnel vision in spirit that vented in a sneering, snarling persona regarding his team, as in, "We don't take what they give us; we take what we want," and "I don't think in terms of rout; I think in terms of domination."

But, was the man in silver and black truly a Darth Vader? For his part, Al Davis has always envisioned himself as an epic figure, not a movie villain. Fair enough. Born in Brooklyn, Davis came of age there at the renowned Erasmus Hall High School. After graduation, he went off to Wittenberg College, in Springfield, Ohio, and later transferred to Syracuse University, where he earned a degree in English, and then boarded the college-coaching carousel, starting at Adelphi and stopping at the Citadel before he got to Southern California. He was working as an assistant at USC when he was invited to join the staff of his idol Sid Gillman with the Chargers in their birth year, 1960. He moved with Gillman and the team down the coast to San Diego, staying for two more seasons.

When the opportunity came to run his own pro team in 1963, the 34-year-old Davis seized the day and became coach and general manager of the Oakland Raiders. It was a fit for the ages, as Al Davis was, at his core, a man of Oakland, the tough seaport and haven for many down-and-out denizens, with all that that entails. Over the next 18 years, he managed to build a championship pro football team, nurture and then slap down his fans, and leave town in a huff, only to return in defiance in 1995, never once displaying self-doubt or regret about the way he treated his loyal fandom.

Oakland's outstanding literary figure was Jack London, one of the few American writers to make a lot of money at his craft and retain a substantial following nearly a century after his death. London's genre was adventure, epitomized in two classics, *The Call of the Wild*, published in 1903, and, a year later, *The Sea-Wolf*. A quarter century before Al Davis's birth on July 4, 1929, London created one of the truly memorable characters in literature, Wolf Larsen, the sea wolf himself.

London's Captain Larsen was a brutal, hard-driving, brilliant, well-read mystic, who took orders from no one. He ran a derelict of a seal-hunting ship, the *Ghost*, which sailed outside the normal shipping lanes and was manned by a crew of the nastiest cutthroats and brigands that ever sailed the high seas. Larsen borrowed his philosophy from Milton's epic poem *Paradise Lost*, in which Satan proclaims, "To reign is worth ambition though in hell: Better to reign in hell than serve in heaven."

Jack London's fictional Wolf Larsen would surface in the physical world in his home port, Oakland, as Al Davis. And he was fated to make life hell for Pete Rozelle.

"Al Davis was Rozelle's bête noire," *Sports Illustrated*'s Paul Zimmerman said. "He was his sworn enemy. It goes back to the merger, when Al felt that the AFL crumbled so easily and believed they shouldn't have done the payoff. Al had been commissioner, and he was left with nothing. So, it was bitterness. Pete was very bitter about Al—wouldn't put him on any of his committees. It was two rivals. For good reason."

"Rozelle had a way of allying people who would normally not be allies to support things in common, mostly in broadcasting and marketing," Pat Summerall commented. "He would get people who didn't want to be together and get them to vote for things he wanted to get passed." An exception, almost at every turn, was the man in silver and black. "Of course, Al Davis was the big thorn after the merger. It never changed," Summerall attested.

"Davis took Pete's job, which he enjoyed and relished, and made him hate it, because he hated all those trips to Washington to testify," Summerall said. "He hated doing that and going into courtrooms."

The depositions and testimony would come years after the merger. Davis was all about football in the '60s as he built the Raiders. When he left for New York in 1966 to make his cameo appearance as American Football League commissioner, he handed the team to his top assistant, John Rauch. Upon Davis's return in the fall as managing general partner, no longer the active coach, the insecure Rauch practically broke out in a heat rash. "Rauch was convinced Davis was going to take his job back, and Davis was notorious for second-guessing anyway," Glenn Dickey said. "In those days, they didn't have fancy stadiums around the league and fancy owner's boxes. So, Davis would be in the press box with us. So, we knew about his second-guessing because he was right there."

Davis, in many ways except for League-think, was the closest thing to George Halas that pro football had ever seen. Nobody else combined the ability to run a franchise, sell his product to the public, judge playing and coaching talent, and understand the game itself. "The one thing you have to realize with Al Davis is he's a football guy, a football coach who is an owner," Tom Flores said. "Like Halas was, he's a football coach that coached and still watches film, and still looks at techniques, and still looks at plays and what would work—weaknesses. That's the way he approaches the game, no different than he did 20 years ago."

Dickey recalled, "I remember one game in Kansas City when all of Stram's wide receivers were hurt, so he went to a tight T, the old-fashioned full house. I think [Lenny] Dawson threw three passes during the game. They killed the Raiders running the ball while the Raiders used a defense suited to stop the pass. Davis kept sending notes down to Rauch to play a basic five-man front, a college defense against a college offense. Rauch wouldn't even read the notes." Dickey chuckled at the memory.

"He did change at halftime. It was too late by then," Dickey continued. "There was always that kind of friction, and Rauch was so insecure. I remember writing when we were in New York before the championship game that Rauch would quit after the season. That basically was what he did and went to Buffalo, but he was not fired; that was his decision. Davis doesn't like to fire people."

Rauch, the head coach of the AFL champions in 1967 and Super Bowl II losers to Green Bay, lasted through the AFL title loss to the Jets in 1968. Once out the door, he shuffled off to Buffalo in time to inherit the most prized draft pick in decades, USC's Heisman Trophy tailback, O. J. Simpson. Rauch blew it, ensuring his firing in 1971, when he foolishly tried to make the best runner in college football history a wide receiver. Simpson would become a Hall of Fame runner after Lou Saban, who had coached the Bills to back-to-back AFL titles in 1964–65, returned to Buffalo in 1972 for a five-season follow-up run.

Davis always has hired the assistants. "Rauch got to name one assistant. That was Mugsy Angleberg, a 23-year-old he signed to be the kicking coach," Dickey said. "He was going to advise George Blanda how to kick."

That experiment fell to earth with a thud in training camp as the hard-nosed, competitive Blanda simply ignored the unfortunate Angleberg. Through his time in Oakland, Blanda, who arrived at age 40, systematically blew away any would-be replacements, year after year. "He had some glory years. Al was always good to him and gave him a chance where nobody else would," said Tom Flores, who was coach John Madden's top assistant during that period. "How many people were going to give a guy in his forties a chance to be part of a team?"

Davis had turned to Madden, his 32-year-old linebackers' coach, when Rauch left Oakland for Buffalo. As Glenn Dickey wrote in *Just Win, Baby*, "He wanted someone who could win with his style, and he wanted someone he could control." If ever two coaches were on the same page, as the cliché goes, the two were Davis and Madden. Madden developed into a wonderful coach in his own right, a Hall of Famer, whom Davis grew to love and respect, then as well as after the big man quit to enter television.

"John was a good guy," Tom Flores said. "He worked hard. He was very loyal, and he was very good on game days as far as managing the clock and game plan. We had a small staff and great players. He was able to get the best out of the players. He motivated them. Then he burned himself out, like many of us do."

"The Raiders always wanted to have the best organization in professional sports," Al Davis said in Canton, Ohio, on August 5, 2006, in his introduction speech for Madden at his enshrinement in the Pro Football Hall of Fame. "We wanted to have the best players, the best coaches, play in the best games, have the best plays, have the best record in professional football." Madden, with 103 victories, seven divisional titles, and one Super Bowl over his 10 years in Oakland, was the great coach of Davis's ideals.

By 1978, Madden was feeling overwhelmed. His fear of flying exacerbated the pressure of NFL coaching, which broke down his system. In an August preseason game that year, Raiders strong safety Jack Tatum collided helmet to helmet with New England's Daryl

Stingley on a pass over the middle. Tatum bounced back up. Stingley lay still, paralyzed from the chest down. He would never walk again before his death in early 2007. From the day of the injury until he was airlifted to Chicago's Rehabilitation Institute later in 1978, Stingley had a constant visitor, one who came every day when he was at home in Oakland: John Madden. During those visits, Madden was able to take his mind off coaching. But he couldn't settle down. "That's when the stress level was highest," Tom Flores said. "He had a great career. He won 10 games, average, every year. In that year, by our standards, we were struggling. We just had to overhaul a little bit. When you get at that level, you get tired. You try to find the energy, and you can't find it."

"At the time when this country needed it, John Madden saw no color," Davis said in his 2006 speech. "The Raiders, more than any other organization—political, sports—led the fight for diversity. John Madden was in the middle of that fight."

Davis made certain his coach had the best possible assistants, all from excellent pro backgrounds. Ollie Spencer, a fine tackle with the Detroit Lions' championship teams of the '50s, coached the offensive line, working with such men as Art Shell, Gene Upshaw, Jim Otto, Henry Lawrence, and Dave Dalby. Tom Dahms coached the defensive lines and developed players such as Ben Davidson and Otis Sistrunk.

Charlie Sumner, a ball hawk and sure tackler at safety in his years with George Halas and the Bears, served two terms as defensive coordinator for Davis, under Madden in Oakland and in L.A. with Flores. He refined the play of fast, hard-hitting guys such as Kent McCloughan, Willie Brown, George Atkinson, and Jack Tatum, as well as the uniquely gifted Ted Hendricks, a rawboned, 6'7", 230-pound former defensive end in college at Miami, who became a prototypical roving linebacker for Baltimore and Green Bay before joining Oakland in 1975 to cement his Hall of Fame credentials. "Sumner could have lasted, but he and Al had a beef," Dickey said. "He was a very good coach, a top assistant. It was his decision again to leave twice. He wasn't fired." According to Dickey, the disruption for the team was minimal: "If you got a coach who's really a strong figure, as Madden certainly was, the players respect him. They don't care if he hires the assistants or not."

It seemed to take forever for the Raiders to reach the Super Bowl again after their climb to the top in 1967. The Pittsburgh Steelers were a constant impediment in the '70s. The teams' first major encounter came in the 1972 playoff at Three Rivers Stadium, when it appeared that Kenny Stabler had engineered a 7–6 Raiders victory, until an improbable stroke of fortune. The Immaculate Reception, the single greatest play in pro football history, came with time running out. From his own 40, Terry Bradshaw threw down the middle of the field. Jack Tatum, on a collision course with receiver John "Frenchy" Fuqua, whacked the ball with doubled fists back toward the Pittsburgh goal. The ball came directly to the trailer, Franco Harris, who caught it off his shoe tops and simply ran by everybody to score, to hand the Steelers a 13–7 victory.

Two years later, the Steelers began their run of four Super Bowls in six seasons, going through Oakland twice in AFC title games, 24–13 in 1974 and 16–10 in 1975. When the Pittsburgh players reported to camp in the summer of 1976, they were coming off defense of their second title, a 21–17 victory over the Dallas Cowboys in Super Bowl X in the Orange Bowl, the best-played Super Bowl game to that time.

Since 1934 when *Chicago Tribune* sports editor Arch Ward persuaded Halas and his defending NFL champion Bears to kick off the football season with an exhibition game against an all-star team of top college seniors at Soldier Field, on Chicago's lakefront, the College All-Star Game had been an established custom. The Steelers were designated to uphold league prestige on Friday night, July 23, for the 43rd edition, against a refreshed Ara Parseghian in his return to coaching after he resigned from Notre Dame at the end of the 1974 season.

The pros no longer wanted to play this contest, nor did they need its promotional value, but tradition was tradition, and Pete Rozelle could not cut the ties that meant so much to the league in its infancy. These Steelers were at their peak, stocked with 10 future Hall of Famers: coach Chuck Noll, quarterback Bradshaw, fullback Harris, center Mike Webster, receivers Lynn Swann and John Stallworth, and the anchors of the "Steel Curtain" defense—tackle Joe Greene, linebackers Jack Lambert and Jack Ham, and safety Mel Blount.

They arrived on game day in a Chicago scorcher, the type of draining heat and humidity that can stoke tempers and leave professionally pressed dress shirts and slacks formless and wrinkled five minutes after they come off their hangers. "The NFL party was Val Pinchbeck, Pete and Carrie Rozelle, and me," Ernie Accorsi said. "They flew out to Chicago for the game. I was already there." Chicago-area native Don Weiss was assigned to work the game for the league.

Late that Friday afternoon, a humid low-pressure system blew in from the prairie to add volatility to the furnace. Just after 5:00 P.M., a cluster of billowing, dark, cumulus clouds unloaded in a downpour that lasted for a half hour, tying up rush-hour traffic. In its wake, the air was superheated, thick and steamy, as 52,595 fans made their way to Soldier Field for the 8:00 kickoff. The teams had just begun their pregame warm-ups when another squall, glinting spasmodic lightning flashes, passed through and disappeared over Lake Michigan. The officials cleared the field, and the teams retreated to the dank tunnels leading to their dressing rooms underneath the stands until it blew over.

It became apparent early that the young all-stars were no match for the world champions. The Steel Curtain rang down on the all-stars from the outset, but the Pittsburgh offense could not get untracked and had to settle for three Roy Gerela field goals, to take a 9–0 lead at the break. "I was down there at halftime trying to find the officials," said retired sports editor Cooper Rollow, who was acting in his capacity as president of Chicago Tribune Charities, Inc. "What was I going to tell them? 'It's raining.' They knew that."

As the teams started play in the third quarter, an unusually hot wind picked up speed as it roared out of the north, directly into the faces of the all-stars. Pinned deep in his own territory, all-stars center Ray Pinney fired a wind-aided snap over the head of punter Rick Engels and into the end zone for a safety. Then, Franco Harris and Tommy Reamon scored touchdowns to make it 24–0 Pittsburgh, when the wind shifted again. The rain clouds were armed and ready to go. The smart fans made tracks for the buses parked at the north end of Soldier Field, but few people got there before the skies opened again in a crushing cascade under flashing lightning. With 1:22 left in the third quarter, referee Cal Lepore ordered the players off the field and then to their locker rooms.

"It was the worst torrential rain," Accorsi said. "We didn't know if it was a tornado, or what." Many in the crowd, mostly young men, charged onto the artificial surface, running frantically, some doing belly flops through the puddles. As the police stood by, the mob mentality kicked in, and hordes stormed both goal posts, bringing them down within seconds. Within a dozen minutes, the last thing on anybody's mind was a football game. Crowd control was nonexistent.

"As elegant and stylish as he was, Rozelle was a man's man," Ernie Accorsi said. "He was careful with his language, but he could get earthy if he had to. Pete called in *Tribune* sports editor Cooper Rollow and decreed, 'We're going to have to call this game off.' "

"This game is the property of Chicago Tribune Charities, and we're not calling it off!" Rollow exclaimed.

As Accorsi recalled, "Pete came back—this is before modern weather forecasting devices like Doppler radar—'Look, Cooper, it's dangerous. There's lightning. My people tell me it's going to last. I think we're going to—' "

Rollow cut him off: "Wait!"

"Pete dug in," Accorsi related. " 'Look, Cooper, the Pittsburgh Steelers are not taking the field.' "

The conversation ended with Rollow shouting, "Do what you want!"

Rollow offered a notably understated account of what transpired next: "When I got back up to the press box, Neil Milbert [the game's director] came up to me and said, 'Hey, Pete just called off the game.' 'He did? Well, good. It seems to be sprinkling a bit.' " By then, the rain was coming down sideways in sheets.

Milbert prodded, "Is that all right with you?"

"Joe Mooshill was there for AP," Rollow recounted. "He jumped in: 'Is it official, Coop?' "

Rollow told him, "Absolutely. Pete says it's off; it's off."

Rollow recalled, "I wrote a piece that night chewing out the cops and fire people. I said something about the police taking sanctuary from the rain, and they didn't like it. They called up my boss, Clayton Kirkpatrick, and asked, 'Does this represent a change in *Tribune* policy regarding crowd control?'"

"No," Kirkpatrick replied. "It's our sports editor making some noise."

The abbreviated game, the first NFL-sanctioned contest ever called for weather reasons, ended in a 24–0 Steelers win. "Rozelle wasn't calling off the series, just the game that night," Rollow noted, "but the series had run its course. The pros were afraid of guys getting hurt. A month later, I was talking to Don Weiss, one of his right-hand men, and I mentioned it to him: 'Up in my own press box, I was told Pete called off the game. That was just fine.'"

"Pete didn't call that game off," Weiss answered. "I called it off."

"You did?"

"Sure. I knew it would be OK with Pete and OK with you, so I went ahead and called it off."

"I attribute that to Rozelle and to you, Don," Rollow told him. It was a distinction without a difference, in Rollow's view. "That's also known as the slickness of the NFL," he said. It was the end of an era for the NFL as well.

"When we left, it was still pouring, and the car was underneath Soldier Field," Accorsi recounted. "We got back to the hotel. The next morning, when we left, it felt like it was 190 degrees, hot, a miserable day. The two of them, Pete and Carrie, not a bead of sweat, looked like they stepped out of *GQ* or *Vogue*. She stood tall and so elegant. Pinchbeck and I were both sweating. We got to the game in Canton for the inductions, which he had to handle in the hot sun."

Mercifully for Rozelle and the sweltering Canton crowd, just three players were inducted in that 1976 Hall of Fame class, the smallest ever. Jim Taylor, the fullback of Vince Lombardi's Green Bay Packers dynasty, was accompanied by the late Cleveland Browns defensive end Lenny Ford and former Redskins end and 1942 championship coach Ray Flaherty.

After the half, the Rozelles, Accorsi, and Pinchbeck rode their limo to the Canton-Akron Airport to board a private plane for the flight back to New York. The plane had not arrived. "We were waiting: me, Pinchbeck, Carrie, and Pete," Accorsi said. "If I was working for Rosenbloom at that moment, my rear end would have been on the line, as in, 'Where's *thaaaat air-plane*? It's your fault, ———!'

" 'Are you guys OK?' Pete asked. 'Are you guys OK? Have you had anything to eat?'

"He was asking *us* if *we* were all right," Accorsi said. "He was worried about Pinchbeck and me. That's just the way he was, and so was she. It was a little LearJet—just seated four people. Going back to New York, Pete and Carrie were in back, with four seats, like a little couch. Carrie was tall and elegant. The four of us just talked. It had been a long two days. They never flinched, complained—nothing. Those are precious moments."

In conversation during the flight, Rozelle related a recent incident between Al Davis and Don Klosterman. Davis and Klosterman had been talking in the presence of Rams owner Carroll Rosenbloom, Davis's friend and Klosterman's boss, when something set them off. Tempers frayed and Davis tore into Klosterman. "Pete," Accorsi recalled, "told how Davis really ripped Klosterman up one side and down the other. Pete heard about it later and went to Al and said 'Why would you do that? What has he ever done to you?' Don didn't dislike Al. They were AFL brothers in the cloth, fought the wars together. 'Why would you hurt Don like that?' Rozelle asked Davis."

"I remember being so touched by Pete's genuine sincerity and sympathy for what Don had gone through," Accorsi said. "I was just a young guy and I had two reactions: why would the guy do something so mean? And Pete was so genuinely concerned, caring about and for an old friend."

Many people insist that the 1976 Pittsburgh Steelers would have pulled a three-peat, until they lost Franco Harris and Rocky Bleier in the 40–14 divisional playoff win over Baltimore. Instead, the Raiders went 13–1 in the regular season, overcame a 21–10 deficit in the fourth quarter to beat the New England Patriots in the divisional playoff 24–21, and ground out a 24–7 win at Pittsburgh to make the Super Bowl at Pasadena. That's where Carroll Rosenbloom gave Davis his "scalping" lectures, with his accusations against Rozelle, before the Raiders routed the Minnesota Vikings 32–14.

A year and a half later, Rosenbloom announced his intention to move the Rams out of the Coliseum and set up shop in Anaheim. "My feeling is, having been around Davis and hearing him talk, he always felt there were only two cities in this country that counted: New York and L.A.," Glenn Dickey said. "He called it 'little old Oakland.' Al LoCosalle, Davis's longtime aide, used to say, if it had been somewhere else, they would have named a street for him, and that sort of stuff. I think he saw his opening in L.A. as soon as Rosenbloom moved out of the Coliseum."

The Rams' Anaheim deal was solid by the meeting in Chicago on October 4–5, 1978. The league had to fashion a defense strategy against the L.A. Coliseum Commission's impending antitrust suit and, at the same time, legitimize Rosenbloom's move to Anaheim. To do that, though, it was necessary to amend or rewrite Rule 4.3, dealing with territorial rights; the 75-mile rule, as written, granted exclusivity to a franchise holder within 75 miles of its stadium.

That was the basis for the Coliseum suit, since Anaheim was within the Rams' territory. However, an Anaheim team would be well inside the San Diego Chargers' territory, a violation in its own right. Also, Rozelle had declared that the move was within the metropolitan area and that expansion was not in the cards for Los Angeles, nor would the city get preferential treatment. To let Rosenbloom move to Anaheim, the league amended the unanimous rule to three-fourths approval for the Rams' move to Anaheim. Davis abstained from a unanimous vote, saying the Raiders were reserving their rights, whatever that meant.

Two weeks later, at 1:00 A.M. on October 19, Davis awoke to find his wife, Carol, lying on the hallway floor between their bedroom and bathroom, unconscious and with no heartbeat. He called Dr. Robert Albo, who hurried over to start cardiopulmonary resuscitation while they waited for the ambulance. She was rushed to Merritt Hospital, in Oakland.

According to Glenn Dickey's account in *Just Win, Baby*, the emergency team administered electric shock jolts three times, twice on the way to the hospital and again in the intensive care unit. Carol Davis lay in a coma for the next 17 days, the first 15 on a respirator. Dr. Albo said her husband took a room next door and rarely left her side or the hospital. Then, Carol revived, rebounded, underwent protracted rehabilitation, and made a complete recovery. Once the crisis passed, Davis resumed his mission with the Raiders.

His universe was jolted again on April 2, 1979, with the news that Rams owner Carroll Rosenbloom had drowned in the surf off Golden Beach, Florida. Georgia Rosenbloom asked Davis to speak at her husband's memorial service at their Belleair estate. "Among the great people in the world," Davis said, "Carroll Rosenbloom was the giant. It will never be over with me. Come autumn, and the roar of the crowd, I'll always think of him."

By late 1979, Rozelle and Davis were locked into battle positions over the Raiders and Davis's L.A. ambitions and intentions. Then, in the week before Christmas, they met again under unfortunate circumstances. George S. Halas Jr.— Mugs, as he was called his entire life—died of a massive heart attack in his Chicago home in the early hours of Sunday, December 16. The National Football League brass came en masse to Chicago to pay their respects to league founder George Halas Sr. and his family in a funeral service at tiny Assumption Church, behind the Merchandise Mart. Jim Finks, Mugs's handpicked choice as Bears chief operating officer, held the distraught George Halas at the elbow as he gently escorted him inside, where friends and NFL colleagues, from Pittsburgh's Art Rooney to George Allen and many other owners, had gathered.

"I made all the funeral and cemetery arrangements for the family. I seated the NFL people," said Jerry Vainisi, who was the Bears' controller at the time. "Inadvertently, I placed Pete Rozelle next to Al Davis. I didn't realize it until it was too late, and I said to myself, oh, Christ! I really felt bad about it, and I apologized to Pete."

"Don't worry, Jerry," Rozelle said. "It's not an issue."

By then, Al Davis was setting up his escape from Oakland to L.A. as he saw fit, not as the other owners would grant it. He would eventually get his wish, patiently enduring the legal process with its depositions, trials, appeals, and league votes against him until, with the aid of his lawyer, the former San Francisco mayor Joseph Alioto, he prevailed.

Before that transpired, Pete Rozelle did all he could to keep the Raiders in Oakland. As Howard Cosell wrote in *I Never Played the Game*, "He pressed his view that it was wrong to vacate a city that had supported its team with twelve years of sellouts. He also held that no prospering team had ever really left its home community." In March 1980, after Davis and the Coliseum agreed on the move, the owners voted against Davis 22 to 0, with 5 abstentions and 1 absentee. He was stuck against his will in Oakland.

Then the Raiders caught fire down the stretch and slipped into the playoffs as a wild card, with an 11–5 record. The key to the Raiders' success in 1980, as it would be through 1983, was the emergence of Stanford's 1970 Heisman Trophy–winning quarterback Jim Plunkett. Having been stuck with losing teams in both New England and San Francisco, Plunkett was physically damaged with a shoulder injury and emotionally drained when the Niners cut him in 1978. The shoulder was healed by the time Davis's personnel director Ron Wolf decided to see if Plunkett had anything left. "He was on the street," former Raiders coach Tom Flores said. "Ron brought him over, and I worked him out. There was nothing wrong with him physically. So, we signed him, made him third string, and let him sit for a year. You could do that in those days. It's a little different arena now."

When Dan Pastorini went down midway through the 1980 season, Plunkett responded as the team finished 11–5. "At the end of their careers, Gene Upshaw and Art Shell reached down and had good years in '80," Flores said. "Jim Plunkett was resurrected because we put him in position to do what he did best. You can go on and on with a lot of these guys. We didn't make a big thing about their pasts as long as they didn't try to disrupt what we were trying to do."

The first playoff game took place in Cleveland in an icy, cutting gale off Lake Erie. The Raiders escaped with a 14–12 victory when safety Mike Davis intercepted Brian Sipe's pass in the end zone. The following week, they withstood a Dan Fouts–led comeback and beat the Chargers 34–27 in San Diego to earn a trip to Super Bowl XV.

"We went to New Orleans," Flores said, "and it was, 'Dick Vermeil and his Eagles'; 'Al Davis and his Raiders'; and 'Al Davis and Pete Rozelle.' We all have egos, and I thought, shouldn't my name be in there? So, I actually introduced myself at a large press conference, saying, 'I'm Tom Flores, coach of the Oakland Raiders.' There was no laughter. One of our local reporters knew what I meant. 'Well, that bombed,' I said. 'Jesus Christ, I am coaching this team.' "

The reporters kept pressing Flores: "Do you think Al will accept the trophy if by any long shot of a chance you guys win?"

"Yes," Flores answered. "Al will do nothing to discredit the moment, and neither will the commissioner. This is important, and they aren't going to do anything."

As Flores mentioned, three years later, with the Raiders ensconced in Los Angeles, the subject came up again at Super Bowl XVIII, in Tampa. "I said the same thing in Tampa if we won: 'They're going to handle it professionally, and that's the way they're going to be.' That's the way they were," Flores recalled. "Did somebody think Pete was going to have somebody else hand over the trophy, or Al have somebody else accept? I couldn't get the trophy away from Al."

During Super Bowl week in New Orleans, Flores and Davis left the players alone at night. Most stayed close to their hotels. John Matuszak was another story. Not only did the 6'8", 280-pound wild man from the Milwaukee suburb of Oak Creek drink copious amounts of liquor and ingest unimaginable quantities of drugs, but he suffered from insomnia as well. Thus, he roamed the streets of the French Quarter all night, offering a unique take on his modus operandi. "I am the enforcer," Big John said. "That's why I was out on the street, to make sure nobody else was."

"Tooz" was the most outlandish character in the league, but this was a team of bigger-than-life eccentrics and oddballs, more than any other in football, a crew that perfectly complemented their Wolf Larsen–like boss. "I think one of the big things in those days, which you will never have again, was the locker rooms took care of themselves a lot," Flores said. "When anybody got out of line, somebody would grab him by the throat or around the shoulders and say, 'Come on, calm down, knock it off.' You don't have that anymore because the locker rooms change every year. That's how you pass on legacies."

Inside the Louisiana Superdome on Super Bowl Sunday, the confident Raiders took full measure of the favored Eagles. Plunkett followed the Al Davis mantra with long passes, the vertical game, as he found Cliff Branch and Bobby Chandler at will. Three of his passes went for touchdowns: one, a hitch to halfback Kenny King that he turned into a Super Bowl–record 80 yards, and two to Cliff Branch. Linebacker Rod Martin was the game's Most Valuable Player as the Raiders won 27–16. "We won and were in euphoria," Flores said. "Everybody wanted the trophy and their rings. Everybody was on cloud nine. In those days, the trophy was given in the locker room, and so it was crowded, with people all over the place. There was never any worry about it: Just enjoy the moment. Respect the moment."

To avoid shaking hands with Davis, Rozelle gave him the Vince Lombardi Trophy with both hands, and Davis held on to the silver Tiffany football for dear life as they displayed their best manners to the world. "I think it's a great credit to you for putting this team together," Rozelle said. "I think Tom Flores did one of the great coaching jobs in recent years and particularly today."

"Thanks very much, Commissioner. This was the Oakland Raiders' finest hour," a subdued Davis said.

"You don't think about it until it's over; then you think back. In New Orleans, after we had gone through all that, Al and I were sitting in the locker room together," Flores recalled. "The coaches had gone. Everybody had left for the party and everything. We were just sitting there reflecting. We were both kind of numb because of the way we had to do it that year, as a wild card—brought in all these players.

"Bobby Chandler stuck his head in the door and just said, 'Thanks' and walked away," Flores said. "That kind of said it all: Here was a guy we picked up from Buffalo. I loved Bobby Chandler. He was a rookie my first year in Buffalo when I started coaching. When we had a chance to get him, I said, 'Yeah, let's do it, if he's healthy.' We got permission to work him out, and he helped us win a Super Bowl as we helped him win a Super Bowl. All he said was, 'Thanks.' He couldn't say anything else. I sat there and got a lump in my throat."

After the victorious team returned to Oakland, Davis went back to work plotting an escape that, in actuality, had been a possibility since the franchise took root there in 1962 following its two nomadic seasons across the Bay. Founding partner Wayne Valley had negotiated the original deal with the city of Oakland and Alameda County. "Every three years, there was an option," Glenn Dickey said. "Valley did it in the early '60s because at the time, there was no guarantee the Raiders were going to stay in Oakland. There was a lot of talk about Portland. It was usually the city most prominently mentioned."

In the original merger proposal, the Raiders were destined for Portland, with the Jets going to Memphis. Through 1965, the Raiders played home games at 22,000-seat Frank Youell Field. "The city built the [Oakland] Coliseum in 1966, but they still had this three-year contract with options," Dickey said. "Davis would drag out every negotiating period to the last minute. This time, he had the opening—didn't have to sign it, and he didn't. The big thing was they had to have luxury boxes. They actually had a plan to build them, and they did build them for the A's. They wanted a 15-year lease to pay for the loan, and he would not sign for anything more than five years."

Then testimony got under way in the long-awaited Coliseum-versus-NFL federal antitrust case in Los Angeles. The jury voted in favor of the Coliseum (and Davis) 8 to 2, with 2 abstentions—a hung jury, which necessitated another trial. The Raiders had to return once again to play in the city that deservedly felt jilted by its unrequited lover. That year, the Super Bowl champions fell to a 7–9 record. On Monday night, December 7, 1981, ABC's telecast opened with an overhead shot of a nearly empty Oakland Coliseum. In an attempt to educate the nation about what was about to happen to their city, most of the crowd stayed outside until the game started. Once the masses took their seats, the team responded with a 30–27 victory. The following week, only 40,000 fans bothered to show up for the finale as the mediocre Chicago Bears beat the dispirited Raiders 23–6.

The retrial in the federal antitrust case began March 15, 1982, over the legality of Section 4.3 of the NFL constitution. The NFL was defending its amended rule that three-fourths of the owners must approve a franchise shift. "What must be decided," Howard Cosell said, "is whether 75 percent is an unreasonable figure, or whether another figure—say, 50 percent—is reasonable under antitrust law." Just before the trial, Cosell reported that Rozelle, in a meeting in Dallas, discussed possible expansion to Los Angeles with several Coliseum commissioners, or even a possible settlement. The case got nasty in court. From that moment on, Davis wanted Los Angeles, come what may, and would do whatever it took to get there, Pete Rozelle be damned.

"I know this took a toll on Pete. It was all one-sided," Glenn Dickey said. "Davis was aiming all his stuff at Rozelle. I got involved. I really wasn't involved, but Davis thought I was. He testified in court down there that Rozelle had called me and told me that they could block his move and that they were going to change the rules so that you had to get 100 percent approval. It was 75 percent at the time. I had indeed written about it, but it was in error. I didn't know they were going to change the rules. Rozelle had not talked to me. I thought it was 100 percent when it was 75 percent. It was strictly an error on my part."

As they walked out of the courtroom after that day's testimony, Davis came up behind Dickey. "I turned around and saw him there, and he said, 'I was talking about you in there.'"

"Yeah, I know," Dickey told Davis.

"That shows you how paranoid Davis is," Dickey observed. "To think that Rozelle would call me up and tell me that. Rozelle was always approachable. If any of us wanted to talk to him, you could call, and if he did not answer, he would get back to you some way or another, but he didn't call people to plant things. He never did any of that. That's what Davis would have done. Davis has always judged people by what he would have done."

"Pete was charged in open court with conspiracy to keep the L.A. franchise for himself," Art Modell said. "I said, 'If that's true, then he's crazier than I thought.' Who'd want an NFL franchise in any market with the post he had? It hurt him. He was absolutely torn apart: depositions, pretrial motions, the trials themselves. He deserved a better shot than that. He did nothing wrong. He did nothing but right for the league. There was nothing underhanded about Pete Rozelle, nothing whatsoever. I can't emphasize that enough. Pete had no personal agenda that he put to use."

That was a minor allegation compared with the one that drew headlines across the country: ticket scalping. Davis had accused Georgia Rosenbloom Frontiere of scalping tickets to Super Bowl XIV in 1980. Several years later, her husband Dominic Frontiere was convicted and sentenced to a year in prison in that case. Then Rozelle got drawn into the case by Davis supporter Mel Durslag, the *L.A. Herald-Examiner* columnist.

"Durslag wrote, 'Rozelle, ticket scalping? Ticket scalper?' That was in the *L.A. Herald-Examiner* during the time of the Raiders' trial," NFL executive vice president Joe Browne recalled. "That really hurt Pete because his dad was still alive at the time. With all the integrity that Pete had built up, that he would be accused of ticket scalping really got him upset. The Raiders, in their depositions and questioning of Pete leading up to the trial, asked Rozelle, 'Have you ever scalped Super Bowl tickets?' " The exchange continued:

"No," Rozelle said.

"Don't you sell Super Bowl tickets to a travel agent?" the lawyer asked.

"No."

"You never sold Super Bowl tickets to Peter Ueberroth?"

"This was in the late '70s," Browne recalled. "Pete sold him four tickets, but the way it came out in the *Herald-Examiner* was Pete was scalping hundreds of Super Bowl tickets. It didn't say it, but it was the implication that Pete was scalping tickets out of our office. Durslag was behind that."

Browne jumped ahead in his story: "So, the trial was over. Now it was '84, and Durslag had another big job. Besides the paper, he was the regular sports columnist for *TV Guide*. One time, I was with Pete when Durslag called Pete to discuss the possibility of having instant replay in the league. 'I'll take the call,' Pete said. I remember him saying that."

Browne couldn't believe his ears. "You mean you're going to take his call?" he exclaimed.

" 'Yeah. Hi, Mel. How are you?' Pete, as I say, was loyal to a fault. When Pete was back in Compton, then with the Rams and his early days as commissioner, Mel Durslag was a big name in Los Angeles. Despite the fact that he turned against us at the Raiders trial, Pete treated Durslag in a civil fashion. It was tough for me, as the younger Irishman, with my Irish temper really getting me. That's the way Pete was. He was loyal to a fault."

On May 7, 1982, a jury of six women found that the National Football League had violated the antitrust laws and also found the league guilty of bad faith in its dealings with Davis. The Raiders were off to Los Angeles. The league appealed and lost again, and Davis collected $35 million in damages, while the Coliseum got $15 million.

"So, he went down to L.A. and signed a 10-year lease," Glenn Dickey said. "They promised him boxes. Bill Robertson said, 'We'll get you the boxes,' but there was never anything in writing, and Robertson didn't have the support of the Coliseum Commission. Davis never did get the boxes."

How could it be that a man as smart and as clever an operator as Al Davis failed to get a written guarantee from the Coliseum Commissioner? "He's really not a very good businessman," Dickey said. "People think he is, and he's been able to get people to throw money at him. In sports, that's not difficult, but when it comes to negotiating a deal, he's not that good. At any rate, I've always been convinced he felt he could go down there and be a big fish in a big pond. Here he was a big fish in a little pond."

Now that they were L.A.-bound, Davis knew the Raiders had to win to get the fans. "When I first became head coach, we had just gotten Ron Wolf back after he spent his time in Tampa," Tom Flores said. "I knew Ron since Al first took the job. We never knew what he looked like because he never came out of the dark room where he looked at film. We became very close. He and I worked together very closely when Al was in court.

"The day we drafted Marcus Allen in 1982, Al was in court and on a pay phone. It came our turn; we went back and forth, and we drafted him," Flores continued. "There were two teams ahead of us that might take him: Minnesota took the little running back from Stanford [Darrin Nelson], and Atlanta took a fullback [Gerald Riggs] from Arizona State. So, Marcus was there, and there was no decision to make, really."

Lyle Alzado was a washed-up free agent when Flores, Wolf, and Davis looked him over and decided to give him a chance. He gave them a big year in 1983 and was a key player in the 38–9 rout of Washington for the Raiders' Super Bowl XVIII victory. "We allowed them to continue being characters as long as they didn't disrupt what we were trying to do," Flores reiterated. "They couldn't come in and disrupt and change the chemistry of the team. We put them in a position where they could do what they did best."

Marcus Allen, USC's Heisman Trophy winner in 1981, was the MVP of Super Bowl XVIII, as he gained 191 yards on 20 carries and clinched it on the final play of the third quarter with a brilliant 74-yard touchdown run, in which he swept left, cut back, and shot through the secondary to put the game away. After the game, Davis couldn't stop talking up his Raiders. "I don't think in terms of rout," Davis told Malcolm Moran, of the *New York Times*. "I think in terms of domination." Then, in front of the commissioner and the National Football League, he uttered the words that would define him forever: "Just win, baby!"

The pressure had been heaviest on Rozelle, the public's sympathetic figure in this personality duel. "Rozelle pulled it off with Davis on those Super Bowl trophy presentations. He never showed the angst," Edwin Pope said.

After that triumph, the last Super Bowl title for an AFC team until Denver beat Green Bay in Super Bowl XXXII in 1998, the Raiders began their long slide. As much as he wanted to make a successful go, Los Angelinos just didn't care. Fortunately for Davis, though, at least one neighboring locale was eager for a chance to play in the big leagues. "People talk about Davis extorting money out of cities, but Irwindale, in the middle of nowhere like most of Southern California is, came to him with $10 million," Glenn Dickey said. "Of course, he took it. It was a stupid deal on their part. They wanted to be on the map, but that wasn't his deal at all. That isn't to say if they had built a stadium there that they would not have played there; it never got that far. They just gave him the money. He pocketed the dough. Ten million!"

In so many ways, the Al Davis–Pete Rozelle contretemps that became all-out war ended, as do so many other feuds, without resolve, and the battle damaged both men. "He was very uncomfortable talking about Al Davis," Frank Deford said. "The subject of Al Davis put him on the defensive, obviously, more than anything else."

"There's no clear-cut winner or loser," Glen Dickey stated. "Pete probably would have stayed on as commissioner longer if he had not been worn down by the constant battle."

"I think he was so furious at Al Davis," Deford said. "Davis broke the compact. Really, you could call it the Rozelle Compact, and they were all in this together."

"Davis won his point by moving the team to L.A., but what did he win by that point?" Dickey posed. "The team was not successful overall, financially. They drew about the same as they did in Oakland. They'd get 90,000 for big games, then 30,000 the next time. He never got what he really wanted out of that: the attention. When I was working on the book in '90, they made it to the championship game. They had a big game in Kansas City and, on Monday, were on page 4 of the *L.A. Times*. They never made any inroads. I asked a cabbie to take me to the Raiders' practice facility, and the guy didn't know where it was."

"Davis beat him on two fronts," Deford said. "First, he's the guy who won the battle and forced the merger. And second, he got inside the tent and changed all the furniture around."

"Now he's back in Oakland, and it's not working out very well here," Dickey said. "I don't think they're going anywhere now. It's hard to say there was a winner or loser."

TWENTY-FIVE

USFL OR USELESS?

"How could they [the NFL] be guilty of what they were found guilty of and we be awarded only a dollar, which was trebled to $3?"

—CHET SIMMONS, FORMER USFL COMMISSIONER, 2005

*I*n a 2005 conversation with the writer Frank Deford, I asked if it was fair to conjecture that Pete Rozelle's life was the stuff of a three-act drama, with the last act not being pleasant at all. "Yes, in a way," Deford answered. "A tragedy is something you bring on yourself. The fact that he didn't get out when the getting was good and the fact that he was a smart enough man to maybe suspect that there were problems ahead are testimony. He thought he could handle them."

Rozelle definitely was in charge during the passage from the '70s to the '80s, despite the brewing storm that had come to a head with Al Davis and increasingly tumultuous player relations. The game on the field itself had become stale and predictable, obvious to fans who fell in love with a game that featured spectacular long passing and comebacks in which no edge was safe unless a team owned a 17-point lead inside two minutes. And even that edge might not be a lock.

By the merger, defenses with the better athletes thoroughly dominated, and as they did, the game took on a dullness—not a full-blown malady, but a malaise. Finally, in 1978, the powers that be realized they had to take steps. "I joined the NFL Competition Committee in 1975 and spent 20 years with it," said Don Shula, the winningest coach in pro football history, with 347 victories for Baltimore and Miami. "Tex Schramm was the chairman, and he and Pete had a great relationship. They later introduced each other for the Hall of Fame."

The Schramm-Rozelle relationship was essential to getting things done, as it combined Schramm's ideas with Rozelle's persuasiveness, along with both men's understanding of the game. Schramm had been Rozelle's mentor and ally in the beginning with the Los Angeles Rams. "Tex was a genius. I think he had more to do with player rules and safety than anybody else in the game," Shula said of the committee's accomplishments. "We never did anything without first running it by the commissioner to see how he felt about it, and whether he felt we could get enough votes from the owners to get things passed. There were times when we got into some controversial things that looked like they weren't going to pass. With Pete's urging in the league meetings, we got the votes to get it done."

They started by liberalizing the offensive blocking rules, legalizing holding within the limits of an offensive player actually tackling a defender. While that helped the offense, the salient change that reenergized the game arose when the Competition Committee successfully attacked the single defensive maneuver that threatened to make pro football as low-scoring as soccer: the bump and run, even more of a detriment than its cousin, the head slap.

"Defensive backs got so proficient at what they called 'axing' the receiver," Shula said. "As a receiver came off the line of scrimmage, they would come up and throw a cross-body block on him. That kept him from getting downfield, enabling the quarterback sack."

If a receiver somehow escaped the "ax," the defender still could take whacks at him all the way down the field until the whistle stopped play. "You couldn't have a real pass offense in those days," said venerable *Los Angeles Times* football writer Bob Oates. "Miami won a Super Bowl one time by throwing the ball seven times. You couldn't throw against a bump-and-run defense."

"The offense was hurting. The passing game was hurting. It wasn't as exciting as it is now," Shula said. "George Allen was a proponent of the defense and axing. At one meeting, he said, 'I don't think there's anything wrong with a 6–0 or 6–3 game.'"

"Rozelle knew passing was the thing that sells the NFL," Oates said. "What Halas was doing 60 years ago was pretty much a running game. Sid Luckman didn't really do much. He gets a lot of ink because he was close to Halas. It was the running—McAfee, Nagurski, and those guys, who made the Bears what they were. Running, in Rozelle's view, was one of the reasons pro football was slow to catch on around the country, because it was smashmouth football. Smashmouth football doesn't sell: I've heard him say that over and over again. He could see that a ball soaring overhead and the guy running it down were the ingredients that sell. He was right about that. That's a principal reason pro football is so popular nationwide: the passing is so damn good."

Schramm and the Competition Committee knew the fans might yell "Dee-fense!" but still wanted offense with spectacular plays and plenty of scoring. Bump and run had come into vogue to counter the wide-open passing attacks in the American Football League, and the team that best exemplified it was also the one that most loved long passing, the vertical game—Al Davis's Raiders. "They had two great corners, Lester Hayes and Mike Haynes," Oates said. "They had the speed and the know-how to take the other team's two wide receivers out of the game. That reduced the game to nine people on the defense against eight on the offense, because the quarterback doesn't count."

After talking it over with the Competition Committee, Rozelle went to Davis, the one man who had the influence to eliminate the bump and run, and told him the rule must be changed. "I really don't know how Rozelle got him to agree," Oates said, "but Rozelle was very good at working with people who had different views than he did or with people who thought he was not on the right track."

To replace bump and run, the committee allowed defenders to knock receivers off balance with a single "chuck," a stiff jolt, within five yards of the line of scrimmage. "That opened it up for everybody," Shula said. "It made the game much more exciting. Our whole emphasis on the Competition Committee was to make the game as exciting as we could make it for the fans without changing the nature of the game."

Rozelle's flexibility enabled him to overlook his deep-rooted difficulties with Al Davis in so many other areas, especially the draining litigation over the Raiders' leaving Oakland for Los Angeles. The commissioner was able to compartmentalize his thinking and set aside those differences to work them out later, if possible. "There aren't many executives who have that ability," Oates said. "It's my way or the highway with most executives and CEOs. Rozelle was terrific at working with people and owners. Rozelle, of course, was upset with the lawsuits with Davis, but that didn't stop him from working on something like this."

The net result was a rebirth of the passing game in the '80s and the emergence of a generation of defining quarterbacks, with Joe Montana, Dan Marino, and John Elway at the top of the list. "The game now is at its height of popularity," Shula said. "It's wide open, and you see great athletes make great plays."

The business of pro football had been flourishing since the merger. Rozelle assured his bosses, the owners, record earnings with the four-year television deals he put together in 1978. "Those television contracts that Pete negotiated through '82 tripled the television revenues on a team basis," said Paul Tagliabue, who served as the league's outside counsel during that period. "They went to $5 million a club from the '78 deal through '81."

In early 1979, after helping NBC secure the 1980 Moscow Summer Olympics, Chet Simmons resigned as president of the network's sports division to become founding president and CEO of a fledgling cable enterprise that one day would dominate sports television, ESPN. He came to ESPN with ideas and ambitions, but nothing to put on the air to attract the few households in America that were wired for cable.

"In the early days of ESPN, we were looking for any and all kinds of programming," Simmons said. "The very first year or year and a half, we couldn't even carry live college football. It had to be done on a delay, starting at midnight on Saturday. We had no NFL. We had to do 'SportsCenter' with news." That's when Simmons went calling with a proposal. As he told it, "We had to get involved, so I went to see Pete Rozelle. We were chatting in his office; then we got into it."

Simmons said, "Pete, I'd love to televise your draft."

Rozelle said, "You want to do *what*?"

"I want to do your draft," Simmons said in as businesslike a manner as he could evoke. "We have a 24-hour network with tons of time. The NFL is a big deal. We'd like to somehow get involved with you. We'd like to televise your draft."

Simmons recalled, "He was incredulous. He couldn't imagine that anyone would want to do that. 'Sure,' Rozelle said. 'Go ahead.' I think he did it with half a smile. We did it, and now look at it. It's the biggest nonplaying event on the planet. It was just something that was going through my head and how we could get involved with Pete. I could have sat with him for two hours on how we could get involved, and we'd have ended up just saying, 'Thanks for the time.' "

With the NFL draft rights in hand, Simmons and ESPN finally had acquired something to showcase for at least one weekend a year, but they still had all that time to fill and lacked material to fill it. Their fledgling "SportsCenter" program, which by the end of the '80s would become the preeminent sports highlights programming in television, needed material. So he went to work.

"We had to negotiate with the networks that were carrying the games to get highlights," Simmons said. "We had problems with that in the early going. Everybody thought we were crazy, but we pulled it off. We did it."

While making inroads with his new venture, Simmons didn't have to feel he'd missed out on the Olympics by leaving NBC Sports. When President Jimmy Carter pulled the United States out of the Moscow Games, citing the Soviets' human rights violations, NBC had no choice but to pull the plug on its ambitious telecast plans.

About that time, New Orleans native David Dixon, the man primarily responsible for gaining the NFL franchise that became the Saints and for building the Louisiana Superdome, came up with another big idea. Dixon, a football-mad antiques and art dealer from the French Quarter, persuaded a dozen like-minded men with money to start up a new football league. Instead of going head to head with the established NFL, Dixon reasoned that spring and early summer was an ideal time for football.

Dixon and his partners needed television, so they lured Chet Simmons from ESPN to become their first commissioner. On May 11, 1982, Simmons announced the formation of the United States Football League, to begin an 18-game season that would run from March to July, 1983. In that first year, Simmons was able to gain television exposure for the league with ABC Sports and his former employer, ESPN, with a two-year deal that paid $18 million in 1983 and again in 1984. The league would operate under a salary cap, $1.8 million a team. The league, incidentally, would end up $160 million in debt. One day shortly after the start-up announcement, Rozelle was holding court with a few writers, and somebody asked him what he thought would happen with the USFL. "They will play," the NFL czar said. "They will start to lose money. Then, they will spend too much money on players and get deeper in the hole. And then, about the time they are ready to go out of business, they will take a lawsuit against us. That is how it has been historically. That is how it will happen again with this league."

The USFL offered two significant playing rules changes: the two-point conversion (the NFL would adopt it in 1994) and, starting in 1985, a system using television instant replay to challenge officials' rulings on the fields. That system was the prototype of the version the NFL uses today.

In those early days of the new league, having Simmons around was a boon in the USFL's dealings with Pete Rozelle and the NFL. "When I got the job as commissioner, I got a really nice note from him," Simmons said. "We went to the same haircutter at that point; we had a nice chat as she finished up with him. I had nothing but the highest regard for him personally or professionally. He was never anything but genuinely gracious when we would talk to each other. I'm sure that he instinctively knew that everything that he said or did with anybody else in the league had to be legally aboveboard. He could never be felt to be doing anything that would be untoward against a new competitor."

Before the USFL opened for business in May 1982, Rozelle announced a new package on March 16, 1982, in which ABC would pay $681.5 million for "Monday Night Football," five Hall of Fame exhibitions, five Pro Bowls, and its first Super Bowl, number XIX, in January 1985. The next day, Rozelle unveiled a CBS package worth $713 million for NFC games, playoffs, and two Super Bowls. Five days later, NBC paid $638 million for AFC games, playoffs, and, like CBS, two Super Bowls. "He trebled it to $15 million a team in the contracts that were supposed to be five years: '82, '83, '84, '85, '86," Paul Tagliabue said. "That was the first time he ever did a five-year contract. It tripled the television revenue." The total price tag was $2,325,000,000! They had come that far since his landmark $28.2 million deal in 1964 with CBS, covering two seasons.

"My own sense is people really began to feel so comfortable with the status quo," Tagliabue said. "Everything seemed to be great, and they stopped being as creative, energetic, and innovative as they had been in the prior 15 years. You had a period of tremendous change, with the merger, expansion to Tampa and Seattle, 'Monday Night Football' coming in. There was so much great energy and so much expansion."

He pointed out, "There were quite a few new stadiums before and after the merger. It started with D.C. Stadium [RFK]; then you had that wave of publicly financed dual-purpose stadiums built for football and baseball in the late '60s and early '70s—Philadelphia, Pittsburgh, St. Louis, Cincinnati, all the way across the country to San Francisco with Candlestick Park, down the coast to San Diego." Seattle, likewise, built the Kingdome. "So, there was this huge wave of energy, culminating with those huge TV contracts in '82," Tagliabue said. "Suddenly, it was, 'OK, here we are. Let's dig in our heels.' It became: fight with the union, fight with Al Davis, fight with the USFL."

The NFL realized how serious the USFL threat had become when, on February 23, 1983, a month before the league played its first game, the New Jersey Generals fired the opening salvo as they introduced 1982 Heisman Trophy winner Herschel Walker, of Georgia. Walker, arguably, the most renowned and important college football player since Red Grange, signed a three-year deal for $3.9 million, most of that coming in a personal services contract with Generals owner J. Walter Duncan, an Oklahoma oilman.

In signing Walker, a college junior with one more year of eligibility, the Generals and the USFL had broken the sacred nonpoaching compact that George Halas and the NFL made with college coaches in 1926 after Halas had signed Grange off the Illinois campus in November 1925. The Walker signing, in comparison, was even more contentious, considering Grange was a senior and had *played* his final college game. Most important, Walker decided to play where he wanted to go, either New York or Dallas, not where he would fall in a draft. That action would directly affect both the NFL and its longtime unsubsidized farm system, the colleges.

The Generals sold nearly half of their thirty-six thousand season tickets in the 11 days between Walker's signing and the March 6 opener. Simmons and his USFL owners knew what they had when the national TV ratings came in at 14.2, just short of CBS's numbers the previous NFL season. Walker delivered consistent performances, as he gained 5,562 yards and scored 61 touchdowns in the USFL's three seasons of play.

The new league attracted scores of outstanding players, coaches, and administrators. Three Hall of Fame coaches served in the USFL: Sid Gillman, George Allen, and Marv Levy. Future Hall of Fame players were quarterbacks Jim Kelly and Steve Young, defensive end Reggie White, and receiver Fred Biletnikoff. Of the total 187 men who eventually played in the NFL, many made significant impacts, most prominent among them being Anthony Carter, Sam Mills, Doug Flutie, and Herschel Walker. Carl Peterson ran the Kansas City Chiefs for Lamar Hunt and Bill Polian, and the Indianapolis Colts for Jim Irsay. To the NFL owners' chagrin, average player salaries rose from $152,800 in 1983 to $225,600 in 1984, a 47.6 percent jump.

After two seasons, the league was holding its own; it was smaller than the mighty NFL, to be sure, but it was entertaining, and it provided good football. The Jim Mora–coached Philadelphia Stars rang up the USFL's best record and one title in those two years. While Mora drew his share of praise, the big noise in the league—and anywhere else he's been, into the 21st century—was Donald Trump.

"He was the best and worst thing that ever happened to the USFL," the late Peter Hadhazy said. Hadhazy worked for USFL commissioners Chet Simmons and Harry Usher throughout the league's existence, which ran from 1982 to '87, and spent much time with The Donald. (The New York tabloids began calling Trump that after his activities flowed from the financial pages into the sports sections and gossip pages.) We spoke at length about his experiences one afternoon in December 2005, just four months before his death.

"In that first season when there was a franchise in New Jersey playing in the Meadowlands, the Generals, people didn't even know it was there," Hadhazy said. "Owner Walter Duncan, who signed Herschel Walker, used to fly in from Oklahoma for the games. Period. Chuck Fairbanks was the coach and general manager, and he really had no interest in promoting the team. He was a coach. Period. And had the title GM. There was nothing newsworthy emanating from their offices, nor did they have any interest in generating some publicity."

The de facto news blackout extended to information as basic as time and date. "This is a true story," Hadhazy said. "You would pick up the *Daily News*, or the *New York Times*, or the *Post*, whatever, the weekend the Generals were playing at home at the Meadowlands, and they wouldn't even have a listing. So, you wouldn't know what time kickoff was or that they were home."

Donald Trump was an ambitious young realtor with growing wealth and no fame outside New York real estate circles when, on September 21, 1983, he bought the Generals from Walter Duncan for $10 million and grabbed the spotlight. He let it been known from the outset that he wanted to build the greatest football team in history. And, as much as he could stand not being the center of attention, Trump informed intimates that he really intended to use the Generals and the USFL to garner a third New York NFL franchise for himself.

"When Donald Trump came in, he was young, he was flamboyant, he was outspoken. He signed 1984 Heisman Trophy winner Doug Flutie," Hadhazy said. "He also made some ridiculous statements, like, 'We can beat the NFL.' But he was quotable. There wasn't a day that went by that didn't mention Trump as owner of the team or of the organization." True to his reputation, one of Trump's first moves when he took charge was firing the coach. "I worked for Fairbanks in New England," Hadhazy said, "but Trump said he didn't want him."

"Who would you hire as coach?" Trump asked Hadhazy.

"I gave him a list of four people," Hadhazy said. "Don Shula, Joe Paterno, Joe Namath, and Walt Michaels, who recently had been let go by the Jets. Namath really wasn't ready to be a head coach, but I said to Trump, 'You know what? You put him up there, and you hire some great assistants, and you let him cut the supermarket ribbons and let the other guys coach, because he wouldn't be dedicated enough to work for 12 hours a day.' Paterno wanted no part of us. We came within a hair's breadth of hiring Shula. Michaels was the last guy left on the board. He hired Walt because he was the guy he could get with the least amount of money."

"Why Shula?" Trump had asked after hearing Hadhazy's list.

"Because Shula might be the next commissioner of the NFL," Hadhazy told him. "He's well respected. He's been on the Competition Committee of the NFL, and that would give our league instant credibility."

"What do you think it would cost to get him?" Trump inquired.

The best-paid coaches at that time were making between $200,000 and $300,000.

"You'd have to offer him a million dollars," Hadhazy replied.

"You're nuts!" Trump said.

"I'm telling you: he's an icon," Hadhazy insisted. "He's not going to leave the Dolphins and the NFL without a guarantee and all that stuff."

"Would you call him for me?" Trump asked.

"Sure," Hadhazy answered, knowing that Shula would listen carefully when he heard how much money was involved.

"I called Don and said, 'Here's the deal: New Jersey, the New York team, has a new owner with a lot of money.'

"At that time, nobody knew Donald Trump," Hadhazy emphasized. "He'd say, 'I make a billion-dollar deal, and I get a little note in the financial section.' Of course, he has a tendency to exaggerate.

This with Shula really was a million-dollar deal. 'If I talk about the Generals and I sneeze, I'm on the front cover of the paper,' Trump would say. He loved being in the limelight."

"Nah, I'm not interested," Shula said when Hadhazy called.

"We knew that Joe Robbie had promised him a new contract before the season," Hadhazy said. "This was in October of '83, because Trump bought the team after that first season. Duncan signed Herschel Walker, not Trump. Trump is the one who signed Flutie. Anyway, what Trump said to me was, 'When you talk to Shula—' " Hadhazy didn't let him finish.

"You have to offer him a million, Donald," he repeated.

"No way!" Trump said. Then he backtracked. "Well, maybe I'll go to a million, but you offer him $750,000, 'cause he's going to jump at that—you know that, you know?"

Hadhazy talked to Shula again. "I have no interest," the Dolphins coach said.

"Let me tell you this," Hadhazy said to Shula. "I'm not supposed to tell you this, but he's prepared to go up to a million dollars."

According to Hadhazy, "That caught his attention." He related, "Shula and I had conversations to the point where he wanted to know where the offices were, what kind of guy Trump was, how active Trump was as an owner, what business he was in. All of a sudden, Shula asked me about real estate in and around New Jersey, Saddle-brook and the like—about schools."

"Trump used to call me Monday nights, because he knew I'd be home watching the Monday-night game," Shula said. "He was getting Herschel Walker [as he bought the Generals from Duncan], and he wanted me to come and coach him."

Hadhazy recalled, "Then Shula's business manager came up and had a meeting with Trump and me. During the meeting, his business manager mentioned, 'If Don is making an appearance in the city and needs a place to stay, would he have the use of an apartment in Trump Tower?' "

"Of course," Trump said. "No problem." So, the meeting ended with the understanding that Shula could have use of an apartment in a need situation, not buy or lease one.

When Hadhazy called back, Shula's mind was totally on his own football situation in Miami. "Look, what I'm trying to do is get this team into the playoffs, and I don't want any distractions at all," Shula told him. "If word gets out that anything is going on, that's it. I'm done."

Those parameters were workable, as far as Hadhazy was concerned. "The object," Hadhazy related, "was to get a contract signed, put it in a safe, and, three or four months later, pull it out and say, 'Here's a contract saying Don Shula is the new coach of the New Jersey Generals.'"

"It got down to his coming down to visit us and talk my wife into going along with it," Shula said.

"He was angry at Robbie because Robbie was supposed to give him a new deal before the season started," Hadhazy said. "Trump and I were supposed to go down there to sign the deal. That's how close it was."

Close, but no cigar. "The game the week before he was going to come down, we played the Colts in Baltimore," Shula said. "After the game, the first question to me was not about the game, but was about Trump. Trump had told the media that the only thing that kept me from agreeing to terms with him was that I *demanded* a suite in Trump Tower. I never had heard about Trump Tower. He was using that to get publicity for Trump Tower. So, I called him that night and said, 'Hey, I don't appreciate what you said. It's not true. Our conversations are over, and I'm staying where I am!' It was typical Trump."

"Then, I got a call around midnight, perhaps later, and Shula was absolutely enraged," Hadhazy said. "Trump was quoted as saying that he could hire Don as his coach if he wanted to; all he had to do was *give* Shula an apartment in Trump Tower. This was quoted on the AP. The Dolphins had played the Colts that afternoon. Shula was livid because all the reporters wanted to hear about was the USFL. So, he told me, 'It's off. As far as you and I are concerned, we never spoke!'"

Hadhazy tried an appeal to reason: "Donald, did you hear *me* being quoted?"

"No, Peter," he acknowledged, but the point was moot. "I don't hold it against you. I hold it against Trump. So, that's done. It's done. I'm going to deny we ever spoke. Tell Trump not to call me. I don't want to hear anything about the USFL anymore." Click.

Hadhazy took some time to collect his thoughts. "I was figuring, at this postmidnight hour, should I call Trump? What the hell! I tried him at Trump Tower. No answer. I tried it at his home in Connecticut, and he picked up," Hadhazy recalled.

"I've got bad news for you," he told Trump, unaware that the coach had already spoken with the Generals' owner in a furious phone call and had slammed the door on further negotiations. "I just talked to Shula, and the deal is done, and he's pissed."

"Why?"

"He's pissed because you were quoted on the wire services that you could hire him and all he wanted to seal the deal was an apartment in Trump Tower," Hadhazy said. "One other thing: Shula told me, 'Not only did this guy break a confidence, he portrays me like I'm some kind of whore, that I wanted a free apartment in Trump Tower.'"

"Why?"

"He's mad because he says that you leaked it, and he didn't want that to happen," Hadhazy explained, "and he's pissed because you made him look greedy and like some kind of whore willing to leave Miami for an apartment."

Hadhazy finished the story: "It was quiet at Trump's end. You'd figure Trump would say something like, 'Damn it!' or, 'What can we do to fix this thing?' You know what he said after a pause of three or four seconds? 'Hey! Is that great publicity for Trump Tower?' And that was the end of it."

By no means, however, was the botched hiring the end of Donald Trump's USFL adventure, which continued to command media interest. Early in 1984, the league added six franchises to the original 12 in an attempt to pump new money to stop the hemorrhaging, and another hot story started making the rounds. "Trump wanted to go to the fall," Chet Simmons said. "He felt he had enough 'friends' that if he put enough pressure on the NFL, a couple of teams would be merged into it. He felt he would be one of them. Blah, blah, blah. He was like the pied piper: he told all those other millionaires he thought they could do it—and you saw what happened."

The league launched its fall-schedule trial balloon on January 19, 1984, under the guise of studying the feasibility of such a move. On September 13, 1984, Simmons sent a letter to Rozelle in which he cautioned the NFL not to interfere with the USFL's planned move to a fall schedule in 1986. He charged in the letter that, concerning a fall schedule, the older league was interfering in television issues and stadium sharing, which tied in with game scheduling; was trying to dissuade players from signing with the USFL; and had issued improper statements and misrepresentations about the USFL.

"They appear to be posturing themselves for an antitrust action, should things go bad for the league," Rozelle said in his verbal reply to Simmons through the media. The letter, Rozelle said, was the third or fourth time the USFL had tried this tactic. "They're making a record of the fact that on this date, they told us about these things." Rozelle said the letter would not force the NFL to change its rules nor its bylaws.

It was during this volatile course of events, in the spring of 1984, as Rozelle was gearing up for yet more court action down the line, that Robert Irsay dropped his bomb on Baltimore and the league. "You had the Colts' move, in the middle of all that, out of Baltimore, which really pained him, because that was such a linchpin of the league, coming out of the liquidation of the old Dallas Texans and ending up in Baltimore," Paul Tagliabue said. "Pete felt his hands were tied on that because of the Raiders' ruling. You had a legendary team moving out of Baltimore and Congressional hearings on that."

The other shoe finally dropped on October 17, 1984, when the USFL announced it had filed a $1.32 billion antitrust suit against the NFL. The suit charged that the NFL had pressured the networks that carried its games—ABC, NBC, and CBS—to not televise the USFL in the fall. One of the bases for the lawsuit was a seminar that analyzed "the NFL versus USFL," given February 29, 1984, at the Harvard

Business School by Professor Michael Porter. Sixty-five NFL executives attended. Rozelle was not one of them.

USFL attorneys, led by Harvey Myerson, described the seminar as a blueprint on "how to conquer the USFL." They specifically charged that the NFL conspired to harm the Oakland Invaders and New Jersey Generals. The lawsuit named the NFL and its commissioner, Pete Rozelle, as defendants. The Los Angeles Raiders and owner Al Davis were not named in the lawsuit, in exchange for Davis's testimony against his own league.

That was the end for Simmons. After enduring constant pressure, mostly from Trump, as the financial losses mounted, Simmons resigned as USFL commissioner on January 14, 1985. "I wanted no part of it," he said in late 2005. "They certainly knew how I felt, I knew how they felt, and we merrily skipped out the door together." Harry Usher, the executive vice president and general manager of the 1984 Los Angeles Olympic Organizing Committee, replaced Simmons as commissioner.

"It's a very tough business, running a sports league," Simmons said two decades later. "It's like sweet and sour. I'm glad I had the opportunity, and I would never consider doing it again. If I knew then what I know today, I would have never even tried it. Very difficult."

Television for Chet Simmons was a far easier proposition than running a three-ring circus under the guise of a football league, led by ringmaster Donald Trump, whose fall-schedule scheme proved to be a disaster. "They [the USFL owners] listened to Trump," Simmons said. "We brought in consultants who recommended against it, and they just wanted to fly in the face of it. They felt Trump knew what he was doing. He had all those rich friends. He knew the president of ABC; he would make calls to Leonard Goldenson, all that stuff." As they soon learned, neither Goldenson and ABC, nor CBS, nor NBC had any intention of going to war against the NFL.

The trial began at the U. S. courthouse in Lower Manhattan's Foley Square on May 12, 1986, with jury selection, a two-day process. The courthouse where the fate of professional football would be decided was the same venue where Ethel and Julius Rosenberg were found guilty in 1951 of nuclear espionage and where, in 1933, an earlier judge had ruled that the James Joyce novel *Ulysses* was not obscene.

Attorney Frank Rothman led the National Football League defense team against the flamboyant, contentious Myerson. In a *New York Times* report on Myerson's opening 87-minute address to the six-person jury, Michael Janovsky wrote that the lawyer referred to NFL owners as "birds and henchman," NFL executive vice president Jay Moyer as "Moyer the lawyer," and to his client as a "little, itty, bitty" league. Myerson upped his damages request to $1.5 billion.

Myerson, according to Janovsky's account, upset NFL partisans in the courtroom when he "sat slouched in his chair, smirking, rolling his eyes, and smiling toward the members of the jury." At one point, he apologized to Judge Peter K. Leisure and the jury, saying, "I'm just an emotional guy. I get wrapped up in this stuff."

Myerson opened his case on May 15 with Rozelle on the stand. "You could see Pete aging," Peter Hadhazy said. "The USFL did a real attack. Like Harvey Myerson said before the trial, if we can discredit the commissioner, we win the suit. So, they went after Rozelle personally, professionally, and every which way."

"That was grueling for him," NFL executive vice president Joe Browne said. "I think he was on the stand for nine days during the trial. Most of it was under cross-examination by Harvey Myerson."

Myerson tried to prove that Rozelle and the NFL had damaged the USFL by negotiating the NFL's first five-year television contract and by placing ABC in the Super Bowl rotation for the first time. That January 1985 telecast of Super Bowl XIX, in Myerson's view, was "further evidence of how the NFL 'tied up' all three networks."

Rozelle testified that neither he nor the networks mentioned the USFL during negotiations and that the contracts were signed *before* formation of the league was announced. He produced a memo to that effect.

When Myerson attacked him on the Harvard seminar, Rozelle said he did not attend the seminar, nor had he read the agenda in advance. "I had nothing to do with planning that seminar," the commissioner testified. Rozelle denied any wrongdoing or impropriety cited in every allegation Myerson introduced.

Donald Trump was next on the stand. "Trump testified how he met with Rozelle at the Hotel Pierre," Peter Hadhazy said. "He said Rozelle stuck a finger in his chest and said, 'Look, you be a good boy and make sure we don't get sued, and I'll make sure you get a franchise.'

"Pete Rozelle had testified that as commissioner, he certainly may have had some influence, but he couldn't guarantee a franchise," Hadhazy continued. "Ultimately, it would be the owners' vote that awards franchises. Knowing Pete Rozelle, to stick a finger in someone's chest was totally out of character. It came out as though it didn't matter: Trump just felt the jury was going to believe him. He thought he could get away with anything he wanted to, because he was Donald Trump. He still had that big of an ego even though he wasn't quite as famous."

"Trump got up there and lied and contradicted Pete," Joe Browne said. "It was on the front page of the *New York Post*. It was all about who called whom to set up their meeting to talk about Donald owning the USFL team. Trump called Pete, and Pete kept notes of the phone call, which were used in the trial."

"Listen," Trump told Rozelle over the phone, "I'll get these USFL owners to drop this litigation if I get an NFL team in New York City."

"What are you going to do about the Generals?" Pete asked.

"I'll get some stiff to buy it," Trump said, as Rozelle recorded in his notes.

"That expression really resonated with the jury," Browne said. "That's the story Pete had told. Trump testified a couple of weeks later, and then Pete came back. Pete actually testified twice: they called him early as what they called a hostile witness; then he came back as our witness at the end of the trial. When Rothman turned his attention to the Trump meeting, he asked, 'Did Mr. Trump say anything about how he would divest himself of the USFL team?' "

"Yeah," Rozelle said. "He said he would get some stiff to buy it."

"You could now see the jury—after hearing Trump, then listening to Pete—nodding, as if to say, 'Yeah, that sounds like Trump,' Browne said. 'Sounds like Mr. Trump who we just heard testify a couple of weeks ago.' "

Roone Arledge was the first network honcho to testify. He took the stand on June 12. In *Roone*, Arledge wrote that while ABC's spring-time USFL telecasts had benefited all, "The Donald, owner of a New York franchise, wanted more." Trump, Arledge believed, saw how the AFL forced the merger in 1966, and he wanted to do the same by playing a fall schedule. When Trump discussed that move with ABC's major domo, Arledge replied, "No way." In Arledge's opinion, "The last thing anyone needed was more fall football." When he reminded Trump that he had a little thing called "Monday Night Football," the USFL filed the lawsuit, charging that the NFL and ABC were "involuntarily conspiring to drive the USFL out of business."

"To this day, I have no idea how one can 'conspire involuntarily,' " Arledge wrote.

"The Raiders' litigation was bad enough, but the one that really astounded Pete—and he didn't get surprised too often—was Al Davis coming back to testify in the USFL against the other NFL owners," Joe Browne said.

In two hours on the stand on June 25, Davis testified that the National Football League tried to destroy the USFL's Oakland Invaders. He maintained that the City of Oakland and the Oakland Coliseum had collaborated in 1980 to destroy the Raiders and continued that collaboration in destroying the Invaders after the team's only season, in 1983.

Rozelle had testified that industrialist and developer Alfred Taubman, owner of the Michigan Panthers and part owner of the dormant Invaders, told him at a dinner in late 1984 that he might be interested in an NFL franchise. Rozelle said on the stand that he told Taubman, "You are the type of person I think we would like to have in the NFL." He told the court, "I didn't go any further than that."

When Myerson asked Davis if he knew about the conversation, Davis said, "I didn't think it was proper. My observation was that, in essence, it was an enticement."

"I think Al Davis got to the point where it was never-ending," Ernie Accorsi commented. "I believe, and this is only my opinion, that Pete's health in '89 would have been better had he stayed, but it was never-ending: there was a lawsuit being contested, a lawsuit being appealed, another lawsuit on the way. There were always lawsuits from within. That's what really hurt him. I don't think it was the labor problems. The great line that people used to utter was, 'We're aware of the enemy. He's in the confines of this room.' Then we went through the USFL, and Davis sided with them."

The USFL's star witness, though, was broadcaster Howard Cosell. In his best bombastic hyperbole, Cosell unloaded on his former bosses at ABC, Roone Arledge and Jim Spence, and the National Football League itself. Bill Nack covered that testimony for *Sports Illustrated*, ending up with a four-page takeout in the July 7, 1986, issue. "Rozelle was smooth on the stand; Howard was the entertainer. He hated the NFL and believed they were breaking the law, had a monopoly, and were manipulative," Nack said.

"I covered the trial along with a guy named Manny Topol, of *Newsday*," Nack told me. "Frank Rothman, the NFL's attorney, at one time represented Cosell. He made a vital error that opened the door for Cosell to barge in and have a field day. The rule for a lawyer is, when you ask a hostile witness a question without knowing the answer to it, it is absolutely swimming in the dark. He did it! Manny Topol nudged me and said, 'He did it!' "

As Nack wrote, "The question to Cosell was, 'Sir, don't you believe the NFL men [owners seated in the courtroom, who included Tex Schramm of Dallas, Wellington Mara of the Giants, Arthur Modell of Cleveland, Alex Spanos of the Chargers, and Leon Hess of the Jets] to be men of high integrity?'

" 'Men of high integrity?' a disbelieving Cosell said. 'I don't think they are villains, Sir. I do think they have been misled and their actions have not been in the public interest.' "

Nack then wrote, "Having led with his chin, Rothman led with it again. 'Do you find them to be truthful men?'

"Now Cosell did not hesitate," Nack wrote. " 'Not in cases involving actions of the National Football League, Sir.' "

Nack summarized, "Then Cosell took off, and that was what my piece was about. He told how dishonest they were and ran a conspiracy." Then:

"I'm not as smart as you are," Rothman said.

"Well," said Cosell, "we have learned that long ago."

Rothman took aim again, saying, "If I ask you a question that you don't understand, you stop me."

"If you ask a question that I don't understand, you will have the biggest story of the century," Cosell replied.

"The courtroom rocked with laughter," Nack reported. "As he strode out the door, he turned to a reporter and said, 'What a performance!'"

Nack recalled, "I was wrapping up my reporting the Friday before I wrote. The trial was adjourned until Monday. The NFL hadn't even presented its case. I came up to Art Modell, who was sitting there. He was kind of a PR guy for the league. 'What do you think?'

"'Well, they're leading by a touchdown and a field goal, but we haven't had our turn with the ball yet,' Modell said. I quoted him with that," Nack recounted, "and the NFL said, 'We hope you're coming back when we're up.' I don't think we ever went back. I know I didn't do another one."

"Yeah, but Cosell was Cosell," Joe Browne said. "He wasn't part of the league. Also, Pete, having been around media, saw what was happening. Prior to '86, Cosell was an Al Davis supporter. Cosell had showed his stripes in the early '80s against the league, supporting Davis's move to Los Angeles. The split [with Rozelle] had occurred before the USFL trial. The fact that Cosell was testifying against us didn't shock us, because he had declared that he was anti-NFL. It really wasn't a bulletin."

In fact, it turned out to be a nonissue in the end. After the trial, the NFL lawyers interviewed the jurors. According to Joe Browne, the lawyers asked, "What did you think about Howard Cosell?"

"Several jurors said, 'He was entertaining, but we had no idea why he was there.' That showed the lack of support of his testimony and how, sometimes, you can overreact," Browne said.

The late Peter Hadhazy, long a loyal NFL man despite his tenure with the USFL, offered a far different slant on Cosell. "Cosell was a damn good man. He was berated by a lot of people who were jealous of him. He was a wonderful human being. I loved the guy. I think he was terrific and a lot of it was put on."

The case went to the jury on July 24, and deliberations took five days. As Harvey Myerson waited for a verdict on July 29, he went to lunch in a Chinatown restaurant. He was delighted at meal's end when he opened a fortune cookie and read the message: "You should be pleased with the answers you are given now." Three hours later, he would listen to the jury issue one of the strangest, if not most controversial, verdicts in the history of jurisprudence.

Rozelle and the rest of the NFL crew, meanwhile, were still on their way back to the courtroom. "They had a Chinese lunch, and they got in the car," Joe Browne said.

Rozelle described the scene to Peter Hadhazy afterward. "He got into the limo, the car, with Val Pinchbeck and a few other NFL employees," Hadhazy relayed. "When you hear the story, about 45 NFL employees were in that limo. What Pete Rozelle told me, they were on their way to the courthouse, and the radio was on. The report said the jury was in, and the USFL was victorious; the NFL was a monopoly. Pete said they groaned and moaned and told the driver, 'There's no sense going down there now. Let's go back to the office.'

"They were all frustrated and down," Hadhazy said. "After going a few more blocks, another report came on the radio: Although they found the NFL guilty of a monopoly, the damages the jury awarded to the USFL was a dollar."

"One dollar. They won one dollar," Browne said.

"Turn this goddamned limo around, and let's go to the courthouse!" Rozelle yelled.

"Absolute depression turned to elation," Hadhazy said. "Former USFL executive Steve Erhart has the check: $3 treble damages, 76 cents in interest—a $3.76 check. Still uncashed. You talk about highs and lows: the high went to millions of dollars, the low to one dollar."

Lowest of all was the USFL, which won the verdict but lost the war. Chet Simmons no longer was with the league, but the mixed verdict continued to bedevil him despite the passage of two decades. "As far as I know about it, and I think I'm pretty accurate, the jury misinterpreted the judge's charge," Simmons said in our interview. "They thought if they found the NFL guilty and wanted a monetary award, he would make the award. If they indicated and said it was a dollar, he then would go from there and make the full award. They were wrong, obviously, but there was nothing that could be done at this point."

The issue of guilt still hangs over the case. "How could they [the NFL] be guilty of what they were found guilty of and we be awarded only a dollar, which was trebled to $3?" Simmons mused. "They had a monopoly, illegal restraint of trade. The jury found them guilty of that and awarded the USFL a buck. The jury system is the greatest in the world, but it also is the worst. The elevator operator, the garbageman, and the clerk: how the hell could they understand that stuff? They didn't. It's like being on a jury for Enron. How the hell does the average guy on the street, not your peers, understand the economics of the sport? The jury was smart enough to know the NFL had been in restraint of trade, but they figured the judge would tell them to award the money, and he didn't."

The USFL pondered an appeal, but Judge Leisure said there was no basis for appeal. One more item remained. The USFL filed for court costs and was awarded $5 million, which was upheld on appeal.

"I worked for a guy, as a consultant after the USFL folded, who wanted to start a new league," Peter Hadhazy said. "His name was Michael Kammerer. He had some business, he had some money, and he was looking for investors and stuff. He had a great idea: he was going to have a corporately sponsored league. In other words, the Pepsis were going to play the Coca-Colas, the Burger Kings would play the McDonalds, and so on. I called Cosell and asked Cosell, who was retired, to meet with him, because I felt he should be the first commissioner of the league. 'Howard, do this as a favor to me.'"

Hadhazy recounted, "The guy came into the city and had lunch with me and Kammerer. He's talked about that lunch every day of his life ever since."

All that litigation culminating in the USFL trial sapped Rozelle's energy. "It wasn't just the trials; it was the depositions and preparations leading up to them," Joe Browne said. "It was so time consuming. I think it gnawed at him because he knew this was time he could use in a productive fashion, and here he was playing defense. In one case, one of our owners [Al Davis] became the first ever to sue our league. In the USFL case, it was a league that couldn't shoot straight that was suing us and blaming us for their going from 12 to 18 teams in one year."

The USFL trial and verdict ended Donald Trump's dream of landing an NFL franchise. "We kept the office open after the trial and went from a staff of 30 or 40 to Harry Usher, who was the commissioner; myself; and one attorney, who was the treasurer," Peter Hadhazy said. "Pending appeal—there was still the question whether we would appeal—we had to stay a business entity. We closed the offices for good in February of '87. I'm told, to this day Trump will not accept a call from anybody associated with the USFL, because he looks at this as a failure, perhaps a personal failure, a failure he does not want to be associated with in his life."

Donald Trump did not return my calls requesting an interview for this book.

After Peter Ueberroth replaced the late Bowie Kuhn as baseball commissioner in 1984, Kuhn returned to practice with his Wall Street law firm, Willkie and Farr. Then in 1988, he joined the USFL's lead attorney, Harvey Myerson, to form Myerson and Kuhn. That firm filed for bankruptcy in 1989. Myerson was found guilty of fraud in 1992 on charges he and his firm had overbilled clients. In his trial, a former partner testified that Myerson went so far as to bill his clients for dry-cleaning his toupees. Myerson was disbarred and went to federal prison for two years. Bowie Kuhn moved to Ponte Vedra, Florida, to shield his home and assets from his former law firm's bankruptcy. He died on March 15, 2007, at age 80.

Those who were around during the USFL trial retain vivid memories of the conclusion and the way Pete Rozelle comported himself after the verdict was released. "We were at practice, and one of the writers was talking to me and said, 'The USFL won the lawsuit,'" Cincinnati Bengals owner Mike Brown recalled. "I about passed out on the spot. I thought that would ruin it for us. I walked back to the dorm room at Wilmington College, our training camp. Somewhere along the way, I found out they had won but won only one dollar, times the three for the treble damages. So, they really had lost spectacularly.

"I called Pete—it might have been presumptuous—and congratulated him and thanked him for seeing us through so successfully," Brown said. "It was a very, very wearing thing for Pete. He realized if we had lost that lawsuit, the league as we knew it would have been undone."

TWENTY-SIX

STRIKES TWO AND THREE AND THEN OUT

"I think the owners' selfishness cost them the ability to overpower the players."

—MIKE PYLE, PAST PRESIDENT OF THE NFLPA, 2006

*M*ajor League Baseball in 1981 was the first professional sports organization to undergo an in-season players' strike. The bitter dispute over free-agent compensation lasted for two months, from June 12 through August 8. It wiped out 713 games and cost $146 million in lost salary, revenue, and concessions, not to mention countless dollars in goodwill. By all reckoning, the players, led by their brilliant executive director, Marvin Miller, came out big winners.

"Marvin Miller might be the consummate union leader, as Ed Garvey, to me, was not," said Jerry Vainisi, former Chicago Bears general manager and protégé of pro football pioneer George Halas. "Miller managed to steal free agency from baseball. Garvey was very militant trying to get something established. He had to be."

The National Football League Players' Association and the owners had operated in a state of "contractual" détente since 1977 when an appellate court upheld the Mackey case and they went back to the bargaining table and agreed on a contract. "We settled and thought we had modified the Rozelle Rule to have some movement of the players," Garvey said. He was soon disillusioned. "The owners had a secret meeting and in essence agreed not to follow the collective bargaining agreement and not to bid for players."

Unlike Miller and baseball after 1981, Garvey and his NFLPA in 1982 still were chasing free agency. "It finally hit me like a ton of bricks that you would never have free agency that meant anything in a closed monopoly," Garvey related. "Therefore, one had to go to a percentage of gross revenue and a wage scale to come up with anything that ever would be equitable."

Talks between the NFLPA and the NFL management council started in the winter of 1982. Pete Rozelle did not participate, as former Browns and Ravens owner Art Modell explained: "For him to be viewed as an impartial person running the whole show, he had to show no favoritism toward player or owner. It was designed that way."

Anytime a reporter asked Rozelle about labor issues, the commissioner would say his hands were tied. "Bill Curtin advised Pete as to where he could and could not inject himself," Paul Tagliabue said. Tagliabue, then with the league's outside counsel, Covington and Burling in Washington, thought Curtin had given Rozelle the wrong legal advice. "[Rozelle] was not chairing the committee. He was not a voting member. If anything, he was a sounding board and less relevant. I think it is a cyclical thing that can happen to organizations if you don't pay attention to what is happening."

Curtin's advice played into the willing hands of the management council's power-hungry lead negotiator, Jack Donlan. "Unlike Tagliabue, Rozelle never thought it was his place to be really the commissioner of all football," said Don Pierson, the *Chicago Tribune*'s veteran national football writer. "Rozelle used to tell Garvey that Jack Donlan was his liaison."

Donlan, who was 47 in 1982, was hired as NFL Management Council executive director in 1980 after 10 years with National Airlines as its labor relations head. He had the reputation of being hardnosed and antiunion. At National Airlines, he worked on 40 contracts with eight unions. Under Donlan-led bargaining strategy, the airline endured four strikes, the longest of which lasted 14 months. His presence sent a clear signal to the union that trouble lay ahead.

On September 12, Donlan, who had rejected every union demand for a pay scale rather than individual negotiations, finally called the talks "futile," saying, "Garvey wants nothing but a strike." The die was cast, and the inevitable materialized. On September 18, Garvey called for a walkout after the Monday-night game on September 20. "Remember the lights went out during that game?" Garvey prompted. "That was at halftime at Giants Stadium. They came back on 45 minutes later. Rozelle was so mad at me. 'Goddamn it, Garvey,' he said, 'leave Monday night alone.' " He added jocularly, "Can't you see Rozelle at the fuse box?" Left unanswered is the obvious question: Who did turn out the lights? "Who knows?" Garvey said. "My lips are sealed. It was an act of God."

By October 2, 12 days into the walkout, Garvey and Donlan were getting nowhere. Since day one of the strike, they had held just four hours of meetings, along with a 90-minute joint session at the bargaining table and, afterward, a nonproductive, hour-long telephone conversation.

In Washington, D.C., Senator Ted Stevens, the Alaska Republican, introduced return-to-work legislation. It called for mediated talks with the owners and, if the talks failed, binding arbitration, to last no more than 30 days. That attempt also went nowhere. The NFLPA, meanwhile, lined up the support of several unions in case the owners resorted to using replacement players, strikebreakers. The use of "scabs," as they're derogatively called by organized labor, wasn't necessary, however, because the owners got paid under the strike clause that Rozelle negotiated into the television contracts earlier that spring. That was the ultimate strike-benefit package for the NFL owners.

As September moved into October and toward November, with spectacular colors in an especially lovely autumn across the Midwest, Northeast, and through the South, Americans passed the time without pro football. The strike continued, with the issues set and hardened. "We said we never would have free bargaining, especially since they shared revenues equally," Garvey said. "There was never an economic incentive to sign a free agent. It wouldn't increase attendance, wouldn't increase TV money, wouldn't increase anything. We were a dog chasing his tail."

The initial suggestion that something had to give came in mid-November when the networks announced they had lost viewers in record numbers as people turned away from their television sets and got to know their families, visited museums, trekked to city parks, and went off on Sunday drives. CBS was down fourteen million viewers on Sundays, while NBC had lost twelve million, and ABC on Monday night was getting whacked without prime-time football, as its viewership dropped from thirty-nine million to twenty-five million. The drop-dead date to salvage the season, November 25, Thanksgiving Day, was approaching.

"Rozelle and the hardliners thought they could break us," Garvey said. "The players were getting about 15 to 20 percent of the gross revenue. We wanted 55 percent, so it would cost them billions of dollars over the course of the deal. That's why the players got behind it."

It all came together when 600 union members, about half the players in the league, met in Albuquerque to discuss the issues, especially gross revenue. "I'll never forget [Cleveland Browns quarterback] Brian Sipe saying, 'What about the stars?'" Garvey recalled.

"Dwayne O'Steen [of the Colts] said, 'Stars? When we played you, you completed one pass; I intercepted one and knocked the others down. I'm the ——— star.'

"'Oh, I wasn't thinking about me,' Sipe said, and everybody there laughed."

Garvey continued, "When you think about going on strike for free agency—the owners would say to the linemen, 'You're out on strike so the quarterbacks can make more money.' And they were right. We listened to what the owners were saying; then we turned it around. We held everybody together."

On Saturday, November 13, Pittsburgh Steelers president Dan Rooney called his NFL colleague Edward DeBartolo Jr., owner of the San Francisco 49ers, to request use of Paul Martha, vice president and general counsel of the DeBartolo family's many sports enterprises, including the 49ers and the National Hockey League's Pittsburgh Penguins, to assist in the negotiations. Prior to earning a law degree from Duquesne University, Martha was a star running back at the University of Pittsburgh and played seven years for his hometown Steelers. He was on the front line as a player in 1968 when a strike was averted in a dispute over pension money. Most important, he knew and got along well with Garvey from the time Garvey tried to organize soccer players whom Martha was advising.

Rooney sent Martha to the St. Regis Hotel, in New York, where he acted as an intermediary, not a face-to-face mediator. Shuttling between rooms where the owners and players caucused separately, Martha told each side which points would result in a final agreement. The deal was reached on Tuesday, November 16, 57 days after the strike began.

"Dan Rooney said when we finally negotiated the contract, 'You're going to get percentage of the gross. We just can't call it that,'" Garvey recalled. "Rooney said, 'You add up the amount for severance pay, minimum wage—and it all comes out to 55 percent or thereabouts.'"

"Fine," the players said. "You can call it a kangaroo so long as we get what we want."

In the spirit of keeping it low-key, Garvey sent the package to his players without a recommendation while the owners voted to return to football. The deal would run five years and enrich the players by $1.3 billion; each team would play seven more games, to total nine, counting the two played before the strike; a 16-team playoff tournament would conclude with Super Bowl XVII on January 30, 1983, at the Rose Bowl, in Pasadena; and the college draft would be extended to 1992. The 1982 NFL strike was more expensive than the 1981 baseball strike, costing the league $240 million. The union did not get its key demand, a wage scale, but the players gained higher minimum salaries and significant benefit improvements, including severance pay and an increase in major medical coverage from $250,000 to $1 million each.

After the settlement was announced, NHL president John Ziegler sent a telegram to Martha: "Congratulations. It took a hockey man to straighten out football with a hockey solution."

It was a basketball solution as well. Percentage of gross revenue has been the model for the National Basketball Association since Larry Fleischer and Bob Lanier negotiated it from 1982 to '83 with the late commissioner Larry O'Brien. "It was our model, and O'Brien followed it," Garvey said. "We produced a pamphlet that had on the front of it: 'Q. Why a percentage of the gross? A. We are the Game.'

"After it was over, Larry O'Brien called me and said, 'Get me that pamphlet, because that's what I want to do in the NBA,'" Garvey said. "I sent him a telegram saying, 'Welcome to the Socialist Party!' Larry called back and said, 'You don't understand. When you propose it, you're a Communist. When I propose it, I'm an enlightened businessman!'

"That's how Larry O'Brien used percentage of the gross to try to control the owners in the NBA," Garvey said. "The guy who was driving him crazy was Ted Stepien, in Cleveland. He was handing out these deferred-salary contracts. O'Brien said, 'You could bankrupt all of us, because we'd have to make good on those contracts.' If you limited the amount they could spend to a percentage of the gross, you could have a rational system. When we established it in '82, the NBA followed."

Ed Garvey turned over his job as executive director to NFLPA president Gene Upshaw. Garvey then returned home to Madison, where he served as Wisconsin deputy attorney general under then governor Bronson LaFollette, grandson of Fightin' Bob. He ran twice for political office as a Democrat, losing narrowly in 1986 to Bob Kasten for the U.S. Senate and, in a 1998 run for governor, by 21 percentage points to four-time incumbent Tommy Thompson. He since has practiced law in Madison.

Pete Rozelle walked away from the 57-day strike with his public esteem intact. That was owing in large part to Dallas Cowboys president Tex Schramm, his friend and mentor. "Tex provided Pete basically with a shield," Jerry Vainisi said. "Tex always was in the forefront and would take on the tough issues and force them ahead while Pete stayed above the fray."

Tex Schramm had been the point man for Rozelle since he started as commissioner and, in return, was granted wide berth to do what he wanted as a leader and detail man. Schramm had guided Rozelle through the television thicket from the beginning, did the National Football League's bidding in the merger talks and settlement with

Lamar Hunt and the American Football League, and pushed through items that have been around so long that they have been taken for granted.

In 1967, after the AFL added two wild card teams, making its postseason a week longer, Schramm persuaded the NFL, then at 16 teams, to break down into four divisions to add that extra week to the playoffs. Finally, starting in 1978, wild card games extended the playoffs by another week. The postseason month of January now features three weeks of playoffs, with a week off before the Super Bowl.

As to the playing field itself, Schramm narrowed the hash marks to align them directly with the goalposts. That made field goal kicking easier from greater distances and helped the running game, allowing sweeps from side to side. He then supported moving the standards back to the end line, to add quality to a long-distance field goal attempt at a time when soccer-style kickers made a 40-yard attempt a virtual chip shot. In addition, he made the field safer by replacing end-zone flags, which carried the danger of puncturing kidneys and lungs and putting out eyes, with foam pylon markers. He also put ribbons on goalposts to let kickers and fans judge wind direction. As previously discussed, Schramm chaired the Competition Committee when it outlawed bump and run, the major change that opened up the offenses.

Then there was 1974, when a little piece of technology came along to bring the fan in the stadium and the viewer at home directly into the action: the referee's microphone. Art McNally was supervisor of officials when Schramm buttonholed him during a Competition Committee meeting. "What do you think about putting a microphone on the referee?" Schramm asked.

"Oh, Tex," McNally said, "I don't want to do that. You know how I feel. I want to keep my men in the background. They do what they have to do. The referee signals when he has to but stays in the background. The players are most important."

"Art, there are times that something happens down on the field and only the officials know what it is," Schramm said. "You can give all the signals you want, but the people in the press box don't know; the people in the stands don't know; the people watching TV don't know."

McNally agreed to give it a whirl. When he returned to New York, he called on NBC Sports executive producer Scotty Connal to discuss the technology involved. A representative from a company called Hollywood Sound was there. "Sure, we do this all the time," the man said. "We can put a transmitter on the official. It will be about the size of a pack of cigarettes."

The next question was where it would go. To protect the transmitter in case the official got knocked down, McNally and the sound technician decided to put the device on the belt line, and because most people are right-handed, it went on the right side. "Look, I'm a neophyte when it comes to that stuff," McNally said, "but there is one thing I ask for. That is, I need a *single* pole switch. Not a button, not something you have to rub. A single pole switch, where up is On and down is Off."

No problem there, the sound expert said. "We can do that." Before then, the referee made the ball spot between plays. Because the ref now had to make the announcements as well as signal the crowd, McNally designated the umpire, the crew member next in seniority, as the ball spotter. Also, the umpire was charged with looking at the referee to ensure that the ref switched off his microphone after an announcement.

They ran a test with veteran referee Bernie Ullman in Buffalo at a preseason game pairing the Bills and Rams. "They would run a tape, and the sound from the microphone would go only to the production truck, not over the public-address system," McNally said.

Ninety minutes before kickoff, McNally went to the officials' dressing room to get Ullman wired. The Hollywood Sound tech was nowhere in sight. Finally, five minutes before the officials took the field, McNally found the man standing by the NBC production truck. "He probably didn't know where to go. So, I grabbed him and pulled him into the dressing room," McNally said.

To install the microphone, the sound tech had to cut Ullman's shirt on the side. "I thought Bernie was going to have a heart attack," McNally recalled. "We had to push the microphone through with the wires. He got that on, and out the officials went." McNally carefully instructed Ullman to follow normal procedures—call penalties, point to the teams, signal the crowd, and anything else he had to do.

A thoroughly confused Ullman was unable to do anything. "Twice in the first half, running backs were illegally in motion, which was Bernie's responsibility to call," McNally said. "He didn't throw a flag at all. It was obvious he was thinking about the mike instead of the game. He had trouble going to his waist, and this was probably confusing him. At halftime, the little guy from Hollywood Sound said, 'Mr. McNally, your referee just took the microphone off.'"

McNally was taken aback. "What?" he asked.

"Your referee just took the microphone off," the sound expert said.

"I got up out of my chair and went down the elevator and then walked to the field," McNally related. "Just as I got to the tunnel, Bernie and the crew were coming out. 'Go back,' I ordered. And he went back and got rewired. I knew this would affect a lot of our referees. When the game was over, I got the tape from the TV truck."

McNally and his associates, Jack Reeder and Nick Skorich, viewed the test in the NFL offices the following Monday morning. "As soon as it got to 9 A.M. in California, I called Hollywood Sound and said, 'I want to order 15 switches,'" McNally recalled.

"What?"

"I want 15 switches," McNally reiterated. "I don't need the transmitters or anything else you have. Just get me 15 switches."

McNally related, "I got them by Wednesday and sent every referee a switch. From that point on, every referee had a switch that he tucked into his belt to his waist. Every time, the umpire was watching. They did it the entire preseason and into the season. Nobody knew about it."

Everything was for real on Thanksgiving Day at Tiger Stadium, in Detroit, where the Lions played host to the Denver Broncos before 51,000 fans in the ballpark and millions of viewers watching NBC and its top announce crew, Curt Gowdy and Al DeRogatis. McNally told producer-director Ted Nathanson what to expect. "We asked them to 'try and tell your announcers working the game that when the referee comes out to give a signal, just hold it for a second, 'cause you're going to hear what he had to say about a penalty.'"

"What?"

"Scotty Connal apparently didn't tell them much about what was going on," McNally recalled. "It was a shock, but it worked and has been great ever since. Commissioner Rozelle knew this would be great for public relations, to give the information to the fans in the stands and at home. This was a great innovation, and he was very much in favor of it. The big thing was, lost in the shuffle, that the idea came from Tex Schramm. He was the guy."

Now that Schramm had the game looking smart for the fans in the stands and at home, he began to devote his attention to the newfound strength the players had gained out of the 1982 strike. He, Tampa Bay owner Hugh Culverhouse, and Donlan, their attack dog, started planning for collective bargaining in 1987. In it for the long run, Donlan would use the owners' 1982 face-off with the NFLPA to learn about his foe the next time they met across the bargaining table.

While they plotted strategy, the league enjoyed unprecedented success on the field, at the box office, and in the television ratings as three old-line NFC franchises came alive to add spice and dominate the rarefied air at the top. The Washington Redskins emerged from the 1982 strike to win Super Bowl XVII behind the masterful coaching of Joe Gibbs; a massive, mobile, hostile, and talented offensive line nicknamed the "Hogs"; a colorful Hall of Fame running back named John Riggins, a fun-loving throwback to the pioneer days; and a swift, talented, fast-receiving corps that quickly gained the name the "Fun Bunch."

The Los Angeles version of the Raiders had their last hurrah in 1983, the last time an AFC team would win until Denver beat Green Bay in 1998. The 1984 San Francisco 49ers proved that their 1981 Super Bowl championship season was no fluke as coach Bill Walsh's superb organization and Joe Montana's magnificent quarterback play led them to an 18–1 record climaxed by a 38–14 rout of Miami in Super Bowl XIX, at Stanford.

The Niners beat the wounded Chicago Bears 23–0 in the NFC championship game at Candlestick Park. That defeat enraged a Chicago franchise whose owner and coach for 40 seasons, George Halas, founded the league in 1920 and dominated it with seven titles in the first 40 years. In fact, in 2007, it still was the league's winningest franchise with the most Hall of Famers, 26. Halas died at age 88 in 1983 as his team, stocked at every position with superior players, was gearing up for a run.

Halas left the club to his heirs, daughter Virginia McCaskey and her children, led by Halas's eldest grandson, Michael. Halas left control of the team itself to two trusted men in their early forties, general manager Jerry Vainisi and head coach Mike Ditka, the tight end who had led the Bears to their 1963 title. Bill Walsh has said the Bears should have won three or four Super Bowls in the late '80s. Injuries and Michael McCaskey's meddling, with his ultimate firing of Vainisi and later Ditka, foiled the Halas plan. Notwithstanding, the Bears did win in 1985 with the most dominant single-season performance in league history, especially on defense.

"In '84, in my opinion, it boiled down to one game and one player," Vainisi said over lunch in late winter 2006. "The game was the Raiders game. We lost five players for the season. They lost seven. We lost Jim McMahon with a lacerated kidney. If we had McMahon in San Francisco, we would have won that game. I think we would have won Super Bowls in '84, '85, and '86, three in a row—possibly in '87. We still had Wilber Marshall." Marshall and the Giants' Lawrence Taylor, he noted, were the two best outside linebackers in the league. "I did a four-year deal—three and an option," Vainisi said. "They lost Marshall, then [speed receiver Willie] Gault and more players, without replacing them. Up to that point, that team was capable of winning the Super Bowl every year."

The '85 Bears reeled off a 12-game winning streak to open the season. The big wins came at San Francisco, when they beat the defending champion 49ers 26–10, and then, in game 10, at Dallas, when they destroyed the Cowboys 44–0. The streak ended on a Monday night in the Orange Bowl, when the Dolphins won 38–24 to honor the glory of Don Shula's undefeated 1972 champions, who won all 17 of their games. The Bears rebounded to enter the playoffs at 15–1.

All season long, when quarterback Jim McMahon came to the sidelines and removed his helmet, fans in the television audience saw him wearing a white headband plugging Adidas. When it was time for the playoffs, the league informed McMahon that he was violating the policy against commercializing a nonapproved product. So,

McMahon wore a new headband with his own custom-designed logo: "Rozelle."

"Rozelle actually liked that," Vainisi said. "McMahon's headband with 'Rozelle' made Pete laugh even more. From that standpoint, Pete enjoyed it, plus it gave personality to the league."

McMahon thrived as the Bears shut out both the Giants, by a score of 21–0, and the Rams, 24–0, to march into New Orleans, where they routed the New England Patriots 46–10 in Super Bowl XX. "That team was completely full of personality, which reflected in the television ratings," Vainisi said. NBC's rating was 48.3, meaning the telecast reached more than forty-one million households—41,490,000 in round numbers. It is the third most watched Super Bowl, after Super Bowls XVI and XVII.

After the Bears took a 23–3 lead into halftime, NBC's host Bob Costas was caught short when writer Pete Axthelm came on to the set. "It's like men playing boys," Axthelm said. Costas did not kick Axthelm under the table, but he probably wanted to.

"When you get a game that's so lopsided, and that game was lopsided early, people stop watching," former NBC game analyst Merlin Olsen said. "To me as a broadcaster, that was my greatest challenge. I went into every game I ever did prepared to handle a blowout on either side. I never needed the 'yellow pages,' the legal pad with all that stuff." Costas need not have worried, however. Viewership did not drop off that day. That Bears team was that special.

"At the league meeting the following March, Pete asked the owners and GMs to rise and give the Bears a standing ovation for bringing the fun back to football and for the interesting dynamic that, in particular, brought women to watch the sport, because of the personalities," Vainisi said. "That year [1985] was a hugely successful year for the NFL. To this day, I run into people all the time who say, 'That team made my wife a fan of the NFL.' For instance, she loved Gary Fencik. If you were fat, you had the Fridge. We had somebody for everybody: Walter Payton—any size, shape, creed, or color you could relate to. We had them all."

After seeing how well instant replay had worked in the USFL, the National Football League opened the bottle in 1986 and let the genie out. "From the time I went in, there always was some individual who wanted instant replay," Art McNally said. "We now could use television facilities on every play. When it first came out, I had a number of people say, 'It's going to be tough on your officials.' I told them, 'This is going to show how good the officials really are: when things happen so quickly on the field, the extreme high percentage of accuracy they have will show you that they really are fine officials.'"

Instant replay went down in flames in 1992, but it would return to stay in 1999 with a more encompassing role. "The next thing was, why doesn't the league use replay to correct errors that people can see at home?" McNally said. "It does work well."

The New York Giants worked extremely well in 1986 as Bill Parcells put together their first championship team in three decades. Lawrence Taylor led a strong defense, and quarterback Phil Simms improved every week in a 17–2 season. He ended with a postseason-record 23 of 25 passes for 268 yards and three touchdowns, to lead the Giants to a 39–20 romp over John Elway's Denver Broncos in Super Bowl XXI.

The Bears and Giants did not meet in '86, but ABC didn't miss the opportunity to pair them in the '87 season opener on September 15 with a Monday-night blockbuster at Soldier Field. McMahon was hurt, but his replacement, Mike Tomczak, passed for 292 yards to lead a 416-yard offense. A savage pass rush, led by linemen Richard Dent and Dan Hampton and linebackers Otis Wilson, Mike Singletary, and Marshall, sacked Simms seven times and his backup Jeff Rutledge an eighth. It would be the last memorable moment on an NFL playing field for weeks.

Negotiations on a new labor contract, by owner design, had been dead in the water for months. "The management council turned to Jack Donlan, the strikebreaker," Mike Pyle said. Pyle, as NFLPA president in 1968, had led the drive to register the association as a union with the National Labor Relations Board. "Donlan, a hard-ass strikebreaker, really beat up Gene Upshaw. He took him to task. Donlan was not going to give in. They had the scabs. The scabs were a terrible thing, in violation of the NLRB."

The specter of scabs that had loomed five years ago now appeared in bodily form, going by the term "replacements," of course, among league officialdom. This time around, the league needed them because, after the situation in 1982 when it got network money despite losing games to the strike, the networks got smart. Under the new television deals, the networks would not pay when the league did not play. "Jim Finks, Tex Schramm, and other hard-liners were part of the management council," the *Chicago Tribune*'s Don Pierson said. "It was Schramm's idea to have the replacement players in '87. I used to argue with Finks that people came to watch Walter Payton.

" 'Bullshit,' Finks said. 'They come to watch football, the Bears. Players come and go. The numbers come and go.'

"That was the argument all those guys made," Pierson said. "They could afford to make it because there was no free agency. If you were lucky enough to make the league, you were owned by your team in perpetuity. Garvey was the guy who said, 'Without us, there is no game.' Finks, who was a player himself, was against that notion. I could see both sides of the argument. In football, you have any number of candidates to play football. It's not like baseball and does not require the skill level of the other sports. So, your labor pool is much wider. You could play with a bunch of fat old policemen in the park."

After a week to get a new crop of players organized and worked into some semblance of conditioning, and to allow them to learn and practice a few plays, the "replacement" games began. Union solidarity was virtually nonexistent. Upshaw had no cards to play and nothing of value to prevent his athletes from crossing the picket line. A total of 86 regular players returned to camp by Friday, October 2, among them Ed "Too Tall" Jones, the Dallas defensive end. Jones came in after one of Schramm's minions in the Cowboys organization told him he was jeopardizing the deferred-annuity payment in his contract if he remained out.

Fans, running counter to Finks's theorizing, had turned in more than 300,000 tickets for refunds. Those who bothered to come saw ragged play that ran from shoddy to poor to worse. Just 12,370 went to Giants Stadium on October 4. Dave Anderson was forced to sit in the press box to cover the game for the *New York Times*. "Imposters in Dallas Cowboy uniforms grounded the winless Jets, 38–24," Anderson wrote. "Tex Schramm, the Cowboys' president, had promised 'competitive, exciting' football in what amounts to rookie scrimmages that count in the standings. But it was more compost than competitive." Nevertheless, the banks accepted the money the teams deposited.

Washington Redskins coach Joe Gibbs, clearly dismayed, protected his regulars, all of whom stayed out, by not commenting on the strike. His regulars appreciated that stance. "Gibbs won both of those strike years, 1982 and 1987," Don Pierson wrote. "He was smart enough to use the scabs to his advantage. In Chicago, Ditka lost the team."

Captain and union rep Mike Singletary kept his Bears in line and away from Halas Hall. Like the Redskins, not one Bear broke ranks. The "spare Bears," as the Chicago newspapers called them, had won their first two of the three games they would play without the regulars, when coach Ditka popped off with postgame words that resulted in killing his relationship with the regulars. "These are the *real* Bears," Iron Mike said.

Jerry Vainisi, whom McCaskey had fired after the Bears lost to Washington in the 1986 playoffs, now was working in Detroit for the Lions, unable to counsel his friend. "Here he grew up in Aliquippa, Pennsylvania, a union town, and his dad was a local leader at the mill," Vainisi said. "You can't accuse Mike of always doing the smart thing. That ultimately led to Ditka's demise with the players."

"They still threw those replacement games out there for three weeks and broke the strike," Don Pierson recalled. "It would have been interesting to see, if the main players never had come back, if the attendance would have come back again. It's not like you're up there striking out every time or missing baskets. In football, the skill level is just not as high. Or take golf: if you're out there shooting bogies, not good. In football, the average fan sees a bunch of fat guys out there running into each other."

Gene Upshaw made one final pitch for some form of free agency, one the obstinate Schramm could not nor would not abide. As Upshaw told it to Bob St. John in *Tex*, Schramm screamed at him across the bargaining table: "You're not going to get it! You're not going to get it in five years, you're not going to get it in ten years, you're not going to *ever* get it. Don't you see? You're the cattle. We're the ranchers!"

On October 15, 1987, the player reps voted to end the strike and send the players back to work. On that same day, the NFLPA filed an antitrust suit in a Minnesota federal court. What would be known as the *Marvin Powell* case, in reference to the NFLPA president at that time, challenged the owners' intent to maintain the right of first refusal in the compensation system. It was the first new round in seeking free agency. The strike was over, but the owners retaliated against the NFLPA for filing the suit by keeping the veterans out of work. That forced those players to miss a third paycheck. In response, the association turned to the National Labor Relations Board and accused the league of using unfair labor practices. The NLRB issued a complaint against the owners, charging that they had discriminated against striking players.

"After the replacement games, when Pete was trying to figure a way to bring the union back to the table, the two people he was relying on most were Dan Rooney and Jim Finks," Paul Tagliabue recalled. "That irritated Hugh Culverhouse to no end because he thought Pete was butting in where he didn't belong. Pete thought the replacement games were an affront to the public and certainly thought they were an affront to the television networks and to their viewers and advertisers."

For the immediate future, the players had to lick their wounds and return to play football. Joe Gibbs's Redskins regrouped and overcame an early two-touchdown lead at frigid Soldier Field to beat the Bears 21–17 in their NFC playoff. Defeated in his final game, Walter Payton sat on the bench after the closing gun, his head in his hands, weeping at the awareness that his brilliant career was over.

"I think that certainly Pete encouraged me and was candid in saying that, with the benefit of hindsight, it had been a mistake to let the management council get out of the league office," Tagliabue said. "By '87, '88, '89, the management council actually had its own office on

Fifth Avenue. They were really separate from the league. Pete said that was a mistake."

"You have to get control of the management council, and you have to deal directly with the head of the Players' Association," Rozelle told Tagliabue.

Culverhouse, Tagliabue noted, "had disappointed Pete because he really didn't seem to be passionate about winning down in Tampa." He added, "They locked horns a lot on the labor stuff."

Tagliabue continued, "One of the things that again irritated Culverhouse and Schramm in '87 was that Pete was talking with Gene Upshaw. Pete and Gene got awfully close. Gene told me a wonderful story about a meeting they had, which Rozelle called to try to pull a deal together. Upshaw felt that Pete was trying very hard with him to get something done and was forcing Culverhouse and Schramm to sit in the room and talk about getting something done."

Then, in January 1989, just before Super Bowl XXIII in Miami, Carrie Rozelle's 26-year-old son Jack Kent Cooke II was found dead in his small apartment in Glendale, California, eight miles north of downtown Los Angeles. It was initially believed that the young Cooke, who was known as a heavy drug user and beset with massive learning disabilities, committed suicide. An autopsy revealed that he had alcoholic liver disease and a chronic heart condition. It was a painful and difficult episode for the Rozelle family.

When Rozelle returned to the office, he resumed the dialogue with Upshaw. "Pete was saying Upshaw was the person you could talk to, and you are going to have to deal with him directly and make it your priority and not leave it to others, not leave it to a committee which you are not the chairman of or a member of," Tagliabue said.

The league held its 1989 winter meetings that March at the Marriott Desert Springs Resort, in Palm Desert, California. On Wednesday, March 22, Ernie Accorsi, then general manager of the Cleveland Browns, was about to leave for lunch when his boss, Art Modell, took him aside and told him to assemble the management team—attorney Jim Bailey, Kevin Byrne, and coach Marty Schottenheimer—for lunch. "You didn't usually do that at a league meeting," Accorsi said. "We were having lunch outside, and Art said, 'Listen, I just wanted to tell you that Pete's resigning in the afternoon session; he asked me, Wellington Mara, Leon Hess, and Dan Rooney to come up to his suite, and he told us.' Among the owners, they were the only people he told."

The meeting resumed after lunch in executive session. Modell told Accorsi to stand at the back of the room. "You worked for him. It's going to be an historic moment," Modell said before they entered the room.

"I was in the room sitting at this long horseshoe table," Tom Flores recalled. In 1989, Flores was president and general manager of the Seattle Seahawks. "Pete was in the front. I looked up, and nobody was paying special attention, and he called it to order. He started talking, and then he started crying. I looked up and was watching this. On one side was Lamar Hunt; on the other was Wellington Mara. I said, "I wonder what they are going to discuss."

"Pete was very brief, and he broke. He later broke at the press conference, and he got up and walked out of the room," Accorsi recalled. He didn't say, 'OK, let's go on with business.'"

"The insiders knew, but I was shocked," said Jerry Vainisi, who was representing the Detroit Lions at the meeting. "Then he said he would stay on until a replacement was found."

"All of a sudden, everybody became quiet, and he was announcing that he was retiring," Flores said. "He turned it over to the presidents of the two conferences. Then he got up. Everybody was in shock. One of my owners said, 'He can't do that.'"

"As I was watching, he walked to the right and to the back right-corner exit," Ernie Accorsi said. "Al Davis always sat in the last seat at the end. As Pete approached, Al got up, intercepted him, and shook his hand. I couldn't hear what he said, but what a dramatic moment. I just felt overwhelmed by the moment."

Tom Flores also was struck. "As he was walking out, he walked to my left," Flores said. "I was on the left side of the room. The first guy who got up and gave him a hug was Al—the first guy. At that point, they were all applauding, and we all stood up. He was a legend. He was leaving, and everybody was stunned. I don't know that anybody knew this was coming."

"At the beginning of the two o'clock session, I, a nobody, walked up to him sitting alone," Accorsi said. "Others had talked to him, and I went up to him and said, 'I don't know what to say to you, but I do know that every day, we should thank the Lord that you made this league what it has been for us to work in.'

" 'I'll always remember your calmness and your sound judgment,' Rozelle replied. There are friends of mine who would fall over and faint at that comment," Accorsi said. "Then he looked at me and asked, 'What exact years were you with us?' "

"Seventy-five and '76," Accorsi answered.

"Boy, does time fly," Rozelle said.

"I remember every word he said," Accorsi maintained. "I have three notes of his framed, plus the last cigar Art Rooney gave to me, encased over my bookcase. They're all handwritten and personal."

"I respected him," Tom Flores said, measuring his words. "I thought he was a great commissioner. He was perfect for the times. We all have a passion for this game. When you have a passion for the game, you do what you think is right for the game. Like I said, it's a unique profession, because you're trying to get along with your friends. As George Young always said, 'The enemy is in this room.' "

TWENTY-SEVEN

PASSING—AND THE REAL INHERITANCE

"You can see how it took its toll. You could see it in his demeanor. He was tired. Just not the same."

—Don Pierson, 2006

$\mathcal{J}$oel Bussert, the National Football League's senior vice president for player personnel, was hired by Pete Rozelle in 1975. Since then, he has been the clearinghouse for every trade and has been held in high esteem by each commissioner he has served, from Rozelle to Paul Tagliabue and, now, Roger Goodell. When Rozelle stepped down as commissioner on March 22, 1989, everyone was caught short. "I was not anticipating it when it happened. I did not see it coming," Bussert said. "He had been commissioner since I'd been there and commissioner almost as long as I had been following pro football."

"I didn't want to die in office like Bert Bell did before me," Rozelle said in an interview with *Sports Illustrated*'s Paul Zimmerman on March 23, the day after his retirement announcement. "I'm 63," Rozelle said that day, adding, "I can't remember the last time Carrie and I had a real vacation. I've got to get out while I can enjoy some years without stress."

Carrie Rozelle told Zimmerman that her husband's life had boiled down to spending his days testifying in depositions or, when he wasn't doing that, meeting with attorneys who had no understanding of sports, let alone football. "He'd come home at night, go to bed at 11:30—he always wanted to watch the 11 o'clock news—and two hours later he'd be up, roaming around, smoking one cigarette after another, working things out on a legal pad." A two-pack-a-day habit really was three, with all the late nights. Thus, with two years and nine months left in his latest term, Rozelle decided to walk away from the job he had held and loved for 29 years.

Stress had been Rozelle's constant companion for a decade that saw Al Davis's defiant actions lead to the move of his Raiders from Oakland to Los Angeles; two players' strikes sandwiched around the United States Football League; and a series of court cases demanding lengthy preparation and testimony, week after week, month after month, year after year. The topper was the unexpected death of stepson Jack Kent Cooke III in January 1989.

"I wonder how much the stress shortened his life," daughter Anne Marie Rozelle Bratton said in 2006. "When you can never leave a courtroom and are constantly battling on the defense, and owners in your own league are battling away—everywhere you look, arrows are coming at you—it's hard to be constantly thinking ahead, when you have to be defensive instead of offensive. It wears you out."

The notion of retirement did not strike Rozelle like some lightning bolt in the night. He dropped hints here and there, often through Carrie. "There were a few occasions when we had dinner with him and Carrie in '87 or '88," Paul Tagliabue said. "Carrie usually was the one who would say, 'Pete's not going to do this forever. You are going to be in the center of the mix going forward.' He would never say, 'You are going to be the next commissioner.' He pretty much deferred to her and played his cards close to the vest."

"He had to be a lawyer of sorts all the time," Anne Marie said. "Being deposed and in the courtroom was not where he was best. He was at his best thinking, where do you want to take the league? How can we make it better?"

By the time he had enough, Rozelle felt a deep weariness from lack of rest, lack of sleep, too many cigarettes. "Is that all there is to life—

work, die, and never experience retirement?" Rozelle said to Zimmerman, as reported in the April 3, 1989, *SI* piece, "He Quit, for Pete's Sake." He got out because he realized that no longer could he get anything done.

What Rozelle did not tell Zimmerman, or anyone else in the media, was revealed by Howard Cosell in 1991 in *What's Wrong with Sports*. According to Cosell, Rozelle realized he had used up his credit with the owners when, on January 22, 1989, the morning of Super Bowl XXIII, he held a labor meeting in which he tried to offer a free-agency concession to the players to end the long, destructive labor dispute. NFLPA executive director Gene Upshaw later told Cosell, "Pete was ready to make us a deal which would have been acceptable to the union, but Hugh Culverhouse killed it on the spot, rebuffed Rozelle, and said he was finished as commissioner." According to Upshaw's recollection, Culverhouse, Tampa Bay's powerful owner and leader of the six-member executive committee of owners, told Rozelle, "Hell, no, we are not making that deal. We are going to crush this damn union."

Culverhouse's penetrating barbs came as Cleveland Browns owner Art Modell was rallying an insurgency to challenge his rule over the management council. "The owners were a house divided," Zimmerman wrote in his April 1989 *Sports Illustrated* piece.

Rozelle had gained weight, maybe 20 or 30 pounds, after he quit smoking, which was close to the time of his retirement, and he no longer sported the perpetual tan that had been his hallmark. He could see the results in the mirror when he shaved, watery eyes and all, and he did not like it. Tom Flores spotted something else at the retirement announcement and paid careful attention every time he saw him afterward. "I also noticed that year, and I mentioned to someone, that there was something not right about Pete," Flores said. "He was always eloquent; now he was stumbling over words. It was early signs. I think he knew it, and unfortunately, it happened."

"I think he had a ministroke then, that he recovered from completely," Anne Marie Bratton said in 2006. But that "incident" foreshadowed the real health troubles.

The commissioner had made at least a tentative decision the previous October to hang it up. He first informed Carrie and then told

Anne Marie and his four stepchildren. Zimmerman reported that Rozelle met with the two New York owners—Wellington Mara, of the Giants, and Leon Hess, of the Jets—in Hess's office on March 14, a week before the league meeting, to work out a consultant's contract. In 2006, a source close to Rozelle confided to me that the commissioner actually balked at the opportunity to negotiate certain favorable provisions in the contract. "No, it's not fair. I don't want to ask for it," Rozelle told a friend, who did not want to speak for the record.

"Pete, I can get you a really good deal," the friend said. "You should get it now. But promise me, if you're not going to do that, before you announce, tell me, so I can negotiate something."

"At the last minute, he told me no," the friend said. "I could have gotten him so much more. He wouldn't let me do it in advance. He wanted to make the announcement. He wanted to go out that way. He didn't care about the money. He wasn't interested."

"I'm just guessing that Rozelle, being human, got tired," the *Chicago Tribune*'s Don Pierson said. "The last 10 years pecked away at his legacy. I remember writing that he had lost a little off his fastball. Joe Browne got pretty upset at me, but it was true. My intention in the piece was to point out why he didn't have the influence or control that he had in the '60s and '70s."

Finding a successor was the top agenda item. A Jack Kemp boomlet rose early and collapsed just as quickly. Kemp still was seeking high political office. So, it boiled down to a single name, the choice of the old guard and league establishment: the highly competent career football man Jim Finks.

Finks, a coal miner's son from Salem, Illinois, who was a T-formation quarterback at Tulsa University, was a man without a position in 1949 when he joined the league's only team that still employed the single wing, the Pittsburgh Steelers. So, he played defensive back until 1952 when Art Rooney hired a new coach, Joe Bach, who junked the single wing and installed Finks at quarterback. He played through the 1955 season, quit in 1956 to coach at Notre Dame under Terry Brennan, and then moved to Canada to run football teams.

"*Reader's Digest* used to have this series called 'The Most Unforgettable Character I've Ever Met.' I've often thought of that when I think of Jim Finks," said Bill McGrane, Finks's longtime associate in Minnesota and Chicago. "He's one of those people who, had he been in the army, would have been a general. Had Jim been a doctor, he would have been a great success. He had that quality about him that inspired people, even casual friends."

Finks returned to the NFL in 1964 as general manager of the Minnesota Vikings and built them into a perennial contender, installing fellow Canadian League alum Bud Grant as coach. He left the Vikings in 1973 to work for the league and then, a year later, became chief operating officer and general manager of the Chicago Bears. "Mugs shouted at his father, 'You've got to get someone in here,'" McGrane said. "Then came Finks. After the Bears won Super Bowl XX, the first thing Mike Ditka said was, 'Let's not forget who put this team together.'"

Finks left the Bears in 1983 to become president of the Chicago Cubs in 1984. He quit a year later and returned to football in 1986 as vice president and general manager of the New Orleans Saints. A chain-smoker like Rozelle, Finks was a formidable negotiator, was antiplayer in labor situations, and was concerned with the game on the field.

Finks was mentor, tutor, and friend to Jerry Vainisi, who joined the Bears as controller in 1972 and became his successor as vice president and general manager in 1983. "In my opinion, he's the one who should have been commissioner," Vainisi said. "I'm not saying that later on you don't go to Paul Tagliabue. I like him." Tagliabue was a year ahead of Vainisi at Georgetown. Vainisi added, "I strongly felt, but I didn't have a voice, that the league needed to name Finks for five years. Let Finks conduct long-range planning to determine how they could generate more revenue and learn where the league was going on the playing field. That way, they could better protect the integrity of the game while they satisfied the younger generation that wanted more money for themselves."

"Jim had great support for commissioner," McGrane said. "I think his support was among the senior clubs, not the younger guys. For a while in the voting, he had the support of Art Modell in Cleveland, Buffalo's Ralph Wilson, McCaskey's Bears, Mara's Giants, and Rooney's Steelers for certain." Other prominent Finks backers included two men who had challenged Rozelle, the Raiders' Al Davis and Carrie's former father-in-law, Jack Kent Cooke, of Washington. Finks had the support of 16 owners. He needed 19 votes, a two-thirds majority.

"You had a coalition of foes," Vainisi said, "Mike Lynn in Minnesota; Eddie DeBartolo in San Francisco; Jerry Jones, then a brand-new owner in Dallas; Pat Bowlen in Denver; Robert Irsay of Indianapolis; Georgia Frontiere of the Rams; and Tampa Bay's Hugh Culverhouse, among them." The antiaxis numbered a dozen in all.

"They were upset that the younger owners had been excluded from the search group that included Mara, Modell, and the old cronies of Rozelle, the old guard," Vainisi said. "They felt they lacked representation in the selection process. So, when the committee came back with one name, Jim Finks, they blocked it by one vote. Jim was not going to campaign for the job. They formed a coalition to block him."

The owners met at the O'Hare Hilton in Chicago on July 5, 1989, on a day when a freak summer thunderstorm delayed flights, several of them carrying representatives to the meeting. Without a quorum, the vote could not be taken. That gave the anti-Finks coalition the time they needed to maneuver. The Finks backers took two ballots on July 6 and quit when it came up short. "Jerry Jones and the new guard blocked it," Don Pierson said.

They tried again in Dallas on October 10–11. Four more ballots failed to produce a winner. "It became apparent Finks was not going to get it, so the rest of them, Modell and the old guard, came around, and it went to Tagliabue," Pierson said.

"I told Finks after Paul got the deal, 'I know you won't agree with me, but I'm glad you didn't get it,'" Bill McGrane related. "I didn't see Jim in that role." Finks returned to New Orleans to run the Saints. He died from lung cancer on May 8, 1994, three months shy of his 67th birthday. He was voted into the Pro Football Hall of Fame the following winter.

"The coalition was formed primarily by new owners who had large mortgages on their franchises," Vainisi explained. "They felt the commissioner needed to have a sensitivity to their problems and that the search committee to find a successor was comprised of old-line clubs that did not have that financial situation. They were looking for new revenue sources. They felt that Pete left more money on the table in the television negotiations, and they needed to get more out of television and other sponsorship situations."

Rozelle would not have been upset had Finks won, but his sympathies lay with the winner, Paul Tagliabue. "Dad was happy," Anne Marie Bratton said. "He wanted Paul to take the position after he did, and I'm sure Dad would be—very sure he'd be—beyond thrilled that Roger Goodell got it now. It's great the league has kept a man with experience with league relationships."

"I didn't know in advance," Paul Tagliabue said. "They looked like they were pretty much at loggerheads. Rozelle called me and told me to come to Cleveland, that I pretty much had the votes." On the 12th ballot, taken October 26, Tagliabue was elected the National Football League's fifth commissioner since its 1920 founding.

"We had a month of transition lunches and conversations in late October–early November of 1989, where he was still around and in the city a lot," Tagliabue said. "To some degree, it focused on the upcoming television negotiations, which were an immediate priority because the contracts were expiring at the end of that '89 season. The broader conversation focused on the league structure—the fact that the management council had gotten away, the fact that NFL Properties was not well integrated into what the rest of the league was doing. Its presence as a promotional vehicle was growing, and it was not really coordinated with the networks, so people were kind of running into each other."

The transfer of power became official on Sunday, November 5, at 12:01 A.M. Now that Paul Tagliabue had the scepter and mace, he went right to work. "For many years, everything Properties brought in was going to NFL Charities. As sport sponsorships and naming rights started to become greater opportunities, Properties was growing," Tagliabue said. "Properties was not really integrated with the TV advertisers. It was not integrated with what he thought was really important. We discussed a lot of those structural issues. After I became commissioner, we got through a resolution that changed the structure of the management council. Those were big concerns of his."

The owners still held tenuous control of the labor situation as Tagliabue entered office, with the action on that front now in the federal courts in Minnesota. In late January 1988, federal judge David Doty ruled in favor of the players in the Marvin Powell case. Certain they would prevail, the owners appealed to the Eighth Circuit Court of Appeals. To hedge their bets and take a safe position in the marketplace of opinion, the owners implemented something they called Plan B. Plan B ordered the teams to maintain a "restricted list" of 37 players under the first right of refusal compensation system. The remaining unprotected roster players then could sign with another team *without restriction* between February 1 and April 1. That allowed the teams to keep their stars even as they claimed they were allowing a form of free agency.

The licensing fees garnered by the NFLPA, which increased from $2 million in 1988 to $11 million in 1990, were enough to keep their litigation active on several fronts. They needed that because on November 1, 1989, the Eighth Circuit Court of Appeals reversed Judge Doty's ruling for the players and stated that players with union representation had no right under antitrust law to sue the owners, nor could they gain trebled damages in court victories.

"Gene was smart enough to know they were breaking lots of laws, but he couldn't sue anybody. So he decertified," Mike Pyle said. That was November 3, 1989. The player reps met in Dallas on December 5 to end the NFLPA as a union. "The NFLPA was an association, and nobody knew how many players would support it. They all could have run or they could support it. He asked for dues. He went to court. Eventually they beat the owners in every court case."

When Tagliabue entered office, he had no television contracts and no labor deal, the union was about to decertify, and the ownership was fragmented. "Looking back, it was not the ideal place to come in where I came in," he said. In one of his first acts, he cut the legs out from under the recalcitrant management council and took personal control of both labor and NFL Properties without firing a shot. Then, on March 12, 1990, the new commissioner announced contracts with ABC, CBS, and NBC and split Sunday-night packages between ESPN and Turner Sports worth a record $3.6 billion. Money, as it always does, talked, and nobody dared challenge him then or ever again.

"You can give Tagliabue credit if you want," Don Pierson said, as preface to registering his own opinion. "The way the league has operated in the last 20 years since 1986 is a vindication of everything that Rozelle did," Pierson declared. "After the rough spot in the '80s, except for free agency, which likely was inevitable, nothing has changed. They've maintained their visionary revenue sharing, everything that Rozelle stood for. It's still, to my way of thinking, Rozelle's league. Tagliabue has done his part in maintaining it, but it's Rozelle's legacy. Definitely."

Pierson's might be an understated view of the power Tagliabue found and exerted. What Tagliabue did was something akin to the way Lyndon Johnson executed John F. Kennedy's blueprint, but, unlike LBJ, Tagliabue did not get mired down in another war.

Free agency was a singular piece of unfinished business that Tagliabue had to address and resolve. The NFLPA had decertified and gone to court. The association's first challenge was the owners' Plan B, which freed players at the bottom of the roster. Clubs could protect 37 players and hold them to the long-standing right-of-first-refusal policy, which meant free agency still did not exist.

Mike Pyle, who served as NFLPA president in 1967 and early '68, has analyzed this issue from stem to stern for years. Pyle has contributed a loud voice in the old-timers' battle with Gene Upshaw and the current union leadership to gain better pensions for men who played in his era and before, many of whom are dealing with serious physical and mental health issues from taking too many hits on too many football fields.

Pyle vividly recalls his first big joint negotiating session with ownership in 1965 when George Halas and the other owners held absolute power. "We got into licensing revenue," Pyle said. "We wanted television money for pensions. Modell made his money in television. Murchison knew money cold. Edward Bennett Williams blew us away on legal issues. The free-agency rep for the owners was Vince Lombardi; Vince threw down his pencil: 'You can't break this down. It will cause terrible things.' There was an expert on every subject to say no.

"Halas never said a thing all day," Pyle continued. "He was taking notes. At the end, Halas went through a 10- to 15-minute story about starting the league, collecting money at the gate, going across the street from Wrigley Field to buy tape. 'We lost money. We deserve to get that back,' the Papa Bear said. Nobody said a word. They all looked at me like, 'What's with this guy who wants us to pay for what happened in the beginning?' "

As Pyle saw the scenario in the late '80s, "The owners figured there was no way the union could finish the court case without required dues being paid. The NFL owners figured to do the money thing and overpower them."

It didn't work the way they calculated it, and Pyle gives Upshaw all the credit for making it work. "Here's my little key," Pyle said. "You know what money funded the court cases that the players won in every instance? It was licensing revenue. When trading cards were the rage, each individual player received as much as $4,000 or $5,000 royalty per season in licensing revenue. Thus, the players let the licensing fees finance the court cases. The union won every one of them. The pension fund was overfunded by $30 million. The owners had promised that $30 million in collective bargaining. They just kept it. Collective bargaining is part of the law; you have to pay in what you promised. They didn't; they kept it. They lost it in court."

In 1990, the union filed the Freeman McNeil case, claiming that Plan B restricted free movement. On September 11, 1992, after two days of deliberations, a jury in Minneapolis struck down Plan B. That led to settlement talks between Upshaw and Tagliabue. "The owners came to Mr. Upshaw and said, 'OK, we're going to have to do this.' And the law said they had to do it," Mike Pyle said. "Gene was not opposed to what they asked. The owners said, 'We must have a collective bargaining agreement, or else you guys will break us.' It was easy to recertify."

The sides compromised, and the owners agreed to free agency providing there was a salary cap. "The players really were chattel when Rozelle was commissioner," Don Pierson said. "Now they are more of a partnership. Ed Garvey wanted a percentage of the gross, and everybody laughed at him. Rozelle told him, 'I don't think the owners are ever going to go for that.' Now they have far more than Garvey wanted. The owners would love 55 percent of the gross now. It's in the 60s now." The players currently get 64 percent.

"The 1993 collective bargaining agreement is the one that still is in effect. It is the underpinning—the principle that Gene Upshaw could go and have dinners with Paul Tagliabue," Pyle said. The troubles were far from over, though, and have continued to this day as the older retirees strongly assert that they have received short shrift while union pension coffers overflow with money that could ensure better lives for them and their dependents.

"In the 1993 collective bargaining agreement, Gene knew what television was going to do," Pyle said. "Upshaw told the bargaining committee, 'Any way I can help you—if there's a work stoppage, they won't pay; I can help you there.' I consider that the greatest leverage a union could have over its ownership at any level of business, and it has earned Upshaw 4 million dollars a year."

In that collective bargaining agreement, Tagliabue, who as commissioner had taken over the NFL Management Council, now gained the power Pete Rozelle had in name but never in fact—the power as sole mediator and arbitrator of league issues and discipline. Roger Goodell has that same power today.

In 1993, Rupert Murdoch's Fox network stole the NFC rights away from CBS, which surrendered without a fight. The owners' coffers were further enriched by more billions.

"I had the advantage of new technologies, satellite, and Fox, the new entrant into the broadcast world," Paul Tagliabue said. "Pete didn't have that. He had a pretty static period in terms of television technology. He did an amazing job through those contracts from '66 through '82 without new entrants, nor new technologies changing distribution. By the time I got in, ESPN got in. They had done that half season in '87. It was not just cable: it was satellite; it was multiple cable players with TNT and ESPN. Then it was Fox coming into the broadcast booth with a new major network that reenergized the next 15 years. You have the Internet now."

Pete Rozelle lived to see free agency, but he no longer had to worry about it. As of November 5, 1989, he was free at last to do what he pleased and what Carrie wanted him to do. Then again, from the time he met Carrie Cooke in the Bel-Air Hotel in early 1973, he was hers.

Before Carrie and Pete Rozelle got married, they sold the Sutton Place apartment and moved to a house in Harrison, in Westchester County, big enough to hold five children. "This is really funny," the late Peter Hadhazy said. "Annie Rozelle Bratton, about two years ago, sent me an e-mail. A friend of hers had sent her an e-mail that a unit was for sale at 16 Sutton Place, which was the building that they lived in. Annie forwarded it to me with a comment: 'This friend of mine sent me this thinking I would be interested in the fact that I grew up in that building, but the picture of the apartment that is for sale is *the actual* apartment that my dad, mom, and I lived in.'

"Annie said they had purchased it in 1960 for $40,000," Hadhazy said. "It was up for sale for $20 million." That was considerably more than Rozelle sold it for when he and Carrie moved to Harrison in 1974. Anne Marie told me he got about $210,000. "He sold at the extreme bottom of the market, I'm sure."

Anne Marie, who was in the middle of high school at the time of the move, missed the wonders and excitement of living in the big city. "I commuted from Westchester to the city throughout my sophomore year," she said. "For whatever reason, when I finished my sophomore year at Marymount School, my father and Carrie decided it wasn't feasible to commute and I needed to go to school out there. So, I switched to Rye Country Day junior and senior years, which is not a great time to switch, after going to a small, Catholic, all-girls, inner-city school all my life, to a large coed school."

She spent one summer in Washington working for Congressman Jack Kemp and other summers working for her godfather, Ken Macker. In 1976, she enrolled at Rollins College in Winter Park,

Florida. She was presented at the St. Vincent Debutante Ball in Rye, New York. "Jack Landry Jr. was my date when I had my debutante party," Anne Marie said.

"Pete got a kick out of that," said Jinny Landry, whose husband, Jack Sr., was Rozelle's best friend.

Anne Marie had dreams of getting into network television. "I worked at NBC on the 1980 Olympics. I worked at ABC News, ABC's 'One Night to Live'—and it was a lot of fun," she said. "I worked so hard on the Moscow Olympics, I wasn't looking for other jobs, and I thought my future was set. Then the Moscow Olympics [telecasts] were canceled for political reasons, and it was back to the drawing board. Our Olympic unit stayed close and still has reunions."

Through the years, Anne Marie experienced many special moments with the father she adored and who nourished her with his love and values, starting in her early days in New York. His humor stood out. "He wrote the wittiest letters," Anne Marie said. "He was just one of the most fun people to be with. When you walked into a room with him, there was always a funny story, there was always a funny joke. He always had a funny take on it. He wore funny hats on his birthday and sang 'Happy Birthday' to himself." Still, Rozelle was never a party animal in public.

"We played a lot of tennis together, my second wife and his second wife," Frank Gifford said. "They would come over to our house. We would spend time at their place in the house I found for him in Harrison. He didn't want any press around him. It was a quiet time. Carrie was very different. She was very out-there gregarious, and the like. Pete went along with it, but he hated black-tie dinners. He'd rather be with his guys—Jack Landry; Dave Mahoney; fortunately, me—hanging out at '21' drinking his rusty nails. He didn't fit into that society."

"My father was very, very generous, especially when it came to tipping," Anne Marie said. "The best stories I hear about my dad were when I was working the U.S. Open. I was working with the ushers a lot. We were down in the basement of the tennis area. The ushers told me stories about the tips he had left for them, the things he had done for them. He did a lot of nice things for people that were never known, just unnamed. He would remember if someone had done something nice for him and figure a way to do something nice for them."

Anne Marie found another wonderful side to her father after he and Carrie moved to Westchester. "He had what he called his 'plantation owner's hat,' a big straw hat that he wore with pride when he walked around the grounds," she said. "He was especially fun at the end of the night, when he would say, 'Let's get suited up.' Everyone put on their bathrobes and met for a nightcap. Then he gave his version of how the evening went. He had funny observations. He made everything an adventure."

And he had Carrie to provide the glamour and live the part as the perfect CEO's wife. "Carrie was very beautiful," Blair Sabol said. "She was of a type, a Joanna Carson. She was a movie star, Doris Day—that ilk. She was classy enough—the big hair. In the beginning, she was great, amusing, kind of funny; she was a courtesan, who knew how to do parties. Her group was Joanna Carson, my aunt Ann Siegel, and a lot of these gals. That's what they did. They went to the hairdresser and had great parties—and big on charity, very big on charity. So, she did the right things."

By 1987, Anne Marie had become director of advertising, publicity, and public relations for Ralph Lauren Home Collections, in New York, and she had met a special young man. Douglas Bratton was in securities investments. Matters got serious by the spring of 1988. "The restaurant was called Nanni Il Valetto. It was a great restaurant," Anne Marie recalled. "My fiancé, Doug Bratton, had called my father and said, 'Let's have dinner.' At dinner, Doug said, 'Look, I'm going to ask only one favor from you. You have always picked up the check everywhere we've ever gone. No matter how hard I try, you do. Now this is my night to celebrate your accepting me for her hand in marriage. Please let me pick up the check.' "

"Sure," Pete Rozelle said.

"They talked about it," Anne Marie said. "Doug was all excited about it. The check didn't come and didn't come. Doug asked for it. The captain said, 'I'm sorry, sir, it's already been taken care of.'

"Doug turned to Father," Anne Marie said. 'I thought we cleared that up.' My father put his hands up in the air and said, 'I didn't pay for it.' Over in the corner was Peter Ueberroth holding the check up in the air. That was the big joke. 'The one time I really wanted to pick up the check, I still get beaten to it!' Doug said."

The couple got married October 8, 1988. They settled in Greenwich, Connecticut, and moved to Texas two years later, where they had two children, Miles and Alexandra.

"When they were here for Super Bowl XXII in 1988, Carrie looked around for property," said Herb Klein, the San Diego newspaper publisher and former director of communications in the Nixon administration. "They wanted to be around San Diego when he retired, as Pete had developed a very close friendship with Gene Klein."

Then came the move to Rancho Santa Fe, just north of San Diego. "The fact is that Carrie wanted to go back to the West Coast, and he went along with it," Joe Browne said. "Gene Klein was his one real friend out there."

"Pete and Carrie designed the house they built here," Herb Klein said. "Gene Klein was developing some property in Rancho Santa Fe, where I lived. Pete bought the lot, and they built the house. The house was peach colored, on a cliff. It had a bar that overlooked the valley and a racehorse training farm below, which Gene owned. Pete had one room with three television sets and three antennas so he could watch all the football he wanted. Once he retired, I don't believe he went to a single game," Klein recalled.

"I thought he was going to have a nice life out there," Blair Sabol said. "He would have a little office and all his people. Thelma Elkjer, his secretary for so many years, moved out there. She was another one who held the keys to the kingdom."

"He grew up in California. He was very comfortable in California," Paul Tagliabue noted. "They were really excited about living near Gene Klein, who Pete had become really close to."

"The whole idea of it was to move to California, travel with friends, and enjoy the last phase of their lives in the house of their dreams that they built from scratch, do all the things they wanted to do, and catch up with the living time they sort of lost with career, and so forth," Anne Marie Bratton said. "The weather in California would have been ideal, allowing them to be outside the year around, play tennis, and do all that stuff." Despite those attractions, she allowed, "I know there were things he missed about New York."

"Prior to Gene Klein's death, we had a custom of having Sunday-evening dinners with Joyce and Gene, Pete and Carrie, and my wife, Marge, and me," Herb Klein said. "We usually went to a Mexican restaurant near here just to have fun. A lot of the time we spent recalling days past in San Francisco, days with the Rams." Underscoring Anne Marie's earlier assessment, Klein stated, "He was someone who had a great sense of humor, someone you could count on whenever you ran into him."

"Pete and Carrie were going to go with Joyce and Gene Klein, travel to the Far East, go to the Olympics with them, everything," Joe Browne recalled. "Then Klein had the heart attack and died the first year Pete was out there." Gene Klein's fatal heart attack on March 12, 1990, dashed the Asian tour plan.

"Gene Klein's death was a huge frustration," Tagliabue said. "One of the main motivations for going out there had disappeared."

"Now Pete was out there wondering, what am I doing out here?" Joe Browne said. So many of his friends of 30 years—Herb Siegel, Bob Tisch, Frank Gifford, Roone Arledge, and Jack Landry—were back east. "They should have kept an apartment here in New York."

"There are people in New York who think it was a big mistake, that he would have been a lot happier had he stayed in New York," Paul Tagliabue said. "I think when you look back, it's not where they were living or who their neighbors were, but the fact that they both developed severe health problems."

"He came back three or four times a year; that was all," Joe Browne said.

"It was pretty rare for him to get back to New York," Tagliabue attested. "Occasionally, there were charitable events. He appeared at a United Way event in San Francisco and an event or so in New York. Carrie tended to come back to New York more than he did. She was involved in her foundation for children with learning disabilities, and they had their big annual event."

In the weeks before March 1, 1991, Pete Rozelle's 65th birthday, Carrie planned a huge party for him at the house, with friends coming in from around the country to surprise him. "Maybe three weeks before the party, Jack Kemp came into town," Herb Klein recalled. "Jack joined the Rozelles and us for dinner at a seafood restaurant. As we were leaving the restaurant, Jack said, 'I look forward to seeing you real soon.' When the Rozelles got in the car with me, Pete was kind of pouting. When he got home, he told Carrie, 'You're trying to throw a surprise party for me, aren't you?' So, she had to call off that party."

Klein continued, "We celebrated his birthday with about 20 of his friends here in San Diego, a small affair. What she did was replan the party, same original guest list, for two months later. One of us had to keep Jack from leaking it. Pete's close friend Don Klosterman took Pete in a private plane to the races at Hollywood Park, then brought him back. Once he left, Carrie moved the furniture around, set up the tables for a party of 60, brought in an orchestra—and when he came back, it worked. It was a surprise. So, Carrie finally got her surprise for him."

An unpleasant surprise for Pete Rozelle came on August 5, 1991, with word that Paul Brown, the Cleveland Browns and Cincinnati Bengals founder, who had pushed so hard for his election as commissioner, had died back in Ohio. Rozelle flew to Cleveland for the funeral in Massillon, 50 miles to the south, the town that Brown put on the football map as a high school coach in the '30s. "I drove down to the viewing," said Ernie Accorsi, then general manager in Cleveland for Brown's bitter enemy Art Modell. "It was like the viewing of some guy in the neighborhood. There weren't that many people there. It was a small funeral home, but standing in there were Dante Lavelli, Otto Graham, Lou Groza—I mean all those great people. I was in a touchy situation with Modell. I would not back off from my devotion to Paul Brown. I told Art he had to go to the funeral: 'You must go.' He went, and I went with him."

Shortly after Super Bowl XXVI in the winter of 1992, Rozelle got the call that Bill Granholm was dead. "Granny" was one of his all-time-favorite NFL people, going back to their meeting in Evanston, Illinois, at the 1946 College All-Star camp, where Granny's lifelong buddy from Wausau, Wisconsin, Elroy Hirsch, got him a job as equipment manager, before they both joined the Chicago Rockets, of the All-America Football Conference. Granholm, a confirmed bachelor, moved with "Crazylegs" to Los Angeles in 1949 and remained with the Rams until Rozelle brought him to the league office in the '60s to be his troubleshooter. Two projects occupied much of his time. He led the NFL troupe in USO postseason tours from 1967 through 1988, and he did advance publicity tasks for Super Bowls. "Granholm was the equipment manager of the Rams when Pete was PR director and later the general manager," Ernie Accorsi said. "We'd ask him a zillion questions about Pete, and he kept his counsel pretty well, but one day he told me, 'A lot of people made the mistake of underestimating his toughness.'"

Granholm told Accorsi: "We were at training camp with Sid Gillman, and Pete was general manager. He was in his motel room at the top of the hill, with the practice fields down below. He was in his bathrobe and pajamas making phone calls. He had left orders that a certain player was not to be waived, not to be cut. Then he got this call from the PR guy: 'Pete, Gillman just cut so-and-so.'"

Granholm continued, "I got this message to come up. It said, 'Pete wants to see you.'" Granholm ran up the hill.

"Get Gillman up here right now," the commissioner ordered.

"He's on the practice field, Mr. Pete."

"I don't give a damn where he is," Rozelle said. "Get him off the practice field, up this hill, and to this room." Gillman went up the hill.

"If I had any doubts in my life how tough Pete could be, they were removed in that moment," Granholm said. "Gillman left that room like a schoolboy, and the player was reinstated."

"Granny's funeral and burial were held in Wausau, which is hard to get to on nice days and especially difficult in the middle of winter," Joel Bussert said. "About a dozen of us from around the league showed up for the funeral, and Pete Rozelle flew in from Los Angeles to be there. That always impressed me that he would make that effort. Sure, he would go to the funeral of an owner, but he had a long relationship with Granny and was there for him, a man he knew for a good 40 years, who worked for him a long time. I don't think he was 100 percent, but he made the effort," Bussert said.

"The night before Granholm's funeral, we went out to eat at a local place," Bussert said. "One of the people there was Jack Faulkner, who was an assistant coach with the Rams when Pete was general manager and was with the team for 40 years. Pete was just peppering him with questions. Faulkner was bringing him up-to-date on the Rams' roster, as in, 'What about this guy? What about that guy?' He was interested in the players and how good they would be. He had an interest in football at the bedrock level."

Looking out for old friends came naturally to Rozelle. "When he retired to Rancho Santa Fe, he saw my name in the paper once, and he called," Al Franken, Rozelle's friend from their post–World War II track-and-field days, said. " 'Why don't you and Shirley [my late wife] come down and join Carrie and me at Del Mar? We have a box there.' " The Frankens took him up on the offer. "He never mentioned a word of what he did, in those four or five hours. He wanted to know about his friends in the track world. That's an interesting measure of the man."

As Franken witnessed in an illustration that day at Del Mar, Rozelle never forgot the position he had held and how others might judge his behavior. "He always had me, Carrie, or someone else take his bets down to the window," Franken said. "Even at this stage, he didn't want to be seen at the betting windows at a racetrack."

"Carrie was a great second marriage for him, and why not? She was beautiful, vivacious, younger than he was, the whole thing, and she was good for him," Joe Browne said. "Then she got sick, and, oh my God, everyone was certain she was going to die. Then he got sick and died, and she's still alive."

Life took a dark turn for both Rozelles. Carrie had a brain tumor. "They sent the information to Art Modell, who sent a brain surgeon from the Cleveland Clinic, who diagnosed her and said she had six months to live," Herb Siegel said.

Life with the Rozelles turned into constant illness as both were afflicted with tumors. "He had a brain tumor; it was removed, and it was fine," Anne Marie Bratton said. "Then she got the supposed death sentence with a brain tumor that's called glioblastoma multiforme. She had the operation. After she had the operation, she was fine and had a good prognosis. Then, screwy things happened. She got a staph infection. Don't forget she had brain surgery. Then there was something where they had cut an artery and they had to go back in with another surgery. After that, she was never really the same. It was so sad. She was so very young, so very beautiful and captivating. She was the type of woman who walked into a room and everybody noticed. She had unbelievable presence. The last surgery, whatever went wrong, absolutely played havoc with her. It was walking, talking, remembering, writing—everything was a struggle. It never was before."

"By then, who knew how sick Pete really was?" Blair Sabol said. "His energy was fading. He sure blew up pretty fast. At the end, the distortion in his face was marked."

The dreaded diagnosis for Rozelle came in midsummer 1996. "He had a couple of small brain tumors on and off during Carrie's illness," Anne Marie said. "When we were given the terminal death sentence, it was about three to six months."

"His last public event was the Republican Convention in San Diego that nominated me for vice president," Jack Kemp said. "He sat with my dad and my brothers. It was great to have him there."

Communication became difficult for Rozelle as the summer wore into fall. Herb Siegel visited him one day and saw signs of trouble within the household. Pete told his friend that one of Carrie's sons was going after his personal possessions. "The gifts the owners had given him with all their names on it were missing," Siegel said. "He had to know it. Paintings were missing. They were robbing the joint. He came down, and we had breakfast together, and he picked up the paper as though to read it, and it was upside down. That also happened to Anne Marie."

"I stayed for the last few weeks," Anne Marie said. "The cruelty of it, the brain tumor. Doctors say that with many, the mind goes first; you're not aware of everything shutting down. His mind never went until the very end, so he was very aware of it. In the beginning, obviously, he could speak with reasonable clarity, but his balance was off—the little symptoms. He knew he was going to die, and he was prepared for it. He kept his sense of humor and went through his ritual and would read his newspaper even though the newspaper might be upside down. He maintained his dignity throughout the process."

"Don Klosterman and I went out with Pete for dinner at Del Mar, and the more we were there, the more he relaxed," Pete Newell recalled. "When we left, I said I was so happy about the way he acted. Don said, 'I've talked to the doctors, and he doesn't have a long way to go.' He was gone within a week. Don died two months later. Heart attack."

"It was not the good time. He didn't fail rapidly," Frank Gifford recalled. "I visited him out there shortly before he died. We had a game in San Diego on Monday night. The last time I saw him, he couldn't talk. We were sitting in the den. He had all these monitors up on the wall. It was a Sunday, and we were watching football. I spent almost the entire day with him. He was watching. I was fascinated as we watched. It spanned the country: the kickoff in the East at 10 out there, 11 in the Midwest, 1 o'clock in the Pacific. It just spanned the country. On the monitors, Kansas City was playing, Dallas was playing, the Jets were playing: it was the most unbelievable thing."

"I just looked at him: 'Pete, did you ever think pro football would be like this, be this important? Here it is, spanning the entire country, and millions and millions of people are watching.' He couldn't really talk, but he got it. He gave me a big smile and then nodded off. I knew I wouldn't see him anymore. But he knew the job was done, and he had done one helluva job."

Anne Marie slept on the floor by her father's bed in the last days and talked to him when she was awake. He died on December 6, 1996. "It's never a pretty sight when someone dies," she said

More sorrow followed. "We had been so close and spent all this time together, and the day after he died, it was just sort of completely understood that I was to move out of the house, and that was it," she said. "It took a completely different turn. They contested the will.

Carrie was in somewhat of a weakened position at that point, and she filed suit. It was very clear that we were on two different courses. I was defending my father's will, and they were contesting it."

Memorial services were held for Pete Rozelle in Los Angeles and New York. Anne Marie delivered eulogies at both services. At the Los Angeles service, held before the Christmas holidays, she told those assembled, "I am most grateful for the real inheritance my father left me: his sense of humor, his compassion for others, his integrity, and his belief that your word is your bond."

The New York service was conducted January 17, 1997, at the Fifth Avenue Presbyterian Church, where owners, league officials, and friends gathered. Carrie was too ill to attend. "Jack Kemp and Ethel Kennedy were there, and I worked with both," Anne Marie told me, calling forth the ecumenical spirit of her father. "I don't know if I'm a Republican or a Democrat. It depends on any given year. I've lived in both camps."

"At the memorial service in New York, Frank Gifford spoke, Well Mara spoke, and Cathy Lee sang Pete's two favorite songs, 'Try to Remember' and 'Edelweiss,' " Ernie Accorsi recalled.

"Cathy Lee sang 'Try to Remember' at the service," Frank Gifford echoed. "She sang it when he retired in L.A. All the NFL gathered. Carrie requested it. He was sick even then. Cathy walked down the aisle singing, and he blushed. She hit the perfect high note then, and she kissed him, and he rode off into the sunset. She sang the same thing at his funeral in New York."

"Wellington had a terrible cold and case of the flu, with the worst throat you ever heard," Accorsi said. "John Mara said to Wellington, 'Dad, why don't you just let me read your remarks?'

" 'No.'

" 'Dad, you sound terrible.'

" 'John, I'm giving the eulogy,' Mr. Mara said.

"That was the end of that," Accorsi said. "Well said, 'When he moved the league offices from suburban Philadelphia to New York, he moved the NFL from the back page to the front page, from daytime to prime time.' "

Mara told the people there how Rozelle, unable to attend Super Bowl XXX in 1996, listened to the proceedings at Paul Tagliabue's news conference by speaker and took a call from New Orleans at home. "At the end," Ernie Accorsi recalled, "Pete said, and Well repeated it at the end of the eulogy, 'We really had a time, didn't we?' "

Anne Marie called him "the best father, best mother, adviser, and friend." She concluded her remarks in New York as she had in Los Angeles: "Dad, thanks for being such a bright spot in what you called life's rich pageantry."

"The service ended in New York, and we were all getting our coats, when Val Pinchbeck walked in and said, 'Kensil died,' " Ernie Accorsi recalled.

It seemed supremely ironic to everyone present that the man who had fueled so much of that pageantry and public relations grit and muscle, the adviser Pete Rozelle called "his offensive and defensive coordinator," died the very morning of the memorial service for his longtime boss and friend.

As close to Rozelle's death as was the death of his professional ally Kensil, even more ironic were the passings of his close business and personal friends Bill McPhail and Jack Landry. "Pete, the product, died on December 6, 1996; Bill, the broadcaster, died in July or August 1996. Dad, the advertiser, died on April 13, 1997," Jack Landry Jr. said. "Those three were so important to the success of the NFL. Jack Sr., Dad, died from lung cancer, the worst kind you can imagine. Horrible."

No single word better exemplifies Pete Rozelle's life and times than *pageantry*. This was a man who took the boy's game that George Halas got men to play for money and turned it into a mass entertainment industry. Yet, he retained a boyish enthusiasm over his product and succeeded as no other sports leader has in the history of fun and games played for money. Although he never lived in the Midwest, he came from a family of Hoosiers who migrated west at the turn of the century. That background helps explain how it was that someone who came of age amid the trappings and bombastic hype of the film industry still loved to share with a mass public such simple pleasures as balloons, marching bands, and hokey singing groups like Up with People!

Joel Bussert was a youngster in Pekin, Illinois, long before he realized he would spend most of his adult life approving contracts and trades for the National Football League. He shared one final story that speaks to the life and legacy of Pete Rozelle: "A couple of years ago, somebody called me from a newspaper to ask me how football had changed through the years. I was a 12-year-old boy 50 years ago. One of the questions was, 'Did you ever think it would be like this?'

"My answer was no, but I was thinking to myself, I bet Pete Rozelle did."

SOURCES

Interview Subjects

Ernie Accorsi general manager, New York Giants, Cleveland
  Browns, Baltimore Colts
Dave Anderson writer-columnist, *New York Times*
Anne Marie Rozelle Bratton daughter
Tom Brookshier defensive back, Philadelphia Eagles; CBS
  sportscaster
Mike Brown owner, Cincinnati Bengals
Joe Browne NFL VP of Public Affairs
Joel Bussert NFL executive
Gary Carter Punt, Pass, and Kick winner, 1961; National
  Baseball Hall of Fame
Dick Cline operations director-producer, NBC
Bill Curry linebacker, Green Bay Packers, Baltimore Colts;
  NFLPA president
Len Dawson quarterback, Kansas City Chiefs; sportscaster; Pro
  Football Hall of Fame
Chuck Day writer, collaborator with Don Weiss
Frank Deford writer, *Sports Illustrated*
Glenn Dickey writer, *Oakland Tribune*, *Pro Football Weekly*
Sonny Eliot broadcaster, WWJ, Detroit

Don Ellis producer, NBC

Dick Enberg sportscaster, NBC, CBS; Pro Football Hall of Fame Rozelle Award

Dan Endy director-producer, Tel Ra Productions, NFL Films

Jack Faulkner coach, Los Angeles Rams, San Diego Chargers, Denver Broncos

Tom Flores quarterback, coach, Oakland–Los Angeles Raiders

Bob Fouts sportscaster, San Francisco

Al Franken track-and-field official, friend

Ed Garvey NFLPA executive director

Frank Gifford running back, NY Giants; sportscaster, ABC, CBS; Pro Football Hall of Fame Rozelle Award

Jerry Green writer, *Detroit News*

Peter Hadhazy NFL executive; USFL executive; general manager, New England Patriots, Cleveland Browns

Paul Hornung halfback, Green Bay Packers; Pro Football Hall of Fame

Sam Huff middle linebacker, New York Giants, Washington Redskins; Pro Football Hall of Fame

Lamar Hunt owner, Kansas City Chiefs; founder, AFL; Pro Football Hall of Fame

Keith Jackson sportscaster, ABC

Bill Jauss writer, *Chicago Tribune*

Charlie Jones sportscaster, NBC, ABC; Pro Football Hall of Fame Rozelle Award

Alex Karras defensive tackle, Detroit Lions; sportscaster, ABC

Jack Kemp quarterback, Buffalo Bills; representative, U.S. Congress; friend

Herb Klein publisher, *San Diego Union-Tribune*; friend

Bowie Kuhn former commissioner of Major League Baseball; friend

Jack Landry Jr. friend

Virginia Landry friend

Rex Lardner producer, NBC, CBS, Turner

Jerry Magee writer, *San Diego Union-Tribune, Pro Football Weekly*

George Mandich NFL security

Jerry Markbreit NFL referee

Bill McGrane NFL executive, Minnesota Vikings, Chicago Bears

Art McNally NFL referee; supervisor of officials

Chuck Mercein fullback, New York Giants, Green Bay Packers

Art Modell former owner, Cleveland Browns/Baltimore Ravens; friend

Lester Munson associate editor, *Sports Illustrated*

William Nack writer, *Sports Illustrated*

Pete Newell basketball coach; executive; friend; Basketball Hall of Fame

Bob Oates writer, *Los Angeles Examiner, Los Angeles Times*

Merlin Olsen defensive tackle, Los Angeles Rams; sportscaster, NBC; Pro Football Hall of Fame

Bill Orr CEO, Tel Ra Productions

R. C. Owens wide receiver, San Francisco 49ers, Baltimore Colts, New York Giants

Bernie Parrish defensive back, Cleveland Browns; union leader

Don Pierson writer-columnist, *Chicago Tribune*

Edwin Pope writer-columnist, *Miami Herald*

Mike Pyle center, Chicago Bears; NFLPA president

Pete E. Retzlaff general manager, Philadelphia Eagles; NFLPA president

Tony Roberts sportscaster, Mutual, Westwood One

Cooper Rollow writer-sports editor, *Chicago Tribune*

Dan Rooney owner, Pittsburgh Steelers

Steve Rosenbloom executive, Baltimore Colts, Los Angeles Rams

Dick Rozelle brother

Blair Sabol friend

Ed Sabol founder, NFL Films; Pro Football Hall of Fame Rozelle Award

Steve Sabol president, NFL Films

Lou Sahadi writer

Joe Schmidt middle linebacker, coach, Detroit Lions; Pro Football Hall of Fame

Danny Sheridan gambling analyst

Don Shula coach, Baltimore Colts, Miami Dolphins; Pro Football Hall of Fame

Herb Siegel CEO, Chris-Craft Industries; friend
Chet Simmons Sr. vice president, ABC, NBC; USFL
    commissioner
Charles "Bubba" Smith defensive end, Baltimore Colts
Bev Snider friend
Edwin (Duke) Snider Brooklyn/L.A. Dodgers Hall of Famer;
    friend
Bert Randolph Sugar writer; raconteur
Pat Summerall NY Giants; sportscaster, CBS, Fox; Pro Football
    Hall of Fame Rozelle Award
Paul Tagliabue NFL commissioner
Jack Teele executive, Los Angeles Rams, San Diego Chargers;
    friend
Rick Telander writer, *Chicago Sun-Times*, *Sports Illustrated*
Jerry Vainisi general manager, Chicago Bears, Detroit Lions
William N. Wallace writer, *New York Herald-Tribune*, *New
    York Times*, *Pro Football Weekly*
Al Ward executive AFL, NFL; general manager, New York Jets
Jack Whitaker sportscaster, CBS, ABC
Ron Wolf executive, Oakland Raiders, AFL, Tampa Bay
    Buccaneers, Green Bay Packers
Robert Wussler television executive, CBS, Turner Broadcasting
Paul Zimmerman football writer, *Sports Illustrated*

Research Sources

Chuck Adams Major League Baseball; friend of Bowie Kuhn
Greg Aiello NFL VP
Kathy Davis NFL Films

Books

Allen, George, with Ben Olan. *Pro and College Football's 50
Greatest Games*. New York: Bobbs-Merrill, 1983.

Allen, Jennifer, *Fifth Quarter*. New York: Random House, 2000.

Arledge, Roone, *Roone: A Memoir*, New York: HarperCollins Publishers, 2003.

Boller, Paul F., Jr., and Ronald Davis, *Hollywood Anecdotes*. New York: William Morrow, 1987.

Brown, Jim, with Steve Delsohn, *Out of Bounds*. New York: Kensington Publishing, 1989.

Brown, Paul, with Jack Clary, *PB: The Paul Brown Story*. New York: Atheneum, 1979.

Buck, Jack, with Rob Rains and Bob Broeg, *"That's a Winner!"* Champaign, IL: Sports Publishing, 2002.

Butkus, Dick, and Robert W. Billings, *Stop Action*. New York, Dutton, 1972.

Butkus, Dick, and Pat Smith, *Butkus: Flesh and Blood*. New York: Doubleday, 1997.

Callahan, Tom, *Johnny U.: The Life and Times of John Unitas*. New York: Crown, 2006.

Carroll, Bob, et al. *Total Football II: The Official Encyclopedia of the National Football League*. New York: HarperCollins, 1999.

Cope, Myron, *The Game That Was*. New York: The World, 1970.

Cosell, Howard, with Peter Bonventre, *I Never Played the Game*. New York: William Morrow, 1985.

Cosell, Howard, with Shelby Whitfield, *What's Wrong with Sport*. New York: Simon and Schuster, 1991.

Curran, Bob, *Pro Football's Rag Days*. New York: Bonanza Books, 1969.

Daley, Arthur, *Pro Football's Hall of Fame*. Chicago: Quadrangle Books, 1963.

Danzig, Allison, *Oh, How They Played That Game*. New York: MacMillan, 1971.

Davis, Jeff, *Papa Bear: The Life and Legacy of George Halas*. New York: McGraw-Hill, 2004.

Dickey, Glenn, *Just Win Baby: Al Davis and His Raiders*. New York: Harcourt, 1991.

Didinger, Ray, and Robert S. Lyons, *The Eagles Encyclopedia*. Philadelphia: Temple University Press, 2006.

Ditka, Mike, with Pierson, Don, *Ditka: An Autobiography*, Chicago: Bonus Books, 1986.

Finks, Jim, Jr., *It's Been a Pleasure: The Jim Finks Story*. Newport Beach, CA: AMO Productions, 2003.

Fortunato, John, *Commissioner: The Legacy of Pete Rozelle*. Lanham, MD: Taylor Trade Publishing, 2006.

Gillette, Gary, and Matthew Silverman, editors, *The ESPN Pro Football Encyclopedia*. New York: Sterling, 2006.

Gruver, Ed, *The Ice Bowl*. Ithaca, NY: McCook Books, 1998.

Harris, David, *The League: The Rise and Decline of the NFL*. New York: Bantam Books, 1986.

Hornung, Paul, as told to William F. Reed, *Golden Boy*. New York: Simon and Schuster, 2004.

Izenberg, Jerry, *Championship*. New York: Scholastic, 1968.

Karras, Alex, with Herb Gluck, *Even Big Guys Cry*. New York: Holt, 1977.

Keteyian, Armen, *Ditka: Monster of the Midway*. New York: Pocket Books, 1992.

Kindred, Dave, *Sound and Fury*. New York: Free Press, 2006.

Klein, Eugene, and Davis Fisher, *First Down and a Billion*. New York: William Morrow, 1987.

Kramer, Jerry, with Dick Schaap, *Distant Replay*. New York: World Publishing, 1985.

Kramer, Jerry, with Dick Schaap, *Instant Replay*. New York: World Publishing, 1968.

Kriegel, Mark, *Namath*. New York: Viking, 2004.

Mackey, John, with Thom Loveroo, *Blazing Trails*. Chicago: Triumph Books, 2003.

MacCambridge, Michael, *America's Game*. New York, Random House, 2004.

MacCambridge, Michael, *The Franchise: A History of Sports Illustrated Magazine*. New York: Hyperion, 1997.

Maraniss, David, *When Pride Still Mattered: A Life of Vince Lombardi*. New York: Simon & Schuster, 1999.

Markbreit, Jerry, and Alan Steinberg, *Born to Referee*. New York, William Morrow, 1988.

Maule, Hamilton B. "Tex," *The Game: Official History of the National Football League*, Revised Edition. New York: Random House, 1964.

McCallum, John D., *Big Ten Football Since 1895*. Radnor, PA: Chilton Book Company, 1976.

McMahon, Jim, with Bob Verdi, *McMahon*. New York: Warner Books, 1986.

Miller, Jeff, *Going Long: The Wild Ten-Year Saga of the Renegade American Football League in the Words of Those Who Lived It*. New York: McGraw-Hill, 2003.

Moldea, Dan E., *Interference: How Organized Crime Influences Professional Football*. New York: William Morrow, 1989.

Mordden, Ethan, *The Hollywood Studios*. New York: Knopf, 1988.

Nack, William, *My Turf: Horses, Boxers, Blood Money, and the Sporting Life*. Cambridge, MA: Da Capo Press, 2003.

National Football League, *75 Seasons: The Complete Story of the National Football League, 1920–1995*. Atlanta: Turner Publishing, 1994.

Nelson, Lindsey, *Hello, Everybody, I'm Lindsey Nelson*. New York: Beech Tree Books, 1985.

Parrish, Bernard P., *They Call It a Game: Shoulders the NFL Stands On*. Lincoln, NE: Authors Choice Press, 1971.

Peterson, Robert W. *Pigskin: The Early Years of Pro Football*. New York: Oxford University Press, 1997.

Pitt, Leonard, *Los Angeles A to Z: An Encyclopedia of the City and County*. Berkeley: University of California Press, 1997.

Plimpton, George, *Paper Lion*. New York: Harper, 1965.

Pope, Edwin, *Football's Greatest Coaches*. Atlanta: Tupper and Love, 1955.

Rein, Irving, Philip Kotler, and Ben Shields, *The Elusive Fan: Reinventing Sports in a Crowded Marketplace*. New York, McGraw-Hill, 2006.

Rice, Grantland, *Tumult and the Shouting*. New York: A. S. Barnes, 1954.

Riger, Robert and Hamilton Maule, *The Pros: A Documentary of Professional Football in America*. New York: Simon and Schuster, 1960.

Smith, Charles "Bubba," *Kill, Bubba, Kill*. New York: Simon and Schuster, 1983.

Smith, Walter W. "Red," *The Red Smith Reader*. New York: Random House, 1982.

Smith, Walter W. "Red," *Red Smith's Sports Annual, 1961*. New York: Crown, 1961.

Sports Illustrated: The Football Book. New York: Time/Sports Illustrated Books, 2005.

Sugar, Bert Randolph, *Hit the Sign and Win a Free Suit of Clothes from Harry Finkelstein*. Chicago: Contemporary Books, 1978.

Sugar, Bert Randolph, *The Thrill of Victory: An Inside Story of ABC Sports*. Chicago: Contemporary Books, 1978.

Summerall, Pat, *Summerall: On and Off the Air*. Nashville, TN: Thomas Nelson, 2006.

Twombly, Wells, *Blanda: Alive and Kicking*. Los Angeles, CA: Nash Publishing, 1972.

Twombly, Wells, *Shake Down the Thunder: The Official Biography of Notre Dame's Frank Leahy*. Radnor, PA: Chilton Book Company, 1974.

Weiss, Don, with Chuck Day, *The Making of the Super Bowl*. New York: McGraw-Hill, 2003.

Whittingham, Richard, *The Bears: 75-Year Celebration*. Lanham, MD: National Book Network, 1994.

Whittingham, Richard, *The Dallas Cowboys: An Illustrated History*. New York: Harper, 1981.

Whittingham, Richard, *Illustrated History of the New York Giants*. New York: Triumph Books, 2005.

Whittingham, Richard, *What a Game They Played*. New York: Harper, 1984.

Yost, Mark, *Tailgating, Sacks, and Salary Caps: How the NFL Became the Most Successful Sports League in History*. Chicago: Kaplan Publishing, 2006.

Articles

Brown, Paul, with Bill Fay, "I Watch the Quarterback." *Colliers*, 136:66–71. Oct. 28, 1955.

Business Week, unsigned, "The NFL Machine." Jan. 27, 2003.

Effrat, Louis, "NFL Official Named NFL Commissioner." *New York Times*, p. 1, Jan. 27, 1960.

Fay, Bill, "Touchdown Target." *Colliers*, 136:301, Nov. 25, 1955.

Furlong, William Barry, "The Last Puritan." *Sports Illustrated*, Jan. 31, 1966.

Internet Sources

Campbell, Jim, "Pro Football History: The 1951 Dons," *Pro Football Weekly* archives, July 28, 1999, profootballweekly.com

Grosshandler, Stan, Professional Football Researchers Association, footballresearch.com.

Newspapers, Periodicals, and Research Sources

Chicago American
Chicago Daily News
Chicago Herald-American
Chicago Public Library
Chicago Sun
Chicago Sun-Times
Chicago Times
Chicago Today
Evanston (IL) Public Library
Program, 43rd Annual College All-Star Game, All Stars vs. Pittsburgh Steelers, July 29, 1976
New York Times
Northwestern University Library
Pro Football Hall of Fame, Joe Horrigan, director of public relations
Skokie (IL) Public Library

INDEX